Macroeconomics

Macroeconomics

4th Edition

JOHN LINDAUER

iUniverse, Inc.
Bloomington

Macroeconomics
4th Edition

iUniverse books may be ordered through booksellers or by contacting:

iUniverse
1663 Liberty Drive
Bloomington, IN 47403
www.iuniverse.com
1-800-Authors (1-800-288-4677)

ISBN: 978-1-4759-6240-6 (sc)
ISBN: 978-1-4759-6242-0 (hc)
ISBN: 978-1-4759-6241-3 (ebk)

Library of Congress Control Number: 2012921895

Printed in the United States of America

iUniverse rev. date: 12/10/2012

CONTENTS

Dedication

To my loves: Dorothy, Susan, John, and Mia. Including, of course, Angelo and Tabriz Oremus-Lindauer and Birdy Sanchez-Lindauer.

PREFACE

*"General Theories and policies that cannot explain or cope
with specific events are not general theories and policies
and must be either discarded or improved."*

This is an updating of an earlier series of books and articles that brought together macroeconomic theories and policies into a pragmatic synthesis integrating the real-world problems, policies, and institutional realities of somewhat-competitive economies such as the United States. The material that follows is as appropriate today as it was years ago because it is an absolute truism of science that *general theories that cannot explain specific events are not general theories and must be either discarded or improved.*

The theories and concepts presented years ago are updated, rewritten, and re-presented after all these years because of my distress at the poor performance of the American economy during the so-called "Great Recession" that began in 2008 and continued unnecessarily for years thereafter—and my increasing certainty that a large portion of the recent unsuccessful economic policy decisions made in the United States resulted from the inadequate graduate student educations and lack of worldliness which characterize some of our PhD granting institutions.

As readers shall see, the current "Great Recession," and the unemployment and deficits it is causing, can be quickly and permanently ended with appropriate monetary policies based on appropriate macroeconomic theories and realities—policies that can be immediately implemented without additional congressional or White House involvement.

The first edition of my earlier *Macroeconomics* series of books and articles introducing the "macro-pragmatic synthesis" appeared in the 1960s and was translated into Chinese, Japanese, Portuguese, and Spanish. Since then, to my amazement, teaching and writing about macroeconomic analysis and its application to problems and realities such as inflation, unemployment, economic growth, monetary and fiscal policies, and governmental deficits, appears to have deteriorated in North America.

Instead of moving up to study the theoretical and policy complexities of the complex real world, and particularly the difficulties inherent in implementing appropriate policies to keep countries such as the United States prosperous, students have all too often moved down to concentrate on unworldly and unrealistic overly simplified quasi-mathematical models that generate over-simplified conclusions and inaccurate explanations and policies.

No wonder the ensuing decades of students became congressmen, journalists, and central bankers who, as a group, all too often purvey absolute nonsense to the public about such macroeconomic conditions as the causes and cures of inflation and unemployment and the significance of governmental deficits.

The decline in the content of macroeconomics is particularly appalling because, absent the complexities of the "real world," it appears to have resulted in policies that have hurt many millions of people—instead of sustained prosperity, growth, and stable prices, the United States has all-too-often pursued policies that have resulted in unnecessary inflations and recessions that have caused unemployment, bankruptcies, business and bank failures, mortgage foreclosures, government deficits, and slow rates of growth.

Worse, if that is possible, twice in the modern era, once in the 1930s and again starting in 2008, the lack of appropriate policy responses has resulted in easily endable recessions morphing into serious depressions wherein the conventional monetary policy no longer works even if it finally starts. All of these problems and failures could have been prevented if the politicians and Federal Reserve governors and regional presidents of the United States had been adequately educated about the complexities of macroeconomics and had had a few real world experiences in business or commercial banking to put them in perspective. They did not.

As one of the earliest of the macro-pragmatic synthesizers I took pride in developing the comprehensive multi-market model presented herein and using it to examine the real world conditions and relationships ignored by the early Keynesians and those who followed: both the neo-Keynesian economists who continue to want a bigger role for government and the neo-classical economists who continue to attempt to integrate micro and macro via a neo-classical synthesis that requires an unattainable economy involving isolated individuals bargaining with one another in free markets unfettered by government activities.

The multi-market model used herein to examine the various relationships and policies epitomizes the "macro-pragmatic synthesis"—because it takes analysts beyond the traditional simplistic models and relationships. It does so via the integration of the various markets and microeconomic considerations associated with aggregate supply with the Keynesian concept of aggregate demand. Then the model is used to depict and explain how the effects of various changes and problems will ripple through the basic markets of an economy as a result of changes in the economy's institutions and policies; when and how conventional monetary and fiscal policies will work and will not work; and the policy alternatives that exist in the real world when the conventional policies become inadequate.

Conceptualizing and understanding the basic interrelationships that exist between an economy's financial, labor, and product markets and knowing what will tend to happen as a result of a specific institutional change or policy is important. It is the key to identifying the policies needed to keep an economy prosperous and growing without inflation and unemployment. Pragmatic analysts reading the following pages will quickly understand why I find it quite depressing that the graduates of many of our best universities are so unworldly that they still cling to the overly simplistic and naïve theories and models and solutions that characterize the early Keynesian and neo-classical generations of macroeconomists and their acolytes.

In essence, the economic institutions of countries differ from one another and are constantly experiencing changes and "unexpected events." These differences and changes make many of the early Keynesian analyses and policy suggestions, and those of many of their neo-classical successors, to put it gently, rather naïve in terms of being applicable to the United States and other modern economies.

Most pernicious of all are the use of unworldly models and inadequate data. This seems to have resulted in both the early Keynesians and the neo-classical synthesizers, and particularly their present-day followers, effectively ignoring or minimizing the significance of problems and policies because their models could not reflect them in an appropriately "scientific" manner—as if the complex concepts and relationships of the real world can be ignored as meaningless if a government or central bank has not collected data sufficient for quasi-mathematicians to analyze. In a word, they have let us down by substituting questionable data and simple models for intellect and reality.

The narrowing of macroeconomics during the past four or five decades is a tragedy because, concurrently with the study of macroeconomics being narrowed in its quest for acceptance as a hard science, the world's ever evolving economic institutions and the burgeoning of ideas, data, and research have, if anything, *expanded* the concepts and ideas and relationships that might be covered in macroeconomic tomes and classes.

Equally, if not more important, the Keynesian decades of overly simplistic theories and models have produced non-economists holding decision making positions who all too often do not have a clue as to how their policies and actions will actually impact the United States economy and its people. Worse, because they do not have a thorough grounding in the pragmatic real world to which macroeconomics applies, they all too often rely on what passes as "common knowledge" from the Keynesian and neo-classical eras and even earlier eras.

The results have been horrendous: tens of millions of Americans have had their lives ruined by inflation, unemployment, bankruptcies, foreclosures, and business and bank failures. These terrible events never should have happened and they certainly should not be continuing to this day.

In essence, many of those who today are presented to the public and our politicians as "business economists" or "economic experts" do not appear to be sufficiently knowledgeable and worldly to understand how the American economy actually operates, let alone how it can be kept prosperous and fully employed without inflation and unemployment. Their acceptance of government positions and media assignments for which they are unqualified and their lack of economic knowledge and understanding have led to everything from bad investment decisions to well-meaning monetary and fiscal policies that exacerbate rather than correct the problems at which they are aimed.

This presentation is for the analysts who will become the investors, managers, and policy makers of the United States. It presents and integrates the basic concepts and pragmatic realities of modern macroeconomics as part of a comprehensive multi-market model describing the basic macro relationships that exist in the real world and how they interact. That is followed by the use of the model to analyze how various basic problems such as inflation and unemployment come about for many reasons and how such problems might be corrected and prevented.

I think it fair to say that analysts and journalists able to understand the concepts of *Macroeconomics* will come away with a better understanding of how the American and similar economies actually function in the real world and be better equipped than most of their peers both to explain what is actually happening, and why, and to make better investment and policy decisions. (A description-only version entitled *Inflations, Unemployment, and Government Deficits: End Them* is available on Kindle and in paperback. It may be useful for members of the public and for students who need additional background; faculty may want to adopt it for their classes and use their own equations and models.)

This edition leaves out certain elements that can still be found in early-oriented macro texts. Specifically omitted is the traditional separate chapter describing the earliest macroeconomists—the "classical economists" who preceded Keynes and his contemporaries. Their ideas such as the quantity theory of money to explain inflation, so beloved and studied to this day in second tier economics departments, and the role of interest rates to equate savings and investment, so there can never be a recession, are merely summarized and debunked. This is done by examining the actual determinants of savings and investment and by using reason, facts, and the multi-market model both to illuminate some of the numerous possible sources of inflation and unemployment that exist in the real world and to analyze the various policies that might prevent them. (*I really thought about leaving in the traditional separate chapter for I have a particular affection for the quantity of money theory of inflation: it's so simple even journalists and the untrained lawyers and bureaucrats posing as qualified Federal Reserve governors can understand it.*)

Also omitted is the traditional chapter describing the national income accounts and the usual extensive source-citing footnotes found in earlier macro texts. These are no longer necessary because the specific concepts which were new in the initial post-Keynesian era are now generally known. Moreover, in this age of Google, Wikipedia, and Kindle readers who want to explore the views of a particular scholar or look up the latest data can easily search them out in much more detail than can be summarized in a few words of text or footnotes.

Because the complexities of the real world and the concepts and policies of the macro-pragmatic synthesis go so far beyond basic ideas and relationships presented in the pages that follow, would-be analysts and journalists should view this material as a starting place. They should also be aware that a model, no matter how complex, merely describes the most basic relationships of the real world in the most oversimplified of terms.

As pragmatic and worldly economists know, and the ever-growing numbers of narrow economic technicians apparently do not, simple graphs and a few hundred simultaneously solved equations populated with the limited and often questionable data that is available can never fully describe the complex economic relationships, institutions, and markets of complex and ever growing and changing economies such as that of the United States and the countries of Europe. In the real world, getting appropriate and accurate data to populate the basic equations is difficult even if writing and solving them is easy. The resulting product is all too often "scientifically sound," totally non-illuminating, and often absolutely useless in evaluating an ever-evolving economy—akin to attempting to drive down the winding road ahead by looking in the rear view mirror.

In this, the fourth edition of *Macroeconomics* the theories and explanations underlying the macro-pragmatic synthesis and its policy alternatives are presented in a more colloquial form and available in both e-book and printed versions. I am doing so because I feel guilty about the poor job I did of informing many of those who became members of our economics faculties of the realities and complexities of macro-pragmatic synthesis—and in so doing left them to mis-educate their now-influential students as to the application of macroeconomic theories and policies to the real world.

Interestingly enough, the theories, policies, and multi-market integrated model contained herein have held up rather well through the years. Indeed, they are even more applicable and unique than I first thought and certainly go far beyond the ideas of Keynes and the post-Keynesians and neo-classical synthesizers who followed him. Unfortunately in my effort to impress my peers and gain academic advancement I obviously wrote too obtusely about the need to fully integrate the concept of aggregate supply and the theories and realities of pragmatic macroeconomies. So some students keep hearing the same old "common knowledge" nonsense and simplistic analysis from the early post-Keynesian era when students learned about *some* of the monetary and fiscal policies applicable to the U.K. and its institutions (Keynes) on the premise that they would also be applicable with a few tweaks to the U.S. and other countries. No wonder we have continually had periods of inflation and unemployment long after they are no longer necessary.

Perhaps it's my fault—after initially developing the ideas and writing to explain the need to fully integrate aggregate supply and the world's pragmatic realities I became bored and moved on, thinking that it was only a matter of time before a worldly rationality would prevail in macroeconomics as it had in the rest of the economics profession and that it would be followed by the adoption of appropriate monetary and fiscal policies in the United States. Instead many of my macroeconomist peers in the United States narrowed their analyzes so they could be "scientists;" assumed that the problems and relationships of the future would be the same as those of the past; and then replicated themselves instead of producing worldly economists to guide our policies and staff our central banks. *Mea Culpa.*

Readers should know that I am indebted to my wife, Dorothy Oremus, for her encouragement and suggestions. Her many years as a director and chairman of a commercial bank provided valuable insights into how the American banking system actually operates in the real world and how it actually responds to monetary and fiscal policies. In a word, it is different from what most of today's journalists, investors, congressmen, Federal Reserve governors, and "business economists" think. The same can be said for my business experiences making decisions about jobs and investments and my political experiences making decisions about taxes, spending and public debt. I surely wish I had known then what I know now about the difficulty people have accepting new ideas! Instead, I feel like a doctor who presented a cure for a terrible disease (think recessions and inflations) and then spent years watching in dismay as his peers continued to prescribe the same old treatments that never worked and never will.

And finally, an invitation. This book contains concepts and ideas that are complex and often run counter to the misleading "common knowledge" typically accepted by those who have not studied the economics and policies of the modern macroeconomic synthesis and/ or have not had experience in the real world of business and commercial banking. The author hopes analysts will understand the material and profit from it—and, as a result, make better policy decisions and be more accurate when they reach decision-making positions or positions of influence. Finally, readers are invited to email their questions and requests for clarification to the author via Facebook or LinkedIn. I won't promise to answer but I will try.

JOHN LINDAUER
Chicago, Illinois

A RECENT LETTER TO THE AMERICAN COLONISTS FROM ADAM SMITH

Glasgow, Scotland 2012

It's been a few years but I'm back for a while. I'm really surprised at how far you've come—and shocked, just shocked, to see where you are headed.

Your wealth and that of your fellow investors is the wealth of your nation. Frankly, I expected to find you much wealthier by now. But in recent years your nation seems to have ignored some of the basic tenets I tried to teach you and stepped well off the high road to prosperity and even more wealth. Something you call a "business cycle" and your election of people who want to regulate your behavior seems to have put you off the road to more wealth.

In a word, your nation seems to have let its politicians and journalists forget or distort all my good advice and those of my successors Ricardo, Mill, Keynes, those pompous Austrians, and, of course, the modern macroeconomists such as Samuelson, Krugman, Davidson, and Lindauer who brought it all together for you. (even if Krugman sometimes writes as if he's in Britain where fiscal policy might actually work).

Instead of listening to us you've been listening to other people explain what we meant, people who apparently never even read our works. No wonder they get it all wrong and the wealth of your nation is stagnating.

Business cycles are bad for a nation's wealth.

One reason I'm writing to you today is because I read about events called "business cycles" that should never have happened because, as all worldly economists know, periodic slowdowns in the accumulation of wealth are not at all inevitable. Strictly man-made as the saying goes.

I still believe in the pursuit of self-interest as a way to drive your economies forward. It works, you know. So why have you let your politicians stifle it with more regulations and those useless monetary and fiscal policies that allow business cycles? Are you really opposed to bigger incomes and higher share prices and people who are healthier and richer? It is quite amazing.

Just think, for example, where the incomes and wealth of your nation would be if you had not been stuck for the past five years in your "Great Recession" or whatever you call it. You and your nation would be a lot wealthier had you taken our advice and taken steps to quickly see it off.

What's to be done.

So what's to be done to get investors going and your nation's wealth growth back on track? Three things.

First, listen to what Keynes really said about the importance of customers and where they come from—and ignore what been made up about him by those who either never took the time to read what he wrote or, more likely, couldn't understand it because of those pesky equations.

And be sure to note that Keynes emphasized fiscal policy because he was writing about our beloved United Kingdom where fiscal policy is workable—perhaps because King James who got the kingdom going was a Scot and had good common sense. In contrast, some of you colonists have set up nations that make fiscal policy totally unworkable by dividing your decisions between something called a President and your parliament, and then re-dividing your parliament into two parts which seem to be unable to act together in a timely manner on anything. So why do you even try to use fiscal policy for such unworkable things such as "jobs bills," whatever they are.

But Keynes was right as I tried to tell you years ago—customers are important. Without enough customers your employers won't hire more workers and produce more to increase the wealth of your nation. Is that so hard to understand? Keynes got it—that's why he became so wealthy as a trader or hedge funder as you apparently call them these days.

It's as I described years ago and Keynes clarified. There are four basic classes of customers for a nation's employers whether they are trying to make profits or non-profits such as charities: consumers, businesses buying plant and equipment, foreigners (those terrible French, for example), and governments buying muskets and roads and schools.

There is nothing inevitable about a nation having a business cycle that is periodically "down" so businesses fail and workers can't find jobs. All a business cycle being "down" means is that your nation's employers aren't keeping all your people working because they don't have enough customers for some reason.

But having a shortage of customers shouldn't be a problem—because everyone's wants are insatiable. Remember that? So it's only a matter of getting money into the hands of potential customers who are willing to spend it.

In the UK we mostly use fiscal policy to keep the wealth of our nation employed and growing. That lets us quickly set things right by spending more or taxing less. (And we often regret it because fiscal policies frequently come with absurd regulations attached as the government's bureaucrats attempt to "fix" things they don't understand.)

A realistic monetary policy is the only answer if a new nation such as the United States is to continually create wealth.

In any event, since Keynes' fiscal policy suggestions will not work in a nation with a government organized as yours is, it means your nation is limited to using monetary policy to encourage the customers your nation's employers must have if they are to keep making investments and creating wealth.

Your central bank can use monetary policy to indirectly encourage customers by creating new money as it is needed and flowing it into your commercial banks which, being the good profit seekers they are, will try to loan it out so consumers and businesses can buy even more than they otherwise would. Or your central bank can create it and directly flow it to would-be customers. In the real world, those are your only two choices.

Some unworldly folk think that creating new money when more customers are needed will cause inflation from too much spending. They are wrong. More money is just fine if it is necessary to generate enough customers, but not too much more so prices generally rise nor too little more so unemployment remains. It's a fine line—that's why every nation uses a central bank instead of gold flows as we did when I first started thinking about the wealth of nations.

Other unworldly folk think that instead of using monetary policy a nation can fix its exchange rates so it sells more to foreigners. These days I hear the Chinese nation is doing exactly that to yours. The problem, of course, is that nations whose customer spending is diverted abroad can and do respond in kind and quickly get it back. So exporting more is really not a policy a nation can depend on to maintain and grow its wealth.

What I am trying to explain here is that monetary policy that gets money into the hands of spenders or selling more abroad are the only two alternatives when fiscal policy isn't feasible. And that selling more abroad is not realistic because of the inevitable retaliation.

But that doesn't mean that a monetary policy that will work for my and Keynes' nation (the U.K.) will work for your U.S. nation.

Here in the U.K. our central bank sets the interest rate at which commercial banks can borrow money from the central bank and loan it to their customers. The rate our central bank sets is, in effect, the wholesale price of money. When it is reduced our banks tend to borrow money from our central bank and then compete to loan it out by lowering their loan rates—and the availability of loan and the lower interest rates encourages more customer spending.

Your central bank is different. The only interest rate your Federal Reserve tries to influence is the rate your commercial banks charge one another to borrow money overnight to meet their reserve requirements.

One has to be daft to think that one of your commercial banks will loan out more money if the Federal Reserve raises or lowers the interest rate for money the bank has to repay in full the very next day—yet I hear your central bank, the Federal something or other, makes much of it and its governors actually think they are doing something when they change that overnight rate. Amazing—no wonder your nation has recessions and depressions.

So not only is your Congress mistakenly and fruitlessly trying to copy our UK fiscal policy, your central bank is mistakenly and fruitlessly trying to copy our monetary policy as well. Probably the result of the poor educations your policy makers got by using textbooks written by economists from my country. In any event, it won't work for you.

Of course, your Federal Reserve can do several things to keep the wealth of your nation growing even if changing interest rates is not one of them. One thing it can do is indirectly flow money into the hands of customers via your nation's commercial banks or your national government. It does this, of course, by buying assets with newly created money or by using newly created money to fund your government deficits so that higher taxes are not necessary.

Another thing it can do is channel newly created money to the recipients of your pension schemes such as Social Security or, God forbid, send it to those abominable bankers in Germany and Greece as your central bank did a few weeks ago.

I just don't understand why you colonists set up your nation's central bank so it does not loan out money to commercial banks to be reloaned. But I am absolutely amazed that the people running your central bank, I think you call them Bernankes or Geithners and they must be from Wales, are so naive and unworldly that they don't realize their central bank is fundamentally different from ours in the U.K. No wonder your nation keeps having those unnecessary "business cycles" cutting into its wealth.

From what I can see today, if your Federal Reserve used the right monetary policies, instead of fruitlessly trying to copy ours in the U.K, your nation's wealth would increase faster, your nation's workers would be fully employed, and your government would probably have surpluses instead of deficits.

Why all the regulations?

Second, if you really want to get your nation back on track to more wealth you really should listen to the Austrians such as Hayek and Schumpeter—encourage investors to add to your nation's wealth. Don't discourage them with silly regulations and laws that help a few of your cronies but generally discourage investment spending and the accumulation of wealth.

Employers making investments are important. They increase the wealth of your nation by building new factories and introducing new technologies. On the other hand, as I pointed out in my earlier writings, businesses that are already in existence will inevitably conspire to fix prices and try to use your government to discourage investors from establishing businesses to compete against them.

Favoring one employer over another is bad for investors and the wealth of your nation for, as John Stuart Mill, Alfred Marshall, and I pointed out years ago, competition tends to drive down prices down and cause inefficient producers to fail—and thus frees up their workers and capital to be employed more efficiently elsewhere and increase the wealth of your nation.

It really is important to resist government interference in the accumulation of wealth or its employment. The self-interest of power-seeking government employees may cause them to seek to expand their personal powers with laws and regulations that impede investors. If you remove those impediments people will be motivated by their self interest to save and borrow more so they could set up new businesses and hire more workers.

For example, I have been told the abominable French and Greek governments restrict the number of coaches available to carry visitors to their cities from one place to the other—so service is horrible, prices are high, and the wealth of their nations is less than it could be. (The difficulty and high price of getting around in such places is why I spend all my time in Scotland.)

And finally, don't be taken in by the unworldly who say that national deficits and the resulting national debt are always bad. Sometimes, of course, they are. It amazes me, but some people wrongly believe they always have the same effect the wealth of your nation as the deficits and debts of people and state and local governments. They aren't the same. And having more of them or less of them really doesn't mean much.

In reality, your nation's sovereign debts are different than all other debts in your nation because sometimes they can be paid with newly created money without causing inflation. That's why responding to them as if they are some kind of great problem as your parliament or whatever it's called ("congress?") seems to do can make things worse for investors and your nation's wealth instead of better. As the Austrians would say "don't let your politicians hurt you by worrying about the little things and making much of them. Keep your eye steadied on what counts—which is the wealth of your nation."

A Final Thought

If you're an investor or ordinary citizen and the politicians and "pundits" have you confused by their inane speeches and silly policies you might want to read one of my successor's, John Lindauer will do nicely, books and articles on the subjects of Keynes, inflation, unemployment, and debt. I understand you can find them at seekingalpha.com and in book-form on the Amazon—though for the life of me I can't understand why books would be on a river.

Hope this helps. Be thrifty and may God keep you from evil.

Adam

CHAPTER ONE

PRAGMATIC ECONOMICS

Millions of people, employers, and governments throughout the world are constantly making innumerable decisions such as whether or not to buy a specific product, or make a specific investment, or put money in the bank, or work more hours if they can find jobs. Sometimes, as is the case in the United States today, their spending does not add up to give an economy's public and private employers enough revenues—so there is a "Great Recession" and people along with their businesses and governments suffer from unemployment, foreclosures, bankruptcies, and business failures. Is it inevitable that such things periodically occur? And, more importantly, what will work to turn things around if and when a recession does occur? And what *won't* work?

Economists once thought that the individual decisions occurring in a relatively free economy such as that of the United States would automatically result in "prosperity" in the form of full employment without inflation—by automatically providing whatever is "enough" customer revenues for its employers, deposits for its banks, encouragements for its investors, stable prices for its products, and jobs for its workers. Obviously that is not the case. But what must a government do (and not do) so that the public and private employers in its economy hire enough people? That is the major economic question that faces every Congress and every administration. How they answer it determines their legacy and their place in history.

The early economists thought a desirable state of full employment would happen automatically if only the economy's government would stop interfering and let nature take its course. Others, the socialists and communists, thought it could only happen if the government and its bureaucrats regulated and planned everything. Both approaches were tried—both failed miserably: There were periodic great recessions and inflations in the former and great stagnations and an inability to grow in the latter, to say nothing of the repression and corruption that accompanied the bureaucrats and their decisions.

Then along came the "Great Depression" of the 1930s and John Maynard Keynes' *General Theory of Employment, Interest and Money*—and the economic science known as "macroeconomics" was born. Subsequent analysts, both supporters and bitter critics, refined and expanded his ideas into what is today the body of thought known as conventional macroeconomic theory and the various monetary policies and fiscal policies it suggests.

In essence, the theories and policies of the Keynesians and their conservative critics are quite elegant, very scientific, and perfectly rational—except for the rather inconvenient problem that they neither explain the real world of the United States economy nor suggest viable monetary and fiscal policies to eliminate its periodic experiences with unemployment and inflation, and the hardships and budgetary deficits they inevitably cause. There is a lot of substance to Keynes. But not all his ideas and policy suggestions apply to countries such as the United States whose economic structures and institutions are significantly different from those of Keynes' Britain. Other ideas and policies are often needed.

Macroeconomics is the area of economics concerned with the prosperity of a nation. It deals with some of the most controversial and challenging problems of our time: inflation, taxes, deficits, unemployment, exchange rates, money, interest rates, and the proper role of an economy's governments and its central bank. In other words, all the things that make politicians reach for microphones and hardware salesmen make impassioned speeches at their Rotary clubs.*

Macro is the Greek word for "whole" as opposed to micro which means something small. Thus macroeconomists study the nature and appropriate policies for a whole economy and microeconomists study the nature and policies appropriate for an economy's individual parts. Thus a macroeconomist might study inflation and an economy's total output while a microeconomist might study the prices and production of a specific item or specific market.

In the years following Keynes his supporters and critics attempted to tie together the then-prevailing economic theories into a synthesized body of macroeconomic knowledge. Then in the 1960s the macro-pragmatic economists came along and added new theories and explanations based on the more complex and ever-changing concepts and relationships of the real world to the simplistic ideas of Keynes' supporters and critics.

In essence, the theories, concepts, and policies of "pragmatic macro-economics" are merely another stage in the continuing development of the field of macroeconomics. In particular, pragmatic macroeconomics deals with the various policies required to keep a modern economy, such as that of the United States, operating at full employment without inflation and undue regulation. As such it goes beyond the theories and ideas and policy suggestions of both the followers and critics of Keynes.

Everyone has a dog in the fight to keep their economy prosperous. When all the billions of individual decisions made daily in a complex economy add up in such a way that prosperity prevails, jobs are plentiful for everyone, including ourselves, and wages tend to be relatively high and growing. When times are hard, on the other hand, the specter of unemployment, bankruptcy, and destitution falls upon millions of men, women, and children—and every one of us is potentially among them no matter how safe we feel at the moment.

ECONOMIC IGNORANCE
OFTEN PREVAILS

As will become increasingly apparent, the general state of a nation's economy is a subject in which passions and prejudices and "common knowledge" often replace facts and pragmatic reasoning as the basis for laws, regulations, and governmental and central bank policies and actions.

Too often well-meaning, but unworldly, theoreticians, congressmen, and central banking placemen advocate and apply simple but unrealistic policies in an attempt to solve complex economic problems in an ever changing world. In essence, they seek prosperity with homemade remedies based on common knowledge and unworldly theories instead of adopting laws and policies appropriate for the real world in which we live.

The consequences of their well-meaning mistakes are horrendous: complex money using economies of prosperous and democratic countries such as the United States and Germany and poor and authoritarian countries such as Russia and China have been plagued and even overwhelmed at times by great inflations, massive unemployment, low or negative rates of growth, and balance of payments deficits.

These are strong terms to be sure, but mild in comparison to the conditions associated with them. People even in the richest countries such as the United States have all too often been periodically unable to afford food and shelter; investments, savings, and pensions have been wiped out or significantly reduced; students have not been able to complete their educations and pay off their student loans; business and banks have failed; and tens of millions of people have lost their jobs and homes.

The tragedy is that all of this suffering was totally unnecessary and could have been avoided by the implementation of the pragmatic macroeconomic policies that are analyzed and explained in the following pages. These are the policies which must be understood by those who would be successful leaders of businesses, banks, and governments—or, after much totally unnecessary human suffering, they will fail and be replaced.

THE ORIGIN OF MACROECONOMICS

The desire to improve the performance of economies and to understand how and why they operate has led economists to probe numerous economic nooks and crannies. They have long examined both the general economic conditions prevailing in an economy and the nature and problems associated with specific parts of the economy.

The study of economics changed forever in 1936 with the arrival of John Maynard Keynes' epic *The General Theory of Employment, Interest, and Money*. It brought macroeconomics to the fore as a separate area of economic theory—and his analysis and explanations established macroeconomics as a separate discipline far removed from microeconomics. In other words, it changed economics and economic policies forever.

Keynes combined being a Cambridge economics professor with being both a very senior governmental advisor and an investor who became one of the world's most successful money managers and philanthropists. He was a director of the Bank of England, the architect of the IMF and the World Bank, and was ennobled as Baron Keynes. A new borough and city was named after him (and the great English poet John Milton): Milton-Keynes. Importantly, *Keynes wrote about monetary and fiscal policies that specifically applied to Britain and its unique political and financial institutions.*

Most importantly, Keynes' policy suggestions for Britain, with their emphasis on rapidly implemented fiscal policies and changes in the interest rate set by the central bank, do *not* always apply to economies such as the United States which have a very different type of central bank and a very different governmental framework.

**The significant errors of
the early macroeconomists.**

The now-called "Austrian" or "Classical" economists who preceded Keynes, and included Keynes himself prior to 1936, thought that there were market forces in existence such that, unless there were government or other interferences which prevented prices from changing, there could never be a long-term recession or depression caused by employers experiencing inadequate customer spending such that they would have to lay off workers.

More specifically, they thought there could never be inadequate levels of spending. Interest rates would adjust to insure it never happened. They saw interest rates as both the primary motivator of savings and the price investors paid to obtain that savings to use for investment purposes. In essence, they thought an economy's interest rates would quickly adjust upward or downward to provide sufficient additional investment spending to offset any additional savings (non-spending) that might occur.

According to them, if interest rates were free to adjust all the money coming into an economy's public and private employers would go right back out to be fully re-spent again—so there would never be a recession or depression with low levels of production and millions of unemployed workers. In essence, according to the pre-Keynesians, an economy such as that of the United States would never suffer from inadequate customer spending, at least not for very long, since the interest rate price of borrowing money would adjust to equate the supply of savings with the investors demand for savings.

To Keynes and everybody living in the real world it was painfully obvious that the Austrians and other Classical Economists were wrong—there *was* a "Great Depression" in the 1930s and it *did* continue for years without ending. And it continued in Britain and the United States despite interest rates reaching all-time lows and despite the forecasts of Keynes' predecessors that such a depression would be short-lived, if it ever came to exist in the first place. Worse, it happened again in the United States when its "Great Recession," which started in 2008, similarly morphed into a prolonged depression.

The idea that recessions and depressions would automatically end led to various policy conclusions: one was that interest rates should be left alone to adjust by themselves; another, that the central bank should not respond to inadequate levels of spending since more money in circulation was not needed because full employment would automatically return. Moreover the addition of such unneeded money would then, it was alleged, cause inflation when prosperity returned. A third was that the only role for government when there is a recession to be the removal of impediments preventing wages and prices from falling—because when wages and prices got low enough everyone will be able to find a job and full employment levels of production would occur.

Very different conclusions.

Keynes rejected and replaced, at least for Britain, the obviously failed analysis and policy conclusions of the Austrians and his other predecessors. He noted, correctly as it turns out, that things were different in the real world: that interest rates were set in the money market by the supply and demand for money rather than by the willingness of people to save and invest; that the amount of savings that occurs in an economy is primarily related to the level of income in the economy rather than the level of its interest rates; and that the total amount of income and customer spending in an economy could be permanently mired at a level too low to generate full employment levels of production—the situation that occurred in the United States both in the 1930s and again starting in 2008.

In essence, the main thrust of what Keynes said is that the total amount of all customer spending in an economy (by consumers, investors, governments, and foreigners) may not be high enough to cause the economy's governmental, non-profit, and for-profit employers to fully employ all the available workers. In other words, as every American business executive and government department head will tell you, revenues are vitally important. Without revenues employers cannot hire employees and goods and services cannot be produced.

Keynes' policy prescription for the depression in the U.K. was 180 degrees different from his predecessors—for more government spending *so that total spending would rise;* and for the central bank to lower the bank rate at which it loaned money to Britain's commercial banks so that they would have more loanable funds which would, in turn, cause them to compete for customers by lowering the interest rates they charged which would, in turn, encourage more investment spending *so that total spending would rise.*

The Keynesians who followed Keynes parsed his words and suggested his fiscal and monetary policy suggestions would also apply to the United States. They were wrong.

Today's pragmatic economists.

The more worldly of the economists of the post-Keynesian era, and today's pragmatic economists who followed them, have expanded and modified almost all of the original and subsequent Keynesian analysis—*except Keynes' main point that there must be enough customer spending in an economy if its public and private employers are to fully employ its workforce.*

Similarly, like Keynes, all macroeconomists including the most pragmatic and worldly are concerned with the aspects and policies of the economy as a whole. And, like Keynes, those among them, at least those who are worldly in their knowledge of how a complex economy actually operates, know that the solving problems such as inflation and unemployment requires policies based on understanding and working within the complex institutions, markets, relationships, and decision making processes that affect an economy's general level of economic activity.

Such knowledge, and the theories that underpin it, together with the study of the problems that can plague an economy and the monetary, fiscal, and other policies designed to solve them, is the domain of today's "pragmatic macroeconomics."

The concerns of pragmatic macroeconomists are multifaceted and, as shall be seen, quite complex and often controversial. Old ideas about problems and policies, it seems, die hard in the academic world and among politicians and central bankers. But macroeconomists as a group, and particularly those that are both "pragmatic" and "worldly" in that they understand there are ever-changing institutions and complexities, want to know about all the *many different things* that might cause the general level of prices to rise (inflation); and about all the *many different things* that cause the general level of employment and production to temporarily recede or be permanently depressed below that which the economy is capable of providing (recessions and depressions); and about all the *many different policies* that could be implemented to prevent such inflations and unemployment.

Worldly macroeconomists, in essence, are concerned with the economic state and general well-being of the many millions of people who participate in the real world of an economy such as that of the United States. As such, they differ significantly both from the microeconomists who study particular economic participants and from today's all-too-narrow macroeconomic technicians who spend time trying to prove their "scientific expertise" and encouraging their students to do likewise—and all too often don't have a clue as to how complex economies actually operate and how they will be affected by various policies and realities.

MACROECONOMIC GOALS AND PERFORMANCE

Worldly macroeconomists often talk of goals; and they evaluate the policies and performance of economies in terms of them. But what are worthwhile goals for an economy such as that of the United States?

First and foremost, an economy must efficiently produce the maximum amount of the goods and services most desired by its people—if it is to attain the basic Panglossian goal of satisfying as many human wants as possible as would be the case in the best of all possible worlds. But the production of the maximum amount of goods and services does not necessarily occur automatically. And there are a number of related goals—low levels of unemployment, stable prices, and economic growth being particularly important ones. There is also the not insignificant question of who is to get whatever is produced.

"Goods and services" is economist-speak for things that can be produced that are important enough to people such that they and their businesses and governments are willing to buy them. They include such thing as medicine and hospitals, food and drink, schools and education, roads and traffic police, banking services, cars and trucks and gasoline, law and order, food, research into new technologies, tanks and planes and their use to defend the country and discourage enemies, new plant and equipment to replace that which has worn out as well as add additional capital items so even more goods and services can be produced in the future. The list goes on and on.

And these things are not produced automatically just because they are needed or because there are savings or because an economy has something of a democracy or a charismatic leader or the necessary workers and capital. No matter whether the economy has a democratic or authoritarian government, there must be someone to buy the goods and services—someone or something that will flow money revenues into the economy's public, non-profit, and for-profit employers so they, in turn, can pay employees and buy the inputs and capital goods needed to produce whatever it is that they are getting money revenues to produce.

Those providing the money revenues are called customers no whether it is someone buying a pizza or the federal government buying a highway upgrade or a city buying a new fire truck or a non-profit buying a new building. They are vital to the success of every economy.

Individuals are customers when they pay the grocery stores money to buy a family's food; grocery stores are customers when they pay money to the food processors to buy foods for their customers and to truckers to have it delivered to their stores; food processors are customers when they buy farm products and machinery and when they pay to have them delivered to their factories; stores and the processors are customers when they pay money to builders and manufacturers to buy new and replacement buildings and equipment; governments are customers when they use the money they borrow or collect in taxes to buy roads and to pay police to write tickets if the delivery trucks and food buyers drive too fast.

The list of potential public and private money using transactions is endless—billions occur in an economy like the United States' every day. The goal is to have "enough" public and private customer spending so the workers and capital of the economy are fully employed producing as much as possible of the medicine, education, food, trucks, buildings, police and defense services, tanks and planes, judges and courts, etc. etc. of whatever it is the people and their businesses and governments want to buy. And we know what they want because it is whatever they and their elected governments buy as they spend the money they earn, tax, and borrow.

In essence, what happens is that money flows into an economy's public, private, and non-profit employers from the spending of their consumer, business, government, and foreign customers and then flows back to the customers in the form of wages, dividends and taxes. But not all of it flows back to the customers and when the customers get the money they may not spend it all. In either event, *there can be a shortfall of customer spending*. If that happens, the economy's employers will not have enough customer revenues the next time around unless something is done to encourage more spending.

Things are obviously much more complex than they are made out to be in this simple description—and understanding those complexities and relating them to realistic policies is the study of macroeconomics.

The first great macroeconomic goal: full employment.

Labor and production capital (plant, equipment, and inventory) are the factors of production whose employment generates the goods and services that are purchased by an economy's public and private customers. Ideally all the labor and production capital in an economy will be employed—unless they are moving between employments or being retooled and retrained so they can keep up with the economy's ever-changing customer preferences, opportunities, and production technologies.

Such a *full employment* of an economy's productive capacity, when coupled with its efficient use, means the level of output of goods and services in the economy is being maximized. Unfortunately, as we shall see, no matter what the philosophies and good intentions of an economy's governments and central bank, a major problem that confronts every economy, whether democratic or authoritarian, is that neither full employment nor the efficient usage of labor and capital occurs automatically. A successful economy, in other words, requires constant care and appropriate policies.

Fully using an economy's labor and production capital is important in the United States and every other country. It means our economy and our workers and production capital are producing the maximum amount of goods and services and *that requires that there be enough customer spending*—not too much spending so that higher prices (inflation) result nor too little spending so that some of our economy's labor and production capacity stands idle (unemployment) due to a lack of customers.

Production capital and financial capital. Pragmatic analysts know that there are two very different types of capital and investments. Production capital in the form of plant, equipment and inventory is acquired by the investment spending of public and private employers and used in their production processes. In contrast, financial capital is money and financial instruments such as stocks and bonds. A company or government may issue a stock or bond and use the proceeds to buy plant, equipment and inventory—or it may use the money for some other purpose such as buying another company or paying dividends or salaries and management bonuses.

Once issued, stocks and bonds can usually be sold back and forth—and those who do so are often called investors even though a more proper term might be "trader" or "speculator." They are very different from the investors who buy plant, equipment, and inventory and use it to produce goods and services.

Pragmatic analysts know that once stocks and bonds are issued their subsequent buying and selling back and forth does not have anything to do with the employer who issued them in the first place or an economy's capacity to produce. Their prices are, however, somewhat of an indicator as to how well an economy is doing: profits and revenues, and thus the prices of stocks and bonds, tend to be higher when an economy is doing well such that its businesses and governments have sufficient revenues coming in that they can pay dividends and interest and redeem their bonds. More important, however, in terms of how an economy is performing are other indicators more directly related to the things that really count:—jobs, price levels, and growth.

Unemployment and underemployment of labor and capital. It goes without saying that if an economy's willing and able workers and other factors of production—its labor force and production capital (plant, equipment, and inventory) are not fully employed there will be unemployment and less-than-possible levels of production. In other words, food and medicine and buildings and police protection and tanks and planes that could be produced and made available will not be produced and made available if there is a lack of customers willing and able to buy them.

Such a shortfall in production and employment resulting from a lack of revenues is bad news for governments since people who are unemployed because employers don't have enough customers tend to be very unhappy voters, and rightly so. Then they must subsist on their savings, borrowings, charity, and any remaining incomes they may still have—until they can turn out the government and its central bank decision makers and replace them with people capable of providing the policies needed to get the economy back to full employment. *It is those policies that will actually succeed in doing this, and those that won't, that are the subject of this book.*

Similarly undesirable is when an economy's labor and production capital is under-employed. For example, when employer revenues are so bad that the only job an engineer can find is delivering pizza, or a factory's production line only runs six hours per day or only three days per week, or a city worker is cut back so he or she only works three days instead of five days, or when only a few floors of a building are occupied, or when some of an airline's planes sit on the ground and some of its pilots idled because there are fewer people flying because the economy is in a recession—because not enough customer spending is occurring so that the revenues of its public and private employers are too low.

Using the rates of labor and capital unemployment for policy purposes. Every country in the world (except perhaps North Korea) constantly tries to keep on top of its labor unemployment and unutilized production capacity. That knowledge lets its leaders and policy makers know the magnitude of their country's idled production capacity and, thus, the size and nature of the monetary, fiscal, or other corrective measures that might be required to get the economy back up to producing at full employment.

For example, pragmatic economists estimate that in the year 2012 as much as twenty percent of the United States' labor force and production capital that might reasonably be expected to be at work was, in fact, unemployed. As a result, the United States' in 2012 only produced about $16 trillion of goods and services even though its economy had a production capacity of about $20 trillion. In other words, production and employment had receded or been depressed so far below the level which the United States economy was capable of providing that it left $4 trillion of production unproduced—*due to a lack of customer spending to buy the goods and services that could have been produced by the United States' public and private employers.*

And, yes, the United States really was that short of reaching its potential. Every month the Department of Labor publishes an "official" unemployment rate for unemployed workers. Throughout 2012 the official monthly rates hovered around 8%. For reasons that shall be subsequently discussed in some detail, the official rate is not worth the paper it is written on. Long ago the White House and Congress realized that people would judge them on how successfully the economy preformed under their leadership—so they "fixed" the estimating procedure to generate a rate far lower than actually exists. As shall be seen, and analysts can calculate, the real rate in 2012 was significantly more than double the reported "official" rate.

In reality, there were almost five million fewer jobs in the United States in 2012 than there had been four years earlier. Moreover, immigration, natural increases in the population, longer lives, and the need of retirees to return to work, had added millions of working-age adults to the potential labor force.

That's a pretty sterile analysis. Think of it in more human terms: it means that due to a lack of customer spending in 2012 the United States' public and private employers did not produce $4 trillion of medical services, education, roads, justice, homes, appliances, and numerous other things that could have enriched and enhanced the lives of its residents—*things that could have been produced.*

Even worse, many of those millions of Americans who were unemployed as a result of that "Great Recession" lost their homes to foreclosures, went bankrupt, used up their savings and could not afford to continue their educations or repay their student loans. Similarly, many businesses and banks closed and, since unemployed people and unprofitable businesses tend not to pay taxes, government revenues plummeted, deficits grew, and many governments were forced to cut back on their spending and services. Some governments, for the first time in the history of the United States, were even forced to join with the millions of Americans and businesses and file for bankruptcy.

As analysts shall see, it was all unnecessary since the Great Recession could have been prevented by proper government and central bank oversight and, when it did occur, could have been quickly ended by proper and immediately available monetary and fiscal policies.

The second great macroeconomic goal: no inflation.

An "inflation" occurs when the prices in an economy move generally higher. In the United States it means each dollar has less purchasing power.

An inflation is generally agreed to be something that is to be avoided: A generally higher level of prices in an economy discourages savings because it wipes out the purchasing power of the savings. It also distorts spending decisions. For example, if a potential saver thinks there will be inflation he or she is likely to spend money immediately before its value, its purchasing power, goes down. Or the saver might put it into financial investments or productive investments in plant and equipment that promise to yield the same or greater returns than the inflation—instead of into the financial investments or productive investments they would choose to make if there is no inflation.

The basic concept of money value is that *the value of the dollar and every other currency is determined by what it will buy.* Inflation in the United States means each dollar has a lower value because it will buy less.

Inflation has a particularly undesirable effect on fixed pensions or bonds and other financial assets with fixed yields—the recipients have same nominal amounts of money coming in but now the recipients cannot buy as much because prices in the economy are generally higher. In other words, inflation not only upsets and discourages savers; it also hurts people on fixed incomes and has a similarly adverse impact on businesses or workers that are selling or working on long term sales contracts or fixed wages.

Many people think that inflation is caused by increases in the money supply—such that "too much money is chasing too few goods." That's a view that prevails even today at a few second-tier economics departments, among most financial journalists and congressmen, and among the lawyers and MBAs running the Federal Reserve and Treasury. In fact, they are wrong. What will be seen in the materials and discussions that follow is that *generally higher prices (inflation) can occur for many reasons* and that "too much money in circulation" is only one of them, rarely occurs, and need never occur—since the Federal Reserve can instantly within hours (yes, hours) remove any money its governors deem to be excess such that it might cause inflation.

The existence of many causes of generally higher prices (inflation) suggests that many different policies may be needed to prevent it. The best policy or combination of policies to fight inflation depends, of course, on what is actually causing the higher prices. In other words, blindly seizing upon on holding down the money supply or implementing any other single "solution" may not stop an inflation. And indeed, as shall be seen, well-meaning efforts to fight inflation may actually cause prices to rise and, thus, the inflation to get worse.

Moreover, not all increases in an economy's level of prices are an indication of a problem or a policy failure. As shall also be seen in the chapters ahead, some pragmatic economists suggest an increase in the general level of prices of two or three percent per year is inherent in the ever changing structure of a dynamic economy such as that of the United States. It occurs as a natural phenomenon in a dynamic economy—as buyers switch their spending to new and newly favored products and cause their prices to rise while the prices of the now-less-favored products tend not to fall.

More specifically, the overall level of prices in a relatively free and dynamic economy such as that of the United States tends to slowly but surely constantly increase as spending patterns change so that the prices of the goods and services gaining favor are bid up by consumers and other buyers anxious to acquire them while the prices of the goods and services losing favor (losing customers who are shifting their spending to the now-favored products) tend not to fall.

The prices of the items losing customers tend not to fall because their production costs which the prices must cover if the employer is to continue producing them, may be fixed due to such things as property taxes and employee wages that do not fall even if the employer is producing fewer items. In essence, if some prices in the economy rise as spending shifts, and other prices remain stable, the overall average level of prices of the goods and services in the economy will move higher—inflation.

Ending the structural changes and economic dynamism responsible for that particular cause of inflation would require either denying individual spenders the freedom to change their spending patterns, or rigid price controls, or clamping down on overall spending so dramatically that some prices fall to offset those that increase—in other words, stopping the economy from constantly growing and changing for the better.

Obviously taking steps to stop an economy from growing and evolving is an altogether absurd policy—which in 2012 was actually advocated by influential members of Congress and members of the Federal Reserve's Open Market Committee. (*Upon working through this material and understanding at least a bit of the pragmatic realities of macroeconomics readers are cheerfully encouraged to run for Congress or apply for positions at the Federal Reserve.)*

The third great macroeconomic goal: economic growth.

Economic growth is traditionally measured in terms of an increase in the total amount of goods and services produced in an economy. A better measure, advocated by the more worldly and pragmatic of macroeconomists, is an increase in the total amount of goods and services produced per capita.

Two basic requirements exist for sustained growth. The first is that the productive capacity of the economy grows so that more *can* be produced. The second is that customer spending (by consumers, employers making investment expenditures to buy plant and equipment, governments, and foreigners) grows so that more *will* be produced.

Merely putting idled workers and production capacity back to work is sometimes referred to as economic growth. In a sense it is because the output of goods and services grows. Thus an economy with a capacity to produce $20 trillion of goods and services that is only producing $16 trillion can have a one-time growth in production of up to $4 trillion just by increasing customer spending.

Thereafter, however, increasing production to some new and higher level, such as $22 trillion, would require *both* some combination of more workers, new technologies, and additional plant and equipment so that capacity grows, and an increase in customer spending of $2 trillion so that the economy's public and private employers take in enough additional revenues so they can pay for the additional workers, materials, and production capital that will be required so that the additional capacity is actually utilized.

Numerous ideas and descriptions have been advanced and published over the years as to what the key elements might be for the growth of an economy's production capacity, its *aggregate supply*. Google, Amazon, and entire library shelves are filled with them.

Among the major determinants of increased production capacity which have been suggested at times, and not in order of importance: increases in the stock of capital via investments in plant, equipment and inventory—which in the broadest sense covers everything from new machines and new technologies to better roads and railroads and more dependable supplies of power and fuel; a growing workforce via population growth or allowing workers to work more years before they forced to retire (hello France) or enabling women to work (hello Japan and much of the Islamic world); better educations for workers so they can better handle the complex production processes of a modern economy (hello United States); and the removal of government laws, regulations, permits, approvals, and taxes that prevent or delay or discourage whatever it takes to get production capacity increases (hello France, Greece, India and just about everyone else).

Many pragmatic macroeconomists with real world experience in business and government have come to believe that the single most important thing enabling and causing economic growth is economic freedom and the "rule of law" reasonably and equitably and uniformly applied. People, it seems, are quite capable of working, investing, and producing more in order to improve their lot in life without a government bureaucracy or authoritarian regime controlling their every effort. If the past is any guide, people will rush to work and invest and become employers—when given an unfettered chance *and there are customers for their products.*

Today the United States, Norway, Britain, Denmark, and Sweden are examples of economies based on economic freedom and the "rule of law;" China, India, Zimbabwe, and Russia are examples of countries whose economic futures appear to be limited due to a lack of economic freedom and the "rule of law."

To paraphrase Adam Smith, the first and arguably the greatest economist of all time, people and employers, particularly in the private sector, will in their pursuit of incomes and stature in their communities constantly make investments and develop new technologies and hire people based on their abilities regardless of their age, race, and sex and increase production and develop new products and produce more and more goods and services—*if they are allowed to do so* and can proceed with confidence that their ideas and properties will not be seized or stolen or prevented or delayed by competitors seeking to prevent competition or by politicians and courts attempting to obtain bribes or curry favor with potential benefactors.

Some macro-pragmatic economists and analysts disagree, but after all these years and experiences a good many of them have come to the conclusion that there is only one "magic bullet" that will enable a country to have sustained economic development—that the most important thing a government can do to cause increases in its economy's production capacity, its *aggregate supply*, and its production of goods and services with that capacity, is to make sure that law and order prevails, that its laws, regulations, and bureaucracy give its people the freedom to work as they see fit and employers freedom to invest as they see fit, that contracts and agreements can be enforced, *and that there will be enough customer spending to keep the production capacity fully employed.*

Adequate roads, banks, schools, dams, and utilities certainly help, whether provided by government or private investors or international donors. But in the real world they do not and can not do much for an economy's total or per capita production unless people are actually allowed by their governments to use the services such capital produces to consume and produce as they see fit.

In other words, the rule of law and the freedom of people and employers to reasonably pursue their interests is required if economies are to progress beyond the relatively low level of per capita production (sorry China, India, Iran, Russia, and the IMF and World Bank) that can be achieved by concentrating on improving the lot of its favored few. To get beyond the minimum requires that the country's laws and regulations and opportunities are both reasonable and applied equally and honestly to everyone.

Analysts can google the per capita incomes and income distributions of different nations and get a pretty good idea as to which countries have relatively honest governments and relative free people and which do not and are run for the benefit of a favored few. (The correlation between the prosperity of a country's people and the honesty and competency of its government appears extremely high.)

In essence, allowing people the freedom to work, invest, and produce as they wish under the rule of law, *and* having adequate macroeconomic policies so that there are customers for their products and no inflation to distort economic decisions and destroy wealth, is the best recipe for economic success for every nation. The U.S. is no exception and neither is China, India, Iran, Russia, Japan, Germany, Norway, Sweden, *et al.*

MACROANLYSIS AND THE PROBLEM WITH GOALS

No economy has ever claimed to attain the obviously unattainable goal of producing and distributing enough goods and services to fully satisfy the diverse and often conflicting desires of all its citizens. All its policy makers can ever do, like the mythical Sisyphus, is forever push the boulder of prosperity further up the hill.

But wait. Even if an economy cannot provide all of what everyone wants it can at least provide as much as possible of it. And, with proper policies, it can provide more and more over time. That is what people rightly expect—*more* and the freedom to pursue it. And "more" tends to happen as our population expands, new technologies and products arrive, plant and equipment is accumulated, education improves, the rule of law is strengthened, and favoritism and discriminatory laws and regulations are removed.

More is not guaranteed. Problems can arise to slow or even reverse an economy's march to ever-higher levels of per-capita production. Things can go wrong no matter how free and well-meaning its people and their leaders may be. For example, the United States economy might be humming along and, all of a sudden, consumers decide to save, or be forced to save, more of their incomes and buy less of the goods and services that our employers are prepared to produce. Then employers in general will respond to having less money coming in by producing less and employing fewer workers.

Or foreigners may reduce their purchasing from the economy's employers or engage in activities, such as devaluing their currency, which result in their country's prices being lower which causes the people and businesses in their economy to switch their buying to their own domestically produced products and away from those produced in the United States.

Or taxes may be increased for some real or imagined purpose, such as reducing the deficit, so that would-be buyers in our economy have less money to spend and less incentive to work and produce.

Or the economy's money supply may be expanded too slowly in response to unfounded fears that inflation is coming from too much spending or not realizing that a trade deficit was sending dollars abroad. Then customer spending may be restricted by the absence of money to borrow and the resulting increase in the level of interest rates and the lack of credit.

Or well-meaning presidents and members of Congress may decrease federal expenditures or implement growth-killing regulations to help their cronies and campaign contributors.

Or the stock and mortgage markets might crash due to a sudden increase in housing foreclosures and wipe massive amounts of financial values—thus causing reduced consumer spending and reduced investment spending to buy production capital.

Or bank regulators may, for all the wrong reasons, impose higher reserve and capital requirements on banks at a time when the economy needs the banks to continue making normal levels of loans to consumers and businesses.

All of these things happened to the United States and contributed to the current Great Recession and its unnecessary continuation.

Measuring success and failure.

We all want our economies to be successful so we can prosper in them. But how does an analyst measure an economy's success? Is it when an economy achieves a three percent rate of unemployment or five percent? Is it the absence of any increases in the general level of prices or is an upward drift in prices to reflect changing spending patterns acceptable? Is success collecting more taxes or collecting less? Is success having a balanced budget or a shorter work week? Is success increased total production or is it increased production per capita? Is success having the interest rate commercial banks charge one another to borrow reserves for twenty four hours conform to a target rate that pleases the Federal Reserve because its governors naively believe there is direct linkage between overnight borrowing and total customer spending?

And how is an economy to be made successful?

Should interest rates be pushed down by increasing the money supply to increase spending or should they be pushed up so pension funds can earn more?

Should Social Security spending be cut back so the federal government can spend the money elsewhere or should it be increased so that consumer spending rises?

Should a more equal distribution of income and purchasing power be encouraged or should inequality be encouraged to grow as it has recently been in the United States?

Should the population be encouraged to grow so there will be a higher percentage of people of working age (United States and India) or is it better to have an aging population which doesn't need more roads and parks and schools but may need more medical and retirement services (Japan and China)?

Should more money be spent by the military and less spent for education or the reverse?

Should more money be spent on public education if the same old unqualified teachers work the same old short school years or should it be reduced and channeled to charter schools?

Should money be borrowed or not borrowed to invest in schools, roads, and dams? To cover government deficits so that government spending can continue?

Should the retirement age be raised so that people can work longer or should the retire age be reduced on the theory that it will somehow create jobs for young people?

Should the retirement age be reduced if it means pension costs will go up and the economy's tax collections and production fall?

The possible alternative goals and the ways to measure them and rank them go on and on and on—and every one of them has sincere and well-meaning advocates and lots and lots of other people trying to feather their own nests or some client's. Perhaps that's why the United States has so many lobbyists and they are paid so much.

The basic decisions as to what an economy's goals should be, and how they are to be obtained and their success measured, come in the form of the policies and decisions implemented by an economy's government and its central bank. And in every economy there are inevitably people who are dissatisfied and attempt to have some form of revolution to dispose the decision-makers who are thought to have failed and replace them. In the United States and other actual democracies it is called an honest election and they are regularly scheduled.

Despite all the questions and problems, as will be seen in the chapters that follow, the basic economic goals of full employment, stable prices, economic growth, and reasonable levels of assistance for people in need are attainable, even after a long period of recession, *if pragmatic rational policies are implemented.*

THE USE OF MODELS

Algebraic and graphic models representing the conditions thought to exist in an economy are often used or cited by economists, central banks, journalists, and financial traders in an attempt to analyze the possible effects various laws and policies might have on the economy. They, in essence, chart this and chart that in an effort to foretell the future by looking at the past. And sometimes it works.

Unfortunately, such models are, at best, hugely oversimplified and incomplete representations of the most basic conditions and circumstances that might exist in a complex economy. Indeed, they are inevitably so grossly oversimplified that they can only be used to help understand the most basic of an economy's relationships and policies. It is inevitably an exercise in folly to attempt to use them, no matter how sophisticated they might appear, to attempt predict the future with great specificity.

In essence, *it's hard to predict the economic road ahead by looking in the rear view mirror at the road previously traveled* with its different conditions, different policies, and different decision makers. Looking in the rear view mirror to drive the ever changing economic road ahead works quite well—until the road bends and the economy goes over the cliff and lands in an economic morass of inflation, unemployment, low rates growth, bankruptcies, and deficits.

And the road ahead inevitably bends. It bent for the United States with the arrival of the prolonged Great Recession which began in 2008 and then, due to the total lack of appropriate monetary and other responses, morphed into the second great depression of the modern era.

What analysts and investors need to understand is that policies and decisions based on using an economy's historical experiences may provide "scientifically" accurate guidance to the policy makers so they can proceed confidently—*until something unexpected happens* that isn't reflected in their models (think mortgage meltdown, Greek collapse, and the adoption of new and sillier Federal Reserve and congressional policies). Then the "scientific" analysis may be absolutely useless and lead to actions and policies that make things worse.

Such unexpected events are often called "Black Swan" events by economic analysts and journalists in homage to the fact that for many years scientists wrote explaining why it was genetically impossible that there could ever be black swans—until they were found flying around in Australia.

The inherent difficulties do not, however, mean that economic models are totally useless. To the contrary, in the hands of trained and worldly experts they can be very useful to show the basic conditions and relationships that exist in an economy. They can also be used to show how reliance on a single explanation or a single policy all too often leads to unnecessary economic disasters. One measure of economic expertise is knowing which models and explanations are useful and which are not.

**The multi-market
model in this book.**

The multi-market model in this book was developed in the 1960s at the dawn of macro-pragmatic economics. Today, as then, it introduces and integrates various heretofore unintroduced and unintegrated theories as to how much production *can* occur in a modern economy and how much of that which can be produced *will* actually be produced—aggregate supply and aggregate demand—and what will happen to the economy's general level of prices as a result. Its purpose is twofold:

First, to give analysts and decision makers a *comprehensive framework* with which to understand the basic macroeconomic interrelationships and problems of a modern economy such as that of the United States.

Second, to introduce and explain the many different causes of inflations and recessions, and government deficits—and the many different outcomes that might be associated with the various policies that might be used in an effort to prevent or fight them. These include various explanations and policies that have been ignored to this very day because they do not fit into the simplistic theories and models and explanations that were developed in the years immediately following Keynes.

The goal of the multi-market model is the same as it was in the 1960s when it was first introduced, to help analysts and decision makers understand complex macroeconomic theories and the basic effects of the policies that might be implemented by the federal government and the Federal Reserve. In other words, to take the understanding of the model's users beyond that which can be obtained via the presentation of a few simple graphs and equations.

Working through the multi-market model and its underlying inter-market relationships and analyses is a challenge. But once readers and analysts "get it" they will be light years ahead of their peers in understanding how a complex economy such as that of the United States operates in the real world—and what will tend to happen to its levels of production, employment, prices, interest rates, tax collections, savings, investment spending, and wages if various policies are implemented either individually or simultaneously. They will, in essence, be a step ahead in the game of life no matter where and how they end up playing it. And if they are politicians and central bankers they might even get re-elected or reappointed.

CHAPTER SUMMARY

I. Modern macroeconomics is the area of economics that deals with how an entire economy functions and copes with its major concerns such as inflation, unemployment, growth, and government deficits.

II. The major macroeconomic goals of most countries are full employment, stable prices, and sustained growth.

III. John Maynard Keynes ushered in macroeconomics as a separate area of study in 1936. The field evolved as the neo-classical economists synthesized microeconomics with the initial post-Keynesian analysis. Then the macro-pragmatists broadened the concepts by adding new explanations and theories that were compatible with the complexities of the real world.

IV. The theories and policy suggestions of Keynes and the post-Keynesian economists who followed him are thought by today's macro-pragmatic economists to be applicable and realistic for Britain—but not applicable to the United States when its economy suffers a prolonged recession or depression such as began in 2008.

V. Macroeconomic models can represent the basic macroeconomic relationships of an economy and be useful in demonstrating, at least in very general terms, the likely effects in its interrelated markets of various basic policies and external forces.

VI. Pragmatic analysts understand that economies constantly evolve as new products, employers, technologies, laws, and policies come on line. Economic analysts and technicians typically attempt to understand the past using data from the past.

VII. Because change occurs constantly in every economy, using data and theories and policies from the past to predict and affect the future is like looking in the rear view mirror to drive the road ahead—it works only until the road bends. It bent for the policies of the Keynesian and neo-classical economists with the arrival of the prolonged "Great Recession" which began in 2008 and, due to the lack of appropriate monetary and fiscal policy responses, morphed into the second great depression of the modern era.

CHAPTER TWO

CONSUMER SPENDING

In the real world, an economy's employers, no matter if they are profit-oriented or non-profits or governmental, are only able to hire workers and produce goods and services if they have enough money revenues coming in from their public and private customers to cover their money costs. And without a doubt, consumers are the biggest and most important customers in every economy including the United States.

Consumers spending the money they earn or borrow or are given traditionally buy about sixty percent of all the goods and services produced in the United States. Employers making investment purchases of capital goods, governments, and foreigners buy the rest. In other words, because employers produce in response to customers, the lion's share of employment and production in the United States occurs in response to consumer spending.

Analysts who want the details can google "national income and product accounts" or search Wikipedia to see the numbers and percentages which show the importance of consumer spending in the United States at a particular point in time. Be sure to realize that the numbers may be slightly overstated if they include consumer spending on goods and services produced outside the country. Foreign-made consumer products such as cell phones produced in Finland and automobiles produced in Japan and Mexico are important but their purchase does not directly generate jobs and production in the United State. It may, of course, generate them indirectly if the dollars the foreign sellers receive enables the exporting countries to import American-made goods and services.

But what determines how much each person or family spends on new domestically produced consumer goods and services? That is something analysts, investors, and policy makers need to know because consumer spending is directly and indirectly the principal driver of an economy's prosperity and growth.

Obviously how much consumer spending people do depends on such things as their wealth, their personal incomes, and the amounts of money and credit they are willing and able to borrow. Some consumers may borrow or use their wealth to spend far in excess of their incomes while others may not spend (save) a good part of it in order to increase their wealth or pay down their debts.

How much of their personal incomes each person or household spends on consumer goods and services depends on each individual consumer's *propensity to consume.* That's economist-speak for the relationship between a consumer's personal income and his consumer spending. It is also used to describe the relationship between the total amount of total consumer spending that occurs in an economy and the total income of the economy—the propensity to consume of the economy as a whole.

Various subjective and objective considerations are thought to influence the willingness of each consumer to spend some portion of his personal income on newly produced consumer goods and services such as groceries, housing, movie tickets, drinks, new cars, TV sets, airline tickets, cell phones, restaurant meals, medical services, etc.

The words "newly produced" are important because analysts are particularly interested in spending that will cause our economy's public and private employers to hire workers and produce goods and services. Any use of personal income that a person does not spend in a way that directly results in the employment of workers to produce consumer goods and services is considered to be personal savings—no matter what it is used for.

And yes there are difficulties and complexities inherent in the consumer spending concept. For example, buying a new TV set at Walmart which was built in China is not, totally, a consumption purchase—because the workers who produced it are not located and employed in the United States. On the other hand, the workers who designed the set, unloaded the ship, trucked the set to the store, put it on the shelves, and rang up the sale at the cash register are employed in the U.S and are producing a service for the consumer.

To a modern macroeconomist that portion of the purchase price which was paid to China for producing the set is savings and that portion which is left to pay the local employees and Walmart for putting the deal together and getting the TV set to its buyer is consumer spending.

Savings is the flipside of consumer spending.

Any use of personal income for other than buying new consumer goods and services produced in the person's own economy is considered personal savings. Thus savings occurs when a person holds cash, puts money in the bank, buys a used car, buys a foreign car, invests in stocks and bonds, gives a gift, pays taxes, or tithes a church. In essence, every dollar of personal income is either saved or is spent so something can be consumed. If a dollar of a person's personal income is not spent for a newly produced consumer item it is considered to be saved no matter how it is used. The more a person spends on consumer products the less he saves and the more a person saves the less he consumes.

What this means is that "personal savings" is very, very broadly defined to include any personal income that is not used to buy newly produced consumer goods and services—and thus does not cause workers to be employed and more of such goods and services to be produced. For some examples, a consumer "saves"—does not spend to buy newly produced consumer products—when he buys stocks and bonds, puts money into a bank or under his mattress, buys a car or other equipment for his business (that's an investment), and pays taxes.

Even the purchase of a used car or a new car or something else built overseas is considered "savings" even if it is for personal use—because such purchases do not directly cause the employment of workers and the production of consumer goods and services in the United States.

This is such an important concept to macroeconomics that it bears repeating: any use of a personal income other than buying new consumer goods and services produced in the person's own economy is considered personal savings. Thus savings occurs when a person holds on to some of his income in cash, puts it in the bank, buys a used car, buys a foreign car, invests in stocks and bonds, gives a gift, pays taxes, or gives a donation to the Salvation Army.

In essence, every dollar of personal income is either saved or is spent so something can be consumed. If a dollar of a person's personal income is not spent for a newly produced consumer item it is considered to be saved no matter how it is used. The more a person consumes the less he saves and the more a person saves the less he consumes.

Don't let the nuances be discouraging—the world is complex and the consumer spending that interests analysts for United States policy purposes is that which causes employment and production to occur in the United States. Every other use of our personal incomes is savings no matter what it is used for—because it does not cause employment and production to occur in our economy.

In essence, we are interested in consumer spending because we are interested in our workers, the wages they earn including their benefits, the taxes they and their employers pay, and prices of the goods and services they produce. In other words, *consumers are important because their spending results in production and jobs.*

SUBJECTIVE INFLUENCES

The decisions people make to spend part of their personal incomes on consumer products, such as restaurant meals and medical services, are based on their spending preferences which are influenced by various subjective considerations.

Economists and pundits of all stripes and varieties correctly pay a great deal of attention to consumers and their motivations because of their importance as purchasers whose spending would cause workers to be employed and goods and services to be produced. A number of economists, economic technicians, and social scientists have written at length about consumers' subjective motivations *not* to spend all of their personal incomes. Among those that have been suggested as causing savings to occur instead of consumer spending: precaution, foresight, calculation, and independence.

Savings as a precaution occurs because individuals want to build up a reserve of wealth to protect themselves against unexpected calamities such as unemployment, injury, illness, lawsuits, and divorce. Savings motivated by foresight occurs so individuals will be able to meet future consumption needs after all or part of their personal incomes end—such as upon retirement. Persons who wish to be able to afford even higher levels of consumer spending at some future time may be motivated by calculation to save part of their income by using it to make financial investments. Similarly, an individual may be led to accumulate savings by his desire to have a sense of independence and an ability to make decisions such as taking a trip or changing jobs.

The psychological drives of enterprise, pride, and avarice are also motivations for persons to allocate a portion of their personal incomes to non-consumption uses. Savings might occur, for example, while an individual is acquiring the financial capacity to enter into some speculative or business enterprise. Or pride might cause him to save some of his income so that he would be able to leave an inheritance; or he may simply be a miser and save part of his income for the sake of savings.

Social pressures. Obviously there are other psychological forces that both offset and promote high proportions of savings out of personal incomes. For one thing, individuals may allocate lots of their income to consumption because they feel the desirability and necessity of maintaining their position in society. In other words, they find it necessary to "keep up with the Joneses."

Individuals' psychological motivations for saving part of their income rather than using it for consumer spending may also be influenced by his community's traditional method of evaluating success and worthiness. Consider the United States: on one hand, consumer purchasing tends to be expanded as individuals seek the recognition and esteem some social groups and media give to the owners of fine clothes, fast cars, big houses, and tables at charity events.

On the other hand, other sectors of the United States' society apparently consider saving or thrift to be desirable. For example, in some quarters people are periodically exhorted by some speaker or publication to emulate the early immigrants who supposedly prospered in the "New World" as a result of thriftily leaving a portion of their incomes unconsumed so that other things such as barns could be produced that would generate even bigger incomes for them in the future.

It is hard to believe there will be no effect on the level of consumer spending in the United States if some of its people consider non-consumption (saving) behaviors to be socially "good" and worthy of emulation and the conspicuous consumption of large amounts of goods and services bring raised eyebrows or even open condemnation.

Consumer expectations. Other subjective or psychological factors that can influence consumer spending are the expectations consumers have about their future incomes or the product prices they will face.

For instance, if a consumer expects his income might be lower in the future he may refrain from making purchases today: first, because any indebtedness associated with the purchase will have to be paid back later out of what may be a lower income; second, because he may decide to save today so he can continue making consumption expenditures if his income declines. People who worry that they might lose their jobs are likely to behave in such a manner.

Conversely, an individual such as a recent college graduate who is just beginning permanent employment may expect higher levels of income in the future; thus he or she may go into debt today—borrow money, run up their credit card balances and student loans—in order to enjoy a consumption level that is in excess of their income. They might do so because they feel they not only can continue that level of consumer spending in the future, but also can pay off any debts incurred as a result of temporarily spending more than their present income. (When they pay off their credit cards an student loans they won't be spending to buy consumer goods and services—so they will be saving)

Similar reactions might occur when product prices are expected to change. For example, when prices are expected to fall consumer spending may decline as would-be buyers wait for the lower prices. And the reverse may occur when prices are expected to rise—people may increase their spending as they rush out to buy before the prices go up. (Interestingly, the increased buying that results from expecting higher prices in the future may cause the prices to be immediately bid up and quickly justify the expectation).

Or just the reverse might happen. If consumers expect price increases in the future they may save more today so that they will be able keep buying in the future when the prices are higher. It depends on how people see things. ("It depends" is a phase important to savvy analysts and worldly economists.)

OBJECTIVE INFLUENCES

Various non-psychological items also appear to influence the degree to which people will use their personal incomes for consumption purposes. They are often categorized as "objective factors" since they are more quantifiable than the psychological or subjective factors. The following are among the forces and factors that have been identified as having an effect on individuals' spending to buy consumer items.

Consumer credit. The availability of credit cards and other forms of consumer credit allows an individual to temporarily make purchases exceeding those he could make if only his income is available. To get some idea of the importance of credit to consumer spending, try to imagine the effect of eliminating credit and debt on the sale of new cars or new houses. Purchases of cars and homes could then only be financed out of cash holdings, or by selling other assets, or by saving from disposable incomes until enough money is accumulated to buy the car or home. Would auto and home sales be hurt—absolutely. And that is exactly what happened during the "Great Recession" when the availability of mortgage financing and refinancing all but disappeared.

Consumer purchases on credit often result in interest charges being the largest part of the monthly payments made to service auto, home and credit card loans. It is now generally accepted that consumers pay little or no attention to the interest rate price of the money they borrow and the amount of credit they owe. Instead their chief concern seems to be with the size of the down payment and the size and duration of the monthly payments. That's what counts to consumers and the sellers of new cars and mortgage lenders know it. Analysts can see this for themselves by reading the ads from new car dealers—the payment terms are typically emphasized; the interest rates are not.

Both the general level of interest rates and the spread of interest rates for different types of loans and credit facilities are discussed in detail in the pages ahead. Suffice to say the higher the risk of nonpayment the higher the interest rate the lender must charge to absorb the inevitable losses that will occur as a result of non-payment. For example, auto loans are relatively high risk so their rates are higher because of the high risk premium and the administrative cost of collecting and processing the monthly payments; overnight loans between banks and savings deposits in insured accounts are relatively low risk so their rates are lower.

The lack of emphasis on the importance of the rate of the interest as a determinant of consumer spending (and thus saving) is important to today's pragmatic economists and analysts—because it contrasts directly with the beliefs and theories of early economists and negates most of the policies they prescribe. To this day, as there has been for centuries, there are analysts, journalists, and "business economists" who maintain that the possibility of earning interest by lending their savings to those who wanted to borrow them to invest is the principal reason savings occurs. Their view is that interest rates dominate consumption and savings decisions. They think the higher the rate of interest, the more that savings will occur.

Similarly, to this day the idea that the level of an economy's interest rates is of extreme important remains the view of the majority of the Federal Reserve's governors, particularly those with little or no relevant professional training as economists and no experience in the real world of business and commercial banking. They naively believe that even the most minor changes in the level of interest rates will significantly affect the performance of the United States' real economy of jobs and production.

Business executives, commercial bankers, and informed analysts and investors know better—they accept the level of interest rates in an economy as just one more of many influences that determine the amount of savings, and a minor one at that. Consumers in general, it seems, are not in tune with the lawyers who are today's Federal Reserve governors and most analysts and journalists—many of them want to consume "now" and are more concerned about the size of their monthly payments than the size of their debts and the interest rates they pay.

The Federal Reserve, of course, is the United States' central bank. As shall become increasingly clear, the seven governors who run it, and particularly its chairman, are arguably more important in determining the prosperity and growth of the United States than the President and the Congress combined. In 2011 and 2012, for example, the Federal Reserve made driving down long term interest rates by a few basis points its primary policy to significantly increase spending in the U.S. economy in an effort to overcome the economy's approximately $4 trillion shortfall in total spending.

To put the most charitable light on the results of that particular Federal Reserve policy, it didn't work. Nothing happened. But it did have a significant effect:—waiting in vain for something that would never occur resulted in the Federal Reserve governors not implementing other more realistic policies that might have succeeded in restoring spending to the levels needed for full employment. So the recession and its associated financial and job losses continued to worsen. Unfortunately, as shall be discussed in some detail, the recession continued to worsen until so many people and businesses were ruined that the United States morphed into a permanent depression wherein conventional monetary policies to expand the supply of money and credit could no long elicit sufficient spending.

More about consumer credit. In the United States the biggest household debts include mortgage debt, credit card debt, and student and car loans. Such debts have steadily risen in relation to the disposable income of U.S. Households. They rose from 85% in the 1990s reaching a peak of 130% at the beginning of the "Great Recession" which began in 2008.

Over ten percent of all the disposable income of the people in the United States is used to pay consumer debt. Because it is not spent to buy newly produced goods and services, that debt service is part of peoples' savings and tends to offset the additional consumer spending that might be enabled by new and even greater household debts.

But wait. Perhaps some of the debt service generates jobs and production—another way of looking at the interest portion of the debt service would be to consider some or all of it as the consumers' purchase of financial services produced by the banks and other recipients of the interest rate payments—so consumers can consume sooner and pay later.

The distribution of income. Another determinant of the extent to which an individual will save his disposable income instead of spending it on consumer goods and services is the size of his income.

Every analyst has seen data showing consumers with relatively low incomes spend less to buy consumer goods and services than consumers with relatively high incomes. For example, it is quite believable that people such a bank president in his extensive Scottsdale home spends more on food, cars, travel, housing, and entertainment than does a bank janitor who has to work two jobs to afford his rented apartment in a Phoenix ghetto.

It is also quite believable that if the janitor and bank president both got major increases in their incomes they would both increase their consumption spending. And it is also quite believable that the janitor spends a bigger percentage of his income, say 95 percent of it, on consumption items such as food, housing and gasoline while the bank president spends a lower percentage of consumer items, say 60 percent of it, because he saves a good deal of his income by spending it to buy stocks and bonds and other financial instruments.

If all the above is an accurate representation of the real world, and the data would suggest it is, then redistributing some of the bank president's income to the bank's tellers and janitors would cause consumer spending to rise. That is exactly what President Obama and some congressmen proposed in 2012 when they proposed increasing the tax rates paid by "millionaires" and using the proceeds to fund more government spending. They saw it as a way to increase consumer spending and generate more jobs in an economy which had about twenty percent of its capacity standing idle due to a lack of revenues from customer spending. Nothing came of the proposal.

Other congressmen and politicians saw it differently—they proposed tax reductions that would particularly increase the disposable incomes of the highest income recipients on the premise that their increased prosperity would "trickle down" to everyone else as they spent their additional incomes. Some of them even claimed that cutting taxes on the highest income Americans would somehow encourage them to make investments and expand the economy's production capacity even though the economy had about $4 trillion of idled capacity at the time.

Taking income and wealth away from some people to give to others is a contentious policy and nothing substantial came of the proposal. In any event, as shall be seen in the pages ahead, such a redistribution of income is not necessary to influence total spending; there are other and quicker ways to get more money for consumer spending flowing to our economy's employers and to people with relatively low incomes.

In other words, unless the goal is to change the distribution of income to make it more or less equal there is no need to take money away from one group of people to give it to another group of people. It is better, most pragmatic economists argue, to concentrate on getting a depressed economy going again and keeping it prosperous so that everyone tends to have higher and higher incomes and everyone can consume more and more. It also takes less time and is less contentious. And if reducing income inequality is the goal it can also be attained by increasing the incomes at the lower end faster—such as restoring jobs by getting the economy going again so their incomes come from wages instead of from welfare and unemployment insurance payments.

Personal wealth. Yet another measurable influence on consumer spending and saving, and it appears to be a major factor, is personal wealth. It impacts in several ways. First, instead of buying consumer items people may use their incomes to acquire personal wealth such as bank deposits, stocks, and land. How each person allocates his disposable income depends on his preferences for accumulating wealth for its future use or the additional income it might generate.

Wealth also tends to influence consumer spending once it is acquired. The greater the value of people's wealth the more consumption spending they seem to do. Most studies of family spending patterns suggest that families with larger amounts of wealth spend more for consumption purposes than families with the same income but less wealth. In other words, wealthy people buy more consumer goods and services than people who are less wealthy.

Perhaps wealth has such an effect because people with relatively large amounts of wealth feel they are closer to having enough purchasing power to meet their future needs—so they do not feel under as much pressure to restrict their consumption spending (save) to build up more wealth. That seems to be particularly true when the wealth consists of liquid assets—the financial assets such as money, stocks, bonds, and anything else a person can quickly convert to cash and use to meet emergencies or take advantage of any good deals that come along or maintain their standard of living even if their incomes fall.

Consumer spending is also affected by people changing their view of wealth. This occurs when the value of their wealth changes or when people reevaluate their need for wealth-provided incomes or for a reservoir of purchasing power. This has happened in the United States on a massive scale at times. For instance, during certain wars patriotism and the lack of consumer goods and service to buy caused people to save relatively large portions of their disposable incomes in the form of money and war bonds. Then, after the war ends, the situation is reversed—many people spend their accumulated savings to buy the consumer goods and services they had foregone during the war years.

A similar change appears to have occurred in the propensity to consume in the United States with the arrival of Medicare which reduced the need for people to accumulate liquid assets to pay for medical services after retirement. In essence, the passage of Medicare caused a permanent increase in consumer spending as the nation's citizens began buying such things as cruises, new cars, and better food and clothing with the money they would previously have held for post-retirement medical services.

Another such change started in 2008 with the collapse of the housing market and the subsequent "Great Recession" and the accompanying massive rise in unemployment, bankruptcies, foreclosures, and business and bank failures. Consumer spending fell as the population became increasingly aware that the federal government and Federal Reserve would concentrate many hundreds of billions of dollars on helping their "favored few," such as Goldman Sachs, General Motors, and Fannie Mae, and do little, if anything, to restore the overall economy to full employment.

More specifically, starting in 2008 the propensity of Americans to make consumer purchases plummeted as they began desperately saving money and foregoing consumer purchases of such things as new cars and better housing. Many Americans apparently behaved in such a manner so they would have the means of survival if they lost their jobs and/or the incomes that previously been generated by their financial assets and businesses. As analysts might imagine, the resulting decline in consumer spending as consumers acted to protect themselves resulted in even more layoffs and business and bank failures as jobs and incomes declined further.

That the federal government and Federal Reserve failed to act adequately during the "Great Recession" is self-evident in that unemployment rose to levels not seen since the Great Depression of the 1930s, banks and businesses failed, tax receipts plummeted and resulted in budget deficits as welfare-related spending skyrocketed, the stock market crashed, and the propensity to consume declined.

In the 1930s the huge decline in the stock and bond markets significantly reduced the nominal wealth of Americans and contributed to a reduction in both their consumer spending and the ability of employers to issue new stocks and bonds.

In contrast, in 2008 the financial markets did not crash. They did not crash because the Federal Reserve adopted various policies to encourage the maintenance of high prices for financial assets in order to help the too-big-to-fail financial traders from having to sell at a loss. Unfortunately, much of the money the Federal Reserved caused to flow into the purchase of financial assets was obtained by diverting it from commercial bank loans to consumers and employers. It primarily did so by various programs that effectively encouraged the banks to make easy-to-liquidate short term loans to the financial community instead of their traditional longer term and harder-to-liquidate loans to consumers and employers.

The tragedy of it all is that appropriate macroeconomic policies could have prevented the 2008 recession from happening and quickly ended it once it did happen. Had our congressmen, Federal Reserve governors, and the "business economists" and journalists who influence them, known what pragmatic analysts know, the "Great Recession" and the depression that followed probably would not have happened. And, if it had started, it would have been quickly ended. Hopefully those who understand the concepts and policies of "pragmatic economics" will take their place and begin to do the right thing.

Transfers. There are many alternative reasons for saving besides accumulating wealth—for example, a person might "save" (not buy new consumer items) by using some of his income to buy a used car or buy stocks and bonds or give money as a personal transfer to a church or school or to someone such as a needy student or unemployed neighbor.

"Transfer," of course, is economist-speak for when a person or organization or employer or financial institution is given unearned income without having produced goods and services to earn it. Welfare recipients get transfers; so do investment banks, derivative traders, and other gamblers if they are "bailed out" when their gambles go wrong.

The stock of durable consumer goods. Another factor influencing consumer spending is the existing stock of durable consumer goods such as cars, TV sets, cell phones, and computers. Its effect goes in two directions and they tend to offset each other. On one hand, the bigger and newer the stock of durable goods the less pressure there is on a consumer to buy more. For example, a person with a relatively new refrigerator or computer or car is less likely to buy another compared to someone who has no refrigerator or computer or car, or has an older and less useful model.

On the other hand, having a large stock of consumer durables encourages increased consumer spending on nondurable consumer items—the presence of a car and computer, for example, encourages the purchase of gasoline and electricity and computer apps. These are consumer products that would not be bought if the car and computer did not exist.

Taxes, gifts, and mandatory pension contributions. Taxes certainly affect the amount of money spent by consumers. You cannot, after all, spend or save your income if a government takes it. It goes without saying that people in countries such as the United States pay numerous and large amounts of taxes—income taxes, property taxes, social security taxes, sales taxes, and many others. Money collected from people in taxes is considered to be part of their personal savings because it is not available to be spent on consumer goods. (Many economists prefer to identify taxes as forced savings or government savings.)

Yes, some of the money people pay in taxes may end up being used to purchase goods and services such as new roads, new tanks, military activities, education, and law and order. When and if that spending happens it will cause production and employment to occur and be counted—but not until it is actually spent to buy things or is transferred to consumers and they actually buy things. Government taxes, spending programs, Social Security and other transfer programs, and budgets and their deficits are considered in the chapters that follow. They and the conditions and policies affecting them are examined in detail because of their real and alleged impacts on production and employment.

Similarly, many public and private employers have pension plans that allow or require their employees to contribute part of their incomes to private pension programs such as 401K plans. Since that portion of people's personal incomes so contributed is not used for consumer spending it too is considered savings. If and when the pension programs subsequently send money to people it will become part of their consumer spending only if and when and they actually use it to buy consumer goods and services. Only then will it be counted as part of an economy's consumer spending. Once again—until money and income is actually spent to buy consumer goods and services it is considered to be saved.

The same reasoning applies to a person's income that is deposited in banks or invested in securities or given as monetary gifts and charitable donations—all income that for any reason is not used to buy new American-made consumer goods and services is considered to be saved until it is actually spent to buy new consumer goods and services produced in the United States economy.

Splitting hairs. There are always gray areas and that is why it is so hard to use economic models to make precise predictions. For example, some economists might consider a donation to a church as a gift and thus part of a person's savings. Others might say it is the purchase of the services the church is producing. Analysts should not let this ambiguity throw them for a loss. What counts is that, no matter how it is measured and counted, consumer spending is darn important to an economy's employment and prosperity.

In summary, analysts know that there are a lot more factors and forces than just interest rates that affect consumer spending and savings. In other words, interest rates do *not* have a particularly significant impact on the amount of saving. The relative insignificance of interest rates is an important concept. Why this reality is important for decision makers to understand will become increasingly clear.

CONSUMER SAVING AND TOTAL SAVING

In the United States not all the dollars spent (by consumers, investors, governments and foreigners) find their way back to potential consumers so they can be spent again to buy more consumer items. Savings occurs all along the way as the money spent to buy goods and services moves to the public and private employers that produce them and then is passed back to potential consumers in the form of wages and other sources of personal incomes.

Employers are big savers. They tend to hold back a portion of every dollar they receive so they can do such things as replace and expand their capital equipment, build up supplies of cash and liquid assets so they have readily available funds, distribute profits to their owners, and pay interest on their bank loans.

Governments are similarly big savers. Their taxes divert another chunk of the money away from consumers to spend —so that governments can buy things such as education and road repairs and transfer money to their beneficiaries such as welfare payments, Social Security retirement benefits, and bailouts for needy investment bankers.

Only what's left over, not saved along the way, gets back to the American people as wages and dividends to be part of their personal incomes along with any earnings from their wealth and any gifts and other transfer payments they might receive. This is the personal income that the American people can either save or use to buy consumer goods and services.

Some of the personal income people receive is also saved. It is certainly saved (not spent) if people pay income taxes so they can't spend it. What's left after paying the taxes is the people's disposable income—the money they can either save or spend. People also save some of the disposable income they receive when they spend it on foreign made consumer goods and services. They save a big chunk of it by buying things such as Volkswagen cars produced outside the United States, French wines, and Chinese-made TV sets. (these are all considered savings because they does not cause production and jobs in the United States).

In the end, only about five percent of the American people's disposable income is devoted to the traditional types of savings most people think of—depositing the money in a bank or buying stocks, bonds, and insurance policies.

Who are the spenders?

In the very roundest of ever-changing numbers: About 10 percent of all American consumer, business, and government spending goes to buy foreign-made goods and services (foreigners, in turn, buy about 8% of what American employers produce); about 5 percent of all spending to buy goods and services is done by the federal government; 10 percent by the state and local governments; and 10 percent by private businesses making investment purchases of new and replacement capital goods and inventories. Consumers buy about 65 percent. Little wonder "the consumer is king" is an oft-used phrase in the American business community and by journalists.

The other major spenders—governments, foreigners, and employers making investment purchases of plant, equipment and inventory, are examined in some detail in the pages ahead. Pragmatic analysts, investors, and policy makers pay particular attention to consumer spending because it is so important.

In the United States only about sixty five percent of each dollar spent to buy American-made goods and services finds its way back to the

American people to be spent on consumer goods and services. The other thirty five cents is saved here and there along the way.

More on the spending and saving process.

Customer spending that flows money to America's public and private employers to buy newly produced goods and services is the key to America's production and employment. The country's jobs and production could not occur without the money such spending brings to its employers. The employers then pass a substantial portion of their revenues on to people as wages in payment for their labor and other contributions. Other monies from the revenues go to people as dividends, rents, and the distribution of profits. The balance of the monies the employers receive are retained for the employers' future uses or paid to the government in taxes and fees.

The money the country's public and private employers pass on to their employees and other people becomes, in turn, a major part of people's disposable income. The cycle then starts again when the people spend their disposable income to buy consumer goods and services and employers, governments, and foreigners again add their buying to the total.

The total amount of money consumers and other customers spend is the total value of a nation's production, its Gross Domestic Product (GDP) or Gross National Product (GNP). Analysts know that it is the value of the economy's production because that is what the customers of its employers are willing to pay for the goods and services they buy.

The total amount of money received by the nation's employers is the nation's National Income. In essence, GDP, GNP and National Income are conceptually equal because what the buyers spend is what the employers receive. For simplicities sake analysts frequently refer to this as the economy's "level of income" or "total spending." More spending will cause an economy's level of income to rise and less spending will cause it to fall.

GDP and GNP are ever so slightly different because GDP includes the buying of foreign made consumer goods and services as part of consumer spending and GNP does not. In other words, GDP looks at spending from the buyers' point of view and GNP looks at spending from the employer's point of view.

For example, if newly produced goods and services worth $25 trillion are purchased each year from United States' employers, the country's GNP is $25 trillion and its National Income is $25 trillion. In economist-speak the $25 trillion is the economy's "level of income" or its "total spending."

Most governments and central banks, including the Federal Reserve, try to get a handle on how their economy is performing by trying to find out both how much spenders are spending (gross domestic product) and how much their employers are receiving (gross national product). The data collection procedures are good but not perfect. So the numbers inevitably differ even though they would not differ in a perfect world with perfect knowledge. But no need to get excited because they differ—it's the concept that total spending is important that counts.

Analysts and investors can Google "National Income Accounts" or look on Wikipedia to find out what actually happened in a particular month or year and see the torturous adjustments that hundreds of federal employees make so our governmental and Federal Reserve policy-makers can have precise information to guide their decisions. The numbers are important and useful—and, as analysts shall see, effectively ignored by most of the United States' policy makers due to their lack of appropriate economic educations and their lack of real world experience in business and commercial banking.

The marginal and average propensities to consume. The addition to consumer spending that occurs as an economy's income increases is the marginal propensity to consume. For example, if for some reason total spending in the United States rises $100 billion and the additional wages and income people receive as a result that increased spending results in

$60 billion more of consumer spending, the marginal propensity to consume is 60 percent.

This would happen as follows: total spending to buy goods and services increases by $100 billion for some reason. The economy's employers receive the $100 billion and pay some of it to their workers and to other people such as their shareholders. That increases their disposable incomes enough so that they, in turn, will spend an additional $60 billion on consumer goods and services.

The marginal propensity to consume of an economy is important to know. It shows how a policy or event that somehow stimulates an initial increase in spending can generate even more spending as the employers pass some of the additional money they receive on to their employees and others in the form of wages and other incomes. Then the employees and other recipients will have higher levels of disposable income and spend more on consumer items—so the total level of spending will rise further. And that additional spending would tend to put even more people back to work if there is unemployment in the economy.

In this example the initial addition of $100 billion of spending will result in an additional $60 billion of consumer spending. But the spending increases won't stop there—the employers getting the additional $60 billion of revenues will, in turn, pass some it on to their employees and owners so that they will be able to do even more consumer spending. In this example economy, the spending and re-spending and re-spending of the initial $100 billion will cause consumer spending to rise by another $150 billion. In other words, the initial spending stimulus of $100 billion is part of, and causes, a $250 billion increase in total spending. Economists call this the "multiplier effect" of an initial spending increase. In this example the multiplier is 2.5.

Moreover, the impact of the initial stimulus will also cause other types of spending to grow. For instance, it might encourages more investment spending if the economy's public and private employers buy plant and equipment to produce the additional $250 billion of products customers now want to buy. If it caused $50 billion of additional investment spending, then total spending would rise to $300 billion. In this case the multiplier is 3.0.

For example, some of the previous increase in consumption spending may be to buy new Ford cars. Then the Ford Motor Company may respond with investment purchasing to buy factories and equipment to replace those worn out so that it can continue to produce cars in the years ahead. Thus total spending will increase and increase until it reaches a new and higher level of total spending—all from the initial $100 billion stimulus. In this example, the initial increase has a multiplier effect on total spending of three times the original increase. The multiplier for an initial spending change in this economy is three.

Consumer spending and savings in relation to GDP and National Income.

The discussion so far has related the levels of consumer spending and savings to the disposable income received by an economy's people. Since the disposable income of the United States is directly related to the money its public and private employers receive—it is also possible directly relate to a nation's consumer spending and savings to the nation's total spending (GDP) or total income. (National Income).

Look at it this way: customer spending goes to the economy's public and private employers. The employers get the money because they are producing the goods and services that are being bought. So what do the employers do with all that money? Obviously a big part of it gets cycled right back to people when it is used pay such things as wages and dividends. But not all of it gets returned to people so they can again decide whether to save or spend it—because some of the money the employers receive from their customers is held back for one reason or another. These "held back" monies are also a form of savings in that they too cannot be spent for consumption purposes—because they are not available.

The "held back" monies are "employer savings" such as retained earnings and "government savings" in the form of the taxes paid by the employers. They join people's "personal savings" to give us the total savings that will occur in an economy at each level of total customer spending.

Here's an example: America's consumers spend $25 trillion and its other customers spend $15 trillion so that a total of $40 trillion dollars this year to buy goods and services produced by the America's employers. The employers then send $30 trillion back to the people in the form of wages and dividends; the employers hold on to $3 trillion so they can buy more capital goods in the future; and they send $7 trillion to the government for taxes.

Now assume that the next time around the American people will spend $21 trillion of the $30 trillion they receive on consumer products and save $9 trillion. These are important facts for analysts and decision makers to know because they mean that America's economy will have to have $19 trillion of investment, government, and foreign spending if it is to again have $40 trillion of total spending the next time around—and more than $19 trillion if the economy has grown so that it now needs an even higher level of spending to keep its labor force fully employed.

Employer savings. This is the money spent by customers that public and private employers do not pass back to consumers in the form of spendable wages, dividends, tax rebates, etc. "Employer savings" occur when employers hold back money for such things as unpaid wages, retained earnings, and depreciation. They are all part of the employer savings which tend to make the disposable incomes of an economy's people smaller than the amount of revenues the employers receive: it represents the money spent by customers that is not passed back by the employer-producers as wages and dividends and bond interest payments to become the disposable income of the people in the economy.

In essence, the more an economy's public and private employers hold on to the revenues they receive from the economy's purchasers (consumers, investors, foreigners, and governments) instead of passing them on to people to spend, the lower the people's disposable income and consumer spending there will be at each level of national income that might occur.

The complexities of a
dynamic economy.

Decision making can be complex for analysts, investors and policy makers. Consider the following real life example from the United States during the Great Recession which started in 2008: there was an encouraging report in the Wall Street Journal from the producers of consumer goods that they had experienced a 3 percent increase in purchases by retailers. The article's author hailed this as an indication the economy was finally turning around and that a further stimulus of some kind might not be necessary.

But wait. At the same time the retailers reported less than a one percent increase in retail sales to consumers. In other words most of the buying that occurred was for goods that were added to the retailers' inventories—they were investment purchases by the retailers to build up their inventories, not consumer purchases.

Note also that in the real world the retailers either had to borrow the money they used to build up their inventories or they used money they had held back instead of passing it on to people as wages and other forms of personal income. In effect, when they held back money and used it to build up their inventories the retailers were engaged in business saving and using the money to invest in larger inventories. This is a normal activity in a complex economy such as the United States.

What is important in this article is that consumer spending did not increase by much. The article got it wrong. The data did not suggest a recovery might have started and, thus, it did not suggest that no additional stimulus was needed. To the contrary, consumer and other spending in an economy such as that of the United States typically has to increase five or six percent each year just to keep its ever-growing and ever-more-productive work force employed. A mere one percent increase in consumer spending is a disaster.

One percent is a disaster because it means the recession was getting worse, that the economy was slipping further and further away from having enough consumer and other spending to generate full employment. In other words the journalist and the paper's editor did not know enough about economics and the real world. They got the story all wrong.

Now assume that you are a congressman or one of the traditional political and academic placeholders that Presidents have appointed as a Treasury Secretary or Federal Reserve governor. Here is a story in a reputable paper that is backed up by facts that suggest the economy is in good shape. Unless you are knowledgeable about macroeconomics and the real world you are likely to traipse off and make speeches about how the economy has finally started to turn the corner instead of taking steps to get the economy going again.

This is exactly what happened throughout the Great Recession that started in 2008—almost every month consumer and other spending, if it grew at all, grew slower than the growth of economy's labor force and production capacity; and almost every month for years journalists, business economists, and Federal Reserve Governors seized on one irrelevant fact or another and cheerful stories were written and speeches given about the latest evidence the recession had ended and the economy was finally turning around.

In fact, month after month and year after year the economy was actually getting worse and worse and worse as production and employment continued to recede further and further below the economy's capacity to produce goods and services and provide jobs. After five years of claiming the recession had finally ended and its journalists and policy makers periodically seeing "light at the end of the tunnel," the United States had five million fewer jobs, its working age population had increased by millions of people, and so many people, businesses, and banks had been wiped out financially that conventional monetary policies would no longer work even if they had finally begun. On the other hand, the stories were well punctuated and some of the speeches were entertaining.

Government savings. This is economist-speak for taxes. In essence, the more taxes governments collect from employers the less the employers have that they can pass back to their employees and owners and other would-be consumers in the form of wages, interest, profit distributions, gifts, and dividends. Similarly, the more governments collect in taxes from the personal incomes of their people the smaller their disposable incomes.

The descriptions are short but the impact of taxes is significant—more government taxes mean smaller disposable incomes for customers to spend. But if total spending is already inadequate to generate full employment, the lower spending that occurs as a result of more taxes being collected means even less production, even more unemployment, and even smaller tax collections and more welfare for the unemployed and, thus, bigger deficits.

The possibility that higher tax rates for the purpose of reducing deficits will actually make the deficits worse is a concept that often escapes politicians and central bankers. The impact of taxes and other fiscal activities on total spending and governmental budgets in the real world will be considered in detail in the chapters that follow.

Public and private transfers. Consumers often get money from other sources in addition to that which is earned as wages and by their assets. This includes the gifts and charitable donations they receive and the pensions they get from businesses and governments. Since this is income that is not earned in the production process it is typically referred to as unearned income. Obviously the receipt of such money increases the recipients' disposable incomes and, thus, affects their consumption spending.

Transfers to people include such things as welfare payments, tax rebates, public and private pensions, the money you drop in a panhandler's cup, the money you send to your children, housing and rent subsidies, and social security payments. They all increase the recipients' disposable incomes and encourage consumption spending. In other words, transfers have exactly the opposite effect of taxes.

Businesses, banks, and foreigners also receive unearned income in the form of transfers. For instance, in response to the United States' "Great

Recession" that started in 2008, $200 was given to each Social Security recipient and many hundreds of billions of dollars of transfers went to each of a handful of to-big-to-fail American and foreign financial institutions to "bail them out" of their gambling losses on derivatives. It enabled them to pay the multi-million dollar bonuses which their trading and gambling employees and their managers claimed to have "earned" from the specific trades and gambles that "won" among their general multitude of losses.

The great mass of America's people, businesses and commercial banks, on the other hand, were virtually ignored. As a result, due to the lack of sufficient consumer and other spending caused by a host of policy failures, including the inadequate size and misdirection of the transfers, the economy sank into the worst recession in years—and then morphed into a serious depression and remained there for many more years.

Taken together, the many types of transfers to people, businesses, and political contributors are a significant part of the disposable incomes of America's people. Many of the people receiving such transfers, such as Social Security recipients, tend to have relatively high propensities to consume because they have relatively low incomes and need to spend everything they receive just to get by.

Such difference in propensities to consume has important policy implications. It suggests, for example, that increasing Social Security benefits to get spending in the economy going again may result in more of a spending increase than if the money is given via subsidies and tax breaks to the high-income people and the traders of investment banks who are less likely to buy new goods and services with it. It is a policy implication that America's decision makers apparently either did not understand or chose to ignore during the recession that started in 2008.

Consumer spending changes and the speed at which they will occur.

How much consumer spending will occur in an economy at a particular level of income is important. It is important because it tells policy makers how much other spending (from investors, governments and foreigners) is needed to move the economy to another level of income and spending. Policy makers also need to know how fast consumer spending will adjust so they can know how soon they must take steps to encourage spending to increase or decrease.

In essence, there may be delays before consumer spending adapts to a new level of income and everything in the economy settles down and stops changing. (Economist-speak for "everything settles down and stops changing" is "equilibrium.")

Economies in the real world, even in the most economically stagnant countries, never actually reach equilibrium because so many things are constantly changing; but they do constantly move towards it as the economy's public and private employers and its consumers and other buyers and governments continually adjust to their ever changing circumstances.

Also important for the policy makers to know is how fast consumer spending will change if there is a change in total customer spending. For instance, will it take many months or just a few days for a particular policy designed to increase total spending to work its way through an economy and get back to people to affect consumer spending? In other words, how long will it take before our policy makers know they have over-reacted and done too much or under-reacted and done too little.

More specifically, how fast and how much will consumer spending fall if an economy starts into a recession and people's personal incomes begin to decline? And how fast and how much will consumer spending rise if an economy comes out of a recession so that people's personal incomes begin to rise?

Analysts and investors looking at the United States economy have a pretty good idea where consumer spending will end up for each level of income (consumer spending has remained stable at about 70 percent of all spending in the United States if you include foreign-made consumer items). But there may be delays in getting there when something changes.

Consider what might happen if a reduction in foreign or government spending causes total spending to fall so that the economy moves into a recession. At first, people whose personal incomes drop because they are laid off or their dividends are reduced may attempt to maintain their previous levels in order to maintain their traditional lifestyles.

If that's the case, consumer spending in the economy will not immediately fall and its decline to its new and lower equilibrium level of will take a while. Thus, for another example, if investment spending to buy new plant and equipment were to suddenly collapse because of a spurt of new anti-business regulations, the full effect of the new regulations on consumer spending (and other spending) might not be felt for some time.

Or go the other way and consider what might happen if something happens to cause total spending to increase so that employers sales and production boom. The employers receiving the additional business may not immediately pass on their higher revenues to people to spend—they may, for example, have more revenues and higher profits but not immediately increase their dividend payments or begin paying higher salaries and hiring more employees

In essence, if employer revenues increase employers may save the additional money by doing something with it other than passing it on to people as personal income. And when the employers finally do begin distributing their additional revenues, the people getting them may initially also save the additional money and continue to consume at their old levels until they can adjust their mode of living to their new and higher levels of disposable income.

What all this suggests is that an economy's consumer spending may be slow to adjust when production and employment in the economy changes. This is important because failing to understand that more changes are coming may cause policy makers to tread too cautiously in response to a developing recession or inflation.

Short run and long run changes
in total consumer spending.

Consider a $20 trillion economy wherein consumer spending normally contributes seventy five percent of all spending and the spending contributed by other buyers is stable at twenty five percent. What will happen in this economy if there is suddenly a $500 billion increase in the foreign or government buying of goods and services?

In this particular economy total spending will initially rise to $20.5 trillion as the additional $500 billion is added to the initial $20 trillion of spending—but then total spending will keep rising higher and higher as more and more the money received by employers is passed on to people so they have higher personal income and increase their spending for consumer items.

More specifically, in this example, consumer spending will keep increasing until the economy settles down (reaches equilibrium) at $22 trillion of which $16.5 trillion is consumer spending. In other words, adding a permanent increase of $500 billion of additional spending to this $20 trillion economy will drive its total spending all the way up to $22 trillion billion as it causes more and more consumer spending. Analysts can work through it and see for themselves.

But how long will it take for the economy to reach its new equilibrium destination at $22 trillion? In other words, how long is the short-run during which the economy's spending will still be moving towards $22 trillion? A month? Six months? A year? In the real world how long it takes an economy to adjust to a spending stimulus depends on the nature of the initial stimulus spending—which buyers and employers get the money and how soon they spend it or pass it on as wages and other payments so peoples' spending on consumer goods and services can increase.

Sooner or later an economy receiving a spending stimulus will work through all the delays and reach whatever is the normal relationship between consumer spending and the economy's income. In this example "normal" is when consumer spending is again equal to 75 percent of the economy's total spending and the economy is at a new and higher equilibrium level of total spending of $22 trillion.

In the real world perhaps the best we can do to describe the relationship between consumer spending and savings and an economy's level of income is: if the level of spending and income in an economy increases both its consumer spending and savings will increase; if the level of income decreases consumer spending and savings will decrease.

THE SIGNIFICANCE OF A DECLINING MARGINAL PROPENSITY TO CONSUME

Is it possible that the marginal propensity to consume of an economy will decline as the level of its personal income gets higher and higher? After all, as an economy's per capita income grows and its residents acquire more and more consumer goods they might be under less and less pressure to buy more.

Consider an economy in which the average family already has two cars, a refrigerator, and four computers. If the family's disposable income doubles over time will the average family increase their consumption spending so they have four cars, two refrigerators, and eight computers? Maybe not. Perhaps as their disposable income increases they will devote higher and higher percentages of it to the purchase of financial instruments such as stocks and bonds and bank CDs.

A declining marginal propensity to consume for an economy as a whole, if it exists, is quite important. It means consumer spending will become less and less important as an economy's income grows higher and higher. And that means that some other type of spending will increasingly have to take up the slack if an economy's total spending is to continue to grow. And total spending must grow if the economy is to maintain full employment in the face of a capacity to produce that inexorably continues to grow. And grow its capacity does as a result of new technologies, sex and immigration resulting in an ever larger labor force, and the accumulation of more and more capital as a result of more and more investment spending.

Policy makers have at times been concerned with the possibility that consumer spending will decline in importance as an economy's income gets higher and higher. In other words, that there will be a declining marginal propensity to consume. After all, once each person in any economy buys one car, food for three meals, one TV and one cell phone they may not buy six meals and a second car, a second TV set and a second cell phone if the level of income in their economy doubles. And if it doubles again will each consumer buy twelve meals, four cars, four TVs and four cell phones? Not likely. They may instead buy stocks and bonds or they may give more gifts to their children and charities. In other words, they may save instead of spend.

The policy implications. It is an obvious truth that if there is less and less additional consumer spending as an economy's income grows higher and higher there will have to be more and more investment or foreign or government spending to take up the slack if the economy's total production, jobs, and the level of income are to continue to grow.

In the late 1930s this was thought to be the case. Various economists and politicians used the suggestion of a declining marginal propensity to consume to explain the need to constantly expand the "New Deal" government spending programs that arose in the United States in response to the "Great Depression" of the 1930s. They reasoned that for the United States to maintain full employment as its production capacity continued to grow, government spending would have to continually grow relative to total spending to offset the decline in consumer spending.

In essence, they concluded that that role of government was destined to increase in the years ahead because the economy's employers would have to produce relatively more for governments and the governments' transfer beneficiaries because they would be producing relatively less for consumers.

Concerns about a declining marginal propensity to consume appear unwarranted.

The fears of the early macroeconomists have, so far at least, turned out to be unwarranted for the United States and other relatively high income economies. Consumer spending as a percentage of income in the United States has remained remarkably stable as the economy grew in both per capita and total production. In other words, so far there appears to be no need for government spending to increase in importance relative to the other sectors of the economy. This is suggested by data which shows that actual consumption has remained remarkably stable over the years in relation to the United States' constantly growing GNP. How can that be?

Delays and offsets. One possible explanation is that things have changed over the past years that offset and delayed the need for government spending to grow in importance relative to consumer and other spending. These, it has been suggested, have offset the decline in the United States' marginal propensity to consume that might have otherwise occurred. Among those that have been suggested for the United States:

1. Credit expansion: An increase in the availability of consumer credit allowed people to make consumer purchases in excess of their personal incomes.

2. More wealth: People in the United States accumulated wealth as their incomes grew and so did not need to save as much to meet their wealth-related goals.

3. Age composition: The proportion of relatively high-saving working age adult in the population declined as medical advances increased life expectancy.

4. New goods and services: Higher propensities of consumer purchasing may have been induced by the introduction of new goods and services such organ transplants, heart stents,

computer apps and digital services, new automobile models, and ever more inclusive cell phones.

5. Structural changes: The proportion of people in traditionally high-savings occupations such as farming declined.

6. Social insurance: The arrival and expansion of programs such as Social Security, unemployment insurance, welfare and food stamps, and Medicare removed some of the incentives to save in preparation for nonproductive retirement years.

7. Migration: Families moved from the high-saving rural sector of the economy to the relatively low-saving urban sector.

8. Income distribution: there was a move towards a more equal income distribution. The proportion of income going to the high-saving relatively rich declined. This trend may have turned around in the past few years as recent tax cuts, regulatory lapses, and financial aid programs in the past decade appear to have favored people with higher incomes and more wealth.

9. Luxuries became necessities: the levels of purchasing required to support a minimum standard of living rose as such things as cell phones, computers, and automobiles moved from a luxury class to a necessity class.

Relative Income and Social Pressures. If the "temporary delays" analysis is correct and there is an ever-declining propensity to consume as the United States' economy grows, then either more of such changes will have to occur in the future or something else such as increased government spending will be required to keep the nation's level of income growing.

Some economists disagree. They say that such changes are not significant because changes in an economy's absolute level of income are not significant. They see a constancy of social pressures that will keep consumer spending stable so that government spending need not grow in importance.

Social pressures make an economy's absolute level of income irrelevant because at every dollar level of income to which the economy might grow, no matter how high, there will always be people who are relatively poor and people who are relatively rich. And it is where the income of each person is in relation to the income of the other people that determines the various individual propensities to consume and save that add up to the economy's total propensity to consume and save at every level of income. In essence, it is a person's relative income, where he stands in his economy's overall income distribution, which determines the percentage of his income that will be devoted to consumer spending.

According to the relative income explanation of consumer spending, the propensity to engage in consumer spending depends on each person's relative income which is always constant rather of the economy's actual level of income which can increase or decrease. An economy's propensity to consume is always constant because there are always the "relatively" rich and the "relatively" poor no matter what happens to the absolute level of income.

In other words, people in an economy's various different income classes always tend to spend the same proportion of their personal incomes because they are always under the same permanent pressure to maintain or advance their "relative" position in society.

The reason relatively poor people and the members of other income classes tend to permanently use the same proportion of their incomes for consumption is that they are always seeing "all those good things that money can buy" being demonstrated to them by people whose incomes are higher. So they always feel the same degree of desire for the relatively good things in life and the same degree of social inferiority no matter what their absolute level of income. After all, the goods and services they are able to obtain with their absolute incomes are always accepted by society as relatively inferior in quality and quantity when compared to those consumed by the relatively rich in the higher income classes.

In essence, the constantly present social inferiority caused by having relatively low incomes, along with the constant desire to overcome the inferior social positions they provide, leads the individuals in all but the very top income classes to use a greater proportion of their incomes for consumer spending than the relatively rich who are not under such pressures.

Consider, for example, what would happen if the national income of the United States doubled and incomes of all the people in the United States doubled. No matter who gets the additional income there would still be the relatively rich and the relatively poor. And each person knows which group he is in and sees the consumption of the other groups (their bigger houses, nicer cars, the pricier restaurants they frequent, etc.)

According to this theory, the propensity to consume of an economy tends to remain the same as the general level of income increases because there are always the relatively rich and the relatively poor and the pressure on them never changes. The overall propensity to consume for the economy is permanent because the social pressures always remain on each class remain the same even if the members of each income class change as some people rise and some people fall.

In essence, no matter which people are in each income class its members are under that class's pressures to consume. In other words, the propensity to consume is constant and permanent because the pressures for consumption are constant and permanent.

The life-cycle explanations of the stable relationship.

People settle into occupations and incomes that go with them. Thus, according to the life-cycle explanation of the stable relationship between consumer spending and total income, people settle into the consumption and standard of living that goes with their occupation and the income and spending that tends to be associated with it. It becomes their "permanent" or "normal" way of life. And they save because they want to maintain their customary lifestyles even when they are not earning incomes for reasons such as retirement or unemployment or illness.

Accordingly, because each household is under the same pressures to spend so that it can maintain its lifestyle throughout its lifecycle, each household tends to save the same percentage of its income so as to accumulate the wealth needed to continue its normal or permanent life-style when there is no income such is the case with unemployment or retirement.

It is true that in subsequent years there will be people entering and leaving the population and incomes may be generally higher. But they will all continue to be under the same pressure to save in order to maintain their customary permanent lifestyles. In the United States, it is explained, that tends to always require people to always save about fifteen percent of their personal income and only devote 85 percent to consumption.

In essence, the life-cycle theories of consumer spending hold that people's propensity to consume remains stable over years because every household in the economy always tends to save the same percentage of their personal income—because everyone at all times is under the same pressures to save since people at every level of income tend to work and live the same number of years and they all want to continue their "customary and permanent" lifestyles after retirement.

The budget studies.

Does a person's income relative to other people's incomes or life-cycle and living standard related permanent income determine how much he spends on consumer goods and services? And does it even matter?

The economic analysts who hold that people tend to save the same percentage of their normal or permanent incomes all have to have their various theories fit the same data—the set of facts provided by budget studies.

Budget studies compare people's consumer spending with the incomes they have received. They inevitably show that people with low incomes spend a higher proportion of their incomes for consumer goods and services than do people with relatively high incomes. How can that be if everyone is under the same pressures to consume?

There are several explanations. One is that the people in these groups have had their absolute incomes temporarily slip below their permanent levels associated with their occupations, wealth, and income class; they are continuing to consume at what are normal levels for them. For example, a highly paid surgeon takes the month off and earns little income but keeps playing golf and spends a lot of money to go driving about the country visiting his children. He buys a lot of consumer goods and services for someone with the low absolute level of income he reports.

Another reason is that the people are in that phase of the income-earning lives where their incomes are below the average that is normal or permanent for their occupation and wealth. For example, the surgeon retires and now reports a low income. But he keeps right on playing golf, eating out, and living in the same expensive house. He consumes a lot for someone with the low level of income he reports receiving.

In economist-speak, consumer spending related to an individual's normal or permanent income may explain the relatively high overall propensity to consume of the people that the budget studies find with relatively low absolute incomes.

Going in the other direction, individuals included in groups reporting relatively high levels of incomes may include people who normally have lower incomes but who have had temporary or windfall increases. These people pull down the proportion of income devoted to consumer spending in the group in which they are placed because their consumer spending is geared primarily to their lower normal or permanent levels of income.

For an economy as a whole any increases in consumer spending resulting when the incomes of some individuals temporarily exceed their normal or permanent levels tends to be offset by the decreases in consumer spending of other people whose incomes are below their normal or permanent levels.

The whole idea that a person's consumer spending is related to his permanent or normal income level is controversial. It assumes, for example, that someone who temporarily jumps to a higher level of income because he finds money on the ground or wins a lottery's grand prize will keep spending as his traditional normal or permanent level of consumer spending instead of, say, spending a lot of it in a wild celebration or spreading it out over time and using it to permanently increase his consumer spending.

**Policy implications of consumer spending
related to normal or permanent incomes.**

During the high inflation years of the 1970s the President's economic advisors thought that the inflation occurring at that time was the result of too much spending. So the White House advanced a plan that would temporarily tax people to stop their excessive spending. The money that was to be temporarily taken from them in taxes would then be returned to them when the inflation ended so they could spend more when the business cycle turned down and more spending was needed to achieve full employment. It was the epitome of a counter-cyclical fiscal policy to maintain a stable level of total spending in order to prevent inflations and unemployment.

The plan was never implemented. But what would have happened to consumer spending if people's incomes had been temporarily increased as proposed? Very little if the permanent income theory is correct. People would have kept right on spending as they had before.

Similarly in the later Bush-Obama administration, one-time increases of a few hundred dollars were given to each Social Security recipient in addition to the hundreds of billions provided to each of a few financial giants in the US and Europe. Most of the Social Security recipients saved it by doing such things as paying down their credit card debts—so it did not do much to cause more consumer spending. Later a temporary reduction in the Social Security taxes deducted from employees pay checks did last long enough that the slightly higher take home pay caused some increases in consumer spending as the increased take home pay became internalized as a part of the recipients' normal level of personal income.

Authors note: The Bush and Obama administrations are often considered to be one and the same by many analysts—because President Obama retained almost all the key Bush economic decision makers at the Federal Reserve, Treasury, and FDIC. Their ineffectual policies which had commenced under President Bush then continued—and so did the Great Recession which began in 2008.

Changes in the rates of growth. It has been suggested that the constancy of an economy's propensity to consume exists because income recipients at all income levels in each age group tend to save the same percentage of their income. But what does it mean for policy makers and investors if the composition of the economy's population changes—either grows younger due to sufficiently high birth rates and immigration (United States) or grows older because of low birth rates and no immigration (Japan).

One thing it means is that the U.S. economy will tend to have a progressively younger population if it enters a period, such as the United States did in the 1990s and early 2000s, when it had relatively high rates of legal and illegal immigration. That, in turn, means a growing number of people of income earning and saving ages in relation to the number of dis-saving people of retirement age. If such rates of immigration continue to accelerate it follows that unless something is done to encourage more consumer spending, the United States economy will always be an ever increasing tilt towards more savings and a lower propensity to consume.

Here's a simplified example to make the point: Consider an economy such as the United States where the amount of consumption spending that occurs is about seventy percent of the economy's income. Assume also that of that sixty percent of the consumer spending comes from wage and income earners and ten percent from dis-savers. If either the number of income earners doubles, say from a surge in the number of working age immigrants, or the amount of income each wage and income earner receives was to double while the pensions and incomes of the dis-savers remain the same, the overall propensity to consume would drop from 70 percent to 65 percent.

A five percent drop might not sound like much until it is recalled that total federal spending to buy goods and services is only about five percent. For increased federal purchasing to make up the slack would require doubling federal spending on everything from roads and education to its spending on the military and health.

What all this means is that if such an economy's production and income is to continue to grow to higher and higher levels at the same time there is less and less of a propensity to consume, there will be more and more need for other spending to make up the shortfall in consumer spending.

Picking up the slack. What are policy makers' options to pick up the slack in total spending if they cannot bring immigration and the birth rate back to their previously lower levels?

Encouraging export sales would pick up the slack as the propensity to consume declines. But such a policy will not work for long because the foreigners will sooner or later take steps to obtain reciprocity before they run out of dollars as a result of buying more from the United States than they are taking in—so Americans buying more abroad would sooner or later tend to offset the increased export sales.

Encouraging more investment spending by employers would pick up the slack. But that also will not work for long because employers tend to only buy enough plant, equipment and inventory to produce for their customers. So they won't need their investment spending to grow even faster than it has in the past as the propensity to consume falls.

Two basic options are left if more export buying and more investment purchases won't pick up the slack when a declining marginal propensity to consume occurs: either more government spending or more government transfers such as increased Social Security payments to encourage more consumer spending. Choices have to be made or else there will not be enough total spending and unemployment will result.

In contrast, an economy whose population is growing ever more slowly and even declining means a progressively older population with relatively fewer people in the higher saving wealth accumulating ages and relatively more people in the dis-saving ages. Under such circumstances the propensity to consume of the economy will tend to rise. Japan, China, and some of the European countries seem to be moving in this direction.

If this is the case, such countries may need to use increased taxes and reduced transfers to hold down consumer spending so that there can be enough of the economy's labor and capital left over to produce exports for foreigners, capital goods for the economy's employers, and governmental products such as roads and military planes for their governments.

Japan is an interesting case in point. Its population is actually declining and its total GNP has remained relatively unchanged for years. Some analysts think this is a great problem. They suggest Japan needs to allow immigration so its economy can grow again and have more working age people to take care of its increasingly elderly population.

What these analysts totally miss, however, is that it is per capita income that counts when evaluating and ranking a country's economic success in producing for its people, not the country's total GNP/income. Thus, Japan's economy was actually a success during the years when many analysts saw it as being in a recession or stagnant: it provided the average Japanese with more and more goods and services as its per capita level of production continued to rise and its production shifted slowly and inexorably towards consumer goods and services.

In essence, in the case of Japan it appears the increased propensity of its population to make consumer purchases as the population aged was offset by the declining need of its governmental and private employers to buy capital items to expand production.

The relationship between consumer
spending and total spending.

The various explanations of the observed proportionality between an economy's consumer spending and its level of income have proceeded on the premise that the consumption spending of the people in an economy tends to be a constant proportion of their incomes. But this explanation, and thus the validity of policies based on it, requires that an economy's disposable personal income and total customer spending (gross domestic product) have a constant relationship so that there is also a constant relationship between an economy's consumer spending and its total spending to buy goods and services (gross national product). This may not be case.

The existence of a progressive personal income tax such as exists in the United States means, if it actually exists which is doubtful due to its many exemptions, greater and greater percentages of personal income will be taken (and thus saved) by the government as the economy grows and people's personal incomes grow with it. Thus the percentage of an economy's total production purchased for consumption purposes would tend to fall as each increase in the economy's level of income occurs and the percentage of it taken in taxes grows.

Consider an economy with $6 trillion of business and government savings coming out of its gross national product of $30 trillion and an additional $3 trillion of personal savings coming out of the $24 trillion that gets back to the people of the economy as wages and other sources of personal income. The economy's propensities to consume are 87.5 percent of personal income and 70.0 percent of GNP.

Now consider a later time period when the economy's gross national product has increased to $40 trillion and business and government savings has increased to $12 trillion. This might be the case if the government has progressive income tax rates being applied to the generally higher level of income in the economy; it might be the case if the business community retains a higher percentage of its earnings (increases its propensity to save) in order to pay for the additional plant and equipment it needs so it can increase production and sell more abroad.

Whatever the cause, in this example economy $28 trillion would get back to people as wages and other incomes and the people would save $3.5 trillion if their propensity to consume remains stable at 87.5 percent of their personal incomes.

In this example, the propensity to consume of the economy's people remains at 87.5 percent of their personal incomes—but the overall propensity to consume in the economy drops from 70.0 percent to 61.25 percent. In other words, if progressive tax rates are maintained and applied to the higher and higher levels of income that occur as an economy grows, other spending is going to have to increase and pick up the slack

In the real world, the possible permutations and changes that might affect consumer and total spending are endless. For example, a tax law or regulation that encourages private employers to use borrowed money instead of retained earnings to fund their investment spending would result in less money being saved (held back) and more being passed on to consumers. That would result in increased consumer spending if people's propensities to consume are stable. The same effect would occur if governments cut taxes and, instead, used more borrowed or newly created monies to pay for their purchases and transfers.

Either way consumer spending would tend to increase because there would be less savings and, as a result, more disposable income for people to spend.

CONSUMPTION FUNCTIONS

In economist-speak the relationship between the various levels of income in an economy and the consumer spending that will occur at each of those income levels is the consumption function. The name is used because, stated in mathematical terms, the level of consumer spending in an economy is a function of (depends on) the level of income in the economy.

A simplistic example of how an economy's consumer spending might occur in relation to the level of income in the economy is presented in figure 2-1. It shows that the higher the economy's level of income the larger the amount of consumer spending that will occur. More specifically, the curve represents an equation relating the amount of consumer spending that will occur in an economy to the economy's level of income (total spending).

Algebraically the basic relationship between an economy's consumer spending and its level of income is often shown as C=f(Y) which simply states in mathematical shorthand that the amount of consumer spending (C) that will be done by people in an economy is a function (f) of the level of income (Y) that occurs in the economy.

Since the level of consumer spending also depends, as we have seen, on various objective and subjective factors, a more complex and accurate consumption function can be presented wherein consumer spending is a function of (determined by) all these influences. Thus, C=f(Y, liquid assets, expectations, tax rates, business savings, credit terms, stock of durable goods, psychological forces, etc. etc.)

In this particular example economy consumer spending is constant at seventy five percent of the economy's total spending. That's an important fact to know if you are a policy maker—it suggests, on the face of it, that an increase in total spending in the economy will cause consumer spending to increase by seventy five percent of the initial increase; a reduction is such spending will cause consumer spending to fall by seventy five percent of the reduction.

A word of warning: don't get hung up on the math—all this curve suggests is that consumer spending will rise and fall as total spending in the economy rises and falls. Obviously how much consumer spending will occur at each level of income depends on a whole lot of different things: such as how employers react to the increases and decreases in their revenues as consumer and other spending increases and decreases, and whether the changes are permanent or temporary.

In other words, this equation and its graphical depiction is very simplistic—using it as part of an economic model to "scientifically" predict the impact of a policy change or any other event may yield very inaccurate conclusions.

A declining MPC. It is possible that the marginal propensity to consume of an economy will decline as its level of total spending increases. After all, as an economy's per capita income grows and its residents acquire more and more consumer goods they might be under less and less pressure to buy more.

Having such a declining MPC is significant. It means obtaining each increment of the additional spending needed so an economy's output can continue to grow will require other types of spending to become more and more important. As might be imagined, using such an consumption function in a macroeconomic model leads to very different policy conclusions such as that government spending will have to constantly increase in importance if the economy is to continue to grow and stay at full employment levels of production.

Today many analysts do not agree with either the concept of a declining MPC or the need for government spending to grow in importance in order to keep the United States prosperous. They believe, as shall be subsequently discussed in some detail, the Federal Reserve already has sufficient power in hand to keep the United States prosperous and growing without constantly requiring congressional action to increase total spending. The concept of a declining MPC is considered here because of the possibility it may at some time begin to occur and because many fine economists think such a decline is inevitable.

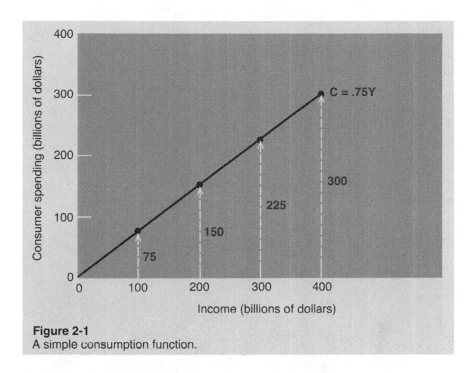

Figure 2-1
A simple consumption function.

Figure 2-2 depicts how an equation representing such a declining MPC consumption function might be depicted graphically. It is not as simple as the equation depicted in Figure 2-1 but it is still a far cry from the reality of the innumerable equations that would be required to precisely depict consumer spending in an economy where billions of individual transactions occur every day. And even if all those equations could be written and solved it would literally be impossible to get the data to populate them. On the other hand, using a representation of the general relationships that *might* exist between consumer spending and total spending is exactly what must be used if potential policy responses are to be evaluated.

Making things even more difficult is that policy decisions based on equations an data from an economy's past experiences may provide "scientifically" accurate guidance to the policy makers—until something unexpected happens that isn't reflected in the equations (think mortgage meltdown, Greek collapse, Federal Reserve policy changes) that makes the equations and the "scientific" analysis of them absolutely useless.

Such unexpected events are often called "Black Swans" in homage to the fact that for many years scientists wrote explaining why there could never be black swans—until they were found flying around in Australia.

The inherent difficulties do not mean that macroeconomic models and the simultaneous solution of large numbers of equations are useless. To the contrary, they can be used and must be used to show the basic nature and relationships of our economy. In reality our policy makers must make decisions on some basis so there is literally no alternative but to use economic models and to continue improving them and to discarding those whose use by policy makers leads to bad outcomes in the real world—inflation, unemployment, and low rates of growth.

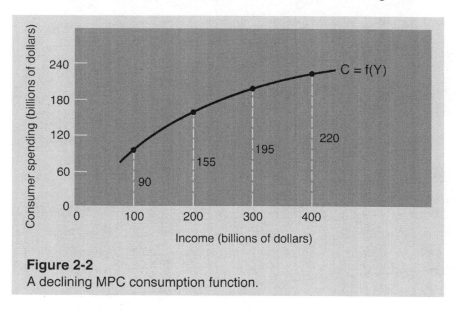

Figure 2-2
A declining MPC consumption function.

Savings and consumer spending.

An alternative to using consumer spending in a macroeconomic model is to use its mirror image—savings, the portion of our economy's total spending that people do not receive as personal income and then spend for consumer purposes. All income not spent to buy consumer goods and services is considered by economists to be savings no matter what use may be made of it. Obviously then, a *savings function*, which depicts the amount of savings that will occur at each level of income, is directly related to the consumption function; as the income of our economy grows, the amount of income our people do not use for consumer spending will also grow.

Since savings occurs when consumer spending does not occur, why and how fast people's savings will grow as their incomes grow depends on the very same set of subjective and objective influences that affect the level of consumer spending. The proportion of each increment in the level of disposable income that is saved is the marginal propensity to save or MPS. Then, since all disposable income is either devoted to consumer spending or "saved," the MPS and the APC total 100 percent. Thus, for example, if an economy's MPC at its current level is 70 percent then its MPS at that level is 30 percent; if the MPC is 65 percent, its MPS is 35 percent.

The savings function and its relationship to the consumption function also can be depicted both graphically and algebraically. Consider an economy where the historical data suggest a consumer spending function wherein there would be $1000 billion of consumer spending even if there is no disposable income and consumer spending then rises by $700 billion for each additional $1000 billion of disposable income. That is the same as saying there will be $1000 billion of dis-savings if people spend their money and other liquid assets in order to survive even if there is no disposable income in the economy and that savings in the economy will grow by $300 billion for each additional $1000 billion of disposable income.

Algebraically. Where consumer spending is related to income and the consumption function has the form C=a + bY, it follows that:

1. $S = Y - C$
2. $S = Y - (a+bY)$
3. $S = -a + Y - bY$
4. $S = -a + (1-b)Y$

The first equation defines savings (S) in an economy as that part of its income (Y) not used for consumer spending (C). Equation 2 reflects C in its more complex form of a+bY. Equation 3 removes the parentheses and rearranges the components. Finally, equation 4 shows that savings (S) is equal to the dis-savings required to provide the consumer spending that occurs when income is zero (-a) plus some portion (1-b) of the level of income (Y). Since b (the marginal propensity to consume) represents the percentage of each increment of income that will be used for consumption spending, the percentage that will not be used (the marginal propensity to save) is 1-b. For example, if the marginal propensity to consume (b) is 75%, then the marginal propensity to save is 25%.

Graphically. Figure 2-3 depicts the relationship between consumer spending and savings. At each level of disposable income the sum of consumer spending plus savings adds up to that level of income. Thus, when disposable income is $200 billion, consumption is $180 billion and savings $20 is billion; when it is $300 billion consumption is $255 billion and savings is $45 billion.

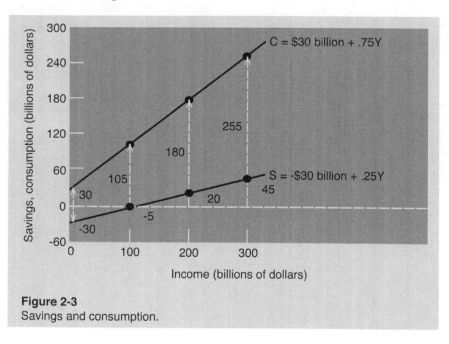

Figure 2-3
Savings and consumption.

Short run and long run consumption functions.

Figure 2-4 is an example of the differences that might exist between consumer spending and total spending in the short-run and long-run. Notice that in the short-run consumption spending will not initially increase or decrease as much as it will in the long run. In this example consumer spending will only contribute the full 75 percent of the economy's income in the long run when the resulting consumer spending changes are completed. More specifically, the economy depicted in Figure 2-4 initially has $200 billion of total customer spending of which consumer spending comprises 75 percent ($150 billion).

Then what will happen in this economy if there is suddenly a $50 billion increase in the foreign buying of goods and services? In this particular economy total spending will initially rise to $250 billion as the additional $50 billion is added to the initial $200 billion of spending—but then total spending will keep rising higher and higher as more and more the money received by employers is passed on to people so they have higher personal income and increase their spending for consumer items.

In this the example economy depicted, consumer spending will keep increasing until the economy settles down (reaches equilibrium) at $400 billion of which $300 billion is consumer spending. In other words, adding a permanent increase of $50 billion of additional spending to this $200 billion economy will drive the economy's total spending all the way up to $400 billion as it causes more and more consumer spending. Analysts can work through it and see for themselves.

But how long will it take for the economy to reach its new equilibrium destination at $400 billion? In other words, how long is the short-run during which the economy's spending will be moving towards $400 billion? A month? Six months? A year? In the real world, as we shall see, how long it takes an economy to adjust to a spending stimulus depends on the nature of the initial stimulus spending—which buyers and employers get the money and how soon they spend it or pass it on as wages and other payments so peoples' consumption spending can increase.

Sooner or later an economy receiving a spending stimulus will work through all the delays and reach whatever is the normal relationship between consumption spending and the economy's income. In this case "normal" is when consumption is again equal to 75 percent of the economy's total spending and the economy is at a new and higher equilibrium level of total spending of $400 billion. Obviously, an economy in the real world never actually reaches equilibrium because so many things are constantly changing; but it does constantly move towards it as the economy's public and private employers and its consumers and other buyers and governments continually adjust to their ever changing circumstances.

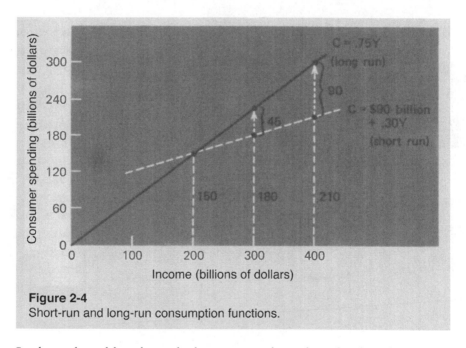

Figure 2-4
Short-run and long-run consumption functions.

In the real world perhaps the best we can do to describe the relationship between consumption and savings and an economy's level of income is: if the level of spending and income in an economy increases both its consumption spending and its savings will increase, but not by as much because some of the increased income will be saved.

GENERAL SUMMARY

The level of consumption spending that occurs in an economy is important to the prosperity of an economy's people, primarily related to the economy's level of income rather than its interest rates, relatively stable, and greatly affected by numerous subjective and objective forces.

SUMMARY

I.   Consumer spending is the largest component of the total spending in every economy because people's propensity to consume is so strong. The propensity to consume is affected by psychological motivations such as precautions, desire for independence, avarice, and pride; by social pressures such as status and community values; and by expectations of the future.

II. Also influencing consumer spending are the amount of consumer credit available, the distribution of income, personal wealth, the stock of durable goods, business savings, and government taxes.

III. Consumer spending depends more than anything else on the levels of the personal and total income (GNP) of an economy.

IV. The proportion of each increment of an economy's income used for consumer spending purposes is its marginal propensity to consume. The MPC differs from the average propensity to consume (APC) which is the percentage of total income devoted to consumer spending.

V.   Savings is the mirror image of spending. Any income not used for consumer spending purposes is considered to be saved. Savings is done by people, governments (taxes), and employers. How much savings occurs in an economy primarily depends on the economy's level of income. Interest rates have, at best, a minor influence on the amount of saving.

VI. Consumption and savings functions may be depicted graphically and in equations.

VII. Studies of people's budgets suggest that when people's incomes rise beyond a certain point they spend less and less of any additional income on consumer goods and services. Nevertheless, the percentage of income devoted to consumer spending in the United States has remained remarkably constant over the years.

VIII. One explanation of the relative stability of consumer spending is that structural changes, the expansion of consumer credit, changes in income distribution, shifting values, and new products have offset the declining MPC that otherwise would have occurred.

IX. Another explanation is that there is always a constant APC and MPC at every level of income because the pressures on people to consume are always constant because they are related to the incomes and consumer spending of other people in the economy.

X. Yet another explanation relates consumer spending to a permanent or normal lifetime level of income and standard of living.

XI. Because of people's tendency to maintain their standard of living despite drops in their personal incomes, tax surcharges may be ineffectual against inflations caused by too much spending and temporary tax reductions may be ineffectual against recessions caused by inadequate levels of spending.

XII. Shifting population characteristics and rising income levels may affect the propensity to consume.

XIII. A constant APC in relation to GNP occurs if people save a constant percentage of their personal incomes and the other forms of savings (as a group) are also a constant percentage of GNP.

XIV. The consumer spending that occurs in an economy is important to the economy's prosperity because consumers are by far the largest buyers of newly produced goods and services. It is directly related to the economy's level of income, relatively stable, and greatly affected by numerous external forces that affect the other spending that occurs in the economy.

CHAPTER THREE

INVESTMENT SPENDING AND
THE STOCK OF CAPITAL

Consumer spending may be far and away the biggest source of customer revenues for an economy's public and private employers, but there are other important types of customers whose purchases have the same production and employment generating effect. Investment spending is one of them. Investment spending to buy newly produced plant, equipment and inventory causes significant amounts of production and employment to occur in the United States—it comprises over ten percent of all customer spending.

Economic investments occur when public and private employers buy products they can use to maintain and enhance their own production processes. They include machinery, tools, plants, warehouses, and inventories. These are the *economic capital items* (aka *production capital* or *real capital)* employers buy so they can employ them to produce goods and services for consumers and other buyers. At any given time a country such as the United States possesses a *stock of capital* its employers can use to produce goods and services for the economy's buyers.

An economy's stock of production capital exists because of previous investment spending. Essentially two things happen to an economy's stock of production capital as time passes: part of it constantly vanishes as it wears out, becomes obsolete, and is destroyed; and new investment spending furnishes a continual flow of new capital assets to *replace* those that have been consumed and to *expand* the size of the stock. Moreover, the new plant and equipment typically embodies new designs and technologies so that it is even more productive than the capital it replaces.

In essence, some of the capital goods acquired by investment spending that tends to constantly occur in an economy may be used to replace worn out plant and equipment so that production can continue. Other capital goods are purchased so that production can increase. For example, an employer such as General Motors might buy new equipment to replace older equipment which it has worn out so it can keep producing cars at its current level as well as buy additional new equipment so it can produce even more cars in the future.

Similarly, a government employer such as a local fire department might buy new equipment such as fire trucks and fire houses to replace older worn out equipment and facilities so it can keep producing fire-fighting services at its current level. It also may buy new equipment and facilities so it can produce even more fire-fighting services.

Because new capital goods tend to embody technological advances, new capital acquired for replacement and expansion purposes tends to be more productive than the capital items it replaces. Accordingly, worker productivity tends to rise when investment spending results in new capital items being introduced into the production process even if they only replace existing older capital.

For example, the purchase of replacement equipment that further automates or speeds up the production lines of an existing Ford or Toyota factory in the United States may result in more cars being produced with fewer workers. Similarly, new digital apps bought for business use are capital items produced as the result of investment purchases and may increase output per-worker because they run faster and have more features than the digital apps they replace.

A significant word of caution.

Much of the following discussion about investment spending directly or indirectly relates it to the rate of interest. That is traditional in economics. It is also often misleadingly wrong because it suggests to uninformed journalists and unworldly Federal Reserve governors and regional presidents that minor changes in the level of interest rates are of great significance to the real economy of jobs and production. They are not.

The importance of minor changes in interest rates appears to be true only for financial assets such as stocks, bonds and derivatives. In the real world of jobs and production, however, relatively minor interest rate changes tend to have little to do with the economic investments that employers make to acquire capital goods such as plant, equipment, and inventory.

The difference between financial investments and real investments is important for analysts to keep in mind—it is only investment spending to buy new capital goods such as plant and equipment that directly affects an economy's prices, production, and employment. In other words, do not be like so many of our journalists and Federal Reserve governors and confuse financial investments and the well-being of investment banks and hedge funds with economic investments and the well-being of our real economy and its workers, employers, and banks.

Finally, astute analysts will notice that nowhere in the following examination of the investment decision-making process is savings even mentioned. Savings is not mentioned because in the real world savings is neither required for investment spending to occur nor does it influence investment spending in any way except negatively—by *reducing* the amount of customer spending employers receive for the goods and services they produce.

The implications of the dual impact of investment spending.

The decisions of employers to invest money to buy new capital goods have two important effects. First, the plant and equipment they acquire tends to maintain and expand their production capacity. Second, the investment spending to buy the capital provides employment and incomes for the economy's capital goods workers and for other people such as the owners of employers' shares (dividends) and debts (interest).

The dual effect of investment spending has definite policy implications. Specifically, policies to encourage investment spending can be used to help the economy's employers get enough customers to fully employ their workers. But the investment purchasing will then result in the economy's employers having even greater production capacities and needing even more spending in the future to keep them fully employed. In other words, more investment today to help maintain full employment means employers will then need even more customers in the future to keep their workers and their now-expanded stock of capital fully employed.

The policy aspects of encouraging investment spending so an economy's public and private employers will have enough revenues so they can remain in operation and continue to hire workers are discussed in subsequent chapters. Here the emphasis is on the rational, and not so rational, investment spending decisions that result in the buying of plant, equipment, and inventory by public and private employers. Notice in particular the influence of interest rates. This is important because, *if* investment spending responds to changes in interest rates, the Federal Reserve System may be able to affect the amount of economic investment spending by using monetary policy to influence interest rates.

On the other hand, if interest rates are not particularly important to the buyers of plant and equipment and to consumers buying products such as homes and cars, the Federal Reserve may *not* be able to greatly influence total customer spending by running interest rates up and down. That is often the case in the real world of consumers wherein the availability of credit and the monthly payments are typically much more important than their rate of interest. It is the case for investment spending as well.

What this suggests is that monetary policies should concentrate on providing enough money and credit for consumers and employers rather than on efforts to affect interest rates and provide special assistance to investment bankers and financial traders.

It is also important to understand the degree to which the expectations of economic investors and the availability and payment terms of credit influence the amount of economic investment spending that will occur when a particular level of interest rates exists. Such expectations and the availability and terms under which loans and credit are made available may change rapidly. This can cause investment spending to rise and fall *even if interest rates do not change.*

In other words, production and employment in an economy's capital goods industries can change rapidly even if interest rates do not change. Then, if such spending changes are undesirable, the federal government and the Federal Reserve will, instead of tinkering with interest rates as its governors have historically been wont to do, need to undertake activities to change expectations and the availability of credit and its repayment terms.

And finally, analysts should notice what is not discussed—savings. It is still an article of faith in some quarters that investment is related to or somehow depends upon savings. That was the prevailing view in the 19th century and the early part of the 20th. Since then numerous studies have shown that savings has little to do with public and private employers making their investment decisions to buy or not buy plant, equipment, and inventory. Indeed, as analysts shall soon see, increased savings *discourages* investment spending by reducing customer spending.

OTHER TYPES OF CAPITAL AND INVESTMENTS

Much of the discussion in this chapter is traditional and greatly emphasized by journalists, in the classes of certain economics departments, and by the Federal Reserve's governors and regional presidents. It assumes that employers rationally analyze each potential investment in plant, equipment, and inventory by comparing the value of its expected contribution to its costs. In other words, it assumes the public and private employers of the United States make rational cost-benefit decisions to buy or not buy capital goods such as plants, equipment, and inventories. In the real world, of course, many do not.

An economy's capital-buying employers come in all kinds of forms and sizes: individuals, partnerships, corporations, limited liability partnerships, limited liability corporations, churches, cooperatives, non-profit organizations, state and local governments, and private schools and colleges are among the most numerous.

Typical investors include profit-oriented businesses such as Microsoft when it buys new offices or spends money to develop new digital apps and other software, the Ford Motor Company when it buys the equipment for a new assembly line, Lee's Corner Cleaners when it buys a new pants press, or a MacDonald's franchise when it buys a newly constructed store building.

Public and non-profit employers are also investors. They would, for example, include state universities when they buy new buildings and stadiums, the Red Cross and city police departments when they buy new vehicles so they can produce more protection and assistance services, and states when they buy new fish hatcheries and highways.

Economists are divided as to whether purchases by governmental employers should be counted as investment spending or as government spending. It really doesn't matter—what is important is that such spending tends to increase production and employment when it occurs, not how it is counted. Pragmatic analysts leave such intellectual nits to be picked by others.

There are also other types of investment spending and other types of capital. An economy's stock of *human capital* is the sum of all the inherent and acquired production abilities of the economy's residents. Investment spending to acquire human capital includes spending on health, housing, medical care, education, on-the-job training, and the aiding of the migration of people to more productive employments. This spending when done by individuals is typically counted as part of consumer spending; when done by governments it is typically counted as part of government spending. In the real world it is an investment no matter how it is counted.

Another form of capital acquired by investment spending is *social capital* or *public capital* such as highways, airports, and public hospitals. Their existence certainly does increase an economy's overall production of services. These investments are often done by governments and, when they are, counted as government purchases. Such investments are often simultaneously being done by private for-profit and non-profit employers—the U.S is full of for-profit and non-profit hospitals, diploma mills, nursery schools, and toll roads.

The investment decision. All capital investments, whether done by non-profits, governments, or for-profit employers, can conceptually be measured and evaluated in terms of the value of the additional production each capital item is expected to contribute if it is purchased and operated. This is the *rate of return* or "yield" each capital investment is expected to generate. In economist-speak it is the *marginal efficiency of investment (MEI)*.

For an overly simplified example, imagine that Amazon or the City of Chicago is considering the investment purchase of a new building or piece of equipment. Rationally, their accountants and analysts would look at the price they would have to pay for each new capital item, the costs they expect to bear by operating it, and the value of the services they expect it to contribute. They might conclude, for example, that a possible new piece of equipment will contribute enough additional revenues and cost reductions to generate a 20 percent annual return (MEI) during each year of its life. Then to cover any contingencies and mistakes and corruption in their analysis their analysts might recommend the purchase of the equipment or facility so long as the interest rate cost for the money required for its purchase is ten percent or less.

In essence, Amazon and Chicago, as described above, would be acting as rational profit oriented investors buying capital. They will buy the new capital item from the employer who produces it *if funds are available* at an annual interest cost of 10 percent or less. Thus, they will make the investment no matter whether the actual interest rate cost to them is 5 percent or 8 percent; and they will not buy it, even if funds are available and the repayment terms acceptable, if they have to pay 11 percent or 13 percent to get them. The decision is the same no matter whether Amazon or Chicago borrow the money or use their own money instead of loaning it out to earn that rate of interest.

Analysts who are considering careers in journalism or at the Federal Reserve should notice something very important here—a minor change in the general level of interest rates such as results in reducing Amazon's and Chicago's interest rate from 8 percent to 5 percent or increasing it from 11 percent to 13 percent will have no impact on Amazon and Chicago making this investment. *In the real world, minor changes in the level of interest rates do not appear to have much of an impact on the decision to buy or not buy capital goods.*

The same type of decision making comparing the expected contribution (MEI) for each dollar of investment to the cost of getting the money to make the investment could conceptually also be made for both social and human capital. That's the rational way to proceed and what most analysts assume occurs—*but it's rarely, if ever, used* by not-for-profit investors such as governments, families, and non-profit organizations when they are considering investment spending to acquire capital goods.

One problem that prevents its use is the difficulty of making the cost and value estimates needed for the MEI calculations. The costs of buying and operating a new police car or new building or new digital app may be known. But how is the monetary value of their contributions to be estimated so that their MEI rates of return can be calculated? In the real world it is virtually impossible to get the necessary data to make a usable estimate so that a valid MEI can be calculated.

Another problem, even when the data needed for making accurate cost and revenue estimates are available, is getting the non-profits and governments to use it to make rational investment buying decisions. For example, various studies suggest that a particular college degree is worth so many dollars of value over one's lifetime. That data, in turn, can be compared to the cost of getting that degree, including the interest cost of getting the necessary money, and rational decisions made as to whether an investment in education is worthwhile.

All this is very "scientific" and precise and, if used, would lead to rational decisions—except, of course, for the not so minor problem that most of the time investment decision makers have other goals. For example, not everyone may want to make the investment expenditures required to go to college no matter how profitable it might be for them later in life.

Similarly, consider a government with limited funds. How is it to compare the value of the benefits that would be derived from each dollar it might invest to buy a new hospital or police car as opposed to the benefits that might be expected from using each of those dollars to repair a road or buy something else? It can't.

Instead, it is much more likely that politicians' investment decisions will be based on how many more votes and contributions they think they will get. For example, should they buy a new school and employ more politically supportive teachers instead of a new hospital that will be staffed by physicians who generally oppose government spending because it may result in higher taxes? In the real world, the investment decision is likely to be based on the political philosophies of the politicians making the decision rather than the estimated rates of return for the projects competing for the available monies.

In essence, the investment spending that occurs in the United States and other economies is not always aimed at getting the capital items that will yield the most valuable bang for each investment spending buck. On the other hand, and this is important, *even if something is not the most profitable capital item to buy, the investment spending to acquire it still causes production and employment to occur.*

FINANCIAL INVESTMENTS AND FINANCIAL CAPITAL

Economic or real capital (plant, equipment, and inventory) is produced by employers in an economy's capital goods industries in response to investment purchasing. It enables an economy's production to continue and be increased. Such real capital that can be employed to produce goods and services is very different from *financial capital* acquired via *financial investments*.

Financial capital includes financial assets such as stocks and bonds, mortgage derivatives, options, puts and calls, etc. All are a form of wealth, have money values, and are relatively *liquid* in that they can usually be easily and quickly bought and sold, in other words "traded," in financial markets such as those of the New York Stock Exchange and NASDAQ—*but in the real world neither the creation nor the buying nor the selling of stock, bonds, and other financial instruments causes production and employment to occur.*

For example, consider what happens when newly issued ownership shares or bonds of Facebook or any other business enterprise are purchased for the first time in an *initial offering*. Facebook creates and issues the ownership shares or bonds and gets the money. But no production or employment of any kind occurs merely as a result of Facebook issuing them. All that has happened is that Facebook has diluted the ownership percentages of its existing shareholders if it issues new shares or has increased its debt and future interest payment costs if it has issued bonds or notes.

Yes, the Facebook company would now have money it can use as its decision-makers see fit and that might include making investment purchases. But investment spending that acquires capital items and affects production and employment does not occur *unless* and until Facebook actually spends the money it has raised to buy new plant, equipment, or inventory to replace or expand its existing stock of capital.

Only when and if Facebook actually spends the money to make investment purchases will that spending be counted as an investment and actually cause capital to be produced and people employed. In essence, no investment occurs by merely raising additional money. The money does not count until a public or private employer actually uses it to make investment expenditures to buy real capital goods and people are actually employed to produce them.

And there is no guarantee the money will ever be used to make investment or any other purchases if money is raised by selling equity or borrowing. Sometimes shares and bonds are issued to pay off company debts, pay dividends or distributions, have funds available for acquisitions, meet loan covenants, or increase the company's working capital so it will always have enough on hand to handle the inevitable ebb and flow of revenues and payments. In other words, money raised by issuing new stocks and bonds might lead to investment spending and more capital items being produced, but it does not necessarily ever have that result.

**Buying and selling in
the after markets**.

After a stock or bond is issued its price can go up or down in the markets where it trades. So what happens to Facebook and the real economy of jobs and production if the prices of Facebook or any other shares and bonds go up or down or if their ownership changes? *Absolutely nothing.*

Most stocks and bonds traded on exchanges such as the NYSE and NASDAQ were issued years ago. So they really don't mean much to the companies that issued them. It is a fact of the real world that most publically traded companies' ownership shares and bonds are widely held—so their executives don't have to pay attention to the "owners" of their shares and bonds.

An exception occurs, of course, when someone such as a company founder or the founder's family has retained enough shares to maintain control. Or, going in the other direction, when an investment bankers or other speculators and opportunists buy up enough of a company's ownership to have a say in what the company does—for example, to force the company to sell some of its assets and distribute the proceeds (to them) or to take over the company and install new managers (them).

In other words, analysts should not make the common mistake of journalists and Federal Reserve governors and think that the stock and financial markets, and the big financial firms and money managers which "advise" companies and buy and sell stocks and bonds, are particularly significant to jobs and production in the U.S. economy. *They are not.* Most of the jobs and financial wealth they create are their own and created at the expense of others who are not as good as they are at gambling in the financial casinos.

As one financial industry insider famously noted—"I know a lot of money managers and investment bankers with yachts but I don't know of any of their clients who own them." His words are prophetic—most studies have concluded that the investment banks and money market funds, so beloved of the Federal Reserve and Congress that they give them loans, bailouts, and tax breaks, contribute little, if anything, to employment and production.

The financial markets' importance is that they provide liquidity by enabling the owners of financial assets to easily and quickly convert their shares and other assets to cash. Even more importantly, in a manner more akin to a Las Vegas casino than to the real world of business and investments, they enable people and firms to gamble on the direction that the prices of financial assets such as specific stocks and bonds will go. Good gamblers and trading desks can thus make money—from those who are not.

In the United States it is estimated that three million shares are bought and sold *every second*. But it is a zero-sum game in that there are no net winners. Worse, every so often there are unforeseen events that turn virtually everyone in the game into such big losers (think mortgage meltdown, euro crisis, and MF Global; Lehman Brothers, AIG, Citi Group, Washington Mutual, and Fannie Mae) that they either fail to survive or wipe out years of earlier gains.

On the other hand, even though the prices of publically traded stocks and bonds do not generally affect the companies and governments that issue them, their performance can affect the market prices of their previously issued stocks and bonds. For example, a company whose products are generating growing revenues and profits is more likely to pay dividends and be able to pay off its bonds and notes. So their shares and bonds may be viewed as more valuable by those who are considering buying them.

Similarly, a city, state, or national government with growing tax revenues and a level of debt that is not excessive is more likely to be able to pay off its bonds and notes (Sorry Greece, Detroit, and California). So traders who have bought the shares and bonds gambling that their value will move higher will win their bet if, for example, their shares and bonds come to be thought of as "more valuable" such that their prices are bid up in the markets where the shares and bonds are bought and sold.

Derivatives. Derivatives are created when the mortgages and other debt instruments issued by borrowers are bought from their original lenders by investment banks and others and packaged together. The investment banks then sell the packages to pension funds and to other banks seeking higher returns than they can earn by making loans to consumers and businesses. The value of each package is "derived" from the assets in the package, the rating given to them by a ratings agency, and the degree to which, if any, the lender or an insurance company will guarantee they will be paid.

The ability of commercial banks and other lenders to package their loans and sell them off as derivatives, at least according to the Federal Reserve and its apologists, encourages consumer and investment spending by enabling the lenders to using the money they receive from selling their loans to make even more loans.

In the real world, however, the ability of commercial banks to engage in creating and "trading" derivatives appears to discourage the banks from making consumer and business loans. This occurs when the commercial banks, instead of loaning the money they receive from depositors to people and businesses to buy such things as houses and cars, use the money they get from their depositors to make loans to investment banks, other commercial banks, and money market funds. Or they may just use it themselves to trade—buy and sell—in the world's financial casinos. The banks do this when they think they can make more money gambling in the financial markets, or making loans to those that do, than they can earn by making conventional loans to consumers and businesses.

Basically the trading-oriented commercial banks, also known as "universal banks," make whatever amount of loans and financial investments they are allowed to make based on the reserves that the Federal Reserve requires them to hold. They then package and sell the loans—and then make *more* loans with the money they receive from the sale of the first batch of loans. The commercial banks' reserves thus support more than one set of loans. Accordingly, the amount of reserves behind each loan gets smaller and smaller as more and more loans are made and sold.

A handful of the very largest American commercial banks such as Citibank, Bank of America and JP Morgan Chase act as both conventional deposit-accepting and loan-making commercial banks and as investment banks creating and trading derivatives and other financial instruments. Such *universal banks* also lend money to investment banks and money market funds to finance their derivative and other trading activities.

The large universal banks do this with their own money—and that of their depositors, so they say, because they are so large they "can't find enough consumers and businesses to borrow it." In reality, of course, they do it because their directors and executives think their bank can make more money (and they can make bigger salaries and bonuses) gambling in the financial markets than they can by making conventional loans to consumers and employers so they can buy goods and services in the product markets.

Lender "leveraging" of their reserves to make more and more loans and sell them for the highest prices and profits works to generate higher profits—right up until enough defaults occur to wipe out the reserves of the lender and any insurance companies which have insured the performance of the assets they are selling. Then the value of the derivatives collapses, the lender and insurance companies fail, and no loans are available for consumers and businesses. The collapse of mortgage derivative prices in 2008 started the Great Recession.

In 2008, on the grounds that they were too-big-to-be-allowed-to-fail, the Federal Reserve provided a handful of the largest universal and investment banks, and the insurance companies which allegedly insured the derivatives they were creating and selling, with hundreds of billions of dollars in emergency loans when the price of mortgage derivatives collapsed. This bailout of their losses saved those who were rescued, and doomed many of the smaller banks who were not rescued to either total failure or huge losses.

The handful of universal banks and investment banks which were rescued responded by continuing to trade and gamble in search of higher profits. Today their trading desks speculating on the prices of financial assets and currencies and their loans to other speculators and gamblers are again a major source of their profits. They also, with additional hundreds of billions of federal government and Federal Reserve assistance, bought up many of the banks and traders who were not bailed out—so that even more bank deposits fell into the hands of the big traders instead of being made available to be loaned out to homeowners and employers in the normal course of banking. This, of course, exacerbated and helped continue the recession.

Are they investors? Journalists frequently refer to the individuals and financial firms that buy and sell stocks and derivatives as "investors." Pragmatic analysts typically consider it a bit more accurate to describe them as "traders"—because they have little, if anything, to do with the investment spending that maintains and expands an economy's production capacity and employment.

Whatever they are called, it is their knowledge, speed, and timing that are the key to their making profits. As one of them said—"We had a lot of companies' shares and used them as collateral to borrow money so we could buy even more. To protect ourselves we had someone in contact with each of our big investments every day. So we usually knew more about what was happening than their executives who were tied up running their day to day affairs. As a result, we were the first to get out by selling our shares, bonds and derivatives if things looked bad and the first to buy more shares, bonds, and derivatives if things were looking up. It worked. We made a lot of money—until the market crashed and we couldn't sell our shares and derivatives for enough to pay our short-term loans. Then we went broke and so did the bank which was loaning to us and one of the money market funds we were using to source funds."

The lack of trading profits over the long term is not unusual: one study estimated that ninety eight percent of all hedge fund profits from the mid-90s through 2012 went to their managers in the form of management fees; two percent went to their investors—less than they would have netted if they had bought low yield federal bonds.

Among the various things this suggests to pragmatic analysts is that the profit and client earnings claims that a money manager or financial advisor or broker makes has probably been carefully "selected" and that investing with them or letting them manage one's money is not likely to do anything except generate sales commissions for the brokers, consulting fees for the advisors, and management fees for the money managers.

It also suggests that depositors and borrowers should consider avoiding the large universal banks that generate a substantial portion of their earnings by letting their deposits be used by their own "trading desks" or making loans and buying financial assets so others can speculate in the financial markets. After all, just because the too-big-to-fail universal banks were bailed-out in 2008 when their derivative gambles and their loans to traders soured does not mean they will be bailed out the next time their trading and gambling gets them in trouble.

Another reason for avoiding them is that it tends to be more difficult for a consumer or employer to get a normal bank loan or mortgage from a universal bank—because instead of making conventional loans it is trading with the monies its customers deposit or using them to make short-term loans to financial traders with the latest "can't miss" electronic trading models that buy and sell millions of shares of stock every second.

One thing an analyst must keep in mind, even if the Federal Reserve governors and regional presidents do not, is that if such trading and loans are actually generating profits for the universal banks, then someone somewhere is making losses and it is a dead wash for the economy as a whole.

In any event, as analysts shall see, the universal banks' diversion of their depositors' money from making conventional bank loans to making short-term trading loans and purchasing derivatives and other financial assets is one of the primary reasons consumer and employer spending has stagnated since 2008 and the Great Recession has continued.

MAKING RATIONAL INVESTMENT DECISIONS

Rational investment spending to buy new plant, equipment, and inventory occurs when the employers who would use them expect returns over each capital item's life which will cover all the costs or purchasing and operating the capital item while also yielding a net return at least equal to the interest that would be paid if the investor borrowed the money to buy it. The return must be that high, so it is often said, or a potential investor would tend not to be willing to borrow money to purchase it.

Similarly, the expected return must be greater than the interest cost even if the investors have sufficient funds of their own so that the money does not have to be borrowed: otherwise a rational investor would choose to lend their money to someone else to obtain the higher interest payment in preference to the lower return that they would earn from purchasing the capital item.

For example, would a profit-maximizing public or private employer be willing to purchase new equipment whose employment was expected to yield $500,000 in revenues (or benefits with such a dollar value in the case of products which have no market price) over its life—if the employer had to pay (or forego earning) $600,000 in interest to obtain the money needed to make the purchase? The answer is would appear to no—rational profit-oriented public or private employers would not make such an investment.

But appearances can be deceiving and mislead unwary analysts and unworldly Federal Reserve governors and regional presidents.

The emphasis on investment spending occurring so that the profits and incomes are maximized is traditional in economics. And it certainly lends itself to elegant statistical formulations. Unfortunately, it is a concept valid only when employers are rationally taking costs and revenues into consideration when they make decisions to buy and employ capital goods. And that is not always the case in the real world of jobs and production. Indeed, it is quite rare.

In the real world, many governments, non-profits, and businesses have goals other than producing high levels of profits and income—such as buying more capital items in order to have higher future levels of production in order to maximize their future revenues or to increase their market share or to enhance their social importance or to attract political support and contributions from specific vested interest groups or to enhance their labor or community relations.

One thing is certain, political speeches and naïve pundits to the contrary, investment spending does *not* occur merely because there have been savings. An individual, for example, may save by putting his money in a commercial bank or money market fund or a hedge fund. But there is no guarantee the bank and other recipients will ever loan it out such that an investment purchase will occur. For example, the bank may instead loan the money to a consumer who wants to take a vacation or pay off a credit card debt.

Or the bank may not lend it out at all, keeping the money in its vaults or on deposit with the Federal Reserve so it can meet its reserve requirements.

Or the bank might use the money to buy easily liquidated federal bonds so it can meet its regulator's capital requirements in case a large number of people wish to withdraw their deposits all at once.

Or the bank might let its own "trading desk" use the money to speculate in the stock, bond, derivative, and currency markets with computer driven high frequency buying and selling based on its latest infallible trading model.

Or the bank might loan the money to an investment bank or financial trading firm so it can engage in such speculations.

Or the bank might loan the money to a money market fund so it can loan it to a currency speculator or use it to buy corporate bonds so that the borrowing corporation can use the money to acquire another business.

In the real world, the list of possible non-investment uses of savings is virtually endless.

Investment spending decisions
In the real world.

To rationally decide whether to make an investment purchase in the face of a given supply price and interest rate, employers must estimate both the additional revenues (or their value equivalent in the case of a government or nonprofit) costs that will result. This requires the employer appraising such things as how many additional products each additional capital item will contribute, how long the capital item will last and its salvage value, what the products it produces can be sold for, and what the effect the sale of the additional products will have on the price and revenues of the products the employer is already producing.

This, in turn, requires the employers assessing such things as how many workers will be needed to operate the asset, how much they will be paid, and the size of any cost changes that may occur in the employer's existing operations as a result of operating the new asset.

Then, if profit-oriented employers are involved, an investment expenditure will tend to be made only if the *expected rate of return* (MEI) of the capital item to be acquired is higher than the interest rate and will not be made if it is lower. For example, if the interest rate an employer must pay to borrow the money needed to make an investment is six percent and the investment is expected to yield the ten percent, the investment will be made; if the interest rate is fifteen percent it will not be made. At least that's the theory.

But the theory does not hold up because not all employers are profit maximizers. Indeed, in the real world it appears that most are not. What if, for example, an employer's goal is to increase market share or its decision makers just plain want to be as big as possible? So long as the employer has enough money or credit the employer could keep making more and more investments and adding more and more new capital even if the additional capital items being acquired have negative MEIs.

What this means is that, in the real world, employers can keep right on investing so long as their total revenues from all sources, including borrowing and selling assets, are not exceeded by the total outlays they have to make in order to stay in business.

In other words, an employer can even keep making investments and expanding until they reach a capital item that takes them past the breakeven point. Indeed, they can still keep right on investing until they reach that capital item whose MEI will cause them to run out of lenders, run out of liquid reserves and run out of assets to sell. Then they are history.

In the real world, it seems, how much investment spending occurs in economy such as the United States depends primarily on the motivations and financial abilities of the employers and only secondarily, on the rates of return (MEIs) which specific new capital assets are expected to earn and the interest rate cost of the money to buy them. Think TWA airlines, Saturn automobiles, and MySpace.

The profitability of each successive capital item may decline as more and more are purchased.

More than one unit of a particular type of capital asset may be considered for purchase. For example, a concrete company might consider buying ten, twenty, or fifty new trucks to help it produce more concrete. Or a city might consider buying ten, twenty, or fifty new police cars or fire trucks to help it produce more public safety or a church might consider buying ten, twenty, or fifty new pews to help it produce more services.

It makes no difference whether the potential employer is public or private, profit or non-profit; to make a rational decision the investment decision makers must not only consider the value and costs that will be contributed by the first new truck or police car or pew but also the value and costs that will be contributed by each successive concrete truck or police car or pew.

The primary question confronting most public, non-profit, and private employers on any given day: do we want the additional capital items we are able to buy and can we get enough money to buy and operate them; the secondary question, if it is asked at all, is what will be each successive capital item's MEI or present value or total costs and revenues?

For various reasons it is reasonable to expect that the MEIs or present values or revenues relative to costs of each successive new capital item might be lower than those that precede it. For example, a city may give a high value to benefits it expects to receive for the first new fire engine it might buy but be not at all sure it really needs the ninth and tenth. Thus it might, at least conceptually, calculate the MEI of the first truck to be fifteen percent, the second to be fourteen percent, the third ten percent, and the ninth to be minus two percent. In the real world all of them might be bought if the city has the money and its firefighters union wants more members.

The same type of declining MEI results could exist for the concrete company looking at the revenues and costs of each concrete truck it might buy or any other employer who considers investment purchases of more and more capital items.

Among the reasons MEIs and present values and profitability of capital goods might decline if more and more are purchased:

Declining revenues and benefits discourage additional investments.
Each subsequent new capital item may yield revenues and benefits that
get lower and lower. This tends to occur if each subsequent capital asset
is expected to result in the production of fewer additional products or
if the additional supply of what is produced causes prices to fall in the
markets where it is sold.

It is not inevitable that the revenues (or the estimated value of what the
additional capital items will produce in the case of public items such
as fire trucks and roads) will decline as output increases. The demand
for the additional production may be perfectly *elastic* in that its price
does not fall if more are purchased by investors. This would be the
case, for example, for an investor considering capital investments to
increase his output of a product such as wheat. A bit more wheat from
an additional farm tractor or two is not likely is not likely to cause the
worldwide price wheat to fall.

Moreover, in the United States the prices of wheat, and many other
products, are often fixed by the government which stands ready to buy
all the output that cannot be sold elsewhere. Similarly an investment in
equipment for one new oil well is not likely to cause the price of crude
oil to fall; and an investment in a new power plant is not likely to cause
the price of electricity to fall.

To the contrary, in the United States a capital investment by a privately
owned public utility such as a power plant or pipeline or water utility
is more likely to initially cause the price of the products it produces to
increase—because utility prices in the United States are regulated to
cover all the costs and still yield a governmentally fixed rate of return
for all capital investments the regulators approve. Thus prices will rise
if buying and operating a new capital item means additional costs
but it does not, at least initially, generate enough additional revenues
to cover them. That is usually the case for major new facilities being
constructed to meet higher demands that are expected to arrive in the
distant future.

A related price-increasing effect occurs when regulators allow a regulated
employer to earn profits that are a percentage of its costs. A good

example is the famous case of the union which threatened to strike a pipeline company because the company wanted to pay significantly higher wages to its workers than the union was demanding—so that the company's government regulator would allow it to charge higher prices and make higher profits. Fortunately, labor peace prevailed—the union capitulated and allowed its members to accept the higher wages and benefits demanded by the employer. (The inflationary impact of prices rising in response to regulatory and other actions not related to spending will be discussed in detail in chapters that follow.)

The union's position was not as stupid as it sounds. It represented workers in other contracts throughout the region and knew they would expect similar wages and benefits—and that trying to obtain them was likely to cause their union employers to move to non-union labor and their union employers' customers to respond to the higher prices that would have to be charged to cover the higher wages by moving to alternative services whose workers were represented by other unions. That is exactly what happened. Moreover, the higher prices that resulted contributed to inflation without there being any increase in spending or the money supply. It also caused unemployment as the higher prices the remaining union employers had to charge resulted in fewer services being sold so that fewer employees were needed.

Increased supply prices discourage additional investment spending. At any point in time the efforts of employers to purchase more and more new capital assets may cause their prices to be bid higher and higher as more and more are purchased—thus causing new capital assets to generate lower and lower yields for the public and private employers who make the investment purchases to buy them. If this occurs, the expected rate of return per investment dollar will decline.

Higher supply prices for capital goods can occur for several reasons. First, the increased demand for the capital assets may cause their prices to be bid up. Additionally, there may be rising costs associated with the higher levels of production needed to produce each subsequent new capital item. This tends to mean that the employers producing the capital items will be willing to supply each subsequent asset only if they can get a higher price for it to cover their higher costs.

For example, to produce ten percent more fire engines and construction cranes each month in response to the existence of increased investor purchases might require the Caterpillar company to begin paying its employees overtime in order to get them to work longer days and on Saturdays and Sundays. In such a case, although the employer is physically capable of building the additional fire engines and construction cranes, it might not be willing to do so unless it can get a higher price to cover the additional and higher costs resulting from their production. This will tend to discourage potential investors.

Increased operating costs discourage additional investments. Another possible cause of declining rates of return at any point in time is an increase in the cost of operating existing capital items as the additional capital items come on line and the demand for workers and other cost items increases. On a national scale the same negative impact on investment spending would be generated by imposing additional operating costs on employers such as requiring all of them to buy health insurance or pay higher employment taxes.

Similarly, employers who are considering expanding their production by investing in new capital assets must consider what will happen to all their costs if they hire more workers and buy more energy and other inputs. If employers expect their need for more workers and inputs will cause their wage and other costs to increase, the rates of return they will expect from the additional new investments will be lower.

Productivity increases. On the other hand, the tendency for the expected rates of return on investment spending to decline (declining MEIs) as more and more capital items are purchased tends to be offset to the extent the new capital items embody productivity-increasing new technologies that require fewer workers and use less energy and other inputs. Then the employers who buy new capital items will end up needing fewer workers and have lower operating costs.

What this means, when employers make profit maximizing investment decsions, is that investment spending to buy new capital items will tend to occur at each level of interest rates so long as the reductions in wage expenses and other costs resulting from using the new technologies exceed the cost of buying and operating the additional capital items.

It also means, in the real world, that employer investment spending that acquires capital goods that make workers more productive can cause unemployment—*unless spending also increases so that the additional production can be sold.*

Diseconomies of scale. The production costs of newly acquired capital items also tend to be higher if they cause employers to reach a size where there are *diseconomies of scale* as they increase production. This occurs when each subsequent capital item an employer buys makes the employer increasingly too large for maximum production efficiency (minimum cost per unit of output). As a result more and more capital and operating costs are needed to achieve the same additions to output. For example, declining productivity might set in at a local Starbucks store if it attempts to squeeze in more and more newly purchased espresso machines, and tables. In other words, the MEI of the investment spending required to buy each such capital item would get lower and lower as more and more are added.

Declining capital productivity and diseconomies of scale are not inevitable as an economy grows. They will not occur if the number of employers increases so that each subsequent capital item can be used by an efficient-sized employer. For example, Starbucks knows about the diseconomies of scale so it is more likely to open another new and highly efficient (low cost per cup) store nearby rather than allow an existing store to become so crowded and overly capitalized that it produces inefficiently (high cost per cup). On the other hand Starbucks management also understands that there are *economies of scale* such that one store that is large enough to be efficient can be better than two stores so close together that each has too few customers.

Overall in the United States, the rising levels of wages and higher product prices for inputs such as gasoline and raw materials have been generally offset by technological advances, capital accumulation, and the ability of the economy to generate enough customer demand to allow full employment and the economies of scale. In essence, despite those cost increases, the motivations of the investors and the expected returns on their investment spending have resulted in the accumulation of more and more capital goods and the production of more and more goods and services.

There is every reason to believe that technological advances will continue. Similarly, there is every reason to believe that employers will be willing to make capital investments so long as they expect that the capital items they buy will generate whatever they feel is "enough" revenues. The big uncertainty is the existence of customers to buy the additional production and, in so doing, provide the necessary revenues. That, as pragmatic analysts know, is not a problem—*so long as appropriate policies are pursued by the federal government and the Federal Reserve*. Without those policies, however, there may not be sufficient investment spending for an economy's production capacity to grow and its wages to increase.

INVESTMENT AND THE PRODUCTIVITY OF CAPITAL

At any point in time in a dynamic modern economy, such as those of the United States and the Scandinavian countries, there will inevitably be a huge number of investment purchasing opportunities available and they will involve various and sundry types and amounts of plant, equipment and inventories. Generally more investments will be expected to be profitable when the economy is booming and employer optimism is high—and less when the economy is not booming and employer expectations are low. And at any point in time the possible investments that might be made would tend to range from capital items with high MEIs to those with relatively low MEIs.

Table 3-1 presents an example MEI schedule depicting the relationship that might exist in an economy at a particular point in time between the amount of capital goods that might be purchased and the MEIs investors think they will generate. It also shows the total amount of investment spending is $15 billion higher than the amount that will be done by the economy's profit-maximizing employers. The total is higher at each MEI rate to depict the reality that more newly produced capital items will be purchased than just those that are profitable because their would-be employers are oriented towards goals such as revenue maximization or market share or self-aggrandizement.

Figure 3-1 presents the Table 3-1 economic data in a graphic form. It gives us an initial look at the possible uses of monetary policy and economic models: It suggests that raising or lowering the general level of an economy's interest rates, something the Federal Reserve may be capable of doing (but not the way most people think), can affect the total amount of investment spending that causes production and employment to occur. As analysts shall see, however, affecting interest rates to affect investment and other spending may not be a realistic solution when total spending in the United States needs to be increased or decreased.

Table 3-1

An economy's MEI and investment schedules

MEI (rate of return expected)	New capital items with this MEI (billions)	Total new capital items bought (billions)
11	$10	$25
10	20	35
9	30	45
8	40	55
7	50	65
6	60	75
5	70	85
4	80	95

Different rates of interest. The construction and use of models using such a single general level of interest rates is common both among economists doing "scientific" analyses of economies and "traders" engaged in high frequency trading. Unfortunately their models inevitably oversimplify the real world to the point of absurdity. In the real world, many different rates of interest exist simultaneously in an economy such as the United States.

For example, an employer with a spotty credit rating might have to pay ten percent to get the funds for the money it needs to buy a new capital item while another with a good credit rating has to pay only five percent to acquire funding to buy the same item.

Similarly, one might have to pay a higher or lower rate of interest depending on the type of capital item being acquired and its collateral value.

What does exist at any time in the United States and every other economy is a general or average level of interest rates. When money is tight the entire level of interest rates is higher; when money and credit are made readily available by the Federal Reserve, the general or average level tends to be lower.

But, once again, as has been seen for consumer spending and shall be seen for all the other major types of spending, minor changes in the level of interest rates are not all that significant in the United States economy—because the spending that causes production, employment, and, rarely, inflation, is much more influenced by the existence of many other considerations. This is particularly the case when an economy's public and private employers have goals other than profit maximization. It is also the case when the economy has an existing stock of capital that is unused due to inadequate levels of total spending.

The existence of other considerations is important. It suggests that lowering the general level of an economy's interest rates may not be an effective way to increase the total amount of spending that causes production and employment to occur in the United States economy.

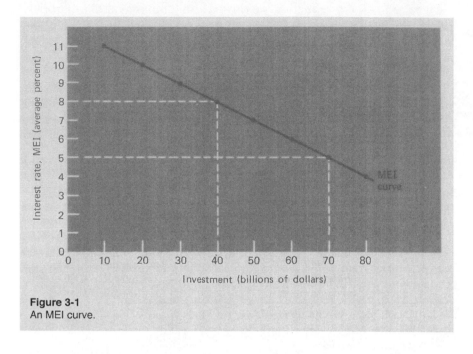

Figure 3-1
An MEI curve.

A word of caution: what analysts shall subsequently find, contrary to the common knowledge repeated *ad nauseam* by journalists, congressmen, and Federal Reserve governors, is that the relatively minor interest rate changes the Federal Reserve periodically attempts to achieve, have virtually no (repeat no) effect on the consumer, investment, government, or foreign spending that might result in production, employment and changes in the level of prices. They are considered here only as a starting point—to help understand where and how and why the Federal Reserve's interest-rate-oriented policies *have gone wrong and always will go wrong when there is a recession or depression.*

New investment opportunities arrive constantly.

In a static and unchanging economy with profit-maximizing investors, once all the potential new capital assets with sufficiently high rates of return (MEIs) have been purchased no further investment spending will occur. It woul only start again when interest rates fall or, more importantly, something happens to raise the MEIs of additional capital items that the economy's employers might acquire. In such a world, only if interest rates fall or something happens so that expected returns (MEI) rise will employers be motivated by the pursuit of profits and income to engage in investment spending to acquire more newly produced plant, equipment, and inventory.

But we do not live in such a static and unchanging world.

Replacement Investment. In the real world things are always changing. For instance, the need for replacement investment tends to occur continuously in every economy as its employers' existing stock of capital is used up in their production processes. The more capital goods the public and private employers of an economy employ and the more intensely they are used, the more capital will wear out and open vacancies for the productive employment of new replacement capital goods that can be acquired with new investment spending.

Whether such worn out equipment and depleted inventories will be replaced via investment spending, however, depends on the goals of their employers, the costs and revenues their employers expect them to generate, and the interest rates the employers have to pay (or forego earning if they use their own money) to get the necessary money.

It is the current level of production in an economy that determines the nature and size of the capital vacancies will open up in any given month. And since the level of production and employment in an economy depends on the total customer spending, the number of vacancies created each month depends on both the size of the economy's capital stock and how intensively it is used to produce the economy's GNP.

Here's the chain of reasoning: an economy's level of production affects how many capital vacancies will occur each month as plant and equipment is worn out; the level of production and the degree to which inventories are drawn down depends on the level of total customer spending; and the employers investment spending as a result of their capital vacancies varies in response to whatever goals the economy's investors are pursuing, the level of total purchasing that actually occurs so that plant and equipment is worn out and inventories drawn down, and what the employers expect for the future.

Complicating things for the policymakers, the plant and equipment which does wear out can often be replaced with idled and underutilized equipment. Similarly, some inventories which are drawn down do not need to be replaced because the sales activities they were supporting have declined.

The relationship between the size of an economy's capital stock and the intensity of its use can result in some interesting circumstances for policy makers to consider. For instance, during a good part of the Great Recession which started in 2008, the United States' economy only produced at about 80 percent of capacity. (at one point it had about $20 trillion of annual production capacity of which only about $16 trillion was being utilized). As a result, plant and equipment did not wear out as quickly as they would have if the economy had been producing at its full employment capacity. In essence, the lower level of total sales meant that some drawn down inventories and worn out equipment did not need to be replaced.

The tendency towards reduced investment spending when there is a recession is important. In the Great Recession that started in 2008 it meant that investment spending to buy replacement plant and equipment and to maintain inventories *fell* at the very time the United States needed more total spending to get back to full employment levels of production.

Moreover, just because plant and equipment wears out or an inventory is drawn down does not guarantee it will ever be replaced. Each investment expenditure for replacement purposes is a totally new decision. The used up plant, equipment and inventory might have originally been purchased even though they had a low or even negative MEIs because interest rates at the time were also low or the employer was pursuing goals other than profit maximization—now the employers may face a different level of interest rates and credit availability and have new goals and new revenue and cost expectations.

In essence, there is a lot more than just an economy's level of interest rates that determines whether its employers will engage in investment spending to replace used up and obsolete capital and drawn down inventories. For example, if business is off at a trucking company because the economy has slipped into a recession the company might not expect new trucks to be sufficiently profitable, particularly if it already has trucks sitting idle or partially used due to a lack of customers. Then the company would not buy new trucks *no matter how low the rate of interest.*

On the other hand, if maximizing profits was not its goal the trucking company might both cut its freight rates and buy more trucks in order to increase its market share or revenues or impress its owner's neighbors. *Profits and profit maximization in response to interest rates are not the only game in town for employers in the real world of the United States.*

Furthermore, things can only get worse once an economy slips into a recession and spending for capital items begins to decline. Things get worse because the reduced investment spending means fewer workers and thus reduced wage payments and personal incomes in the capital goods industries. That, in turn, causes consumer spending to tend to decline even more as the capital goods workers stop buying haircuts, houses, and cars. And that, in turn further reduces the need for more capital goods. All these spending-reducing forces feeding on each other tend to occur. In essence, *once a recession gets started it may well continue and worsen unless something is done to turn things around.*

For example, an economy operating at a $30 trillion full employment level of production and employment might have $3 trillion of investment spending for replacement purposes if the average interest rate in the economy is 4 percent. It is then reasonable to expect more investment spending for replacement capital if interest rates are lower and less if they are higher. Thus if the economy's level of income drops to $25 trillion so that less capital wears out, or its average rate of interest rises to 10 percent, its employers might reduce their replacement investment spending to $2 trillion; if it drops to $20 trillion its employers might cut their replacement spending to $1 trillion or even to zero.

The example is simple but the concepts are real and have serious policy implications when an economy moves into a recession.

Figure 3-2 simplistically depicts the kind of situation that tends to exist over time as an economy's public and private employers accumulate larger and larger stocks of capital. It illustrates the different levels of investment spending that might occur in an economy when there are different levels of total spending creating different levels of replacement investment opportunities at each rate of return.

More specifically, this simplistic example depicts the different amounts of investment spending that might be done to replace capital in this example economy at three different levels of spending and production: a GNP of $800 billion is full employment; $600 billion is the economy in a serious recession; and $400 billion is the economy in a terrible depression.

Since the economy's level of production determines how many vacancies will occur each month, and since the level of production depends on the level of total customer spending, the amount of capital vacancies created and the level of replacement investment spending (Ir) to fill them depends on the level of total purchasing that actually occurs so that plant and equipment is worn out and inventories drawn down.

The example economy operating at its $800 billion full employment level of production and employment would have $60 billion of investment spending for replacement purposes if the interest rate in the economy is 4 percent—and, as analysts might expect, more investment spending for replacement capital if interest rates are lower and less if they are higher. If the economy's level of spending drops to $600 billion its employers would reduce their replacement investment spending to $40 billion; if it drops to $400 billion its employers would drop their replacement spending to $20 billion. The example is simple but the concepts are real and, as analysts shall see, have serious policy implications.

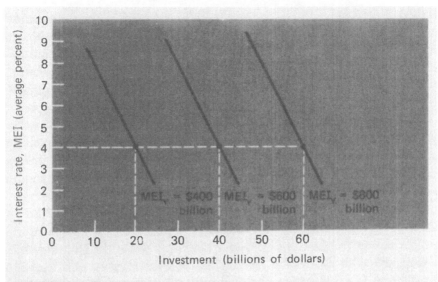

Figure 3-2
Investment demand at different GNP levels.

Autonomous investment spending. New capital items that might be profitable for investors to buy arrive and encourage investment, no matter what an economy's level of income. They arrive as a result of circumstances that are "autonomous" or unrelated to employers' replacement needs. In other words, companies such as Apple or Toyota can make the autonomous investments needed to bring out new products and expect to make a lot of money or create a lot of value even if the country is in a recession and unemployment is rising. So can governments, churches, and anyone else.

**Among the possible autonomous causes
of higher MEIs and more investment:**

1. *New products*. New products often require new and different types of capital to manufacture. Employers anticipating profits from the sales of such goods and services may then expect high returns from investments made to acquire the plant, equipment, and inventory needed to produce and sell them. The invention of each new wave of more-advanced cell phones, pharmaceuticals, cars, surgical procedures, and computers, for instance, undoubtedly

required additional new investment expenditures on the part of employers who wanted to manufacture and sell them. Every so often for centuries a pundit gets a bit of notoriety by proclaiming that "everything has been invented" or "investors are running out of opportunities." In the real world, however, new ideas are continually being built on old ideas so there is no reason to expect the introduction of new products and services to slow down.

2. *Additional customer spending.* Additional customers might arrive for both existing and new products. Apple's introduction of the iPad and iPhone, for example, generated unexpectedly large and profitable sales; Apple and its suppliers responded by rushing to buy plant, equipment and inventory so Apple would be able to produce and sell more of them. Apple made the investment spending to acquire the additional capital items because it expected, rightly as the results showed, that their employment would be highly profitable. In other words, Apple's decision makers expected the MEIs of the additional capital to be very high and they were right. But it was not just the prospect of high rates of return relative to the rate of interest that drove Apple's leadership to make investment needed to develop and produce its products. There were obviously a great deal of non-monetary motivations involved in the decisions as well.

   More customers spending to buy existing goods and services can have the same effect. For example, a housing boom might cause a window glass and lumber manufacturers to open new factories and to buy new capital equipment for its existing factories. In a broader vein, the rise in consumer spending each time the United States has come out of a recession has tended to motivate employers throughout the economy to rush to make capital investments both to replace capital that has been depleted and add even more so they can increase their sales of goods and services to even higher levels than previously existed.

3. *New technologies.* The MEIs of potential new capital assets will rise if more efficient (lower cost) methods of operating them are devised. The same effect occurs if a new type of machine embodying

technological advances results in a new and more efficient (lower cost) method of production. For example, the expected profits and values of capital equipment used in water distillation will rise with every new technique lowering the cost of producing a gallon of water. Alternately, new technologies can also affect MEIs by lowering the supply price of capital items. For example, the move to the computerized manufacturing of solar panels and machine tools reduced both the need to employ skilled workers and the wastage of costly materials. The resulting lower manufacturing costs drove down their prices as their manufacturers competed for sales.

4. *Lower noncapital costs.* The noncapital costs of production such and wages and energy may decline because of a reduction in the cost of some ingredient used in a production process. For example, the government might remove some excise taxes that had previously been levied on some input required in the operation of certain types of capital item. Or perhaps the price of a fuel might decline due to the collapse of a pricing cartel or because, as was the case in the United States, new technologies for extracting natural gas results in a reduction in its price that not only reduced the costs to its users but also motivated users of other energy sources such as coal and oil to begin using it in order to reduce their operating costs.

5. *Lower capital costs.* The possible effects of improved technologies on the supply prices of capital items and the noncapital costs of production have already been noted. It should also be noted, however, that the supply prices of capital goods can also be reduced for other reasons. For example, the demand for capital goods might decline, and thus their prices tend to fall, with the ending of the burst of investment spending that tends to occur as an economy comes out of a recession.

6. *Lower interest rates.* Interest is a major cost of employing capital goods. Thus the level of an economy's interest rates helps determine the amounts of both income-related and autonomous investment spending that can be done by profit and quasi-profit maximizing employers under a given set of supply prices, revenues,

and operating costs. It can also affect the investment decisions of employers with other goals because interest is a cost that, like all the others, must be covered no matter what the investors' goals. Furthermore, when the level of interest rates in an economy rises or falls it can cause capital to be substituted for labor or labor to be substituted for capital. For instance, the level of the economy's interest rates could decline and cause more investment spending so that capital replaces labor in employers' production processes. Such investments are considered to be autonomous investments because they are not related to changes in the economy's level of income.

7. *Increased availability of loans and credit.* Lenders and vendors feel more comfortable about making loans and extending credit when an economy is expected to grow or is growing—because they think they are more likely to be paid. Employers similarly tend to be willing to use their reserves and go into debt if they expect the investments they make will generate enough revenues because the economy is or will grow.

8. *Changing employer goals.* The move of some of an economy's employers from attempting to maximize profits to other goals, such attempting to maximize growth or maximize revenues or just plain spend all the money they can get, may increase the amount of investment spending they are willing to undertake at each level of interest rates. In effect, investment spending in the economy then tend to increase because the employers are now willing to sacrifice profits, assets, and credit lines in order to purchase capital goods with MEIs below the interest rates that have to be paid to finance their purchases. (That is the same as saying the employers are willing to buy capital items with present values below their supply prices or that the capital items would yield additional revenues below their supply prices, operating costs, and interest costs).

United States' legacy airlines and legacy automobile manufacturers are notorious examples of private employers pursuing goals other than profit maximization; most governmental and non-profit employers do not even attempt to quantify and compare the costs and benefits that will occur when they buy capital goods such as police cars, roads, drug recovery programs, homeless shelters, and military aircraft. They tend to spend all the money they receive and, often, all they can borrow.

9. *Changing employer expectations.* Investment decisions made today often result in capital items being purchased that will be operated many years into the future when the revenues and costs they contribute cannot possibly be known. Investors are therefore, it is suggested, primarily motivated by what they know of the past, see today, and expect in the immediate future. Accordingly, if today is gloom and doom, such as when the economy is in a recession or has an anti-business government, they may assume the distant future will be equally bad and pass on potentially viable investments even though supply prices and interest rates are low; if things are booming they may assume the distant future will be equally bright and proceed to invest with an almost "irrational exuberance" even if it means paying above average interest rates and supply prices.

The instability of investment spending.

Investment spending is similar to consumption spending in that both contribute to the total amount of spending that occurs in an economy. They also tend to track together in that both tend to be higher as the level of income in the economy increases—consumption because higher and higher levels of disposable income tend to occur when there are higher and higher levels of production and employment; investment because more and more capital goods will wear out at the higher and higher levels of production associated with higher and higher level of spending.

Similarly, at each higher and higher level of income there will tend to be different total amounts of consumer spending at each level of interest rates just as there will be different levels of investment spending at each level of interest rates.

Surveys of investment spending in the United States indicate that the amount of investment that goes on at any point in time tends to fluctuate proportionally more than fluctuations in the amount of consumer and total spending. The instability appears to have many causes. The causes are related to the autonomous changes listed above—because they may not arrive smoothly. For example:

Changing interest rates and financing opportunities. Changes in the level of interest rates and the supply of credit and loanable funds may be caused at any time by Federal Reserve actions *or the actions of other central banks and other creators and lenders of money and credit.* This would change the amount of investment spending even if it does not affect employers' expectations about the profitability and revenues of the capital items that might be purchased.

Changing expectations. Changing investor expectations are an important cause of instability, perhaps the most important cause of all. In the real world expectations are much more important to the investment decision than interest rates. And they can be quite volatile. The basis for the instability is that no employer can ever know for certain what revenues it will obtain from new capital items it might purchase or what the costs of operating them will actually turn out to be. Instead the employer can only estimate them as best it can. The estimates may be based on experience, knowledge, and even contractual agreement—but there is always an element of uncertainty.

Furthermore, since employers cannot predict the future with any certainty, it appears that the expectations of investors are heavily guided by the present of near-past circumstances, even when they are virtually irrelevant. For example, unexpected losses and the immediate political uproar from a nuclear power station being wiped out in a flood is no guide to how profitable a new nuclear power facility will be forty years from now. But, if experience is any guide, it is likely that the revenue and cost expectations for forty years out will be hardly considered at all.

For another example, anxieties today about the policies advocated by the current occupant of the White House may discourage expectations as to the revenues and costs that will be generated years after the current occupant has retired to write his memoirs and cash in on his fame. Or just the reverse, a pro-investment congress or White House might cause high expectations for the future and result in investment increases even though there is no certainty at all as to the policies of the next inhabitant.

In essence, today's immediate business and political conditions tend to disproportionately affect the things that influence an investment decision to buy or not buy a new refinery or steel mill or highway or government office building or anything else that will not be operational until years in the future—when the business conditions and governmental policies might be quite different.

The accelerator effect.

Higher levels of income are associated with higher investment spending because the higher income levels are associated with increases in the amount of capital that will wear out. But moves to a higher level of income do not always occur smoothly. Often they are subject to political and central bank changes as well as changes in foreign behavior. The resulting jerky moves to or from a higher level of spending and production can themselves cause dramatic changes in investment spending. It is called *the accelerator effect* because an initial increase or decrease in investment spending or total spending may move or accelerate an economy to even larger or smaller levels of investment and total spending.

Consider an economy that starts out with its labor force and its $10 trillion capital stock fully employed with ten percent of its capital wearing out in each time period. Assume the economy is at full employment with $3 trillion of investment spending of which $1 trillion is replacement investment and $2 trillion is autonomous investment spending. That means that in the next year $1.2 trillion of replacement capital will be needed to replace ten percent of the economy's now higher $12 trillion capital stock.

But what if in the next year no new products or other changes come along to cause another $2 trillion of autonomous investment? If nothing else happens to encourage even more investment, total investment spending in the next year will decline from today's $3.0 trillion to only $1.2 trillion.

But the decline in investment spending may not stop at $1.2 trillion—because the decline in investment spending may result in a decline in the wages and other incomes that had previously been earned by producing capital goods. This, in turn, might result in a decline in the wages and other incomes of people in the capital goods industries. Also there may be less state and local government spending as their tax collections fall. Indeed it is possible that by the next time period arrives total spending will have declined so much that there will be no need for any replacement investment because the capital stock that remains is more than enough to produce everything that can be sold at the new and even lower level of total spending. So total investment spending will drop to zero and consumer spending and state and local spending will fall even more.

In this example, the initial reduction in investment spending causes the economy's production of goods and services to recede (aka *recession*) or be depressed (aka *depression*) below that which would exist at full employment. As a result, production in the economy will be reduced, unemployment and welfare spending will rise, tax collections will decline so that governmental services will either have to been reduced or there will be deficits, and the inevitable foreclosures and bankruptcies that befall unemployed people and employers with fewer and fewer customers will occur.

If nothing is done to reverse or prevent the decline the economy will *sooner or later* reach some point at which investment spending begins to increase. This could occur because of something such as the Federal Reserve making additional money and credit available; or because of the arrival of new "must have" products; or perhaps so much capital finally wears out that the employers expect profitable opportunities for replacement capital even if the economy remains seriously depressed.

The additional investment then triggers a move in the other direction—it drives total spending upward as workers and governments respond to the additional jobs and revenues. Their additional spending will then, in turn, cause even more production so that even more capital is worn out and even more spending is generated by the resulting higher and higher levels of personal incomes and governmental revenues.

The upwards move in total spending will continue until investment stops expanding. Then once again the level of total spending will stop growing. Then once again there will only be replacement investment and the level of investment spending will again begin to decline and the cycle will begin again.

This helps explain a number of economic observations: that investment spending tends to be the most volatile of the major spending components; that how investment spending proceeds as expectations and the level of income change greatly affects both the appropriateness and timing of monetary and fiscal policies and their effectiveness; and, most important of all for analysts to keep in mind, *there is no reason to think that the amount of total spending that occurs at any point in time during the spending oscillations will somehow automatically be high enough to cause full employment.*

INTEREST RATES, INVESTMENT SPENDING, AND THE STOCK OF CAPITAL

Once they are purchased capital goods become part of an economy's stock of capital. The "optimum stock" for an economy includes all the capital goods an economy's public and private employers will want to have when the economy is at an equilibrium level of income. The size of that optimum stock, at least when rational investors are involved, is determined the same things that affect investment spending: the contribution the capital can make to production, interest rates, the supply prices of capital items, and the product prices and the non-capital costs that the employers confront.

Accordingly, with such investor rationality an economy's stock of capital will tend to be expanded whenever the additional capital goods that might be purchased are expected to be productive enough to yield rates of return sufficiently high relative to the rates of interest that must be paid or foregone to finance their purchase.

But what determines the total amount of capital that will tend to exist in an economy at any point in time *if there is adequate customer spending in the economy* and its employers are free to buy whatever amount of capital items they desire to employ? The basic answer is that the amount of capital is related to the expected net revenues and costs associated with operating the capital, the supply prices that have to be paid to buy each successive capital item, the level of interest rates and the availability of credit in the economy, and, most importantly of all, the motivations of those who employ it.

More capital tends to be wanted by profit-maximizing and other employers when interest rates are lower because lower interest rates mean a reduction in the cost of using capital in the employers' production processes. Thus, when an economy's interest rates decline, the production processes economy's employers tend to become more capital intensive. This occurs as the employers find it reduces their production costs to increase their stock of capital and substitute the relatively inexpensive capital for the labor they have been employing. This allows them to increase their profits (or, in the case of employers who are not profit maximizers, to increase their production levels until they can no longer cover their production costs.)

Whether an employer will be able to do so, of course, depends on the degree to which the available technologies and institutions (labor unions, governmental regulators, suppliers) will allow them to do so. No such substitutions will occur if there is only one possible combination of capital and labor.

For a simplistic example of how lower interest rates result in a larger optimum stock of capital, consider the two production processes whose cost aspects are described in Table 3-2. They both provide the same level of production, but one (Process C) uses more capital and less labor than the other (Process L) which is labor intensive and uses less capital.

The data in the table indicate that at the highest of the three interest rates, the relatively labor intensive production process will be preferred by profit maximizing and revenue maximizing and output maximizing employers—because its lower costs will let them produce more output before they reach their goals and are motivated to stop adding more machines; the employers can go either way with the middle rate because the costs will be the same; and the production process employing relatively large amounts of capital will be preferred at the lowest rate of interest.

It all appears very rational and suggests that investment spending will increase to buy more capital if interest rates are reduced. At least, that is the theory. In the real world, however, there are things such as unions and labor laws and human non-economic goals and financial considerations. For example, if the labor laws are strongly pro-union they may be able to force the employer to use the labor-intensive process no matter what the interest rate might be.

Similarly, once the capital items for one type of production process have been purchased it may be too expensive to rip them out and make the investment purchases needed to replace them with the capital required for the other process when the interest rates change. And management may be too lazy or uninformed of the facts or insufficiently financed to make the investments needed to change to the other process even if it is not too expensive to do and there are no labor impediments.

Even more importantly, during periods of recession and slow growth, the time when more spending is needed to get the economy going again, is the time when capital tends to be idled—the time when employers are most likely *not* to add more capital items to increase their production capacities or replace their workers.

Table 3-2
Interest Rates, Production Process, and the Optimum Stock or Capital.

Interest rate	Production process	Stock of capital	Annual depreciation	Annual interest cost	Annual labor cost	Total cost
8%	Process C	$50,000	$5000	$4000	$2000	$11,000
	Process L	$10,000	$1000	$800	$8400	$10,020
6%	Process C	$50,000	$5000	$3000	$2000	$10,000
	Process L	$10,000	$1000	$600	$8400	$10,000
4%	Process C	$50,000	$5000	$2000	$2000	$9000
	Process L	$10,000	$1000	$400	$8400	$9800

What all this means is that driving down the interest rates in the United States during a recession is *not* likely to cause employers such as General Motors and Joe's Corner Cleaners to respond by making investment expenditures to replace their current lightly used automobile assembly plants and clothes cleaning machines with more highly automated capital-intensive plants. In other words, *once an employer's capital stock is in place interest rate changes, even big ones, are not likely to have much effect on the employer's investment spending.* This is an important reality analysts must keep in mind when evaluating policy alternatives, particularly during a recession when more spending is needed.

The optimum stock of capital.

The "marginal efficiency of capital" (MEC) is the rate of return expected from an increment in the economy's stock of capital. It contrasts with the MEI which is the rate of return expected from an additional increment of investment spending. They tend to converge but at any point in time they may differ for several reasons:

First, an investment expenditure may merely be replacing an existing capital item with a higher MEI instead of adding to the stock of capital.

Second, the MEI of a possible investment may be affected by short term prices and costs—for example, when the price of the capital item is temporarily bid up by an accelerator-caused bubble in demand or is affected by higher costs such as when it requires workers to work overtime to build it.

The MEC, in essence, is the long-term expected rate of return when the economy is in equilibrium; the MEI is the short-term expected rate before prices and costs and revenues settle down.

Whether or not profit-maximizing and other employers will actually want to spend money to buy and employ a particular capital item depends on whether or not the item is expected to be at least productive enough to cover the interest and other expenses of its employment. In essence, the higher the interest rates of an economy, the fewer the capital goods that employers will see as productive enough to cover all the costs associated with their ownership and employment.

Table 3-2 also depicts the way the optimum stock of capital for an economy's public and private employers might relate to lower or higher interest rates. In this example economy, a permanent reduction of the average rate of interest from eight percent to four percent would increase the optimum stock of capital from $1000 to $5000.

The data are a reasonable depiction of the interest rate and capital relationship in the sense that some employers will want to employ more capital when interest rates are lower—because the lower interest rates mean lower overall costs of production. It then logically follows that lower interest rates will result in more capital items being purchased and the capital stock expanded so that capital can be substituted for labor in the production process.

The substitution of capital for labor occurs because lower interest rates can result in lower production costs for goods and services when the additional capital is employed. Higher interest rates tend to have the opposite effect—encouraging the use of less capital and more labor by employers throughout the entire economy.

Initial pragmatic conclusions.

Table 3-2 is a reasonable depiction of the interest rate and capital relationship because some employers will want to employ more capital when interest rates are lower—because the lower interest rates mean lower overall costs of production. It then logically follows that lower interest rates will result in more capital items being purchased and the capital stock expanded so that capital can be substituted for labor in the production process. This occurs because lower interest rates can result in lower production costs for goods and services when the additional capital is employed. Higher interest rates tend to have the opposite effect—encouraging the use of less capital and more labor by employers throughout the entire economy.

This analysis suggests that higher interest rates will generate more jobs in an economy by discouraging the use of capital in the economy's production processes. That is true if higher rate cause employers to substitute labor for capital. But generating jobs during periods of recession by discouraging the use of capital with high interest rates or regulations is neither desirable nor necessary for an economy's labor force to be fully employed (sorry France). To the contrary, most pragmatic analysts see the best policies for an economy such as the United States to be low interest rates so that each worker will tend to have more capital to use *and* appropriate monetary and fiscal policies so the economy's public and private employers have enough customer revenues to keep *all* their workers and capital fully employed.

In other words, high interest rates and make-work "jobs bills" and "retraining projects" for which there are then no subsequent employers may *not* be the best way for rational policy makers to obtain full employment. In the real world 100 men on one hundred bulldozers (large amount of capital per worker due to low capital costs) producing in response to road buying are likely to produce more roads than 100 men leaning on shovels (small amount of capital per worker due to high capital costs) in response to a make-work jobs bill.

Most pragmatic analysts see the best policy combination for an economy such as the United States is to keep its interest rates as low as possible so that the average worker has as much capital as possible to produce with *and* have appropriate monetary and fiscal policies so the economy's public and private employers have enough customer revenues to keep *all* their workers and capital fully employed.

THE REAL WORLD OF INVESTMENT AND CAPITAL ACCUMULATION

What has been examined so far is a bit of the conventional macroeconomist's traditional analysis of rational investment spending and capital accumulating decisions. It basically assumes investment spending and the resulting capital accumulation occurs in response to employers' earning expectations and the interest rates they have to pay or forego earning in order to obtain the necessary funds. Such an assumption is traditional in the study of macroeconomics. It is also very naïve.

In the real world of jobs and production in the United States, the people, governments, and companies who act as the economy's employers and make its investment expenditures frequently *pursue goals other than maximizing their earnings or the value of the benefits to their constituencies.*

Buying more than the optimum amount of capital.

Some employers buy more capital than is needed to maximize their earnings. It's quite common and they do so for numerous and often interrelated reasons: For example, because they want to increase their market share;

Or because they want to maximize their revenues; or because they want to maintain or increase their social importance as an employer in their community;

Or because the employer's decision maker wants to have an organization that is as big as his neighbors or competitors;

Or because the employer's union threatens to strike if the employer doesn't improve their working conditions by buying air conditioners and safer equipment;

Or because some government threatens to withdraw a favorable regulation or impose an unfavorable one if they don't;

Or because they have some money and don't know what else to do with it;

Or because they see it as a way to help some crony or family member or politician;

Or because they just plain make a mistake;

Or because they want to employ capital near where the CEO likes to golf so he can justify investing in a company plane that can be used to fly there to "check things out."

The list of potential motivations that might cause a public, non-profit, or for-profit employer to buy more or less capital than is needed to maximize earning is endless. Important among them:

Market share and maximum revenues. United, American, US Airways, Delta, Pan Am, TWA, and other past and present legacy airlines are classic examples of investing far beyond the levels needed to maximize their earnings. They each pursued gross revenues and market share rather than efficient production and profits—and all went bankrupt doing so. Then the value of their shares and bonds plummeted and many of the excess capital items they bought to increase their sizes and market shares can be viewed where the planes are parked in the Arizona desert.

A similar fate almost befell the plants and equipment of similarly oriented Chrysler and GM in 2008 except that their unions prevailed upon the Obama Administration and Congress to bail them out when they bailed out some of the too-big-to-fail financial intermediaries. The Detroit landscape is littered with their excess plants and equipment and America's junkyards are filled with the brands federal bureaucrats required them to terminate as a condition of the financial aid they needed to survive—Mercury, Saturn, Dodge, Pontiac, and Hummer.

Investing by mistake. Investor mistakes are another major reason not all investment spending occurs because capital purchases are expected to yield high enough returns or other goals are being pursued.

Consider inventories. They are treated as capital items acquired via investments because they are needed for employers' operations. For example, consider an employer that produces 1000 units because it anticipates selling 800 to its customers and desires 200 more for its own use in order to increase the size of its inventory. If the employer foresees incorrectly and sells only 700 the employer's inventory holdings of this product will be expanded by 300 instead of 200.

Inventories buildups and drawdowns are things analysts and policy makers watch closely. In this case it will appear to the unsophisticated that the economy is doing well in that its employers and workers have produced and sold 1000 items. In fact, the subsequent sale of the 100 excess items merely requires drawing down the inventory—no additional production and employment will occur.

In essence, the existence of production and employment associated with the buildup of inventories across a broad spectrum of employers is not necessarily a cause for press releases and speeches suggesting a depressed economy has turned the corner and its recession is finally ending—*rather it can be an early warning signal that the economy is performing even more poorly than its employers expected and that policies to increase total spending to induce production and employment need to be quickly implemented.*

Inadequate decision-making information. Lack of information is a major problem that leads to investment spending that is too large or too small or involves buying the wrong capital items. The supply prices of potential capital investments are fairly well known for private, public, and non-profit investors. So are the interest rate costs. And the operating costs of an additional capital asset can be estimated though even the most sophisticated employer may find it hard know with any degree of certainty what a capital item's future wages and other operating costs might be—particularly if the capital item whose investment is being considered has a long life such as a road or refinery or army tank.

The big question is how to value whatever it is that a potential new capital item will produce. A profit-oriented employer can, at least conceptually, even if it rarely happens in the real world, make an estimate of the value of the contribution that a capital will make by estimating the additional units of output the new capital item will contribute and the prices buyers will be willing to pay for its output.

But how does one value the services that will be produced by a road or school or halfway house? Traditional macroeconomic analysis assumes that such values can be estimated and the rates of return (MEIs) computed for each additional investment that might occur. In reality it is virtually impossible to estimate the "dollar value" of the goods and services which might occur as a result of an investment if they are not bought and sold in a market.

The inability to determine the value of what will be produced is the problem faced by governments and non-profits when they try to decide whether to invest in and employ such things as police cars, roads, schools, women's shelters, military planes, etc. They can know the supply prices; they can estimate the operating costs; but the best a potential employer of such *social capital* can do is guesstimate the value of whatever it is the capital will produce if the employer buys and operates it. And who is to do the guesstimating in the case of government investments—the bureaucrats whose empires will grow? The elected representatives whose supporters want jobs and contracts? The president, governors, or mayors?

So far it has been assumed that rational calculations can be made by employers who are deciding whether or not to buy a capital item, and that interest rates play an important role. But is this even possible, for example, if the employer of the capital is the street maintenance department of your local city and the $50,000 potential investment spending is the purchase price of a new street sweeper?

The supply price and interest rate costs are knowable and the operating costs are potentially calculable. What is totally lacking is an estimate of the value of the cleaner streets the sweeper will generate. In the private sector the expected revenues from the operation of a capital item can be based on estimates of the additional output it will contribute and the price the output will fetch. But this isn't the private sector. The street sweeper might have some quantity component such as tons of trash per week or miles of additional streets cleaned or streets cleaned every five days instead of every seven days. But what's that worth?

In the real world the value of many things is often impossible to calculate in money terms. Sometimes it is possible to make an estimate if the same services can also be bought from a private employer. Then a very specific rate of return can be calculated *if* it is assumed that the price the government is willing to pay reflects the value of the additional services the capital will provide—and not a rigged bid to help someone's crony or relative or to help a bureaucrat expand his empire.

Many observers feel that little, if any, effort is made by public and non-profit employers to make rational investments. Others are not sure. They suggest that elected officials try to make the most valuable investments—"get more bang for the taxpayers buck"—because they will be voted out of office if the public thinks their money has been badly spent.

Buying less than the optimum amount of capital.

Some employers, particularly those influenced by shareholders who have short-term objectives such as higher share prices in the immediate future, may deliberately not make potentially profitable investments in order to meet their influential shareholders desires for more immediately available cash to distribute and higher immediate profits. Such firms are frequently also characterized by cost cutting so excessive that the ensuing lack of service and quality discourages future customer revenues.

The usual goal of such activities is to push up short term profits and cash availability at the expense of the capital investments and customer service that would result in even greater profits in the future. This tends to generate cash the advocates of short term changes can strip out of the employer. It also tends to temporarily increase the value of the company's stocks and bonds as unwary financial investors misinterpret its earnings reports to think that the company's profits are growing and that even higher profits will follow. *

In the United States, Home Depot, eBay, and Chrysler have been suggested as companies with short term oriented managements and owners who have periodically limited their investment spending and customer service to levels below those needed to maximize their companies' profits over the long haul of time.

Hedge funds, investment and universal banks, and other corporate raiders routinely engage in such activities. They typically use their own funds, including as much borrowed money as possible, to buy enough of an employer's shares to get seats on its board of directors and a say in its policies. Then they force the employer to eliminate the current costs associated with the employer investing to get future profits.

Such actions provide the employer with a short term increase in reported profits and cash. The short-term "investors" are then able to take the cash via special dividends and distributions or sell their shares to unwary financial investors who have been seduced by the short-term increase in the profits. The corporate raiders then use the proceeds to repay their lenders, retaining what is left as the profits from their investment-killing raid. Alternately, they may take control the company, sell off its assets, and take as much of the proceeds as they can get.

And it works for them—until there is a black swan event such as mortgage collapse or euro crisis. Then the value of all shares and other financial instruments may be lower so that theirs cannot be sold for enough to repay the money they have borrowed to finance their raids. Then they tend to fail—unless the federal government or the Federal Reserve buys their "troubled assets" and bails them out.

Governments, of course, have their own version of investment-killing raiders. Better hospitals and more police services, for example, might well provide tangible benefits far in excess of the cost of buying and operating them—but not be purchased because the philosophy of those making the decisions is that "all government spending is bad" or "government debt is bad even if the value of the resulting services exceeds the interest rate expense associated with obtaining them.

Non-economic considerations. Non-economic considerations can motivate public and private employers to buy capital in excess of the amount needed to maximize their earnings. Among the many investment motivations that have been suggested: political pressures to create jobs, cronyism, corruption, nepotism—create employment for family members, and travel to destinations unsuitable for the efficient employment of capital.

Consider, for example, the experiences reported by an analyst who served on the board of a well-known nonprofit employer. He also served a term in a legislature as a reform candidate from the university district and had a seat on the Finance Committee where such decisions are made. It was a time of budgetary surpluses and thousands of capital expenditures were authorized involving billions of dollars. Not once at either the non-profit or the legislature were interest rates considered or attempts made to estimate the MEI or net benefits or anything else of the various capital items whose purchases were funded.

Other considerations such as cronyism, campaign contributions, and geographic location ruled the day. The basic investment goals of the elected decision makers and the non-profit's board were to keep their jobs and to spend every available dollar so that nothing would carry over to be spent by the next legislature or the non-profit in the next fiscal year.

Some pretty silly investments were funded. They were the public and non-profit investment equivalents of U.S Airways and American Airlines, before *and after* they went bankrupt, investing for market share and buying airbuses because their executives preferred visiting Paris to visiting Chicago and Seattle. His favorite was a multi-million dollar highway-related project to fund tunnels under a highway so that wild animals (moose) would not be hit by cars as the animals crossed between the wild areas on either side of the road. He questioned the agency representative as to how the wild animals would know to use the tunnels—and was assured that the agency's capital budget included signs so the animals would know where to go. The money was appropriated.

FORMULI FOR MAKING RATIONAL INVESTMENT CALCULATIONS

The emphasis on the expected rate of return is traditional in economics. There are, however, other conceptual approaches employers can use in an effort to make rational profit-maximizing investment decisions to purchase specific new capital goods. One involves computing the potential new capital good's "present value" and comparing it to the price that must be paid to buy the item; the second involves the comparison of total costs and total revenues expected from operating the new capital item.

Present value. The *present value* of a potential new income-yielding capital item that might be acquired with an investment expenditure is whatever amount investors are willing to pay to get its expected *net revenue*, the revenues in excess of its costs that an capital item is expected to generate if it is purchased and employed. If what an employer is willing to pay for those net revenues, the item's present value, is more than enough to buy the item, investment spending will occur and the production and employment of the capital item will result.

More specifically, net revenue is defined for investment purposes as the dollar value of whatever is produced by a capital item minus the additional costs caused by its employment. But, as analysts know, many public and human capital items such as police cars, educations and military planes do generate operating costs but do not directly generate actual dollars of revenue to which they can be compared. Then the best that can be done is to estimate the value of the benefits that will be produced by operating the capital item and comparing them to the cost of operating it.

In essence, the term "net revenues" means both the actual dollars of revenues if such revenues exist and, in the case of public and other capital items where they do not exist, the estimated value of the benefits as if they existed. The estimated values are typically obtained by assuming the amount of money spent to acquire them is equal to their value.

Investors find the present value of something they are considering purchasing and employing by comparing the dollar value of the additional goods or services it is expected to contribute minus its expected operating costs including interest but excluding depreciation.

Consider equipment whose employment is expected to produce goods or service worth an additional $500,000 during its one year of life and cost $401,000 to operate; left is $99,000. Now assume the investor is able to borrow money at ten percent (or earn ten percent if he loans out his money elsewhere).

If this is the case a rational profit-oriented investor would be willing to buy the equipment if its *supply price* is $90,000 or less: $500,000 of additional revenue minus $401,000 of additional operating costs minus $9,000 of interest equals $90,000, the item's present value to the investor. The investor would make the investment purchase and buy the capital item if he could get it for the $90,000 price or less. He would not make the investment if

The formula for finding the present value of any asset is as follows:

$$V = \frac{R1}{(1+i)} + \frac{R2}{(1+i)2} + \ldots + \frac{Rn}{(1+i)n}$$

Another example, assume that an investor is considering the purchase of a new capital item, a piece equipment or facility improvement he expects to yield $800,000 in excess of its operating costs in the one year of its life except interest and depreciation (R). Also assume it will cost 6 percent interest to finance the purchase. Applying the formula for determining the present value (V) to these data we see that:

$$V= \frac{\$800,000}{1.06} = \$754,716.98$$

Put another way, the present value of the capital item whose purchase is being considered is the maximum amount on which the investor can pay six percent interest if he expects the item to generate $50,000 to cover its capital costs. The required interest payment is then equal to:

6% x $754,716.98 = $45,283.02

The computation shows the present value of the potential capital item to be $764,716.98 at 6 percent. That means that if the investor buys the asset for $754,716.98 and pays $45,283.02 in interest to borrow that amount to make the purchase, he breaks even.

But what if the supply price of the item, the price at which the investor can buy it, was lower, such as $600,000? A rational investor would borrow the money at 6 percent and make the purchase because the asset has a higher present value at six percent than the $400,000 it costs to buy it. In fact, he would be paying out a total of $636,000 ($600,000 plus 6% interest on the $600,000) and receiving $800,000 of revenues for a profit of $164,000. The present value exceeds the supply price so investment spending will occur to purchase the item.

Consider the same investment opportunity except that the potential investor does not expect to get the $800,000 until the end of a two-year period. The approach is the same except he will now have to pay the 6 percent *compounded* for two years. This means he will pay six percent on the amount he borrows for the first year and then another six percent on the amount he borrows for the second year plus another six percent on the first year's interest. Thus:

1. $V = \dfrac{\$800,000}{(1.06)2}$

2. $V = \$711,997.15$

Which means a rational benefit maximizing employer will purchase the item if its supply price is less than $711,997.15

Now expand the example to an asset that will yield $400,000 in each of the two years of its life and for which our investor will again have to pay six percent interest. The present value of the item then is the sum of the one-year and two year present values. Or:

$$V = \frac{\$400,000}{(1.06)} + \frac{\$400,000}{(1.06)2}$$

= $377,358.49 + $359,595.81

= $736,954.30

Clearly the length of a capital item's life, the interest costs of financing its purchase, and the additions to the revenues it is expected to generate and how soon they are generated all affect the investment spending decisions of a profit-maximizing employer to buy plant, equipment, and inventory.

Total cost vs. total revenues. A second conceptual approach to profit or value maximizing investment decisions weighs total costs against total revenues. The total cost of buying and using a capital asset is the sum of the additional noncapital operating costs including the *normal profits* associated with its employment, the interest expenses of financing its acquisition, and the actual cost of its purchase less any salvage value.

Normal profits is economist-speak for the additional profits an employer must earn to make an investment "worth it" for the employer to proceed. For example, making millions of dollars of investments because it is calculated that they will generate a few thousand dollars of additional income may not be enough additional profits to offset the additional risks, hassles and uncertainties that might come as a result of buying and operating the capital. To a pragmatic analyst, normal profits are one of the costs of an employer operating a capital item.

Consider an employer already operating five machines producing 80,000 items that will sell for $120 each. This employer's investment purchase of a sixth machine will only occur if the expected additional costs associated with the sixth machine are less than or equal to the additional revenue the machine is expected to generate for the employer.

Assume the employer with his expertise and knowledge of his industry and competitors expects the sixth machine to last two years and add $1,279,159.80 to his total costs: $740,000 of direct operating costs for the supplies and workers to run the machine; $10,000 of normal profits to induce the employer to bear the additional burdens of an expanded operation; $40,000 of additional cost because the labor and materials for the first five machines will rise 50 cents per unit of production because of the employers efforts to hire the additional labor and buy the additional material for the sixth machine; $450,000 for the use of the sixth machine because it can be purchased for $500,000 and is expected to have a salvage value of $50,000 after two years; and $39,159.80 of interest to finance the purchase of the machine over its two year life.

Under these conditions the sixth machine will be purchased only if it is expected to produce more than the $1,279,159.80 in revenues at which the employer will break even. That would be the case if the sixth machine is expected to produce 14,000 units of production that can be sold for $110 each. In which case, the addition of the sixth machine would add $1,540,000 to the employer's revenues. It would be purchased.

But wait. There are other cost and revenue considerations that have to be considered. For example, the employment of the sixth machine may only increase the employer's total output by 13,500 units if its installation and operation in close proximity to the other five machines causes their combined production to fall by 500 units. And the increase in the employer's revenues that the 13,500 additional units add at $110 may not all be a net addition to the employer's revenues if the sale of the additional units drives down the market price for the output of the first five machines from $120 to $110 and thus reduces the employer's revenues by another $800,000 for an actual increase of $645,000 in the employer's revenues compared to the $1,279.80 it will add to his total costs. It won't be bought—*unless the employer has goals other than profit maximization.*

Calculating the marginal efficiency of investment (MEI). The MEI is the rate of return that a potential new capital item is expected to earn after all its costs, except interest, are covered. More specifically, the MEI is the rate of return that equates the expected flow of revenues and benefits in excess of expected operating costs including normal profits (efficiency) from one additional (marginal) newly constructed capital item to the cost of buying the item (investment).

Consider again the new machine that could be purchased by a public or private employer of capital with an investment expenditure of $10,000 and whose employment is expected to yield $61,000 of additional revenues (or estimated benefits) and add $40,000 of additional wages and other operating costs, including normal profits, to the employer's costs in the one year of its life after which it expires with no salvage value.

Under these circumstances, after covering the operating costs, the potential employer of the capital item expects to be left with $11,000; that's enough to cover the $10,000 purchase price with $1000 left over as profit—a return of 10 percent on the employer's $10,000 investment purchase of the machine. The MEI of this capital acquisition is ten percent.

The MEI of potential new capital asset that might be purchased can be calculated if its supply price is known, and it is possible to estimate the value of its production and its operating costs in each of the time periods of its life. The following algebraic formula, in which "r" represents the MEI, can be solved for the value of a capital item's MEI:

$$\text{Supply Price} = \frac{\text{Return over operating costs in period 1}}{(1+r)}$$

$$+ \quad \frac{\text{Return over}\ \text{operating costs}\ \text{in period 2}}{(1+r)2} \text{(continued . . .)}$$

$$+ \quad \frac{\text{Return over operating}\ \text{costs in last period (n)}\ \text{of asset's life}}{(1+r)n}$$

Consider a new capital asset costing $10,000 which is totally worn out without salvage value at a uniform rate during its life span of two years. It is expected add enough production to cover its operating costs plus yield an additional $5000 in the first year and $6050 in the second year (maybe its productivity rose in the second year because the employer's work force finally learned to use it; maybe its depreciation was larger the first year when it was first used). In any event:

$$\$10,000 = \frac{\$5000}{(1+r)} + \frac{\$6050}{(1+r)2}$$

Solving this equation yields an expected rate of return, its MEI, of 10 percent for the capital item whose investment purchase is being considered. Whether this capital asset will actually be purchased depends upon the interest rate that must be paid (or foregone if the potential investor uses his own funds) to acquire the dollars necessary to make the purchase.

CHAPTER SUMMARY

I. Public and private employers (businesses, non-profits, and governments) are the investment spenders who buy capital items such as the plant, equipment and inventory that are employed in an economy's production processes.

II.   Every economy has a stock of capital goods. Each day some capital items wear out or become obsolete while others are being added as a result of investment spending by their employers. It is an on-going process.

III.   Investment spending tends to maintain and expand an economy's capacity to produce. It also provides customers for employers who produce capital items and their suppliers. An economy's capital goods industries are a major source of both capital items and wages and income.

IV.   Savings has nothing to do with causing investments. It can only effect investment spending negatively.

V.   nvestments in plant, equipment, and inventory are very different from financial investments in financial assets such as stocks and bonds. The buying and selling of stocks, bonds, derivatives, and other financial instruments has little effect on the economy even though how the economy's employers perform has a great effect on them.

VI.   Investments, at least supposedly, occur because the employers who make the investments expect the revenues (or the benefits that are the equivalent of the revenues) they will add to exceed the cost of buying and operating the capital items being purchased.

VII.   There are three conceptual approaches to investment decision-making that profit oriented public and private employers can apply: present value, revenues in excess of costs, and the marginal efficiency of the investment (MEI).

VIII.   Employers considering the purchase and employment of more than one unit of a capital item must consider the possibility that each successive unit will yield a lower present value or expected return—because as more are employed operating costs may increase, supply prices may increase, and revenues from the sale of their product may decrease.

IX.   New investment opportunities arrive constantly. At any given time there are a numberless replacement and autonomous investment possibilities in an economy such as that of the United States. They can be presented in relation to the level of interest rates as a schedule or graphically.

X.   There are two types of investment spending: replacement investment spending that is related to the total spending and employment in economy which determines how fast the existing stock of capital will wear out; and autonomous investments that occur regardless how fast the existing capital wears out—as a result of such things as new products, changed expectations, and lower interest rates.

XI.   Investment spending in an economy is functionally related to investors' goals and expectations, the economy's level of interest, and the economy's level of income. It tends to be higher when interest rates are lower and higher when the expectations and the level of income are higher.

XII.   Investment spending is relatively unstable compared to the other types of spending, rising and falling more than total spending. This occurs because investment spending is dependent on expectations, information that may be faulty or misleading, and the accelerator effect on investment induced by changes in the level of the economy's income. (An economy's income is the money received by its employers from the economy's major purchasers—consumers, investors, foreigners, and governments.)

XIII. The MEI, the marginal efficiency of investment, is the expected rate of return on investment spending. It increases or decreases in response to changes in investor expectations about the revenues, costs, and supply prices that an additional investment expenditure will generate. The MEC, the marginal efficiency of capital, is the expected return for an additional capital item when investment spending is in equilibrium—not being run up or down by the accelerator effect or other causes.

XIV. In the real world the rate of interest is often not a key factor in an investment decision. Many investment decisions are made for reasons other than the rate of return the investment is expected to generate—to maximize revenues, maximize growth, spend every available penny, be seen as important, increase market share, etc.

XV. Lower and lower interest rates tend to encourage employers to use more and more capital instead of labor—to substitute the employment of capital for the employment of labor.

XVI. Capital can have a long life. For example, planes, bridges, buildings, and machines may last for years. Accordingly, relatively minor interest rate reductions are unlikely to cause employers to rush out and buy more plant and equipment. That is particularly true when employers have capital sitting idle due to a lack of customers as might be the case in a recession or depression.

Chapter Four

IMPORTS AND EXPORTS

Goods and services are exported when foreigners buy them from an economy's employers. Such *export* sales to foreigners have exactly the same effect as the purchases of consumers, governments, and employers—they cause production to occur and labor and capital to be employed.

For example, American autoworkers and the Ford Motor Company obtain the same amounts of jobs and incomes producing a Lincoln automobile whether it is produced because of the spending of an American lawyer (consumption), a limousine service (investment), an Arab oil sheik (exports), or Detroit to be the mayor's official car (government).

Similarly, employers producing aircraft and farmers producing wheat obtain the same amount of jobs and income if the fighter planes and wheat are sold to foreign buyers as they would if they were instead sold to customers in the United States. *Sales to foreigners are important and growing. They now provide over ten percent of the customer spending that causes United States employers to produce goods and services.*

Conversely, goods and services are imported when an economy's customers buy foreign-made services and products. The difference between buying imports and buying domestically produced goods and services is, obviously, that buying imports means the jobs and incomes created by the import spending go to the foreign employers and their workers and capital.

For example, an American who buys a new Toyota instead of a new Ford causes Japanese employers and autoworkers to have jobs and income rather than American autoworkers—unless, of course, the Toyota is produced in South Carolina and the Ford in Mexico or Germany. In the real world the component parts of imports and exports may be produced in multiple countries, and thus generate wages and incomes worldwide.

UNITED STATES EXPORTS AND IMPORTS

The United States economy is one of the world's largest and most successful. Its public and private employers produce about twenty percent of the value of the world's production with less than five percent of the world's population. The countries of the European Economic Community as a whole produce also about twenty percent with more than seven percent of the world's population; China produces about sixteen percent with almost twenty percent of the world's population; and India produces about two percent with seventeen percent of the world's population.

Sales to foreigners are important. Typically over ten percent of all customer purchases that cause production and employment to occur in the United States are the result of U.S. employers producing goods and services that are sold to foreigners. To put that in perspective, the America's employers produce and export goods and services with a total value equal to all the goods and services produced by Russia or India.

What is unique about the United States and other large economies such as the EEC, Russia, and China is that they are relatively self-contained—their employers can and do, with varying degrees of efficiency, produce almost every kind of good and service. Accordingly, they tend to have a wide range of goods and services available to export and relatively little they need to import.

In contrast, the smaller economies of other relatively prosperous countries such as Switzerland, Sweden, and South Korea cannot produce everything in amounts sufficiently large to be highly efficient in the sense of getting highest possible levels of output value per worker. They tend to be much more specialized and limited as to what their employers produce. As a result, they need to import a wide variety of goods and services produced elsewhere—so their consumers, employers, and governments tend to do a significantly larger proportion of their spending to buy goods and services from foreign producers.

The consumers, employers, and governments of the smaller economies tend to buy a wide range of items from the United States because U.S. employers are able to efficiently produce a relatively wide range of products and sell them at competitive prices. The foreigners primarily get the dollars to pay for their purchases by selling assets and products to American buyers and others with dollars. They, in effect, trade with the United States, selling to American buyers and buying the goods and services American employers produce. In essence, trade is important to the United States and even more important to countries with smaller economies.

And sales to foreigners have been growing in importance for the United States in recent years. Today approximately ten percent of the goods and services produced by United States employers are sold to foreign buyers. That's a big increase over what it was in the late twentieth century but exports are still the smallest of the four major spending categories affecting United States employers.

THE AMOUNT OF EXPORTS AND IMPORTS

Imports of foreign made goods and services into the United States occur because of spending decisions made by American customers (consumers, employers, governments) to buy things produced by employers located in other countries; exports from the United States are based decisions of foreigners to buy goods and services produced by our employers. They are done by different people for different reason so there is no reason to expect them to be equal in size. Today the United States imports more than it exports.

There are many causes of imports and exports. Some are simple and obvious. Others are not. Basically, however, buyers tend to purchase goods and services produced by employers in a foreign economy because they are unable to buy them at comparable prices in their own economy.

Analysts can find the facts as to how important exports and imports are to various countries and the composition of such exports and imports via Google or Wikipedia. It is unexpectedly easy to analyze and compare the imports and exports of different countries—because the United States economy is so dominant that many international transactions are done with dollars and almost all data are available in terms of United States dollars.

The determinants of imports and exports.

Unique products. French wines are a unique to France. Close substitutes may be produced elsewhere but if you are an American the only way you are going to get French wines is to either spend money to import them or go to France and buy them there—and that is also considered to be import spending. Similarly unique are Jaguar automobiles and the specialized financial services produced in the U.K.; the military training aircraft and cane-based ethanol produced in Brazil; the rare earth metals mined and processed in China; and the Ford and General Motors automobile models produced in Mexico. They are all imports because they are produced by employers located outside the United States.

Products and services produced by United States employers become exports when they are sold to foreign buyers even when the foreigners are in the United States. California wines and Cadillac cars are only produced by employers located in the United States and that's where they have to be initially bought from their producers. And if foreigners want to ski Park City or spend an evening at the Grand Canyon hotel, or have a medical procedure done or be a foreign student at the University of Chicago, or buy F-35s for their air force, they too will have to spend their money in the United States and what they buy will be considered as exported to them.

In the real world, although it does not show up in the data, the American dollar is one of the United States' biggest export items. The dollar has become the standard currency of much of the world's international trade, finance, and tourism. So virtually every bank and currency exchange in the world typically has a stock of green dollars and dollar bank deposits on hand, with additional billions in reserve at their central bank in case the commercial banks and currency exchanges need more.

In essence, every year the United States government and the Federal Reserve manufacture billions of green paper dollars and bank deposits that are exported along with wheat, California wines, Cadillac cars and all the many other goods and services produced by United States employers and sold to foreign buyers. Dollars are arguably America's biggest export item. Including them in the data would dramatically reduce or eliminate the United States' trade deficit.

The dollars are exported because they are generally accepted in payment everywhere—because those who accept dollars know they can buy things with them in the United States as well as almost everywhere else. In essence, foreigners buy dollars with their own currencies because they know dollars have purchasing power virtually everywhere, *not* because dollars are "backed" by gold or some other asset.

Lower costs. It is a fundamental principle of economics that buyers *tend* to buy where the price is lowest. And since an employer's cost to produce something tends to be the minimum price that the employer must receive if it is to continue to be produced, the prices of some things may be less in one economy than they are in another. Wheat, for example, could be produced in Saudi Arabia—but the cost to a Saudi employer of producing a bushel of wheat in the desert would most probably be much higher than the cost of an efficient American farmer producing a similar bushel in Kansas. So Saudi bakers and millers are likely to buy wheat from the United States and import it. Similarly, India has a relatively large English-speaking labor force available to work at wage levels significantly below those of the United States. So, other things equal, call center services and computer programming services are likely to be produced in India and sold to American buyers instead of the other way around.

Wage levels and natural resource endowments, however, are not the only considerations affecting imports and exports. Employers in the United States, for example, are able to export certain products produced with relatively expensive labor because they employ their labor more efficiently than their foreign competitors: through their utilization of the latest technology they get more output per worker, and thus lower production costs, than do the foreign employers with whom they compete. Many U.S. factories and airlines, for example, produce twice number of planes and passenger air miles per worker as their European counterparts.

Exchange rates. A country's employers inevitably pay their workers and local costs such as electricity, rent and taxes with their country's own currency. Thus the European company producing Airbus airplanes pays it workers and European suppliers in euros but prices and sells the planes it produces worldwide priced in dollars. This allows its potential customers to both compare the prices of Airbuses with those of the comparable planes of the Boeing Company, its principal competitor, and seek financing worldwide for the dollars needed to buy them.

Other exporters similarly do business in the currencies of other countries—such as when Swiss watch manufacturers accept rubles when they sell to Russians and Israeli drone manufacturers accept Japanese yen when they sell drones to Japan.

And it can get quite complicated. A Swiss watch manufacturer, for example, may have borrowed dollars in London and exchanged them for euros so it could open a warehouse and display store in Rome in order to sell to visiting Russian oligarchs, Chinese princelings, and various and sundry African and Middle Eastern buyers—all of whom variously might use currencies other than Swiss francs with which to pay, usually dollars because it is the most widely accepted currency in the world.

When exporting employers accept a foreign currency they then have to exchange some or all of it for the currency which they have to use to pay their workers and suppliers. For example, the drone manufacturer may need to exchange some of its yen revenues for shekels in order to pay its workers and some for dollars and euros to pay the suppliers of some of its components that are produced in China and Europe. Similarly, a European buying the latest Apple electronics or two nights in a Chicago hotel is likely to have to pay for them with U.S. dollars instead of Euros or Swedish krona.

Exchange rates are very complex since there several hundred currencies in use in different nations around the world. As a result, there are active currency markets throughout the world, the largest being based in New York and London. They are where most of the world's different currencies are exchanged as they are bought and sold. Today, as a result of the current and future values of many currencies being unknown or unstable, many export items are priced and sold and paid for in U.S. dollars even when the United States is not in any way involved other than producing the dollars.

The rate of exchange is significant. Some governments such as the United States let the market for currency determine the exchange rate. Then the rate freely fluctuates as supply and demand for their currencies changes in the world's currency markets. Other countries such as China fix their exchange rate by using their currency and the dollar reserves to buy and sell dollars in the currency market as needed to keep their currency at the exchange rate they specify. Countries' currencies have either freely *fluctuating exchange rates* or *fixed exchange rates*.

When currencies' exchange rates are allowed to fluctuate, a currency's exchange rate is said to have *appreciated* if it goes up or *depreciated* if it goes down. If a country's exchange rate is fixed (also known as *pegged*) at one rate and then that fixed rate is subsequently changed, its currency is said to have been *revalued* if it goes up so that it can be exchanged for more of a foreign currency or *devalued* if it goes down so it can be exchanged for less.

However it is set, the rate at which one currency exchanges for another, its *exchange rate*, is significant because it affects where goods and services will be purchased and produced. For instance, the exchange rate for the Chinese yuan is 100 to one if it takes 100 Chinese yuan to buy one United States dollar or one dollar to buy 100 yuan.

The rate is important because it determines where the costs of buying or producing comparable goods and services are the lowest. And the rates relate to one another. For example, if the exchange rate of the Indian rupee is 50 rupees to one dollar and the Chinese yuan rate is 100 to one, it means the exchange rate between the rupee and the yuan will tend to be two to one—or else, within seconds, canny currency traders will push the rate back to two to one by selling the currency that is overvalued and buying the currency that is undervalued. In essence, *the exchange rate represents the value of each currency being exchanged—because it is the price of a currency that someone with another currency is willing to pay in order to get it.*

Consider a product that employers are producing and selling for 1000 yuan in China and for ten dollars in the United States. If the exchange rate is 200 to one, all the buyers will tend to buy it in China; if the exchange rate is 50 to one, all the buyers will tend to buy it in the United States; only when the exchange rate is 100 to one will the price be the same in either country. That is because at 200 to one a buyer from Europe or elsewhere looking at the two sources would know he could buy in China with yuan he can buy for $5 or in the United States for $10 of dollars; at 50 to one the European and other buyers would buy it in the United States because they would have to pay $20 to get the yuan needed to buy it in China.

How are exchange rates set?

How the rate of exchange between two monies is established depends on whether their exchange rates are fixed or floating. Some countries such as China *fix* the rate at which their currencies exchange for dollars by using their currency to buy and sell dollars in the currency market as needed to keep their currency at the exchange rate the Chinese government specifies.

Other governments such as the United States let the market for their currency, the supply and demand for it, determine the exchange rate—thus *the dollar's exchange rate with other currencies floats up or down in response market forces*. What this means for the dollar is that the rate at which the dollar exchanges with every other currency is sometimes set in response to market forces as the supply and demand for the dollar changes and sometimes fixed by the other country because of its willingness to provide either its currency or dollars at the rate it fixes.

There are also variations between the extremes of fixed and floating. Some countries let their currencies float so long as they stay within a narrow band of fixed rates. For example, the Chinese might not intervene by buying or selling dollars so long as the yuan to dollar rate stays within one percent of fifty to one. Other countries let their currency's exchange rate fluctuate but periodically step in to buy or sell in order to smooth out any changes due to temporary events. Basically, however, *countries either have freely fluctuating exchange rates or fixed exchange rates*.

Market forces cause exchange rates to change.

Fluctuating exchange rates. Fluctuating exchange rates exist when the rate at which two types of money exchange is allowed to float up or down in response to market pressures. Thus the rate of exchange between the euro and the US dollar might be 1.0 to 1.30 today, 1.0 to 1.29 tomorrow, and 1.0 to 1.32 the next day. In other words, today it takes $1.30 to get one euro; $1.29 tomorrow; and $1.32 the next day.

When currencies are free to fluctuate, the exchange rate between currencies is set by the traditional market forces of supply and demand in the financial markets where those currencies are bought and sold. How much the exchange rate will be between two currencies depends on the willingness of those who have one currency and want another are willing to give up to get it; and how much those who have the wanted currency are willing to supply at each exchange rate. In essence, the exchange rate of a currency is its price (value) in terms of the currency for which it is being exchanged.

For example, the exchange rate between Swiss francs and the dollar would be 3 to 1 if the holders of $30 billion of U.S dollars were willing to exchange them for 90 billion Swiss francs and the holders of Sfr90 billions of Swiss francs were willing to exchange them for $30 billion of U.S. dollars.

The next trading day in the currency market the holders of Swiss francs may want another $20 billion of U.S. dollars at yesterday's rate of 3 to 1 and be willing to give up sixty billion Swiss francs for them. But what if the holders of dollars are today only willing to supply $15 billion dollars at that rate? Then those who want more than $15 billion of dollars will have to compete to buy the available dollars by offering a better exchange rate than 3 to1; For example to get $20 billion they might have to pay 61 billion Swiss francs, a rate of 3.05 to 1. And some of the holders of Swiss francs may not be willing to buy dollars at the 3.05 to 1 rate because that is a higher price for dollars.

Finally, the rate for dollars in the market will float high enough so that the holders of francs will be able to get all the dollars they are willing to buy. Thus, for example, the market for dollars might end with a transaction wherein the holders of Swiss francs buy $18 billion dollars for $54.72 billion francs, for an exchange rate price of 3.04 to 1.

In this example, the dollar's higher exchange rate price causes the holders of Swiss francs to buy $2 billion less than they would have bought if the dollar's exchange rate price had been lower at 3.0 to 1.

Increasingly, the exchange rates between the world's currencies have come to be freely set in the so-called currency markets in response to the supplies and demands of the currencies that people and employers and governments wish to exchange.

Fixed exchange rates. Fixed exchange rates occur whenever a government or its central bank is willing to exchange two different types of money at a fixed rate. There is no need for agreement between the two countries. Either or both can fix the rate at which they want their currency to exchange with the other, at least for a while. For example, the rate between the yuan and the dollar will always be fixed at 200 to one *so long as the Chinese central bank is willing to provide 200 yuan for each dollar it is offered.*

In terms of our example, that would result in all the buyers buying in China and China accumulating an ever growing stock of dollars. That is exactly the policy of undervaluing its currency that enabled China to begin its long (and doomed for reasons that shall subsequently be considered) export-fueled move towards higher wages and production.

In essence, China's economic policy makers accepted the basic macroeconomic concept that customers are important and that employers will keep hiring until everyone is employed *if they have enough customers.* In other words, to get jobs for its people so they would not revolt and overthrow its authoritarian government, China undervalues its currency and, in effect, accepts little green pieces of paper with dead presidents' pictures on them in exchange for its people being able to produce and sell a myriad of products to the West.

Looking at it cynically, China's leaders held off the threat of a workers revolution caused by massive unemployment by accumulating closets and bank accounts full of green paper dollars in exchange for China sending hundreds of thousands of boatloads of valuable products to the United States.

Some countries try to fix rates in the other direction—trying to keep their people satisfied by overvaluing their currency so their people can buy more imports with less of their country's money. South American countries are famous for such efforts. Consider a Venezuelan example where the exchange rate between its bolivar and the dollar is fixed at ten bolivars to one. At that rate there is neither a net inflow nor net outflow of dollars because at that exchange rate the Venezuelan employers are selling as much in dollar terms to foreigner buyers as the Venezuelan buyers are buying from foreign employers.

Now consider what might happen if for some reason inflation or political instability threatens in Venezuela. Perhaps the government embarks on major spending programs that result in prices and wages doubling as inflation occurs from too much total spending. Foreign buyers might cut back on spending dollars to buy Venezuelan products because at ten to one it takes twice as many dollars to get enough bolivars to buy the Venezuelan products at their now-higher prices. As a result Venezuelan exports decline and the amount of dollars coming into Venezuela declines; at the same time Venezuelans whose incomes in bolivars have increased due to the inflation can now get more dollars with the additional bolivars they earn if the exchange rate remains ten to one—so they are likely to increase their buying of imports.

In essence, the combination of inflation and a fixed exchange rate causes Venezuela to have fewer dollars coming in and more going out. In other words, Venezuela now has a *balance of payments deficit* because it has overvalued it currency by fixing its exchange rate at 10 to one.

How long can such a country's overvalued currency and the negative dollar outflow associated with it last—until the country's central bank runs out of dollars (and other assets that it can convert to dollars) for those who offer ten bolivars to get them. Then the amount of imports will be reduced to the new lower levels possible with whatever dollars, if any, are obtained from the reduced exports.

More likely, at some point the exchange value of the Bolivar will be re-fixed to a new and less-valuable-in-exchange level such as twenty to one. Then it would take so that twenty bolivars to get a dollar and a dollar gets twenty bolivars. In that case, the dollar price of the Venezuelan exports will be restored to the same level it was when the exchange rate was ten to one and the amount of Venezuelan exports will return to the original levels and generate the original amount of dollar inflows.

In essence, a country which attempts to overvalue its currency can only succeed temporarily until it runs out of reserves. Then it tends to move its exchange rate to where it would have gone if ithe rate had been free to fluctuate—because that is the only rate at which there will be equilibrium with neither inflows nor outflows.

Analysts, of course, should not make the common mistake of inexperienced journalists and politicians and confuse changes in exchange rates with changes in the value of a currency. The dollar's exchange rate, for example, may change in response to forces in the financial markets—but the actual value of each dollar, its purchasing power, remains stable unless prices in the United States change so that more or fewer good and services can be purchased with each dollar.

Intervention and the real world. Government leaders of countries with fixed exchange rates are typically embarrassed and threatened when they run out of reserves and are forced to change their currency's exchange rate. Often such countries do not have politicians capable of understanding why it is happening. So they flail about blaming their political opponents and foreign plots rather than curing the problem that caused it to occur in the first place (in the above example, inflation from excessive government spending and consumption generating welfare programs). Sometimes they try to hold off changing the exchange rate by borrowing or confiscating dollars, or assets that can be converted into dollars, and exchanging them for the their local currency—until they can't borrow or confiscate anymore and again run out.

Swings in exchange rates can also occur when the rates are allowed to fluctuate. This might occur, for example, when crops fail or tsunamis wipe out production capacity or political upheaval or anything else raises questions about the ability of the country to sell its exports or pay for its imports. Normally, however, wide to-and-fro swings, such as a move from 10 to one to 20 to one, tend *not* to suddenly occur with floating exchange rates. The activities of eagle-eyed speculators and central banks stop this—they smooth out the fluctuations by stepping in to buy currencies when they feel the exchange rate price is below what they think is normal and to sell them when they think their exchange rates are above what is normal.

In essence, speculators accumulate dollar reserves and their use of them smoothes out the fluctuations as they buy and sell currencies in an effort to make money for themselves.

Central banks and governments similarly accumulate reserves and use them to smooth out fluctuations in their currencies' exchange rates. They do so in order to allow their employers to hire workers and produce products for export without having to worry about sudden massive changes in their currencies exchange rates that might suddenly and dramatically change their ability to buy and sell abroad. (e.g. going from 10 to one to 20 to one overnight)

Central banks and governments whose currencies have fixed exchange rates are often aided by loans from their political allies and the International Monetary Fund (IMF) when they need reserves to exchange for the dollar and other currencies in order to defend their fixed exchange rates. Indeed, the IMF was set up (by Keynes incidentally—because he clung to the notion that fixed exchange rates were desirable for Britain) for the purpose of helping countries with fixed exchange rates avoid having to make unnecessary changes in their rates.

Today the IMF is staffed by politically appointed government bureaucrats from around the world and its primary function is to loan additional reserves, frequently dollars, to the countries it is "helping." The IMF does this so the recipients can keep their current fixed exchange rate while they fix their "temporary problems." It also provides the countries it is helping with the kind of economic and fiscal "expertise" that only a career government bureaucrat from a third world country could possibly provide.

The IMF has been primarily and continually funded by the world's richer countries such as the United States. It is famous for its highly paid bureaucrats giving advice that is always accepted to get the money and then disregarded once the money is in hand. But it rarely makes bad loans even when the money is used to buy yachts and Ferraris for dictators' sons. Instead, it tends to keep rolling its unpaid loans over and making them larger and larger to cover the ever accruing interest—until it gives up and years later writes the whole loan off as uncollectible, and then starts again with new loans when the United States and its other donors come through with more money.

The impossibility of continuing to find the additional reserves needed to maintain a fixed rate for a currency whose exchange rate is hopelessly overvalued typically means there is no "greater fool" to provide them after the IMF. In any event, the post-IMF move of most currencies to fluctuating exchange rates has basically eliminated the need for the IMF's services and increased the importance and volume of the world's currency markets.

Today the IMF has two major problems. The first is that it has rarely been successful because the problems of the countries it attempts to help are rarely temporary—for example, inflation caused by too much government spending or too little taxation, the diversion of businesses to cronies who are incapable of running them, and excessive and counterproductive regulations. Think Greece, Italy, and Spain.

The IMF's second major problem is that fixed exchange rates have been abandoned by many countries. This occurred as their decision makers, such as those of the United States in the 1970s, finally came to realize that small incremental changes associated with fluctuating exchange rates upset their economies' buying and selling abroad much less than the periodic big changes associated with fixed rates. It also occurred as countries clubbed together to share the euro as a common currency with its own advisors and loan programs. Today many pragmatic analysts consider the IMF to be a highly paid irrelevant bureaucracy desperately searching for something to justify its existence—such as giving advice to Greece to cut its spending and raise its tax rates in such a way that its tax collections fell so much that its budgetary and balance of payments deficits actually increased.

In contrast to the IMF, whose loans can delay changing a fixed exchange rate, speculators and currency traders tend to hasten the inevitable devaluations of currencies with overvalued fixed rates. They tend to move very quickly when they think a currency is overvalued and on course to run out of reserves if its fixed exchange rate continues. For instance, in the case of the Venezuelan example they might rush to borrow Bolivars and exchange them for dollars at the 10 to I rate. Then, when Venezuelan government quickly runs out of dollar reserves and the Bolivar is devalued to 20 to 1, they exchange some of the dollars for Bolivars needed to repay the Bolivars they borrowed—and keep the rest.

Fixed exchange rates that overvalue a currency do not last long in the digital age of speculators and currency trading if they are out of line with the rate that would occur if the currency was allowed to fluctuate in response to market forces (Venezuela). In contrast, fixed exchange rates that undervalue a currency can last indefinitely *so long as the exporting country is willing to continue accumulating reserves* (China).

Lots of money has been made in such speculations—and several major investment banks and hedge funds such as Baring Brothers and MF Global have gone broke or lost billions when their currency traders bet wrong. In the long run, however, all exchange rates are flexible except the fixed rates which undervalue a currency: they either adjust constantly in response to market forces or, if they are fixed, periodically when they run out of reserves as a result of political and economic forces that the currency market speculators reinforce and accelerate.

Balance of trade and balance of payments.

A country's balance-of-trade is the difference between the total amount of money coming in from foreigners to buy goods and services produced by the country's employers and the total amount the economy's consumers, employers, and governments spend to buy goods and services produced abroad. On balance, particularly if its exports of dollars are excluded, the United States has a *balance of trade* deficit—its buyers spend much more for things produced abroad than foreigners spend to buy things produced in the United States.

More specifically, and excluding the dollars shipped abroad for foreign use, over ten percent of all sales of U.S. made goods and services are to foreigners and about fourteen percent of all American spending is done to buy foreign-made goods and services.

Keep in mind that trade is complex and multi-national. Thus, for example, the United States might have a huge trade deficit with China while simultaneously the Chinese are using the surplus dollars they receive from the United States to cover a huge trade deficit with Europe which is using the surplus dollars it receives from China to spend more than it buys in the United States. *What counts is a country's overall trade deficit, not its deficit with a particular country.*

Having an overall trade deficit does not mean that a country has a problem. Money goes in and out of a country for many more reasons besides buying and selling newly produced goods and services. Some countries such as Mexico receive billions in remittances sent to families by Mexican citizens working in the United States. Similarly, billions of dollars come into the United States from abroad from Americans working overseas and from foreigners buying U.S. real estate for vacation purposes or in case they need to flee their current residence.

Money also tends to go abroad and come from abroad in the form of loans to and from businesses and governments; or to buy the stocks and bonds of foreign corporations; or to buy the bonds and currencies of foreign governments; or it moves back and forth as dividends, interest payments, bond and loan repayments, and profit distributions.

Other dollars go abroad because foreign governments, central banks, financial institutions, and others want dollars to hold as reserves in order to cope with unexpected dollar needs and to take advantage of purchasing and financial opportunities that might arise anywhere in the world where the dollar is acceptable.

Hot money. Typically billions and often trillions of dollars of "hot money" constantly rushes from one country to the next as financial intermediaries, traders and speculators move their dollars and other currencies (aka "financial capital") from place to place in a constant search for higher interest yields and for currencies, stocks and bonds that might rise in value and be quickly sold for a profit.

Central banks such as the United States' Federal Reserve attempt to keep a close eye on such short term "capital inflows and outflows" because they change the amount of money in circulation in their economy. This can be serious—changes in the supply of money may mean an economy has too much or too little money in circulation to maintain full employment levels of production without inflation.

For example, every so often troubles around the world cause money to flow into Switzerland and the United States and other "safe havens." Sometimes the inflows have been so great that the Swiss central bank has required the Swiss commercial banks to charge interest on bank deposits instead of paying interest on them.

Similarly, but in reverse, upheaval and turmoil in a country may cause such large amounts of money to rush out in search of safety that the country is left with inadequate amounts of money in circulation to handle the day to day transactions of its businesses and their customers.

United States balance of payments deficits. Each year the United States government typically reports a balance of payments deficit. *And that is impossible!* It is impossible because countries such as the United States with freely floating exchange rates cannot have balance of payments deficits and surpluses—because their currency's exchange rate constantly adjusts on a minute to minute basis in the world's money markets to equate the supply and demand for their currency.

Accordingly, any reported United States balance of payments surplus or deficit is actually a measure of the inaccuracy of the government's data—the inflows would be exactly equal to the outflows if the government's numbers were accurate.

In other words, if an analyst hears some politician or Federal Reserve governor or journalist talking or writing about a U.S. balance of payment deficit and suggesting that it is a problem or could be a problem, the analyst can be absolutely sure they are not experts and do not know what they are talking about.

How long can an exchange rate last?

There are advantages and disadvantages to each approach so some countries choose one and some the other. The advantage of fluctuating rates is that the rates are set by market forces and change relatively slightly minute by minute without requiring any governmental or central bank activities.

The advantage of a fixed rate is that it is very stable so that export and import activities and contracts can be made without worrying about constant changes in the value of the country's currency—until, of course, the fixed rate gets hopelessly out of line and is then either changed to a new fixed rate or freed up to float in response to market forces. And, of course, when it changes downwards those holding the currency lose big—unless, of course, they have bought insurance or hedged against the possibility, in which case their insurance company or counterparty loses big.

Fluctuating rates, on the other hand, change constantly on a minute to minute basis as the demand for a currency and the available supply of it changes in the world's money markets. There are entire companies devoted to constantly buying currencies whose rates appear undervalued and constantly selling those whose rates appear to be overvalued. They are currency traders and they perform a valuable function—smoothing out exchange rates and keeping them closely aligned to their true value in terms of other currencies.

Such currency traders can make serious amounts of money buying and selling to keep currencies exchange rates close to their true values—until they make a big mistake. For example, for several centuries the venerable London-based British investment bank Baring Brothers succeeded in being a highly profitable currency trader. Then over a short period of time one of its minor traders located in Hong Kong bought huge amounts of currencies whose exchange rate price did not move in the direction he thought. Baring Brothers could not repay the money it had borrowed and owed—so it failed. More recently America's MF Global went down for the same reason.

Fixed exchange rates can be either temporary or permanent. It depends on whether the rate is fixed above or below the rate that would exist if it was set in the market by the forces of supply and demand. A rate that is set too high is inevitably doomed to fall sooner or later. As previously discussed, its fall occurs when whoever is trying to protect the high rate runs out of reserves.

On the other hand, a rate which is fixed below the rate which would exist in a free market can continue so long as the country is willing to soak up the foreign currency that is supplied in excess of the country's need for the foreign currency and add it to its reserves.

China is a good example. In its efforts to fuel exports by holding down the yuan's exchange rate so that its products have relatively low prices to foreign buyers China has accumulated huge amounts of dollars and other currencies rather than let the exchange value of the yuan rise. In effect, it is importing dollars and exporting products. So long as China is willing, in effect, to accumulate more and more little green pieces of paper and dollar deposits in bank accounts the yuan will continue to be undervalued and China will tend to continue to have surpluses in its balances of trade and payments.

Technically China could keep the yuan undervalued forever. It could then keep exporting more than it imports and continue build up its dollar and foreign currency reserves to ever higher levels. In so doing, of course, it will deny its people and employers the opportunity to buy foreign made products at the lower yuan prices that would exist if they could get more dollars for each yuan.

On the other hand, such an accumulation of dollars and dollar related assets is risky for China because political tensions exist between the United States and China on a number of issues. Indeed if the United States becomes sufficiently irked with China for some reason, it could cancel or impound the dollar assets China has accumulated—as the United States has done at times to numerous other countries when they have fallen out of favor with the United States (think Iraq and Iran).

Alternately, at least conceptually, the U.S. could monetize the Chinese-held dollar assets so that they no longer earn interest. Indeed it could even print large denomination green dollar bills for the total amount of dollar assets China is holding and pay them off in full. Either way, in addition to being more than a little aggravated and confused, the Chinese would be even more liquid and likely to begin buying more goods and services produced by United States employers or anyone else who would accept dollars.

Export and import instability.

Imports and exports, despite their relatively small sizes, are important to the United States because fluctuations in their sizes may originate abroad and cause unexpected changes in the size and nature of an economy's production and thus in the employment of the U.S. labor force, the incomes of its employers, and the tax collections of its governments.

There are many sources of United States export and import instability originating abroad. Among the possibilities:

1. *Interest rate changes.* A foreign central bank such as the Bank of England can tighten up the money supply in its economy to fight inflation from too much spending by increasing the interest rates the U.K.'s commercial banks pay for deposits or for the U.K.'s government and private bonds. The higher interest rates and reduced availability of credit would tend to discourage consumers from buying at home *and abroad.* So imports from the U.S. and elsewhere might decline. Moreover, the higher interest rates and resulting lower bond prices would, and traditionally have, attract dollars from the United States that might have otherwise been spent in the United States to buy products or make real and financial investments.

   On the other hand, a foreign central bank might do just the reverse. The Bank of England might create new money and pour it into the British economy to encourage more consumption spending by the British people and more investment spending by British employers.

Interest rates in Britain would then tend to go down and the prices of British stocks and bonds go up. So some people and financial institutions, both British and foreign, might sell their British stocks and bonds and withdraw their deposits—and move their money to the United States to buy things such as American-made products and American-issued stocks and bonds (which would now tend to yield higher rates of return relative to those of Britain.)

The resulting increases in United States exports, and the amount of money in circulation in the United States and the increased value of U.S. financial and other assets resulting from the additional spending from the U.K., would tend cause spending in the U.S. to increase—all without the Federal Reserve or Congress lifting a finger.

2. *Exchange rate changes.* A foreign economy can change its exchange rate by fixing them against the dollar at a new rate or, if its currency has a floating rate, by buying additional dollars for its reserves or selling additional dollars from its reserves. That changes the dollar price of whatever the economy is buying or selling without the United States doing a thing. If it has the effect of raising the prices of things bought from the United States then U.S. exports will fall; if it has the effect lowering the price of things bought from the United States then U.S. exports will rise—again without the Federal Reserve or Congress lifting a finger.

3. *Tariffs and quota changes.* A *tariff* is a tax a country levies on imports to raise revenues and discourage imports. Local manufacturers can conjure up many reasons why a particular tariff is desirable, but it inevitably boils down to fact that they want to be protected from foreign competition so they can sell more themselves and get higher prices for what they sell. For example, Detroit has long advocated tariffs on Japanese-made cars; the corn state governors on ethanol from Brazil.

Quotas limiting the number of imports have the same effect and are used for the same reason. Japan is famous for negotiating mutual tariff and quota reductions with the United States to increase its exports and then imposing *de facto* quotas to protect its employers from foreign competition. Many economists think Japan's policy of protecting each of its employers from the competitive pressures of imports in the domestic market is the main reason its economy's total output stagnated in the later decades of the twentieth century and the first decades of the twenty-first.

The effect of such tariffs and quotas was aptly summed up many years ago by a famous American economist:

"Trade does not require force. Free trade consists simply of letting people buy and sell as they want to buy and sell. It is protection that requires force, for it consists in preventing people from doing what they want to do. Protective tariffs are as much an application of force as are blockading squadrons and their objective is the same—to prevent trade. The difference between the two is that the blockading squadrons are a means by which nations seek to prevent their enemies from trading; protective tariffs are means by which nations attempt to prevent their own people from trading. What protection teaches us, is to do to ourselves in time of peace what enemies seek to do to us in time of war."(Henry George 1886)

4. *De facto quotas.* A *de facto* quota is a government action that has the effect of a quota. It can be achieved by custom officials taking months or years to clear an import or subjecting them to spurious tests and barriers. Japan is famous for them. Among them: preventing imports of American apples and pears at the request of Japanese growers because there was fruit rust in the United States (there also is fruit rust in Japan); keeping small fiberglass boats out at the request of Japanese boat builders by testing them with the same test applied to large concrete boats—dropping each from a height sufficient to destroy them; keeping ski equipment out at the request of Japan's ski equipment manufacturers because it is dangerously unsuitable for the "unique type of snow" that exists in Japan; and keeping Dutch tulip bulbs out at the request of Japanese growers by testing each bulb for insects by cutting it in half. It is little wonder that the Japanese consumer pays particularly high prices for ski equipment, recreational boats and tulip bulbs.

5. *Changes in prices.* If one economy's level of product prices changes more rapidly than the price level of another economy, the total amount of purchasing in both economies will be affected. For example, consider what would happen if the euro zone countries and the United States were each initially buying the same amount of products from each other and then, over time, product prices rose ten percent in the United States and two percent in the euro zone. Euro zone buyers would tend to stop buying from United States producers and switch their spending to the now relatively less expensive goods and services of Europe. Additionally, U.S. consumers, employers, and governments would also tend to switch to European products.

   Whether the money amount spent by foreign purchasers would go up or down in either economy when their purchase of imports changes depend, of course, on the *price elasticity* of the foreign buyers purchasing desires. The dollar amount of European spending to buy American products, for instance, would rise if the French demand for U.S. produced goods and services is *price inelastic* so that a ten percent increase in United States prices results in a one percent reduction in the number of products sold to the Europeans. European spending in the U.S. would fall, on the other hand, if the French demand is *price elastic* so that the ten percent price increase caused a fifty percent reduction in the amount of products purchased by the Europeans.

6. *Non-economic events.* Everything from boycotts and revolutions to weather changes and tsunamis can change an economy's level of exports and imports. Japan's economy, for example, suffered a great blow when a 2011 tsunami devastated part of the country and the supply chains of its employers. It dramatically changed Japan's exports to and from the United States and, thus, Japan's balance of trade. Revolution and upheaval in the Middle East has periodically had the same impact—U.S. sales to Syria, Tunisia, Yemen, Syria, and Egypt were reduced at one time or another by the chaos. U.S. sanctions and embargos on buying and selling with Iran and North Korea have had the same effect and resulted in those countries switching their import spending from the United States to China and Russia.

The benefits of exports and imports.

There is more to imports and exports than just keeping just keeping an economy's labor and capital employed. Countries encourage trade for other reasons as well.

Specialization. International trade allows countries which can't do everything for themselves to specialize in what they can do best. Thus Australia particularly emphasizes the production of raw materials for the world's industrial employers, something Japan cannot do. Japan, on the other hand, has employers that specialize in the production of automobiles, the United States in airplanes and wheat, the Saudis in oil, the French in truffles and tourism, and the Bahamas in servicing cruise ships. By specializing in what they can do best, and exporting what they can do best and do not use for themselves, the world as a whole ends up getting more and better of everything that can be traded.

Economies of scale. The efficient use of workers sometimes requires a huge scale of plant and suppliers. Every small country probably could produce automobiles and wheat. But each of their employers would be too small to efficiently use their labor and capital if it could only sell in its domestic market. Export sales solve that problem. It enables Finland to be an efficient producer of cell phones, France of fine wines, Canada of lumber products, the United States of digital technologies, and Germany of high tech machinery.

Competition. One of the greatest positive impacts of buying and selling abroad is that it forces and economy's employers to be efficient users of labor and capital; if they are not efficient other employers in other countries will step up and take their customers. The other employers do not even have to exist. Just the possibility that they will develop and their exports take the customers of inefficient employers is often enough to keep employers investing in new capital and technologies and pricing competitively.

Peace and Relationships. International trade has benefits in addition to providing more products at lower costs for the participating nations.

Among them is the possibility it will bind the nations together in a mutually beneficial relationship to replace one that might otherwise be antagonistic. For example, the historic animosity and warfare between France and Germany caused the leaders of both countries and their allies after WWII to enter into an extensive array of economic and political relationships.

Among their actions: the establishment of the European Economic Community (EEC) which removed barriers to trade and enabled the free movement of workers and capital; the adoption of the euro as a common currency with a common central bank (ECB) to create it; shared tariffs and other trade restrictions; common business and environmental regulations; common bank regulations; and the Schengen Agreement which allows visa free travel among a number of European countries.

Despite its excessive (by United States' standards) bureaucracy and all its other problems, particularly those associated with its excessive regulations and the sharing of the euro, the EEC seems to be working: the countries of Europe have become more economically dependent on each other and at peace.

Similarly, the United States and Japan, once bitter antagonists, appear to be embarked on a somewhat similar relationship as regards to trade. The United States has opened its doors to Japanese products, winked at the huge trade imbalance and dollar outflows resulting from Japan's undervalued currency, and become a major force in Japan's prosperity and growth. It later embarked on a similar relationship with China: accepting products China can sell as a result of its undervalued currency and winking at the dollar reserves China is accumulating.

So far it appears to be working. China and Japan have each accumulated dollars and dollar-related assets worth about two trillion dollars and the United States has gotten goods and services worth trillions of dollars in exchange. (two trillion is the equivalent of about 37 days of United States production when the economy is at full employment.)

**Export sales and
the level of income.**

Foreign spending is an important source of customers for United States employers. And just as the level of consumer and investment spending is related to an economy's level of income, so too is foreign spending. For many years the United States data emphasized the total foreign spending that occurred to buy goods and services produced in the United States (GNP). Then it switched to an emphasis on *net exports*, the difference between the country's exports and its imports (GDP).

The United States switched because it was easier to identify the total amount of spending consumers and investors were doing if it included goods and services produced abroad. In any event, both GDP and GNP are useful because they enable analysts to see the different categories of spending in a slightly different light. Astute analysts and policy makers consider them both because they each reveal conditions that are important for policy decision makers to know.

Consider consumer spending. The act of buying a bottle of French wine by an American consumer is an import. As such it is an act of personal savings in that it is not part of the consumer spending that causes production and employment to occur in the United States. Similarly, the act of buying a European Air Bus or German machine tools is an import but not part of the investment spending that causes production and employment to occur in the United States. Using the GNP approach and not counting these as consumer and investment purchases lets analysts see where the actual buying is coming from that is results in production and employment occurring in the United States.

On the other hand, since such investment and consumer spending is not counted as part of the economy's consumer and investment spending, the United States' GNP data tend to understate the total value of the consumer and investment goods and services its people and employers are obtaining. The GDP approach is to add the spending for these imports to the domestic spending for consumer and investment items. That gives analysts a better picture of how well the economy's consumers are actually doing and how much capital goods its employers are actually buying to add to the United State's stock of capital.

More specifically, to avoid double counting, each dollar spent on imports is added to its appropriate GDP category and subtracted from the total amount of imports reported in its GNP estimate. Consider an example economy with $3 trillion of imports and $2 trillion of exports. The $3 trillion of imports is allocated to the respective GDP components. This shows analysts the value of the products received by the economy's consumers, investors, and governments. In this case the economy's balance of trade, its net exports, is minus $1 trillion. It is getting $1 trillion more goods and services from foreigners than it is sending to them. In other words, its GDP is $1 trillion higher than its GNP.

Both approaches are important and are related—because the dollars foreigners spend to buy American exports tend to be obtained by the foreigners when their employers sell the goods and services that the Americans import. In other words, no matter how they are counted and allocated for analytical purposes, the export sales of American employers are a function of the United States' level of income and tend to rise as the level of income in the United States rises.

An export function.

To represent the possible repercussions from abroad when an economy's income changes, total foreign buying (F) can be subdivided into two parts: autonomous foreign spending (Fa) whose size is not affected by the level of income in the exporting economy and induced foreign spending (Fi) whose size grows as the economy's level of income grows and people have more income to spend at home and abroad. Algebraically: $F = Fa + Fi$

For example, if autonomous foreign spending in an economy is $300 billion and income related exports are ten percent of the economy's level of income: total exports will be $1.3 trillion when level of income is $10 trillion and $2.3 trillion when the level of total customer spending received by the economy's employers is $20 trillion.

Analysts can develop very impress models to scientifically project future imports and exports with such historical numbers. In the example above, for instance, it appears that when example economy reaches an income level of $30 trillion will have $3.3 trillion of exports.

But such projections and models can lead to problems. For example, not too long ago foreign spending only comprised about five percent of the revenues received by United States employers. Economists built various models that used that historical data to scientifically predict what United States exports and imports would be in the future as the incomes of the United States and its then-trading partners evolved.

But then a couple of black swan events occurred. China changed its economic policies in an effort to provide jobs for its people by increasing its exports and the United States' Congress suffered a sea change in its traditional efforts to protect American employers from foreign competition and approved various trade liberalization treaties and agreements. As a result, the international trade models turned out to be very scientific and very elegant and based on data that were very accurate *and yielded projections of import spending that were very wrong.*

CHAPTER SUMMARY

I.   Exported goods and services are produced by an economy's employers and sold to foreign buyers. They mean jobs and incomes, but not goods and services, for the people in the producing economy. On the other hand, imported goods and services are bought from other economies where they are produced; they mean goods and services for the people in the receiving economy but not jobs and incomes. They tend to balance out but sometimes counties have trade surpluses or trade deficits.

II.   The main advantage of buying and selling abroad is that it provide access to unique products and allows specialization, price competition, and lower production costs. The resulting mutual benefits may help alleviate hostility between nations.

III. The United States exports about ten percent of the goods and services produced by its employers and imports the equivalent of about fourteen percent. The difference is made up by financial flows such as when dollars go abroad to facilitate trade among other countries and act as currency reserves.

1V. Foreign-made goods and services are typically purchased because they are unique or less expensive than those produced in the buyers own economy. Exchange rates determine the dollar price of buying things abroad.

V. When a customer in one economy buys goods and services from a seller in another the two must not only agree on the price but also on the exchange rates between their currencies. Such rates may be fixed so each currency has a specific value in exchange or floating which allows the rate at which they are exchanged to rise or fall in response to market pressures.

VI. The total amount of money sent abroad and received from abroad for all purposes is recorded in a balance of payments account. An economy can have a payments surplus or deficit if its money has a fixed exchange rate; it will always be in equilibrium with a zero balance if the economy's exchange rate is allowed to fluctuate.

VII. Balance of payments deficits caused by overvaluing an economy's currency can be temporarily covered by the economy drawing down its currency reserves, selling or borrowing against its assets, and "borrowing" from the IMF or a donor country. Exchange rates change no later than when the money and assets a country is using to maintain the fixed rate run out. On the other hand, surpluses resulting from an undervalued currency can continue so long as the country whose currency is undervalued is willing to accumulate reserves and its trading partners are willing to run trade and payments deficits.

VIII. Both imports and exports may fluctuate because of such things as interest rate changes, exchange rate changes, the imposition of tariffs and quotas, changes in prices, and non-economic events such as political upheavals and natural disasters.

IX. An economy's export sales are related to its level of income because the more income its employers receive, the more money that that is available to be sent abroad to enable foreigners to buy its exports. An export function depicts the relationship between the size of an economy's exports and its level of income.

CHAPTER FIVE

GOVERNMENT SPENDING,
TAXES AND DEBT

Governments are among the largest buyers in most economies. At every political level they spend vast sums of money to buy new goods and services such as tanks and missiles, roads and airports, school buildings and public hospitals, agricultural products, and the services of soldiers, teachers, police, and government officials. In the United States governments do approximately twenty percent of all the customer spending that causes production and employment to occur. Of that, *the lions share is done by the state and local governments.*

The federal government only buys about seven percent of the nation's production and the great majority of that is for the defense services produced by the military and the equipment it buys and employs to produce defense services. Perhaps more significantly, *federal non-defense spending only comprises about one and one half percent of the total spending that causes production and employment to occur.*

To put the relative unimportance of the federal government's non-defense spending in context—total federal non-defense spending to buy goods and services is only enough to buy about seven months of the *growth* in the amount of goods and services the United States economy is capable of producing. Looking at it yet another way—both foreign buyers and state and local governments are six to eight times as important as the federal government's non-defense buying in terms of creating jobs and producing products. Even with military spending included the state and local governments are more important sources of jobs and production.

Governments also disburse money for purposes other than the purchase of job-generating newly produced goods and services—for example to *transfer* money to social security recipients for having worked in the past, to farmers for not growing food, to help investment banks and lenders when they make bad loans or have trading losses in the securities markets, and to state and local governments to help them finance their own governmental spending. Such transfers, of course, will themselves subsequently cause production and employment to occur *if and when* they are used by their recipients to buy goods and services for consumer, investment, and governmental spending purposes.

In addition to their purchases of new goods and services and their provision of transfers, governments also collect taxes and borrow money to finance their expenditures. All four of these major fiscal activities affect the level of total spending that goes on in an economy to buy things. Thus, they affect the level of production and employment that occurs.

All four fiscal activities are considered in some detail in this and later chapters, both in terms of why they occur and their impact of total spending. One reason they are considered in detail is because governmental spending and budgets, particularly federal spending and federal budgets, are often erroneously blamed when an economy has problems such as inflation, unemployment, and inadequate rates of growth. Another is that it is believed in some quarters that fiscal activities can be successfully implemented to prevent and control inflation and unemployment. And another is so the journalists, politicians, and Federal Reserve governors and regional presidents who subsequently replace those who stood idly by while the economy collapsed will know what to do and what *not* to do in the years ahead when they are in power.

GOVERNMENT PURCHASING

It is a characteristic of certain types of goods and services such as streets and highways, sewer and water lines, school buildings, national defense, and police protection that their benefits can be received by more than one person. Thus there is no necessity for each person to act alone to buy these products and services. Instead, the potential beneficiaries of these goods and services have a vested interest in banding together (forming a government) to buy them so that each person can receive benefits from them but will have to bear only a portion of their purchase price.

Goods and services whose benefits can be shared are "public" or "social" products. They are different from "private" goods and services such as soft drinks, shoes, and cell phones whose benefits accrue to only one user so that there is no incentive for joint purchasing. A list of the various public goods and services that governments might buy is quite extensive and goes far beyond such things as roads and schools and military planes—such as the need for the services of the Treasury, the Congress; various offices to study and implement fiscal activities to promote full employment and prevent inflation; actions to influence and regulate otherwise private transactions that involve social costs and social benefits; and courts and police services so the rule of law is maintained and equally applied.

Sometimes, as in the case of road construction or military aircraft, a government buys from a private employer. In many cases, however, *governments are both the buyer of the services and the employer who produces them.* For example, the federal government is both the buyer of military services and the employer which produces them; state governments buy and produce the services of state universities and mental institutions; city governments buy and produce police services and street repairs; school districts buy and produce public education; and sewer and water districts may both buy and produce water and dispose of waste.

Whether a government should or should not be both the buyer buying goods and services and the employer producing them is an eternal debate: should the streets and sanitation department pick up the garbage and fill the potholes or hire private employers to do it; should the school district produce all the educational services or pay charter and religious schools to produce them; should state operate mental institutions, hospitals, and prisons or pay private employers to operate them; should state universities produce football teams or should they be privately operated.

But one thing is absolutely certain—*it is that governmental spending money to purchase such goods and services causes them to be produced and workers to be hired* no matter whether the employer that produces them is public or private.

The argument as to whether something should or should not be bought or produced by a government has been going on for ages and has often been quite witty. Consider this wry quote from the great University of Chicago and Stanford economist Thorstein Veblen commenting on colleges and universities spending money to buy new stadiums and running quasi-professional sports programs—*"football is to higher education as bull fighting is to agriculture."*

How much should governments buy?

Some people think governments should buy more and some people think governments should buy less. The rational answer is rather Panglossian—in the best of all possible worlds the appropriate amount of government purchasing (and transfers) is neither more nor less than whatever will acquire the amounts and types of goods and services which the people in the economy, acting together through the governments they elect, choose to have the governments buy and help others to buy.

In the real world, of course, government spending always ends up with a great degree of imperfection and compromise due to failures and imperfections inherent in the political process and among the politicians and bureaucrats who make the decisions. On the whole, however, the tendency is for democratically elected politicians to at least pretend to provide the amounts and types of spending that the people want—or risk being ousted in the next election.

Authoritarian governments, on the other hand, so long as they can stay in power can buy whatever they see fit: statues and billboard pictures of themselves; luxury palaces for their family members; handouts and subsidies for their supporters; grandiose parades and extravaganzas to impress visitors; and big security apparatuses to keep them in power. Their spending inevitably continues until they are assassinated or replaced in the next revolution. It has been suggested that, as a general rule, the bigger the statues and posters of the current leader, the sooner and more violent the revolution and the less the likelihood the next government will buy things and make transfer payments in accordance with the wishes of the people it is governing.

Needless to say, the willingness of people to authorize governmental expenditures may change as the circumstances confronting them change. Thus it is quite possible that as the United States economy grows Americans may come to want more of the increased production to be devoted to government purchases and transfers. Or they might want less.

Why government spending increased. Recently, since the Great Recession began in 2008, it appears governmental spending and transfers have been increasing in importance at every level of government. A few observers have decried this as an "indication of national weakness" and even "creeping socialism" despite the fact that the products purchased have been produced by governmental employers in accordance with a government plan.

It is not "socialism" to have government spending. The essence of socialism is production throughout the economy by governmentally owned and operated employers in response to a plan—as opposed to production by privately owned employers producing in response to buyers who are buying in markets what they want instead of what the government plans call for them to have.

In essence, the United States economy today remains fundamentally non-socialist in nature; even government-purchased products such as roads and military equipment are produced primarily by private employers responding to government purchases rather than produced in government owned and operated plants in response to the directives and plans of government bureaucrats.

Fortunately there are more lucid explanations of the growth in the absolute amount of government outlays in countries such as the United States. Among them: the population of the country has risen over the years both from births exceeding deaths and from high levels of immigration—more people require more roads and schools; people are living longer and older people require more hospital and care services.

Another reason government has grown is that the private sector has periodically been hit hard by recessions such as the one that started in 2008 and resulted in welfare assistance for wealthy financial traders and for the increased numbers of unemployed people who qualified for one or more of the various welfare programs.

Another reason federal spending has grown is war and terrorism, the threat of war and terrorism, and the use of the military in an effort to impose friendly governments and "democracy" on heretofore real or imagined enemies such as Iraq and Afghanistan and to protect the American public from terrorists.

Defense spending in a country such as the United States is relatively large. The military employs over a million people and its buying in the private sector has resulted in the employment of millions more. It has been suggested that technology advances are a major reason its spending has increased. In any event, the military seems to require ever more expensive planes and equipment that can go faster and faster and carry more and more weapons.

Recently, as a result the 9-11 attacks by terrorists from Saudi Arabia, fighting terrorism, providing military services, and attempting to impose a new way of life on other countries all became growth industries with more and more revenues and employees. That growth was associated with the United States invading Iraq which was not involved in the 9-11 attack but was "unfriendly" and run by a megalomaniac. It also invaded Afghanistan which became peripherally involved as the place where the terrorists' leader may have hid for a while until he was killed in Pakistan which could not be invaded because it was an ally.

Whatever the reasons for the invasions and subsequent military occupations to "build nations," military purchases rose by many hundreds of billions of dollars, military careers were extended and enhanced, generals and admirals awarded each other bushels of medals and retirement jobs, and business boomed for our military suppliers, hospitals, and contractors.

Various inventions have also contributed to a perceived need for more and more government activity: the advent of the automobile and the huge increase in its numbers created an ever growing need for more streets and highways; the growth of air travel introduced the need for more airports and government regulations to insure that planes do not fly to the same place at the same altitude at the same time; the growth broadcasting and digital services introduced the need for government action to insure that only one company tries to provide digital services on the same frequency.

In addition, rising aspirations for health and education led people to act together through their governments to buy and operate more schools and hospitals; and the growing urbanization of the country caused a growing need for large-scale sewage and water systems and modern police and fire facilities and services.

The relative stability of government purchasing. Despite the growth in the absolute size of government spending and the tendency of politicians and journalists to blame government spending, and particularly federal spending, for causing inflation, the proportion of the United States' total production bought by the federal government has actually *declined* for both military and non-military goods and services over much of the past thirty or forty years. It is the more rapidly growing and significantly larger spending of state and local governments that kept the overall share of United States production bought by governments relatively constant in the range of plus or minus twenty percent.

Where federal government expenditures have particularly grown is in the area of transfers. Social Security, Medicare, CHIP (Children's Health Insurance Program), and various safety net programs grew and their coverage was extended to a larger and larger percentage of the population.

A more prosaic explanation is that people, in general, may be confusing the growth in importance of federal spending which did not start until 2009, and then primarily in response to the recession, with the growth of federal regulations which has occurred almost continually and seems to have accelerated in recent years.

Despite the transfer programs that have grown, and even with the Bush and Obama wars to impose a new way of life on the people of Afghanistan and Iraq, total federal expenditures remained remarkably stable, oscillating around twenty percent of gross domestic production until the Great Recession caused federal transfer spending to skyrocket in fiscal 2009. For example, total federal spending, all purchases and transfers, was equal to 21.6 percent of the value of all production in the United States in 1990 and 20.9 percent in 2008. Then, after years of relative stability it jumped to 25.1 in fiscal 2009 when the Great Recession started and transfers increased to help unemployed workers, needy speculators and investment bankers, and a handful of the President's political supporters.

On the other hand, though it appears less likely, it may be that the 2009 increase in federal purchases and transfers resulted from the American people and their elected representatives suddenly wanting a greater portion of the goods and services being produced in their economy to go to those in need and for government-purchased goods and services such as education and highways and police protection.

But then how does an analyst reconcile the idea that Americans want government spending and transfers to become relatively more important with the reality of the long years of stability? That is an important question for if actual government purchasing and transfers remain proportional and the public's desire for government financed services is actually growing faster than peoples' desires for consumer goods and services, it means that as its economy's income grows the United States will tend to have an ever-increasing backlog of unproduced public goods and services.

Such a "social imbalance" of production could exist due to noneconomic restraints such as public fears of losing individual freedoms to "big government" and its bureaucrats. In essence, the economy's people may want more of such goods and services but be motivated to oppose governmental spending to buy them in order to prevent the power of governmental administrative bodies from growing in importance relative to those of individuals.

In other words, it may be that Americans want more government services but want the spending to get them held down in order to avoid the onerous regulations and favoritism that seems to accompany such spending.

GOVERNMENT TRANSFERS

Government transfers are monies which governments give for one reason or another to people, employers, organizations, campaign donors, and other governments. They include all federal, state, and local government expenditures other than those used to buy newly produced goods and services. Among them: interest on government debt, bloc grants to other governments, and Social Security payments to retirees, disabled people, and widows and orphans. What they have in common is that none of these expenditures directly result in jobs and production—they merely transfer purchasing power to recipients who may or may not use it for that purpose.

Transfers are an important source of many people's disposable incomes and *a very big part of every federal budget.* Among the most important transfers are Social Security, Medicare, various "safety net" programs, and CHIP (children's health insurance program).

Other transfers occur on a one-off basis to meet special problems and requests. For example, at the start of the 2008 Great Recession the Congress and White House transferred an additional $200 to each Social Security recipient to encourage consumer spending an effort to encourage consumer spending. They simultaneously transferred many hundreds of billions to Goldman Sachs and a few other large financial traders so they could continue distributing profits to their partners and continue paying billions of dollars of annual bonuses that their employees earned creating and trading the mortgage derivatives which failed.

The "favored few" received the special help instead of America's unemployed workers and its failing businesses and commercial banks, so their White House and Federal Reserve apologists allege, because their failure as a result of their financial trading gambles gone wrong would cause commercial banks and other financial institutions around the world to "melt down." This, they said, would cause even more unemployment and business failures because consumers and other spenders would then have been unable to obtain normal levels of loans and credit from their commercial banks. They would not be able to get them, it was said, because the traders owed so much to the commercial banks that they would be ruined and forced to close if the traders could not pay.

And what they allege appears to be true. It seems the Federal Reserve and other regulators had indeed allowed the universal banks other depositories to loan and use so much for trading purposes, instead of for loans to the consumers and employers in their communities, that without the bailout of the "favored few" they would have either failed or been forced to cut back even further of their conventional loans and credit lines.

Basically, in essence, the Congress and Federal Reserve rescued the handful of too-big-to-fails. Then they stood idly by while the supply of money and credit in the economy collapsed and the resulting reduction in total spending pulled the economy ever deeper into what became known as the Great Recession and then morphed into a permanent economic depression with massive permanent unemployment and government deficits.

Other transfers.

The federal government is not the only source governmental transfers. For example, a state may transfer money to its welfare recipients or as revenue sharing to municipalities or to its state universities or cities so they can pay interest on their construction bonds; a city may transfer funds to a non-profit organization operating a woman's shelter or to the Salvation Army to help pay for an alcohol abuse program.

To an economist, *any money that a person, public or private employer, or government receives that is not been earned producing goods and services is a transfer.* Thus students receive transfers when they get money from home or scholarships from a school or government; the elderly and disabled when they receive Social Security payments; military and other retirees when they receive pensions; people, banks and the Federal Reserve when they receive interest and dividends from the securities and bonds and bank deposits they own; financial traders so they can cover their trading losses and still pay bonuses; farmers when they receive payments for not growing crops; and state universities when they are given state and private monies so they can offer more athletic scholarships and build bigger football stadiums.

The Federal Reserve is the biggest single recipient of federal transfers (except when too-big-to-fail financial institutions get them so they can cover their trading losses and maintain their profits and bonuses). Specifically, the Federal Reserve receives many billions of dollars per year in the form of unearned interest on the federal debt it holds as a result of creating new money at no cost to itself.

In fairness it should be noted that the Federal Reserve, unlike the hedge funds and the too-big-to-fail financial institutions which are given both periodic bailouts and special tax rates below those of other businesses "because they are so important," pays a 100 percent tax rate on any income it receives in excess of its operating costs. In effect, the Federal Reserve receives the interest payment transfers and then immediately signs them over to the Treasury as a tax payment.

The reasons for transfers.

One fundamental basis for government transfers is the inability of some individuals to obtain "enough" goods and services because of a lack of earnings due to circumstances related to their age, physical condition, unemployment, occupation, or location. Of course, transfers are also given for less humanitarian reasons such as improving the lot of certain types of voters and lobbyists or rewarding financial institutions for loaning the government money or for their political contributions and willingness to provide sinecures when a "friend" leaves government service.

Another fundamental basis for governmental transfers is the previous savings individuals undertook by saving some of their incomes by paying Social Security and Medicare taxes. In a sense, people's income from such things as Social Security and Medicare and state pensions is "earned" by their earlier work—but such governmental transfers, along with monies from private pensions and gifts and monies people receive from their financial assets and the sale of their real estate, are all counted as transfers when they happen.

And when they happen they are counted as transfers *because such government spending does not cause production and employment to occur.* The money and income provided by such transfers will, of course, subsequently count as spending that causes production and employment to occur *when and if* it is used to buy newly produced goods and services—for example, when a Social Security recipient uses his one-time transfer of $200 to buy food or a stock market trader uses his too-big-to-fail bailout millions to buy a new Ferrari and a home in the country.

A third fundamental basis for government transfers is political manipulation and favoritism. This typically takes the form of obscure footnotes and obtuse verbiage buried in spending and tax bills to favor important sources of political campaign contributions and post-government employment opportunities. As anyone who has lived in Chicago or worked in government knows, executive orders and legislation requiring appropriated monies be given or loaned to specific recipients is common in Washington and in state capitols and city halls around the country.

In essence, the fact that money is appropriated to help people and employers in need of temporary assistance because of a recession or mortgage meltdown does not mean that the intended recipients will always get it. All too often it is diverted to the "favored few" by political insiders. The actions of Congress and White House in response to the Great Recession are a classic example.

GOVERNMENT TAXES
AND REVENUES

Governments obviously need money in order to make purchases and transfers. Most, with the possible exception of Greece, obtain a major part of their revenues from taxes and fees—the various required payments that governments levy on public and private employees, the for-profit employers of the private sector, and on some of the goods and services produced in the economy.

Only one thing is certain about taxes—*they reduce the taxpayers' disposable income and wealth and thus the taxpayers' ability to buy goods and services.* To the extent taxes reduce spending they reduce the amount of production and employment that will occur in the economy.

Of course, governments could spend such monies to offset the adverse effect of their taxes on production by themselves buying goods and services. But governments do not always do that. They may, instead, use it for such things as transferring money to people in need or to pay interest on their debts or to help traders and speculators who can be counted on to make political contributions. On balance, the taxes collected in an economy have a negative impact on its levels of production and employment.

The reduction of consumer, employer, and foreign spending that tax increases tend to cause has important implications for policymakers—*it means that well-meaning efforts to raise taxes to reduce a governmental deficit may backfire by reducing the tax base of income and profits and taxable transactions so much that it makes the deficit worse instead of better.*

Alternately reducing tax rates may encourage such a growth in the tax base as to cause total tax collections to rise. What will actually happen, of course, depends on whose taxes are cut and how they respond to the resulting increases in their disposable incomes.

Governments have other sources of revenue besides taxes and fees. They can also borrow, receive grants from other governments, and, in the case of a national government, literally create money or have it created for them by their central bank such as the United States' Federal Reserve or Europe's European Central Bank or the United Kingdom's Bank of England.

Taxes are rarely neutral: different taxes can distort behavior in different ways. If income taxes are high enough, for example, businesses and people, may be discouraged from working and producing; consumers and employers may change what they buy if they have to pay taxes on some items and not on others; collecting taxes on profits and incomes earned abroad when the money is repatriated may cause the money to be held abroad; high taxes in one jurisdiction and not in another may cause employers and customers to migrate to the low tax jurisdiction; reducing taxes if assets are held longer before they are sold is virtually certain to cause some of them not to be sold before the lower taxes kick in. The list goes on and on.

GOVERNMENT BORROWING
AND GOVERNMENT DEBT

Governments big and small sometimes, rightly or wrongly, do not take in as much money in taxes and fees as they spend. In other words, they have budgetary deficits and have to borrow money to cover them. How and where they borrow can affect and distort total spending. It can also result in an ever increasing debt that requires ever more interest payments. Sometimes the interest burden gets so large it cannot be sustained (Greece, Detroit) and the government becomes bankrupt and effectively collapses.

Popular folklore and congressional speeches to the contrary, bankruptcy and non-payment due to excessive deficits and governmental debt need never be the case, at least not when a government has its own central bank. Then it can always, if necessary, create whatever money it needs and pay whatever needs to be paid. Whether or not it is best for the economy to do so is another matter entirely. It needs to be considered in great detail before the borrowing proceeds.

State and local borrowing
and debt.

State and local government obtain money from a wide variety of sources to finance their spending. Among the biggest are transfers from the federal government, sales taxes, property taxes, income taxes and the sale of interest-bearing bonds. They also frequently act as employers and produce in response to their own spending: School districts employ teachers and produce education services; cities employ police and firemen and produce public safety; state universities employ professors and produce higher education and football games. The list is endless.

Almost all state and local governments from the biggest states to the smallest sewer districts have issued bonds so they can buy now and pay later. And using debt to pay for something can be a reasonable thing to do, particularly if the debt is issued to pay for capital items that will generate production for years into the future. That is because the *bonds can be structured to be repaid over the useful life of the items their money buys so that the beneficiaries of the items are the ones who pay for them.*

Consider a highway bond or school bond that is used to buy roads and schools that might reasonably be expected to provide benefits for the next thirty years. Spreading out the interest expenses and payments over thirty years is a way to insure that those who will benefit during those thirty years will be the ones who pay. But pay they must because state and local bonds are just like the debts of people and businesses—they must be paid or at some point it will be impossible for the government issuing them to borrow any more money.

The day of reckoning arrives if and when lenders and bond buyers see a government's revenues as being insufficient to service any additional debt. Then they will no longer be willing to make loan and buy bonds. When this happens the overly-indebted governments have to either cut their spending to the levels that can be financed with their revenues or go bankrupt. And, when the debt is so large, servicing the debt may take so much of the government's revenue that little, if anything, is left over to pay for normal expenses such as police, street maintenance, fire protection, and schools. (Hello California, Detroit, and Greece)

In the end, no matter whether it is to buy capital items with long lives or just to skate over a budget deficit until next year, *for state and local governments the basic choice is between taxing now or borrowing and taxing even more later.* (More has to be taxed later because not only will the original amount have to be repaid but also the interest charged by the lenders.)

Federal borrowing and the Federal Reserve.

The position of the federal government is *totally different* from that of the state and local governments—because the money for federal spending can also be obtained in ways other than tax-now or borrow-and-tax-more-later. Moreover, and hugely important for policy purposes, the most appropriate levels of federal taxes and federal spending may result in either surpluses or deficits.

What the United States' federal government has that the state and local governments do not have is its own central bank, the Federal Reserve System. The Federal Reserve System is controlled by seven governors appointed by the President and confirmed by the Senate. It has several important and interrelated goals and duties. Its primary duty, enshrined in law, is to insure that there is enough total spending so that the public and private employers operating in the United States are producing at full employment levels of production.

In other words, the Federal Reserve's primary job is to keep the United States prosperous by making sure there is enough revenues flowing into coffers of its public and private employers so that they fully employ the United States' labor force.

The Federal Reserve's legal but all-to-often-ignored charge to maintain full employment contrasts with that of other central banks. The European

Central Bank, for example, is charged with preventing inflation and forbidden to finance government spending. Unemployment in the euro zone is the responsibility of the individual countries.

The Federal Reserve basically carries out its duty to keep the country prosperous by increasing and decreasing the supply of money and credit as it governors and regional presidents deem appropriate. It is supposed to increase the supply of money and credit as needed so there will be enough total spending—not too much as it cause inflation from excess spending nor too little so as to cause unemployment from not enough total spending. This is a constant challenge as the economy constantly grows and the spending needed to maintain full employment constantly changes.

In effect, the President and Congress control the composition and structure of the economy by establishing the taxes, rules and regulations under which its employers and workers operate. This establishes the economy's total capacity to produce, its *aggregate supply*. The Federal Reserve then, supposedly, responds to the resulting economy's production capacity by doing whatever its governors and regional presidents deem necessary to cause total customer spending, the economy's *aggregate demand*, to be high enough maintain full employment without causing inflation from too much spending.

That, at least, is the plan. As historians know, and as shall be examined in the chapters that follow, efforts to keep total spending at a desirable level is often talked about by Federal Reserve officials—but rarely realistically attempted; and when it has been attempted, the policies employed have often been too little and too late. Moreover, they often do not work because they are inappropriate and unrealistic because they are not based on macroeconomic knowledge and the conditions and realities of the real world.

The Federal Reserve is also a significant player in the fiscal process. The laws and regulations coming from Congress and White House often create a situation wherein federal revenues fall short of federal spending. Then the Treasury must either sell bonds in the financial markets to get the necessary funds *or obtain the money directly from the Federal Reserve*. Either way requires the Federal Reserve to coordinate with the Treasury and to integrate any financing assistance it might provide with its efforts to keep total spending in the economy at the level needed to generate full employment without inflation.

The federal government can always obtain the necessary funds to cover a federal deficit and pay off any national debt that comes due because, if necessary, both it and the Federal Reserve can literally create the money for the federal government to spend. But will such money creation to finance a deficit or refinance the national debt cause inflation (as some fear) by resulting sooner or later in too much spending because more money will now be in circulation? *Absolutely not.*

As shall be seen in great detail, the Federal Reserve can create money to help finance the federal government and *simultaneously* take that much money, or even more if it wishes, out of circulation using the various money-supply-reducing tools in its arsenal.

In other words, the Federal Reserve's financing of a government deficit, if it should do so, does *not* mean the total money supply of the economy will increase and cause inflation. The federal government could, at least conceptually, should Congress and the White House so desire, run a deficit (or surplus) in perpetuity. What this might do to the economy and whether it is the best way or a realistic way for the Federal Reserve to proceed is another question.

What all this means, however, is that because it has its own central bank—the Federal Reserve—with the ability to create and destroy money and credit, the federal government does *not* face the same "tax now or tax more later" alternative that state and local governments face.

Unfortunately, even though the President appoints, and the Senate confirms the Federal Reserve governors, and each new President selects the Chairman from among them, the federal government has never been able to count on the Federal Reserve to do the right thing *whatever that might be.* Federal Reserve has all too often failed to perform. It has neither appropriately helped finance the federal government nor appropriately increased and decreased the supply of money and credit as needed to keep the economy prosperous without unemployment and inflation.

To the contrary, the Federal Reserve has consistently adopted naïve and unrealistic policies—apparently because the majority of its governors typically have neither the appropriate training in macroeconomics nor the real world experiences required to understand which policies will succeed and which are unrealistic and will fail.

The root source of its failure appears to be that the Federal Reserve governors are typically lawyers, cronies, and bureaucrats from the Treasury, the Federal Reserve, and a handful of too-big-to-fail Wall Street traders. The results have all too often been comparable to what one might expect if an economist who never studied law or medicine was appointed as a federal judge or heart surgeon—bad. For example, as we shall see, the Federal Reserve frequently pursues interest rate actions in the mistaken belief they will significantly affect total spending and, thus, production, employment, and prices.

It has also been suggested that the Federal Reserve has behaved so badly for so long because its governors, at least the minority who have actually studied economics, are all sufficiently aged to have studied Keynes and British-oriented monetary and fiscal policies in their economics classes when they were students—but not sufficiently worldly to be aware of the significant differences between economies of the United Kingdom and the United States that make reasonable policies for the UK totally inapplicable and unworkable for the United States.

In essence, as shall become all too abundantly clear, even today the Federal Reserve's governors and regional presidents are the modern day macroeconomic equivalent of the elderly physicians who in some countries still use leeches instead of modern medicines to reduce high blood pressure—living and working with inappropriate theories and cures based on "common knowledge." So patients die and the United States has periodic periods of inflation, unemployment, and large and unnecessary amounts of national debt. On the other hand, the governors and regional presidents are always well dressed.

Borrowing from the financial markets.

Sometimes the Federal Reserve increases the money supply by buying bonds directly from the federal government. The federal government then spends it and the money supply begins to increase as the newly created money get into circulation and becomes part of the monetary base. In fact, most federal borrowing is *not* done via the Federal Reserve. What normally happens when the Treasury needs more money to cover a budget deficit, or to pay off bonds whose payment date coming due, is that the Treasury prints up new bonds and openly sells them in the financial markets. The bonds then end up in the hands of whoever buys them and the Treasury has money it can spend as it sees fit.

There is an active market for U.S. bonds. Sophisticated buyers and analysts know they are secure and will always be paid because the U.S. always has the Federal Reserve. So they tend to be snapped up by commercial banks, pensions, speculators and traders, and anyone and everyone else wanting an absolutely secure asset that yields a bit of interest income. Moreover, in the unlikely event the Federal Reserve does not come through with the necessary funds, the Treasury itself can print enough money to promptly pay whatever is due.

Less knowledgeable "analysts" and investors, on the other hand, are not so certain of the soundness of United States bonds. One major rating agency, for example, is so devoid of economic expertise that it actually lowered the rating of U.S. bonds because they might not be paid when they mature. To put the degree of ignorance of its "analysts" in perspective—it lowered its rating of no-risk federal bonds below the top rating it had assigned to mortgage derivatives up until the day they collapsed.

Pragmatic analysts attribute the rating agency's blunder to a lack of knowledge about economics and the workings of the U.S economy, and to the "fees" the traders issuing the derivatives paid for their ratings. It would be slanderous, of course, to claim that the "fees" the derivative issuers paid to Moody's, Standard and Poor's, and Fitch to rate the derivatives higher than federal bonds were bribes.

Among the biggest buyers of the U.S bonds sold in the open market are countries such as Japan and China. They each own about seven percent of the United States' national debt. They have been able to accumulate dollars and use them to buy federal bonds and other highly liquid dollar-denominated assets because they have balance of payments surpluses. China's surpluses, for example, are the result of China fixing the yuan's exchange rate so Chinese employers can sell more abroad for dollars than the Chinese buy abroad with dollars; Japan's because of its de facto quotas to prevent imports.

The Chinese and Japanese could, of course, just keep selling more abroad than they buy and let the dollars and federal bonds keep piling up. But that might invite U.S. retaliation. So there appears to be an "understanding" between the United States and China that the U.S. will not retaliate for China undervaluing the yuan so long as the Chinese use the surpluses to buy U.S. bonds. There apparently is a similar understanding with Japan.

How long can the trade imbalances and the Chinese (and Japanese) bond buying continue? Forever if that's what both parties desire. But what happens if one or the other decides to stop? Not much except that China loses some of its ability to sell in the United States and the U.S. bond market loses a major buyer.

But wait. What if China decides to dump its bonds on the market? No problem. The Federal Reserve could buy them all if it wanted to do so—then the Chinese would have very liquid dollars instead of very liquid federal debt. And those dollars would not cause inflation even if they flooded into the U.S. economy—because the Federal Reserve has the power to instantly (repeat instantly) soak them all up. The process the Federal Reserve uses to remove money from circulation is examined in detail in subsequent chapters.

Alternately, of course, the Federal Reserve could stand idle and let the Chinese sell their federal bonds in the world's financial markets. Such a major increase in the supply of bonds would certainly tend to drive their prices down and, thus, their interest rate yields up. That would certainly please the banks and pension funds and insurance companies that tend to buy such financial assets in order to obtain the interest they pay.

On the other hand, it would certainly displease those other banks and other financial intermediaries which also have such bonds because it would cause the bonds already in their portfolios to be worth less if they had to be sold.

Moreover, at least on the face of it, the resulting lower bond prices would make it more expensive for the Treasury to sell its next batches of bonds unless they are priced to yield a higher rate of interest. But wait. The Treasury does not have to sell bonds in the open market to raise money—it has the Federal Reserve.

In an ideal world, if the Federal Reserve was functioning appropriately, its governors and regional presidents would look at the state of the American economy and decide for themselves whether it is in the best interest of the economy for the Federal Reserve to buy the new bonds issued by the Treasury or go into the open market and buy existing bonds owned by others including the Chinese.

Thus the Federal Reserve could, for example, tell the Chinese and the Treasury to sell their bonds on the open market and then provide the commercial banks with additional reserves and encourage them to buy the bonds. Or it could buy them itself. In the real world the Treasury rarely sells its bonds directly to the Federal Reserve—it sells them in the financial markets and then the Federal Reserve takes whatever steps its governors and regional presidents deem necessary to help that happen smoothly, typically by providing potential buyers with enough money to buy them.

Borrowing affects total spending.

Governments do have an alternative to financing their deficits by selling their bonds and other debt instruments to their central bank or into the financial markets or to foreigners—they can sell them directly to people and businesses. Until recently the United States federal government did this by selling assorted "savings bonds" and "war bonds." It did not do this primarily to raise money, but rather to encourage savings and, in so doing, discourage consumer spending so that fewer consumer goods and service would be produced. Then there would be more labor and capital available for employers to use to build such things as tanks and planes for the military.

In essence, the possibility of people lending money to a government means they have an alternative use for their disposable incomes. If they make such loans they will have to either reduce their consumer spending or devote less of their disposable incomes to other forms of savings. In effect, federal government borrowing tends to "crowd out" the borrowing of the banks' traditional customers.

Sales via the financial markets can have a somewhat similar effect—to the extent banks and other intermediaries buy government debt they will have less money available to buy private debt by making loans to consumers and others. In essence, *government bond sales, no matter whether they are made directly to potential spenders or indirectly via the financial markets, tend to "crowd out" private borrowers. Thus they tend to reduce people's propensities to consume and to cut into employers' abilities to produce.* Pragmatic federal policy makers try to structure and schedule their bond sales to minimize such effects.

The important role of deficits and the national debt.

Federal taxes hold down spending. So does federal borrowing that soaks up money that would otherwise be spent or loaned to those who would use it to spend. And there is no question but what the federal government must borrow when it has a deficit. It legally could, but generally does not, create money to cover its deficit. It does not do so because it has effectively delegated that power to the Federal Reserve.

When the federal government runs a deficit it typically uses the Federal Reserve to directly or indirectly finance the deficit. The Federal Reserve cooperates in the process because it uses the buying of bonds issued by the federal government as its primary method of putting additional dollars into the United States economy and into the rest of the world.

This goes on continually because the United States as an economy with an ever growing capacity to produce needs an ever growing supply of money. Sometimes the Federal Reserve creates the additional money and gets it into circulation by directly buying the bonds; sometimes by buying them in the open market. Either way the monetary base tends to be expanded and the United States' money supply tends to grow.

Since the Federal Reserve buys bonds when it wants to create new money and expand the money supply, and sells them when it wants to destroy money and reduce the money supply, analysts can follow what the Federal Reserve is doing by tracking its holdings of federal bonds. In essence, the amount of bonds the Federal Reserve holds is equal to the amount of monetary base it has created.

In other words, as shall be seen, federal deficits and the national debt are very important because they are used to affect and track the size of the United States' money supply—and the size of the supply of money and credit is typically *much more important* to maintaining prosperity and full employment than the amount of federal spending and how that spending is financed.

GOVERNMENT AND THE LEVEL OF INCOME

Government tax collections, spending, and transfers are affected by the level of income in an economy just as is consumer spending, employers' investment spending, and foreign spending. Accordingly, governmental fiscal activities can be related to the level of income in the economy just as consumer spending, employer investments, and foreign spending can be related.

Table 5.1 depicts the types of fiscal relationships that are possible for an example economy. This economy, as we first observe it, has a balanced budget, an income level of $30 trillion, a full employment level of income of $50 trillion; and a progressive tax structure such that tax collections will grow faster than income grows when the economy comes out of the recession. In other words, the economy is in a serious recession, comparable to that of the United States in the early 21st century, with its attendant higher transfers and lower tax collections compared to those that would exist at full employment.

The table specifically depicts an economy whose government purchases will remain a steady twenty percent of the economy's level of income; transfers are initially five trillion and will be reduced $.5 trillion for every gain of five trillion in production and employment as the unemployed find jobs and go off welfare; and tax collections will take a bigger chunk of each income increment if the economy's level of income increases towards the $50 trillion full employment level of spending.

Table 5-1
Government spending, transfers, and
tax collections (trillions of dollars)

Income.....	20	30	40	50
Taxes........	7	11	15	20
G..............	4	6	8	10
Tr.............	5.5	5	4.5	4
Budget	-2.5	0	+2.6	+6

In this particular economy there is $2.5 trillion deficit if the level of income is $20 trillion; a balanced federal budget when the economy has a $30 trillion level of income; a $2.5 trillion surplus if the economy reaches $40 trillion; and a $6 trillion surplus if the economy is able to return to full employment at $50 trillion.

The numbers are overstated but this is a pretty good depiction of how the U.S. economy looked in the second decade of the 21ˢᵗ century. A budgetary surplus and full employment, not a deficit and the unemployment of the Great Recession, is what would have tended to happen if the Federal Reserve had been run by professional macroeconomists and engaged in the monetary policies necessary to achieve enough total spending so that the United States returned to full employment.

Food for thought about balanced budgets. Consider what might happen if something such as the Federal Reserve providing a monetary expansion or more sales to foreigners or new laws that increase investor expectations or anything else induces more spending so that the example economy comes out of its recession and reaches the $50 trillion full employment level of income and the $6 trillion surplus. There are politicians who are devoted to balanced federal budgets. They might prevail. So what will happen to this economy if Congress and the White House decide to increase government spending or reduce taxes by $6 trillion because "balanced budgets are good?"

Obviously taking such an action to "balance the budget" will pour trillions of additional dollars into the hand of consumers and employers—and cause more spending at a time when there is already enough spending to buy everything the economy's public and private employers can produce. As a result, the additional spending will tend to bid up prices. In other words, *inflation can be caused by the adoption of a balanced budget.* Balanced budgets are not always good for an economy even if they do make for great political speeches by people who don't know any better.

CHAPTER SUMMARY

I.   Governments typically buy new public goods and services whose benefits are widely shared and, therefore, don not lend themselves to individual purchases. Furthermore, their prices are often quite high so that purchases of them are possible only when their costs are shared.

II. Governments are major buyers of goods and services. State and local governments are much more important buyers than the federal government. In the United States almost twenty percent of all buying that causes production and employment is done by governments. Non-defense federal buying is inconsequential in terms of causing production and employment to occur. State and local buying is twice of the federal purchases even when defense is included.

III. Governments can be both the buyer spending money to buy goods and services and the employer receiving the money to produce them. For example, the federal government spends money to buy national defense and uses the money to employ military personnel to produce it; similarly, a city may both spend money to buy clean streets and keep its sewers open and operate a streets and sanitation department to employ people to produce those services.

IV. The importance of governments buying goods and services has remained remarkably stable over the years at a bit less than twenty percent of all the buying that causes production and employment to occur in the United States.

V. Government spending includes "transfers" to people, employers and other governments. Most federal spending involves transfers. They range from Social Security and Unemployment Insurance payments to the retired and unemployed to the periodic big bailouts of too-big-to-fail financial speculators and the President's political supporters.

VI. Taxes are the major source of government revenues. They are a form of "forced savings" in that they reduce spendable incomes and wealth and thus have a negative effect on total spending. They can have other effects such as discouraging the use of taxed items.

VII. Governments which do not collect enough taxes to pay for their spending can cover their budget deficits with borrowing. Borrowing to buy capital items with long lives can be a way to make the future beneficiaries pay their share of the costs.

VII. How governments borrow to cover their deficits can affect the level of spending that occurs in an economy.

VIII. State and local governments have limits on how much they can borrow because lenders will stop lending to them if they think they may not be repaid. Thus state and local governments have only two choices: tax now to pay for their spending or tax even more in the future to repay their borrowings plus interest. Such a delay tends to push the burden of the taxation on to future taxpayers in future generations.

IX.   The United States and other countries with their own central banks do not have limits on the size of their deficits and national debts. If necessary they can always cover their deficits by with new created money provided by their central bank. Thus, unlike state and local governments, the federal government can always borrow money and always repay it. Such borrowing need not cause inflationary increases in spending or the increases in the money supply. It is not a burden on future generations.

X.   Federal deficits and the national debt are important because their financing and ownership is used by the Federal Reserve to create the additional dollars that a growing United States economy needs to constantly add to its money supply.

XI.   Balanced budgets, contrary to the received wisdom of politicians and journalists, can be associated with spending increases that cause inflation. They can also be associated with total spending that is so low that there is massive unemployment.

CHAPTER SIX

MONEY AND INTERMEDIATION

Economies such as that of the United States are exceedingly complex with billions of transactions occurring every day. They produce enormous amounts of different good and services with enormous amounts and varieties of labor and capital. Barter, exchanging one item or service for another, would be absolutely impossible in such a complex economy because there are so many intertwined levels of transactions ranging from buying raw materials and components such as screws and boxes and chips, to assembling the finished goods and services, to financing the transactions in such a way as to minimize risk, to selling them.

In other words, in today's world the endless variety of economic activities and products necessitates some medium of exchange—money. In essence, *money is anything that is generally accepted in payment.*

The medium of exchange in the United States, and for many transactions in the rest of the world, is the United States dollar. Dollars are the money of the United States and are exchanged for products, labor, and other things in billions of dollar-denominated transactions every day. But who determines how many dollars there are in circulation and how does the quantity of money grow and decline?

THE FEDERAL RESERVE SYSTEM

The Federal Reserve System is the United States' central bank. It shares the power to create dollars with the Treasury and it is explicitly charged by law to create whatever amount of money is needed to maintain full employment. That is the Federal Reserve's *principal* charge although, as the nation's central bank, it is implicitly charged with preventing inflation and acting as the federal government's banker and as a lender of last resort for the nation's commercial banks. It is the Federal Reserve, and only the Federal Reserve, that is responsible for controlling the money supply of the United States.

All national banks in the United States are required to be members of the Federal Reserve System. They and other depositories such as state chartered banks, savings and loans, and credit unions are subject to its rules, regulations and reserve requirements.

The Federal Reserve is independent within the federal government. Its monetary policy decisions do not have to be approved by the President or anyone else in the executive or legislative branches. Its authority and independence are derived from laws enacted by Congress. It is only subject to congressional oversight in the sense that it can be called before congressional committees to explain its activities.

Congress levies a one hundred percent tax on its income so that the Treasury receives all of the Federal Reserve's profits after a statutory dividend of six percent on the relatively token capital investment required of each of its member banks. The Federal Reserve is a major holder of federal debt as a byproduct of its money-creating powers and the "backing" requirements imposed by Congress. The backing requirement means the Federal Reserve is required to hold a dollar's worth of assets for every dollar it creates—so the "asset" "backing" each dollar is inevitably federal bonds which the Federal Reserve buys with its new created money.

More specifically, the Federal Reserve literally creates new money with the stroke of a pen and uses it to purchase federal bonds. Then the newly created money is put into circulation when the sellers of the bonds spend it or deposit it in the bank. Because of the many hundreds of billions dollars of federal bonds it has acquired as a byproduct of creating money over the one hundred years of its life, the Federal Reserve is the largest single owner of U.S. Government's national debt and the largest single taxpayer as a result of its interest income.

The managers and structure.

The Federal Reserve is run by a seven member Board of Governors. Its members are chosen by the President and confirmed by the Senate. Professional training in macroeconomics and relevant experience in business or commercial banking is *not* required. Governors are appointed for fourteen year terms. Each newly elected President of the United States gets to select, and the Senate gets to confirm, the board's Chairman from among the seven governors.

At this time a majority of the governors are lawyers and former state regulators. Only two or three of the seven appear to be qualified as professionally trained economists and none of the seven has had experience in the real world of business or commercial banking.

The Federal Reserve System operates with twelve regional Federal Reserve banks of which the New York bank is the most important because it is located in the New York financial district and houses the staff charged with implementing the Federal Reserve's policy decisions. The presidents of the regional banks are chosen by the regional banks' directors who are typically prominent people in their region's commercial banking and business communities. They are usually selected from among the regional banks' bureaucrats. No professional training or relevant experience in business or commercial banking is required for appointment as a regional president.

The regional banks were established a century ago for political reasons in order to get enough congressional votes to pass the legislation setting up the then-new central bank. The regional banks are of a little consequence—except that a rotation of five of the twelve regional presidents, always including the New York regional president, sits with the seven governors to make the policy decisions that determine whether or not the United States economy will have full employment and stable prices. They sit on the Federal Reserve's Open Market Committee. The committee is appropriately named because its twelve members periodically decide whether the Federal Reserve should be expanding the money supply by buying bonds in the open market—or selling them in the open market to reduce the money supply.

The current president of the New York regional bank was formerly a long-time employee of Goldman Sachs. The former president was one of the four principal architects of the Federal Reserve's response to mortgage crisis wherein Goldman Sachs and a few other large traders were bailed out with hundreds of billions of dollars of Federal Reserve assistance and the economic distress of rest of the nation effectively ignored. The other three were the Bush-appointed Federal Reserve Chairman who had been a Princeton professor, the Bush-appointed Treasury Secretary who had previously been chairman of Goldman Sachs, and the Bush-appointed lawyer who headed of the FDIC.

As a reward for their efforts to save Goldman Sachs, Citibank, and a handful of other big New York based traders the New York regional president was promoted by President Obama to be Secretary of the Treasury; the Federal Reserve Chairman was reappointed by President Obama for another four year term; and the head of the FDIC was retained by President Obama for several years until her term expired. The Secretary of the Treasury, who had previously been a long time employee and chairman of Goldman Sachs, was allowed to return to investment banking and enjoy the wealth he had saved for himself and his cronies without being arrested.

In essence, the architects of the current economic disaster were rewarded for saving Goldman Sachs, Citibank, and a handful of big New York based traders and causing the "Great Recession" that began in 2008. They then stood by relatively idly and let it continue for years until it morphed into a permanent depression.

Independence and institutional capture.

The Federal Reserve is one of several commercial bank regulators in the United States. The principal others are the Comptroller of the Currency and the Federal Deposit Insurance Corporation. The other regulators can, and periodically do, implement regulations and requirements that negate or offset the efforts of the Federal Reserve to control the supply of money.

The Federal Reserve's ostensible headquarters is located in Washington, D.C. Its most important site, however, is the New York regional bank where its policy decisions are implemented by its open market desk which operates every minute of the banking day to buy and sell federal bonds in the financial markets. Other than the chairman, the New York regional president is traditionally the most influential of the decision makers because he is alleged to be "in touch" with the financial community; or, as cynical analysts suggest, in their pocket.

Most analysts agree that the lack of relevant professional training, the personalities required to rise through academic and governmental bureaucracies, and the lack of experience in business and commercial banking, leaves the Federal Reserve governors particularly susceptible to "institutional capture" by the Federal Reserve staff and the Treasury Secretary who inevitably represents the New York financial community. In the absence of a fully qualified chairman with a strong and decisive personality, or the chairman's domination by a Treasury Secretary with a strong personality (who actually has relatively few powers), the entire board tends to adhere to the policy recommendations of the Federal Reserve's bureaucracy.

The capture of the Chairman by the Treasury Secretary and the Federal Reserve bureaucracy, it is alleged, has all too frequently resulted in decisions being based on obsolete economic theories and oriented towards meeting the needs of a handful of large financial institutions even when their needs conflict with those of the country as a whole. This will become increasingly apparent to analysts.

MONEY AND THE MONEY SUPPLY

The traditional nineteenth century definition of an economy's money supply, the one still used by the Federal Reserve System and cited by most journalists and used in most economic "studies," is that it is the total amount of coins, currency and transactions (checking account) deposits in the economy. The Federal Reserve and its staff continually collect and parse this and other money-related data. From it they develop equations and formulas to "scientifically" relate the size of the money supply to everything from inflation and unemployment to population growth and the installation of false teeth.

Yes, analysis using the Federal Reserve's vaunted "scientific techniques" shows that the growth of the money supply, as narrowly defined by the Federal Reserve staff and used to guide its policies, correlates better with how high airplanes have flown and the installation of false teeth than it does with inflation and unemployment. It seems the United States money supply has constantly increased over the years and so has the size of the population, the heights to which planes have flown, and the number of false teeth installed. Wags have suggested that this proves "scientifically" that the Federal Reserve would be more effective fighting inflation and unemployment if it would just increase the money supply at some constant rate and concentrate its efforts on grounding airplanes and eliminating sex and dentists.

All economists and the Federal Reserve agree that the United States' money supply includes the transactions (checking) deposits in United States banks and other financial institutions—because checks and digital instructions make such deposits instantly available for use to buy things and they are generally accepted throughout the economy for payments. The payments are primarily made by writing checks or sending digital instructions via cell phone swipes and computers. They are simply their owners' instructions to the bank or other holder of their deposits regarding the disposition of their money.

Similarly, all economists and analysts exclude savings deposits and certificates of deposit and credit lines from the money supply *if* their available balances cannot be immediately and automatically transferred when their owner writes a check or issues electronic payment instructions. Other things are similarly not included in the money supply because they too cannot be instantly used to buy goods and services. For instance, jewels, cigarettes, gold, and houses are not included in the United States' money supply because relatively few sellers of goods and services or anything else are willing to instantly take them in payment.

Even if there are withdrawal limitations so they cannot be instantly used to buy things and pay debts, savings deposits and certificates of deposit do provide their owners with a great deal of *liquidity* in that they can be quickly converted to instantly spendable dollars. Similarly liquid are stocks and bonds, various financial instruments, gold, and anything else that has an active market where they can be quickly sold to convert their value to dollars. Houses, gold mines, and cattle ranches on the other hand, are *illiquid* because it typically takes time to convert their value to dollars by selling them or borrowing against them.

The official definitions: A number of definitions of money and liquidity are traditionally used in the United States. Their sizes are calculated and published by the Federal Reserve and used to provide data for the staff and other macroeconomic studies that, allegedly, guide the Federal Reserve's policies:

MB is the monetary base which determines the maximum amount of transactions deposits that can exist in the Federal Reserve System's commercial banks and other depositories. It consists of the coins and currency in circulation, and the reserves of the commercial banks and other depositories;

M1 is the total of coins, currency, and transactions (checking and debit card accessible) deposits of the non-bank public;

M2 is M1 plus the savings deposits and certificates of deposits in the banks and other depositories that the Federal Reserve believes can be immediately spent via check or debit card because they are likely to be automatically transferred to a transactions account prior to the contracted maturity date.

The dollars of the real world.

The money supply of the United States according to pragmatic economists is more inclusive than that of the nineteenth century version of the money supply used by the Federal Reserve. They see money as *anything that is generally accepted in payment by the sellers of goods and services*. Accordingly, to the pragmatists, the money supply also includes Paypal and Square balances; the available credit on all widely accepted credit cards such as those in the Visa and MasterCard systems and American Express; immediately accessible deposits in money market accounts; the amount of "overdraft protection" offered by depositories, credit card companies, and money market accounts; the unused balances of working capital and personal credit lines; and the instantly transferable dollar deposits and unused dollar credit lines at foreign financial institutions.

In other words, pragmatic economists and analysts do not go along with the Federal Reserve governors by pretending the world of today does not have such things as the Internet, credit cards, foreign-held dollars, foreign financial institutions with dollar accounts and fractional reserve requirements, Paypal and Square digital deposits, swipeable cell phones, international money markets, credit cards issued by foreign financial institutions that are accepted in the United States, money market accounts accepting dollar deposits, business working capital lines, personal credit lines attached to real property and other assets, and anything else that is widely and instantly accepted in payment.

In essence, the Federal Reserve and the analysts who rely on its data tend to ignore a significant portion of the money supply of the real world. Perhaps they do so because accurate data about it is not systematically available. Perhaps they do so because ignoring the recent additions to the money supply makes it easier to "scientifically" analyze the relationship between money and the performance of the economy.

Whatever the reason, looking at the money supply and analyzing data from the perspective of the nineteenth century seems to have led the Federal Reserve governors and many journalists and "business economists" to some rather foolish conclusions, concerns, and policies.

THE MONEY OF
THE REAL WORLD

Coins. The total amount of coins in an economy tends to expand when new coins are minted; it tends to decline when coins are lost, placed in coin collections, sent abroad, or melted down. The general policy of most countries is to produce all the coins that are requested by banks and businesses. That is certainly the policy in the United States.

The mere existence of a common sense policy, however, does not mean it will or can always be pursued. Indeed, the retail trade in some countries has been periodically constrained by the lack of coins when inflation makes their purchasing power inconsequential. Other times, and it has happened in the United States with silver and copper coins, the face value of the coins is exceeded by their commodity values so they begin to be illegally melted down. Then they have to be replaced by new coins with lower commodity values. In the absence of small denomination coins, paper currencies with low face values and alternative forms of money, such as postage stamps and cigarettes, are often used to make change in small denominations.

Currency. The United States is somewhat unique among countries in that its green paper dollars can be issued by two different entities: Treasury Notes by the Treasury and Federal Reserve Notes by the Federal Reserve System. It's just tradition—both are actually printed by the Treasury's Bureau of Engraving and Printing. Both are "legal tender" in that they can be used to pay taxes and debts and both are "backed" by the "full faith and credit" (whatever that is) of the United States. The Federal Reserve notes are additionally "backed" by the Federal Reserve's holdings of national debt of an equal or greater value. In the real world, of course, *the value of the American dollar exists because it can be used to buy things (it has "purchasing power") and because it is accepted in payment of taxes and dollar denominated debts.*

Stated more plainly, the value of a dollar is whatever can be bought with it and dollars have value because things can be bought and paid with them. It is the policy of the United States to print as much currency as the country and world require. Somewhat surprisingly, the Federal Reserve only uses the vault cash numbers reported by U.S. depositories when it estimates the size of the money supply. It ignores the dollars held abroad even though they inevitably come zipping back when better opportunities are thought to exist in the United States.

Gold. Gold is *not* money because it is not widely accepted in payment. Even so, for many years it has been an article of faith among certain members of the public, and most gold dealers and gold miners, that dollars should be "backed" by a commodity such as gold. In essence, the "gold bugs" want the federal government and Federal Reserve to hold some amount of gold for each dollar that is created and require that dollars be freely exchangeable for gold at some fixed price.

The advocates of "gold backing" claim it would "give the dollar real value," and some even claim that it would prevent inflation, though they have never quite been able to explain how or why the existence of gold would prevent an economy's prices from rising. What "backing" the dollar with gold would do, of course, would be to force the government or the Federal Reserve to buy gold and thus tend to push up the price of gold and encourage more gold mining.

Some wags have suggested that an even better commodity to "back" the dollar would be exchange-traded commodities such as pork bellies and wheat since they, at least, can be both sold and eaten. But it hardly matters—in today's digital world coins and currency in the form of green paper dollars are an incredibly insignificant portion of the total money supply, far less than one percent.

Transactional deposits. Transactional deposits, also known as checking account balances, are a large component of the United States money supply. They consist of dollars that have been deposited in United States and overseas commercial banks and other deposit-receiving institutions such as credit unions and savings and loans. They are money because they can be immediately transferred digitally or by check or debit card to pay for things. Today such balances comprise the lion's share of the traditional supply of dollars even if the Federal Reserve ignores the dollars deposited in foreign checking accounts and created by foreign banks.

The amount of demand deposit dollars in the checking accounts of commercial banks and other United States and foreign financial institutions is affected by the actions of the institutions and their depositors, and by the laws and regulations governing their operations.

How these actions and regulations combine to influence the total amount of money can be examined by tracing the effect of someone's depositing $100,000 of dollars newly created by the Federal Reserve or wired in from abroad into a checking account at a commercial bank or other deposit-accepting financial institution.

Consider, for example, the impact of the Federal Reserve creating $100,000 and using it to buy a federal bond that a pension fund or bank or someone else wants to sell. The seller of the bond gets the $100,000 and inevitably deposits the money in their bank. The initial deposit means that the bank owes $100,000 more to its depositors and that it has $100,000 more in *reserves*. But the institution is not required to hold all the $100,000 so that it is available in case the depositor wants to make a withdrawal. It is only required to have enough reserves to cover some proportion of its total deposits. For example, suppose depositories are only required to hold ten percent.

If that is the reserve requirement, and it is in today's United States, $10,000 is the amount of *required reserves* that will have to be held by the bank or other financial institution receiving the $100,000 deposit. As a result of the fractional reserve requirement the institution has $90,000 in *excess reserves* available to lend to borrowers, and the depositor simultaneously has $100,000 available to spend.

The monetary reserves an institution is required to have immediately available need not all be in the form of coins and currency (vault cash). Most bank reserves are themselves deposited into a depository which acts, in effect, as bank for other banks. In the United States most large banks are members of the Federal Reserve and use the Federal Reserve as their bank.

In essence, each large American bank has an account at the Federal Reserve where it tends to deposit most of its reserves instead of holding them in its vaults. Other commercial banks such as state chartered banks may deposit such reserves at the Federal Reserve regional banks or at Federal Reserve member banks if they do not want to keep them at the Federal Reserve or in their vaults in the form of coins and currency.

Savings and Loan associations, credit unions, and non-member commercial banks, primarily mutual banks and state-chartered banks, are also subject to the Federal Reserve's reserve requirements; they too are required either to hold their reserves in the form of coins and currency (vault cash) or deposit them at the Federal Reserve or in a Federal Reserve member bank. Significantly, however, the Federal Reserve has no control over increases and decreases in foreign dollar holdings; or the reserve requirements and creation of dollars by foreign financial institutions; or the size of credit card lines; or the existence and size of money market funds and their reserves, if any, to cover possible depositor withdrawals; or the existence and size of consumer and business lines of credit, etc.

Commercial banks and other depositories are inevitably for-profit businesses or, in the case of credit unions, act like one in order to earn incomes for their members. They typically try to stay *loaned up* in order to earn as much income as possible. Accordingly, the bank receiving the $100,000 initial deposit will try to lend the $90,000 in excess reserves in order to earn the interest its borrowers will pay. The lending of these excess reserves has the effect of turning the original $100,000 into $190,000: the borrower will now have $90,000 to spend and the original depositor will have $100,000 in his account which he too can spend.

But it does not stop there. The borrower or whoever ends up with the $90,000 is also likely to deposit it in a financial institution until he wants to spend it. When this occurs, the bank or other depository receiving the $90,000 would have to hold $9,000 to conform to the ten percent reserve requirement. It would loan out the remaining $81,000 to another borrower. So now the total money supply is even higher at $271,000 ($100,000 available for the first depositor to spend, $90,000 available for the second borrower to spend, and $81,000 for the third).

The cycle of expanding deposits and the resulting expansion of the supply of money will continue until the total amount of loans and deposits reaches some multiple of the original deposit. Specifically, it will keep expanding until the entire amount of the original deposit of

$100,000 is all held as required reserves somewhere in the world. In this case, with the reserve requirement being ten percent (as it actually is in the United States today), the initial $100,000 increase in the money supply will tend to keep increasing until the total demand deposits increases tenfold to reach $1,000,000. This will occur even if some or all of the depositors and institutions are located abroad.

The example is quite simple. But that's exactly how the Federal Reserve *usually* acts to increase the money supply when it determines the economy needs more money. Thus, for example, the Federal Reserve might create ten billion new dollars with a stroke of a pen and use the new dollars to buy ten billion dollars of federal debt from the Treasury or in the bond market. Then, without lifting a finger or bearing any costs, the Federal Reserve will have the bonds and whoever sold it the bonds will have the money.

What is virtually certain is that the bond sellers will deposit the money they receive into a United States or foreign bank or some other financial institution such as a money market fund. Then, if the reserve requirement is ten percent, the initial $10 billion of newly created money becomes part of the monetary base and will grow to as much as $100 billion as the deposit to loan to deposit cycle proceeds.

In essence, the result of the Federal Reserve creating an additional $10 billion with the stroke of a pen is an increase in the total money supply of $100 billion. *It also results in the Federal Reserve accumulating another $10 billion of unearned assets.*

The result is the same whether Federal Reserve funds the federal government which then spends the money so that the recipient of the money deposits it in a bank or the Federal Reserve buys existing bonds or other assets in the open market so that the recipient deposits the money in a bank or elsewhere—however the newly created money is routed into the economy, it is inevitably deposited somewhere and the money supply is increased.

In the real world during the past century of the Federal Reserve's existence, the United States and other economies have needed ever increasing amounts of dollars to facilitate the operation of their ever growing economies. They are used for both transactions and as reserves by banks and nations. As a result, during the hundred years or so of its existence the Federal Reserve has accumulated trillions of dollars of unearned federal bonds as a by-product of using bond purchases to expand the supply of dollars. T

In essence, the amount of such "national debt" the Federal Reserve holds at any point in time is a measure of the amount of the dollar reserves supporting the total amount of dollars and dollar denominated financial assets in the United States and abroad.

Such a money supply expansion when new money is created by the Federal Reserve only occurs if the depositories receiving the new money loan it out; and the maximum increase occurs only if every depository is "loaned up." That's usually the case—*except* when there is a recession or depression that is so severe that the banks and other depositories won't make loans to consumers or anyone else at any interest rate because they are afraid they won't be repaid or because they are constrained from doing so by regulators who want them to hold more reserves. (Such a trapping of liquidity during a recession is an important reality and analysts would be well-advised to keep it in mind.)

The amount of available credit card credit. Today in the United States credit cards are used much more than coins and currency to make purchases. They are instantly accepted by most merchants and, from the point of viewer of the card user, being able to pay with a card is the same as carrying a wad of currency in one's wallet or purse. What affects the spender is the same—how much coins and currency is in his pocket and how much spending power is available via his debit and credit cards. They are all money because they all can be immediately used to buy things.

It is more than a bit surprising that the Federal Reserve counts the instantly spendable currency in people's wallets and purses as part of the money supply but does *not* count the instantly spendable credit on credit cards, bank credit lines, Paypal and Square accounts, and overseas dollar accounts. In other words, the Federal Reserve's data, and the policies, analyses and the "scientific" scholarly articles based on its data, became obsolete long years ago with the arrival of widely accepted credit cards and the various other parts of the United States' money supply whose descriptions immediately follow.

The amount of electronic money. The rise of digital and electronic commerce has resulted in money creating companies such as Paypal and Square. They credit a seller's account if something is sold and charge a customer's account if something is bought.

Paypal is a good example. When something is sold on eBay or by any of the many other merchants accepting Paypal payments, Paypal takes the money into its own bank account. It then effectively creates new dollars by increasing the seller's Paypal account balance. As a result, Paypal has dollars it can spend and the seller also has the same amount of dollars that the seller can spend.

Paypal balances are money because, like credit cards, they tend to be immediately accepted in payment by both on-line and conventional sellers. Paypal even issues credit cards and debit cards linked to Paypal accounts. A retail store, for example, accepting a Paypal credit or debit card or cell phone swipe neither knows nor cares that the payment comes from someone's Paypal account; if the store has an account with Paypal the payment is deposited into the store's Paypal account. If it does not have a Paypal account the store gets cash from Paypal (from the initial $100 it has been holding) deposited in its bank account just as it would from processing any other credit card.

For example, consider what happens if if you sell golf balls for $100 on eBay and agree to take payment via Paypal (eBay requires Paypal be used by eBay sellers). Buyer Sam Smith uses his bank credit or debit card and pays $100 to buy them. Paypal accepts the money and increases your Paypal account balance by $100. Now Paypal has $100 in its bank account that it can spend and you have $100 in your Paypal account that you can either spend to buy things from another Paypal seller or have Paypal deposit into your bank account. The money supply has increased.

When you spend your Paypal balance it goes down and the Paypal balance of the person or company you are buying from goes up. Meanwhile Paypal still has the initial $100. In essence, the $100 initially paid to buy your golf balls has just turned into $200 of immediately spendable money; the size of the United States' money supply has grown and the Federal Reserve had nothing to do with it.

There are two types of electronic commerce. A *hard electronic currency* is one that does not provide services to dispute or reverse charges. In other words, it only supports non-reversible transactions, even in the case of unauthorized use, legitimate error, or the failure of the seller to supply what was purchased. In essence, it's just like handing someone cash. The advantage of hard electronic currency systems is that their operating costs are greatly reduced by not having to resolve payment disputes. It also makes the funds immediately available to the recipient as soon as the transaction is made.

A *soft electronic currency* is one that allows for reversal of payments in the case of fraud or disputes. Such reversible payment methods generally have a "clearing time" to enable reversals if there is a product or payment dispute. Paypal and credit cards are examples of a soft electronic currency.

Soft electronic currencies are assumed to be safer for customers and sellers because their transactions are reversible. But that is not necessarily so. Certain credit card processors have been periodically accused of falsifying claims of fraud to justify withholding funds from businesses in order to pump up the cash reserves of their too-big-to-fail owners. This is particularly alleged to have happened at times of turmoil in the financial markets when their universal bank owners were desperately searching for liquidity to cover the effects of their trading losses. The banks needed the money because they faced closure or regulatory actions due to their lack of reserves and capital and their inability to pay their debts as they came due. The money supply is reduced when such an taking of depositors' money occurs.

Similarly, eBay and Paypal have been similarly accused of holding monies to pump up their monthly and quarterly liquidity and sales reports in order to impress potential financial investors in order to prop up the prices of the eBay's share and bonds. This routinely occurs when a Paypal payment is made, products shipped, and then Paypal holds the money for many weeks even though the buyer acknowledges receipt and even writes a favorable review of the transaction. This too reduces the money supply—and again without Federal Reserve's knowledge and participation.

The amount available on business and personal credit lines. People and businesses are not only limited to writing checks and making electronic transfers when they have money on deposit in transactions accounts. They may have overdraft protection or business and personal lines of credit. Such an arrangement automatically honors their check or transfer or debit card transaction. Often the lines are secured by second mortgages on real estate. Whatever the collateral, the result is immediately spendable via check, debit card or digital transfer. So such lines are just another form of money created by financial institutions over and above those that which the Federal Reserve creates and reports in the money supply data used by analysts. When such credit lines are created the size of the money supply changes without the Federal Reserve having anything to do with it.

The amount of dollars foreigners move in and out of the economy. The Federal Reserve's money supply data and money supply policies are based on information reported by United States banks and other financial institutions. That is the way it has always been done. But in the years since the Federal Reserve was established just prior to the First World War the United States dollar has grown in importance. Today the dollar is widely used and deposited in other countries as well as in the United States. Foreigners, for example, may have dollar bank accounts and dollar credit lines in foreign banks. And they can use those foreign dollar deposits and debit and credit cards to make payments in dollars to buy things in the United States and elsewhere.

Recent United States trade deficits have merely accelerated the overseas supply of dollars so that today many hundreds of billions of dollars are held abroad. Some are held by governments and banks as reserves but often they are held overseas in the hands of universal banks such as Citibank, Chase, and Credit Suisse, those that make loans to both foreign and United States consumers and employers in addition to accepting deposits and trading in derivatives and currencies.

Those dollars do not appear in the Federal Reserve's data but they certainly exist and are available to return to the United States. And they will certainly do so if opportunities in the United States suddenly appear to better than those abroad.

What is important for analysts to realize is that it is possible for the Federal Reserve and journalists to look at the quantity of money the Federal Reserve reports to be in the United States' economy and think that the money supply is expanding and that this will encourage spending—when, in fact, imports and overseas financial investments are sending more dollars abroad than are coming from abroad and the money supply is contracting.

Money market funds, shadow banks, and leveraging. Money market and various other investment funds act like banks in that they accept interest earning deposits, hold a small amount of cash reserves in case of withdrawals, and make loans with the rest. They create additional new money in the process just as if they were commercial banks. Indeed, they are so similar to banks they are commonly referred to as "*shadow banks.*"

The main difference between shadow banks and regular commercial banks is that the shadow banks have no reserve requirements, no deposit insurance, and no regulatory oversight. So they can take more risks to earn higher interest rates on their loans and are able to pay a slightly higher rate of interest for their deposits.

Some commercial banks are *universal banks* in that they both operate their own money market funds (and also act as investment banks trading in derivatives and currencies) in addition to accepting conventional deposits and making conventional loans. Indeed, some of them routinely encourage depositors to put their deposits into the bank's money market funds instead of into the bank's checking and other deposit accounts. The universal banks can then, instead of making conventional loans to consumers and employers, speculate and trade with the money and make the more risky higher-interest loans that their bank regulators might not approve—loans to money market funds and derivative traders, for example.

Consider a hundred dollar deposit into a *shadow bank* such as a money market fund: The one hundred dollars goes into the shadow bank. It loans all one hundred out to a borrower such as a currency trader who gives a note or other IOU in exchange for the money, and deposits the borrowed money in the bank. The money market fund then uses the IOU as collateral to borrow another one hundred dollars. This new one hundred can then be loaned out for another one hundred dollar IOU.

The process is repeated and repeated over and over again so that, in effect, the shadow bank is *leveraging* the initial deposit into more and more and more loans and creating more and more and more dollars and credit in the process. It works very well and generates higher profits than a regulated commercial bank could earn making loans with the money it has left over after meeting its reserve requirements—until loan defaults or depositor withdrawals unexpectedly occur in such larger-than-anticipated amounts that the shadow bank, with zero or limited reserves, has assets that can be sold for less than it owes its depositors. It is bankrupt and its depositors, if and when they are paid, inevitably only recover part of their deposits.

That is exactly what happened in the United States during the Great Recession. Americans who were encouraged by their bankers to make deposits in uninsured bank-owned money market funds to earn higher rates of interest lost many millions of dollars when the funds failed; and the money supply of the United States declined by trillions of dollars as their leveraging unraveled.

The Federal Reserve data, however, showed that the monetary base had not declined. As a result, the members of the Federal Reserve's Open Market Committee apparently did not realize that the money supply of the United States had collapsed—they looked at the modest increases they continued to provide to the monetary base and thought the money supply was growing. That was years ago and, if their continuing lack of response to the resulting shortage of money and credit is any indication, they still do not understand what happened.

THE SUPPLY OF DOLLARS IS NOT TOTALLY CONTROLLED BY THE FEDERAL RESERVE

In the United States business and personal credit lines are an important part of the money supply. They are comparable to the available balances on credit cards. Indeed the personal lines are often drawn down and spent via the use of credit and debit cards. The withdrawal and reduction of business working capital lines that accompanied the "Great Recession," for example, not only caused numerous businesses to reduce their production and employment, and many to go bankrupt, it also caused a dramatic reduction in the supply of money.

Another great reduction in the money supply occurred simultaneously as dollars poured overseas in response to trade deficits.

Another great reduction in the money supply occurred when banks and other institutions reduced and cancelled hundreds of billions of unused personal credit lines based on real estate.

Another great reduction in the money supply occurred simultaneously as commercial banks refused to renew credit cards and reduced credit card lines.

Another great reduction occurred as both the universal and commercial banks held their reserves rather than loan them out. One reason this occurred is because they and their regulators were concerned about their borrowers' ability to repay. Another reason it occurred is because the Federal Reserve and other regulators required them to improve the quality of their assets by holding more federal bonds. Another reason it occurred is because the Federal Reserve encouraged them to hold excess reserves by paying interest on reserves deposited at the Federal Reserve that in some cases exceeded what the banks could earn with conventional loans.

All of these reductions occurred during the Great Recession when the Federal Reserve's governors and journalists were looking at MB, M1, and M2 and reporting that the Federal Reserve's "quantitative easings" were increasing the quantity of dollars in the United States' money supply. What they did not report, because the data did not include the entire money supply, was that the expansionary effects of the Federal Reserves quantitative easings (QE1, QE2, and QE3) were overwhelmed by reductions everywhere else.

Worse, as analysts shall see, when the recession did not end and certain irrelevant interest rates reached all time lows the governors and journalists, and even some Keynesian economists, mistakenly concluded that the Federal Reserve and its monetary policies had done all they could do and that something outside the monetary realm would have to be done to get the economy going again.

In other words, the Federal Reserve governors and regional presidents mistakenly thought they had expanded the economy's money supply to encourage more spending and driven down interest rates as low as they could go. In fact, the money supply was contracting such that money and credit was not available to consumers and employers at any rate of interest. In essence, they had expanded only part of the money supply and by far less than its other parts declined. No wonder consumer and other spending and the United States' economy did not recover.

FINANCIAL INTERMEDIATION AND INTERMEDIARIES

Not all the dollars people, employers, and businesses receive is deposited in American banks and not all dollar borrowers turn to American banks when they need dollars and credit. There are, in the real world, many different forms of financial intermediaries which stand between those who have dollars and those who want to borrow them.

They include foreign and domestic credit unions and savings and loans, mortgage companies, credit card companies, hedge and buyout funds, money managers, Paypal and Square, investment bankers, and financial brokers, governmental lending agencies, quasi-governmental agencies such as Fannie Mae and Freddie Mac, investment banks, pension funds, universal banks, and money market funds are all examples of non-bank intermediaries.

Also accepting dollar deposits and making dollar loans are foreign central banks and foreign commercial banks and other financial intermediaries; they have been increasing acquiring, creating, and using United States dollars and dollar deposits instead of their own currencies.

Financial intermediaries exist wherever an economy has (1) people, employers and governments with money "deficits" in the sense they desire to spend more money than they have; and, (2) people, employers, and governments with money "surpluses" in the sense that they have more money than they want to immediately spend. The intermediaries, often multiple intermediaries working together via financial markets, bring them together and this, it has been alleged, allows more spending to occur than would otherwise occur.

Commercial banks and shadow banks are "financial intermediaries" because they accept money and, in exchange, issue intermediate financial assets in the form of checking account and other deposit balances that their owners can instantly withdraw and use to make payments. The banks then use whatever portion of the deposits they are not required to hold as reserves to make loans to borrowers in exchange for assets such as the notes, mortgages, and other securities that the primary borrower might issue in exchange for the money. The banks might then sell the mortgages or notes on to an investment banks which in turn might sell them to a pension fund or foreign bank.

Intermediaries, both commercial banks and the others, are alike in that they each create their own "intermediate financial assets" and offer them to whoever has money in exchange for the money, and then use to money, sometimes via other intermediaries, to acquire more *primary financial assets* such as mortgages and notes from the initial borrowers that they can package and sell. Together the intermediaries comprise the financial markets of the United States and the world.

In other words, financial intermediaries exist because they facilitate the loaning and borrowing that occurs in an economy, and thus the higher level of spending this allows with a given supply of money, by standing between the ultimate borrowers with the money deficits and the ultimate lenders with their money surpluses. For their efforts the intermediaries earn an interest differential. For a simple example, they may charge borrowers ten percent and pay their lenders and depositors six percent—and so end up with four percent for themselves.

The intermediaries get the differential because they provide the necessary administrative services and reduce the risk of the lenders and any subsequent assignees not being repaid. In effect, they add their knowledge and expertise, and sometimes even their guarantees of repayment, to the primary assets (e.g. the mortgages they buy) which spenders use as collateral to obtain the money they borrow. The size of the differential depends on degrees of risk and the administrative costs associated with the financial instrument.

Of course, things are very much more complex in the real world where there are numerous financial instruments ranging from bank deposits to mortgages to stocks and bonds and derivatives, resale agreements, and repayment insurance. At times, they all play a role in someone ultimately getting money to buy a house or finance a business. And with so many different types of institutions and trillions of dollars involved, minor differences of just a few *basis points* may cause trillions of dollars to flood into one type of security or another or into one country or another.

The complexity also enables astute financial institutions to creatively mobilize monies and use it to make loans and financial investments via the use of extreme *leveraging* (buying financial assets with little or no money by using the assets they buy as collateral). This can yield big profits for traders and speculators such as Citibank, Chase, and Goldman Sachs.

On the other hand, the leveraging can also result in big losses if relatively minor price adjustments wipe out the traders' equity and cause their collateral to be dumped on the market and drive down prices. Then their assets cannot be sold for enough to repay their depositors and lenders. The financial damage to the lenders, in turn, can cause major losses for others who were not involved and did not even know they are at risk—such as the uninvolved home owner whose mortgage cannot be refinanced when it becomes due because their lender has failed and their home is "under water" in the sense it cannot be sold for enough to payoff what is owed against it.

Long-time investment banks such as Baring Brothers, Bear Stearns, and Lehman Brothers were wiped out by such losses. So too were go-go hedge funds such a MF Global. Their failures triggered major economic declines as they rippled through the world's financial markets and caused breaks in the web of financial relationships that get money from where there is a surplus and move it to where there is a deficit. And the ripples and profits and failures can come fast in a digital world where, for example, as many as three million shares trade electronically *ever second*.

Such activities are not tracked as part of the narrow data the Federal Reserve collects. As a result, they are not considered by the Federal Reserve's staff and advisors when they use the data generated by the Federal Reserve to "scientifically" analyze the economy. Little wonder the Federal Reserve was blindsided in 2008 by the arrival of the Great Recession triggered by the Lehman Brothers collapse and the failure of mortgage derivatives despite their being "rated" as equal to federal bonds in safety.

The collapse began with Lehman's huge losses on its highly leveraged gambles on mortgage derivatives. The reduction in the market value of its derivative-related assets meant that they could not be sold or borrowed against for enough to pay its debts. Lehman's inability to pay its banks and other lenders quickly rippled through the economy as its inability to cover its trading losses and pay its debts caused losses at other financial institutions including many commercial banks.

The commercial bank losses were particularly devastating to the real economy of jobs and production as they forced the commercial banks to cut back on their lending to consumers and businesses. This, in turn, resulted in production and employment receding throughout the entire United States and the rest of the world.

Reality check. Analysts will recall that the "investment banks" such as Lehman Brothers, MF Global, Goldman Sachs, and Morgan Stanley are not to be confused with the commercial banks that accept deposits and make loans to consumers and businesses or with the "universal banks" such as Citibank and JPMorgan Chase which the Federal Reserve and other regulators allow to simultaneously act as both commercial banks and investment banks.

The health of an economy's commercial banks is important to the general prosperity of the economy; the health of its investment banks acting as it traders, speculators and merger and acquisition advisors is not important—except that their gambling failures in the world's electronic "financial casinos" can cascade to their lenders and counterparties that include commercial banks.

Some large too-big-to-fail commercial banks such as Citibank, JPMorgan Chase, and Bank of America are universal banks because they also function as investment banks and traders. The Federal Reserve and their other regulators have, until recently, increasingly let them use significant amounts of their capital and deposits to trade and speculate on their own account and to make loans to other traders and speculators—instead of loaning it out to consumers and businesses in the communities they are licensed to serve.

The outcome of the efforts since 2008 to limit the ability of the universal banks to use their deposits and capital to finance speculation and trading, instead of making conventional loans, is still uncertain.

Intermediaries and financial assets.

The trend in the United States and most countries has been for a relatively constant percentage of total consumer and employer spending to be financed with primary debt instruments such as notes and mortgages. But the percentage of total financing provided by commercial banks and other transaction depositories such as universal banks and savings and loans, whose reserve requirements are also regulated by the Federal Reserve, has been declining for years. They have, in essence, been increasingly replaced by non-depository intermediaries acting as shadow banks: insurance companies, money managers, stock brokerages, money market funds, and pension funds—the financial intermediaries and traders whose reserves the Federal Reserve does not regulate. This is significant because the less regulated and unregulated non-depositories tend to have lower, or non-existent, reserve and capital requirements.

Consider another version of the earlier example wherein an initial $100 deposit resulting in an increase in the money supply of $1000 because the reserve requirement was ten percent. Now consider the fact that non-depositories are increasingly able to create financial assets, such as a credit in a brokerage account or an insurance policy, that are more appealing to the owner of the initial $100 than a bank deposit. Everything now changes.

If the money had been sent to an insurance company for a policy instead of to a bank for a deposit, the insurance company would have the initial $100 dollars instead of the bank. The insurance company might, for example, only hold $5 dollars in reserve to meet its immediate cash needs to pay out benefits as its policies mature. That means it can loan out or invest the other $95 dollars. If the $95 dollars goes to a financial speculator who puts it into a brokerage account which also holds a five percent reserve, then $90.25 dollars would be available for the brokerage firm to lend out. In the end, if the loanable portions of the initial $100 dollars keep tracking through intermediaries that hold five percent reserves, then the initial $100 dollars would generate $2000 dollars of highly liquid assets. And every one of the $2000 dollars could be part of the money supply if their owner could instantly transfer it to someone else by digital order.

Since the trend in the United States has been to move away from the regulated relatively high reserve requirement commercial banks and other depositories located in the United States to shadow banks and other non-regulated intermediaries with lower reserve requirements, both in the United States and worldwide, there has been a constant increase in the amount of money and liquid assets available to buy goods and services. This has been enhanced by the ever increasing supply of dollars going abroad and being created abroad as a result of dollar deposits in foreign banks.

The trend to the non-depositories and foreigners also works in the other direction. If the web of financial transactions between the unregulated intermediaries and their lenders suddenly breaks down, it raises questions as to who among them is safe to deal with. When this happens, as it did with the failure of Lehman Brothers, there may be a "flight" of liquidity to the relatively safety of the regulated and insured banks and other depositories. Then the $2000 of our example would collapse towards $1000. *In other words, there could be a massive reduction in the supply of money and liquidity in the United States without the Federal Reserve lifting a finger.*

And then the reduced supply of money might not be loaned out, no matter what interest rates and Federal Funds rates the banks might be able to command, because of "stress tests" and the banks not knowing who could be trusted to survive the resulting recession and ensuing depression.

That's exactly what happened before and during the Great Recession that began in 2008 and the depression that followed. And, as might be expected when analysts only look at a narrowing slice of an increasingly broad spectrum, the Federal Reserve and its staff and consultants missed it; their simple models using the too-narrow data and irrelevant short-term interest rates, suggested the commercial banks were doing okay in terms of deposits and reserves and thus, to the Federal Reserve governors and regional presidents, that the total amount of money and liquidity in the economy had not collapsed. *So they underestimated the magnitude of the problems facing consumers and employers and the size and appropriate injection techniques of the money supply increases needed to eliminate it.*

THE FEDERAL RESERVE AND THE
SUPPLY OF MONEY AND CREDIT

The key to how much an economy's supply of money and credit can expand or contract as a result of the activities of the financial intermediaries is the percentage of each deposit in a commercial bank or other intermediary that must be held as reserves and the preferences of the economy's participants for the various financial assets that can be created for them.

More specifically, the smaller the proportion of the value of the financial assets that must be held in reserve by their issuers, the larger the amount of money they have to loan out or use to buy other financial assets. In other words, since excess money tends to be put to work earning income, the lower the reserve percentages the greater the supply of money and liquid assets that can be created.

Various state and national regulatory bodies determine the reserve requirements of certain types of financial intermediaries in the United States. State insurance commissions, for example, may determine how much reserves companies selling insurance in their state must hold. The most important regulator, however, is *usually* the Federal Reserve System. It sets the reserve, capital, and loan requirements of the commercial banks, savings and loans, and all other check issuing depositories located in the United States—unless some other regulator sets them higher.

The Federal Reserve does not, however, set the reserve, capital, and asset requirements of financial intermediaries such as money market funds, hedge funds, Paypal and Square, and "investment bankers" even though they are doing business in dollars and, in some cases, creating dollars. It similarly does not set the reserve, capital, and asset requirements of foreign commercial banks and other foreign intermediaries even though they create and destroy dollars if they accept dollar deposits and make dollar loans.

THE ROLE OF THE
FEDERAL RESERVE

Even though it is technically owned by the commercial banks that participate in its programs, the Federal Reserve is much more than a servant of the commercial banks which provides the banks with a safe place to hold their reserves. Its primary function is to be the nation's central bank and, as such, provide whatever its governors and regional presidents consider to be the most desirable supply of money needed to achieve its mandate to keep the United States labor force fully employed.

What this means, since there are other intermediaries and reserve-setting regulators outside its control both in the United States and abroad, is that the Federal Reserve's governors must be aware of, and ready to act, to offset the effect of any undesirable changes caused by the activities of other regulatory bodies and unregulated intermediaries.

Unfortunately The Federal Reserve has all too often ignored them. Thus, for example, the Federal Deposit Insurance Corporation (FDIC) has periodically usurped the reserve-setting and capital-setting roles of the Federal Reserve by pressing banks to increase their reserves and capital so that the FDIC will not have to put up so much money if it closes the banks. This has reduced the money supply and, thus, supply of loanable funds available to the economy's consumers and businesses—*all, it seems, without the Federal Reserve's untrained and inexperienced governors and regional presidents realizing what was happening.*

The Federal Reserve has a number of tools at its disposal to accomplish its basic goal of seeing that the United States has enough money in circulation to generate full employment: reserve requirement changes, open market activities, rediscount rate changes, federal funds rate changes, and special lending facilities. It typically engages in these actions to *indirectly* affect total spending by changing the amount of money the economy's financial institutions have available to lend to consumers and employers.

The Federal Reserve also can undertake, but has rarely used until recently, other actions such as the direct injection of money into the financial system via flowing it *directly* to needy beneficiaries such as Goldman Sachs and Deutsche Bank in hopes that such gifts to maintain their prosperity and bonuses will "trickle down" to main street America.

What the governors did not do, *and probably should have done* given the magnitude of the recession, was directly flow the many hundreds of billions of newly created dollars to high propensity to consume consumers such as Social Security recipients so that it would "trickle up" to the Federal Reserve's favorites.

Reserve requirement changes.

A change in the percentage of deposits that an economy's transaction depositories hold in the form of immediately available reserves affects the economy's money supply by affecting the amount of excess reserves that its banks and other depositories have available to lend.

For analytical purposes, consider a situation where the United States economy's commercial banks and other depositories have $50 trillion in deposits, $5 trillion in reserves in their vaults and on deposit at the Federal Reserve or its member banks, and a reserve requirement of ten percent. Under these conditions, all the immediately available bank reserves are *required reserves*, and the banks and other depositories have no *excess reserves* that can be loaned out to increase the supply of money. The depositories are fully *loaned up*.

But what if the Federal Reserve lowers the reserve requirement to eight percent? The depositories will then be required to possess only $4 trillion in immediately available reserves. Then, the depositories will have $1 trillion in excess reserves they can loan out. Being dedicated profit seekers as most bankers are, the commercial banks and other depositories will then, under normal circumstances, immediately seek borrowers for their available money even if they have to lower the interest rates they charge. The money supply will then begin increasing as the $1 trillion is deposited and re-deposited until the economy's money supply reaches the new and higher level that can be supported by

$5 trillion in reserves and an eight percent reserve requirement—$62.5 trillion.

An increase in reserve requirements tends to have an opposite effect. Consider what would happen if the reserve requirement was increased to twelve percent. The depositories would now not have enough reserves to meet the Federal Reserve's new requirement. They could no longer make loans. So when their existing loans are repaid the money will be held instead of being loaned out again. This would continue until the money supply contracts to the level that $5 trillion of reserves can support when the reserve requirement is twelve percent—$41.667 trillion.

Open market operations.

The Federal Reserve's purchase and sales of government bonds, and sometimes other assets, in the financial markets are known as its "open market operations." The Federal Reserve's buying and selling of federal bonds goes on continuously every minute of the banking day. It is the most common tool the Federal Reserve uses to control the United States' money supply. It works by indirectly working through the financial community to change the amount of dollar reserves and excess reserves in the hands of the depositories.

To increase the money supply and encourage customer spending, the Federal Reserve creates new money and uses it to buy bonds in the bond market from whoever is willing to sell them. If banks and other depositories sell the bonds they give up the bonds to the Federal Reserve and get the money; so the Federal Reserve owns more of the national debt and the depositories have more reserves—and it is all loanable excess reserves.

The same thing occurs if someone else sells the bond to the Federal Reserve. The sellers give up the bonds so the Federal Reserve now owns more of the national debt and the sellers get the money—which the sellers inevitably deposit in their banks or other depositories both in the United States and abroad. Again the depositories now have both more deposits and more reserves of which most are excess and loanable.

In essence, when the Federal Reserve creates new money and uses it to buy bonds the depositories get more reserves and the money expansion process continues until all the newly created money is held as reserves and there is a new and larger supply of dollars in the United States economy and the world.

The process works in reverse when the Federal Reserve wants to reduce the money supply and discourage customer spending. It sells bonds in the bond market, thus giving up the bonds and accepting money in payment. When the money is received it comes out of the money supply and the reserves of the bank on which the payment is drawn are reduced. The U.S. and world supply of dollars then begins dropping to the new and lower level that can be supported by the new and lower level of reserves.

The Federal Reserve's buying and selling to affect the United States' and world money supply is directed by its Open Market Committee (FOMC) and is conducted by the its Open Market Desk located at the New York Federal Reserve Bank. The Open Market Desk operates every minute of the New York banking day by buying and selling federal bonds in the open market via twenty or so "primary dealers" who act as the FOMC's trading counterparties. Each of the primary dealers then buys and sells the bonds on its own account in the financial markets around the world.

The FOMC committee is composed of the Federal Reserve's seven presidentially appointed governors plus five of its regional bank presidents of whom one must be the president of the Federal Reserve's New York regional bank. The other four rotate from among the other eleven Federal Reserve regional banks.

There are no educational or business or commercial banking experience requirements for appointment. Typically the governors come from the academic world or are career government employees who have served in the Federal Reserve and Treasury bureaucracies and whose candidacies are supported by the leaders of a handful of major New York investment banks. Similarly, the regional presidents typically come from the regional bank bureaucracies. Rarely, if ever, have any of the governors or presidents been trained macroeconomists with real world experience in business or commercial banking.

Traditionally the committee's decisions are dominated by its presidentially appointed chairman. It is the Chairman who determines the monetary policies of the United States and, thus, the degree to which the United States will be prosperous *or not*. Accordingly, because the United States economy and the dollar are so important both domestically and internationally, many pragmatic analysts consider the Chairman to be the most powerful and important person in the United States—more powerful than the President and Congress combined because what he or she does is much more important to the prosperity and international standing of the United States.

Reality. Pragmatic analysts understand that the newly created money the Federal Reserve flows into the economy is particularly important because each new dollar the Federal Reserve injects into the economy becomes part of the economy's "monetary base." Each such newly created dollar then, depending on the reserve requirements of those who receive it, results in an expansion of the total money supply. Thus, conceptually, a Federal Reserve creation of $1 billion additional dollars and its injection into the economy via an open market purchase can result in a $10 billion increase in the money supply— if the reserve requirement is ten percent as it is today in the United States.

Such an injection of newly created money would, of course, have no effect at all if the banks for some reason were simultaneously required to hold $1 billion more as reserves. And it would be associated with a decline in the money supply if the banks were for some reason, such as the action of another regulatory agency, simultaneously required to hold even more money as reserves. *The possibility that a depository will hold money instead of loaning it out, or that it might loan it out for purposes other than to finance consumer and employer spending, is an important concept for analysts to keep in mind when considering the causes and potential cures of a "Great Recession."*

The Federal Reserve discount rate.

It is a common misconception of journalists and non-economists that commercial banks and other depositories hold reserves in case they must cover unexpectedly large withdrawals. That is not the case: the basic reason the Federal Reserve requires the banks and other depositories under its jurisdiction to hold reserves is so the Federal Reserve can control the size of the money supply, not so the depositories can cover unexpected depositor withdrawals. Instead, the Federal Reserve stands ready, at least on paper, to help depositories cover unexpectedly large depositor withdrawals in another way—by giving them access to instant and virtually unlimited borrowing from the Federal Reserve via the "discount" process *if they are seriously in trouble*.

In other words, unlike the banks in Keynes' Britain, commercial banks in the United States are not allowed to borrow from the Federal Reserve for the purpose of making loans.

Discounting. "Discounting" is a process which supposedly enables banks and other depositories to obtain monies they can use to cover unexpected withdrawals and other financial needs. Basically it allows qualified depositories to put up their assets such as the notes and mortgages resulting from its loans as collateral to borrow money from the Federal Reserve. The banks can then use the borrowed money to cover their reserve requirements and depositor withdrawals.

The rate of interest the depository borrowers pay for such emergency needs money is known as the *discount rate* and is set by the Federal Reserve. It is often confused by "business economists," and journalists with the *Federal Funds target rate* which is the rate the Federal Reserve would like to see banks charge one another to borrow reserves for twenty four hours.

The terms "discounting" and "discount rate" arise from the way banks and other lenders typically lend and borrow; because they typically compute their interest charges on loans on a discount basis to increase their revenues. Thus a borrower who borrows $100 from a bank for one year at four percent interest rate tends to receive $96. Of course, the borrower is paying more than four percent—because he is actually selling or discounting his note to the bank; paying $4 to borrow $96. In any event, to get money the bank would then take the $100 note to the Federal Reserve and discount it for to get money from the Federal Reserve just as the borrower got money from the bank. Thus, if the rediscount rate is three percent, it would get $97 for it; $95 is the Federal Reserve's discount rate is five percent; $92 if the Federal Reserve's rate eight percent, and so on.

It's all very interesting and much discussed, *but in the real world none of this ever happens*. The discount rate is totally meaningless—because along the way it came to be understood in the financial community and among depositors that a commercial bank only went to the Federal Reserve to rediscount its loans and assets when it had absolutely no other options and was about to fail.

In other words, the Federal Reserve's discount rate is virtually irrelevant since a commercial bank or other depository would *never* voluntarily engage in such borrowing. It would never do because it would be a signal to its customers and regulators that the bank is in such serious trouble due to a lack of reserves that that it is more likely to be closed than have loanable funds for its customers to borrow. In essence, it would be a signal to the FDIC and the Treasury's Comptroller of the Currency that the bank should be closed.

Today it appears the primary function of discount rate changes is for the Federal Reserve to periodically announce them so the public will think the Federal Reserve is "doing something" about the economy and be encouraged about the future. Cynical pragmatists disagree. They think the main function of discount rate changes is to generate speaking engagements for the Federal Reserve chairman and give journalists and talk show "experts" something meaningless to talk about. Others suggest discount rate changes may be a "signal" of the governors' intentions. It's probably a little of both. *More importantly, it is totally irrelevant as a policy tool because it is never voluntarily used.*

Then why is much written by journalists and "business economists" about the discount rate? The answer appears to go back to Britain where the interest rate the Bank of England charges commercial banks to borrow money is extremely important. It is extremely important because British banks do use their loans and other assets as collateral to borrow money from the Bank of England so they can loan it to their customers. It is, accordingly, the wholesale price of the money which British consumers and businesses borrow from their banks.

It is also important because it sets the interest rate floor under the interest rates which British consumers and employers will have to pay. This occurs because, in addition to borrowing from the Bank of England at that rate, the banks can also deposit their loanable funds with the Bank of England and earn that rate.

In other words, the inadequate educations and unworldliness of journalists and Federal Reserve decision makers cause them to confuse the Bank of England rate which Keynes wrote about, and is important, with the Federal Reserve discount rate which has no purpose and does not mean anything.

Interbank borrowing and the "Federal Funds" rates.

The *Federal Funds rates* are the interest rates commercial banks, universal banks, and other depositories charge one another to borrow reserves overnight. Under normal circumstances, when there is no recession, they all walk a tightrope—trying to loan out their excess reserves in order to earn as much income as possible while still maintaining enough reserves to meet the reserve requirements set by the Federal Reserve.

Each bank and depository handles numerous transactions every day—some of them tend to expand their reserves and others to reduce them. The problem is that it is not until each depository tallies up its reserve requirements and reserve position at the end of the day that it knows for sure how its reserves stand in relation to its reserve requirements. Inevitably, no matter how hard they try, some are a bit over and some are a bit short. But no problem. Those who are over and have excess reserves can loan them overnight to those who are short.

In essence, *the Federal Funds rate is the interest rate reserve-borrowing depositories pay to borrow reserves for twenty four hours from depositories which found themselves with excess reserves at the close of each banking day.* It allows the lenders to squeeze a few more dollars of income out of their deposit bases and the borrowers to cover the Federal Reserves' reserve requirements.

The Federal Reserve does not set the Federal Funds rates charge one another. The banks negotiate the rates among themselves. What the Federal Reserve does do is set a "target rate" for the Federal Funds rates which the Open Market Desk. In essence, the "target rate" is what the Federal Reserve wants the various interest rates negotiated between the banks for the overnight borrowing of excess reserves to average out to be.

The Federal Reserve's use of the target rate. The Federal Reserve's basic theory is that banks and other depositories will negotiate higher Federal Funds rates among themselves for borrowing overnight reserves when they are short of having "enough" money to meet their customers' requirements. It tends to occur, as a result, when the banks are raising interest rates to ration the limited amount of funds they have available to loan out.

Accordingly, if one accepts this theory, when there is full employment and the actual Federal Funds rates start to pull ahead of the target rate, it means the banks customers want additional loans to engage in spending that will cause inflation from too much spending. Thus the existence of actual rates above the target rate is a signal for the Federal Reserve's Open Market Desk to sell assets in the financial markets to reduce the money supply. Then interest rates will rise to choke off the move towards additional spending.

Similarly, when the average of the Federal Fund rates moves below the target rate it means consumer and employer demand for loans of money to spend is falling and spending may need to be encouraged. The target rate being above the actual rates is, thus, a signal to the Open Market Desk to buy bonds and other assets in the financial markets in order to put more money in circulation in order to drive interest rates down in order to encourage more spending in order to obtain the level of total spending needed in order for the economy's labor force to remain full employed.

The Federal Reserve also uses the target rate both to guide its policies and announce its intentions when there is inflation or unemployment. For example, when the American economy is in a recession the Federal Reserve traditionally lowers the target rate blow the then-existing actual rates. That is the signal to the banking community and the Open Market Desk that the Federal Reserve is going to increase the supply of money because it wants the banks to charge lower interest rates and make more loans so that their consumer and employer customers will buy more goods and services.

The Federal Reserve's use of the Federal Funds target rate to guide its policies is based on a wonderful and widely accepted theory about the relationship of the Federal Funds rates to the interest rates and spending in the economy. It is an excellent theory *except for the not so minor problem that it has no basis in reality*:

First, in the real world the commercial and universal banks do not borrow money for twenty four hours in order to make loans to consumers and employers that will not be repaid for months and years—if they did such twenty four hour borrowing would be considered to be the equivalent of discount borrowing from the Federal Reserve and they would likely be closed by the FDIC.

Second, there is a very weak relationship, if it exists at all, between the rates banks and other depositories charge one another to borrow overnight reserves and their supply of loanable funds and the interest rates they can charge their customers.

Third, just because the banks get more loanable money as a result of the Open Market Desk responding to the spread between the target rates and the actual rates does not mean they will loan it to consumers and employers and, by so doing, cause an increase in spending. They may lend it all to financial traders or use it for their own trading purposes.

Fourth, in the real world the banks look upon the target rate as merely an indication of what the Federal Reserve staff thinks they *should* charge one another for twenty four hour loans.

Fifth, the entire relationship between the Federal Funds target rate and the state of the economy totally breaks down, if it ever even existed, when all the commercial banks have excess reserves due to pressures from the FDIC and the Federal Reserve's own regulators. Then the demand for overnight reserves to meet their legal reserve requirements is nil and the rate banks willingness to pay to borrow reserves approaches zero no matter what target rate the Federal Reserve establishes.

Sixth, and most important in terms of today's Great Recession, the existence of minimal Federal Funds rates for overnight loans does not mean that there is nothing more the Federal Reserve can do to restore prosperity and full employment when the United States is in a recession or depression. To the contrary, as analysts will see, it is more likely to mean that it is time for the governors to stop making excuses and begin ding whatever needs to be done to get spending increased so that the United States returns to full employment.

Using the target rate. What the Federal Funds target rate does do is act as a buying and selling instruction to the Open Market Desk and as a signal to the commercial banks and other depositories as to the Federal Reserve's intentions:

Raising the target rate sends the message that the Federal Reserve will be tightening up on the money supply and they should start rejecting and reducing loans;

Lowering the target rate sends the message is that the Federal Reserve will be loosening the money supply. That means they can expect more deposits and should start looking for even more loans to fund if they want to stay loaned up;

Leaving the target rate unchanged in relation to the actual rates sends the message that no special efforts will be made to change the money supply in either direction and the banks should keep lending as before.

In the real world, the banks and other depositories increasingly ignore the "signal" because the Federal Reserve has not always followed through with what it signals; instead, they look at their customers' loan requests and price their loans as they always have—to earn as much as possible for the bank with whatever reserves, capital, and deposits they have available to loan.

As an instruction to the Open Market Desk, the Federal Funds target rate particularly fails because a minor move of the actual rates between depositories to borrow reserves overnight above or below the target rate is neither a good surrogate for the general state of the economy nor a good indication of the direction it is moving nor how far it will go.

It also fails because relatively minor interest rate changes primarily affect the financial markets, not consumer and employer spending in the product markets.

In essence, the problem is that there is little or no connection between the Federal Funds rates and the state of the economy (or between the Federal Funds rates and the level of interest rates in the economy or between the level of interest rates and the level of total spending needed for full employment)

In any event, and particularly important during a severe recession or depression, whatever connection does exist is virtually obliterated when the banks have excess reserves such that they are not willing to pay to obtain more. In essence, market forces related to a reduced demand for reserves may cause the Federal Funds rates for overnight reserve loans to be extremely low at the very same time the Federal Reserve is setting the target rate extremely low. Then no signal exists to either the banks or the Open Market Desk.

That is exactly the case when there is a severe recession so that banks are willing to hold more reserves than they are required to hold because they are fearful of lending to anyone including other banks. And it is particularly the case if the Federal Reserve begins paying interest on bank reserves so the banks are encouraged to hold excess reserves rather than making conventional loans to consumers and employers.

And that is exactly what happened during the Great Recession. The Federal Reserve set the target rate at all-time lows approaching zero and the actual Federal Funds rates were also at all time lows because the banks did not need to borrow reserves. So the differential between them did not signal the Open Market Desk to increase the money supply—so it did not do so even though the United States economy was as much as $4 trillion short of having enough spending to achieve full employment.

Simultaneously, the low Federal Funds rates coupled with the low yields on federal bonds led the Federal Reserve governors and regional presidents to conclude that interest rates in the real economy had gone as low as they could go given the risk differentials between the borrowers in the real economy and the yield on federal bonds—and that, since they wrongly assumed based on a long-ago-rejected theory that interest rates are a primary determinant of savings and investment, meant there was nothing more that monetary policy could do to end the Great Recession.

Summarizing the basic problem. In essence, the basic problem with the FOMC using the Federal Funds rates in any manner is that they have little or no relationship to either the economic conditions in the United States or the amount of money and loanable funds needed to keep the United States prosperous.

The Federal Reserve's actions during the Great Recession are a case in point. The Federal Reserve lowered the Federal Funds target rate and the Open Market Desk dutifully added some new money to the economy and the banks and depositories dutifully renegotiated the rates they charge each other to borrow reserves for 24 hours—and the economy remained mired in a recession for years because there were not enough loans and credit available in the real economy.

There was not enough lending in the real economy because not enough money and credit was created as a result of the failure of the target rate instruction in conjunction with all the other things that caused the banks to cut back on their conventional loans—opportunities abroad, opportunities in the financial markets, Federal Reserve interest payments on reserves, capital requirement increases that encouraged banks to hold more federal bonds and short-term securities in relation to conventional assets such as mortgages and working capital lines, and the decline in the number of eligible borrowers due to business failures, unemployment and millions of bankruptcies and mortgage defaults.

The American military has a profane word to describe the situation caused by the Federal Reserve governors and regional presidents naïve reliance on the Federal Funds rates during a recession—it begins with cluster.

Things might have been different if the Federal Reserve's governors had been sufficiently trained and worldly to give the Open Market Desk a more realistic target for its buying and selling to affect the size of the monetary base—such as some combination of inflation, labor force participation, and capacity utilization; or moved decisively as the European Central Bank once did to provide long term loans in whatever amount the banks wanted for the purpose of serving their consumer, business, and other customers.

Such possibilities will be considered in the pages ahead along with the reasons why the Federal Reserve, and particularly its Chairmen, have so frequently failed to keep the United States prosperous and growing—and free of the ravages of unemployment and inflation.

Misleading the public. Despite their irrelevance to the functioning and financing of the real economy, the discount and target rates are the rates which, when increased or decreased, for example, cause journalists to write, and TV reporters and talk show hosts to breathlessly announce, that the Federal Reserve has increased or decreased interest rates; or, if the discount and target rates are maintained, to write and announce that the Federal Reserve is not going to raise or lower interest rates. As analysts shall subsequently see, nothing could be further from the truth or more misleading or a better indicator of journalistic ignorance and bad monetary policies.

Indeed, one of the most pernicious and misleading things the Federal Reserve and journalists do is write and talk about the Federal Funds target rate in a way that gives it great and positive significance. In the real world, only a seriously unworldly financial journalist or Federal Reserve governor could possibly believe that a commercial bank or other depository would respond to a reduction in the target rate by borrowing money overnight and loaning it out for consumer and business loans if the money has to be repaid the next day. It does not happen.

And a reduction similarly does not mean that the overall money supply will be increased; or that, if it is increased, there will be more loanable funds and credit available for consumers and employers; or that, if there is more money and credit available for consumers and employers that it will be enough to sufficient to end the recession.

Special facilities and other Federal Reserve responses to the Great Recession.

Because of the severity of the situation from the perspective of Citibank, Goldman Sachs and other big traders, the Federal Reserve initially took various other actions that had the secondary effect of increasing the monetary base so there would be more reserves and to encourage the universal banks, commercial banks, and other lenders to make more loans to both the financial and real sectors of the economy. Among them:

Term auction facilities wherein the Federal Reserve auctioned off short term reserves wherein investment and universal banks could get the cash they needed to honor their commitments by collateralizing their borrowings with acceptable securities;

Term securities facilities wherein the investment banking traders and universal banks could exchange their mortgage-backed derivatives for federal bonds to strengthen their balance sheets to meet the new capital requirements which were being imposed; and

Commercial paper funding facilities wherein the Federal Reserve loaned money against commercial paper to encourage the renewal of expiring business lines of credit.

Special facilities. The Federal Reserve also made direct emergency loans to influential traders such Citibank, Goldman Sachs, Morgan Stanley, and AIG, and to certain of their creditors who owed them large amounts, particularly those who owed money to Goldman Sachs whose former chairman was the Treasury Secretary and held great sway over the Federal Reserve chairman.

The European Central Bank subsequently did something somewhat similar: it periodically created, and let Europe's banks borrow, as many euros as they wanted at a low interest rates for the purpose of making loans to consumers and employers. But there was a big difference—the ECB's loans were for three to five years instead of overnight or for one or two weeks. Thus the ECB periodically poured many hundreds of billions of euros loanable for spending purposes into the European commercial banks which were experiencing a loan-killing sovereign debt collapse comparable to the loan-killing mortgage debt collapse going on in the United States. The European commercial banks then had all the money they expected to need for reserves and to make conventional loans in the years ahead.

As a result, the European Central bank saved many of the European commercial banks and accomplished in minutes what the Federal Reserve failed to accomplish in years with its emphasis on the Federal Funds rates and all its many short term programs tailored to aiding a certain handful of influential universal banks and financial traders.

Even worse, if that's possible, the Federal Reserve also created new programs that had the effect of discouraging the commercial banks from using their capital and deposits to renew loans and make new ones: the Federal Reserve began paying daily interest on reserves that were deposited at the Federal Reserve so they would be able to earn interest without having to make loans to their regular borrowers; and a *term deposit facility* was established which gave financial institutions a safe interest-earning place to deposit money instead of loaning it out.

Overall, to put the most charitable possible spin on the failures of its Chairman, governors, and regional presidents, the Federal Reserve's activities during the Great Recession were concentrated on saving a handful of large universal banks and financial traders so the worldwide financial system and its counterparty relationships would not "melt down." Unfortunately, and at the same time, the Federal Reserve effectively ignored both the declining actual size of the United States money supply and its mandate to maintain full employment—so it did *not* engage in substantial monetary easing.

Indeed, the Federal Reserve did not even do enough to offset the money supply reductions occurring elsewhere in the economy, let alone increase it to encourage and maintain private sector spending. As a result, many commercial banks and other depositories failed, consumers and employers could not renew their mortgages and credit lines, and the economy continue to decline until what would have been a temporary recession morphed into a permanent depression—wherein, as analysts shall see, conventional monetary policies to set things right will not work.

And even worse, if that's possible, the assets of the smaller banks and other institutions which failed were quickly snapped up by the influential too-big—to-fail institutions—which had access to the facilities and the ability to personally contact and influence the governmental and Federal Reserve decision makers. They even received Federal Reserve special funding and assistance to do so. This had the effect of moving deposits from the control of smaller locally-oriented banks which traditionally use their monies to provide loans and credit to local businesses and consumers to the larger banks that tend to ignore the local needs and, instead, use their deposits for their own trading and speculation purposes and to loan them to other large financial traders.

What the Federal Reserve faced.

In essence, the Federal Reserve faced two major problems when the Great Recession of 2008 began:

First, it faced a world financial system with a handful of too-big-to-fail trading institutions whose failure would "melt down" the financial system because they owed so much to their "counterparties," the commercial banks and other participants in the financial system. In essence, if the "too-bigs" failed, their counterparties would suffer such great losses that they too might well collapse. It basically solved this problem.

Second, The Federal Reserve faced a collapsing economy and failing universal and commercial banks caused by the refusal of the banks to use the discount process, the banks' increased capital requirements, the rigidity of the Federal Reserve's reserve requirements, the inadequacy of the Federal Reserve's open market operations because they were guided by the federal funds rate instead of the state of the economy, the collapse in the value of the banks' mortgage and other financial assets, and the failure of banks to loan to one another or anyone else for fear they would not be repaid. It totally failed to solve this problem.

Instead of doing something significant, the Federal Reserve responded by reducing its irrelevant Federal Funds target rate and with several relatively minor "quantitative easing" programs of open market purchases to increase the quantity of money and credit in the economy. It also used its emergency powers to set up a number of *special facilities* to get money into the system where it appeared to be most needed to save the "too big" trading and universal banks from failing. It also allowed certain favored "too-big" investment banks such as Goldman Sachs and Morgan Stanley to proclaim themselves to be commercial banks so they could receive a significant portion of the special financing and loans that were channeled to the commercial banks so they could continue making their traditional loans to consumers and employers.

So, yes, during the Great Recession the Federal Reserve governors used open market operations and "special facilities" to pour dollar reserves into the economy and the world both on a daily basis in response to the federal funds rates and in three relatively minor "quantitative easings." But although the additional dollars increased the monetary base—*they did not increase the excess reserves available to be loaned to consumers and employers:*

First, because huge amounts of dollars were being sent abroad, particularly to China, to buy Chinese and other foreign-made products;

Second, because concurrently the Federal Reserve and Federal Deposit Insurance Corporation (FDIC) conducted "stress tests" and effectively raised the reserve and capital requirements of the commercial banks and other depositories by forcing them to hold more and better reserves and assets upon threat of closure. This forced them to cut back on credit card lines and personal and business loans;

Third, because the Federal Reserve and the other regulators did not enforce the Community Reinvestment Act which supposedly requires banks to extend loans to the communities of their depositors. Instead, they stood idly by while the banks continued to fund their trading operations, reduced credit card and personal lines, raised mortgage interest rates and foreclosed on mortgages instead of rewriting them, and reduced and refused to renew business working capital lines.

Fourth, more of the available money supply was held by people and employers for precautionary purposes because of the uncertain future they faced.

Fifth, because the reduced bank lending to other financial institutions such as money market funds resulted in a massive deleveraging and, thus, a massive reduction in the supply of money and credit despite the increase in the monetary base.

In essence, the shipment of dollars overseas, the increased capital requirements associated with the stress tests, the deleveraging, and the increased holdings for precautionary purposes absorbed additional monetary base the Federal Reserve added to the economy *and more*.

That left the commercial banks and other depositories in the United States rightfully worried that they still might not have enough reserves if the economy continued to worsen in the future. As a result, throughout the first five years of the recession the commercial banks and other depositories responded to their lack of reserves and higher capital requirements by reducing the amount of new loans they issued to consumers and employers and by not renewing existing loans as they matured.

The banks' responses. The universal and commercial banks stopped making loans so their total current and potential liabilities would shrink to the levels that their managers thought could be supported with whatever reserves and capital they had in hand. Incredibly, the Federal Reserve governors and other FOMC members looked at the low Federal Funds rates and thought the commercial banks had access to all the money they needed to meet the loan requests of their consumer and business customers. Even more incredibly, the governors and regional presidents somehow came to believe that creating additional money would somehow cause inflation from too much spending even though the economy was trillions short of having enough spending. It was a perfect recipe for the Federal Reserve to cook up a prolonged recession that would eventually morph into a permanent depression. And that is exactly what happened.

The results achieved by the Federal Reserve programs.

Lending by the universal banks, commercial banks and other depositories virtually collapsed at times during the Great Recession which began in 2008. The collapse in lending, and the recession it caused by cutting consumer and employer spending, was triggered by the collapse in the mortgage and housing markets and the resulting collapse in the size of the money supply as credit card lines and consumer credit were reduced for fear of non-repayment.

In essence, the banks and depositories suddenly found themselves without money to lend at a time when everyone including themselves needed more cash. They stopped their normal pattern of lending to consumers and employers because of the recession, the higher capital and loan requirements imposed on them by the regulators, and the fear that they would need more reserves. Instead, they were motivated to try to collect whatever was due them, to sell the collateral before its value fell further, and to not make any loans that might go bad. Since almost every loan is at risk of going bad in a collapsing economy they reduced and, in some cases, stopped renewing maturing loans and making new ones. The economy, of course, collapsed even further.

The depositories could have gone to the Federal Reserve and discounted their good assets to get the money and reserves they needed—but that would have brought in the FDIC and other regulators and virtually guaranteed their failure; and:

They could not loan or borrow from other banks and depositories for fear their counterparties would fail;

They could not sell their assets except at prices so low that the losses they would have to book would eat up their capital and force them to close;

They could not loan to businesses and consumers because the regulators were pressuring them with "stress tests" to hold their assets is safer and more liquid forms such as federal bonds and would close them if they did not;

They had alternatives to making consumer and employer loans because they could deposit their reserves with the Federal Reserve and earn interest or loan the money for shorter terms to financial traders.

And, throughout it all, they could not loan out their reserves because they were being held by the rigid reserve requirements of the Federal Reserve to control the money supply.

Summarizing the results.

A handful of big bank and non-bank financial traders and foreign commercial banks were saved and their executives and traders rewarded with bonuses for selling the derivatives that failed; loans and credit dried up so that millions of people became unemployed and used up their savings and pension assets; growth stagnated; bankruptcies skyrocketed, many commercial banks and businesses failed, government deficits grew as tax collections fell and businesses failed; and *the people who were responsible for the debacle got retained and reappointed by the newly elected President and reconfirmed by the Senate.*

SUMMARY

I.   Money is whatever is generally accepted in payment by the sellers of goods and services. The total amount of money available to be spent is the money. In the United States that would traditionally include all coins, currency, transactions deposits. Macro-pragmatic analysts additionally include the available credit on widely accepted credit cards such as Visa and Mastercard, Paypal and Square balances; the total amount of available "overdraft" protection issued by financial institutions, the unused balances on working capital and personal credit lines, and the instantly transferable dollar deposits and unused credit lines at foreign financial institutions.

II.   The Federal Reserve System is the basic creator of new money in the United States. When it expands the monetary base (MB) by creating new money it increases the quantity of money in circulation grows as it passes through the fractional reserve deposit system.

III. The use of newly created money to increase the monetary base, and thus the money supply and total spending, by buying bonds from the Treasury or in the open market has resulted in the Federal Reserve accumulating trillions of dollars of federal debt. The amount of debt it holds is a good estimate of the size of the monetary base.

IV.   The total amount of transactions deposit money an economy depends on the size of the monetary base and the percentage of each deposit that must be held in reserve to cover withdrawals.

V.   Financial intermediaries stand between those who have money and those who are willing to pay interest to borrow it. Typically they accept money in exchange for something such as a bank deposit and then lend it out in exchange for something such as a mortgage.

VI. The Federal Reserve typically controls the United States supply of money by buying and selling bonds and other assets in the open market. It can, but rarely does, also affect the total money supply by changing the reserve requirements and implementing various special facilities.

VII. The rediscount rate is the interest rate banks pay to borrow money if they are in trouble. It is never used because banks do not want to admit they are in trouble.

VIII. The rate of interest banks charge one another to borrow reserves for 24 hours is the Federal Funds Rate. The Federal Reserve has traditionally used the Federal Funds rate to guide its open market buying and selling on the assumption that the rate closely reflects the economy's need for more or less money. It does not.

IX. During the Great Recession that started in 2008 the Federal Reserve established "special facilities" and other programs to provide funds directly to a handful of large financial trading intermediaries. It assumed that helping them survive the recession would somehow help the real economy recover. It did not. Many of the too-big-to-fail recipients used the money they received from the Federal Reserve to buy up the assets of the smaller financial institutions that failed due to the Federal Reserve's negligence.

X. The Federal Reserve engaged in several large "quantitative easing" to pour additional money into the economy during the Great Recession to increase the monetary base and encourage the additional spending needed to end the recession. It did not work because dollars flowed abroad and reserve, capital, and loan requirements were simultaneously increased so that the additional money could not be loaned out.

CHAPTER SEVEN

INTEREST RATES AND THE FINANCIAL MARKETS

Interest is price of using or holding money. For the possessors of money it is the price that can be earned by lending their money to those who want to borrow it. For borrowers it is the price they must pay for the privilege of borrowing it. For example, if an employer wants to purchase a new machine or facility but does not immediately have all the money needed to buy it, he may be able to offer a payment, interest, to induce some of the possessors of money to lend him the amount he needs to make the buy.

Merely repaying borrowed money at some future time is not enough. The possessors of money would gain nothing by letting the employer, or anyone else, use their money on those terms. The borrowers must agree to pay an additional amount (*interest*) that is high enough to induce the possessors of money to temporarily forego possessing it and accept the risk that some or all of it might not be repaid.

Furthermore, interest is not just the price that has to be paid to obtain someone else's money. There is also an interest cost inherent in possessing or using one's own money. It exists because holding your own money means giving up the opportunity to lend it out and earn interest. In other words, *all holders and users of money directly or indirectly pay an interest price for any money they hold or use, whether it is their own or someone else's.*

Interest rates. The interest price of using or holding money for a given period of time typically is expressed as a percentage. For example, if one borrows $100 and has to pay back the $100 plus $5 of interest at the end of one year, the price of using or holding money for one year is five percent of the amount borrowed. That percentage price is the *rate of interest* (i).

The advantage of using interest rates, when considering the interest price of using or holding money, is that it is possible to compare the interest prices of different quantities of money. For instance, an interest payment of $5 to obtain the use of $50 for a year means an interest rate of ten percent; that is half the twenty percent price paid when $80 of interest has to be paid to obtain the use of $400 for one year.

The general level of interest rates in an economy is set by the demand for a money such as the dollar and the supply of it. Money demand refers to the different amounts of money people, employers, governments, and foreigners are willing to borrow or hold at each interest rate. The money supply is the amount of money that is available to hold or be loaned out or spent at each general level of interest rates. They come together in the world's *money markets* where the level of interest rates that will prevail for a particular type of money is established by the forces of supply and demand.

Accordingly, since the interest price of each currency is set in its markets, if the supply of a money such as a U.S. dollar increases or the demand for the money decreases, the interest rate price of money will tend to decline; if the supply of money decreases or the demand for money increases, the interest rate price of that money will tend to increase.

Some macroeconomists consider the general level of interest rates that exists in the United States for dollars at any point in time as being set by the total supply of all dollars, including those held abroad, and the total of all the demand for dollars including those desired by foreigners; others by the supply and demand for the loanable dollars that are available from the commercial banks and other lenders; and others by the supply and demand for money as defined by the Federal Reserve.

It really does not matter where the specific rates are set that establish the general level of interest rates in an economy—because in today's digital world any differences between different markets are quickly eliminated by traders moving money from where it earns lower rates to where it will earn more. In any event, no matter how and where its various rates are set, *an economy such as the United States only has one general or average level of interest rates at any point in time.*

The Federal Reserve governors and many economists think that the level of an economy's interest rates is a very significant determinant of its total spending. Pragmatic analysts disagree. They believe that expectations and the availability of credit and its repayment terms are much more important than its interest rate price. All agree, however, that interest rates are enough of a factor in spending decisions and policies that they need to be considered and understood.

Obviously there are lots of different interest rates occurring simultaneously in an economy such as that of the United States. What is being considered here, however, is the concept of interest rates as the price of obtaining money and credit and the reality that the establishment of the general level of that interest rate price occurs in the financial markets where the use of money is bought and sold.

The fact that money markets establish interest rates is an important concept both because interest rates do somewhat affect consumer, investment, and government spending, even if they don't dominate them, and, more importantly, because efforts to change the general level of interest rates are often implemented by the Federal Reserve in an effort to affect the level of total spending that occurs in the United States.

THE DEMAND FOR MONEY

The money in an economy's money supply does not have to be instantly spent to buy newly produced goods and services or anything else. Indeed at any point in time *all the money in the economy is being held somewhere for some purpose.* How much each person or employer or government or financial institution wants to hold is determined by their views as to how holding money, instead of spending it or loaning it out, will help them maximize their incomes, utility, or whatever other goals they are pursuing.

There are three basic reasons people, commercial banks, and employers want to hold money in spite of the foregone interest and lost spending opportunities involved in holding it instead of spending the money or loaning it out. These are the so-called *transaction*, *asset*, and *precautionary* uses of money.

The total demand for money in an economy is the sum of the amounts of money that are desired for these purposes at each general level of interest rates and level of income. It is important because money that is held is *not* loaned out or spent to buy goods and services. It is also important because it constitutes the demand side of the money market where, in conjunction with the supply of money, the general level of interest rates is set. The resulting general level of interest rates then, in turn, is one of the many things that influence consumer, investment, and other spending and, thus, the economy's production, employment and prices.

In essence, the demand for money is important because it helps determine the level of interest rates in an economy; the level of interest rates is important because it helps determine the total amount of spending in an economy; and the total amount of spending is important because it determines the levels of production, employment, and prices that will occur in the economy.

Money demanded for transactions purposes.

The transactions demand for money refers to money held in wallets, checking accounts, cash registers, and unused credit lines so that money can be spent in the future. It is held for such purposes primarily because there may be a lack of correspondence between money inflows and money outflows.

Many households, for example, tend to receive money on periodic paydays but make their outlays such as for food and housing on other days. Obviously, when such differences occur, these households need to hold certain sums of money in their wallets and checking accounts for a period of time after payday.

Similar circumstances exist for businesses and governments. They may not receive revenues for their products at exactly the same time they must pay their bills. Furthermore, there is an inevitable element of uncertainty in their transactions; they may not know when payments to them will arrive and when they themselves will have to make payments. Similarly, they may not receive payments in exact amounts and, as a result, must hold a supply of money in their cash registers and bank accounts and credit lines in order to make change.

How much money is desired for transactions purposes depends, of course, on both the number and size and nature of the transactions occurring in the economy and the amount of time expected to elapse between money inflows. The latter is important since the more time between inflows, the greater the tendency for transactions involving money outlays to fall between them, thus increasing the amount of money desired for transactions purposes.

The money holdings required for transactions in an economy tend to be larger when the economy's level of income is higher. This is because the higher levels of income tend to mean an increase in the number and size of its transactions. Accordingly, it is possible to relate the amount of money demanded for this purpose to an economy's level of income. For example, if the households and employers generally want to hold money equal to ten percent of their total spending they will want to hold $2 trillion of money if the economy is producing at the $20 trillion level and $3 trillion if it is at $30 trillion.

Algebraically, the amount of money demanded for transactions purposes in an economy (Mt) depends on (f) the level of income in the economy (Y), or $Mt = f(Y)$.

Influences other than income levels. The proportion of each level of income that an economy's households and employers will desire to hold in the form of money for transactions purposes depends on more than just the amount of time between inflows and outflow and the amount of money outlays involved. Among the other influences:

1. *Vertical integration.* Employers that are vertically integrated have fewer buying and selling transactions, and thus need less money for transactions than do un-integrated employers. Employers are vertically integrated when they perform more than one of the subsequent steps required in the process of producing and selling an item. For instance, a steel making employer is not vertically integrated when it buys iron and coal from other employers and then sells the steel to other users; it is integrated if it mines and processes its own coal and iron, uses the coal and iron to make steel, and then uses the steel to produce products which it sells. The point is that integrated employers do not need to engage in money-using transactions to buy coal and iron or to sell steel, whereas the unintegrated employer does.

2. *Use of credit.* Credit reduces the amount of cash and transactions deposits needed for transactions at every level of income. It allows payments associated with transactions occurring between money inflows to be delayed until the money inflows take place. When such delays are possible there is no need to hold money from earlier inflows to make payments when the transactions occur. For example, the use of credit cards and digital money has virtually eliminated the need for many individuals to hold cash in order to buy meals, travel, and consumer durables.

3. *Sales of financial assets and used goods.* Money also has to be held for transactions involving used goods or financial assets such as stocks, bonds and derivatives. The more used goods and financial assets are being bought and sold, the larger will be the proportion of the amount of total purchasing for new goods and services that will tend to be held for transactions purposes.

4. *Barter.* Barter involves the exchange for one item for another; it does not require money. The greater the amount of bartering in an economy the smaller will be the amount of money held for transactions. Not much barter occurs in a money-using economy such as the United States. But it grows rapidly, even to the extent of companies being set up to facilitate it between the owners of small

businesses, when money and credit become generally unavailable to them.

5. *Rate of interest.* There is an interest expense in holding money for transactions or any other purpose. That expense is the interest income that is foregone if the money can be loaned out. People, employers, and governments and behave rationally when they try to keep their interest expenses as low as possible. They tend to hold the minimum amount of money needed for their transactions and other economic activities.

There are several reasons why smaller amounts of money may be desired at higher rates of interest. On the demand side, smaller amounts of money are desired when the interest costs of holding or borrowing money are higher than additional costs of avoiding such transactions through the use of credit, barter, and vertical integration. In essence, the higher interest rates are, the more an economy's transactions tend be handled without money in order to avoid the higher interest costs.

On the supply side, larger amounts of money are supplied when the interest that could be earned by lending it out is higher than the administrative cost associated with such lending.

Finally, the difficulty of obtaining money to hold for this and other purposes at high rates of money may cause the use of more and more substitutes, such as owner financing, foreign currencies, and barter certificates, at higher and higher rates of interest. This reduces the amount of money demanded.

6. *Foreign uses.* The United States dollar is used extensively outside the United States for transactions and other purposes. In some countries the dollar is the primary currency. The number of foreign transactions in dollars, and thus the foreign demand for dollars, has been growing for years.

Transactions demand curves. A transactions demand curve depicts the amount of money that would be desired in an economy for transactions purposes at each level of income. How much money is actually desired at each level of income is affected by the factors listed above.

Figure 7-1 presents such a curve. The level of income in the economy is measured on the horizontal axis and the amount of money desired for transactions purposes on the vertical axis. The curve rises to the right in order to depict that more and more money will be desired for transactions purposes at higher and higher levels of income. It indicates, in this example, that $45 billion of money will be demanded for transactions purpose when the level of income in the economy is $300 billion and that more money will be demand for this purpose at higher levels of income; less at lower levels of income.

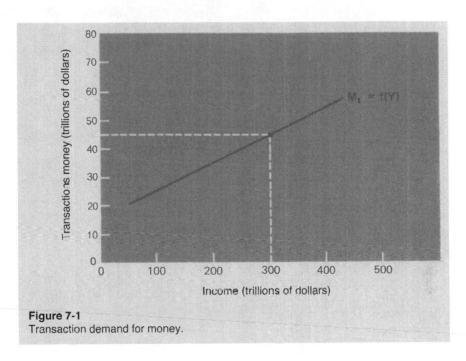

Figure 7-1
Transaction demand for money.

Money Demanded for Asset Purposes.

The owners of an economy's wealth may want to hold some of their wealth in the form of money even if they do not need to do so for transactions or other purposes. How much each wants to hold depends on the size of his or her wealth, the level of interest rates in the economy, and his or her expectations regarding the future prices of assets and other things that might be bought including newly produce goods and services.

For example, individuals and others who *expect* the prices of goods and services and assets such as stocks and bonds and real estate will be lower in the future may wish to hold a significant portion of the wealth they own or can borrow in the form of money so they can buy more assets and products in the future when prices are lower. Conversely, those who *expect* prices to by higher in the future may want to hold no money; they will spend it now before it loses its purchasing power.

People and employers and financial institutions hold their assets in various asset forms such as money, mortgages, bonds, stocks, and real property. The rate of return the assets earn is the price their owners receive for not holding their wealth in the form of money.

In a rational world the owners of wealth will hold it in assets other than money only as long as the incomes the assets generate exceed the brokerage fees associated with getting into and out of the assets, the implicit interest costs, and the risk of losses from possible reductions in their prices. In other words, the owners of an economy's wealth tend to continually adjust out of and into money and into and out of non-money assets until the expected returns on all the non-money assets are at least equal the interest rate which could be earned by loaning the money out.

Crucially important, at least to the thinking of the Federal Reserve governors and regional presidents, at some very low rate of interest it won't be worthwhile for banks and other lenders to hold wealth in the form of spending-related assets such as mortgages and credit card advances—because of the fees and other administrative costs of acquiring them and the possibility they will lose some or all of their value. This means that once some low level of interest rates is reached an infinite amount of money will be held by the commercial banks and other lenders rather than being loaned out to acquire mortgages and make other loans.

Equally important, again primarily to the Federal Reserve governors and regional presidents, all the spending that consumers and others will want to do at that low interest rate will already be being done—since the interest rates cannot go lower consumer and other spending will not increase.

In other words, according to this theory, money may be held in unlimited amounts once an economy reaches a point where its interest rates are as low as they can go. That occurs when the prices of financial assets are so high, and thus their yields so low, that everyone with money is wants to hold it rather than buying financial assets and risking a big loss in exchange for a low interest rate. Then, even if more money is made available to the commercial banks by the Federal Reserve, it will not be loaned out to consumers and others to spend—because it is not worth the risk of loss to do so. So spending does not increase and the level of interest rates does go lower. This is the Keynesian *liquidity trap.*

Because of the liquidity trap and the belief that savings (and thus consumer spending) and investment spending are heavily influenced by interest rates such that lower rates are needed to get more spending, the Federal Reserve governors, journalists, and even to this day some trained economists, believe that expansionary monetary policies cease to be effective when interest rates such reach a minimum. They are right, of course, *if* monetary policy primarily affects spending through interest rate changes. They are also right *if* loans and credit stop being available when interest rates reach some minimum. They are also right *if* consumer and other spenders are primarily motivated by interest rates instead of the availability of credit and its repayment terms. They are also right *if* loans and credit will no longer be made to consumers and other spenders because of the costs of administration and the risk of non-payment exceed the interest rates that could be charged.

The Federal Reserve governors and regional presidents, and even some analysts, thought such an interest rate minimum was reached during the Great Recession. The governors then rationalized their failure to further expand the supply of money and credit on the premise that interest rates could not fall further—and that, as a result, there was nothing more that monetary policy could do. *They were wrong* and

America's people and businesses, and America's standing in the world, paid a terrible price for their mistakes.

They were wrong because, as shall become increasingly clear, the liquidity trap is not just an interest rate phenomenon: and interest rates are not the major determinant of consumer and employer spending. Moreover, the interest rates available to consumers and employers had not come close to reaching a minimum such that lenders and sellers would no longer offer loans and credit to buyers.

In essence, the American economy was left in a terrible economic malaise by a perfect storm of Federal Reserve ignorance about the conditions and economic relationships of the real world of business and commercial banking. The buyers whose spending was needed to pull the economy out of the recession were there in droves as homeowners sought to vain to refinance their mortgages and businesses desperately sought to renew their working capital lines of credit—*but the money and credit was not made available.*

Graphic depiction of the asset demand for money. A graphic example of an economy's asset or wealth-holding demand for money is presented in Figure 7-2. The curve slopes down to the right from eight percent to indicate that the owners of the economy's wealth will want to hold more and more of their wealth in the form of money when the economy has lower and lower rates of interest. In this economy, for example, $50 billion will be desired for portfolio purposes when the level of interest rates in the economy average four percent.

The curve becomes perfectly elastic at a minimum interest-rate level averaging two percent. This is where the Keynesian "minimum level of interest rate" liquidity trap kicks in. It occurs, allegedly, because at such a low level of return the banks and other owners of the economy's wealth would prefer to hold any money they might have rather than bear the risks and transactions costs associated with loaning it out. Since there will be no lenders competing to buy mortgages and provide other types of loans and credit, the prices of such interest generating assets will not be bid up and the level of the economy's interest rates will not decline further.

What this means according the Keynesians is that if additional money is subsequently made available to the banks via the Federal Reserve buying federal bonds in the financial markets, it will all be held rather used to make loans to consumers and employers. In essence, it will all be held because the low rates of interest are not sufficient to cover the risks of non payment and the administrative costs of the loans.

What this ignores, of course, is that some of the newly created money flowing into the economy might be spent to buy goods and services instead of deposited in the banks. It also ignores the possibility of funneling the newly created money *directly* to potential spenders instead indirectly to them via bond purchases that route money, at least some of it, to the banks who, in turn might loan some of the money to consumers and employers.

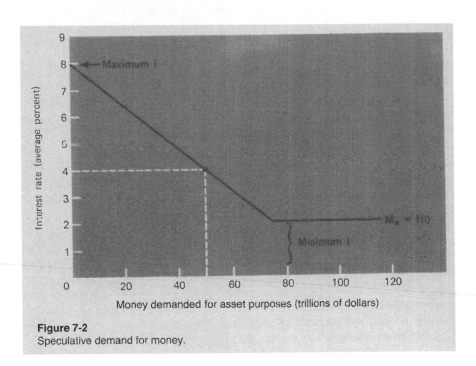

Figure 7-2
Speculative demand for money.

Money demanded for
precautionary purposes

Money is held for precautionary purposes so that anticipated outlays can continue despite the arrival of unexpected circumstances, such as those that require unexpected spending or caused reduced incomes. Examples, of such unexpected circumstance include the loss of income due to illness or unemployment or the need for money to spend caused by an auto accident.

The determinants of precautionary demand. Money demanded for precautionary purposes is related to the confidence that the economy's employers, financial institutions, and people have in their ability to make all the outlays of money that they may desire; the less confidence they have in their ability, the more money they will wish to hold. For example during the United States' Great Recession people who had not yet lost their jobs and homes began rapidly building up their money and liquidity reserves in fear the worst was yet to come.

Various things can influence the level of confidence. For instance, the availability of credit means that unexpected additional outlays or reductions in income can be temporarily covered without having precautionary money holdings available. Similarly, the loss of credit such as when banks reduce credit card lines, stop making personal loans against homes and property, and tighten up their credit requirements has the reverse impact.

Another factor that may affect the level of confidence is the level of income in the economy. At relatively high levels of income, individuals and employers may, as a group, be receiving more money and thus be better able to meet unexpected situations without having to dip into their previously accumulated holdings. Also, with such high incomes they may have better chances of obtaining credit when need arises because of their better ability to repay debts.

Finally, a high level of income tends to means more jobs for employees and customers for employers, so that if someone losses a job they may be able to quickly find another without having to use the money they have put aside for precautionary purposes. Similarly, if a business losses a customer it may be able to quickly find others.

On the other hand, and going in the other direction, it is also possible that a move to higher consumption and sales levels associated with an economy having higher levels of spending and income may cause consumers and employers to want to hold even more money so they can continue their normal spending patterns if something goes wrong—until they find another job or more customers.

Graphic depiction of the precautionary demand for money. Figure 7-3 depicts some of the infinite number of ways that the amount of money desired for precautionary purposes in an economy might be related to the level of income in the economy.

Curve number 1 slopes down to the right to represent an equation indicating that less and less money will be held for precautionary purposes at higher and higher levels of income. This will be the case if the net effects of higher incomes and the higher employment associated with them is to increase the confidence of people and employers that they will be able to keep spending if something goes wrong without relying on money held back for precautionary purposes. This particular curve indicates, for instance, that $30 billion will be desired for precautionary purposes when the level of income in the economy is $500 billion.

An entirely different situation different situation would exist if higher levels of income cause people and employers to desire to hold more money at higher levels of income. The curve depicting the equation relating the amount of money held for precautionary purposes and the level of income would slope upwards as income increases. The curve designated #2 is an example.

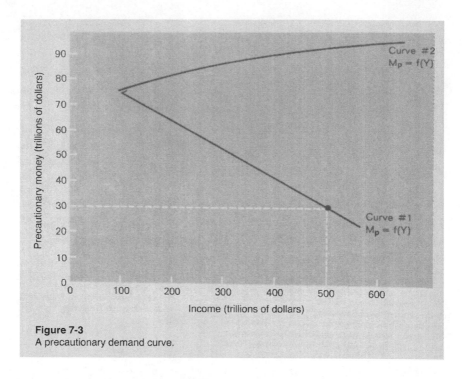

Figure 7-3
A precautionary demand curve.

THE MONEY MARKETS SET THE LEVEL OF INTEREST RATES

The idea of a single "money market" or "financial market" where money and liquidity is bought and sold is simultaneously both true and absurd. In the narrow technical sense there is no single "money market" where the holders of dollars and those that want to borrow them come together to buy and sell their use for some interest rate price.

What the real world has is a complex web of numerous highly competitive interrelated financial institutions. They range from local community banks and savings and loan associations to hedge and money market funds to great international financial giants operating in numerous financial areas to sovereign wealth funds and the central banks of other countries.

As a group these financial institutions create and buy and sell just about every conceivable financial instrument from checking account deposits in a local bank to esoteric gambles tied to various market indexes to complex insurance instruments that insure payments will be made on other instruments. Moreover, since the dollar is one of the most important currencies in the world's financial markets and international trade, the web of financial institutions conducting dollar based transactions extends throughout the world.

Taken together these intertwined institutions are the participants in the "money market" as they create, loan, borrow, buy, and sell dollars in all the ways described above, and many more. Their combined desire for dollars in conjunction with the combined supply of dollars determines the general level of interest rates that will exist for dollars in the United States and abroad at any point in time.

On the other hand, in the real world, the worldwide existence of the Internet and automated currency trading means that is effectively a single market for dollars.

The total demand for dollars.

No matter how money is defined, the total amount of money that will be desired in an economy at each level of interest rates is the sum of the amounts desired for transactions, asset, and precaution purposes. More and more money is held as interest rates get lower and lower because the lower rates result in an increased willingness on the part of owners of wealth to hold their wealth in the form of money while they wait for opportunities to spend it or earn more with it.

Similarly, the amount of money for transactions and precautions purposes is determined by the level of income in the economy (and the rest of the world in the case of the dollar which is used worldwide) and is relatively unaffected by the rate of interest. More money is wanted when the level of income is higher because there are more transactions and they may have higher dollar values.

Algebraically, the total amount of money holdings, no matter how money is defined, that will be desired in an economy at each level of interest rates (Md) is the sum of the amounts desired for transactions, asset, and precaution purposes: $Md = Mt + Ma + Mp$. A money demand curve representing that basic equation shows the amount of dollars that will be demanded at each interest rate price that must be paid to obtain dollars to use or hold.

An example of a money demand curve showing the amount of dollar holdings that will be desired at each general level of interest rates with the current combination of income and wealth is depicted in Figure 7-4. The curve slopes downward to the right to indicate that the participants in the dollar money market will desire to hold more money at lower rates of interest.

Notice also that the money demand curve for the example economy appears to have three distinct portions. Above an interest rate of ten percent the curve depicting the total demand for money becomes almost inelastic. This occurs because all the money in the economy is needed for transactions and precautions purposes. As a result, the level of interest rates gets bid higher and higher until a level (10% in this economy) is reached such that no money is desired for asset purposes because the interest the owners of wealth can earn with it is so high.

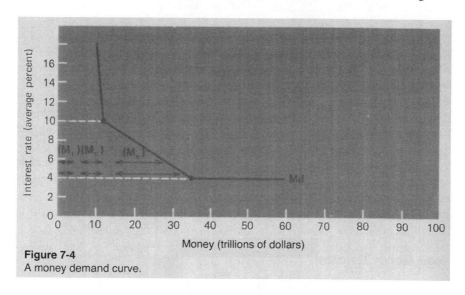

Figure 7-4
A money demand curve.

In other words, to make change and scheduled payments a fixed amount of money has to be in store tills and checking accounts no matter what the interest rate price of holding it. In this example economy approximately $10 trillion is needed to conduct normal business operations and personal spending no matter what the interest rate; it declines ever so slightly at even higher interest rates to the extent the higher rates induce the holders of money for transactions and precautions purposes to reassess their needs to hold money and try to find viable alternatives.

The total amount of money holdings that is demanded at interest rate levels below twenty percent then increases at lower and lower rates of interest mainly because the owners of wealth increasingly want to hold it in cash so they can avoid the risk of losses and be able to take advantage of future buying opportunities that might come along.

Finally, at some minimum average interest rate, four percent in this example, the curve depicting this particular economy's demand for money becomes perfectly elastic because at such a low average interest rate (and high prices of financial assets) the economy's wealth owners are willing to hold infinitely large amounts of money rather than bear the risk and pay the brokerage costs of loaning it out or using it to buy financial or other assets.

Complications and complexities. Complicating any attempt to analyze the total demand for a money such as the dollar is the likelihood that different amounts of money will be demanded for transactions and precautions and asset purposes at different levels of income and different levels of wealth and interest rates. Thus the total amount of money that will be held, not spent to buy things such as newly produced goods and services, at each level of interest rates will also change from one income level to the next and one wealth level to the next.

Further complicating the demand for money are price and income expectations. Smaller money holdings may be desired when prices are expected to rise. Then buyers will tend to use more of their money try to buy now and beat the increase. For example, by using it to buy houses if they expect their prices to rise. Expectations of lower prices would have the opposite effect—more money would be held so it is available to spend when prices are lower.

What this means is that a complete algebraic description of an economy's demand for money requires a different equation and money demand curve for every possible combination of income and wealth. Figure 7-5 depicts an extremely simple example of such a state of affairs. The curves in the figure merely depict the reality that more and more money will be demanded at each level of interest rates when the economy has higher and higher levels of income.

In reality, of course, the world is infinitely complex when it comes to determining how much of the money supply created by the Federal Reserve will be held or loaned or spent. Moreover, the demand for money to hold is but one of the many economic relationships and realities in a complex economy such as the United States. How those relationships and complexities interact is the subject matter of macroeconomics, not something one learns in law school or by supervising bank inspectors or by studying other types of economic ideas and concepts (sorry governors).

The policy implications of having different demands for money holdings at different levels of income and wealth and interest rates will become increasingly apparent. At the very least, however, it should be becoming more and more obvious that the economic and political structure of the United States is so complex it is virtually impossible to model with precision.

The modeling problems are significant. They suggest that analysts using sophisticated models involving a few hundred simple equations populated with data of questionable validity may not be able to explain what happened in the past, let alone "scientifically" predict what will happen in the future. Rather, using such models is likely to result in inaccurate and misleading conclusions even if they are solved with scientific rigor by the most well-meaning of analysts. Pragmatic analysts understand this.

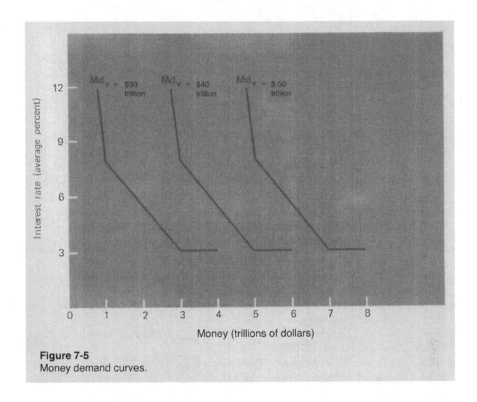

Figure 7-5
Money demand curves.

INTEREST RATES AND
THE SUPPLY OF MONEY

The amount of money available to be held as reserves (the monetary base) in an economy such as the United States determines the total amount of money and financial assets and the level of credit that can be generated by the economy's financial intermediaries. In the United States it is usually determined by the reserve influencing activities and regulations of the Federal Reserve.

More specifically, in the United States *it is the Federal Reserve, and only the Federal Reserve, that is charged with determining the size of the money supply and ensuring the proper availability of loans and credit to consumers and employers.* And the Federal Reserve does act to establish the supply of United States dollar—except when other regulatory agencies such as the FDIC and Comptroller of the Currency effectively override its decisions by establishing higher reserve, capital, and credit requirements.

Target rates and bank rates.

In the United States, unlike Keynes' Britain, the commercial banks do not *directly* obtain newly created money for the purpose of obtaining money to loan to consumers and employers—they obtain newly created money to make such loans *indirectly* via deposits and loans from whomever sells the bonds to the Federal Reserve. In essence, the British put newly created money directly into the banks by loaning it directly to them; the United States puts newly created money into the economy indirectly by buying bonds in the open market. In essence, in the United States newly created money reaches the banks and becomes available for them to loan out when and *if* it is deposited in the banks or loaned to them.

In essence, the British central bank, the Bank of England, knows for sure when Britain's banks want more money to loan out because they come to the Bank of England to borrow it; the Federal Reserve neither knows for sure the banks want more money to loan or that the money the Federal Reserve creates will ever reach them.

Despite the great differences, the Federal Reserve governors and regional presidents have historically acted as if the target rate the governors set for the borrowing and lending of overnight reserves is comparable in to the "bank rate" at which Keynes' Bank of England stands ready to make loans to British commercial banks.

In essence, the governors and regional presidents act as if the Federal Fund rates banks charge one another to borrow reserves for twenty four hours is the best indicator that the banks want and/or need more or less money to loan out. In contrast, the commercial banks believe and tend to act as if the Federal Reserve target rate is merely what it is—the rate at which they can borrow and loan reserves from each other for twenty four hours to meet unforeseen fluctuations in their reserve requirements.

It is so important that it bears repeating: T here is an important fundamental difference between the target rate and the bank rate: The Bank of England creates new money and it all goes *directly* to the banks as the banks borrow it from the Bank of England. In contrast, the Federal Reserve creates new money and some of it goes *indirectly* to the banks—via open market purchases that put money into the hands of whoever is selling bonds. The new money is then deposited into the banks *or used for other purposes* such as being sent abroad or deposited in money market funds or used to fund financial speculations.

Because it causes newly created money to reach the banks indirectly, pragmatic analysts disagree with the governors and regional presidents as to the importance of the target rate. They note that the Federal Funds target rate as a guide to setting the size of the money supply has frequently provided the banks with insufficient funds to loan to consumers and employers. In other words, the Federal Reserve's reliance on the target rate has all-too-often resulted in inadequate monetary policies that have repeatedly caused unemployment.

Pragmatic analysts conclude, based on the relationships they observe in the real world and the results the Federal Reserve has achieved, that the Federal Funds rates banks charge one another for overnight reserves are neither good indicators of the appropriate size of the money supply nor an appropriate way to get loanable funds into and out of the commercial banks. To the contrary, they see the target rate as not directly related to the general level of interest rates in the economy; not directly related to the country's monetary needs to achieve full employment levels of spending; and not always an appropriate guide for the actions of the Open Market Desk.

In the real world, according to the pragmatists, commercial banks and other lenders to consumers and employers do not relate the interest rates and volume of their loans to employers and consumers to the Federal Reserve target rate. Rather, they ignore the Federal Funds rates and price and distribute their loans and credit lines to maximize their profits. The pragmatists also point out that commercial banks and other depositories do not borrow reserves overnight for the purpose of making loans.

In other words, pragmatic analysts see the Federal Reserve as basing its money supply policies on target and actual Federal Funds rates that have little, if any, relationship to either the total spending needed for full employment or the availability of loanable funds for consumers and employers or the level of interest rates or the banks need for more or less money and credit.

Using alternatives to the Federal Funds rates to guide monetary policy.

The pragmatists say interest rates on personal and business loans, loan renewal and turndown rates, the availability of mortgage and consumer credit, and, particularly, the economy's rates of inflation, unemployment, and growth, are all much more significant indicators as to whether or not the supply of money and credit should be increased or decreased.

In essence, pragmatists think real world conditions are better indicators of what should be done to affect the money supply rather than barely used and largely irrelevant rates related to the overnight borrowing of reserves.

The Federal Reserve's apologists disagree. They think the pragmatic economists are unfair. They say the Federal Funds target rate is merely the device by which the governors give the Open Market desk their orders to change the supply of money—lowering it when the governors want the money supply expanded; raising it when they want the expansion to slow.

The pragmatists respond by pointing to the Federal Reserve's use of the target rate during the Great Recession and the recessions that preceded it. If the target rate's relationship to the actual Federal Funds rates really is an appropriate guide to monetary policy, they ask, why has it repeatedly failed to give the correct orders to the point of being proven useless? They note that if the Federal Funds target rate was significant and applicable as a guide to monetary policy there would have been a quick end to the Great Recession and all the recessions that preceded it.

But one thing is certain—no matter how appropriately or inappropriately it is set, there is only one quantity of dollars in existence at any point in time and it is greatly impacted by whatever monetary base is established by the Federal Reserve. Accordingly, a curve representing the supply of money in the United States at any point in time would indicate no change in its size no matter if interest rates are higher or lower. Such a curve is depicted in Figure 7-6.

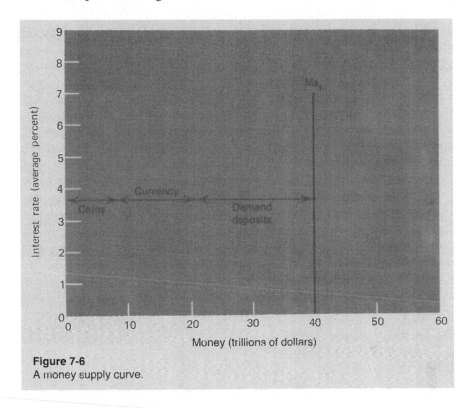

Figure 7-6
A money supply curve.

Foreign dollar holdings.

The level of interest rates in an economy may affect the supply of money and financial assets in the economy if its interest rates influence the willingness of foreigners to provide or obtain dollars. The United States is an "open" economy—it allows the dollar to freely fluctuate and does not attempt to encourage or restrict monetary flows. Accordingly, dollars held abroad for precautionary purposes and the financing of local and international trade will tend to be returned if the interest rates they can earn are high enough.

Moreover, it is also possible that, whenever interest rates are relatively high, foreign currencies will flow into the United States and be used for some of its economy's transactions, precautions, and asset purposes. In essence, as the interest rate price of holding dollars gets higher and higher, more dollars and other currencies may be attracted from abroad by the higher rates to return. Then hedge funds, traders, businesses, and other financial institutions and employers will increasingly use other currencies in their transactions and to hold for precautionary and asset purposes. When this happens, the economy's supply of dollars can facilitate the transactions associated with a higher level of spending.

Figure 7-7 depicts such a situation. In this example, the money supply in the United States is $40 trillion of dollars, and will be larger and larger if the general level of interest rates are in excess of an average of six percent. The increase occurs as foreign-held dollars return in pursuit of the higher interest rates. Moreover, it is also possible that whenever interest rates are relatively high, foreign currencies will come into the United States to be used for some of its economy's transactions, precautions, and asset purposes.

In essence, as the interest rate cost of holding dollars gets higher and higher, dollars may return from abroad and hedge funds, businesses, and financial institutions, may increasingly use other currencies in their transactions.

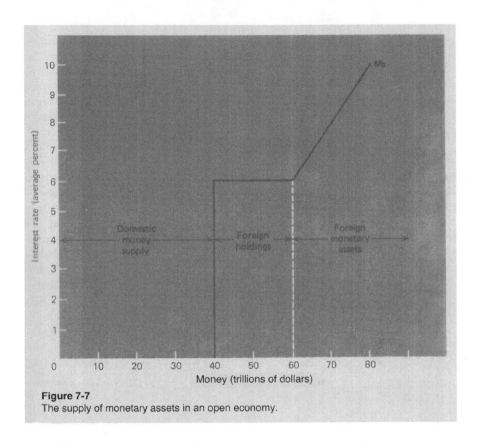

Figure 7-7
The supply of monetary assets in an open economy.

MONEY MARKETS AND THE GENERAL LEVEL OF INTEREST RATES

The currency markets, also known as the money markets, are where the supply of dollars and the demand for dollars come together. The interest rate price of money that results is the general level of interest rates, the level of rates at which the amount of dollars demanded will equal the amount of dollars supplied.

Various interest rates. Does that mean there is only one interest rate for a money such as the U.S. dollar or the euro or any other currency? Of course not. What exists for every currency including the U.S. dollar is a *spread* of rates for different purposes around the general or average rate for that type of money. It is the spread that moves up and down as the general level of interest rates rises and falls in response to supply and demand changes in the money markets.

The specific rates for specific uses vary according to their risks of non-payment, length of time involved, and the administrative costs of lending the money out and collecting it when the payments are due. Thus, for example, money for high risk loans with high administrative costs, such as credit card loans, may be available at rates far above the average while at the same time money for overnight loans between strong financial institutions or short-term certificates of deposit might involve substantially lower rates. In essence, the general or average rate of interest for the dollar is the average rate about which all the various interest rates spread.

Where are interest rates set?

Perhaps there may have been a time when the general level of interest rates on dollar loans was set in the United States by the demand for loans and the supply of loanable dollars in its commercial banks. That time is long past due to the arrival of non-bank financial institutions and foreign dollar balances—even if the Federal Reserve and many economists still cling to the notion and use only U.S. balances in their analyses and models.

The Federal Reserve's MB, M1 and M2 data to the contrary, today the market for dollars is worldwide; any differential in the rate of interest price which dollars can earn in different places and markets is instantly eliminated by electronic transactions as the owners of the money relentlessly pursue the highest rates of interest wherever they might be located and those who want to borrow money pursue the lowest rates. In other words, you may borrow dollars or loan them out by depositing them in a U.S. commercial bank or other depository, but the interest rate that you earn or pay is set by the worldwide supply and demand for dollars.

The market forces.

There can be only one general or average rate of interest in an economy at any point in time; at any other rate there will be either a surplus or money or a shortage. The differences between the amounts of money demanded and supplied at rates other than those associated with the equilibrium level of rates ensures that such rates can only exist temporarily, very temporarily.

Today interest rates adjust rapidly—because in the digital age interest rates are constantly known and responded to instantly, often automatically, as holders and users of money pounce on the opportunities associated with any interest rate outside what their models show to be the normal spread around the equilibrium rate. In other words, the laws of supply and demand govern the various dollar rates of interest because they constantly push the dollar's general level of interest rates towards its equilibrium level.

For instance, consider what would happen if for some reason the worldwide dollar market suddenly has a surplus at whatever is its current level of interest rates. This, for example, would happen if the Federal Reserve creates new money and injects it into the economy by buying assets. It could also occur if political problems in China or Europe cause the holders of dollars in Europe or China to send them to safety in the United States. There would then be a surplus of dollars in the United States at the current level of interest rates.

But neither the surplus nor the current level of interest rates could continue—since the possessors of this surplus would now have some of their wealth in a form that they may not desire, they will exchange their surplus dollars for existing assets by using their surplus money to buy such as bonds and other financial instruments. Then as their buying of such assets bids up their prices and their yields accordingly decline, more and more dollars will be held for asset purposes until a new and lower level of interest rates is reached at which all the money in the economy is in the hands of those who want to hold.

Of course those who had the initial surplus could also use some of it to buy goods and services. Then the level of income in the economy would increase and the dollars would be in the hands of the employers who produce the goods and services bought by the surplus dollars. All these results tend to occur concurrently—dollars flow into the financial markets and banks, interest rates tend to decline, and spending tends to increase. And that can result in an inflation caused by too much spending if the economy is already at full employment.

In any event, when there are surplus dollars both the level of spending in the economy will tend to increase and its interest rates decrease as the prices of financial assets are bid up. That will continue until the level of spending and the general level of interest rates and all its component rates are such that the amount of dollars held in the economy are equal to the amount of money that is wanted for some purpose. That is the equilibrium rate of interest for the economy.

In our example, it has just changed, the amount of money in circulation in the economy has just changed, the amount of loanable funds available has just changed, and spending in the economy has just changed—and all without the Federal Reserve lifting a finger.

Figure 7-8a depicts such a situation. The money market for dollars is initially in equilibrium with all $40 trillion dollars being held at an average interest rate of six percent. Then, for the sake of an example, assume the supply of dollars increases by $20 trillion due to dollars being repatriated from China or an increase in the level of available credit card credit or any of the many other ways the supply of dollars can be increased. If this occurs in the example economy, the average level of interest rates will fall until it reaches a new and lower equilibrium rate of three percent.

A similar decline in the general level of interest rates would occur if the demand for dollars for transactions purposes declines—such as when the level of total spending in the economy recedes because of some event such as the federal government reducing its spending because it has been running deficits and the voters have just elected leaders who are determined to end them.

Figure 7-8b depicts the effect of a reduced demand for dollars. As before, the general level of interest rates falls from six percent to three percent *and again the Federal Reserve had nothing to do with it.*

Astute analysts will notice that it is a recession in the economy that causes the demand for money and the level of interest rates in the example economy to fall. If the federal funds rate agreements between banks track with interest rates in the economy, as the Federal Reserve assumes, then the federal funds rates will decline and thus tend to be below whatever was the Federal Reserve's previously established target rate; and that is the signal to the Federal Reserve that the banks do not need more loanable funds—*at the very time the economy is moving into a recession.*

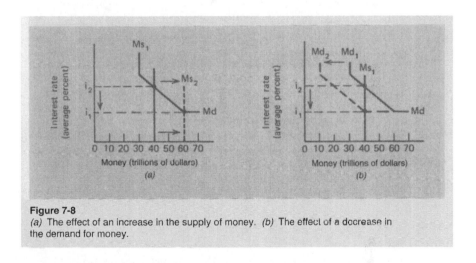

Figure 7-8
(a) The effect of an increase in the supply of money. *(b)* The effect of a decrease in the demand for money.

If such a recession were to occur and drive down the economy's interest rates it would be hoped that the Federal Reserve governors and regional presidents would notice that the economy is in trouble. Then the next time they set the target rate (typically eight times per year) they will set it far below the new and lower federal funds rates—and that would be a signal to the Open Market Desk to expand the money supply to drive down interest rates and encourage more spending.

But wait. That might not occur if the Federal Reserve governors think interest rates have already reached the minimum so that a further expansion of the money supply could not bid asset prices higher and drive down the level of interest rates even more.

Interest rates and the
Keynesian "liquidity trap."

The Figure 7-8b example economy illustrates an important concept, the Keynesian *liquidity trap*. The average level of interest rates in example economy reached its absolute minimum of three percent. Interest rates won't go below that minimum level because of the administrative costs of loaning and borrowing money.

But what if the interest rates charged by the commercial banks are already at the absolute minimum and the United States still does not have enough spending to generate full employment? That appears to be exactly the position of the United States during the Great Recession?

Obviously, under such circumstances an increase in the money supply cannot drive down interest rates any further. Instead, when the minimum is reached any increase in the money supply will be "trapped" in the hands of the commercial banks and other lenders who would prefer to hold it rather than loan it out and bear the administrative costs and the possibility of big losses when interest rates next increase and the prices of bonds, mortgages, and other financial assets decline.

Today the Federal Reserve governors and regional presidents and many journalists and "business economists" assume monetary policy has its primary effect through interest rate changes. Perhaps they assume this because that is what was alleged in the British-oriented first macroeconomics textbooks; perhaps because that is what Keynes and his followers suggested would be the case for Britain and American economists thought his theories and policies would apply to the United States; and perhaps because that is how the U.K. central bank of operates—it posts a rate and allows commercial banks to borrow at that rate and make loans.

Whatever the reason, the belief that monetary policy works primarily through changing interest rates lead to the conclusion that the effectiveness of monetary policy ends when interest rates reach rock bottom. Then, it is said, other policies, such as more government spending and lower taxes, are required if more spending is needed is needed to generate production and employment.

Indeed, well into the second decade of the 21st century the Federal Reserve's chairman and governors were still touring the country explaining how they had done all they could by forcing interest rates to their absolute lowest possible level. According to them, fiscal and other policies were needed if the United States was to ever get out of the recession which started in 2008.

Where the Federal Reserve governors and other analysts went wrong is that *the existence of a minimum level of interest rates does not mean that further increases in the supply of dollars will have no effect on the level of spending.* To the contrary, the recipients of the additional money may use it to buy additional goods and services even if the economy is at some minimum rate of interest. Indeed, increasing the amount of liquid assets in an economy is likely to cause spending to rise—because the availability of money and credit and its repayment terms are more important to potential spenders than the rate of interest.

What analysts will find, when monetary policies are considered in the chapters that follow, is that if an appropriate monetary expansion occurs, total spending will tend to rise even if interest rates are at a minimum. In essence, as analysts will see, and despite the views of the Federal Reserve's governors and regional presidents to the contrary, the Federal Reserve can expand the money supply in such a way as to absolutely insure that whatever increase in spending is required to reach full employment will occur.

In other words, in the chapters ahead analysts will see why there was no reason for the Great Recession and its associated unemployment and budgetary deficits to last so long that it morphed into a permanent depression. To the contrary, at any time the recession could have been quickly ended and prosperity and governmental budget surpluses restored without causing inflation or requiring increased government spending or lower taxes. *Even today it can be quickly ended with appropriate Federal Reserve actions.*

A regulatory liquidity trap. Start again with the economy at full employment. Now assume that consumer and other spending falls and a recession begins, and that the Federal Reserve responds with "quantitative easing" so the money supply is increased—*and* that at the same time the economy's regulators require the banks to raise their loan requirements so that they hold the additional money instead of loaning it to consumers and employers. The new money is then "trapped" by the new regulatory requirements so that it cannot be loaned out to consumers and employers. The recession then continues despite the quantitative easing. This actually happened during the Great Recession.

Or perhaps the regulators ignore or change the banks' Community Investment lending requirements and, instead allow the banks to use the new money for purposes other than funding consumers and employers. The recession then continues despite the quantitative easing. This actually happened during the Great Recession.

Or perhaps the FDIC sees bank failures being caused by the recession, and changes the capital requirements of the commercial banks so they tend hold all the additional money as reserves or use it make short term loans to other financial institutions and buy federal bonds. The price of bonds goes up, their interest rate yields go down, and consumers and employers do not get any additional financing. The recession then continues despite the quantitative easing. This actually happened during the Great Recession.

Or perhaps the Federal Reserve starts paying interest on bank reserves. As a result, the commercial banks deposit some or all of the additional money in their accounts at the Federal Reserve instead of loaning it to consumers and employers. The recession then continues despite the quantitative easing. This actually happened during the Great Recession.

Or perhaps the federal government decides to pay six percent interest on all its bonds in order to improve the earnings of pension funds. Some or all the additional money is used to buy bonds instead of making loans to consumers and employers. The recession then continues despite the quantitative easing. Raising interest rates paidon federal bonds was advocated but did not happen during the Great Recession.

Or perhaps the Comptroller of the Currency sets consumer and employer loan requirements so high that relatively few borrowers can qualify. The recession then continues despite the quantitative easing. This actually happened during the Great Recession.

Or perhaps the FDIC conducts "stress tests" and decides the commercial banks should hold more short-term assets, such as loans to money market funds, that are not loans to consumers and employers. The recession then continues despite the quantitative easing. This actually happened during the Great Recession.

Or perhaps the Federal Reserve directly sends some of the newly created money overseas to help foreign universal banks such as Deutsche Bank instead of making it available for U.S. banks to loan to consumers and employers. The recession then continues despite the quantitative easing. This actually happened during the Great Recession.

What this means. What this means, of course, is that in the real world additional money created by the Federal Reserve can be trapped from being spent by many more circumstances than just the existence of a minimum rate of interest—such as by being diverted by regulators to uses other than the provision of loans and credit to consumers and employers; or never reaching the banks in the first place; or being diverted by the banks to financial-related loans instead of product-related loans.

In other words, an expansionary monetary policy can work to end a recession only if it is implemented in such a way that the Federal Reserve and banks get the additional money into the hands of the consumers and employers who are willing to spend it to buy newly produced goods and services.

Money market equilibrium curves.

Figure 7-9 depicts a "money market equilibrium" curve representing the equation for the relationship between equilibrium income levels and the equilibrium levels of interest rates is a *money market equilibrium* curve. Often designated as the LM curve, it represents the various combinations of interest rate levels and income levels that will result in the amount of money demanded in the economy equaling the supply of money. No other combinations can exist, except in passing, because they would not result in equilibrium in the economy's money market—they would, instead, cause the economy's level of interest rates to change. This, in turn, would cause changes in the economy's level of income. These changes would continue until both the level of income and the level of interest rates are in equilibrium.

In essence, the LM curve shows what the equilibrium level of interest rates would be at each level of income that the economy might obtain.

Notice the curve's four distinct segments. First, at low levels of income the curve depicts the economy in which the level of interest rates will be as low as they can possibly be given the structure of the economy and its regulations. This occurs because the amount of dollars demanded for transactions and precautions purposes is low at low levels of income. In this example, the level of interest rates in the economy will be at its four percent minimum level at all income levels below $25 trillion.

The second portion of the economy's LM curve indicates that if the economy's level of income is $25 trillion or higher, the increased demand for dollars to hold for transactions and precautions purposes will reduce the amount of money available to be held for asset purposes. As a result, the economy's level of interest rates will be bid up above the economy's minimum rate as the economy's income increases. In this example, the economy's equilibrium level of interest rates will rise higher and higher as higher levels of income are reached until an income level of $45 trillion is reached at an average interest rate of twenty percent: Twenty percent is rate of interest at which this particular economy's interest rates are high enough (financial asset prices low enough) so that no dollars are being held for asset purposes.

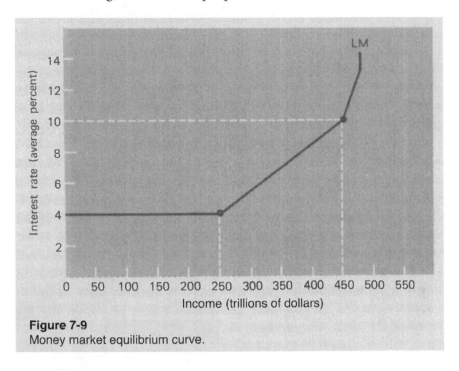

Figure 7-9
Money market equilibrium curve.

The third portion of the economy's LM curve begins at levels of income above $45 trillion. In essence, the higher and higher rates over twenty percent will continue to reduce the amount of money held for transactions and precautions purposes at every income level. In so doing, the existing supply of dollars will be able to support higher and higher levels of income as interests get higher and higher. This section of the curve is more inelastic than the $25 trillion to $45 trillion section because its higher interest rates are no longer freeing money previously being held as assets.—the rates are already so high and asset prices so low that no money is being held for asset purposes. But the money supply of the economy available for additional spending transactions is still increasing as the higher and higher interest rates do such things as attract dollars from abroad, motivate employers to hold fewer dollars in their cash registers and bank accounts, and encourage barter and the use of money substitutes.

Finally, at least conceptually although the possibility is far fetched except in a grossly mismanaged economy, it is possible that a maximum level of income may be reached wherein all foreign dollar holdings have returned, all holdings of money for asset purposes have ended, all possible degrees of barter are occurring, and the maximum use of foreign monies and dollar substitutes has been attained. This is the absolute highest level of income the economy can attain with its current supply of dollars. It is $50 trillion in the example economy. Any tendency for spending to move past that level will merely cause interest rates to rise until the level of spending in the economy is forced back to $50 trillion where the amount of dollars demanded will again equal the amount of dollars supplied.

Generating Money Market Equilibrium Curves. An economy's LM curve can be constructed graphically, as it is in Figure 7-10, by using curves that represent the various basic conditions in an economy's money market. The curves are the income-related *transactions* and *precautions* curves, the central bank related *money supply curve*, and the interest rate related *asset demand curve*.

Figure 7-10 shows that it is conceptually possible to derive an economy's LM curve if an analyst knows the size of its money supply and can write equations describing the transactions and precautions demands that will occur at each income level and the asset demand that will exist at each interest rate.

The resulting LM curve shows the various combinations of interest rates and spending levels that can exist in the economy. Why knowing the various combinations of interest rate levels and spending levels that are possible is important for policy makers will soon become clear.

An example of curves depicting basic money market conditions can be found in Figure 7-10. Together they can be used to generate an LM curve:

a) the transactions & precautions curve slopes upward to the right because more money is needed for those purposes as the level of income in an economy increases; and

b) the money supply curve depicts the fixed supply of money that exists in an economy at any point in time. The curve is a straight line to ensure that when the total amount of money going to one use is measured on one axis, the total amount of money available for a second use is measured on the other access; and

c) the asset demand curve slopes down to the right to show that more and more money will be held at lower and lower rates of interest and that at some low rate the economy will be in the liquidity trap and all the money available to be held as an asset will be held.

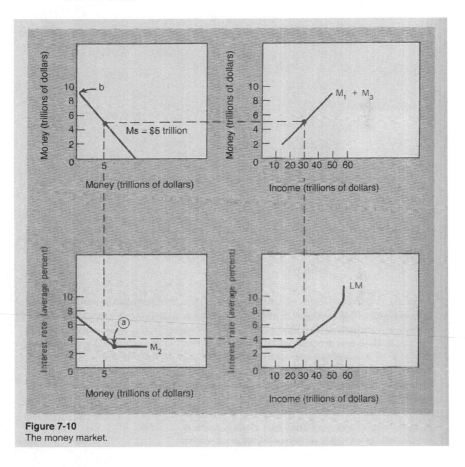

Figure 7-10
The money market.

Deriving money market equilibrium curves. Start with the economy's existing supply of money and any given level of income. Then find the level of money needed for transactions at that level of income and subtract it from the money supply. That leaves the amount of money available for precautions and asset purposes. Finding and subtracting the amount that will be held for precautionary purposes at that level of income leaves the amount available to be held for asset purposes. The resulting point on the LM curve depicts the level the equilibrium level of interest rates that will occur as a result of the demand for money associated with that specific level of income.

Subsequent points on the LM curve can be found by repeating the process. The curve slopes upward to reflect the fact that more and more money will be demanded for transactions and precautions purposes at higher and higher levels of income. The level of interest rates is initially at a minimum. It stays there until the level of income reaches a high enough level to generate a demand for money that is high enough to begin causing the level of interest rates to rise.

CHAPTER SUMMARY

I.   Interest is the price paid by borrowers to obtain money to spend or hold. It is also the price paid by the holders of money in that by holding money they are foregoing the interest income they could earn by loaning it out.

II.   There are three basic motives for holding money rather than spending it: to use it for transactions, to have it available for precautionary purposes, and to hold it as an asset.

III. Money is held in wallets, cash registers, checking accounts, and credit lines for transactions purposes such as to make change and enable spending to occur between money inflows.

IV.   Affecting the amount of money held for transactions purposes are the level of income, the time span between inflows, the extent to which credit is available from sellers, the purchasing of used goods and financial assets; and the extent to which barter and money substitutes are used.

V.   Those who hold money as an asset forego any income they might earn from bonds or other assets and any utility they might gain from using it for consumption.

VI.   Money is held for precautionary purposes so its holders will be prepared for unexpected circumstances.

VI1. The amount held for precautionary purposes has a great deal to do with confidence which in turn by the amount of credit available and the level of income.

VIII. The total demand for money holdings is the sum desired for transactions, precautions, and asset purposes. Curves depicting the demand for money are relatively inelastic above a certain high level of interest rates and relatively elastic below a certain low level of interest rates.

IX.   The total supply of money in an economy or the entire world is fixed at any point in time. Since money can move between economies, dollars held abroad will return to the United States as the interest rates that can be earned by bringing them home increases. The total supply of dollars will not change but more of them will be in the United States.

X.   The equilibrium level of interest rates is the level causing demand and supply for money to be equal. It may change if there is a change in either the demand for money or the supply of money.

XI.   Lower levels of interest rates encourage investment and other spending.

XII. There is a minimum level of interest rates in every economy. At that level, those with money prefer to hold it rather than loan it out. This is known as the Keynesian "liquidity trap." It occurs when lenders at some low rate of interest hold money because loaning it out yields a rate of interest insufficient to cover the costs of administering loans and the risks of nonpayment.

XIII. When the money supply is increased more money is available to hold and loan. If the economy is not in the Keynesian liquidity trap, interest rates will tend to drop and total purchasing to rise.

XIV. A regulatory liquidity trap can occur even when interest rates are not at a minimum. This occurs when the money supply is increased and the additional money is not loaned out for consumers and employers to spend due to regulatory requirements or the existence of fears that the money will not be repaid no matter what interest rate is charged or the existence of borrowers who will not spend the money to buy newly produced goods and services.

XV. Determining an economy's equilibrium level of interest rates is difficult because interest rates both affect the level of income and depend on it. Nevertheless, it is possible to construct money market equilibrium curves (LM curves) depicting the interest rate that would occur at each level of income

XV. The shape of the LM curve reflects the fact that interest rates will be at a minimum at low levels of income. This occurs because lower levels of income require little money for transactions and precautions, leaving enough for asset use such that the prices of financial assets are maximized and the interest rates they yield minimized. Interest rates begin to rise as income rises so that more and more money is needed for transactions and precautions purposes. The curve then becomes relatively inelastic at some high rate where no money is held for asset purpose and all the money held abroad has been repatriated. It becomes perfectly inelastic when it becomes physically impossible for the existing money supply to handle more transactions.

Chapter Eight

TOTAL SPENDING, INCOME FLUCTUATIONS, AND THE SPENDING MULTIPLIERS

The total amount of spending that occurs in an economy to buy newly produced goods and services is popularly known as an economy's *level of income*. Using the term "income" in place of "total purchasing" or "total spending" is traditional in economics. The interchange of names is valid because the amount of money consumers and other customers *spend* to buy goods and services is conceptually the same amount of money that is *received* as income by the sellers of the goods and services—the sellers being the public and private employers who produced them. More specifically, an economy's level of total income is equal to the total amount of buying done by its various types of buyers.

The total level of spending that occurs in the United States, and what affects and determines it, is important to know because it is total customer spending (C+I+G+F) that determines how much will be produced. Thus it determines whether the United States will have full employment or unemployment, stable prices or inflation, and economic growth or a recession.

But what determines the amount of total spending that will be done by the various buyers? And how does an analyst cope with the fact that a change in the size of each of its basic spending components will cause changes in the sizes of many others?

The answer for professional analysts when many things simultaneously affect each other is algebra. This has the additional advantage of making the analysis appear "scientific." The disadvantage, of course, is that it may be the first time in many years, if ever, that readers and policy makers have written a computer program or used algebra since college.

Adding up the various types of spending to get an economy's equilibrium level of income.

One way to determine an economy's level of income is to just add up the various amounts of spending being done in the economy by the various types of customers. Consider a simplistic economy in which investment buying of new capital goods is $2.0 trillion, foreigners buy $1.5 trillion, governments buy $3.5 trillion, and consumer spending is $1.0 trillion plus sixty percent of the level of income.

This economy looks a lot like a simplistic version of the United States in the second decade of the 21st century. Under these circumstances the economy's level of income will be $20.0 trillion of which consumption will be $13.0 trillion. That is the only level of income that can be maintained under these conditions. And it will be maintained as long as there are no changes in any of the spending that is being done to buy goods and services. It is the economy's *equilibrium level of income*—the one and only level of total spending that can exist unless something changes.

All other levels of income are disequilibrium levels, levels that cannot occur except temporarily which the economy is moving toward the equilibrium level of income. For example, consider the impossibility of the economy maintaining a higher level of spending such as $30.0 trillion. With an income of $30.0 trillion, the economy's consumer spending would be $19.0 trillion. That means there would be only a total amount of spending of $26.0 trillion when there is $7.0 trillion of other spending.

But a spending level of $26.0 trillion also cannot be maintained—because when the economy's income is $26.0 trillion, its consumer spending will be $16.6 trillion so that the economy's total spending will drop to $23.6. The level of income in the economy will continue to decline until total spending reaches $20.0 trillion.

On the other hand, a level of income lower than $20.0 trillion also cannot be maintained. Consider what would happen to the example economy if the level of income was only $10.0 trillion: consumer spending would only be $7.0 trillion at such a low level income. Add in the government, foreign, and investment spending and total spending is only $14.0 trillion. But at $14.0 trillion there would be more consumption. And total spending, and thus consumer spending, would grow and grow until total spending reaches the $20.0 trillion equilibrium level of income.

The basic equation.

Consider the example economy algebraically. As described above, it is an economy in which investment buying of new goods and services is $2.0 trillion, foreigners buy $1.5 trillion, governments buy $3.5 trillion, and consumer buying is $1.0 trillion plus sixty percent of the level of income. Determining that the level of income in this economy will be $20.0 trillion during the time period under consideration requires the following steps:

1. $Y = a + bY + I + G + F$ (basic equation)
2. $Y = \$1.0 + .60Y + \$2.0 + \$3.5 + \$1.5$ (putting in data)
3. $Y = .60Y + \$8.0$ (combining numerical values)
4. $Y - .60Y = \$8.0$ (combining values of Y)
5. $.40Y = \$8.0$ (relating Y to numerical values)
6. $Y = \$20.0$ trillion (of which C=$13.0 trillion since it is $1.0 trillion plus 60% of Y)

Using the propensity to save to calculate total spending. The example economy above is in equilibrium when its income is $20.0 trillion. That is the only level of buying that can occur so long as the propensities to consume and save and the government, foreign, and investment purchases remain unchanged. The $20.0 equilibrium level of spending will recur over and over again in every subsequent time period because the $7.0 trillion that is saved when the level of income is $20.0 trillion is balanced by the addition of $7.0 trillion from the non-consumption components such as investment, foreign, and government purchasing.

In other words, *an economy's equilibrium level of income occurs at the one and only level of income that causes or generates a total amount of savings that is exactly offset by the amount of non-consumption spending occurring in the economy.*

Astute analysts know that the equilibrium level of income can be too large or too small to result in full employment without inflation They also know that whatever level of total spending occurs is attained without specific regard to the existence of deficits, the size of the national debt, the level of federal spending, presidential speeches, political platforms, the Federal Funds target rate, money market funds, the existence of unions, the size of the money supply however defined, or any of the other innumerable causal influences so dear to so many who are typically so wrong.

In the real world each of these things can and does influence the total amount spending that occurs in one or more of the spending categories in some way—but it is the totality of *all* the relationships and *all* the activities that counts. And the result may not be pleasing—with or without a balanced budget total spending may be so low as to result in massive unemployment or so high as to result in a massive inflation.

The fact that an economy's equilibrium level of income is the only one generating a total amount of savings just equal to the size of the economy's non-consumption spending is important. It means that the one and only level of total spending that will occur in an economy is the one, *the only one*, at which all the dollars spent that are not subsequently re-spent once again for consumption purposes is *exactly* made up by all the other spending so that the *total* amount of spending remains unchanged.

Analysts will recall from the previous discussions of savings that not all the dollars employers receive as income go back to people so they can be spent again. Some of the revenues employers receive are saved along the way instead of being re-spent—for various reasons such as the government takes them in taxes or people get them but decide not to buy new goods and services with them or employers retain them so they make investments at a later date to buy more plant, equipment, and inventory.

Another way of looking at it is that the portion of an economy's income that is saved for any reason (not re-spent for consumption purposes) is said to have leaked away from the economy's total spending while non-consumption spending is said to be injected into its spending. The equilibrium condition is then "saving leakages" equal "total injections." The only difference between these equilibrium conditions is terminology.

Simplistic texts often lump together investment, government, and foreign spending and call it "total investment." Then the economy's total savings is equal to its total investment. The equality sometimes confuses politicians, journalists, "business economists," and high school students into erroneously thinking savings causes investment or is necessary for investment. That is not true as analysts have seen in the preceding discussions of consumption and investment.

What happens is that the level of total spending tends to change until it reaches the level of income that yields enough savings to exactly offset the investment and other non-consumption spending that is occurring. Then there is nothing to cause further spending changes—*that is the economy's equilibrium level of income*—and it may not be high enough to buy enough of the economy's production to cause full employment. Or it may be so high that inflation results despite the money supply not increasing.

$20 trillion is the only total amount of spending that tends to occur in the example economy. It means there would be massive unemployment if the economy had a capacity to produce of $25 trillion but only produced $20 trillion because that is all that its employers can sell.

That the equilibrium level of income is indeed the only one generating a total amount of savings just equal to the size of the non-consumption purchasing is demonstrated algebraically by the following steps:

1. $Y=C+I+G+F$
2. Thus $Y-C=I+F+G$
3. and since $Y-C=S$
4. Then $S=I+F=G$
   (because both are
   equal to $Y-C$)

More about the savings-income-investment relationship. Quite often the equilibrium requirement that savings be exactly offset by the amount of non-consumption purchasing is analyzed in terms of an overly simplistic economy in which investment is the only purchasing component other than consumer spending. Then the condition existing when the economy's level of income is in equilibrium is that the total amount of savings is equal to the total amount of investment ($S=I$).

Analysts will recall that "savings equals investment" is the condition that the early "classical" economists thought existed because the interest rate was the primary determinant of both savings and investment. That equality morphed into the even greater inaccuracies such as "savings results in investment," "savings causes investment," and "savings is necessary for investment."

Perhaps the silliest extrapolation of the inaccuracy inherent in "savings equals investment" is an influential politician's recent statement "we need more investment so we need to encourage more savings." Astute analysts recognize that more savings would mean even less spending and thus even more idled production capacity and thus an even greater reduction in the need for investment spending to buy the additional plant and equipment required if the economy is to grow.

In essence, just because savings equals investment when an economy's level of spending is in equilibrium does not mean savings causes investment or is required for investment to occur. Both are important but they occur independently of one another.

In the real world, the amount of savings that occurs in an economy depends the level of income and the degree to which savings occurs at each level of income is caused by numerous factors including the rate of interest—such as people's propensities to consume, governmental taxes, the purchases of imports and used goods, and the desires of employers to accumulate money for their future investments instead of borrowing it.

Similarly, investment is affected by many factors other than savings such as expected sales revenues, the existence of idled production capacity due to a lack of customers, and expected costs of which the interest rate is but one. The many factors being such things as wages, taxes, employee benefits, utilities, litigation and regulatory expenses, and cost of material inputs.

Identifying the equilibrium level of income.

Since it is known that an economy's equilibrium level of income occurs when the economy's non-consumption purchasing (I, F, G) equals the amount of income that the economy's consumers do not use for consumption purchases (total savings), the equilibrium level of income also can be identified if the amount of total savings is known. Examples of how this can be accomplished both algebraically and graphically follow.

Algebraically. Since an identity exists between savings and non-consumption spending, it is possible to substitute the amount of non-consumption purchasing into an economy's savings function and solve for the equilibrium level of income—the only level of income at which the decisions of savers yield the same amount in savings as the amount of government, foreign, and investment purchases.

Consider the example economy described above where the propensity to consume is described as $1.0 trillion plus sixty percent of the level of income, investment purchasing is $2.0 trillion, foreign spending $1.5 trillion, and government purchases $2.5 trillion.

The savings function is S = -$1.0 + .40Y. Since it is known that the level of savings at equilibrium will be equal to the total amount of non-consumption spending, the appropriate equation is $7.0 = -$1.0 +.40Y. Solving this equation yields Y = $20.0 trillion; this is the only level of income for this economy that will provide the required $7.0 trillion of savings.

This is an excessively simple example. In the real world numerous complex equations would be needed to even crudely approximate an economy such as that of the United States. Such a simplistic equation is useful, however, in that it illustrates how a substantial change, such as an increase in spending by foreigners due to changes in exchange rates or by governments such as might accompany a new administration or Congress, will tend to impact the spending that occurs in an economy and result in effects such as increased production and employment. In the real world billions of decisions are made every day and equilibrium is never attained—but the economy constantly and inexorably moves towards it.

Graphically. It is also possible to determine an economy's equilibrium level of income with a graphic depiction of its savings function. Figure 8-1 presents a savings function for the simple example economy. It represents the savings that would occur in the economy at each level of income. The other line in the figure represents the non-consumption spending that will occur. It is perfectly horizontal in the figure to indicate that the total of non-consumption spending in this example is not affected by the level of income.

The equilibrium level of income in this economy ($20.0 trillion) is identified at the intersection of the savings function representing the amount of savings that will occur at each level of income and the I+F+G line representing the amount of investment, government, and foreign spending that will occur in the economy at each level of income. The level of income associated with the point on the savings function where the two lines intersect is the only one that will generate an amount of savings equal to the level of non-consumption purchasing.

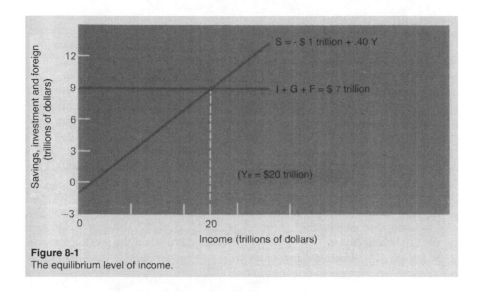

Figure 8-1
The equilibrium level of income.

The forces that move an economy's
level of income toward equilibrium.

The move of the level of income of an economy such as the United States towards equilibrium is inexorable. It is the spending increases and decreases made by the hundreds of millions of individual customers—people, foreigners, employers, and governments—that constantly moves the level of spending towards equilibrium. Basically, total spending changes any time consumers, foreigners, governments, and employers adjust their actual spending to buy new goods and services to bring it in line with changes in their desires and circumstances.

It is such adjustments and spending changes that cause the total level of spending in an economy like the United States to change—until the economy reaches equilibrium and once again savings is exactly offset by the injections of foreign, investment, and government purchases. Then the spending changes stop. The economy's level of income is again in equilibrium.

Moving a bit closer towards reality.

In the real world employers tend to make more investment expenditures when customer spending is higher. They do this both to produce the higher level of goods and services that can be sold and because more capital goods wear out when there is more production.

Similarly, higher incomes tend to result in more imports. That sends dollars abroad that can then be spent to by foreigners to increase the economy's exports.

Similarly, the higher tax revenues generated by increased spending and higher incomes give governments more money to spend—and if there is one thing known about politicians it is that if they have money to spend they will spend it. In other words, all the various major spending components tend to increase as an economy's income rises.

More specifically, every major type of purchasing has two parts: an autonomous sub-component that occurs no matter what the level of income (Ia, Fa, Ga) and an income-related sub-component that changes in size as the level of income increases. (e for employers' investment, f for foreign, g for government)

Thus:
$$Y = a + bY + Ia + eI$$
$$+ Fa + fF + Ga + gG$$

Using the previous data with autonomous government spending reduced to \$2.5 trillion and the addition that replacement investment occurs at the rate of ten percent of the level of income, foreign imports at three percent of the level of income, and government spending at seven percent of the level of income, we see that the equilibrium level of income in the example economy becomes \$35.0 trillion:

1. $Y = a + by + Ia + eI$
$+ Fa + fF + Ga + gG$

2. $Y = \$1.0 + .60Y$
    $+ \$2.0 + .10Y + \$1.5$
    $+ .03Y + \$2.5 + .07Y$

3. $Y = .80Y + \$7.0$

4. $Y - .80Y = \$7.0$

5. $.20Y = \$7.0$

6. $Y = \$35.0$ trillion

The same results can be obtained by setting the savings function ($S = -\$1.0\text{tr} + .40Y$) equal to the sum of the income-related and autonomous non-consumption spending components (I, F, G) and solving algebraically for the level of income that yields an amount of saving just equal to the sum of the non-consumption buying. Thus, using the same data:

1. $-a + (1-b)Y = Ia + eI$
    $+ Fa + fF + Ga + gG$

2. $-\$1.0 + .40Y = \$2.0$
    $+ .10Y + \$1.5 + .03Y$
    $+ \$2.5 + .07Y$

3. $.20Y = \$7.0$

4. $Y = \$35.0$ trillion

The saving function can also be used graphically to depict the equilibrium income level when the income-related investment, foreign, and government spending occur. Figure 8-2 presents this for the example economy. Notice that the savings function has the same form depicted in Figure 8-1. The only difference is the I + F + G line slopes upward to reflect that more of these expenditures will occur when the economy has higher levels of income.

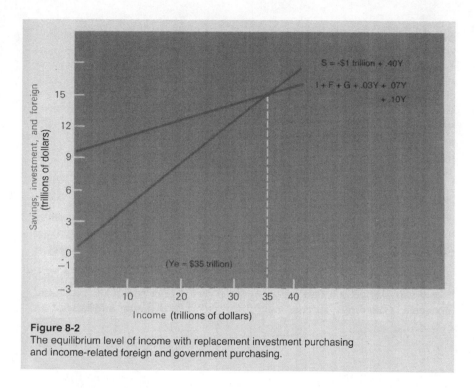

Figure 8-2
The equilibrium level of income with replacement investment purchasing and income-related foreign and government purchasing.

THE MULTIPLIERS

A change in the amount of spending done by some of the customers of an economy's employers will have a greater effect on the equilibrium level of income than just the amount of their own changes. For instance, consider what might happen if investment spending rises in the United States due to increased profit expectations resulting—such as might result from the introduction of simplified taxes and regulations that increase employers' profit expectations:

Total spending would rise as investment spending increases. Then, as the initial increase in investment spending goes into the hands of the employers producing the additional capital goods, they will tend to have higher incomes and employ more labor and pay more wages. Then, as a result of their people having bigger wage and other incomes, consumption spending in the economy will also rise.

The additional consumer and investment spending will also tend to mean more imports—so foreigners will have more dollars to spend and export sales will tend to rise. And everyone will tend to pay more taxes because they have higher incomes so governments will have more money and their spending will tend to rise.

But it does not stop there: the employers and workers who produce the additional consumer products, exports, and government goods and services will also receive greater incomes and so they too will tend to spend more. And the spending increase will continue as the employers then produce even more goods and services. In essence, spending will continue to increase until a new and higher equilibrium level of income is reached. In other words, *total spending will change by some multiple of an initial change* as the dollars of the initial spending increase move from hand to hand.

Consider what would happen in our example economy if foreign or government or investment or consumption spending permanently increases by $1.0 trillion for some reason: the equilibrium level of total spending would rise from $35.0 trillion to $40.0 trillion—a fivefold increase results from an initial $1.0 trillion increase. In other words, the *multiplier* for this economy is five.

This is significant—*it means that an economy that needs an increase in the level of customer spending to achieve a full employment needs only an initial stimulus; the subsequent spending and re-spending of the initial stimulus will do the rest.* Or, going the other way, it means an economy that needs less spending to avoid inflation needs only a relatively small initial reduction; the subsequent reductions in other spending will do the rest. Algebraically:

1. $-a + (1-b)Y = Ia + eI$
   $+ Fa + fF + Ga + gG$
   $+ additional\ spending$

2. $-\$1.0 + .40Y = \$2.0$
   $+ .10Y + \$1.5 + .03Y$
   $+ \$2.5 + .07Y$

+ $1.0 add'l spending

3 *.20Y = $8.0*

4. *Y = $40.0 trillion*

The nature and size of an economy's spending multiplier.

The size of an economy's *spending multiplier* depends on how each type of spending responds to changes in the economy's level of income. The size of an economy's multiplier can be computed with the following formula where the MPC is the marginal propensity to consume; the MPI is the marginal propensity to invest: the MPX is the marginal propensity to export and the MPG is the marginal propensity for government spending:

Multiplier (K) =

$$\frac{1}{1 - MPC - MPI - MPX - MPG}$$

Or, the same formula with the notation representing the MPC, MPI, MPX, and MPG:

Multiplier (K) =

$$\frac{1}{1 - b - e - f - g}$$

Thus, for the example economy in which the MPC is 60 percent, the MPI is 10 percent, the MPX is 3 percent, and the MPG is 7 percent:

$$K = \frac{1}{1 - .60 - .10 - .03 - .07} = 5$$

The nature and size of an economy's transfer multiplier.

Consider what would happen in our example economy if government transfers permanently increase by $1.0 trillion for some reason: the equilibrium level of total spending would rise from $35.0 trillion to $38.0 trillion—a threefold increase results from an initial $1.0 trillion increase. In other words, the *transfer multiplier* for this economy is three.

This is significant for several reasons. First, it means that an economy that needs a change in the level of customer spending to achieve a full employment level of income needs only an initial stimulus and that the stimulus can be either additional purchase or additional transfer; the subsequent spending and re-spending of the initial stimulus will do the rest. It also means that if additional transfers are to be used to get the economy going again there will have to be more of them.

1. $-a + (1-b)Y = Ia + eI$
   $+ Fa + fF + Ga + gG$
   $+ bTr$

2. $-\$1.0 + .40Y = \$2.0$
   $+ .10Y + \$1.5 + .03Y$
   $+ \$2.5 + .07Y + \$.6$

3. $.20Y = \$7.6$

4. $Y = \$38.0$ trillion

The size of an economy's transfer multiplier depends on how each type of purchasing responds to changes in the economy's level of income. Its size can be computed with the following formula where the MPC is the marginal propensity to consume; the MPI is the marginal propensity to invest: the MPX is the marginal propensity to export and the MPG is the marginal propensity for government spending:

Transfer Multiplier (Ktr) =

$$\frac{MPC}{1-MPC-MPI-MPX-MPG}$$

Or, the same formula with the notation representing the MPC, MPI, MPX, and MPG:

$$\text{Multiplier (Ktr)} = \frac{b}{1-b-e-f-g}$$

Thus, for the example economy in which the MPC is 60 percent, the MPI is 10 percent, the MPX is 3 percent, and the MPG is 7 percent:

$$Ktr = \frac{.60}{1-.60-.10-.03-.07} = 3$$

The important thing for policy makers to note when considering fiscal alternatives is that transfers do not yield as much bang for the government buck as government buying. In other words, *roads and other purchases are better for increasing total spending, and thus production and employment, than welfare and bailouts.* On the other hand, increasing government purchases may take longer to implement than transfers. If that is the case, transfers may still be a better way to go if an economy needs more spending to increase its production and employment.

The size of an economy's tax multiplier.

One important way taxes affect the level of spending in an economy is by reducing the disposable income that people have available to spend on consumer items: first, all spending to buy newly produced goods and services may not be received as income because of indirect business taxes such as sales taxes and excise taxes such as those on gasoline and cigarettes. For example, a $40 excise tax on a product that costs $100 leaves only $60 dollars for the employer producing the product to receive as income.

Furthermore, not all of this $60 may become personal income because of business taxes such as corporate income taxes and inventory taxes. If business taxes are $10, for instance, there will only be $50 available for distribution to individuals as part of their personal incomes. Finally, not all of the $50 may be disposable income because of the imposition on individuals of personal income taxes and personal property taxes. Thus, if the governments' taxes take $15 of the $50 of personal income there will only be $35 for the individuals to either save or spend on consumer goods and services.

Consider what would happen in our example economy that has a $38.0 trillion level of income if the economy's governments then levy $1.0 trillion of taxes and the tax payers have the same sixty percent propensity to consume as everyone else—the equilibrium level of income would fall from $38.0 trillion to $35.0 trillion. In other words, this economy's *tax multiplier* is three:

1. $-a + (1-b)Y = Ia$
$+ eI + Fa + fF + Ga$
$+ gG + bTr - b'Ix$

2. $-\$1.0 + .40Y - \$2.0$
$+ .10Y + \$1.5 + .03Y$
$+ \$2.5 + .07Y + \$.6$
$-\$.6$

3. $20Y = \$7.0$

4. $Y = \$35.0 \ trillion$

Of course, taxes can also influence an economy's equilibrium level of income in other ways. Consider three of the many possibilities:

First, taxes may cause a decline in investment spending if they cut the flow of revenue which the potential new capital assets are expected to yield.

Second, taxes on exports may discourage foreign purchasers because the foreign buyers will have to pay both the tax and the price of the product.

Third and going the other way, taxes on imports may discourage domestic purchases of foreign-made items and cause an increase in the purchase of similar domestically produced products.

Additionally, taxes may directly affect an economy's ability to produce: Since taxation absorbs a portion of disposable income, it may lessen taxpayers' incentives to work and willingness to act as an employer. Thus the long-run effect of taxes could be to cause a gap between an economy's potential and actual production capacity.

The balanced budget multiplier.

It is a commonly, but wrongly, held belief in some quarters that a balanced federal budget is not inflationary and will not cause unemployment or inflation. Those who believe that are wrong. Consider what would happen in our example economy with the $35.0 trillion level of income and full employment if the economy's government, as a result of being dedicated to a balanced budget, increased its spending by $1.0 trillion to buy new roads and military planes and levied an additional $1.0 trillion of taxes to pay for them: the equilibrium level of income would rise from $35.0 trillion to $37.0 trillion.

1. $-a + (1-b)Y = Ia$
   $+ eI + Fa + fF + Ga$
   $+ gG + bTr - bTx$
   $+ \text{new } G - b(\text{new } Tx)$

2. $-\$1.0 + .40Y = \$2.0$
   $+ .10Y + \$1.5 + .03Y$

$$+\$2.5 +.07Y +\$.6$$
$$-\$.6 +\$1.0 - \$.6$$

3. $.20Y = \$7.4$

4. $Y = \$37.0 \text{ trillion}$

The source of the increased level of total spending when government spending and taxes increase in equal amounts is that all of the government spending is used to buy new goods and services whereas some of the increased taxes may be paid out of income that would have not have been spent. Thus the initial effect is a $1 trillion increase in government spending and a $1.0 trillion tax increase that reduces disposable income and cuts consumption by $.6 trillion. So there is an initial spending increase of $.4 trillion that ripples through the economy and drives up total spending by $2.0 trillion. In other words, this economy has a balanced budget multiplier of two.

What this demonstrates, among other things, is that if the $35.0 trillion economy had been at full employment the "balance the budget" $1.0 trillion of additional spending and $1.0 trillion in additional taxes would have increased total spending to $37.0 trillion and caused inflation from too much spending. This economy's *balanced budget multiplier* is two.

Similarly, had the Congress gone in the other direction, a $1.0 trillion cut in federal spending balanced with a $1.0 trillion tax reduction would result in a $33.0 trillion level of spending and result in a recession.

In other words, *balanced budgets affect total spending and can cause inflations from too much spending or recessions from not enough spending.* What they do depends on the condition of the economy when the fiscal changes are implemented.

The importance of the multipliers.

The spending and other multipliers are significant for several reasons. First, they mean that an economy that needs a change in the level of customer spending to achieve a full employment level of income needs only an initial stimulus and that the stimulus can be either an additional purchase or an additional transfer or even involve a balanced budget; the subsequent spending and re-spending generated by the initial stimulus will do the rest.

On the other hand, if additional transfers are to be used to get the economy going again there will have to be more of them—because they won't all be spent to buy goods and services. Some might be used, for example, to pay down credit card debt and farm mortgages.

One important reality for policy makers to keep in mind when considering fiscal alternatives is that transfers do not yield as much bang for the government buck as government buying. In other words, *roads and other purchases are better for increasing total spending, and thus increasing production and jobs, than welfare and bailouts.*

On the other hand, increasing government purchases may take longer to implement than transfers due to the lack of "shovel ready" projects. If that's the case, transfers may still be a better way to go if an economy needs more spending to increase its production and employment.

Another important reality for policy makers to keep in mind is that matching spending and transfer changes with tax changes in order to have a balanced budget can cause total spending to change.

Fiscal Drag and balanced budgets.

It is often suggested by congressmen, journalists, and "business economists" that when the United States has a level of income and job creation that is inadequately low, that such as state of affairs exists because the economy's income is being held down by the "fiscal drag" of having tax rates set higher than would be required to have a balanced budget at full employment.

But would an economy's level of spending be "just right" if the fiscal drag is eliminated so that there would be a balanced budget when the economy operates at a full employment level of income? In other words, *are the advocates of this policy rational when they call for the economy's tax rates to be set so they will yield a balanced budget at full employment?*

Consider the economy whose total spending rose to $37.0 trillion because it had the balanced budget increase of $1.0 of additional government spending and $1.0 of additional taxes. What if this economy had a capacity to produce $45.0 trillion of goods and services? Obviously there would still be a lot of unemployed production capacity and a lot of unemployed people if the economy is only operating at a $37.0 trillion level of production.

This example of a balanced budget causing an increase or decrease in total spending is a pretty good general depiction of the situation that confronted United States' policy makers during the Great Recession when about twenty percent of its available labor force hours were idled or under-employed by inadequate levels of customer spending. Prominent congressmen called for a balanced budget reduction in federal spending and taxes to help end the recession and restore full employment; others wanted only a major reduction in spending—to cut federal spending back to the level needed to balance the budget and "restore prosperity."

Both proposals would have cut total spending and production, and increased the deficit and unemployment. Other congressmen pointed this out and proposed merely eliminating the "fiscal drag" by cutting tax rates back so they would yield a balanced budget at full employment.

It is absolutely true that the United States' federal government would collect more tax revenues if there was full employment so that its tax rates were applied to the wages, profits, and sales of a $45.0 trillion economy. Similarly, its transfer payments to the unemployed and the make-work spending for "jobs bills" would be reduced and subsequently tend to disappear as people and businesses go off welfare and back to work.

So consider some of the various alternatives the federal policy makers would have if the economy is operating with only $37 trillion of spending even though it has a capacity to produce $45 trillion of goods and services and its current tax rates would yield a $4 trillion surplus if the economy reaches the $45 trillion of total spending.

The policy makers might decide to balance the budget by spending the full employment surplus to buy stuff. Pork barrel projects would boom, lobbyists would salivate, and federal spending would increase would increase $4 trillion. The spending multiplier in this economy is five as the initial increase is spent and re-spent so there would be a $20 trillion spending increase to a total of $57 trillion.

As a result, the budget would be balanced, unemployment would be ended, and the $57 trillion of spending would undoubtedly cause a massive inflation since the economy's employers are only capable of producing $45 trillion of goods and services. It would also cause another budgetary surplus when the tax rates are applied to $57 trillion instead of just the $45 trillion of spending needed for full employment.

Alternately, the policy makers might decide to cut taxes by $4 trillion. That would certainly balance the budget—or would it. What a tax cut actually does to a budget deficit and the rest of the economy depends on whose taxes are cut. If the taxes are cut on hedge funds and investment bankers, a real possibility because their lobbyists are so influential and campaign-supporting that they already pay lower tax rates than other businesses, they might use all of it to increase their buying and selling of derivatives and currencies. Then the economy's total spending would remain at $37 trillion.

Or perhaps the employment taxes of the poorest Americans would be cut. They tend to have relatively high propensities to consume. If their propensity to consume is eighty percent, consumer spending would increase by an initial $3.2 trillion and cause an increase in total spending of $16 trillion for a total spending level of $53 trillion. Then total spending will be so high that there is an inflation. Also there is likely to be a budgetary surplus as the rates that would have resulted in a balanced budget at a $45 trillion dollar level of income are applied to the $53 trillion that occurs.

Or perhaps corporate taxes are cut by $4 trillion. The corporations might not use any of it to invest in new plant and equipment because they already have more than enough idle capital because total spending is only $37 trillion. Total spending would not change.

Or perhaps the lower tax rates might raise employer expectations and cause some of them to make $1 trillion of additional investment spending. That would increase total spending by $5 trillion to $42 trillion. That level of spending would increase production and reduce unemployment, but leave the economy with some unemployment. There would also tend to be a budget deficit because the tax rates are being applied to a level of income that is below $45 trillion.

Or employers might be so encouraged about the future that they increase their investment spending by $3 trillion and cause total spending to rise to $52 trillion and cause inflation and budgetary surpluses.

No one can know what the elected representatives and president of a vibrant democracy such as the United States will do or exactly how people and employers will react. But the one thing that is certain is that merely balancing the budget or eliminating "fiscal drag" is not a solution that is guaranteed to work or even improve things at all. *It depends* on the structure of the economy and how the budget is balanced and how the full employment surplus is eliminated.

The automatic stabilizers dampen income changes.

An initial change in an economy's customer spending tends to cause the economy's level of income to change by some multiple of the initial change. But a change in the size of a spending component that affects the level of income may not have a full multiplier effect—because of the offsetting changes it induces in the spending of other customers.

For example, consider the effect of a $2 trillion increase in investment or government spending in the $37 trillion economy: there will be a $10.0 trillion increase in the equilibrium level of income to $47.0. It would have gone even higher except that as income increases there tend to be offsetting increases in both taxes and business savings, and decreases in the level of transfers as people come off of welfare and go back to work.

Since these subsequent changes occur automatically and tend to keep an economy's level of income stabilized closer to its original level by offsetting the effect of any initial change, they are often referred to as *automatic stabilizers*. The term is particularly applied to governmental fiscal activities such as income taxes and transfer payments that automatically work against the prevailing spending trend.

And it works both ways—the decline in tax collections and increased welfare transfers to the unemployed which automatically result from a fall in an economy's level of income are automatic stabilizers that prevent the level of income from falling even further than it would otherwise fall; the increased tax collections and reduced welfare transfers which automatically occur as spending increases are automatic stabilizers that prevent the level of income from rising even further than it would otherwise rise.

The multiplier time period.

The various multipliers indicate the degree to which an economy's equilibrium level of income will change when there is a permanent change in the size of one of its spending components. But what time will elapse between the initial change and the attainment of the new equilibrium level of income? That is a significant question because it would be best for the economy if a change in government spending or taxes or monetary policies to change the supply of money fixed the problem quickly instead of taking years and years.

The past responses of the United States economy to various different changes that affect spending suggest that some take only a few months to impact total spending while years and years may pass before the effects of others are felt. *It depends* on the nature of the initial change and the conditions and relationships that exist in the economy when it occurs.

The length of time obviously depends on the speed with which individual spenders react to the income changes they experience and forecast. But changes in consumption and the other types of spending when there is an initial change may not wait until spending actually occurs. Instead, consumers and other spenders may see an initial change and quickly adjust their spending to the income levels they expect to subsequently occur as a result of it. Obviously, the better their forecasts and the more spenders are willing to act on their expectations, the faster the multiplier effect will be completed and the faster the economy will attain the new equilibrium level of income.

The differences between some alternatives seem fairly clear. For example, the federal government or the Federal Reserve putting $100 billion more into the hands of Social Security recipients every year would seem likely to increase spending and employment faster than putting the $100 billion into the hands of the states to build new roads or into the hands of nuclear power plant manufacturers and operators to build new nuclear plants—which might need years of planning and permits and litigation before production and employment finally begins.

Permanent and one-time changes.

The full multiplier effect of an initial spending change only occurs when the initial change is permanent. Thus, in the previous example the initial spending increase of $2.0 trillion would have to recur over and over again each year in order to permanently increase the annual level of income from $37.0 trillion to $47.0 trillion. But what if the $2.0 trillion was a one-time shot to "stimulate" the economy or "prime the pump?"

Obviously total spending in the economy would initially jump *towards* $47.0 trillion as the additional $2 trillion is spent and re-spent. But in the next time period the $2.0 trillion would go away. So spending would begin dropping back towards $37.0 trillion. What this means is that *the effect of a one-shot stimulus soon fades away*. In essence, temporary tax cuts and the government spending associated with a one-time "jobs bill" or "bail-out" can, at best, trigger a temporary bump in the level of income and employment but will not do much to take an economy out of a "Great Recession" and keep it out. In other words, "priming the pump" is a great political slogan but not a workable solution when an economy is in a recession.

Equilibrium is never reached.

Finally, it is important to note that the circumstances and relationships influencing consumer and other customer spending in an economy are continually changing: they are dynamic rather than unchanging or static. For example, new markets and products are located, new production processes developed, the labor force grows, propensities to consume change, and capital is consumed through use or accident. Changing circumstances such as these make it impossible to believe that all spending will remain constant long enough for a specific level of income to ever be attained. They also make it difficult to believe that the level of income observed at any point in time is actually an equilibrium level.

The most that can be expected of a dynamic economy such as that of the United States is that the level of income is always moving *toward* its equilibrium level. Analysis of the levels of purchasing and attempts to understand the equilibrium level of income and what influences it are important, however, even though they cannot be precisely estimated; they provide a general idea of the state of an economy, its direction and how much further a particular change will tend to carry it than it would otherwise go.

THE RELATIONSHIP BETWEEN INTEREST RATES AND THE LEVEL OF INCOME

An economy's equilibrium level of spending is determined by the spending of its customers—which can be influenced by many different things—including the interest rates which the various types of spenders confront. To the extent interest rates actually affect consumer and other types of spending, a different equilibrium level of income will exist for each general level of interest rates that might occur. The fact that changes in an economy's general level of interest rates primarily affect financial assets does not mean that interest rate changes are totally inconsequential for the real economy.

Major interest rate moves can affect spending by doing such things as changing the relationship between labor and capital in the production process and significantly changing the monthly payments that have to be made to buy housing and automobiles. Minor interest rate changes, in contrast, tend to primarily affect financial assets and have a negligible effect on total spending. In any event, the relationship between an economy's level of interest rates and its level of income is important for journalists and analysts to understand, if only because irrelevant efforts to change interest rates continue to be used by the Federal Reserve in its efforts to affect the consumer and other spending that generates production and jobs.

IS curves. The various combinations of interest rate levels and equilibrium incomes that can occur in an economy can be depicted graphically with a curve. Such a curve is the economy's *product market equilibrium curve* (IS) curve. It's a simple model of the reality that more and spending will tend to occur a lower and lower interest rates. The slope ("elasticity) of the curve reflects the responsiveness of an economy's total spending to changes that will occur in response to changes in the economy's general level of interest rates.

Analysts and model builders traditionally designate such a curve with the abbreviation IS because it depicts each combination of income and interest rates that fulfills the income equilibrium condition that the amount of investment (I) and other non-consumption spending equals the total amount of savings (S). Whatever its name, the curve is important to policy makers *because it represents the different levels of spending that will occur in an economy at different levels of interest rates.*

The shape and position of an economy's IS curve can be constructed in several ways. One approach uses the equilibrium income-determining formula Y= a + bY + I + F + G. Each level of income estimated with this formula and the level of interest rates associated with it provides one point on the IS curve. For example, when the various interest rate levels and income levels are those depicted in the Table 8-1 IS schedule, the economy's IS curve will be as it is in Figure 8-3 which depicts higher levels of income at lower levels of interest rates.

Table 8-1

A Hypothetical IS Schedule:

Interest Rate (percent)	Level of Income (trillions of dollars)
20%	10.0
15%	20.0
10%	30.0
5%	40.0

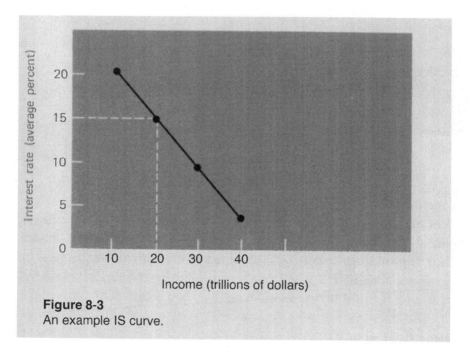

Figure 8-3
An example IS curve.

For modeling purposes an economy's IS curve can be generated with the aid of three other curves representing conditions in the economy. Together these curves represent the product market portion of the graphic model that is being developed.

The three curves include MEI curves which show how much investment purchasing will occur at each level of interest rates; 45-degree lines that help to aggregate graphically the various types of spending that must be offset with savings before an equilibrium level of spending can be reached; and savings functions which, as they indicate the level of savings that will occur at each level of income, provide the basis for identifying the level of income at which non-consumer spending will be offset by an equal amount of savings.

All the curves depicting conditions in the product market have been discussed previously except the 45-degree lines. These are merely graphical tool to move the amount of spending being measured on the vertical axis to the horizontal axis.

In the model all non-consumption spending is measured on the vertical axis and only the economy's investment spending that will occur at each level of interest rates is measured on the horizontal axis. Thus, for example, the model shows that the $40 billion of investment spending that occurs when the economy's interest rate is three percent will be added to $15 billion of foreign and government purchases for a total of $55 billion of non-consumption spending when the economy's average level of interest rates is three percent—and that this is enough to offset the savings that will occur at an equilibrium income level of about $580 billion.

In other words, the various spending-related equations being graphed in this simple model show that the investment and other non-consumer spending that will occur in the example economy when the interest rate is three percent will result in an income level of about $580 billion.

The IS curve is constructed for each interest rate in the following manner from the relationships depicted in the figure. First, the economy's savings function at a specific interest rate is used to determine how much savings will occur at a specific level of income such as $600 billion when the economy's money market yields a specific interest rate such as nine percent. The level of savings at that level of income tells you how much I+F+G will need to be injected into the economy at that interest rate to yield that income level. The MEI for that income level tells you how much investment will occur *at that interest rate and income level, and thus how much foreign and government spending will be needed to achieve that income level if the economy has that level of interest rates.*

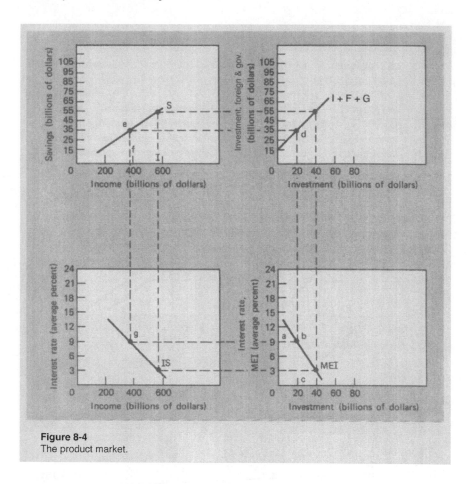

Figure 8-4
The product market.

Adding a bit of reality: the impact of replacement investment.

The tendency for more and more capital goods to be used up at higher and higher levels of production means there will be a different MEI curve for each level of income and, thus, that different levels of investment spending will occur at each level of interest rates. The Figure 8-5 MEI curves depict the higher and higher levels of investment spending that will occur at each level of interest rates when the economy has higher and higher levels of income.

The tendency for higher interest rates to discourage consumption and other spending and result in more savings is similarly depicted in Figure 8-5. It shows more savings at every level of income as interest rates get higher and higher. Putting the spending components together for the conditions depicted in this particular example yields an IS curve depicting an economy that will have an income level of $200 billion if interest rates average nine percent and $600 billion of total spending if they average three percent.

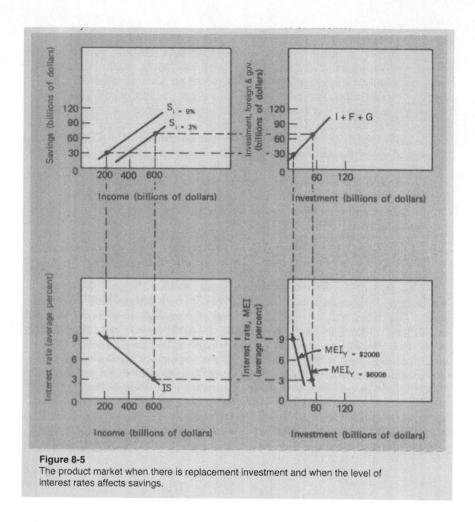

Figure 8-5
The product market when there is replacement investment and when the level of interest rates affects savings.

Changing government spending or sales to foreigners.

An economy's IS curve depicts the equilibrium levels of income that will occur in the economy at different levels of interest rates. But the amount of spending occurring in an economy can certainly be changed by doing more than just increasing or decreasing interest rates. For instance, export sales to foreigners or government spending may increase for reasons that have nothing to do with interest rates.

Consider the effect of an increase in export sales such as might accompany a trade agreement between the United States and Korea or a group of South American nations. Such an increase, unless it's a temporary one shot affair, will cause an even greater increase in the level of income as its multiplier effect generates additional consumption and other types of spending. The basic impact is depicted in Figure 8-6 for an economy in which, for the sake of exposition, there is no change in the level of interest rates or anything else.

Delta F represents the increased foreign spending and its impact is depicted by an upward shift in the 45-degree line. The resulting new IS curve lies to the right of the original IS curve since there will now be a higher equilibrium level of income at every level of interest rates. Similar results will occur with any other change that tends to increase the level of spending at each interest-rate level. Exactly opposite effects occur when something tends to drive the level of spending lower.

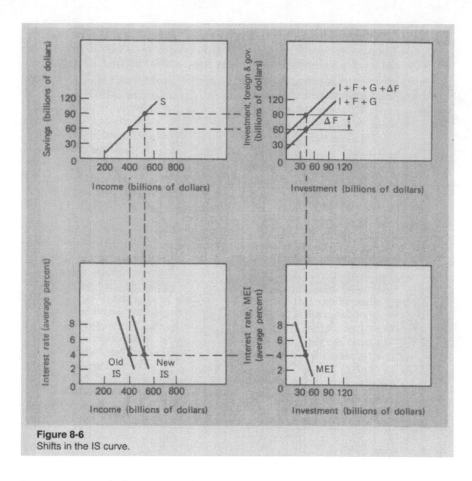

Figure 8-6
Shifts in the IS curve.

Long-run and short-run changes.

The analysis up to this point has proceeded as if an economy has only one set of interest and income combinations to depict with an IS curve. But both consumer spending and investment spending have long-run and short-run relationships with the level of income. This means that the equilibrium level of spending may be at one level in the short run and somewhere else when in the long run.

Knowledge of how an economy's level of income relates and responds to various levels of interest rates is important to policy makers, particularly those at the Federal Reserve who seem to be focus their policies on interest rate changes. For example, if an economy's interest rates are reduced and maintained at a new and lower level, the total of investment and other spending in the economy may initially increase *but, then, subsequently decline to only replacement levels of investment spending as employers complete their efforts to build up their stocks of production capital.*

But similarly important is the reality that consumer and other spending may differ in the short run from the amount that will occur in the long run Thus it is similarly important for policy makers to know the extent and speed with which consumers will expand their consumption spending as they become accustomed to the higher levels of income that might result from the lower interest rates. For instance, will consumer spending rise fast enough to offset the decline in investment spending as the economy's capital stock reaches the equilibrium level associated with a new and lower level of interest rates?

Figure 8-7 depicts the short-run and long-run savings functions, MEI curves, and IS curves for an economy that is initially in long-run equilibrium at an interest rate of nine percent and an equilibrium level of income of $400 billion. Notice that the tendency for larger short-run levels of investment spending at interest rates below nine percent is partially offset by the short-run delays of consumers in adjusting to the higher levels of income. What this suggests is that policy makers and their economic modelers need to keep in mind that consumer and other spending may or may not lag in responding to changes in the level of income.

Modelers and policy makers should particularly note that the conditions and relationships in an economy may be such that a temporarily higher level of spending may occur in the short run if interest rates are reduced. They need to keep in mind that once the capital stock reaches the levels appropriate for a new level of interest rates investment spending, and the additional consumer spending it generates, will stop increasing once investment spending declines to the replacement levels associated with that new and larger stock.

In other words, don't make the mistake of recent Federal Reserve officials and claim your monetary policies are sufficient if there is an initial burst of spending and job gains because your policies have driven down interest rates—only to see most of the initial gains quickly disappear as the effects of the initial increase fall away.

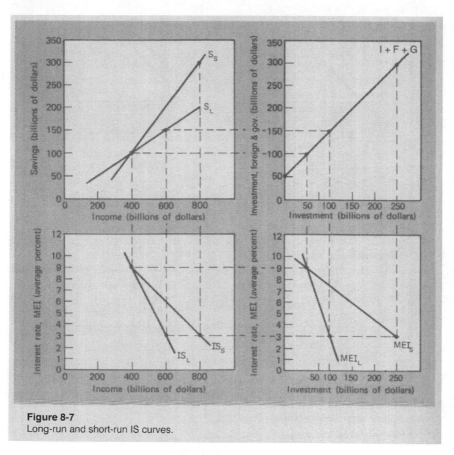

Figure 8-7
Long-run and short-run IS curves.

Consider the economy depicted in Figure 8-7. If interest rates decline to three percent, for example, the long-run equilibrium level of income would rise from $400 billion to $600 billion while in the short-run the level of income could reach as high as $800 billion. If the policy makers' goal is a level of spending such as $800 billion to obtain full employment, and they take steps to get spending to that level, the policy makers need to realize that the economy is going to end up short of having enough spending after the initial burst of increased spending occurs.

Thus, for example, a one-time payment of a few hundred dollars to Social Security recipients to "jump start" or "prime the pump" of a flagging economy may result in an initial surge of consumption spending but its impact will soon be over with consumption spending returning to its normal level for the current state of the economy. *In other words, short-run changes in an economy's level of income associated with one-time events are not likely to hold up in the long run.*

COMBINING THE MONEY AND PRODUCT MARKETS

Figure 8-8 brings together both the money market and the product market of an economy. On the money market side the LM curve shows the various combinations of interest rates and income levels that can exist in the economy that will put its money market in equilibrium. On the product market side the IS curve shows the various combinations of interest and spending that will put the economy's total spending for the products of its employers in equilibrium. Bringing the two markets together illustrates a very important concept: only one level of interest rates and one level of total spending can exist in an economy at any one point in time—*that is the equilibrium combination of interest rate and spending levels towards which the economy constantly moves.*

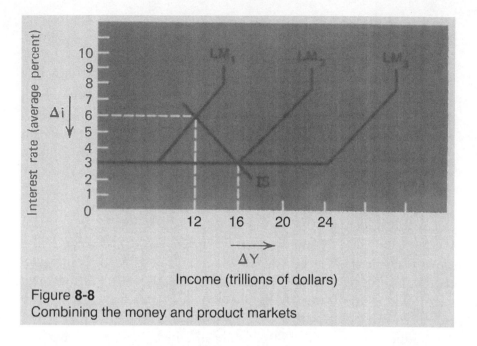

Figure **8-8**
Combining the money and product markets

No other combination of interest rates and total spending can be maintained because either or both of the level of interest rates and level of total spending will not be in equilibrium. In other words an economy such as that of the United States will inexorably move toward that one and only level of income and one and only level of interest rates that can exist in an economy at any point in time with the conditions and relationships that exist in the economy.

For the purposes of analysis consider the impact on the example economy when the monetary conditions are those depicted by LM1. Then the equilibrium level of interest rates will be six percent and the equilibrium level of spending is $12 trillion.

But what if the level of total spending required for full employment in the economy is $20 trillion?

If this is the United States economy the Federal Reserve could engage in quantitative easing. It might, for example, engage in quantitative easing (QE1) and increase the money supply so extensively that LM2 represents the new and lower level of interest rates that will tend to exist at every level of total spending.

When spending increases as a result of such a money supply increase the United States would move towards a new economic equilibrium with more production and more people at work. In this example the additional money provided by the Federal Reserve drives down the average level of interest rates to three percent and total spending increases to buy $16 trillion of newly produced goods and services. Monetary policy works!

But wait. The economy has a labor force and supply of plant and equipment capable of producing $20 trillion. Innumerable journalists, "business economists," and Federal Reserve governors will quickly see the answer: the economy needs a third round of quantitative easing (QE3). So again the money supply is increased and there is a new LM3 curve to depict the results—absolutely nothing.

This time the additional money pours into the financial system and some of it finds its way to the commercial banks—and is *not* loaned out because interest rates are already as low as they can go. Any lower and they would not even cover the cost of administering the loans. The economy is in the Keynesian version of the liquidity trap!

In essence, QE1 increases spending, and production and employment and QE2 increases spending and production even more. But another quantitative easing (QE3) won't work because the economy will be in the liquidity trap after the first two.

But wait. The economy may not be doomed to remain forever in a recession or depression with twenty percent of its production capacity is unemployed. Perhaps something can be done to encourage more spending at every level of interest rates—more spending by governments or foreigners or investors or consumers would work. And, at this point, more spending that is not related to interest rates is the only possible answer.

Figure 8-9 depicts the effects of such an increase in the buying of goods and services. The IS curve shifts to the right to reflect that more newly produced goods and services will be bought at every level of interest rates.

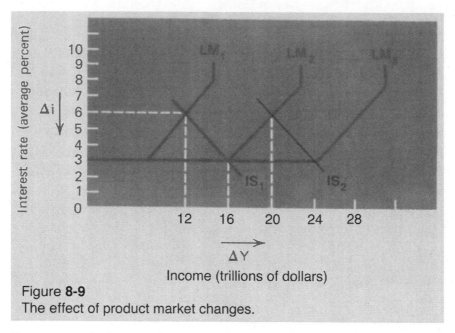

Figure 8-9
The effect of product market changes.

But even with the spending increase this economy is in the Keynesian liquidity trap and still short of having enough spending to generate full employment.

This is exactly the situation the United States found itself in during the Great Recession. Obviously more needs to be done to increase spending and get people back to work. The question, of course, is how to get the required spending increase—and the quicker the better because unless spending is increased there will be a tendency for more and more businesses and banks to fail and for unemployment, foreclosures, bankruptcies, and deficits to grow.

But all is not lost even though lowering interest rates is no longer a viable option because they are already as low as they can go. Even if the economy is in the Keynesian liquidity trap of minimum interest rates or the recessionary liquidity trap caused by repayment fears and regulatory requirements, the Federal Reserve can still generate the changes needed to increase total spending.

In other words, it is possible for the United States to get out of a recession or depression without government "jobs bills" and lower taxes that result in bigger deficits; without new laws and regulations to spread the available jobs around; without more selling to foreigners; and without inflationary increases in the money supply. How the Federal Reserve can accomplish this will be discussed in detail in the policy chapters that follow.

In essence, in terms of the graphic model, even when their traditional quantitative easings fail the governors and regional presidents still have the power to move the IS curve as far to the right as it needs to go. What this means, as analysts will subsequently see, is that monetary policy can work even when there is a Keynesian or a regulation-related liquidity trap. Whether the Federal Reserve's decision makers are sufficiently knowledgeable to do so, of course, is another question entirely.

The basic combination of money and product markets.

Figure 8-10 provides a more complete picture of the relationship between the money and product markets. If an analyst had viable equations and data for each of the curves the analyst would, at least conceptually, be able to solve them and determine the impact on total spending of any policies that might be instituted.

In this particular example economy the equilibrium level of income is $12 trillion and the equilibrium level of interest rates is six percent. That is where the economy's total spending and interest rates are inexorably headed—and *there is no reason to believe that $12 trillion is the right level of total spending for the economy at this or any other point in time*: it may be too little and thus result in massive unemployment; or it may be too large and result in inflation.

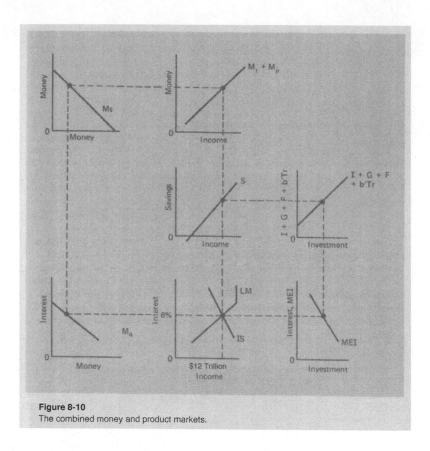

Figure 8-10
The combined money and product markets.

CHAPTER SUMMARY

I. The sum total of all customer spending to buy newly produced goods and services from an economy's employers is known as the "level of income." That is a reasonable definition because, conceptually, all the money spent to buy the goods and services is received by the public and private employers who produce them

II. Consumer and other customer spending not only affects the level of income but also depends on the level of income.

III. The equilibrium level of income is the only one that can be maintained. It will continue until there is a permanent spending change in one or more of the major customer categories.

IV. The equilibrium level of income can be identified using either the consumption portion of purchasing with the consumption function or the non-consumption portion with the savings function.

V. Customer moves to bring the actual amounts of their spending into line with amounts they want to spend each level of income are the forces that move an economy's spending towards its one possible equilibrium level and the specific customer spending that will occur at that one level.

VI. Because money can be spent and re-spent, an initial change in customer spending can cause the level of income to increase or decrease more than the amount of the initial change.

VII. The amount of the multiplier effect of an initial permanent change in spending, taxes, and transfers can be determined with the multiplier formulas.

VIII. Government transfers do not have the same impact on production and employment as government purchases. This occurs to the extent the transfer recipients save rather than spend the transfers they receive.

IX. Balanced budgets are not neutral. They can result in increased total spending if federal spending and taxes are increased in the same amount. As a result, the spending associated with a balanced budget can cause inflation from too much spending.

X. One-time spending increases do not stimulate the economy to move to a permanently higher level of income.

XI. "Fiscal drag" is the budgetary surplus that will exist at full employment levels of income. Eliminating fiscal drag does *not* guarantee that an economy will have enough spending to reach full employment levels of production.

XII. Automatic stabilizers are the fiscal actions that occur automatically to mitigate spending changes that would cause changes in an economy's level of income.

XIII. Because economies such as the United States are dynamic and conditions within them ever changing, the equilibrium level of income is only the level towards which economies move but never reach.

XIV. Different equilibrium levels of income exist at different interest rate levels. An equilibrium level of income may exist that is insufficient to generate the revenues needed for full employment levels of production

CHAPTER NINE

INCOME FLUCTUATIONS AND THE BUSINESS CYCLE

It is a historical fact that spending has at times fluctuated in economies such as the United States and that this has periodically caused inflation and unemployment. Little wonder then that over the years various economists have attempted to explain why income fluctuations occur. Frequently they are discussed in terms of the "business cycle" in response to the fact that business revenues rise and fall as customer spending rises or falls.

Some of the more common of the business cycle explanations as to why and how spending fluctuates are described below. They need to be understood if an economy's decision makers are to knowledgeably consider the various policies that might be implemented to stabilize an economy's spending at whatever levels will result in minimal rates of inflation and unemployment.

In essence, responding to inflation and unemployment requires understanding why spending fluctuates. It also requires understanding the policies that might reasonably be implemented to stop the fluctuations and the many more income stabilization policies that have been advocated but have never worked and never will—because they are not applicable to the conditions and realities of the real world.

Monetary theories of income fluctuations.

Domestic and foreign central banks, commercial and investment banks, and other financial intermediaries, trading houses, and speculators may all modify their behavior in some way and cause changes in an economy's level of customer spending. This, in turn, may change the revenues and incomes of the economy's public and private employers—thus, affecting their workers and governments and others that end up receiving and spending the money the employers receive. Other holders and users of money and credit can also change what their behavior and similarly affect total spending.

The pre-Keynesians, early Keynesians, and neo-classical analysts date themselves, and the state of their economic knowledge and understanding of the real world, by referring to income fluctuations as "business cycles" and discussing them as if each is an inevitable phenomenon that occurs naturally such that it can be charted and predicted. Pragmatic economists, on the other hand, attribute income fluctuations primarily to poor monetary and fiscal policies—and they do not believe incompetent policy makers arrive and perform poorly in a predictable or cyclical pattern. They are also aware that research by Vernon Smith and Steven Gjerstad suggests the income fluctuations of the past have been misattributed to business-related changes in investment spending; that the income fluctuations are much more closely associated with changes in consumer durable purchases, particularly housing, such that the "business cycle" would be better named as the "consumer durable cycle."

Among the changes, for example, that might cause spending to rise and fall are the arrival and departure of new credit arrangements and new forms of derivatives. These could change the demand for an economy's money and credit and affect its spending both directly as well as indirectly by affecting its interest rates; or an economy's central bank and other domestic and international depositories and holders could change the amount of money available to be held as reserves and, thus, change the quantity of the money; or its foreign customers of its employers might find a new and less expensive source of the products they had been buying.

Alternately, various participants in an economy may modify their activities in response to the economy's existing monetary conditions and characteristics. For example, a major trading firm such as Morgan Stanley might wake up as it did not long ago and find itself highly leveraged with $58 trillion (yes, trillion) of derivatives and credit default swaps. It had so many that its bond rating was about to be reduced to junk status because of the growing likelihood of defaults which would destroy Morgan Stanley and, most probably, many of its customers and counterparties.*

Wags among pragmatic analysts have suggested that the rating agencies' untrained "experts" have been so consistently wrong in the past that the fact that they were considering such a move probably indicated that Morgan Stanley's risks were not as excessive as they appeared.

Morgan's response was to petition the Federal Reserve to let it transfer the derivatives to the commercial bank it established to get bail out money when the mortgage crisis hit. The transfer would allow Morgan to retain its bond rating and, thus, be able to keep borrowing money to "trade" with. That would be the fair thing to do, Morgan argued, because the Federal Reserve had already allowed a similar large transfer of potential derivative losses to another new-so-we-can-receive-more-bail-outs commercial bank of one of its competitors (Goldman Sachs).

Fairness aside, a slight blip in the derivatives market and both those newly minted make-believe commercial banks are more likely to need another bailout than to keep (read start) making significant amounts of loans to consumers and employers.

In other words, lots of complex money-related things can and do continually happen that might cause spending fluctuations in a modern market-oriented economy such as the United States—so long as the country's monetary and fiscal decision makers orient themselves to the problems of the *financial markets* instead of taking action to maintain the level of spending needed in the *product markets* to maintain full employment without causing inflation.

And that, of course, requires that the members of Congress and the Federal Reserve's governors and regional presidents have at least a clue as to why total spending changes, and how monetary and fiscal policy can operate in the real world to stabilize total spending at the ever-changing and ever-growing best possible level of income.

Interest rates and inventories. One of the earliest explanations of income fluctuations emphasizes the effect of inventory changes in response to changes in the general level of an economy's interest rates. The main villain in these explanations is a lowering of the economy's interest rates by the economy's central bank: that lets the commercial banks make loans at lower interest rates. That, in turn, encourage retailers and wholesalers to build up their inventories; so total purchasing increases. The increased inventory purchases mean higher incomes for both the employers and their workers and the other recipients of their revenues—which leads to even more spending increases.

The additional purchasing then leads to even more purchasing as even larger inventories are needed to handle the new and higher levels of business the employers are experiencing. The upturn is then further fueled by the price increases that occur as a result of the increased purchasing. Moreover, the higher prices result in higher profits for both the producers and retailers because increases in their wages and other costs lag behind the price increases—and because the retailers and wholesalers can sell products from their inventories which were bought earlier at lower prices. The entire business community is, therefore, encouraged to buy even more goods to further build up their inventories before prices rise.

The upturn comes to an end when the central bank stops making low interest loans and the commercial banks start to run out of excess reserves and begin to increase their interest rates. The higher interest rates reduce the stock of inventory that is desired and, as a result, goods are sold out of inventories and not replaced. As a result the sales of the economy's employers begin to decline and their retailers and wholesalers need to hold even smaller inventories—so there is a decline in both purchasing from manufacturers and the desire to borrow money from banks.

Finally, enough loans are repaid, the amount of money needed for transactions and precautions purposes is sufficiently reduced, and the banks have such excess reserves that they begin to lower their interest rates to compete for loan customers. Inventory buildups are then encouraged and the income fluctuating interest-inventory cycle begins anew.

Underinvestment and overinvestment theories. Another early "business cycle" explanation of the fluctuations in an economy's level of income is that the spending fluctuations occur as a result of business investment purchasing rising or falling below the levels needed to offset the savings generated by the economy's level of interest rates or income. In this explanation, the business cycle begins when the central bank creates money for banks to loan out in addition to the money provided by the economy's savers. This results in more being spent for investment purchases than is saved, so the level of spending increases.

More specifically, the interest rate-inventory cycle starts when a central bank is encouraged by the commercial banks to provide them with more reserves so they can make more loans and increase their profits. Injecting the additional money into the economy then results in lower interest rates which, in turn, encourage employers to adopt more capital intensive methods of production. The investment spending the businesses make to buy the additional capital goods then launches the economy into a spending-related cycle of inflation and unemployment.

It works like this: when the additional investment spending increases, it drives the level of total spending higher until a new and higher equilibrium level is reached—the level which generates enough additional savings to offset the new and higher level of investment spending. But only so much production can occur in an economy at any point in time. Thus, if the economy is already at full employment, only prices in the economy will be increased as a result of the additional investment spending and the other spending increases it causes.

The higher prices caused by the *"overinvestment"* spending triggered by the lower interest rates means that fewer noncapital goods and services can be purchased by the other purchasers in the economy whose money incomes lag behind the increases in the prices. Such a lag is assumed to occur so that the higher prices reduce the amount of production that is bought for non-capital purposes and, thus, frees up more of the economy's labor and capital to be devoted to the production of plant and equipment.

But the lagging wages and other incomes do eventually rise and, as they do, there is more and more demand for non-capital goods and services so that prices and profits rise in these industries. Simultaneously, the rising wages and other incomes mean higher costs of production in the capital goods industry so that the profits of its employers tend to be reduced. With their rising profit margins the employers in the non-capital industries are then able to bid workers back from the capital goods industry.

Furthermore, as prices and the level of income rise the banks begin to run out of the additional reserves provided by the central bank; so interest rates begin to rise and the level of investment purchasing further contracts. The higher interest rates and lower profit margins then discourage further borrowing and investment begins to decline below the level needed to maintain the new and higher level of income.

The economy is now in a condition of "*underinvestment*" and its level of total spending declines until the reduced demand for investment loans causes interest rates to fall while simultaneously profits from the production of capital goods rise as a result of the reduced demand for consumer and other noncapital goods and services leads their producers to be less competitive for the available labor and capital. Then investment spending begins to rise and the spending cycle begins again.

Where they fail. What is wrong with these business cycle theories? Changes in investment spending and interest rates can and do occur as a result of central bank activities that affect the supply of money and credit. Astute analysts, however, question the underinvestment and overinvestment explanations of income fluctuations because they assume relationships and conditions that do not exist in the real world.

The analysts know, for example, that savings is more related to income than to interest rates; that the outflow of savings from the spending stream is offset by the total of foreign, government, and investment purchases, not just investment;

They also know that the Federal Reserve need not make one-time additions to liquidity so that the banks will run out and start raising interest rates; income equilibrium wherein savings is equal to investment (and more) can occur at a level of income that is so low that spending increases do not cause inflation from too much spending;

They also know that savings is all income that is not spent and thus much more than just the money that is deposited into banks; that production costs per unit may not change if the size of the stock of capital changes; and they know that the Federal Reserve can adjust the supply of money and credit so that interest rates in the economy need not change as the level of income changes.

In essence, the problem with such business cycle explanations is that they overstate the importance of investment spending and assume an economy will be in equilibrium at full employment levels of income so that an increase in spending will cause inflation and change factor prices. In essence, the overinvestment and underinvestment explanations fall apart when there is unemployment so that people go back to work and produce more instead of prices rising.

They also fall apart because: they require that wages and prices be flexible; they assume the central bank will only make a one-time injection of money and then leave the economy to rise and fall instead of continuing to add money as needed to maintain full employment without inflation; they assume the central bank will put the interests of the commercial banks ahead of the interest of the economy's workers, employers, and governments; they assume that there are no other spenders such as foreigners or governments to influence total spending or to offset the effects of the changes in investment spending; and they assume that all employers making investment purchases are profit oriented.

In other words, such explanations of the "business cycle" are scientifically sound and immensely logical—they just don't fit the real world.

Entrepreneurs and innovative changes.

Innovation, the introduction of something new, is not the same as inventing it. Examples of innovators and innovations might be Steve Jobs introducing personal computers even though Xerox invented them first; Sony introducing digital cameras even though Kodak invented them first; Microsoft introducing software and desktop computer concepts that IBM invented; fracking changing the use of natural gas relative to other energy sources; and Walmart selling large amounts of goods produced in China.

Innovative changes in the structure of an economy are the source of both growth and income fluctuations according to economists such as the late Joseph Schumpeter. They typically start their explanations with an economy in equilibrium with full employment, every employer producing efficiently, and product prices being equal to average and marginal costs. Then, in an effort to obtain profits, an entrepreneur disturbs the equilibrium by introducing an innovative modification such as a new technique of production or financing, or introducing a new product even if someone else invented it, or finding unserved customers, or establishing or reorganizing a business or industry, or finding a new source of supply.

If the innovations introduced by entrepreneurs are successful, the entrepreneurs make profits. And the profits attract imitators who seek to share them by duplicating the original innovations. It is the subsequent alteration of an economy's structure that flows from an entrepreneur's initial innovation that is the essence of economic progress.

But innovation has cyclical effects as well. The initial spending by the entrepreneur must bid workers and capital products away from other uses and the subsequent increases in investment purchases by the imitators drive the economy's income, and sometimes its prices, even higher. Finally, the increases in prices and income are reversed by both the tendency for the imitators to complete their wave of additional investment purchasing and the increase in production that may begin to flow from the new facilities and processes. The economy then turns back toward equilibrium at a lower level of income with a new and more productive structure.

Further influencing an economy's price and income movements is the possibility that the optimism generated during the period of expansion may lead both to the innovation of other modifications and to an expansion of production in the unmodified sectors as a result of the general increases in purchasing. In other words, the newly employed and affluent Apple and Microsoft engineers and programmers will tend to buy more cars, homes, and haircuts.

However, once the upswing in income stops a decline sets in; certain employers whose success and existence are based on producing goods and services for the expansion become overextended and fail. Lenders become pessimistic in view of the receding income levels and the business failures. Loans and other financial advances to entrepreneurs are held in abeyance so that the downturn becomes a period of net borrower repayments.

The economy then turns itself around when the repayments cause loanable funds to pile up in the hands of lenders and financial institutions and more and more inventions keep occurring to open up additional innovative opportunities for entrepreneurs. Finally the economy's entrepreneurs begin to be able to get the funds they need to introduce new innovations, and another upturn occurs in the economy's income cycle.

The principle of acceleration.

The accelerator principle is an early business cycle theory that explained an economy's fluctuating level of income in terms of the investment changes occurring in response to changes in the economy's optimum stock of capital goods. Specifically, it starts with investment spending only occurring for replacement purposes because an economy's employers already have the optimum stock of capital goods needed to produce their share of the production. Under such circumstances, investment spending in excess of replacement needs will occur only if the level of income in the economy is increased so that more capital is needed to produce the additional goods and services that can be sold.

Then something happens to increase total spending. Then investment spending rises above of the original replacement-only investment spending. The increase occurs because employers now need a larger stock of capital to produce the larger amount of goods and services they can now sell. The additional investment spending then itself further increases total spending which then causes employers to need even more plant and equipment and make even more investment purchases.

But the increased level of income is difficult to maintain because it is based on investment purchasing in excess of replacement needs. If there are no spending-increasing forces to keep the level of income expanding fast enough, investment spending will begin to decline. Then the level of income will tend to fall. Then, since a smaller stock of capital is needed to produce the goods and services that can be sold at the lower level of income, capital assets that wear out may not be replaced so that investment spending, and thus the level of income, will decline further.

Finally, enough capital will wear out and investment purchasing will begin again for replacement purposes. Then even more investment purchasing will have to occur in order to provide the capital stock needed to produce the now higher level of production that can be sold.

An example of the acceleration effect on investment and income is depicted in Table 9-1 for an economy with a 2:1 capital-output ration whose level of income permanently rises $10 billion in time period T3 due to some extraneous change such as an increase in foreign or government purchasing. Investment spending in each time period is based on the capital consumption and changes in the optimum stock of capital that occurred in the previous time period. It is also assumed that $1 of capital will have to be replaced for every $5 of production and that, except for the initial$10 billion income increase, all subsequent changes in the economy's level of income will be caused by changes in the level of investment purchasing. (this totally unrealistic restriction will be removed in the next section which adds the multiplier effects, which were discussed earlier in some detail.)

In this example economy an initial $10 billion increase in purchasing in time period T3 results in a two percent increase in the economy's level of income. This, in turn, increases the amount of capital needed by the economy's employers so in the next period they add $20 billion of additional investment spending to the replacement investment spending they are already doing.

The employers make that additional investment expenditure to tool up to produce for the increased customer demand. The result, in this case, is a twenty two percent increase in the economy's investment spending in time period T4. The economy's level of income in time period T4 thus rises by the amount of the additional investment purchasing and, as a result, even more investment purchasing occurs in subsequent time periods.

The income increases continue to result in even greater investment increases until the economy reaches an income peak in time period 6. Then income begins to decline as the growth in the economy's level of income is insufficient to encourage enough additional investment spending so that the higher level of income is maintained. The level of income then declines as a result of the reduced investment spending. The lower income then reduces the amount of capital needed by the economy's employers and so further reduces their investment spending.

Finally, the level of income bottoms out in time period 9 and begins to rise again in period 12 when the economy has finished consuming the capital stock that is not required at the low levels of income and begins to again experience investment buying. The resulting increase in the level of income accelerates investment spending and the cycle begins anew.

Table 9-1
The Acceleration Effect (Billions of Dollars)

Time Period	GNP	Optimum Capital Stock	Desired Net Capital Addition	Replacement Investment	Total Inv.
1	500	1000	0	100	100
2	500	1000	0	100	100
3	510	1020	0	100	100
4	532	1064	20	102	122
5	560.4	1120.8	44	106.4	150.4
6	578.9	1157.8	56.8	112.1	168.9
7	562.8	1125.6	37	115.8	152.8
8	490.4	980.8	−32.2	112.6	80.4
9	410	820	−144.8	98.1	0°
10	410	820	−160.8	82.0	0°
11	410	820	0	82.0	0°
12	448.5	897	0	82.0	38.5°
13	576.7	1153.4	77	89.7	166.7
14	825.7	1651.4	296.4	119.3	415.7
15	1033.1	2066.2	458.0	165.1	623.1
16	1031.4	2062.8	414.8	206.6	621.4
17	612.9	1225.8	−3.4	206.3	202.9
18	410	820	−837.0	122.6	0
19	410	820	−405.8	82.0	0

* Total investement is less than the economy's replacement requirements because capital comsumed need not be replaced since the economy's actual stock exceeds its optimum stock.

The accelerator-multiplier interaction.

The trouble with a simple accelerator explanation of income fluctuations is that it ignores the multiplier effect caused by an initial change in the level of spending. What actually happens to an economy when something causes an initial change in spending depends on the resulting interaction between the economy's multiplier and accelerator effects.

The change in total spending that occurs when there is an initial spending change depends on the size of the multiplier and the size of the capital-output ratio which tells us how much investment spending will occur so that employers can both replace capital that wears out and produce the additional goods and services that can now be sold.

There are four major types of multiplier-accelerator combinations, and each has a different effect on an economy's level of income when there is an initial change in customer spending. They vary according to the accelerator and multiplier values and are depicted graphically in Figure 9-1.

Each of the figures shows the effect of one of the combinations of an initial increase in the level of income beginning in time period 3 when the economy is initially is in equilibrium at $1000 billion of income. Notice that the different combinations have different effects. Notice also that the economy moves to new and higher equilibrium levels of income with multiplier and capital-output combinations of types in cases I and II and that it will explode to infinitely high levels of income with combinations III and IV *because each increase in income will result in an even greater increase in investment spending in the next period.*

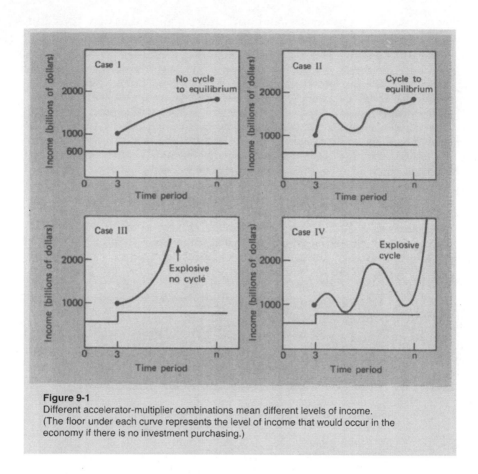

Figure 9-1
Different accelerator-multiplier combinations mean different levels of income.
(The floor under each curve represents the level of income that would occur in the
economy if there is no investment purchasing.)

The various multiplier and accelerator values in each of the four basic
combinations are identified in Figure 9-2. The "k" on the horizontal
axis of Figure 9-2 is the accelerator value relating investment spending
to changes in the level of income. It is the economy's marginal
capital-output ratio. For example, k is 0.1 if it takes $2 billion of
additional investment purchasing to provide the additional capital to
produce $20 billion of additional goods and services in each subsequent
time period.

The economy's income multiplier is measured on the vertical axis of
Figure 9-2 and is the sum of the economy's marginal propensity to
consume and the economy's marginal capital output ratio. Thus, if
the economy's marginal propensity to consume out of total income is

0.5Y and 0.2Y of replacement investment is required to maintain the economy's stock of capital, the multiplier component on the vertical axis would be 0.7 and the economy's income multiplier would be 1/(1.0-.0.7)=3.33.

Thus, for example, an increase in government spending in an economy with "k" value of 0.1 and a multiplier component of 0.7 (a 3.33 income multiplier) would have a Case I "smooth climb to equilibrium" effect on income; with a "k" value of 0.5 it would be a "cycle to equilibrium" effect on income; With a K value of 1.5 it would be an explosive cycle of spending to an infinitely high level.

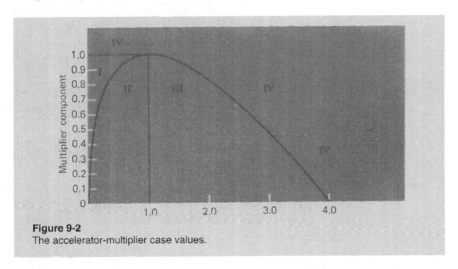

Figure 9-2
The accelerator-multiplier case values.

Tables 9-2, 9-3, and 9-4 are examples of the period by period spending changes that occur in a $1000 billion economy as the multiplier and accelerator forces interact in response to a $100 million increase in government purchasing. The tables show the period by period changes that will occur in total spending and how they are affected by the economy's marginal capital-out ratios (the "k" value).

"I" is the total level of investment spending initially occurring and is composed of "Ir" which is the replacement investment required as a result of the production that occurs in the previous period; "Ia" is the investment spending required to build up the economy's capital stock so its employers can produce more in response to a spending increase that occurs in the previous period t-1; c is the propensity to consume; Ii is the investment spending to replace capital worn out during the previous time period; and r is the percentage of the level on income in the previous time period that must be devoted to replacing capital consumed during the previous time period in order to maintain the economy's stock of capital.

Algebraically, Y=C+G+F+Ii+Ia and the example economy is initially in equilibrium with a $1000 billion level of income consisting of:

C = $500 billion
Ir = $200 billion
Ia = $0
G = $200 billion
F = $100 billion
c = .5
r = .2

Begin, for the sake of an example, by assuming that for some reason the level of government spending rises from $200 billion to $300 billion in time period 3. This initial increase in customer spending then has both a conventional multiplier effect and induces the economy's employers to buy more capital goods so that then can produce the additional goods and services they can now sell. How customer spending responds in subsequent time periods then depends on the size of the economy's multiplier and its capital-out ratios (see tables).

Table 9-2
Case I Multiplier - Accelerator Interaction K = 0.1

Period	Y	C	I	G	F	I_r	I_a
1	1,000	500	200	200	100	200	0
2	1,000	500	200	200	100	200	0
3	1,100	500	200	300	100	200	0
4	1,180	550	230	300	100	220	10
5	1,234.0	590	244	300	100	236	8.0
6	1,269.2	617	252.2	300	100	246.8	5.4
7	1,292.0	634.6	257.4	300	100	253.8	3.5
8	1,306.6	646.0	260.7	300	100	258.4	2.3
9	1,316.1	653.3	262.8	300	100	261.3	1.5
10	1,322.2	658.1	264.2	300	100	263.2	.9
11	1,326.2	661.1	265.1	300	100	264.4	.6
12	1,328.7	663.1	265.6	300	100	265.2	.4
13	1,330.4	664.4	266.0	300	100	265.7	.3
14	↓	↓	↓	↓	↓	↓	↓
15							
n	1,333.3	666.67	266.66	300	100	266.66	0
(equilibrium reached)							

Table 9-3
Case IV Multiplier - Accelerator Interaction K = 60

Period	Y	=	C	+	I	+	G	+	F	I_r	I_i
1	1,000		500		200		200		100	200	0
2	1,000		500		200		200		100	200	0
3	1,100		500		200		300		100	200	0
4	1,770		550		820		300		100	220	600
5	5,659		885		4,374		300		100	354	4,020
6	27,695.3		2,829.5		24,465.8		300		100	1,131.8	23,334
7							↓		↓	↓	↓
8	↓		↓		↓						
n	∞		∞		∞		300		100	∞	∞
(No equilibrium reached)											

Table 9-4
Case II Multiplier - Accelerator Interaction k = .9

Period	Y	C	I	G	F	I_r	I_a
1	1,000	500	200	200	100	200	0
2	1,000	500	200	200	100	200	0
3	1,100	500	200	300	100	200	0
4	1,260	550	310.0	300	100	220	90.0
5	1,426	630.0	396.0	300	100	252.0	144.0
6	1,547.6	713.0	434.6	300	100	285.2	149.4
7	1,592.8	773.8	418.9	300	100	309.5	109.4
8	1,555.6	796.4	359.2	300	100	318.6	40.6
9	1,455.4	777.8	277.6	300	100	311.1	−33.5
10	1,328.7	727.7	201.0	300	100	291.1	−90.1
11	1,216.0	664.3	151.6	300	100	265.7	−114.1
12	1,149.8	608.0	141.8	300	100	243.2	−101.4
13	1,145.3	574.9	170.4	300	100	230.0	−59.6
14	1,197.6	572.6	226.0	300	100	230.1	−4.1
15	1,285.4	598.8	286.6	300	100	239.5	47.1
16	1,378.9	642.7	336.1	300	100	257.1	79.0
17	1,449.3	689.4	359.9	300	100	275.8	84.1
18	1,477.9	724.6	353.3	300	100	289.9	63.4
19	1,460.2	738.9	321.3	300	100	295.6	25.7
20	1,406.3	730.1	276.1	300	100	292.0	−15.9
21				300	100		
22				300	100		
23				300	100		
n	1,333.3	666.66	266.66			266.66	0
(equilibrium reached)							

Incompetency cycles.

The various explanations of why total spending in an economy has cycled up and down in the past or will do so in the future are all very interesting and, in some cases, quite elegant. There is no doubt each reflects important aspects of the infinite number of forces and relationships at work in somewhat-market-oriented economies such as the United States. But once again the question is whether the various income cycle theories and econometric studies of the past can predict where an economy's level of income will be in the future and how it will get there? In other words, can an analyst see the road ahead by looking in the rear view mirror?

The question of whether the cycle theories and studies of past experience can predict the future is an important question for, if the answer is "no," then charting or explaining an economy's past income experiences and projecting them to continue into the future may be an exercise in futility, more likely to mislead the economy's analysts and decision makers rather than guide them.

And the answer is "no." In the real world, what actually happens to the level of income of an economy such as the United States will depend on the decisions of a relative handful of people—the congressmen on the relevant committees, the Federal Reserve governors and regional presidents on the Open Market Committee, and the White House and its appointees.

If the past is any guide, the decision makers will periodically be so unknowledgeable and unworldly that they will make particularly bad policy decisions. Then the level of income will go up or down in the wrong direction. But this does not happen on a systematic basis because policy makers are human and thus variable in their ethics and abilities. In other words, it is not likely incompetents will come and go according to some predictable schedule. And that means a systematic explanation of income fluctuations is not possible.

In other words, business cycle theories and past experiences cannot be used to predict the future because the levels of income that occur will be heavily influenced by the actions of decision makers who may come and go with diverse qualifications, ethics, and degrees of worldliness.

The ethics of the decision makers. Pragmatic analysts look at the ethics of decision makers from two perspectives. The first is that of qualified decision makers who act to feather the nests of their cronies, supporters, and potential employers while leaving the great bulk of the economy to suffer the distresses caused by their lack of appropriate policy actions. They are despicable and are all too often appointed to be Federal Reserve governors and Treasury secretaries.

The second is that of decision makers and "business economists" who claim to be qualified and are not. One of the economics profession's great problems is that, unlike medicine and law, it does not have an enforceable code of ethics. In medicine or law someone who never studied or practiced in the field and provided legal advice or medical treatments would be arrested. In economics, in contrast, anyone can claim to be an economic expert and be appointed as a Federal Reserve governor or regional president—even though they have neither appropriate educations nor appropriate real world experiences.

The problem becomes particularly severe when such people are so unethical that they accept positions such as that of a governor of the Federal Reserve for which they are patently unqualified. And then do not know what to do. So they fall back on "common knowledge" to guide their policies. Their policy failures then periodically ruin the economy and destroy millions of people, banks and businesses. They also tend to be a real threat to the re-election chances of those who appoint and confirm them.

CHAPTER SUMMARY

I.   Income fluctuations, and their accompanying periods of inflation and unemployment, are sometimes said to occur in predictable patterns called "business cycles." Some explanations as to why spending fluctuates focus on how and when banks and other financial intermediaries modify their behavior; others relate spending changes to consumers and investors modifying their spending in response to conditions in the economy's markets.

II. Some fluctuations may be the result of entrepreneurial efforts to introduce innovations into the structure of an economy. The initial investment spending of the innovator is then temporarily increased by the burst of additional investment spending that tends to occur as imitators rush in an effort to share the innovator's potential revenues. Then spending falls back towards normal until the next new innovation arrives.

III. The accelerator principle explains income fluctuations in terms of fluctuations in investment spending that occur in response to changes in the size and use of an economy's stock of capital. The expansion is triggered by an initial increase in investment spending that triggers further investment increases that continue until employers again have sufficient capital to produce all the goods and services they can sell. Then investment spending declines until enough capital wears out such that investment spending again begins to increase.

IV. Because the accelerator effect does not disclose the impact of new investment spending on consumers and the economy's other buyers, modern analysts combine the accelerator effect with the multiplier in order to better model the effect of an initial spending change.

V. Business cycle theories and past experiences cannot be used to predict the future because the level of spending that occurs in an economy such as that of the United States is greatly influenced by the human imperfections of the economy's decision makers.

CHAPTER TEN

PRODUCT PRICES AND THE AMOUNT OF GOODS AND SERVICES THAT WILL BE PURCHASED

An economy's levels income and production are traditionally analyzed in terms of the nominal amounts of money that are spent by customers and received by employers. But ultimately what counts are the goods and services themselves, the things that are produced by the workers of the economy's public and private employers and sold to their customers. It is the actual goods and services obtained by the spending of the economy's consumers and other customers that help satisfy human needs, not the money that changes hands as the products are bought and sold.

That does not mean that money is unimportant. To the contrary, in the real world public and private employers must take in enough nominal revenues if they are to continue to be able to pay for their workers and other inputs. So the total amount of production occurring in an economy is determined by *both* the prices of goods and services and the nominal amounts of money customers spend to buy them.

In effect, merely looking at events and relationships in terms of money is not enough. An increase in spending, for example, may result in breathless announcers talking about an "increase in GDP." But it means absolutely nothing to output and employment if prices simultaneously rise at the same or a higher rate so that production and employment remain unchanged or decline. In other words, don't make mistake of "seeing light at the end of the tunnel" if a journalist or government agency reports that total dollar spending (GDP) has finally begun to increase.

The aggregate demand concept.

"Aggregate demand" is economist-speak for the total amount of goods and services an economy's customers will purchase at each level of product prices. An economy's aggregate demand is thought by journalists and others to be rather conventional in that more and more products will be purchased at lower and lower prices. That makes sense, at least on the face of it, because it is logical that the nominal amount of dollars in an economy will buy more and more goods and services as their prices get lower and lower. But is that really what would happen if prices fall?

The early macroeconomists disagreed about the effects of a "deflation." One school of thought, from those who evolved into today's market-oriented neo-classicists, was that if wages and prices got low enough everything the economy's employers could produce would be sold and there would be full employment. Thus, in the event of a recession or depression, prosperity and full employment could be restored by a deflation without increasing the money supply or government spending and without reducing taxes and causing the government's budget to be unbalanced.

More specifically, they thought that wages and prices would fall in response to market pressures and, as a result, the recessions and depressions would resolve themselves by more goods and services being purchased. The role of the government, if any, was thus to remove any laws and regulations preventing wages and prices from falling. And, since full employment would then be assured, the role of the central bank was to stabilize the supply of money so that inflation from too much spending would not occur when full employment was restored.

Another group of economists, those who evolved into today's Keynesians and included Keynes himself, was not so sure. They analyzed the various components of aggregate demand and came to a different conclusion—that *deflation* (generally lower wages and prices) might not end a recession. They noted that at some point, when interest rates get as low as they can go, a further lowering of prices would not increase aggregate demand. Accordingly, there is no reason to wait around for a deflation that will not work—fiscal and other non-monetary expansionary policies should commence immediately, particularly if interest rates are already at minimum levels so that monetary policies cannot work by causing further interest rate reductions.

In essence, the two schools of thought do not agree as the extent to which customers will buy more when an economy's prices are lower and buy less when its prices are higher. Their disagreement is based on the effects they see lower wage and price levels having on the various product and money market determinants of the amount of goods and services that will be purchased. Their views are examined below so that both schools of thought and their policies can be properly debunked.

Modern economists disagree with both schools of thought; they observe that wages and prices in an economy such as the United States' are generally not flexible downward, despite individual exceptions to the contrary, such that relying on a policy of deflation to restore prosperity is a fool's errand; that assuming monetary policies will not work when interest rates are at a minimum is just plain wrong; and that calling for rational fiscal actions from a Congress whose constituencies do not understand macroeconomics is the advocacy equivalent of pissing into the wind on one of Adam Smith's sailing ships. Analysts will find that there are better and faster and more certain ways to go about restoring and maintaining full employment.

Considering variables and outcomes in real terms instead of money terms.

Up to this point, an economy's money and product markets have been discussed in terms of nominal amounts of money. For example, the money market has been discussed in terms of the amount of nominal dollars held for transactions and precautions purposes and the product market in terms of the amounts of money spent by consumers, investors, foreigners and governments.

Converting the analysis of an economy from nominal money to real terms can be accomplished by dividing the money amounts of each market component by the average level of the economy's product prices. Looking at things in the resulting "real" terms is important for analysts and policy makers—because they will be less likely to be misled by changes in the amount of money being spent or saved if prices also change.

Consider an economy in which the average product price is $200. Instead of showing that $200 billion in consumption spending occurs, the curve depicting conditions in the economy, its aggregate demand curve, will show that one billion products will be purchased; when the level of spending is $300 billion, the total amount of products being purchased and produced is 1.5 billion. Similarly, rather than showing that $20 billion of investment purchasing will occur at a certain interest rate, the curve representing investment spending will indicate that 100 million goods and services will be purchased by employers when the average product price in the economy is $200.

With such a conversion from "nominal" amounts of money to "real" amounts of products, there are no changes in either the nature of the components that affect these markets or their relationships. The advantage of describing the market components and the resulting levels of real income in such terms is that it is then possible to identify the way that changes in the level of prices affect the amount of goods and services being purchased. After all, *if generally lower prices, a deflation, are to cause an increase in the number of products being purchased, they must cause one or more of the different types of purchasers to buy more goods and services.*

Deflation: the Keynesian analysis.

The early Keynesians considered the possibility that unemployed workers could find jobs producing goods and services if they would but accept lower money wages. This, the advocates of encouraging deflation explained, would result in employers having lower costs and being willing to produce and sell their products at lower prices. But, the Keynesians asked themselves, would such lower wages and prices increase the amount of goods and services that would be purchased in an economy and thus increase the number of jobs available for the economy's workers? *If* the answer is yes, it means deflation may be a viable solution when an economy is in a recession or depression. If the answer is no, it means that deflation will not end a recession such as the Great Recession of the United States which began in 2008 and morphed into the depression that continues to this day.

To find the answer the early Keynesians examined each of the components of the money and product markets to see if there are any customers whose purchases might be affected by lower prices and lower wages. The only influence they found that would tend to expand the amount of products being purchased (when their reasoning is put in real terms) is that a decline in the level of wages and prices in an economy has the effect of increasing the real size of the economy's nominal supply of money. *In other words, a deflation has the same effect as expanding the money supply.*

An economy's real supply of money increases when its wages and prices fall because the existing nominal amount of money in the economy can then handle a greater amount of transactions. This is important because it means the transactions associated with the purchasing of a given amount of goods and services will no longer require so much of the economy's nominal money supply. Consequently, there would tend to be a surplus of money when prices fall.

The monetary surplus, the early Keynesians reasoned, would be used to bid up the price of the economy's financial assets and thus reduce the average rate of interest in the economy and cause more goods and services to be purchased. How much the economy's level of real income would rise as the result of such a "general deflation" would then depend upon such things as the responsiveness of investment spending to interest rate changes and the multiplier effect of any initial change that occurs in the level of income.

The early Keynesians saw interest rate changes as the only impact of lower wages and prices. Everything else would remain unchanged because the lower wages and prices would not change the other determinants of purchasing such as the propensity to consume, the MEI, or the amount of products obtained with government buying or transfers.

They pointed out that the consumer's positions would not change if wages and prices are lower—because the lower wages and prices mean that they would receive proportionally less money for what they sell as well as pay proportionally less money for what they buy;

Similarly, governments would still need, and thus purchase, the same number of products such as planes and ships and roads as before.

Similarly, employers would not change their willingness to make investments at each rate of interest because the percentage return on each potential new capital investment would remain the same since supply prices and expected costs and revenues would all tend to decline together in the general deflation.

The more astute early members of the Keynesian school of thought did acknowledge, however, that there are other possible effects of a general wage and price deflation which might under certain circumstance influence the level of purchasing in addition to cause an increase in the real size of the money supply and drive down interest rates. Some of them:

1. *Redistribution of income*: Money wages are only one of the costs of production that must be covered by the prices of products before employers will actually be willing to produce them. Thus, to lower the cost of producing goods and services enough so that the employers will be willing to produce them at lower price levels, money wages might have to fall proportionally more than any decline in the product prices (this would be the case, for example, if some of the inputs are coming from abroad where there is no deflation driving down prices).

But a decline in money wages in excess of the decline in product prices means a decline in the purchasing power of workers and thus an increase in the income left to the recipients of income other than wages. This may mean that purchasing power is being redistributed from high propensity to consume workers to business and asset owners with higher incomes and lower propensities to consume. *If so, total purchasing would fall and things would get worse instead of better.*

On the other hand, reductions in money wages could have just the opposite effect. This would occur if a reduction in wages results in the now cheaper labor replacing machines and other capital items so that a proportionally greater number of workers are employed. Then a larger proportion of the economy's real income would go to people with relatively high propensities to consume and the level of purchasing might rise.

2. *Foreign purchasing.* A decline in prices in the economy relative to those in other economies may lead foreigners to buy more. It depends on whether the foreign economies retaliate against the possibility of losing sales at home by changing the exchange rate or imposing tariffs or quotas in order to prevent their buyers from switching to the economy with relatively lower prices.

3. *Expected future prices and wages.* Both the propensity to consume and the MEI of an economy may be affected if a wage and price decline is not expected to be permanent. If prices and wages are thought to be temporarily low the proportion of the economy's production devoted consumer goods may rise as consumers act to take advantage of temporarily low prices. Investment purchasing also may increase as employers take advantage of the temporarily low prices for capital goods and buy inputs that can be stored for future use.

On the other hand, the reverse is true if wages and prices are expected to fall further in the future; consumers will tend to save more from their present incomes in order to buy later when prices are lower, and investors will not purchase as many new capital goods because those they obtain will have to compete with similar assets that will not have to earn as much to cover their supply prices.

Depicting aggregate demand.

Figure 10-1 brings together both the money market and the product market of an economy together in real terms. On the money market side the LM curve shows the various combinations of interest rates and income levels that can exist in the economy at different price levels that will put the money market in equilibrium. On the product market side the IS curve shows the various combinations of interest and income that will put the economy's total spending in equilibrium at different price levels.

Bringing the two markets together for the various different prices levels that might exist illustrates an important concept—that the amount of goods and services that will actually be purchased may not always be affected by the economy's level of prices.

The Keynesian view of aggregate demand.

The effect of lower prices changing the real size of an economy's money supply is presented in Figure 10-1. The figure depicts the effects of the larger and larger real supply of money that would exist in an economy as its prices move lower and lower such as from P4 to P3 to P2; it indicates that the economy's LM curve is shifted more and more to the right as prices get lower and lower and the real money supply increases.

What this figure shows is that the amount of goods and services that will be purchased as prices fall will continue to rise *only* until prices in the economy decline to the P3 level and the level of income reaches Yr200. Then any further decreases in the general level of prices, such as to P2, will merely increase the real supply of money and result in conditions in the money market wherein interest rates reach an absolute minimum. Then further reductions in the level of prices will *not* cause more goods and services to be purchased.

In this example, the effect of lower and lower price levels is depicted by the LM curve shifting further and further to the right. The level of real income stops increasing when prices drop below price level P3. In other words, *the liquidity trap means there is a limit to the positive effects* *of a general wage and price deflation in terms of increasing an economy's production and employment.**

Some of the components in the example economy's two markets have "r" superscripts. This denotes that they are depicting the economy's macroeconomic relationships in real terms. The basic procedure for constructing an economy's aggregate demand curve involves determining the economy's equilibrium level of real income at one level of prices and then repeating the income-determining process for other price levels. When the points representing each combination of real income and prices are joined they form an aggregate demand curve like that in Figure 10-1 wherein each point on the curve represents the amount of goods and services that will be purchased at a particular level of prices. The aggregate demand curve for the economy reflected in Figure 10-1 slopes down and to the right to indicate more and more goods and services will be purchased as deflation occurs—until the economy gets into the liquidity trap and deflation no longer is a viable policy.

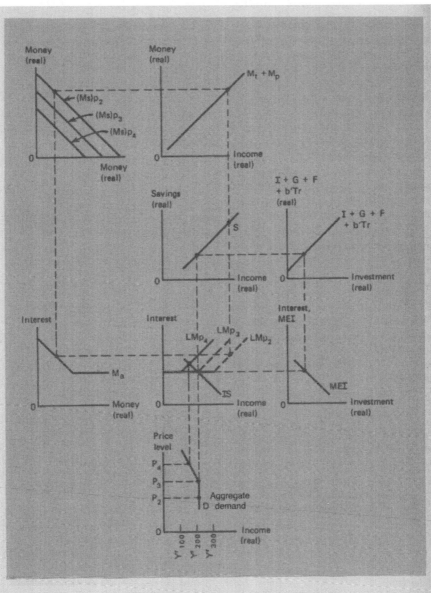

Figure 10-1
Aggregate demand with the Keynesian liquidity trap.

A different view of the effects of deflation

Not all early neo-classical analysts agreed that deflation has its limits because of the liquidity trap. Some noted that when product prices are lower, the savings individuals had accumulated in the form of financial assets with fixed money values (debt instruments, fixed income streams such as pensions, and money assets such as coins, currency, and demand deposits) will have higher real values since they then can be used to buy more goods and services.

Moreover, they noted, the higher real value of the financial assets which occurs when product prices are lower means that the owners of such asset will not have to save as much of their real incomes in the future to attain their savings goals. In other words, they see deflation as causing both an increase in the real supply of money and an increase in the propensity to consume.

Unfortunately, other economists pointed out, such a view of deflation is not very realistic. The expansionary effect of a wage and price deflation due to increases the real value of assets may be offset by the effect of lower wages and prices on those who are in debt. The basis for this effect is that smaller money incomes will be received by employers and their employees when the goods and services they produce are sold at lower prices. Then those who have payment obligations such as mortgages and other debts with fixed amounts of money payments will have to save a *larger* portion of their smaller money incomes to pay their obligations as they come due.

In other words, the real size of the consumers' debts increases and offsets any tendency for more to be purchased because prices are lower. Similarly, governments with debts and unfunded pension obligations may have to increase their tax rates so they can collect enough to service them from the taxpayers' now-smaller money incomes.

What this means is that the increased propensity to consume on the part of the holders of private and public debt and the recipients of fixed money pensions may be offset by the reduced propensities to consume of those who owe those obligations or have to pay a bigger percentage of their smaller money incomes in taxes to service them.

In other words, the positive aspects of deflation on consumer spending tend to be limited to assets in the form of government liabilities such as money, federal debt, and pensions that do not require additional savings in order that they can be paid—*which is only the case if the consumers in the economy has access to borrowing or its central bank has money creating powers.*

Those who make such an argument for deflation assume prices and wages will fall and the expansionary impact of the increased purchasing power of their money balances and financial instruments will not be offset by the redistribution of income or expectations of further price declines. They also assume that the tendency for spending to increase will not be offset by the increased real indebtedness of those of debtors or taxpayers with obligations fixed in money terms.

They may be right. If so, the possibility of deflation successfully eliminating a recession or depression does exist, at least conceptually.

The potentially positive effect of deflation seen by its advocates is depicted Figure 10-2. Notice that the economy's aggregate demand curve no longer becomes perfectly inelastic at some low level of prices as it does when only deflation's impact on the real money supply is considered. *It is the increased propensity to consume resulting from deflation that is the essence of the argument of those who propose deflation as the cure for a recession instead of central bank or government actions.*

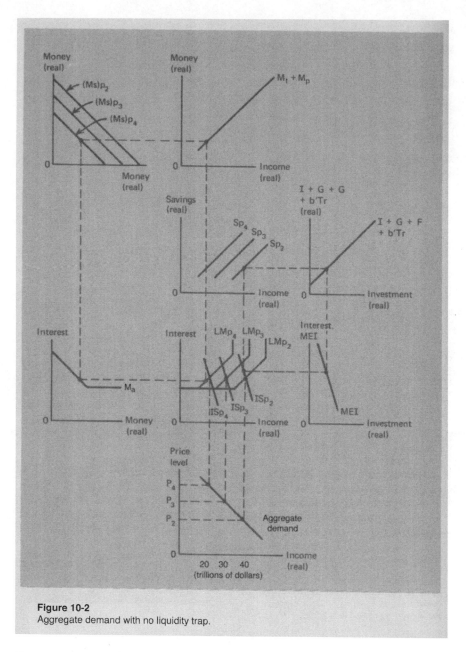

Figure 10-2
Aggregate demand with no liquidity trap.

Pragmatists and aggregate demand.

Which aggregate demand curve best depicts the reality of the American economy? The short answer according to pragmatic analysts is *neither*.

In the real world, at any point in time, an economy such as that of the United States has a specific quantity of money and a general level of prices and wages that are generally inflexible downward; specific levels of interest rates, wages, and labor productivity; and a specific level of total spending and the production and employment that is associated with that level of spending and the economy's price level.

So, yes, a simplistic aggregate demand curve can be generated from the basic information and relationships that are known. But, since the general levels of prices and wages in an economy such as the United States are not flexible downward, *every part of the curve below the current price level can be disregarded.* In other words, waiting for deflation to end a recession or depression is a fool's errand.

Aggregate demand and inflation.

The discussion of aggregate demand in terms of deflation is quite traditional, if only because a major depression with massive unemployment was the problem at hand at the time many of the original authors were writing—just as it is today. But the concept of aggregate demand can also be applied to analyze inflation.

Consider, for example, what will happen in the economy depicted in Figure 10-2 if an expectation that price controls were going to be levied to "fight inflation" caused employers to rush to increase their prices (so they would be frozen at a higher level) such that the overall level of prices in the economy increases from P3 to P4: prices rise, the money supply in real terms is reduced and interest rates rise, and production declines from $30 trillion to $20 trillion in real terms.

In other words, there is a move to a higher level of prices, an inflation, without a money supply or spending increase. There is also an interest rate increase without the central bank taking any steps to tighten up the money supply. Worse, the amount of goods and services being purchased is less at the higher price level—it is an inflation that results in unemployment and less production.

So should the policy makers wait for a deflation to get the economy back to $30 trillion of production and employment? Tighten up on the money supply to increase the level of interest rates to fight inflation by reducing the amount of spending to buy goods and services—which will make the economy's recession even worse? Increase the money supply to drive down interest rates and increase spending? And what can be done if $40.0 trillion of spending is needed because that is the economy's production capacity at full employment? *These are the things analysts will consider in the material that follows; aggregate demand will play an important role in those considerations.*

CHAPTER SUMMARY

I.   How much consumers and other customers spend, and the prices they pay, determines how much of an economy's potential production will actually be produced. When there is not enough customer purchasing there will be unemployed workers and idle production capacity.

II. One possible solution when production is not at full employment levels is to reduce the prices consumers and other customers pay for the products they buy.

III. The total amount of goods and services customers will buy at every price level is depicted by aggregate demand curves. Deriving those curves requires that purchases and whatever influences them be converted from money to real terms. This is accomplished by dividing the money amounts of total spending, and the various money market and product market components that affect total spending, by the level of prices.

IV. Some analysts think the primary effect of lower prices is an increase in the supply of money. The lower prices reduce the amount of money needed for transactions purposes which frees up money that is used to buy financial assets and drive down interest rates. The lower interest rates then cause spending to increase. The effectiveness of deflation ends when the liquidity trap is reached.

V.   Other analysts think lower prices will result in more consumer spending, even if the liquidity trap is reached, because those with currency and other financial assets will have increased purchasing power and be closer to their savings goals.

VI.   Some analysts think any tendency deflation has to cause more consumer spending will be offset by the resulting redistribution of incomes, expectations of further price declines, and the increased debt, contract, and pension burdens that are fixed in money terms.

VII.   Pragmatic analysts think that it is meaningless to analyze deflation because prices and wages tend to generally be inflexible downward. As a result, lower levels of production and employments occur when there are inadequate levels of total spending, not lower prices.

VIII.   The concept of aggregate demand may be useful in analyzing inflation and its effects even if it is not realistically useful in analyzing deflation.

CHAPTER ELEVEN

THE LABOR MARKET AND AN ECONOMY'S CAPACITY TO PRODUCE GOODS AND SERVICES

The maximum amount of goods and services an economy's public and private employers *can* produce if the economy's labor force and capital is fully employed is important. It is the maximum "real income" that the economy's workers and other participants can share. Its size depends on the amount of labor available to be employed by the economy's public and private employers and the productivity of that labor.

To the extent that an economy's employers attempt to maximize profits and are free to employ as much of the economy's labor force as they desire *and can generate sufficient revenues for whatever they produce*, employers will tend to employ workers who will add products to the employers' total production that can be sold for at least enough to pay for the workers' services and for any other additional costs of production. Thus an employer would be willing to hire a worker who is paid $2000 per week whose employment would raise the employer's production by ten units of a product that could be sold for $400 each and would not cause the employer to bear any other additional costs.

It is rational for the employer to do this because, even though the worker costs the employer an additional $2000, he or she adds an additional $4000 to the employer's revenues. This is the same as saying that the employer hires the worker because he can produce ten additional units but has to be paid wages that are equivalent to only five of them.

Complicating the determination of how many workers the employers of an economy are willing to hire is the possibility that some of the employers are pursuing goals other than profit maximization. Another possible complication is that the employers may not be allowed to pay the wages they wish to pay or to employ the workers as they wish to employ them.

Also complicating the determination of how many workers employers will want to hire is the possibility, at some point, that diminishing returns will set in so that each subsequent worker begins to add fewer and fewer units of product to the employers total production.

Consider, for example, a plant that could be operated by an employer except that there are no workers in it. Now picture a line of potential new workers walking into the plant (or office or mine or school or police station or church).

At first, each subsequent worker takes his place by an idle machine (or squad car, or podium or desk or pulpit or truck) and commences producing so that the capital item is no longer idle. But after a while, all the machines are busy. New workers may then assist the already employed workers and relieve them so that production can continue when they take breaks. Sooner or later, however, a new worker is going to walk in whose presence does not add anything to the employer's total production; every idle machine is producing at maximum capacity using all the labor it can productively employ.

Profit-oriented employers will not be willing to keep hiring workers until they come to the one who contributes nothing of value. Instead, such employers will only add workers until they reach the last worker who contributes enough to production to cover his wages and whatever other additional costs are associated with his or her employment. In the example above, that would be the worker whose employment yields five additional units of product. Subsequent workers who add less than that would not be employed because to do so would cost the employer more than they contribute. For example, the employer would not hire an additional worker who cost $2000 per week but only contributed four additional units of production that could be sold for $400 each.

Complicating the question of how many workers employers will be willing to employ, and thus how much they will be able to produce, is the possibility that some, and perhaps most, employers in an economy such as that of the United States will have goals other than profits, such as rapid revenue growth or revenue maximization or increased market share if the employers are for-profit employers; or souls rescued or educated if they are non-profit employers such as churches or school districts; or reelection by hiring as many voters and campaign donors if they are government employers.

In such cases the employers may be willing to hire additional workers and use the revenues that would otherwise be earned or received as taxes or contributions to cover any revenue deficiencies caused by hiring workers who add more to costs than they generate as revenues or are able to borrow.

It is also possible that an economy's employers will not be able to find all the qualified workers they would like to employ no matter what wage they want to pay or they will be allowed to pay. In such cases, the amount of goods and services produced would be determined by the number of workers who are employed and their productivity.

Still another possibility is that highly productive workers will not be employed because the additional goods and services they produce cannot be sold. That is an important possibility but at this point the only thing being examined is the maximum amounts of output and employment that *could* be produced by an economy's employers at a particular point in time. What an economy has the capacity to produce is being considered in detail because it provides the basis for evaluating an economy's performance and policies by comparing what *could* happen with what *does* happen.

For example, an economy would be doing quite well if its public and private employers have the capacity to produce of $16 trillion of goods and services and they have enough revenues coming in so that they actually produce the $16 trillion; on the other hand, the economy would be doing quite poorly if it has a capacity to produce $20 trillion of goods and services but only produces $16 trillion because its employers do not have enough revenues or are somehow prevented from hiring all the workers they wish to employ or are forced to inefficiently employ them.

An economy's production capacity: the aggregate supply concept.

An economy's aggregate supply is *the maximum level of output that can occur in the economy at different price levels* if there is a sufficient level of customer purchasing. Thus, and more specifically, an aggregate supply curve depicts the maximum amount of goods and services which the economy's public and private employers are willing and able to produce at each of the levels of product prices that might exist in the economy.

The maximum amounts will differ at different price levels to the extent higher or lower product prices cause more or fewer workers to be employed, and thus more or fewer goods and services to be produced. For instance, the additional worker who would have to be paid $2000 per week and would not be employed because he only contributed four extra units of production that could be sold for $400; he would be employed if the four units could be sold at a higher price such as $600 each.

In essence, the key determinants of an economy's capacity to produce at each price level (the economy's aggregate supply) are the availability of workers, the productivity of the workers, the goals of its employers, the non-wage costs associated with each workers employment, and the general level of wages that the economy's workers are paid.

Whether all the goods and services that employers are willing and able to produce will actually be produced, however, depends on the willingness of customers to buy the products at each price level (aggregate demand). After all, Regardless of prices or productivity or production capacity or the willingness of workers to work for lower wages, employers can only employ workers and produce goods and services if their total production can generate enough revenues to cover their production costs.

Yes, temporarily employers may be able to borrow money or use retained earnings or sell assets to pay for workers and inputs—but in the end they must take in enough revenues to cover their costs even if they are government owned or non-profits or pursuing goals other than profit maximization. Police and clerics and autoworkers and pizza cooks may produce different goods and services but in the real world they all have to be paid.

Labor productivity.

The maximum amount of goods and services that can possibly be produced and distributed in an economy depends on the number of workers employed, their skills and habits, the quantity and quality of the capital and other materials that they use, and the level of technology with which they work. That maximum is important because it determines the real income that is potentially available to be distributed to the economy's workers and other participants.

A curve depicting the different levels of production that would occur in an economy at a point in time if different numbers of workers are employed using the economy's existing stock of capital and other materials is often referred to as the economy's *production function*, since the level of production that can occur in an economy is a function of the number of workers employed in it.

Figure 11-1 presents an example of an economy's production function. The amount of goods and services that might be produced and distributed in the income (Yr) is measured on the vertical axis, and the number of workers (N) that might be employed to produce the products is measured on the horizontal axis. For example, the employment of N6 workers means the production of Yr35 goods and services.

Notice the shape of the production function: because there is a fixed amount of capital and other productive materials and technology in the economy at this or any other particular point in time, additional workers will tend to add increasingly smaller amount of additional products to the economy's total output until worker N9 is reached whose employment would result in no additional production. In other words, just as a line of workers filed into one plant and added diminishing amounts of additional products until one further worker added nothing, so additional workers can be added to the capital, materials, and technology possessed by all the employers in an economy.

The employers, conceptually at least, will continue hiring and increasing their output until a worker is reached at N9 whose employment adds nothing to the economy's real income no matter how he is employed. If they hire more than N9, and they could if they are pursuing goals other than production maximization, production in the economy will decline.

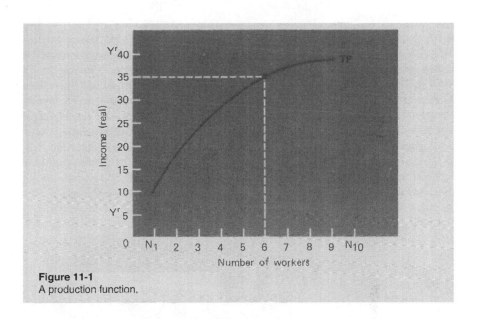

Figure 11-1
A production function.

Analysts know some employers such as profit-maximizers will stop adding workers before the employers' output is totally maximized—they will stop hiring when additional employees add less to the value of the employer's production than it costs to hire them. Governments, non-profits, and private employers with other goals such as maximizing market share or revenue maximization are not so constrained so long as they can acquire enough money to pay their workers and cover all their other costs.

What this means, of course, is that the economy might not employ as many as N9 workers. On the other hand, its employers may employ even more if they have access to enough money to pay them and are not constrained by the pressures of profit maximization or the losses their employment causes.

Money wages.

Workers ordinarily are compensated for their services with monetary payments such as wages, salaries, benefits, commissions, bonuses, and pensions. These are usually lumped together and discussed as *money wages* (Wm). It is also possible to convert such money wages into *real wages* (Wr) which represent the amounts of products that can be purchased with money wages.

Employers effectively pay real wages because the money wages they pay represent products that the employers produce and give up to purchasers in order to obtain enough revenues to pay their workers' money wages. Similarly, workers receive real wages because their money wages can be used to buy the goods and services that the economy's employers produce. In essence, an economy's workers and employers exchange labor services for products.

The level of real wages in an economy can be computed by dividing workers' money wages by the price level of the products they buy. For instance, if the average level of money wages in an economy is $100,000 per year and the average price for the goods and services produced in the economy is $50, then the real wage of the average worker is equivalent to 2000 goods and services per year.

Alternately, money wages can be converted into real wages that represent relative purchasing power. For instance, if the level of money wages is $100,000 per year and there is an inflation such that the average price doubles to $100, the number of products the employers must sell to pay their workers is reduced to the equivalent of 1000 goods and services per year.

For analytical purposes the relationship between real wages and money wages can be depicted by a curve that allows the level of money wages paid for the use of labor to be converted into the different levels of real wages occurring with each price level. Such a *money wage curve*, appears graphically with the various possible levels of product prices on the vertical axis and the various possible real wages on the horizontal axis; the curve itself is a rectangular hyperbola sloping downward to the right so that a change in the level of prices is associated with a proportional change in the level of real wages.

An example of such a curve is presented in Figure 11-2 for an economy with an average general level of weekly money wages of $5000. It shows, for example, that if the general level of product prices in the economy is doubled (eg. from P2 to P4) the workers' real wages (and the number of goods and services the economy's employers must sell to pay their workers) will be halved.

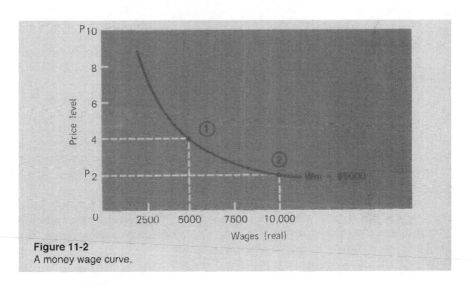

Figure 11-2
A money wage curve.

Individual wage differences.

There is no conflict between the use of a single general level of wages for an economy and the obvious fact that workers in different locations and occupations may receive different sizes and types of wages for their services. What is being considered here is the general or average level of wages that an economy's labor force receives. There is no conflict because the general level of wages is based on, and determined by, the diverse wages actually received by the individuals who compose an economy's labor force. Thus, just as the average level of interest rates is used to represent the general level of the various different rates that exist in an economy and the average level of product prices is used to represent the general level of all product prices, so the average level of wages represents the pay received by the average worker in the economy.

THE LABOR MARKET

The public and private employers of an economy employ workers to produce goods and services when those products are expected to generate at least enough revenues to cover all of the employers' costs of production. Profit-maximizing employers, at least conceptually, will only desire to employ additional workers so long as each additional worker produces enough additional output to cover their wages and the other costs associated with the production they contribute; other employers such as governments, non-profits, and private firms with goals other than maximum profits may hire beyond that level so long as whatever it is that they produce generates enough revenues from sales or borrowing to cover their costs. Every employer has an employee hiring limit of some sort at each general level of wages that might exist in an economy such as that of the United States.

The determinants the general level of wages that will exist in an economy are the conditions that exist in the economy's labor market—the supply of workers and the employers' demand for them.

The demand for labor.

The amount of labor employers will want to hire depends on the wages the workers must be paid. In general, the lower the wages the more employers will want to hire additional workers. Thus a curve representing the demand for labor by an economy's employers will slope down and to the right to depict the fact that more and more workers will be demanded by an economy's employers at lower and lower wage levels.

The elasticity of the employers' demand for labor, as with their demand for equipment and other capital goods, is affected by many things. Among them: the extent to which the employment of more labor results in additional production that drives down product prices; the extent to which diminishing marginal productivity and increased non-labor costs cause the additional workers to produce less and less production in excess of the non-labor costs that result from their employment; and the goals of the employers and, thus, their ability and willingness to hire additional workers who will contribute less to revenues than they add to costs.

More labor also tends to be demanded when real wages are lower because the lower wages result in labor being substituted for capital in the employers' production processes. Thus, the amount of labor employers will demand at each price level is influenced by the degree to which it is technically possible to substitute labor for capital and the response of the prices of the employers' other costs to the adoption of production techniques that employ more labor. For example, if wages are low enough four workers might be hired to pick up boxes in a factory to replace one worker and a forklift; or ten cotton pickers hired instead of a farmer employing a cotton picking machine and one driver; or cashiers used in a grocery store instead of self-checkout machines.

An example of an economy's labor demand curve (Nd) is presented in Figure 11-3. It shows that employment of a maximum of N6 workers will be desired by employers when the general level of money wages paid to its workers is the equivalent of Wr15 units of production. Even if more goods and services could be sold, no more workers will be employed because the employers cannot or will not pay any more for additional workers in view of what such workers contribute.

On the other hand, the level of employment will not be lower under such circumstances because it would mean employers were foregoing the employment of workers who would contribute more production than the employers need to get from the workers to be willing to employ them.

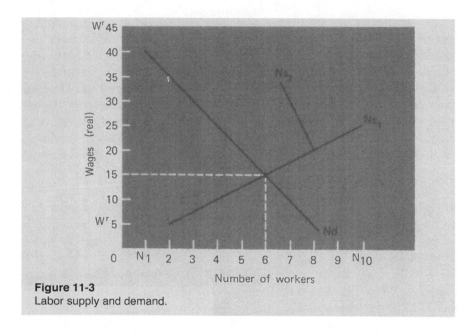

Figure 11-3
Labor supply and demand.

Product purchases and the demand for labor.

It is important to keep in mind that aggregate supply and all its components such as the demand for labor are related to an economy's production capacity and represents what an economy's employers are willing and able to do *if they have sufficient revenues for their products.* The actual amounts of workers an economy's employers will desire to employ at each level of real wages can be below the levels represented by such a labor demand curve. This occurs because no employer will employ workers to produce goods and services for which it cannot obtain revenues to pay for the labor and other inputs required to produce it.

If the employers in the economy depicted in Figure 11-3, for example, are unable to sell more products than those produced by N3 workers, they will hire no more workers than that at real wage level Wr15 even though they would be willing to hire as many as N6 workers if they could sell or otherwise obtain sufficient revenues for the additional goods and services that would be produced.

The supply of labor.

The supply of labor in an economy (Ns) depends on the size of the working age population and their desire to be in the labor force—their *labor force participation rate*—if there are jobs available. As analysts might imagine, the labor force participation rate varies greatly by age and sex. It is generally accepted that the more goods and services an economy's workers are able to purchase with the money wages they receive for their services, the more that the economy's working age population will be willing to give up their leisure and production of non-market products such as household services and, instead, work for wages.

Curve Ns1 depicts this type of situation in Figure 11-3; it shows more and more labor being supplied in the example economy at higher levels of real wages.

Another possibility is that as real wages get higher, workers will begin to desire more and more leisure because they feel that they will be able to obtain enough goods and services to satisfy their needs even if they work less. In such circumstances, the quantity of labor supplied in an economy will fall to the level of the economy's real wages rise past the levels needed to obtain some desired level of goods and services.

This possibility is depicted in Figure 11-3 by labor supply curve Ns2. It shows the amount of labor supplied declining as real wages exceed Wr20. Similarly, less labor may be supplied at higher wage levels because spouses and other family members may get out of the labor force if the incomes of those who work are high enough to support the household.

Yet another possibility is that a prolonged period of unemployment and business failures may result in savings being wiped out and pensions lost or reduced. That could increase the number of people who want to work past whatever they considered to be their normal retirement age.

Such a situation would be depicted with a rightward shift in the labor supply curve to depict that more people are willing to work at every level of wages. In other words, the size of an economy's labor force, and thus the economy's production capacity, would grow as an adverse by-product of a long recession.

This is exactly what happened in the United States as a result of the Great Recession: senior citizens whose pensions and saving were wiped out or reduced returned to the workforce, retirements were delayed, and heretofore non-working household members returned to the labor force so their households could maintain their standards of living.

Equilibrium in the labor market.

The general level of wages that exists in a relatively free economy such as the United States is determined in the labor market by the supply of workers and the demand for them. In essence, workers tend to move to where wages are higher; employers tend to move to wherever wages are lower.

Figure 11-3 depicts the labor market of an economy wherein the average level of real wages received by its workers is Wr15 and the number employed is N6. That general level of wages and level of employment is the only combination wherein, in general terms, every worker who wants a job can find one and every employer who wants to hire workers can hire all they want.

A lower general level of wages such as Wr10 cannot exist because the employers would want more workers than are willing to work. As a result, competition from the employers for the available workers would bid the wage price they are willing to pay higher until it reached Wr15. Similarly, any wage price higher than Wr15 cannot exist because more workers would be supplied than are willing to work. As a result competition among the workers for the available jobs would bid the wage price lower. Wr15 and N6 workers are the equilibrium levels of wages and employment for this economy.

Of course, such a "perfect" labor market does not exist. In the real world there are inevitably numerous imperfections in every economy's labor market. For example, the government could pass a minimum wage law requiring that no wage be lower than Wr20; or it could encourage or require everyone over a certain age to retire in an effort to provide jobs for younger workers; or it could push up the general level of wages by mandating employers provide medical insurance; or it could enact child labor laws to prevent anyone under the age of 18 from working; or it could enact Social Security benefits for retirees that are higher than the wages that they could earn if they remain in the labor force. The list of potential labor market imperfections is endless.

AN ECONOMY'S AGGREGATE SUPPLY

An economy's "aggregate supply" is the maximum amount of goods and services which the economy's employers are capable of producing when the economy's labor force is fully employed. It depends on such labor market considerations as the level of wages that have to be paid, the amount of workers willing to work at those wages, the productivity of the workers, and the other costs that have to be covered if they are employed.

And just because there are workers and employers in an economy does not mean that the maximum or any other level of production will occur. How much is actually produced, and thus how many workers will be able to find jobs, depends on the existence of sufficient customer spending—employers are only able to continue employing workers and producing if they receive sufficient revenues to cover both the wages of their employees' and their other costs.

Aggregate supply curves.

An aggregate supply curve represents the maximum amount of goods and services that an economy's employers will be willing to produce at each level of product prices. Such a curve can be determined in the following fashion:

First the general level of product prices and the general level of money wages determine the level of real wages.

Then the number of workers who will be employed at this level of real wages is determined in the labor market; it will be the smaller of the number of workers willing to work at that level of real wages or the number of workers employers will be willing to hire at that level of real wages. *It must be the smaller amount because employers will not hire workers just because the workers are willing to work and the workers will not work just because job vacancies exist.*

Finally, the total output which this number of workers can produce is determined by the nature of the economy's technology and stock of capital. It is represented by the economy's production function. That output is the maximum amount of goods and services that the economy's employers can be supply at that price level—and the combination of that price level and that output is represented by one point on the economy's aggregate supply curve. Subsequent points represent the maximum possible production that can occur at other price levels.

An economy's maximum possible aggregate supply at various price levels can be obtained graphically with the aforementioned procedure by placing graphs containing the four curves in the particular relationship depicted in figure 11-4 and proceeding in the manner described above for different price levels.

RELATING AN ECONOMY'S CAPACITY TO PRODUCE TO ITS PRICE AND WAGE LEVELS: THE SHAPE OF AGGREGATE SUPPLY CURVES

The supply and demand components of an economy's labor market determine the shape of its aggregate supply curve because they determine the maximum level of employment that can occur at each level of real wages. There are three basic possibilities and they all relate to the flexibility of the economy's money wages; each results in an aggregate supply curve with a different shape and, as analysts shall subsequently see, *each has significant policy implications.*

Flexible money wages.

Economies with highly competitive labor markets such that money wages rise when there is a shortage of workers and fall when there is a surplus, have aggregate supply curves such as that depicted in Figure 11-4.

If there is unemployment in the Figure 11-4 economy the unemployed workers will bid the wage price of labor lower and lower until they find jobs (or permanently leave the labor force). For example, if the level of real wages in the Figure 11-4 economy is Wr30 because the level of product prices is P1 and the level of money wages is Wm2, less labor will be demanded by the economy's employers than its workers are willing to provide.

On the other hand, since money wages are flexible, the unemployed workers will compete for the available jobs by offering to work for money wages lower than Wm2. Money wages will fall until they reach the level of Wm1 which yields a full-employment level of real wages (Wr15) when the price level is P1 so that there is neither a labor surplus or labor shortage in the economy's labor market.

In essence, *if there are enough customers in this economy* as many as N4 workers will be employed at price level P1. In other words, basically everyone who wants to work when the average wage is Wr15 will be able to find a job, and they will produce Yr18 of products which is the full-employment level of production.

The existing labor force cannot produce more than the Yr18 level of output with the existing capital and technology and with its own abilities and preferences. So the combination of P1 and Yr18 is one point on the economy's aggregate supply curve; it represents the maximum that this economy's employers can produce when the economy is at full employment with real wages of Wr15, N4 workers employed, and money wages of Wm1.

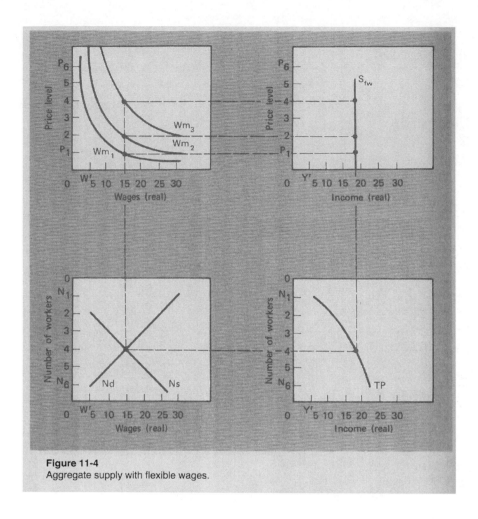

Figure 11-4
Aggregate supply with flexible wages.

On the other hand, when prices are higher (P4) so that the level of real wages in the economy is lower than Wr15 when money wages are WM2, more workers will be demanded at the lower real wages than are willing to work. The shortage of workers at that price level and the real wages associated with that money wage level will then cause the economy's employers to bid for the available supply of workers by offering higher money wages. Money wages, and thus real wages, will rise until a real wage of Wr15 is reached when the money wage level reaches Wm3.

When Wm3 is reached, N4 workers will be employed and, if the employers have customers for their products, they will produce Yr18 of goods and services which is the maximum level of output for such an economy. Thus P4 and Yr18 is another point on the economy's aggregate supply curve—which will be perfectly inelastic since competition in the labor market will cause money wages to adjust until real wages reach the level at which everyone who wants to work is employed. It is designated Sfw to denote that it is for an economy in which there are flexible wages.

Reality: money wages flexible upward and inflexible downward.

In an economy such as that of the United States it is realistic to expect that a shortage of workers will lead the employers to offer, and the workers to accept, higher money wages. Things might be quite different, however if there is a surplus of workers who are willing to work but cannot find jobs; it is quite possible that many individual money wages are inflexible downward, or at least "sticky" and slow to fall; because of such things as legal restrictions imposed by minimum wage laws and long-term labor agreements calling for the maintenance of specific rates of pay and benefits.

Figure 11-5 is an example of the effects of such a situation. It depicts the production capacity of an economy which initially has a general level of money wages of Wm2 and a price level of P2. Since that price level is associated with full employment, price level P2 and real income Yr18 are one point on the economy's aggregate supply curve.

Price levels above P2 in this economy (such as P3) mean that the real wages associated with the initial money wage level of Wm2 will be so low that there is a shortage of workers. Employers will then offer, and workers undoubtedly accept, higher money wages such as Wm3 wherein real wages will reach Wr15 and there is again no shortage or surplus of labor to cause money wages to be bid up or down. Thus price level P3 and the Yr18 level of production is another point on the economy's aggregate supply curve.

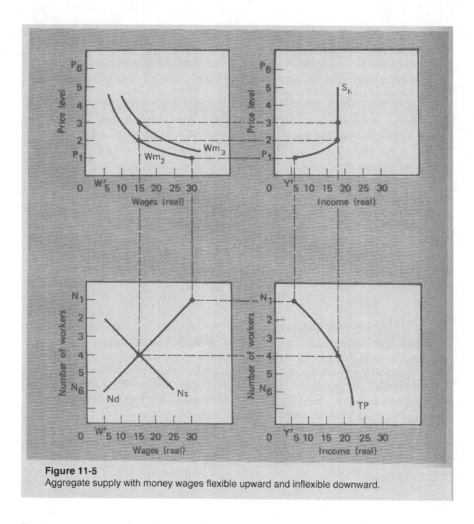

Figure 11-5
Aggregate supply with money wages flexible upward and inflexible downward.

In contrast, price levels lower than P2 (such as P1) will mean real wages when the money wage in the economy is Wm2 will be so high that more workers are willing to work than the employers are willing to hire. And yet money wages will not fall because they are inflexible downward for reasons such as minimum wage laws and union contracts. Accordingly, if the level of money wages remains at Wm2 in the example economy, the employers will only be willing to hire N1 of workers and produce Yr5 of goods and services. P1 and Yr5 are another point on the aggregate supply curve and it is designated Sfi to indicate that money wages in the economy are flexible upward and inflexible downward.

Astute analysts will particular note the shape of the resulting aggregate supply curve. It slopes upward to indicate that the economy's employers are willing to produce more and more goods and services at higher and higher prices, until full employment is reached and they cannot produce any more no matter how high prices go in the economy. The upward slope is related to the declining contribution to productivity of each additional worker as they go to work. The employers have to be able to charge higher and higher prices for the products each additional worker contributes in order for the employer to take in enough additional revenue to be able to hire them.

Wage freezes: money wages are inflexible upward and inflexible downward.

Finally, consider the impact of the government imposing a wage freeze such that money wages cannot be increased or decreased. This is the kind of thing a well-meaning government might do to help "fight" inflation or achieve some other goal. China did this during its "great leap forward" under Mao in the twentieth century—and it helped turn China into one of the poorest countries in the world. It was also seriously considered, though not implemented, during the inflation of the Carter and Nixon administrations: wages were to be frozen so that they would not increase and raise the costs of production that would have to be covered with even higher product prices than those that already existed.

This particular inflation will subsequently be discussed in some detail because it was one of the worst and most unnecessary inflations in the history of the United States—because it was primarily caused by unwarranted inflation fears on the part of Congress and the Federal Reserve and the foolish policies they implemented to head it off. In essence, as analysts will see, the inflation of that period was primarily caused by the naïve and inappropriate policies that were intended to prevent it.

Figure 11-6 depicts the aggregate supply curve of an economy whose money wages are frozen. In essence, when product prices are high the level of real wages will be so low that workers are unwilling to supply their labor to employers, preferring instead to remain on their farms and communes outside the money economy; when product prices are low the level of real wages will be so high that, even though lots of workers are willing to work, the economy's employers are not willing to hire them. The aggregate supply curve in Figure 11-6 depicts such a situation—production will be below that which would occur at full employment at every level of prices except P2.

Reality check. *It is important to reiterate that these levels of production and employment will only occur at each level of prices if there are enough customer and that such a "full employment" level of real wages does not mean that every single person of working age is employed; it means that if there is enough customer spending everyone in the labor force will be employed except people in the process of normally moving between jobs and individuals who, though willing to work, are not able to work due to reasons of health, location, or ability.*

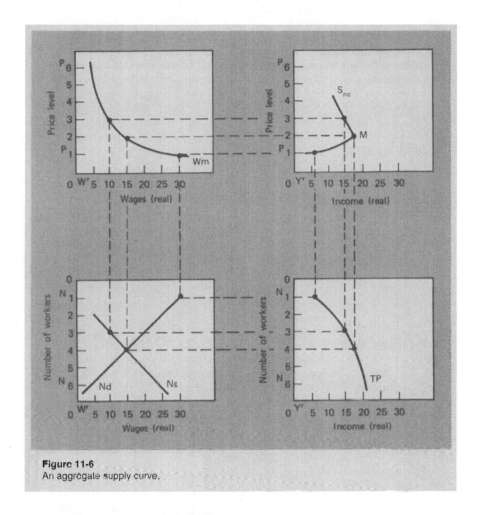

Figure 11-6
An aggregate supply curve.

COMBINING AGGREGATE DEMAND AND AGGREGATE SUPPLY

A large and dynamic economy such as that of the United States is incredibly complex with billions of transactions and conditions constantly occurring and changing. Analysts understand that any effort to model the basic relationships of such an economy is useful only in understanding how the most basic of economic forces and relationships come together and how they might react to monetary, fiscal, and other policies implemented to affect them.

A good starting point for any analyst is the fact that at any particular point in time an economy can only have one general level of prices, one general level of wages, one level of employment, and one level of production. They are determined the forces and conditions that determine the economy's aggregate demand and aggregate supply. The economy's price level and the various market forces that bring it about are important because they simultaneously determine the levels of employment and output that the economy's public and private employers will produce, the general level of the economy's interest rates, and the level of the real and money wages that will occur. That, in turn, determines the distribution of the economy's production between its workers and others.

For the purpose of considering the most basic of an economy's relationships, consider the Figure 11-7 economy and its various markets. This economy's price level is P6 and its production level is Yr30 even though its employers could produce twenty percent more (Yr36). Those are the equilibrium levels of prices and production for the economy. This particular economy is in equilibrium producing at less than full employment levels of production.

This particular economy appears stuck in a recession with no light at the end of the proverbial tunnel given the various conditions and relationships in the economy. And it will stay stuck until something changes. Price levels below P6 cannot be maintained because there would be a larger amount of newly produced goods and services purchased by consumers and other buyers than the employers are willing to supply—then prices would be bid up by competition among the buyers until the general level of prices reach P6 and the buyers can buy all they are willing to buy. Similarly, the general level of prices would not be bid up above P6 because there would be no reason for buyers to pay more since they are already able to buy all they want to buy.

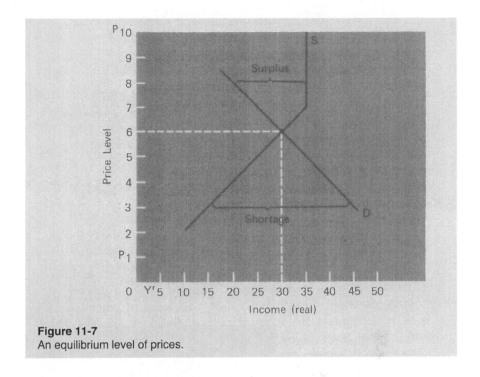

Figure 11-7
An equilibrium level of prices.

An economy with its product, labor, and money markets in equilibrium: the basic model.

Simultaneously occurring with the determination of an economy's equilibrium level of real income and product prices is the determination of the equilibrium levels of all its basic money market, product market, and labor market components.

For instance, the determination of an economy's equilibrium level of income means the determination of the number of workers who will be able to find jobs; the amount of money that will be used for transactions and precautions purposes; and the levels of interest rates, consumption spending, investment spending, and government spending, taxes, and transfers.

Bringing together the basic markets (labor, money, products) of an economy and relating them to one another makes it possible to construct a complete model. The value of such a model is that it can be used to examine how a change will ripple through the economy and affect the level of its prices, wages, production, employment, interest rates, and all the many other components of its markets.

Figure 11-8 presents an example of such a comprehensive model with a price level of P2 and money wage level Wm. The money wage level represents the current level of wages and they are inflexible downward. The amount of each component can be identified by working back from the equilibrium levels of production and product prices as demonstrated by the broken line in the figure. The relevant consumption function and money supply curve are those for the equilibrium price level P2.

This economy is in equilibrium with substantial unemployment. Its production is far below capacity because total spending in the economy is not high enough to enable the economy's employers to fully employ its work force. In other words, it is a representation of the United States during its long years of the Great Recession when those in power let the economy stagnate without adequate levels of total spending.

Another version of a similar situation is depicted in more detail in Figure 11-9. In this economy, the amounts of goods and services purchased and produced are equal at Yr15 and the average level of prices in the economy is P2. Even if prices were generally flexible downward, which they are not in an economy such as the United States, no further price declines will occur even though the Yr15 level of output is less than the economy's employers are capable of producing—because the economy's employers are already selling all they are willing to produce and the economy buyers are already buying all they are willing to buy.

In essence, *this economy is in equilibrium even though there is substantial unemployment:* only N3 workers are required to produce the Yr15 amount of goods and services that can be sold even though N5 is number of workers willing to work at the Wr20 level of real wages that exists in the economy and N4 workers would be employed if the economy was operating at full employment.

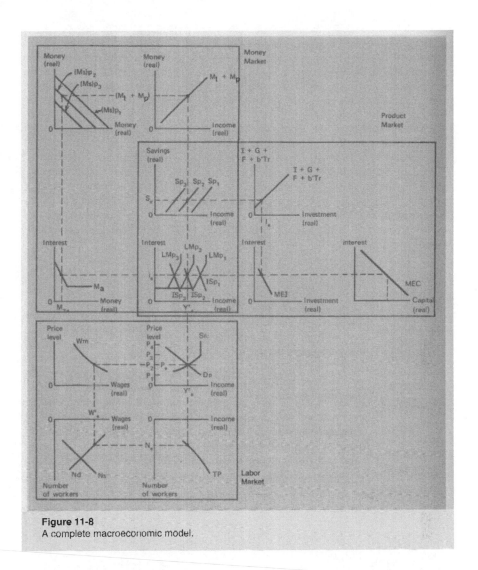

Figure 11-8
A complete macroeconomic model.

The impact of flexible wages. There are unemployed workers in the Figure 11-9 example economy—only N3 are employed whereas N5 are willing to work when real wages are Wr20. And in the real world wages tend to be inflexible downward in economies such as that of the United States. But what if wages were flexible and competition for the available jobs caused wages to fall? In this particular example economy, the general level of wages will be bid down until enough people leave the labor force so that only N3 workers are willing to work. Then there will be no official unemployment—just a lot of early retirees, discouraged workers sitting at home, welfare recipients, and people claiming Social Security disabilities. They will, of course, immediately rejoin the labor force as soon as jobs are again available at wages above Wr8. Sound familiar?

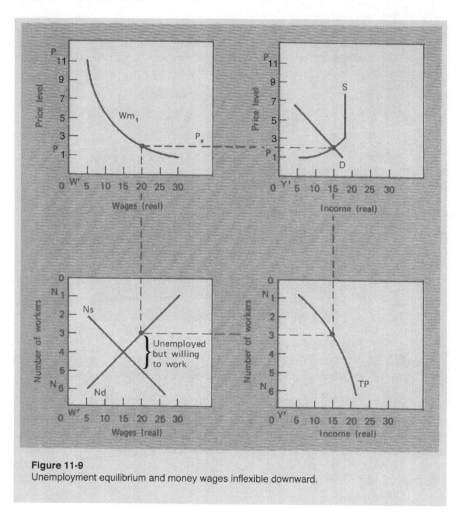

Figure 11-9
Unemployment equilibrium and money wages inflexible downward.

CHAPTER SUMMARY

I.   Governmental, non-profit, and for-profit employers will employ workers and capital and buy other inputs only when the employers can obtain enough revenues to pay for them. What is produced, therefore, only tends to be whatever can be sold for a price high enough to cover the employer's costs.

II. Different price levels may result in employers being willing to produce differing amounts of goods and services because of their effect of the employers revenues—higher prices tend to mean greater revenues and, thus, make it more likely an economy's employers will be able to cover their production costs. An aggregate supply curve represents the maximum possible amounts of production that could occur in an economy at each possible level of prices.

III. The total amount of production possible depends on the number of workers who are employed and their productivity.

IV. Employers tend to hire workers as long as what they produce generates enough revenues to cover production costs. Thus a curve depicting the productivity of labor, the production in excess of that needed to cover all the other costs, represents an economy's demand for labor and shows that more workers will be employed at lower wages.

V.   The supply of labor depends on the level of wages; more workers are willing to work at higher and higher wages.

VI. The maximum amount of goods and services an economy's public and private employers can produce, its aggregate supply, depends on whether wages are flexible, flexible upward and inflexible downward, or inflexible.

VII. An economy's general level of wages is the average of a wide range of individual wages.

VIII. Aggregate demand and aggregate supply represent only the most basic of the macroeconomic conditions and relationships that exist in every economy. Aggregate supply is the production an economy's employers can produce. Aggregate demand determines what they will produce. If aggregate demand is insufficient an economy will move towards an equilibrium wherein its employers are not willing to hire more workers, pay higher wages, and produce more goods and services.

IX. If money wages in an economy are inflexible downward, an economy with inadequate customer demand will move towards an equilibrium with unemployed workers and its employers producing less than the maximum levels of production they would be willing and able to produce *if they had more customers*.

X. If wages are flexible downward an economy with inadequate customer demand will move towards an equilibrium with lower wages and no unemployment—but with fewer workers working and the economy's employers producing fewer goods and services than they would be willing and able to produce *if they had more customers*.

CHAPTER TWELVE

THE GROWTH OF JOBS AND INCOME

A growing economy is one in which the employers produce more and more goods and services *per capita* in each successive time period. One way growth occurs is when available but unused productive capacity in the form unemployed workers and idle capital is restored to work by increases in the amount of goods and services that are purchased.

In the long run, however, growth occurs only if the productive capacity of the economy's employers grows *and if the customer spending to buy the additional production also grows*. In essence, an economy's equilibrium level of spending must be high enough and continually growing if it is to result in full employment and the continually utilization of the economy's constantly growing production capacity. In economist-speak both aggregate supply and aggregate demand must grow if an economy's employers are to produce ever increasing amount of goods and services.

Growth in capacity and spending is important for several reasons. First and foremost, growth means that more and more goods and services will be available to meet the needs of the economy's people. Furthermore, and particularly for the United States, growth and the rate of growth are important because of the competition between different political and economic systems; many countries are apparently willing to emulate and befriend whichever form of government and economic system is most successful in producing and distributing ever-increasing per capita amounts of goods and services.

But will production capacity rise and, if it does, will customer spending (aggregate demand) grow enough so that it is fully utilized?

Per capita production versus total production. Even when an economy's capacity to produce grows and customer spending grows so it is all purchased, there is still the possibility that production will not grow on a per-person or per-worker basis. For instance, there may be investment purchases that expand the stock of capital but if the labor force grows at the same rate that the capital stock expands it means that each worker in the economy is still using the same amount of capital. Thus, unless the workers have become better trained or the new capital embodies new and more productive technologies, there will be no reason for increases to occur in the amount of goods and services produced by each worker.

Increases in the stock of capital accompanied by similar increases in the labor force are often referred to as "capital widening" additions to the economy's capital stocks. They tend to result in increased total production without increasing output per worker. This contrasts to the "capital deepening" which occurs when an economy's stock of capital grows faster than the size of the labor force so that, over time, the average worker in the economy's labor force has more capital assets with which to work.

And, of course, the worst case of all is a situation in which total production and the stock of capital rises, or at least so its government claims, but the population rises even faster. (hello India?)

The sources of production capacity growth.

A host of factors influence the amount of goods and services and the size and quality of an economy's capital stock with which its labor force works. Among them: The level and quality of the education of the labor force, the cultural standards of the economy regarding the desirability of work (pay attention Japan and the Islamic countries—women are capable of making significant contributions); the degree to which competition exists to force employers to produce efficiently in order to keep their costs at competitive levels (pay attention Japan, India and Greece); and the level of the technology with which labor and capital are combined in the productive process;

But arguably the three most important conditions if the production of a country's economy is to grow:

1. The degree to which the economy's public and private employers can, as a group, expect that if they produce they will receive enough revenues so that they can pay for the workers and other inputs they use in their production processes. (Pay attention United States—unless your central bank keeps total spending high enough your economy will stagnate no matter what the federal government does to encourage your economy's production capacity to grow);

2. The degree to which economic freedom and the rule of law exists. Without freedom and the rule of law the leadership of a government and its bureaucracy inevitably steps in to enhance their powers and extract the unearned rents of corruption by blocking or discouraging new employers and delaying employer decisions that would result in production growth (Pay attention India, China, Russia, and South Africa. There is something to be learned from the Soviet experience—government bureaucrats are inherently incapable of making significant positive contributions; their efforts to enrich themselves and their cronies by giving them control of businesses and industries discourages everyone else; pay attention United States—promulgating regulations that can be used by to spuriously delay economic decisions for years discourages investment spending and production.)

3. The degree to which competent decision makers are appointed or elected to implement the policies necessary so that there are customers to flow enough revenues to the employers so that the capacity is utilized. (Pay attention United States. Appointing lawyers who never studied economics to the Treasury and Federal Reserve is not a likely road to good economic policies.)

Capacity growth is possible.

Over time it is possible that an economy's *capacity* to produce, its aggregate supply in economic-speak, will be able to increase because of changes that occur in either the size or the productivity of its labor and capital. For instance, so many newly produced capital items such as plant, equipment, and inventory might be purchased by an economy's employers that there is a net addition to the stock of capital in the economy and the technology inherent in it.

Alternately production capacity may grow if an economy adopts laws and patterns of behavior that are conducive to higher levels of production. For example, judicial procedures may be strengthened to protect property rights and encourage timely and exact contract performance;

or the economy's labor force may become more educated and more accustomed to the punctuality required by such things as showing up for work or engaging in preventive maintenance;

or the useless permits and licenses most countries require may be issued more quickly without employer-discouraging bribes or extensive procedural delays;

or the economy's culture may evolve so that women and minorities are allowed to obtain educations, obtain employment, and open businesses.

or potential new employers may no longer be discouraged or prevented because some crony or supporter of the "President" or influential member of the government does not want a competitor;

or potential new employers are no longer discouraged because they must give bribes or part of the ownership and management to the "friends" and families of the rulers.

Can an economy's production capacity continue to grow?

Pragmatic macroeconomists have long attempted to determine how much an economy's production can grow, how fast it will grow, whether it will at some point stop growing, and what it will be like when and if growth stops. They are generally optimistic about the possibility for countries with the rule of law, somewhat surmountable bureaucracies and regulations, and the ability to implement the monetary and fiscal policies needed to generate higher and higher levels of spending as their economy's production capacity gets larger and larger.

In other words, countries such as the United States, Canada and some European and Asian countries have no upper limits on their potential growth and prosperity. They and countries like them appear to be capable of continual growth and a reasonable distribution of the production that does occur.

Pragmatic analysts are not so sanguine about the rest. They see little chance of sustained growth in countries with insurmountable bureaucracies and corruption such as India. In these countries and in countries without economic freedom and the rule of law such as Russia, India, and China they see per capita growth permanently plateauing at relatively low levels of per capita production and income.

They acknowledge, however, that at any given point in even the most advanced economies such as the United States there is an absolute limit to the amount of goods and services that an economy's workers can produce. The limit is set by the existing quality of the economy's labor and its willingness work, the quantity and quality of the capital which is available for the economy's labor force to use, the level of technology, and the impediments imposed by government.

On the other hand, most economists generally see no inherent reason to expect such an upper limit on capacity to remain unchanged over time *if* an economy's production capacity is allowed to grow and *if* total spending grows so that the additional capacity is employed. Both conditions must be met—and they can be met. Firstly, modern monetary and fiscal policies can ensure that there will always be sufficient customer spending. Secondly, human forces and ambitions exist in every economy that will, *if allowed*, result in capacity-expanding increases in the quality of the economy's labor force and the quality, amounts of capital, and the level of technology with which the labor force works.

Labor as the source of continuing growth. The quality of an economy's labor force rises as its workers learn to use larger amounts of capital and higher levels of technology. Workers ranging from clerks and laborers to top management and technical specialists are under continuous pressure to develop their abilities to do this because of the larger incomes that increased productivity tends to bring.

On the other hand, the workers may prevent the economy from growing if they or those supposedly acting on their behalf resist implementing productivity increases because they think it threatens their jobs. This would be the case if they believe, rightly or wrongly, that the increased productivity means fewer workers will be needed and, thus, some of them may lose their jobs. "Protecting" workers from such layoffs by maintaining "work rules" that prevent the introduction of labor saving machines and technology is a major function of many unions and the politicians who support them.

The basis for the continual efforts of the members of a labor force at all levels to improve their productive abilities is rooted in the fact that the size of their incomes tends to determine both the amount of goods and services they will have to meet their infinite needs *and* their social positions in the economy. Consequently, a person can satisfy more of his needs as well as tend to improve his position in society if he increases his ability to produce.

Furthermore, people who do not want others to move ahead of them socially must also improve the quality of their own labor merely to keep their relative positions. In essence, *competitive pressures exist at every level of society to induce people to become more productive.* Not everyone responds, of course, but it appears that in every economy there are enough do to move its labor force, as a group, forward over time—*if* they are free to do so.

Technology and capital as the source of continuing growth. New and productive technologies tend to be sought by individual members of the labor force; they endeavor to enhance their value by increasing the amount and value of the products they can produce via the acquisition of educations and experience. New technologies are similarly introduced by employers who see it as a way to improve their profits and abilities to compete or reach other goals by increasing the productivity of the labor and capital they employ.

Workers know that their productivity makes them more valuable—that is why they attend schools and training programs. Similarly, employers know that productivity is important. That is why they tend to hire appropriately educated and change-receptive people, introduce new technologies, and make capital investments in plant, equipment, and inventories. Indeed, the new technologies are often embedded in new capital goods and are a major reason investment spending occurs.

An additional cause of the present optimism of pragmatic analysts is the belief that the employers of most economies can produce or import whatever amounts of additional capital assets their employees may be able to use as a result of improvements in labor quality or technology. The stocks of capital can grow because savings is not a problem—the existence of business savings, taxes that reduce spendable income, and personal savings means that in economies such as the United States not all income will be used to buy consumer goods and services such that no labor and capital is available to produce replacement and additional capital goods.

Indeed, it is more often the case that taxes, business savings, and personal savings are so high that the primary problem of the policy makers of an economy such as the United States is having enough spending, and keeping it growing, so that employers can continually sell more and more goods and services and thus have an incentive to make more and more investment purchases such that more and more capital is accumulated and production constantly grows. Savings, in other words, is not a problem.

Astute analysts will recall that the role of taxes at the national level is to hold down spending so that there is enough of the economy's production capacity is left available to produce more capital goods. This is possible because governments with central banks have their central bank as an alternative non-inflationary source of funding for whatever level of government spending is desired.

The existence of an alternative funding source is significant for countries such as the United States—because efforts to use only taxes to pay for government spending may at times result in excessive total savings and thus not enough total customer spending to cause employers to make the investment expenditures needed to increase the economy's capital stock so that even more can be produced in the future.

In other words, the basic question the United States and every other economy must answer is—how much taxes need to be collected so that there will be sufficient total spending and enough labor and capital available for employers to buy so the economy can produce even more in the future?

The answer may somehow be that magically the correct amount of taxes is always exactly enough to exactly pay for the government's spending and balance the budget—such a Panglossian optimum has never happened but it is always a possibility even though the prospects of it happening would seem less likely than winning the Irish Sweepstakes.

More likely to be the case is that the optimum level of taxation to generate full employment will either be lower or higher than the amount of government spending and transfers—and thus result in either a deficit or surplus.

One recurring problem has historically arisen when the United States economy has been at full employment: It is that the Congress and the White House see a deficit or surplus and then, because it is "common knowledge" that balanced budgets are "good," decide to either raise taxes and cut spending to end the deficit or cut taxes and raise spending to end the surplus.

The results are inevitable—responding to the deficit by increasing taxes or cutting government spending cuts total spending. The result tends to be unemployment and a lack of customers to incentivize the employers to make investment purchases of the additional capital needed to grow the economy's production capacity. After all, employers won't hire workers and buy more capital goods if they can't even sell all the goods and services they can produce with the plant and equipment they already own.

Similarly, responding to the surplus by reducing taxes under such circumstances will result in increased consumer spending and thus, potentially, a demand-pull inflation. It is also likely to cause a possible bidding away to produce consumer products of the labor and capital that are needed to produce the additional capital products required for growth.

Impediments to capacity growth.

Inadequate employer revenues. Just because total and per capita growth is possible does not mean that either will occur. There are many reasons why various economies have not grown, stopped growing, or grown more slowly than they could. One of the very biggest impediments, an absolute killer of growth, is a lack of sufficient customer revenues.

For example, the periodic absence of sufficient aggregate customer demand due to the failures of the Federal Reserve governors and regional presidents has periodically discouraged the public and private employers' of the United States from making capital investments and introducing new products and technologies. After all, no public or private employer will be able to continue producing additional products for very long if those products do not in generate sufficient revenues to cover the employers' costs. Similarly, public and private employers certainly will tend not to be interested in expanding their plant and equipment and introducing new technologies and products if they expect those facilities to stand idle due to a lack of revenues.

The United States' "Great Depression" of the 1930s and its Great Recession that started in 2008 are classic examples of economic stagnation and low rates of growth caused by inadequate aggregate demand.

Production impediments. On the supply side, the production capacity of economies may not grow because the quality of their labor force remains unchanged; or new technology and additional capital might be available but not acquired and used because the people in the labor force are unmotivated due to such things as the lack of education or the existence of a social structure which prevents or discourages them from improving their productive abilities.

For example, in some societies women are effectively not allowed to work outside the home (Saudi Arabia) or are discouraged from working outside the home (Japan); other societies have powerful caste and cultural codes that encourage people to accept their lot without trying to improve it (India); and other societies have imposed such rigidities, through laws and regulations, to protect politically favored people and employers in virtually every industry and occupation from change and competitors that nothing can be changed or improved (Greece, India).

Still other economies might not grow because they cannot produce or import the additional capital goods needed to increase the productivity of their workers. This lack of capital is often observed in economies with low per-capita levels of production and high rates of population growth. The people in these economies must consume just about everything to survive (Somalia, Zimbabwae, India). Consequently, only a few products can be produced and sold to employers to replace their capital that wears out and expand their stock of capital. It is in these economies that a shortage of savings can impede growth.

Worse, the populations of these economies also tend to increase despite their low levels of per capita production—and the additional people tend to consume the few additional products that can be produced. Thus, such an economy is back where it started, having few goods and service left that can be used as capital. This is the classic case of an economy in which the lack of savings prevents growth.

Still other economies slowly grind to a halt and their per capita output stops growing, or never really starts, because their governments adopt policies that prevent or discourage capital additions, cultural changes, and the introduction of new technologies and employers. This particularly occurs where the government attempts to protect a large portion of its existing employers and workers from the pressures and uncertainties of competition and change (India, China, Greece, and France). Their peoples are doomed to a life of economic stagnation and less overall prosperity than the people in economies such as those of North America and Northern Europe where change and competition are more likely to be allowed.

No upper limit on growth
For relatively free economies.

Pragmatic macroeconomists today accept the idea that it is always possible for an economy such as the United States to have enough customer spending to cause full employment and economic growth—because the wants of people for goods and services are thought to be so infinite in scope and quantity as to be insatiable. Consequently, there is no upper limit to the total amount of goods and services desired by the residents of an economy; thus, there is no limit on the amount of customer purchasing that can occur *if consumers and other customers have sufficient purchasing power.*

This is an important concept—it means that with proper monetary and fiscal policies there can always be enough spending. Then, if there is enough spending, how much the per capita real income of an economy increases over time will be determined by the growth of the production capacities of the economy's governmental, non-profit, and for-profit employers.

The idea that with proper monetary and fiscal policies there can always be enough customer spending is not universally accepted. To this day the type of people who get elected to Congress and appointed to the Federal Reserve seem to be in thrall to the ideas of the early Keynesians—whose writings and media interviews suggest that there is an upper limit to total spending due to a declining marginal propensity to consume and a minimum rate of interest which makes monetary policy ineffective when it is reached.

Some of them also accept the Keynesian conclusion that the existence of a declining marginal productivity of capital means that there is a limit on the investment spending that will occur.—that an economy can become so stocked with capital that its investment spending stops growing because the rate of return expected for any increment to the capital stock would be less than the minimum rate of interest.

Under these circumstances, they wrote and taught (and their students still write and teach), monetary policy will not work because interest rates cannot be lowered. Then something such as more government spending must be done about the situation. If it is not, the level of income in the economy could be in equilibrium at less than full employment with investment maximized and interest rates at the lowest possible level.

What this means, in essence, is that there would be idled production capacity and no reason for employers to expect sufficient additional revenues if they make additional investment purchases to add even more capital. The economy would, in effect, be at a "full investment" level of income without full employment. Capital accumulation, and thus the growth of the economy's productive capacity, would stop at that point.

The Keynesians' answer to the liquidity trap. According to the Keynesians, the only thing that can be done to restore full employment when an economy's interest rates are at a minimum and there still is not enough spending, is to have make-work government spending in the form of "jobs bills" to restore the unemployed workers "dignity."

Here is the condition they foresaw. The level of interest rates has reached the minimum possible level and total spending is still not high enough to reach the amount needed to fully employ the economy's labor force and maximize its production. The economy is in the Keynesian version of the "liquidity trap" in the sense that the level of interest rates can be driven no lower in order to encourage more spending.

This is exactly the state of affairs that existed in the United States during the 2008 Great Recession. It existed because, as group, the governors and regional presidents of the Federal Reserve neither understood their own powers to add and subtract money from circulation nor the reality of how an economy's commercial banks and businesses operate. So, in their sincerely held, but erroneous, beliefs that 1) inflation will somehow result if they increase the money supply when there is inadequate spending, and 2) that monetary policy works through interest rate changes and they had done all they could to drive interest rates down, the governors and regional presidents of the Federal Reserve effectively sat on their hands for years. As a result, production stagnated and more and more Americans could not find work and lost their homes and businesses.

Simultaneously unemployment additionally grew both because the population expanded and because new technologies inexorably arrived to increase the productivity of the workers who could find jobs.

The governors and regional presidents on the FOMC could have, at least during the initial years, ended the recession by appropriately increasing the money supply—because it is the availability of credit and its repayment terms, not the rate of interest, that primarily affects spenders. But they did not; they could have used the community investment and related rules that were in place to see that the commercial banks used their reserves to make loans to consumers and businesses instead of holding them or using them to make financial speculations and fund others to make them. But they did not.

The list of their failures goes on and on and will be continually examined in detail in the chapters ahead in the hope that future analysts and Federal Reserve appointees will not repeat their mistakes.

Does growth inevitably grind to a halt in authoritarian economies?

The per capita production of countries such as China and Russia appear to be growing at a rapid rate. Can their rapid growth continue until they too reach the levels the United States and Northern Europe? Can countries such as those of India, Greece, Italy, France, and most of Africa ever shake off their current self-inflicted stagnations and even begin to grow from where they are today?

Many pragmatic analysts believe that, as things stand today, none of them will ever succeed—that the economies of countries such as China and Russia are more likely to join India and most of the African countries with permanently low per capita incomes. In essence, the analysts see the people in such countries as doomed to being relatively poor and the gap between their peoples' incomes and those of the United States and Northern Europe continuing to widen—until they overthrow their governments implement economic freedom and the rule of law.

Political speeches and charismatic leaders to the contrary, in the real world massive internationally financed capital projects and minor interest rate and regulatory changes have very little impact on the investment decisions that lead to increases in an economy's capital stock and the growth of an economy's per capita output. Infinitely more significant are the laws and regulations provided by an economy's governments that are actually implemented and, most important of all, the expectations of existing and potential workers and employers as to the existence in the years ahead of revenues, economic freedom, and the rule of law.

Countries with high growth rates are often referred to very positively as "Economic Tigers" because their rapidly growing incomes may open new opportunities for existing employers to invest to expand their production capital and new employers to make the investment purchases necessary to commence operations. Before its economy collapsed due to its banks speculating in such "sure things" as Greek debt and mortgage derivatives Ireland was hailed as a "Celtic Tiger."

China was, and perhaps erroneously still is, thought of as an "Asian Tiger" whose economy will continue to grow. Its total and per capita production initially soared as its centralized government allowed its communist party officials and their families to take over its politically paralyzed and grossly inefficient industries.

The percentage increases in China's total production were initially impressive because they started from such a base level. But then corruption and the lack of the rule of law caused China's growth to slow to a virtual halt even though the average Chinese citizen was still significantly poorer than his counterparts in the United States, Japan, and Northern Europe.

Indeed, in absolute terms the citizens of the modern economies actually were pulling further and further ahead even when China's growth rates were peaking—their smaller growth percentages applied to their much higher income levels resulted in the average citizen of the world's higher income countries getting bigger absolute income increases than the average Chinese.

Similarly, before its bureaucracy-imposed economic stagnation and paralysis came to be realized as permanent, India was also thought to be a fast growing "Asian Tiger" because of the high rates of growth its bureaucrats inevitably reported in response to their targets in India's latest five-year-plan—in the best tradition of the Soviet Union where many of them were educated.

Unfortunately government press releases and extrapolations from questionable data can be misleading indicators of how an economy has been performing and can be expected to perform in the future. That is particularly the case if the data are "cooked" by the bureaucrats to show that a government's five year plan or other goals are being met (sorry India—no pragmatic analyst can believe your economy grew fifty percent without a comparable increase in the production of electricity).

Identifying economies with growth prospects.

Various efforts have been made to systematically forecast and compare the investment opportunities of different economies in an effort to identify those that are potential growth tigers as opposed to the economic "pussycat" countries which are tiger poseurs.

One such effort, the Lafarge Index, has proven remarkably accurate in predicting the economic prospects of various economies. It focuses on the incomes and prospects of the economy's non-elite masses, the people who, as a group, provide the employees and the greatest portion of its consumer and other spending. The index is used to guide the internal investment decision making of more than a few large multinational corporations. It is also is useful "shorthand" tool for analysts to use to evaluate and compare the likely economic futures of different countries. In essence, the higher the number generated by the Lafarge equation, the lower the chances of the economy growing and the greater the likelihood of significant investor losses via political instability, theft, and expropriation.

Astute analysts will note that the Lafarge equation and its components focus on long run expectations in relation to the negative impact of governmental interferences. They will particularly note that it ignores the aspects more commonly discussed at Junior Chamber of Commerce lunches, congressional hearings, and Federal Reserve board meetings—such as minor interest rate changes, the need for more savings in order to have more investment, and the condition and size of the government's budget.

In other words, the Lafarge index attempts to pragmatically relate investment spending and the chances of an employer being successful in a specific country to the conditions and impediments that actually exist in the country.

Lafarge index =—150 + 90P + 30(D-90) + (J-180) + 5B + 50(Br x Br) + 800S + 30(2000-WW) + 20CR+ 20XW where P is the number of outdoor pictures of the country's leaders and political party; D is the estimated number of days it will take to obtain all the licenses and permits to build and operate a cement manufacturing plant; J is the average number of days required to obtain a final court decision in a contract dispute; B is the percentage likelihood of being required to pay a bribe to open such a business and operate it during its first 365 days; Br is the estimated number of bribes that will have to be paid during the entire process through the first 365 days of operation; CR is the percentage estimate that the necessary permits will not be forthcoming unless a crony or relative of a political leader is given an ownership interest; S is the number of statues in the country of the existing leader or deceased members of his family; WW is the average number of hours private sector employees actually work per year;

XW is the average number of days needed to discharge an incompetent or dishonest employee.

CHAPTER SUMMARY

I.   A growing economy is one in which the employers produce more and more goods and services *per capita* in each successive time period.

II.   There is in every economy an absolute limit to the amount of goods and services that can be produced at any given time; it depends on such things as the quantity and quality of labor, the quantity and quality of capital, and the level of technology. Growth can occur on a one-time basis merely by putting unemployed production capacity back to work.

III. Growth is potentially continuous over time with no upper limits. Workers can become more productive with education, experience and the use of additional capital and improved technologies; impediments to growth can be removed; and customer spending can continue to grow because the wants of man are insatiable.

IV. Growth tends to be limited in countries which do not allow personal freedom and the rule of law.

V.   Growth is not inevitable. Governments may interfere to protect existing employers from competition; consumer and other customer spending may not increase; the quality of labor may not improve if the educational system is static or in decline; there may be a shortage of capital goods and key inputs such as electricity; government regulations and corruption might discourage capital accumulation and the introduction of new employers, products, and production techniques; and population increases may offset any increases in production.

VII. Governments desiring growth have alternatives such as the removal of onerous regulations and improving the rule of law; offering tax and subsidy incentives; supporting education and technological advances; and insuring that there will always be sufficient total spending. Often such efforts are negatively warped by efforts to assist existing employers resist the arrival of potential competitors and provide favors to cronies, family members, and political supporters.

CHAPTER THIRTEEN

THE MANY CAUSES OF
INFLATION AND UNEMPLOYMENT

Inflation and unemployment, and the circumstances and policies that cause them, are more than just matters of intellectual and political interest. They determine whether or not men and women will be vainly roaming the streets looking for employment to earn the wages needed to provide food and shelter for their families or whether the slim pension of an elderly couple or the trust fund of a disabled child will be adequate to provide the necessities of life.

The equilibrium level of income is the level of total spending toward which economies constantly move, not one they ever attain. In the real world, economies such as that of the United States are too complex and dynamic for all the contributing factors to attain such an idealized state at the same time. And while economies are constantly evolving towards equilibrium their ever changing conditions and policies may generate spending levels and other circumstances that result in either inflation or unemployment and less than maximum levels of production.

In today's common usage the term "inflation" means an increase in an economy's general level of prices increase so that consumers and other buyers have to pay generally higher prices for the goods and services produced by an economy's public and private employers. The term "unemployment" is typically used to mean workers who are willing and able to work but cannot find jobs. Capital in the form of plant, equipment, and inventories can be similarly unemployed as well. The term "economic growth" is typically used to mean increases in an economy's total or per capita real production.

A number of different indices are used to indicate how the United States' economy is performing and guide its policies—such as the GNP deflator which is an index based on prices of all the goods and services produced by employers and the oft-cited Consumer Price Index which is based on the prices of a relatively small number of consumer products. These and other indicators are so important for policy purposes that an entire chapter is devoted to them.

There is no question that inflation and unemployment are disastrous for people and their politicians. In the case of high levels of unemployment, it means millions of people and businesses going on welfare, being forced to retire early or close their businesses, going bankrupt, losing their homes to mortgage foreclosures, exhausting their savings, ruining their credit. Increased unemployment also means governments will tend to have deficits because fewer taxes will be collected and more transfers paid.

Similarly, in the event of inflation, it means a reduced value of one's monetary assets such as pensions and financial instruments such as bonds and bank deposits. It also means a reduced value of wages and incomes that are not indexed to the price level.

In essence, when the federal government or the Federal Reserve allows or causes inflation it is effectively levying a 'tax' on the purchasing power of the dollar and dollar denominated assets such as bonds and business receivables, and dollar denominated incomes such as wages, rents, dividends and interest.

Little wonder, then, that *full employment with stable prices and ever-growing levels of per capita production are the basic macroeconomic goals* of the United States and almost every other non-authoritarian country. Accordingly, inflation and unemployment and low rates of per capita growth are conditions to be avoided—and that requires decision makers and analysts who understand how and why they occur.

So what are the basic causes of inflation and unemployment?

EXCESSIVE SPENDING
CAN CAUSE INFLATION

One of the most commonly discussed economic events that *may*, under certain circumstances, cause inflation and unemployment is an increase or decrease in the total spending done by consumers, investors, foreigners and governments—the customers of the economy's public and private employers. If total spending, *aggregate demand* in economist-speak, gets beyond the levels needed for full employment the economy's prices will be bid up as buyers compete to buy the limited amount of available goods and services; if total customer spending is too low, employers will lay off workers and reduce their production to the output levels that can be sold.

Pragmatic analysts understand that *customer spending increases can be caused by a multitude of factors* in a country such as the United States—not just the popular and easily identifiable ones such as increases in the money supply. They also understand that the various other causes of inflation and may be occurring simultaneously along with changes in total spending.

Among the many things other than increases in the money supply that could cause changes in total spending:

Foreigners may buy more goods and services as a result of a foreign government changing the exchange rate between their economy's money and the United States dollar;

Or state and local taxes may be reduced to increase people's disposable incomes and their ability to buy consumer goods and services;

Or political speeches and events may change employer profit expectations and cause them to increase their investment purchases;

Or tax and other laws may change to encourage the purchase of more new homes or anything else;

Or the stock market might boom and affect the propensity to consume by increasing the value of people's stocks and bonds.

Or new products and services such as medical advances may be developed and cause people to increase their consumption spending;

Or the distribution of income might change to give more to people with higher or lower propensities to consume;

Or people might feel they have to save less because they no longer mistakenly believe Social Security will run out of money;

Or state and local governments might raise their spending;

Or fears of inflation may cause people with money to run out and spend it before prices rise; fears of a price freeze may cause employers to raise their prices so that if they are frozen they will be frozen at a higher level;

Or there might be a balanced budget increase in state and local government spending;

Or new financial instruments might be developed or so that more money gets to those who would spend it.

The list of things that might cause the size of an economy's total spending to change and cause inflation or unemployment is endless and ongoing. Pragmatic analysts will note that, once again, nowhere is there any mention of the usual inflation suspects so beloved of journalists, "business economists," Federal Reserve governors, and the speakers at Junior Chamber of Commerce lunches—deficits, national debt, and federal spending. Analysts know that in the real world, inflation and unemployment can be caused by numerous forces and events, many of which are occurring simultaneously and pushing the economy in opposite directions.

Demand-pull inflations.

Consider an economy whose public and private employers are, at least for the moment, employing everyone who is willing to work. They are then, in effect, producing as much as the economy can possibly produce—as, for example, the United States was producing in 2007.

Of course, "full employment" does not literally mean everyone of working age is working at an income earning job. There will always be those who decline to work for some reason such as raising children or retirement or pursuing an education; those unable to work because of illness, incarceration, injury, and age; those in the normal process of moving between jobs; those beset by structural changes in the industries where they used to work who are unable to find jobs because of their location or lack of training and experience; and a few lazy bums.

Typically about seventy percent of the working age population is in the United States workforce at any point in time. The "working age" and propensities to work tend to increase as people live longer or if their retirement savings are wiped out by unemployment, inflation, or illness.

For the sake of an example, and to make the point that the usual suspects do not have to be involved, assume that the Federal Reserve does not increase the money supply and that federal spending and the deficit do not increase, but that one or more of the many other things that could cause spending to increase does occur. For instance, exports rise because China changes its import policies and starts buying more products that are made in the United States; or state and local governments stop sending so much money to their employee pension plans and start using more of it to buy roads and education; or new energy sources are identified and investors rush to increase their investment spending to develop them.

Whatever the reason, total spending obviously tends to rise when such changes occur. Moreover, the initial increase has a multiplier effect as the dollars of additional spending are passed on to consumers and governments to be spent and re-spent. But what if the economy's employers already have enough revenues so they are already producing all they can produce? The result is inevitable; the increased customer spending results in inflation—by causing the prices of the goods and services its employers produce to be bid up to higher levels.

More specifically, the inflation occurs because total spending has increased above the level that was already high enough to produce everything the economy's employers and labor force are capable of producing. Thus, some of the spenders who want to buy goods and services will find none available at the current level of prices. These would-be buyers will then have to compete for the available products by offering to pay higher prices for them.

The market system works—the buyers' efforts will cause the economy's prices to rise so long as more goods and services are demanded by the economy's customers than are supplied by the economy's government, non-profit, and for-profit employers. In effect, prices in the economy will keep rising until everything that can be produced is rationed out among the buyers—there will be an inflation.

The level of money wages in the economy will also tend to increase as a result of the inflation caused by the increased demand. The fully employed workers are now worth more to their employers because of the higher prices at which their output can be sold. Any employers who do not increase their employees' wages will soon find the employees moving to other employers who can and will pay more. Only when the level of money wages is bid up to a new and sufficiently higher level will there be no shortage of workers at the employers who were initially hiring them.

Such an inflation is typically referred to as *demand-pull* inflation—because the increase in spending "pulls up" the economy's general level of prices as the purchasers bid up the prices of the various goods and services produced by the economy's public and private employers.

No impact on jobs or production. Inflation caused by too much spending does not change the amount of workers employed or the amount of products they produce. Even though an economy's levels of money wages and product prices rise when spending increases under demand-pull conditions, there tends to be no effect on either the amount of goods and services purchased or the number of workers employed and the level of real wages they receive—they do not change because the economy is already at full employment and money wages will rise to restore whatever is the general level of real wages associated with the full employment.

Importantly, once such an inflation occurs, there is no going back to the earlier level of prices and wages—because, in general, money wages tend to be inflexible downward due to such things as union contracts, employment agreements, minimum wage laws. This means there will now be higher costs of production at every level of output.

Prices also tend to stick at the higher levels once they are reached; after all, once the level of money wages and the prices of inputs increase, the economy's employers will only be willing to produce the various possible levels of production at the higher prices that will generate the now higher revenues needed to cover the now higher production costs that will now occur at each level of real income. There is, in other words, a "ratchet" effect—because prices in general can only increase.

Inflation's other effects. A demand-pull inflation tends to be benign in the sense that total production continues to be maximized and its labor force continues to be fully employed. But it's not totally benign; it may have other effects on the behavior of an economy's participants.

First, it may change the participants' propensities to save if the inflation is expected to continue. After all, why should an individual save if he or she expects to buy less in the future with his savings and financial investments than he can get now?

Second, and going in the other direction, higher prices may encourage savings because they reduce the real savings (purchasing power) of savings individuals have accumulated in form of money and financial instruments. People who want to maintain their lifestyles when they quit working will now have to save more.

Third, higher prices tend to cause a redistribution of purchasing power away from people such as pensioners who are living on fixed incomes; they cannot get as many products with the disposable incomes they receive, and thus more goods and services are available for individuals whose disposable incomes rise as prices rise.

Inflation is not inevitable when spending increases. Demand-pull inflation is not the inevitable result of increased spending any more than increased spending is the inevitable result of an increased money supply.

First, there may be no effect at all on an economy's overall level of prices *if* the increased spending occurs when the economy's employers have idle production capacity and are producing less than maximum levels of output—the kind of situation that existed throughout the United States' Great Recession. Then the additional spending tends to increase production and jobs instead of prices.

Second, the increased spending may occur over time and be accompanied by an increase in the economy's production capacity—its aggregate supply—so that there is never a shortage of goods and services to cause prices to be bid up.

In either case, production and employment will rise without prices necessarily being bid up. In the first case it will rise as the existence of additional customers motivates the economy's employers to reactivate their idle capacity and hire more workers to produce the additional goods and services which they can now sell; in the second case the additional production capacity will absorb the additional spending.

In essence, neither an increase in consumer or other spending nor an increase in the money supply nor any of the many other things that might cause spending to rise and have a multiplier effect on total spending tend to be inflationary—*so long as the employers have production capacity and workers available to employ.*

Using the model to depict inflation caused by excessive spending.

The basic effect of increased customer buying on an economy's production, employment, prices, and wages depends on the initial state of the economy. Consider Figure 13-1 as an example of the United States economy. Initially all is well. The economy is in equilibrium at price level P10 and money wage level Wm1. There is enough aggregate spending (D1) so that the economy is operating at full employment levels of production (Yr18) and employment (N20) and is initially in equilibrium at price level P10 and money wage level Wm1.

Now assume that for some reason the economy's consumers or other buyers increase their spending in an effort to buy even more goods and services. As a result, aggregate demand increases to D2. Now the economy's customers are willing to buy more goods and services at price level P10 than the economy's public and private employers have the capacity to supply. The result is inevitable—there will be a demand-pull inflation in this economy as the prices of the goods and services its employers produce are bid up to higher levels by the additional spending.

The higher level of the economy's prices (inflation) will occur as customers desiring to purchase additional goods and services find none available since the economy's producers are already selling all the goods and services they are willing to produce at the existing level of prices. These would-be buyers will then have to compete for the available products by offering to pay higher prices for them. Their efforts will cause the economy's prices to rise so long as more goods and services are demanded by the economy's customers than are supplied by the economy's governmental, non-profit, and for-profit employers.

For example, if customer spending rises from D1 to D2 in the Figure 13-1 replica of the United States economy, the result will be inflation as the increased purchasing bids up the level of prices. Specifically, the price level will rise from P10 to P20.

The level of money wages in the economy will also tend to increase—since the higher price level and the initial level of money wages (WM1) would otherwise result in a lower level of real wages so that more workers are demanded than are supplied. Only when the level of money wages is bid up to Wm2 as a result of the tendency toward a shortage of workers will the level of real wages be restored to W15. Then the economy's employers will no longer desire to employ more workers than are willing to work.

Moreover, once such an inflation occurs there is no going back to the earlier level of prices—both because prices tend to be inflexible downward and because of the resulting increase in the money wages employers will thereafter have to pay their workers. Money wages also tend to be inflexible downward. And so do the prices of everything else including the prices of the inputs used in the production process. That means there will now tend to be permanently higher costs of production at every level of production that might occur. So prices will have to stay high to cover the higher costs that will now exist at ever level of production.

The effects of such cost increases is depicted in the Figure 13-1 replica economy by a shift in the economy's aggregate supply curve from S1 to S2; it shifts upward to the extent that higher product prices are needed at each level of production to cover the now higher production costs caused by the increase in the level of money wages. After all, once an economy's money wages and prices increase, the economy's employers will be willing to only produce the various possible levels of production at the higher prices that will generate the higher revenues needed to cover the higher production costs that will now occur at each level of real income.

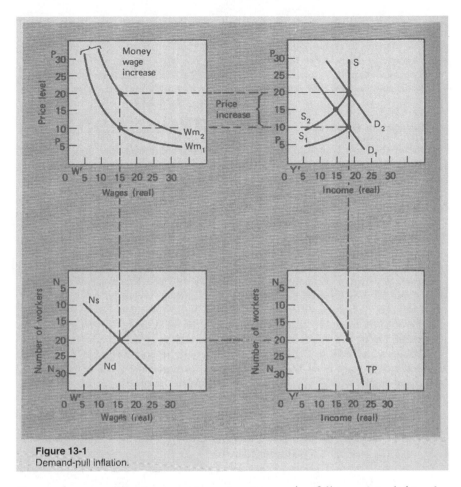

Figure 13-1
Demand-pull inflation.

Customer spending does not just rise. It can also fall just as it did in the United States in 2008 after years of full employment and ever-growing levels of production and higher wages. Reductions in the amount of goods and services customers purchase can result from a variety of causes. For instance, employer expectations may decline and cause a reduction in their investment spending for plant and equipment;

Or the supply of money might be reduced by foreign banks and governments deciding to hold more of the dollars they receive when American consumers buy abroad—then there would be a smaller money supply in the United States and interest rates might rise and discourage consumer spending and the borrowing of money by governments to finance road and school construction;

Or the Congress might raise tax rates in an effort to balance the budget and cause less consumption spending and a multiplier effect as people's disposable incomes decline;

Or the euro zone banks might get in trouble and reduce the loans they make that result in the foreigners importing American-made products;

Or mortgage derivatives might collapse and cause banks to cut back on their loans to each other and to consumers and businesses.

Or the Chinese and Japanese may cut back on their spending to buy American-produced wheat and products.

Or a reduction in total spending may be caused by tax increases and government spending decreases to "balance the budget." Indeed, this may well result in such low taxable profits and transactions and such increased unemployment that there are even bigger deficits and a larger national debt.

The European Central Bank and the IMF experienced this when they tried to force Greece and other countries to reduce their deficits by raising their taxes and cutting their spending. The Greek deficit rose instead of falling—because the higher taxes and lower government spending had multiplier effects that resulted in such a large decline in total spending that it caused massive unemployment and a great reduction in taxable wages, business profits and sales. So tax collections collapsed, transfers to the unemployed increased, and the deficits grew instead of falling.

What actually happens when there is a decline in the level of spending in an economy depends on the flexibility of the economy's wages and prices. Those of the United States and other advanced economies appear to be flexible upward and inflexible downward.

Consider an economy in equilibrium with full employment, stable prices, and a full employment level of production. Now assume that something happens to reduce total spending. This would be the case, for example, if Congress raises taxes to balance the budget or the Federal Reserve tightens up on the money supply or euro zone countries reduce their imports because their banks are being hit by a sovereign debt crisis.

An example of such an economy is depicted in Figure 13-2. It starts with the economy in equilibrium at full employment with demand D1 resulting in the economy having a full employment level of production Yr18 and price level P15, money wage level Wm1, and the employment of N20 workers.

Now assume that something happens to reduce total spending so that aggregate demand declines from D1 to D2. This would be the case, for example, if Congress raises taxes to balance the budget or the Federal Reserve tightens up on the money supply, or the countries in the euro zone reduce their imports because their banks are being devastated by a sovereign debt crisis.

When spending in the Figure 13-2 economy falls from D1 to D2 only Yr11 of goods and services will be purchased at price level P15. Thus, if the economy's prices are "sticky" downward and do not fall, as would certainly be the case in today's United States, employers would only be willing to employ the N10 workers that would be needed to produce the Yr11 level output that can be sold. In essence, production and employment would recede or be depressed by the decline in the level of total spending.

In other words, if the prices of the products produced by an economy's public and private employers are inflexible downward and a spending reduction occurs, production in the economy will fall and its unemployment rate will rise.

Figure 13-2 is a good example of what happens in the United States when spending recedes for some reason as it did in 2008. In the United States, both prices and wages tend to be inflexible downward as a result of long-term price agreements, non-competitive producers, government-determined prices, and production costs such as wages that do not decline due to minimum wage laws and the long-term employment contracts such as are traditionally negotiated by unions, awarded to professors.

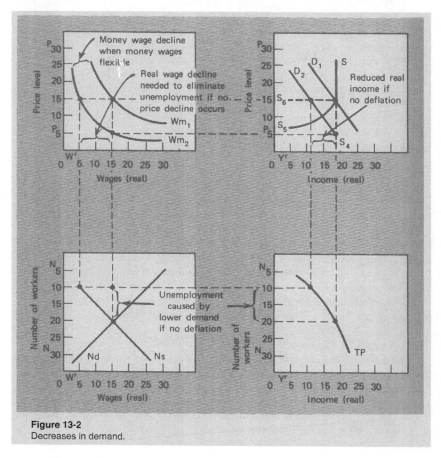

Figure 13-2
Decreases in demand.

Recessions and depressions. When decline in production and employment when customer spending recedes or is depressed are popularly known as a "recessions" or "depressions." And they have all-too-often been inflicted on the United States. Several of them have been particularly severe. One in this century, now known as the Great Recession, occurred when the initial and easily endable 2008 recession morphed into a prolonged depression due to inadequate policy responses. A similar situation occurred in the 1930s and is known as the Great Depression.

Whatever you call the result, in the real world grossly inadequate levels of total spending mean a huge loss of production and a massive increase in unemployment with all the human distress and hardships that exist when people cannot find jobs. It also tends to result in unbalanced government budgets as welfare and unemployment expenses skyrocket and taxes collections collapse. That is exactly what happened in the United States during both depressions.

What is so sad and depressing is that such adverse events are totally unnecessary and can be easily and quickly cured. How that might be accomplished will subsequently be discussed in some detail. Suffice to say it requires something the United States and other countries frequently seem to have in uniquely short supply—competent fiscal policy and monetary policy decision makers.

Flexible wages as a solution. Wages do not tend to be flexible downward in countries such as the United States—but what if they were? Obviously if an economy's labor market is highly competitive and wages are flexible, the unemployed workers in the economy will compete for the available jobs by bidding down wages until they get so low that anyone who still wants to work can find a job.

Consider again the example economy depicted in Figure 13-2. If wages in the economy are totally flexible, the level of money wages will decline to Wm2—the level at which all the workers who want to work (N10) can generally find jobs while the others stop participating in the labor force and, at least, temporarily, retire.

In essence, if wages in an economy are totally flexible, the level of money wages in the economy will decline to the level at which all the workers who want to work can generally find jobs while the rest stop participating in the labor force and, at least, temporarily, retire. Then there will be full employment but the smaller number of workers who are employed will produce less—the economy's production will still have "un-grown" or "receded" or been "depressed" as a result of the decline in total spending.

If wages are not downwardly flexible, however, wages will not fall and more workers will be willing to work than will be employed. That is generally what happened in the United States during both the Great Recession and the Great Depression. It seems that laws, labor agreements, tradition, and general inertia combined to keep the general level of wages from falling.

In other words, in countries such as the United States widespread wage reductions are not likely to occur when spending is inadequate to generate full employment. Instead, there is every reason to expect that a reduction of total customer spending will result in both unemployment and less than maximum levels of production.

This is exactly what happened in the United States during the Great Recession and the depression that followed: Product prices remained relatively stable; labor force participation rates fell as millions of workers temporarily dropped out or were forced out of the labor force; the hours in the average work week declined; and some wages fell but most did not. The dropouts, forceouts, and lower wages were not enough to eliminate all the unemployment.

PRODUCTIVITY INCREASES
CAN CAUSE UNEMPLOYMENT

An economy's productive capacity tends to be constantly rising in response to improvements in such things as the size, skills and quality of its labor force; the quantity and quality of the capital and other materials used by its labor force; the work rules under which employees work; and the technology or way its labor force uses the economy's stock of capital.

If productivity rises, it means fewer employees will be needed to produce the same levels of production. In other words, productivity increases will cause unemployment—*unless additional spending occurs.* On the other hand, if spending does rise as productivity increases there will be more goods and services produced and even higher levels of wages and other incomes.

Looking at it another way, increased productivity accompanied by increased spending means the existing labor force can continually produce more and more goods and services.

In other words, for productivity increases to continually cause higher levels of production means that spending will have to continually be higher and higher if production is to grow and the economy's labor force is to be fully employed.

Importantly, if spending does grow, the productivity increase will also tend to mean that the economy's workers will be more and more valuable to employers because they can contribute more and more to their employer's. As a result, productivity increases mean the average worker will now able to command a higher wage—and if they don't get it from their current employers they will tend to be able to move to other employers and get it. In other words, market forces insure an economy's wages reflect the productivity of its labor force.

The reality of increased productivity is that more goods and services *can* be produced in the economy at every level of prices and wages can be increased. Whether more *will* be produced and wages will increase, however, depends on whether or not there are buyers for the additional products. If spending does not increase to keep pace with the increased productivity, there will be unemployment and idle production capacity instead of higher wages. Wages will not tend to rise because there will be no need for employers to pay more to get all the workers they wish to hire.

An example of the effect of a productivity increase without a concurrent increase in spending is depicted in Figure 13-3. The curves representing the conditions in the economy prior to the productivity increases are identified with the subscript 1, and those for the various conditions that might exist after a productivity increase with the subscript 2. The demand for workers increases from Nd1 to Nd2 to reflect the increased value of each additional worker now that each is more productive.

In this example economy the aggregate supply curve representing the new and higher levels of maximum production that can result from the productivity increase lies to the right of the economy's original aggregate supply curve. It depicts the reality that increased productivity means more goods and services *can* be produced in the economy at every level of prices. But, once again, whether more *will* be produced depends on whether or not there are buyers for the additional products. On the other hand, there will be unemployment and idle production capacity if spending does not increase to keep pace with the increased productivity.

In the Figure 13-3 example economy the increase in productivity from S1 to S2 as a result of productivity increasing from TP1 to TP2 means that fewer (N10 instead of N20) of the now more productive workers are needed to produce the goods and services that can be sold. In other words, productivity increases can cause unemployment.

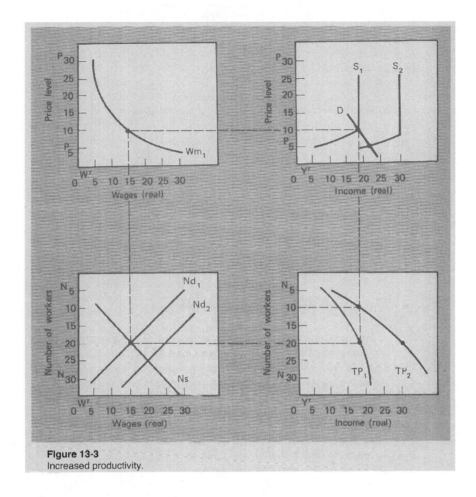

Figure 13-3
Increased productivity.

The effects of productivity increases.

Merely increasing the productivity of an economy's labor force is not enough to ensure that a higher level of production will actually occur and that the now-more-productive workers will earn higher wages. To the contrary, productivity increases can and will cause unemployment if customer spending is not sufficiently increased. After all, employers will only produce goods and services if they can sell them or otherwise generate enough revenues to cover their production costs.

What this means for an economy such as the United States is that if its worker productivity continually increases, and total customer spending increases more slowly, production will only rise to the extent that more can be sold and the economy's public and private employers will employ fewer of the economy's now-more-productive workers. In other words, *there will be growing unemployment even though production rises.*

This is exactly what happened in the United States during the Great Recession: the labor force and worker productivity continued to rise and total customer spending rose more slowly and sometimes not at all. Unsophisticated analysts, journalists, and Federal Reserve appointees looked at the slow growth when it began and said such things as "the recession has ended" and "the recovery has begun." In fact, unemployment was rising and production was receding or being depressed further and further below the economy's capacity to produce.

It is the willingness to confront such realities and to try to understand and explain them and to implement pragmatic policies to keep economies prosperous that is the defining difference between today's pragmatic macroeconomists and the "business economists" and journalists who spend time writing about interest rate changes and the need for "make work" jobs spending.

More spending is the only rational response when productivity increases.

Unemployment, less than maximum levels of production, and stagnant wages are not the inevitable fate of an economy that experiences productivity increases. Instead, the level of product purchasing may rise at the same time. Then the economy's employers will increase workers' wages so they can increase their output of goods and services to the new and higher levels that the increased productivity enables them to produce. After all, if employers do not raise the wages to reflect their increased productivity the workers in a free society such as the United States will tend to take their services to other employers who will pay them wages that reflect their contributions.

Figure 13-4 depicts the effect of adding spending increases to the effect of productivity increases. In this example, total spending increase from

D1 to D2. As a result production in the economy increases from Yr18 to Yr30 and the number of employed workers increases from N20 to N30.

In this example, the labor supply has increased as people return to the labor force and immigrants arrive in response to the higher wages employers are now willing to pay for the now-more-productive workers. Real wages increase from Wr15 to Wr20 as money wages increase from Wm1 to Wm2. Money wages increase because the labor shortage that now exists at Wm1 will cause the economy's employers to compete for employees by offering higher and higher money wages until employers are able to hire all the workers they wish to employ.

All workers tend to benefit when productivity increases.

Even if the productivity gains only occur in certain industries the entire labor force benefits from the increased general demand for labor and the desire of employers to hire enough workers so they can produce all they can sell. Here's how it works. The demand for more labor in some industries means there will be a general shortage of labor at the original level of money wages and its associated real wage level. Thus employers seeking more workers will bid up money wages as they compete to hire the available labor. Furthermore, even more of the economy's population may willing to work if the wages they are offered increases—thus increased productivity may also increase the number of workers employed and paying taxes increases.

These are the outcomes of productivity increases that an economy such as the United States can enjoy—*if* the Congress approves appropriate fiscal and trade legislation or *if* the Federal Reserve governors appropriately increase the supply of money and liquidity. Such policies would result in the increases in total spending needed to keep pace with the productivity increases. The initial spending increases they generate, of course, would then have the usual multiplier impact on total spending.

Analysts should also note that the higher profits that will tend to be associated with the increased production and the higher wages and increased number of workers receiving them. These, in turn, will tend to mean increased tax collections and less transfer spending—a move towards budgetary surpluses.

In essence, as productivity increases governments will move further toward a condition of budgetary surpluses—*if* appropriate policies are implemented so that spending increases as productivity increases. With the right macroeconomic policies and decision makers it is possible for wages, employment, production, and tax collections to rise without causing inflation.

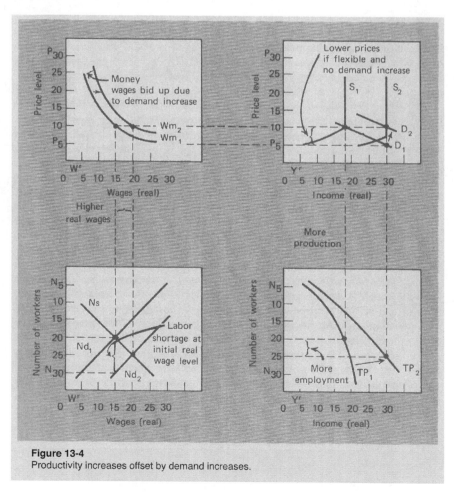

Figure 13-4
Productivity increases offset by demand increases.

The policy alternatives when productivity increases.

Two basic policy alternatives exist when unemployment results from increased productivity. The first alternative is to increase customer spending so that the additional goods and services are produced. This is typically accepted as the most desirable course of action since it results in a larger amount of goods and services being available, more employment opportunities, higher wages, and no unemployment problems. It also tends to increase taxable incomes so that the economy's governments move toward budgetary surpluses.

The other alternative is to ignore the possibility of increasing production and, instead, prevent the unemployment by eliminating or offsetting the increased productivity. This is typically accomplished by such techniques as legislating shorter work weeks, forcing early retirements of workers and machines, preventing workers from working over-time, and insisting on the retention of traditional work rules and methods of production.

It is interesting to note that a substantial portion of the labor union movements in the United States and Europe have consistently advocated such policies. Apparently their leaders and political allies believe there is only so much work to be done such that any improvement in worker productivity means that fewer workers will be needed. The advocates of such policies, in essence, ignore the possibility that demand can be easily and quickly increased with appropriate monetary policies.

More surprisingly, since they claim to have the interests of workers at heart, they ignore the higher wages that tend to accompany productivity increases when production is allowed to increase. In the real world of countries such as the United States and those in the European Common Market, the only way working people can get higher wages so they can buy more goods and services, and thus have higher standards of living, is for the economy's public and private employers and their employees to produce more so that the economy's total production increases—*and that requires both productivity increases and spending increases.*

HIGHER PRODUCTION COSTS
CAN CAUSE INFLATION AND
UNEMPLOYMENT

One of the many conditions that can arise to *simultaneously* cause both higher prices and unemployment is an increase in the employers' costs of producing goods and services. Employers will still be able to produce if their costs increase—but only if they can charge higher prices to cover their now higher costs.

Higher production costs can be caused by numerous events such as increases in wages, property taxes, interest rates, utility prices, federal benefit mandates, energy prices, union activities, the prices of imports, restrictive legislation and regulations, safety requirements, and the list goes on and on and on.

The initial effect of cost increases that are not offset by lower costs elsewhere is that while the economy's public and private employers may still physically be able to produce as many goods and services as before the increase, they will now only able to produce them if they can get the higher prices that are needed to generate the higher revenues needed to cover their now higher costs.

The willingness of an economy's employers to supply the same amount of goods and services but only at higher prices is the inevitable effect of higher costs that are not offset by productivity increases.

Consider the effect that an increase in one important cost, the level of money wages, might have on the prices and production of an economy such as that of the United States in 2007. It is initially in equilibrium with money wages such that all the workers who want to work can find jobs and there is a full employment level of production.

Now assume the general level of wages in the economy rises as would be the case, for example, if the government tries to "help workers" by requiring all employers to provide more medical benefits to every worker; or if there is a burst of successful union wage-raising activities due to changes in the government's laws that encourage union organizing; or if the government increases the employers' social security and unemployment insurance contributions in the mistaken belief that such an increase is needed to "save" Social Security.

If such things happen the capacity of the employers to produce remains the same—but the higher costs would tend to cause inflation by forcing the employers to raise their prices in order to cover their now higher costs. The rules associated with the United States' adoption of universal medical care had exactly this effect.

The result such efforts to "help workers" is an inflation as prices move higher to cover the now-higher wage costs. But at the same time, because the current level of spending now buys fewer products at their now higher prices, production will tend to decline and workers will be laid off or encouraged to retire because employers now need fewer of them to produce the goods and services that can be sold.

But that is not the only effect. The higher wages and benefits may also increase the willingness of people to work. Some people who were previously not working might look at the additional medical and other benefits and decide they would like to work to get the new and higher real wages that the government action caused. As a group, they would join with those being laid off and unemployment would grow even larger. In other words, *the government's efforts to "help the workers" can result in higher prices and, unemployed workers.*

Such a state of affairs is traditionally referred to as *cost-push* inflation and unemployment and sometimes as *wage-push* inflation and unemployment, since both prices and unemployment have been "pushed up" as a result of the higher costs.

The level of an economy's prices and its rate unemployment tend to rise when its employers have higher wage and other costs because the cost of some of the products they have been producing can no longer be covered by the prices they fetch. The employers are forced to stop producing them—are not willing to supply as many goods and services at the initial price level as their customers are willing to buy. As a result, the purchasers bid up the price level as they compete to buy the fewer goods and services the employers are willing to supply.

In essence, other things equal, government efforts to force up wages without a concurrent productivity increase also tends to "help" some of the workers to lose their jobs. And that, of course, tends to lead to budgetary deficits to the extent welfare and unemployment costs go up and tax collections go down. On the other, other things may not be equal as shall soon be evident.

Modeling the effect of a general Increase in an economy's wages.

The willingness of an economy's employers to supply the same amount of goods and services but only at higher prices is depicted in the basic model by a new and higher aggregate supply curve; it shifts upwards to higher prices by the amount of the additional costs that must be covered if production is to occur.

Figure 13-5 suggests the effect that an increase in one important cost, the level of money wages, might have on an economy's prices and production. It depicts an economy such as that of the United States in 2007. It is initially in equilibrium at price level P10, money wage level Wm1, and a full employment level of real income Yr18 with all N20 of the workers willing to work at Wm1 fully employed. Aggregate supply curve S1 represents the maximum amount of goods and services the economy's government, non-profit, and for-profit employers are willing to produce at each price level—*if their output can be sold.* In 2007 there were enough consumer and other customer spending so it could all be sold.

Now assume the general level of wages in the economy rises from Wm1 to Wm2 as would be the case, for example, if the government tries to "help workers" by increasing their wages and benefits. The productivity of the workers and the capacity of the employers to produce remain the same but the higher wage costs force the employers to raise their prices in order to cover their now higher costs. In this economy aggregate supply increases to S2.

In this instance, the result the efforts to help workers is an inflation as the general level of prices move higher from P10 to P15, lower production as output drops from Yr18 to Yr15, and unemployment as the number of workers who can find jobs drops from N20 to N15. Simultaneously, the higher wages and benefits increase the number of people willing to work from N20 to N25. In other words, in the example economy *the government's efforts to "help the workers" by pushing up their wages and benefits has resulted in higher prices and unemployment.*

In the Figure 13-5 economy, for instance, prices will tend to be bid up beyond the initial price level of P10 because at that price level the employers will now only be willing to supply Yr6 of products when they have to pay the higher Wm2 level of wages—while at that price level the customers still desire to purchase Yr18. As a result, the price level will rise to P15, output will drop to Y15, and employment will drop to N15. In other words, the government's well-meaning effort to "help" the workers has indeed helped those who remain employed—but at the cost of causing inflation, unemployment, and lower levels of production.

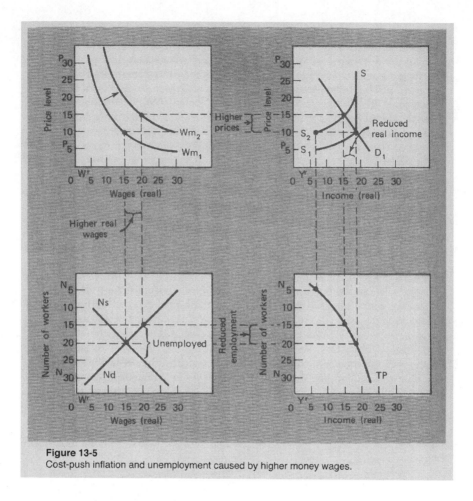

Figure 13-5
Cost-push inflation and unemployment caused by higher money wages.

Cost increases other than wages.

Cost increases that are not directly related to the level of wages in an economy tend to have the same effect. They too result in inflation and unemployment. For instance, consider workers whose employment will result, on average, in the production of ten additional product units as well as costs in addition to their wages that are equivalent to four product units. Since the workers makes a net contribution of six units of output, the workers will tend to be hired if they will work for a real wage equivalent to six or fewer products.

But what if the other costs associated with the output their employment contributes rises to the equivalent of six products because of such things as increases in taxes or the cost of material inputs? Then the workers will be employed only if they will work for a real wage equivalent to four units of product or less. In other words, non-wage cost increases tend to result in a decline in the demand for labor by the amount of the additional costs associated with each subsequent worker's employment.

Lots of things happen in the real world that will cause this effect: higher energy prices because the government shuts down nuclear or coal burning power plants or OPEC takes steps that raise the price of petroleum imports; the government subsidizes the production of ethanol so that corn and other agricultural prices rise as cropland is diverted to growing corn for ethanol; property taxes rise so that new federal or state education mandates can be met; and anti-trust actions are weakened so that monopolies and cartels are formed and can increase their prices because they are no longer subjected to competition. The list is endless.

Then the employers will not produce as much because fewer workers will be able to make net contributions equal to or larger than the real wages that will exist at the higher price level. Furthermore, the equilibrium level of income in the economy will decline and unemployment will occur as the number of employees at work falls.

The higher price levels and unemployment will have a secondary effect. Prices are higher but the existence of unemployment means wages will tend to rise less than the prices rise, if they rise at all. And that may mean that fewer workers are willing to work at the lower level of real wages. Then less production will occur in the economy at the new and lower full-employment level of real wages. In essence, *higher costs not only cause inflation and unemployment, they may also reduce the economy's production capacity by inducing workers to leave the labor force.*

The effect of such cost increases on an economy's prices, production, and employment is depicted in Figure 13-6 for an example economy in which S1 represents the maximum amount of goods and services that will be produced initially in the economy at each price level. The economy is in equilibrium at price level P10, money wage level Wm1, and a full employment level of income of Yr18 produced by N20 of workers.

Aggregate supply curve S2 represents the maximum amount of products that would be supplied by the economy's employers if the additional costs associated with the employment of each subsequent worker rise to the extent depicted by the decline in the labor supply curve from Nd1 to Nd2. Examination of the latter aggregate supply curve indicates that if the production costs rise in the manner depicted the level of prices will rise from P10 to P12—"pushed up" by the higher costs because the economy's employers will no longer hire workers and produce all the goods and services purchasers desire to buy at price level P10.

The employers will not produce as much because fewer workers will be able to make net contributions equal to or larger than the real wages that will exist at price level P10. Furthermore, the equilibrium level of income will decline from Yr18 to Yr13 and unemployment will occur as the number of employees at work falls from N20 to approximately N12.

Notice also that fewer workers are willing to work in the economy at the lower level of real wages which are caused by the higher price level; as a result, the new aggregate supply curve lies to the left of the initial curve to indicate that less production will occur in the economy at the new full-employment level of real wages. In essence, *the higher costs have not only caused inflation and unemployment, but have also reduced the real wages of the workers who remain employed and reduced the economy's production capacity by inducing workers to leave the labor force.*

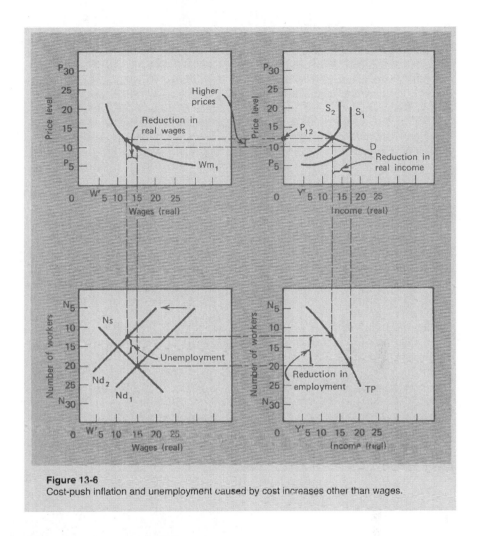

Figure 13-6
Cost-push inflation and unemployment caused by cost increases other than wages.

Changes in costs and changes in the distribution of income.

It is not just inflation and unemployment that tends to occur when costs rise in an economy such as the United States. For example, the level of money wages (which include benefits) might double while the employers' other costs remain unchanged so that the economy's price level at full employment is only pushed up sixty percent.

Under such circumstance there would be a redistribution of the total purchasing power generated by the economy *away* from individuals, employers, and governments whose money incomes either increase less than the increases in prices or are greatly reduced if they become unemployed; it would go *toward* the individuals, employers, and governments whose incomes increase more than sixty percent.

There would be no change in aggregate demand if both those receiving additional purchasing power and those losing purchasing power had same the same propensities to spend. But that might not be the case if workers have higher propensities to consume than the others who might receive the increases in purchasing power. For instance, if those who receive the increases have lower propensities to buy goods and services than those who experience reductions, there would tend to be a decrease in aggregate demand at every price level.

The reverse, of course, would be true if those who receive it have higher propensities to consume. In other words, *in addition to causing inflation and unemployment, higher costs may help certain types of income recipients increase their incomes and hurt others.*

This is exactly what happened in the United States during its Great Recession. Wages did not increase as fast as other incomes because the demand for workers and number of jobs was falling as spending receded. So there was a constant redistribution of the economy's total income away workers and towards their employers' owners. This reversed the long preceding trend associated with years of relatively full employment wherein wages increased tracked with the incomes of non-workers.

The slower increases in wages inherent in a recession or depression also tends to affect total spending by changing the distribution of income. This would be the case if the beneficiaries of the redistribution had lower propensities to spend as might be the case if the lagging wage increases raised the incomes of the employers. In other words, aggregate demand will be unchanged only if both the beneficiaries and those whose incomes are reduced have the same propensities to use their incomes to buy newly produced goods and services.

The cost-push policy dilemma.

There is a basic policy dilemma when cost-push inflation and unemployment occurs in an economy. *The policy choices are rather clear and which one is selected says a lot about the corruption and competency of an economy's government and central bank.* The three basic choices open to the economy's decision makers are simple:

Do nothing and accept the inflation and unemployment, lower levels of production, and the slower growth caused by the slower introduction of productivity increases associated with idle capital not being replaced; or

Take steps to increase spending to fight the unemployment and put people back to work and maintain labor's share of the economy's income even though it may cause *even more inflation* before wages and other costs readjust to full employment; or

Take steps to decrease spending to fight the inflation and protect people on fixed incomes and those who are holding large amounts of money and financial instruments even though it may cause *even more unemployment and an even greater reduction is the share of production going to the economy's labor force.*

Consider the two economies described above. In both of them, as a result of higher money wages in one and higher non-wage costs in the other, there is inflation as the level of prices rises and unemployment as the level of production that generates revenues falls. Under these circumstances, the maximum level of real income can only be regained by increasing increasing spending in the economy—the economy's aggregate demand.

The increased spending could be achieved, for instance, by monetary ease, more government spending and transfers, selling more abroad, or any of the many other things that might cause consumer and other spending to increase. Prices will then tend rise to even higher as wages and other costs are bid up as the economy moves back towards full employment levels of production.

Alternatively, the initial level of product prices can be retained and inflation prevented if total spending in the economy (aggregate demand) is sufficiently reduced concurrently with the increases in costs—so that the prices of some goods and services decline enough to offset the prices that increased because of the cost increases. This could occur via such actions as tightening up on the money supply and reducing government purchases and transfers. That, of course, would tend to prevent inflation but cause an even greater increase in unemployment and a bigger decline in production and slowing of capital accumulation.

The basic dilemma is depicted in Figure 13-7. As a result of higher money wages, there is inflation as the level of prices rise from P10 to P15 and unemployment as the level of production (real income) falls from Yr18 to Yr15. Under these circumstances, the maximum level of real income Yr18 can only be regained by increasing the economy's aggregate demand from its initial level of D1 to D2. This could be achieved, for instance, by monetary ease, more government spending and transfers, or any of the other things that might cause total spending to increase; prices will then rise to P20 and full employment levels of production and real wages will be regained.

On the other hand, the initial price level of P10 can be maintained if the economy's aggregate demand is reduced from D1 to D3 via such actions as tightening up on the money supply, restricting export sales, and reducing government purchases and transfers. That would prevent inflation but cause a massive increase in unemployment and a decline in production to Yr6.

In essence, once cost pressures arise, whether from external forces such as increase in the price of crude oil or domestic forces such as tax and wage increases, an economy's government and its central bank have to choose between protecting the work force from unemployment even though it may mean more inflation; or protecting the holders of cash and financial assets from inflation at the expense of even more unemployment; or doing nothing and accepting some of each.

To complicate things even further, the government and central bank might pursue conflicting goals: for example, one might try to choke off spending to fight inflation on behalf of the financial institutions and other large holders of financial assets who are its campaign donors while the other tries to encourage spending to fight unemployment in order to keep people employed and economy's per capita production ahead of that of other countries.

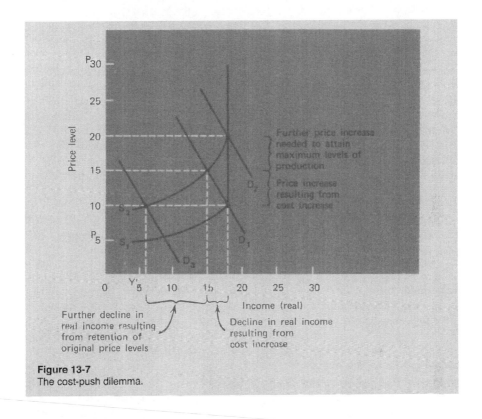

Figure 13-7
The cost-push dilemma.

CHANGES IN THE SUPPLY OF LABOR

The working age population of a country such as the United States tends to increases two or three percent every year as a result of more young people reaching working age, immigration, and people working longer because they live longer and because previous periods of inflation or unemployment wiped out some or all of their retirement savings and pensions. Such increases in the size of an economy's labor force *may* cause unemployment and *may* or *may not* affect the size of the economy's employment and production. It depends, of course, on whether spending increases so there are more jobs available.

Moreover, the labor force may increase for other reasons. One is that the higher wages associated with the benefit increases that result in cost-push inflation and unemployment may induce non-workers to leave their homes and retirements and to be willing join the labor force and work if jobs become available; or the spouses and partners of those who lose their jobs because of the benefits increases may begin to seek work; or those whose retirement lifestyles are threatened by the higher prices may re-join the work force to bolster their assets.

Similarly, the Great Recession wiped out assets, and particularly housing values, such that many older people delayed their retirements or were forced by their losses to be willing to return to the labor force as soon as jobs became available. All of this actually increased both the unemployment rate and the capacity of the economy's employers to produce goods and services—if they could find more customer revenues.

Whatever the cause of an expansion of an economy's labor force, an increase in either the number of workers or the number of hours worked by each worker may cause unemployment to increase if aggregate demand does not increase. On the other hand, such increases in the supply of labor may also cause increased production and a growth of governmental tax revenues.

What actually happens in a particular economy such as the United States when its labor supply increases depends on the flexibility of its wages and prices *and whether the customer spending to buy the additional goods and services also increases*. If spending does not increase the unemployment will continue until it does.

Consider an economy that is initially in equilibrium at full employment level of production. Now consider that the economy experiences an increase in its labor force—perhaps just its natural annual increase or perhaps it has just come out of a Great Recession such that the labor supply increases substantially because foreign workers who had left or been forced out during the recession return and millions of people who had retired or gone off to school to wait out the recession flood back into the workforce seeking jobs. Whatever the source of the larger labor force, the number of workers willing to work increases and so does the economy's maximum production capacity.

Such an economy is depicted in Figure 13-8. It is initially in equilibrium at full employment level of production Yr21, an average product price level of P7, aggregate supply and demand of S1 and D1, an average level of money wages of WM2 which yields a real wage of Wr20, and N15 of workers employed.

Then the labor supply increases to Ns2. In this example, the number of workers willing to work at the real wage Wr20 increases from N15 to N35 and the economy's maximum production capacity represented by an aggregate supply curve representing becomes S2.

The first possibility of what will happen is: absolutely nothing; *all of the increased labor force is unemployed.* In essence, the economy now has the capacity to produce more than its initial level of Yr21 but its employers will not produce more because their customers are already buying all they want at price level P7. In other words, because they do not have more customers the employers in the economy continue to need only the original full employment level of workers even though more workers (N35) are willing to work.

The second possibility is that customer spending will rise (to D2) and put the additional workers to work—resulting in more production, more employment, *and inflation* as prices are bid up from (P7 to P15) to cut the real wages low enough so that everyone who wants to work is hired. How much output and employment will increase depends on what happens to wages in the economy's labor market as the unemployed workers compete for the available jobs.

If money wages are generally inflexible downward, as is the case in the United States, product prices would have to be bid up to P15 by the increased customer spending to whatever extent is necessary to cut the real wages low enough (Wr10) for the economy's employers to be able to hire all the workers (N25) who are willing to work.

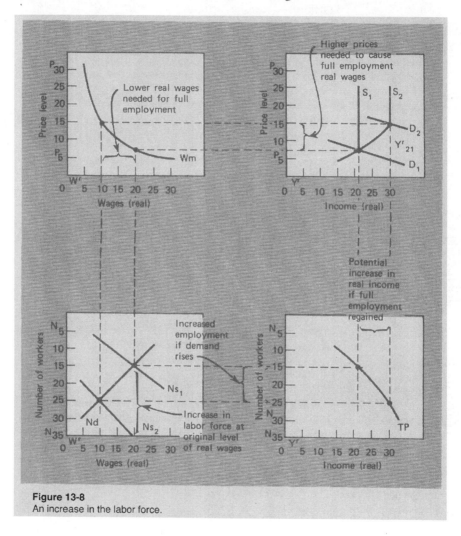

Figure 13-8
An increase in the labor force.

INCREASES IN NON-COMPETITIVE PRICES CAN CAUSE INFLATION AND UNEMPLOYMENT

In the real world, the prices of many goods and services are set by the arbitrary administrative decisions of governments and non-competitive employers rather than determined in competitive markets by the forces of supply and demand. And if some prices in an economy are arbitrarily set higher by some type of administrative decree or the exercise of monopoly powers, then the average level of prices in the economy will rise (*inflation*). That will also tend to result in unemployment to the extent that fewer of the now-higher—priced products are sold so that fewer workers need to be employed.

Americans like to believe they live in a highly competitive market-oriented economy. And while it may be true that there is a lot of competition in the financial markets, it is certainly *not* true about about many of the goods and services produced by it public and private employers. In the real world, however, there are governments, regulators, monopolies, and cartels that can set prices higher without worrying about competitors stepping in to take their customers by charging lower prices. As a result, there can be inflation and unemployment despite the best efforts, if they occur, of the federal government and the Federal Reserve to prevent such undesirable outcomes.

Consider an economy is initially in equilibrium with full employment and stable prices and wages. Then a governmental or action occurs that increases certain product prices. If some prices increase and others remain the same, it means the average of all the individual product prices in the economy will increase—inflation. And it can and does occur even though there are no increases in the costs of production, no increases in the money supply or customer spending, and no changes in the labor market or worker productivity.

The result of establishing higher prices for some of an economy's products while others remain unchanged is clear—the average level of the economy's prices will increase. There will be an inflation. There is also a reduction in the economy's level of production and employment since fewer goods and services can be sold at the now-higher general level of prices. The unemployment, of course, occurs because the economy's employers need to hire fewer workers in order to produce the goods and services for which there will still be customers. Moreover, unemployment may rise even more as spouses and partners enter the labor force in an effort to obtain jobs in order to maintain their families' incomes and lifestyles.

Figure 13-9 models the basic situation that might occur in economies such as the United States. The economy is initially in equilibrium at price level P10, real income Yr18, and there is full employment with N20 workers receiving a money wage that generates a Wr15 level of real wages. Now assume a governmental action occurs that increases certain product prices so that the average of all the individual product prices in the economy increases from P10 to P15 even though there are no increases in the costs of production, no increases in customer spending, and no changes in the labor market or worker productivity.

The result of establishing higher prices for some of the economy's products is clear: inflation occurs as increases in specific prices cause the average level of prices in the economy to increase from P10 to P15, there is a reduction in the economy's level of production from Yr18 to Yr12 since that is all that can be sold at the now-higher general level of prices, unemployment occurs as the number of employed workers drops from N20 to N10 because that is all employers need to hire in order to produce things for which there will be sufficient revenues, and the real wages of the economy's workers who can find jobs declines form Wr15 to Wr10.

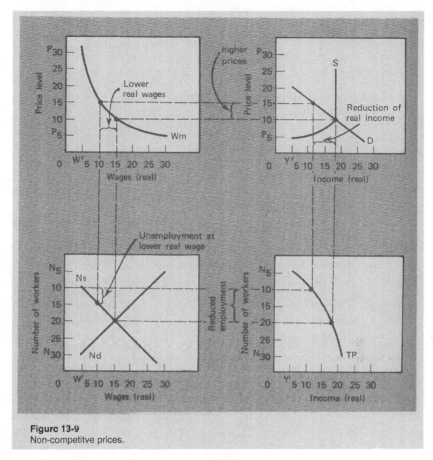

Figure 13-9
Non-competitve prices.

The many sources of non-competitive price increases.

Various conditions and institutions can cause price increases and unemployment when prices are set by public and private administrative or political decisions rather than by competition in the market place. Often these conditions and institutions are interrelated with each other and with other causes of inflation and unemployment. They include non-competitive private employers arbitrarily setting their prices higher and regulatory agencies setting prices higher for employers who have "captured" them. They also include governmental price-increasing actions when the governments are themselves the employers—for example, school districts raising the price of housing by raising property taxes so they can pay higher wages and benefits to their teachers; or government-owned utilities raising the price of electricity they sell; or water districts raising the price of the water they sell.

Here are but a few of the types of things that might cause specific prices to be set higher and thus cause the average of all prices to rise (inflation) and unemployment to occur. Each may have a minor effect but, taken together as major part of the fabric of the American economy, they are a mighty force—together they tend to constantly push up almost every individual product price. Analysts should once again note that none of these inflation-causing actions involves increasing the money supply or increasing government spending or increasing budgetary deficits:

1. *Illegal employer combinations.* For example, even if it is illegal, five or six large book publishers or cement manufacturers might come together and agree to actions that would cause the price of the books and cement they sell to increase. If they get away with it those particular product prices would increase and the average level of prices in the economy would tend to rise—inflation. The threat of non-competitive price increases is so pervasive that the United States has for over a century promoted competition with anti-trust laws and regulations. They prohibit private employers from coming together to even discuss increasing the prices of their products or reducing competition among themselves.

2. *Monopoly and price leader pricing.* Many goods and services do not have competitors who will swoop in and take their customers and revenues if they increase their prices. For example, due to its patents and copyrights Apple has a monopoly on the production and pricing of the software run on it devices. Accordingly, it can increase the price of its software and operating systems at any time. The City of New York has a similar ability as the only provider of bus and subway services to increase their prices.

   Similarly, there does not need to be overt price-fixing collusion between employers with competing products if one of them is the price leader and the others increase their prices when leader does. United States' airlines are famous for announcing fare increases in the hope that the other airlines will follow—and rescinding them if they don't.

3. *Relaxation of anti-trust scrutiny.* The President appoints the Attorney General and decision makers of the various regulatory agencies who are charged with regulating prices and promoting competition. Little wonder that the country's business community constantly supports having a "friend of business" in the White House, someone who will either appoint regulators who will set their prices higher or look the other way when they do so themselves.

4. *Government price mandates.* Congress has a long history of setting crop prices higher to "help" employers such as large corporate farmers; states and their university regents and trustees have a similar history of raising the tuition price of education so the schools will have enough revenues to hire well known athletes and coaches for the athletic events and educational services they produce.

5. *Governments pursuing other goals.* Governments at every level may take steps that increase prices. For example, they might increase excise taxes on certain products such as gasoline and cigarettes so consumers have to pay higher prices to buy them. Or they might prevent pipeline construction and drilling on government lands for environmental reasons, which would have the effect of reducing the supply of gas and oil and forcing their prices higher.

6. *Restricting competition.* Politicians at every level of government are motivated by their friends and campaign contributors to take steps to protect them from competition and the lower prices that might tend to result: requiring "certificates of necessity" before new hospitals can be built to compete with those already existing; outlawing or limiting charter schools to protect public schools from competition; requiring the "prevailing union wage" be paid to highway and construction workers so that non-union employers cannot bid lower prices; requiring would-be competitors to meet spurious requirements such as local residency; requiring licenses for certain occupations and establishing meaningless training requirements such as "education" classes before teaching certificates

can be issued; preventing electric and cable companies from offering services where such services already exist; and issuing high priced sole source contracts to friends and supporters.

The list of actions governments and bureaucrats might take to restrict competition in order to support higher prices for their friends, constituents, and potential campaign contributors and future employers is virtually endless.

7. *Generating additional revenues.* Governments seeking additional revenues increase the general level of prices when they do such things as increase sales tax rates and the fees they charge for everything from garbage collection to parking permits.

8. *Regulatory inflation.* Governments typically allow utilities and other employers whose product prices are regulated to increase their prices as needed to earn "fair rate of return" on their capital. Typically, the return is in excess of the interest rate cost of borrowing money ("fair," of course, being as high as they can coax out of their regulators). This encourages the regulated employers to buy and operate more capital than they need and to pay higher prices for the capital they buy.

A similarly inflationary form of pricing has periodically been used by government purchasing agents and regulators wherein employers are allowed to earn profits that are a fixed percentage of their production costs. Employers then have both an incentive and the ability to raise the prices they charge by paying higher wages to their employees and higher prices for the capital they employ and the goods and services they use as inputs in their production processes.

9. *Inflation expectations.* Employers may increase their prices, or request their regulators to allow them to do so if they have regulated prices, if they expect inflation or can convince their price regulators that one is coming. They typically justify the increase on the premise that the coming inflation means they will have to pay more for their inputs and, thus, need the higher prices to maintain their profits

and stay in business. In other words, expectations of inflation may cause it.

10. *Responses to recessions.* Large employers such as Boeing, the Southern Pacific Railroad, and the Los Angeles School District tend to enter into labor and supply contracts that cover long time periods of time and specify the specific wages and prices that are to be paid. Their employees are hired on the expectation that what they will contribute to production can be sold. But what if a recession occurs so that the revenue coming in is not as great as was initially expected?

Traditional supply and demand theory assumes prices will tend to fall when demand falls. The analysis which leads to these conclusions can be presented most eloquently. Unfortunately it does not always conform to the realities of the real world. Normally, an employer in such a position would attempt to stay in business by drawing down its cash reserves or borrowing money or selling assets. That would tend to provide the money to tide the employer over until it can cut its costs or increase its revenues. But sometimes such money is not available. Then the employer must either cease operations or raise its prices in hopes of taking in enough revenues from the customers who remain so it can survive until the recession ends. Inevitably management's choice is for higher prices instead of closing down and losing their jobs.

11. *Sheer stupidity*—Inadequate customer spending and the ensuing unemployment and starvation in the United States during the 1930s Great Depression caused certain prices to fall. Congress and the President were much taken by an "economic advisor" who pointed out that prosperity was associated with higher prices. So the National Recovery Administration was set up to establish higher prices. It did so, for instance, in the midst of widespread hunger, by destroying crops, killing livestock, and discouraging food production—so that supply would fall and prices rise. It also set various product prices higher and required employers to sell their production only at the higher prices. The higher prices made the unemployment and starvation worse.

12. *Union-government collusion.* Governments act as both the customer who pays for the service and the employer who receives tax and other revenues for such things as local schools, police and fire departments, and streets and sanitation services. Little wonder that unions and their members constantly advocate that more money should be spent (higher prices paid) to acquire such services—and constantly support the politicians who are willing to have the government pay more to get them.

And it is not just the prices of the government services that increase. For example, state and local governments tend to get the money they need so they can pay more for the services they produce by raising property and sales taxes—so the price of buying housing services and consumer goods also rises.

The non-competitive price dilemma.

The existence of higher prices and unemployment caused by increases in non-competitive prices leads to the same dilemma as the inflation and unemployment caused by higher costs—how should the economy's government and central bank respond? There are same three basic alternatives that face policy makers when there is a administered price inflation as there are when they face a cost-push inflation: one is to do nothing and accept the inflation and unemployment; the second is to implement policies to increase customer spending to eliminate the unemployment even though it might cause even more inflation as some industries reach full employment before others; and the third is to implement policies to reduce demand in order fight the inflation by offsetting the higher administered prices.

In other words, inflation caused by administrative actions that raise some prices can, at least conceptually, be offset by cutting spending so much for the goods and services whose prices have not increased that their prices fall enough to offset those which did increase. And that might take some serious cutting and even more unemployment if prices are generally inflexible downward.

So, yes, an inflation caused by increases in non-competitive prices might be contained by cutting spending in general just as a cost-push inflation might be similarly contained—but at a similar cost of even fewer people with jobs and an even greater reduction in the level of output. Unemployment is the inevitable outcome of fighting inflation by reducing demand in an economy such as the United States.

Figure 13-10 depicts the three basic alternatives an economy's policy makers face when costs increase or non-competitive prices are increased:

If customer spending is left unchanged there will be inflation and unemployment:

If customer spending is increased to D2 the unemployment is eliminated and the general level of prices rises even more. Money wages will then increase to Wm2—and the economy's production and real wages will be back to where it started—except that its prices and money wages will be higher;

If customer spending is cut to D3, the price level will be held at P10 so that inflation is avoided—but at a cost of fewer people with jobs (N10 instead of N20), substantial unemployment, and a reduced level of output which drops from Yr18 to Yr12.

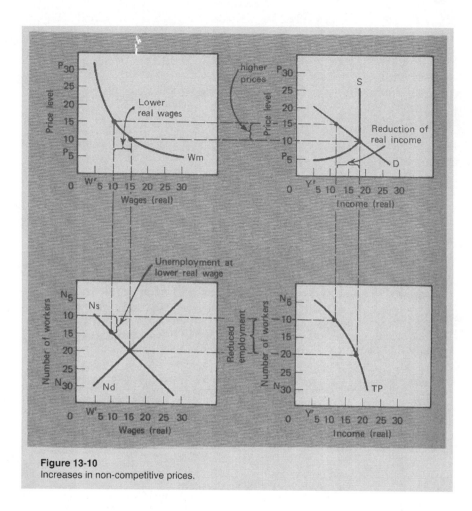

Figure 13-10
Increases in non-competitive prices.

STABILIZATION INFLATION
AND UNEMPLOYMENT

One of the least considered aspects of governmental and central bank efforts to fight inflation is that the efforts themselves may cause the very inflation they are intended to prevent. This occurs because the imposition of higher interest rates, and increases in certain taxes, directly affect the prices and production costs of many goods and services. In other words, *efforts to prevent inflation by raising taxes and interest rates to hold down spending may cause the very inflation they are intended to prevent.*

Such a *stabilization inflation* occurs because certain taxes such as sales taxes, excise taxes, and property taxes directly affect the amount of consumer and other spending that must occur to buy the taxed items. Thus the impact of such taxes being levied is correctly reflected in the Consumer Price Index as an increase in the price that must be paid to acquire the consumer goods and services. Furthermore, the increased price of such items caused by the taxes may then increase the costs employers must cover to produce other products and so result in additional inflation of the cost-push variety.

Higher interest rates, such as might occur in an effort to prevent an inflation caused by too much spending, would have the same effect. Higher interest rates, for example, cause greater amounts of consumer expenditures to be needed each month to buy housing and make the payments necessary to buy such things as automobiles and expensive appliances. In other words, the effect of certain taxes, higher interest rates can themselves cause the very inflation that they are intended to prevent. Moreover, the higher prices caused by the efforts to fight inflation will tend to cause unemployment to the extent the higher prices reduce the amount of such things as houses and cars that are purchased.

The policy implications of stabilization inflation.

The possibility that well-meaning government anti-inflationary efforts may themselves directly cause inflation and the unemployment associated with higher prices is important. It means that each potential policy aimed at preventing inflation, such as tax and interest rate changes and money supply changes, must be evaluated both in terms of its ability to counter inflation and unemployment and the degree to which it will itself directly cause inflation and unemployment.

In essence, care must be taken that the degree of stabilization efforts that could offset the forces that would cause one level of inflation and unemployment do not directly cause even greater levels of inflation and unemployment.

Modeling stabilization inflation and unemployment.

Figure 13-11 depicts the trade-off between the direct and indirect effects of different degrees of stabilization effort. D5 represents the economy's initial level of aggregate demand and the various supply curves represent the willingness of the economy's employers to produce goods and services at different levels of production costs. The economy is initially in equilibrium at price level P100 with the economy's labor force and other factors of production fully employed producing a real income of Yr500.

Now assume that for some reason there is an increase in customer willingness to buy goods and services as reflected by an increase in aggregate demand to D0 so that the economy's price level will rise to P112.5 unless some degree of additional monetary and fiscal restraints are implemented. Aggregate demand curves D2 and D3 represent two of the different degrees of monetary and fiscal restraint that might be implemented in response to those demand-pull influences while D5 represents the restraint on total spending that would keep the economy's prices stable at P100 in the absence of any cost or direct price effects from such efforts.

Unfortunately, in the real world such cost and direct effects may exist. And if they do, efforts to prevent inflation by holding down total spending may result in both unemployment and an even larger increase in the level of prices. In other words, fighting inflation by raising interest rates and increasing tax collections to cut spending may make the inflation worse and cause unemployment.

Consider the economy depicted in Figure 13-11. The various aggregate supply curves such as S2 and S3 depict the cost effects of the various degrees of stabilization efforts that might be implemented. The extent to which costs change with different types of stabilization efforts depends on which monetary and fiscal activities are undertaken.

In the Figure 13-11 example economy, stabilization to degree 5 is associated with cost increases that would tend to push up the economy's price level to P105 and reduce its level of output to Yr450.

The direct price effects associating the various degrees of stabilization efforts to the other determinants of prices and employment are depicted by the A, B, and C points in the figure.

The A points represent the cost effects of each degree of stabilization effort.

The B points represent the higher levels of prices that will result from adding the direct effect on prices of the various stabilization efforts; they indicate that the greater the degree of stabilization effort, the more the level of prices will be above the level that would exist in their absence.

The C points indicate the amount of production which will be purchased at the higher levels of prices associated with each degree of stabilization effort. Thus a curve joining the C points would represent the trade-off between prices and unemployment under the new conditions assumed to exist in the economy.

In this economy, the cost changes and direct price effects of the policies to degree 5 that would be implemented to restrict demand and prevent the level of prices in the economy from rising to P112.5 will result in an even higher price level of

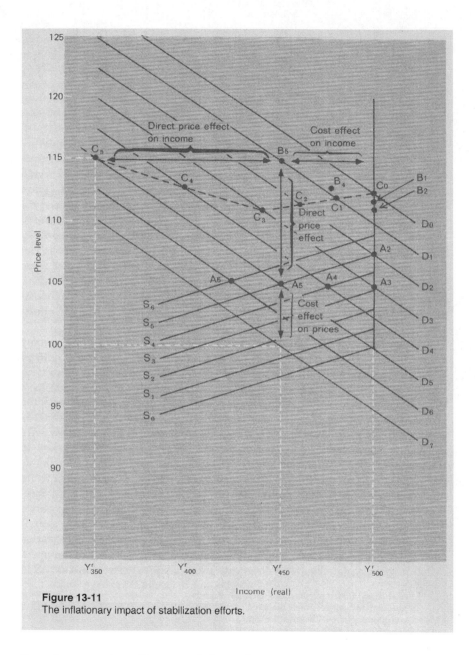

Figure 13-11
The inflationary impact of stabilization efforts.

In other words, efforts to fight inflation may cause an even worse inflation. In this particular economy, stabilization efforts to degree 3 would result in the lowest possible price increases, but at the cost of a significantly lower level of real income. It is one of the many trade-offs between inflation and unemployment available to the economy.

What this importantly means is that an economy's government and central bank, if they cannot adopt a set of monetary and fiscal policies that will have less of a cost and direct effect on prices (*they can*), could provide their economy with a greater degree of price stability if they would do nothing to stop a demand-pull or other inflation from occurring. In essence, the more an economy's policies to prevent inflation and unemployment take forms that actually increase the economy's costs and prices, the more likely the policies will be unsuccessful in stabilizing the economy's at full employment levels of production without inflation.

Finally, it should be noted that a CC curve depicts the combination of inflation and unemployment available to an economy at a particular point in time. It shows the present trade-off between various degrees of inflation and rates of unemployment that was once thought to be depicted by curves depicting the inflation—unemployment trade off (in the next chapter) first suggested by Samuelson and Solow. Their curves, however, do not represent the inflation-unemployment tradeoffs presently confronting an economy such as the United States as a result of its current circumstances and menu of policy choices—they are merely lines fitted to an array of points, each of which represents the specific inflation and unemployment combination that existed *in the past* as a result of the unique and ever changing conditions and policies existing at that point in history.

In other words, *the CC curve represents the inflation and unemployment effects that will occur today as the result of today's policy choices whereas curves fitted to past combinations of the rates of inflation and unemployment represent the historical results of past policy choices.**

The article that first presented this theory is Lindauer's "Stabilization Inflation and the Inflation-Unemployment Trade-off." Indian Economic Journal (Spring 1973). It is derived from an earlier paper of the same title delivered at the 1967 Western Economic Association meeting to report the results of an earlier econometric analysis. As an interesting aside, the paper was initially submitted to the Journal of Political Economy but was rejected with a reviewer's note that "this cannot possibly be about the causes of inflation for nowhere does it mention an increase in the money supply."

An American experience with stabilization inflation and unemployment.

During the late 1960s and early 1970s inflation was not great, but it was feared to be coming. It was a time of war and the conventional wisdom of journalists and the punditry was that "you cannot have both guns and butter." So Congress and the Federal Reserve's governors, believing that inflations would be caused in the future by the increased federal spending, undertook the traditional spending reduction steps of raising taxes and cutting the money supply.

The Federal Reserve governors reduced the money supply and the economy's interest rates dutifully rose so that the monthly payment price to buy housing and cars *increased*; and Congress raised excise taxes on everything from tires and gasoline to theatre tickets so the prices that had to be paid to get them *increased*.

To the great surprise of the Federal Reserve's governors and regional presidents, the tighter they turned the screws, "to squeeze inflation out of the economy," the more the prices in the cost of living index increased and the more unemployment grew. The "inflation" only ended when they finally stopped tightening the money supply and interest rates began to decline.

Subsequently, pragmatic macroeconomists led by Professor Lindauer disaggregated the Consumer Price Index for that period and closely examined its components. They found that almost all of the higher prices resulted directly from the higher interest rates and higher tax rates. It seems that the "economic experts" at the Federal Reserve and advising Congress had overlooked the fact that in the real world interest rates and excise taxes directly increase the prices that have to be paid to buy many consumer goods and services. They also overlooked the fact that the production capacity of the American economy was growing fast enough to produce all that the additional war-related federal spending was buying—and a lot more—so that there was no threat of a demand-pull inflation.

In other words, Congress and the Federal Reserve "fought" an inflation that had not yet started and would never have started. Yet to this day the then-chairman of the Federal Reserve claims that what he did was necessary to "wring inflation out of the economy."

What the Chairman and his fellow governors really did, as a result of their naive belief that inflations are caused by federal spending increases, was cause a massive inflation, the failure of numerous businesses and banks, huge budgetary deficits, and the unemployment and impoverishment of millions of Americans. (If you understand this, please run for Congress or apply for a job at the Federal Reserve.)

CREDIT CRUNCH INFLATION AND UNEMPLOYMENT

What happens if unwarranted Federal Reserve fears about inflation cause the Federal Reserve to implement an unexpected reduction of the availability of credit? Obvious the effect of such a "credit crunch" would cause the revenues the economy's employers receive for their products to be not as great as they initially expected. Traditional economic theory has always assumed that prices will tend to fall, or at least remain stable, when there is not enough customer demand. The analysis which leads to these conclusions can be presented most eloquently. Unfortunately it does not always conform to the cost rigidities and other realities of the real world. Normally, an employer in such a position would borrow money or sell assets to tide it over until it can cut its costs or increase its revenues.

But sometimes money and credit is not available if the Federal Reserve is tightening up because it fears inflation from too much spending. Then the employer must either close their doors or raise their prices in hopes of taking in enough revenues from the customers who remain.

Setting their prices higher instead of closing is the inevitable choice of employers when they have inadequate revenues and cannot sell enough assets or borrow enough money. After all, they have nothing to lose—if the higher prices fail to generate enough revenues they can still cease production; if the higher prices do succeed, however, the decision makers keep their jobs and any ownership or options they might have. In essence, the decision of employers to raise their prices to at least try to survive is a no-brainer when the Federal Reserve and Congress implement policies that cut their revenues.

And inflation is not the only effect of a credit crunch: the higher prices will tend to result in even fewer goods and services being purchased—so unemployment grows even more, growth slows even more, and budget deficits tend to rise even more. And as things worsen the employer may increase prices even more in an effort to survive.

Such a sad state of affairs has tended to occur periodically in the United States whenever the Federal Reserve fights inflation by tightening up on the money supply to such an extent that it causes a recession. In other words, in the real world the result of Federal Reserve efforts to fight inflation can force a number of employers to increase their prices in the hope that enough of their customers will pay the higher prices needed to meet their revenue needs.

PRICE FREEZE INFLATION AND UNEMPLOYMENT

Sometimes governments of economies react to the threat or existence of inflation by "freezing" prices—literally ordering or pressuring employers not to raise them. But the government announcement and pressures may have just the opposite effect. This happens if the employers respond to the possibility of such an announcement by rushing to increase their prices in order to claim the increases occurred prior to the freeze.

Why do they do this? They do so in case they will need to have higher prices in the future to cover the higher costs of inputs whose prices were not frozen. This tendency is reinforced by the fact that if the cost conditions they fear do not develop, the employers can always lower their prices to reestablish the pre-freeze levels.

This is exactly what happened to the United States in the 1970s when the White House attempted to stop inflation by ordering a price freeze; the policy makers were surprised to find that the greatest monthly increase in the price level in over twenty years occurred in the month immediately *following* the freeze. The higher prices resulted in fewer goods and services being purchased and resulted in unemployment.

FULL EMPLOYMENT AND FRICTIONAL UNEMPLOYMENT

Is it actually possible for full-employment to occur such that everyone who is willing and able to work has a job? Certainly not. In a dynamic economy such as the United States there will always be some workers and capital unemployed because they are moving between available jobs. Unemployment for this reason is typically referred to as "frictional unemployment" because it is caused by various interference or "frictions" that prevent job seekers from instantaneously leaving on job and starting another.

Among the possible frictions that cause temporary delays in reaching available employments are such things as the need to move to another geographic location or an inadequate dissemination of information about available jobs.

STRUCTURAL INFLATION AND UNEMPLOYMENT

Various changes are constantly occurring in the markets and structure of a dynamic economy such as that of the United States. Among them: new products that make old products obsolete; new production technologies; new labor skills, new foreign competitors and markets; new financial instruments; new consumer preferences; and new laws and regulations.

The changes, for example, might involve a shift in consumer preferences from the products of one automobile or durable goods manufacturer to the similar or better products of another; or a change in the optimum location for producing a product from the industrial north to the non-union south or a lower wage overseas destination; or a technological development that changes the type of labor and plant and equipment required by employers; or a new law that encourages or discourages the employment of younger or older workers; or a new energy source or an energy source that is newly forbidden. There are others.

Such changes have various possible effects. First, there may be "structural unemployment" as the labor and capital associated with certain types of goods and services or geographic areas become unemployed due to structural changes. For example, the decline in the purchasing of products such as coal and railroad passenger services may mean that that less labor and capital will be needed to produce them. Furthermore, the labor and capital that are no longer needed may remain permanently unemployed because they are not adaptable to other locations or production techniques.

What structural change means in the real world, for example, is that farm workers and auto workers may lose their jobs due to the development of crop picking machinery and automated assembly lines and then not be able to find comparable employment in those industries or where they live; similarly miners in West Virginia's coal fields and oil field workers in Texas may lose their jobs because of played out reserves, new safety and environmental regulations, and the discovery of new and less expensive ways to produce natural gas and nuclear energy.

A second possible effect of structural change is inflation. A general rise in the level of an economy's product prices will occur if increases in the demand for newly favored goods and services cause an increase in their prices at the same time that business practices and the need to cover unchanging costs of production prevent an offsetting drop in the prices of the now relatively unfavored products.

In other words, inflation tend to occur continuously in a dynamic and ever changing economy. After all, a continual increase in the prices of some of an economy's goods and services without offsetting decreases in the prices of other goods and services means a continual increase in the general level of prices.

An economy faced with such structural problems has choices. It can attempt to solve the problem be resisting the development of new products or methods of production. For example, a team of electricians working to turn the lights on and off every day at a newspaper printing plant or automobile assembly plant could continue to be employed if the plants are forbidden to install computer driven light switches or allow other workers to flip the switch. Or it can encourage competition so that the prices of products that become relatively undesired will fall to offset any increases in those that become favored. Or it can encourage structurally unemployed workers to retrain or to move to new locations.

One thing is certain, however, that increasing aggregate demand is unlikely to result in enough additional demand for the products they used to produce to put them back to work—in the real world, railroad firemen, cotton pickers chopping the ground with hoes, and the employees who used to make film for cameras and the tubes for television sets are not going return to their old jobs no matter what happens to aggregate demand. *They are structurally unemployed and some of them are likely to remain so no matter what happens in the rest of the economy.*

The natural rates of inflation and unemployment.

Obviously an economy such as the United States will always have some inflation and unemployment because frictional and structural changes are inherent in a modern dynamic economy. They will always exist even though they can be minimized by anything that causes the rapid communication of job information and the rapid transportation of workers and the capital assets of plant, equipment, and inventory to the site of new jobs.

Accordingly, pragmatic analysts consider an economy to reach a state of "full employment" when everyone who is willing to work is able to find a job *except* those who are moving being between jobs and people who are permanently unemployable because they have been left behind by structural change.

In essence, continuous structural change and frictional unemployment are a natural outcome of dynamic and relatively free economies such as those of the United States and Northern Europe. Such economies will *always* tend to have frictional and structural unemployment and *always* tend to have a modest amount of inflation.

The rate at which such inflation and unemployment occurs in a dynamic economy are often referred to as the economy's "natural rate of inflation" and "natural rate of unemployment." Both are signs of an economy's success and continuing economic progress, not signs of failure that require monetary and fiscal changes to affect total spending.

ECONOMIC GROWTH IS POSSIBLE WITHOUT INFLATION AND UNEMPLOYMENT

Is it conceptually possible for an economy such as the United States to constantly to grow without periodically or permanently suffering from inflation and unemployment other than the natural rates inherent in a dynamic economy? The answer is absolutely *yes*. It is also possible that productivity increases can cause the demand for labor in such an economy to rise even faster than the economy's labor supply. Then the real wages of the average worker will also constantly increase. In essence, the continual introduction of new technologies and the accumulation of more better capital, *if* they occur, will increase the productivity of the economy's workforce so that its per capita production and wages will continue to rise—*if* customer spending rises sufficiently so that the country's government, non-profit, and for-profit employers take in the necessary revenues to cover their costs of production.

On the other hand, if customer spending rises too much there will be inflation and if it does not rise enough as the economy's work force and its productivity rises, as has periodically been the case in the United States, there will be unemployment.

The overall experience of the United States throughout its modern era has been favorable—the labor force and the general level of its real wages have continued to increase despite major depressions in the 1930s and again in the early part of the 21st century. And, since the wants of man for goods and services is insatiable so that the willingness of man to buy them is unlimited, the growth and prosperity of the United States can continue ad infinitum as new technologies and capital are added to those which already exist.

In other words, even if the population and labor force grows, *so long as customer spending and labor productivity increase sufficiently, there can be higher and higher wages without inflation and unemployment even if the size of the population and labor force grows.* This conclusion is valid even if an economy's wages and prices are inflexible or "sticky" downward as appears to be the case in the United States and other highly productive economies.

Such a conclusion is also too good to be true. In the real world of a dynamic country such as the United States there will always tend to be an upward drift of prices and structural and frictional unemployment. Even more significantly, such a full-employment-without-inflation state of affairs requires appropriate monetary and fiscal policies so that total spending appropriately increases as the economy's production capacity grows. That, as pragmatic analysts are well aware, is a major problem—because it requires competent policy makers in Congress and at the Federal Reserve.

CHAPTER SUMMARY

I.   When an economy is producing all the goods and services it is capable of producing, an increase in customer purchasing will be inflationary as buyers compete for the available products. This is a demand-pull inflation wherein prices are "pulled" up by excessive total spending. An increase in the money supply is one of the *many* possible causes of increased spending.

II. Inflation affects all aspects of an economy: buyers have to pay more to buy things; money and financial instruments lose purchasing power; workers want hire wages; the propensity to save may change.

III. Reducing customer spending tends to cause unemployment because employers tend to produce only those goods and services for which they expect to receive revenues sufficient to cover their costs.

IV. When productivity increases, real wages can rise without causing inflation and an economy's consumers and other buyers can obtain more goods and services. There is a tendency for unemployment to occur if productivity increases and customer spending does not. To eliminate unemployment when productivity increases, purchasing can be increased via monetary and fiscal policies or the productivity of workers can be lowered by such techniques as cutting the work week.

V. Higher wages and other production costs can cause cost-push inflation and unemployment. When costs rise employers tend to be forced to increase their prices in order to be able to cover their higher costs and remain in business. The higher prices tend to mean that fewer goods and services will be produced resulting in unemployment.

VI. When a cost-push situation occurs the only choices are to increase customer spending to restore production, which may cause even higher prices, or reduce customer spending which may hold down prices but result in even less employment and production.

VII. An increase in the supply of labor will cause unemployment unless customer spending increases.

VIII. Higher prices can be established for goods and services that do not have competitors even though costs and customer spending do not increase. Inflation and unemployment tends to result when this occurs. Then the dilemma is whether to increase spending to put the unemployed back to work or decrease spending to fight the inflation.

IX. Collusion among employers may cause price increases and unemployment. So can price freezes, changes in expectations, government decrees, and the reactions of employers in response to cash-flow pressures that develop when their sales decline and there is a "credit crunch."

X. Efforts to fight inflation with certain taxes and monetary policies that result in higher interest rates may cause inflation, sometimes even than if the inflation is not fought.

XI. Structural changes in an economy can cause unemployment and reduced production in certain sectors of the economy and higher prices, more employment, and more production in others.

XII. Full employment exists when all the workers in an economy are employed except those moving between jobs or permanently unemployed because of structural changes in the economy.

XIII. With appropriate policies a dynamic economy can have constantly higher levels of production and wages without experiencing inflation and unemployment other than the inflation and unemployment associated with the economy's structural changes and frictional unemployment.

XIV. The natural rates of unemployment and inflation are the rates inherent in a dynamic economy as it evolves in response to an economy's new products, technologies, and locations.

XV. So long as customer purchasing and labor productivity increase sufficiently, an expanding labor force, higher wages, and increased spending and production will result in neither inflation nor unemployment in excess of their natural rates.

CHAPTER FOURTEEN

ADDITIONAL INCOME AND INFLATION CONSIDERATIONS

Pragmatic analysts understand that inflation, unemployment, and a lack of growth can result from inappropriate levels of total customer spending as well as a number of other circumstances such as cost increases, administered prices, and structural changes.

They also know that poorly chosen efforts to stabilize an economy's inflation and unemployment can themselves cause the very inflation and unemployment they are intended to prevent.

They also know that total spending may fluctuate so that the magnitudes of the problems, and thus of the corrective monetary, fiscal, and other measures that might need to be implemented, may vary from one point in time to another.

Finally, and most importantly, they know that inflation and unemployment cause distress. That means that it is in the best interest of an economy's people and future that its total spending be constantly fine tuned to be at whatever level of income will best enhance the economy's price stability, employment, production, and growth.

Pursuing such a spending goal is easier said than done. One reason is that each economy has unique structures and institutions that influence its wages, prices, employers, and customers. For example, the United Kingdom has a rather unified and centralized governmental structure that allows it to move rather quickly to make fiscal changes. The United States is different. It has a governmental system of checks and balances associated with two legislative houses, a President with veto powers, and numerous state and local governments.

Similarly the United Kingdom has a professionally run central bank that sets the bank rate which the wholesale interest price of money. This is the rate at which British banks can borrow money to loan to consumers and businesses. The United States is different. Its central bank, the Federal Reserve System, tends to be operated by political appointees and offers no such wholesale rate. It primarily operates by changing the Federal Funds target rate and via open market and other operations that affect the money supply. It uses them to affect both the less-important level of interest rates and the all-important amount and repayment terms of the money and credit which is available to consumers and employers.

Making rational decisions.

In order to make rational policy decisions to stabilize an economy's level of income, it is necessary for policy makers to know how their economy's prices and production are related to what happens both in their economy and outside of it in other countries. Only when these relationships are known can reasonable combinations of policies be promulgated to provide the appropriate levels of prices, wages and customer spending.

Various efforts have been made to identify useful key relationships; some of them are discussed below. When considering them, analysts should keep in mind that one reason it is difficult to identify proper policies to appropriately influence total spending is that various different relation-ships may exist at different points in time—so that no one relationship exists and no one best "solution" is always possible.

For example, inflation can be of a demand-pull nature at one point in time and primarily the result of higher wages or other costs or administrative actions or foolish spending-influencing policies at another. It follows logically that different policies may be needed for different problems. It also follows, from the fact that in the real world there are a variety of causes of inflation and unemployment, that *anyone advocating a single cure-all policy such as controlling the money supply or balancing the budget will be wrong most of the time.*

Choosing between inflation and unemployment.

Economists have for years used historical data to suggest that a relationship exists between inflation and unemployment. The data clearly show that in the past unemployment has been lower when price levels increases have been greater. In other words, the data seem to suggest that inflation is the price an economy must pay to have low levels of unemployment. This, in turn, has been used to suggest that policy makers bent on stabilizing and economy's income *must choose between some combination of inflation and unemployment.*

Figure 14-1 depicts the basic finding that in the past unemployment has been lower when prices are higher.

Okun's Law. The relationship between inflation and unemployment has given rise to various rule of thumb summaries based on regressing historical output data against employment changes and other data. Arthur Okun, in what is now known as "Okun's Law" suggested that a three percent decrease in output corresponds to a one percent increase in the official rate of unemployment; a one half of one percent decrease in labor force participation; a half of one percent decrease in hours worked per employee; and a one percent decrease in output per hours worked. Subsequent studies have suggested that Okun was a bit pessimistic and that it would take a two percent decline in output to get those results.

Analysts can also turn around the above relationships, as Okun himself did, and suggest that they mean it will take a two or three percent increase in income to reduce official rate of unemployment by one percent. They also need to consider how technological advances (and the required increases in aggregate demand associated with them) that result in a two percent increase in total output, or any other increase, can reduce the rate of unemployment if the economy is already at full employment so that everyone who is willing to work has a job except people frictionally unemployed who are moving between jobs and people structurally unemployed because they are unemployable in their current geographic locations and unable to move.

What some of this suggests, and pragmatic economists accept, is that when an economy such as the United States has unemployment ten or fifteen points higher than its natural rate of unemployment, it is leaving many trillions of dollars of goods and services unproduced. What this means, of course, is that an economy in such a depressed state will need many trillions of dollars of additional spending to get back to full employment.

But is the historical relationship between inflation and unemployment, and the policy tradeoff it suggests, a valid guide to policy?

Most pragmatic macroeconomists do *not* think so. In a nutshell, they think that past experiences when inadequate or inappropriate monetary and fiscal policies periodically resulted in unstable levels of customer spending and periodic spurts of inflation are no guide to the inflations and unemployment that will occur in the future in dynamic economies if they have adequate monetary and fiscal policies. In other words, past experiences during periods of unnecessarily unstable levels of income may not be much of a policy guide to preventing inflation in economies enjoying periods of sustained full employment.

Moreover, there may be no such tradeoff between inflation and unemployment once appropriate monetary and fiscal policies are implemented on a sustained basis. Then there will only be relatively constant "natural rates" of unemployment and wage and price increases as the structure of the economy continuously evolves.

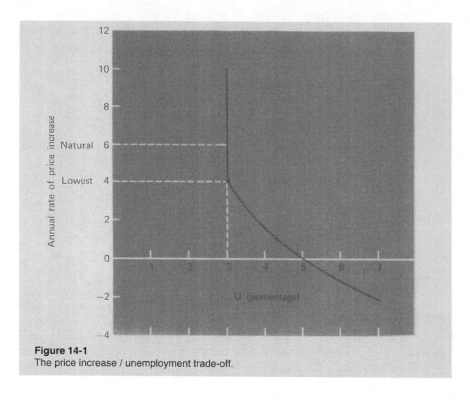

Figure 14-1
The price increase / unemployment trade-off.

The ratchet effect of cost and price increases. The policy conundrum of choosing between higher prices and full employment on one hand and price stability and more unemployment on the other is exacerbated by the "ratchet effect" of inflation. It occurs because prices and wages are inflexible downward. As a result, inflation and wage increases tend to be a one-way street—once wages and prices rise they tend to stay at the new and higher level until they rise again for some reason; deflation (lower prices) is conceptually possible but never-realized because of the institutional forces which discourage lower wages and prices. What this means is that the levels of an economy's nominal wages and prices tend to be constantly ratcheted upwards as an economy changes and evolves.

The redistribution of income and the natural rates of inflation and unemployment.

As analysts will recall, the natural rate of unemployment is the proportion of an economy's frictionally unemployed and structurally unemployable workers are of its total labor force; and the natural rate of inflation is the upward drift in prices that tends to occur as some prices rise in response to changes in the structure of the economy while the economy's other prices tend not to fall. They are going to exist no matter what is done to fight inflation or unemployment.

With the proper monetary and fiscal policies an economy can choose to operate at its natural rate of unemployment. That is the same as saying that the rest of its labor force is fully employed and the economy is maximizing its production.

But what if the natural rate of inflation, the natural rate of wage increases, and the natural rate of unemployment are not compatible with a stable distribution of income? Consider, for example, an economy where there is a three percent natural rate of unemployment, the rate of money wage increases associated with full employment is nine percent, and the lowest possible rate of structural price increases associated with permanently continuing full employment is four percent? If this economy's annual increase in productivity per worker is three percent and the economy's decision makers choose to operate it at its natural rate of full employment with ninety seven percent of its labor force employed, and they want to keep its rate of inflation minimized to its natural rate of four percent, there will be a steady redistribution of the real income the economy produces to the economy's workers at the rate of two percent of labor income per year.

If this is the case, and some analysts think it is representative of the United States in the early 21st century, then *the policy makers must choose* between increasing spending so that it is high enough that the economy's rate of inflation rises to six percent and prevents the redistribution or holding spending down so that the inflation is only four percent and allowing America's workers an ever larger share of the increased output. In the example economy, six percent is the natural rate of inflation that allows *both* maximum production and the wage and price increases needed to obtain the structural changes and the reallocation of labor and capital to where their contributions to production will be the greatest.

Many pragmatic economists think the United States' natural rate of inflation associated with continuous full employment will be in the range of two to three percent per year if and when appropriate income stabilization policies are ever permanently implemented. It is, of course, impossible to accurately predict—both because economic forces and relationships are constantly changing and because there has never been a sustained period of appropriate monetary policies. As the late economist Milton Friedman noted: "the Federal Reserve has been remarkably consistent in its major policy decisions to affect total spending—always wrong."

On the other hand, redistribution could also work in reverse. During the Great Recession, for example, the productivity of American workers continued to increase as new technologies came on line, money wages remained relatively stable, and the general level of prices rose very slightly. Accordingly, the real wages of the workers who still had jobs declined and a larger and larger share of the economy's total production went to the holders of wealth, the recipients of income from financial trades and rents, and all the other people who derived their incomes from sources other than the labor they provided to employers to produce goods and services.

The relationship between wage changes and unemployment.

The Phillips Analysis. Professor A.W. Phillips' famous charting of the historical relationship between wage changes and unemployment found that the rate of changes in money wages in the U.K., and thus the changes in the production costs of the economy's employers, depended primarily on the level of unemployment. Similar studies were done for most other economies.

As analysts might expect, studies in the United States and elsewhere tended to confirm the findings for Britain. They show that, in the past at least, wages have increased more when unemployment was lower. They also found that the rate of change in the economy's wages was influenced by the cost of living, as indicated by changes in the consumer prices and state of the economy's "business cycle" as indicated by the direction and rate of change of the unemployment rate.

The Phillips procedure. A Phillips analysis plots points representing each year's combination of the percentage change in money rates (w) and the annual rate of unemployment onto a scatter diagram and fits a curve to it. Examples of the type of relationship they found are presented in Figures 14-2(a) and 14-2(b). The dotted loops around the fitted curve trace out the move from one year's observed combinations to the next. The loops also indicate the degree to which the actual combinations deviate from the curves at any particular time during the time periods being consideration.

Nature of the curves. Most curves fitted to actual wage and unemployment data for the U.S., Canada, and the U.K. have the basic shape depicted in the Figure 14-2 examples. Their positions to the right of the vertical axis are explained by the frictional and structural unemployment whose existence ensures that some unemployment will exist no matter how anxious employers are to hire workers and how fast wages rise.

The curves for small and relatively slow growing economies such as the United Kingdom lie closer to the vertical axis than do those of larger and more rapidly growing economies such as the United States because they have less frictional and structural unemployment. There are several possible explanations for the observed difference between economies. Among them:

When the geographic size of a nation is smaller it takes less time and effort to move from one employer to another;

Job stability in the form of long term occupation and employer relationships may be more binding in some countries due to traditions and legal encouragements;

Some economies have political impediments to change that make them less dynamic so that fewer changes occur to leave workers behind and raise wages to lure them to move;

And, finally, some economies' labor forces are better prepared by culture and education to handle alternative employments. Then fewer are left behind as unemployable when the structure of an economy changes.

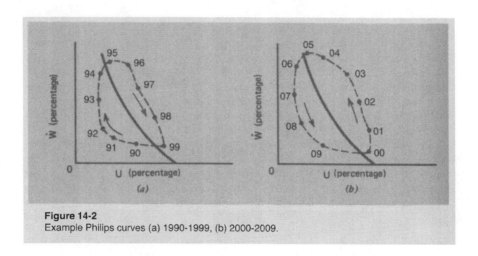

Figure 14-2
Example Philips curves (a) 1990-1999, (b) 2000-2009.

Shape of the Phillips curves. Rapidly rising wage rates tend to be found in all relatively-market-oriented economies when they have relatively low rates of unemployment. This can be explained, in the best market tradition, as occurring because wages tend to be bid higher when the supply of unemployed labor becomes relatively low. Most economies (North Korea may be an exception as China was during its Mao-inspired Cultural Revolution) do not have government restrictions against raising wages, and their employers have generally been unable to organize themselves to stop competing for workers.

On the other hand, and contrary to the best market tradition, wages have also risen at times when unemployment apparently existed significantly in excess of the structurally and frictionally unemployed. This could be caused by the upward pressures on wages from unions and governments that continue even when there is unemployment. For example, the government might increase the minimum wage or require employers to provide their workers with more medical insurance or increase employment taxes to cover retirements and unemployment insurance or increase teachers' salaries even though there are one hundred applicants for every vacancy.

The same thing would occur if an economy's labor submarkets have temporarily different levels of labor unemployment—so that a general increase in the demand for workers puts workers back to work in some markets where there is unemployment but only bids up wages in other markets where the available labor force is already fully employed. In other words, the average level of wages rises if some wage rise and some remain stable.

This was the one of the euro zone's problems during its sovereign debt crisis. Germany opposed efforts to increase aggregate demand because its labor force was fully employed. German decision makers understood that more spending would both bid up prices for its products and increase the demand for its labor which would result in higher wages and permanently higher costs. The Germans did not want inflation and they did not want higher costs so that Germany's employers would have to charge higher prices and risk losing export sales. In contrast, other euro countries were suffering from high levels of unemployment. They wanted the aggregate demand to be increased in order to increase the demand for their workers and put them back to work.

Wage increases and income fluctuations. The historical wage and unemployment data also suggest employers in market-oriented economies are more willing to pay higher wages if they expect to hire more workers than if they expect their sales and revenues to decline. Thus the degree of wage increases and decreases in an economy not only depends on the level of unemployment but is also influenced by the direction and speed of changes in the level of economic activity in the economy.

Various studies have been made relating the rate at which unemployment levels have changed to fluctuations in the level of income. The studies generally suggest that both cyclical position and the length of length of each cyclical upturn major factors influencing the rate at which the general level of an economy's money wages change.

Astute analysts will note the policy implications implicit in such findings—that removing impediments to capacity expansions and maintaining full employment via a sustained growth in total spending are more important to the general prosperity of an economy's labor force than efforts to redistribute income and legislation and regulations that enable unions to push up the wages of specific workers.

**The internal versus external dilemma if
an economy has fixed exchange rates.**

Both monetary and fiscal policies may be used both internally to stabilize an economy at full-employment levels of spending and, externally, to repair a balance of payments that has a surplus or deficit. At one time or another almost every country has attempted to either affect the total spending in its economy or attempted to fix the rate at which its currency exchanges with the currencies of one or more other countries, or both. Even today many countries such as China try to maintain a fixed exchange rate against the United States dollar or only allow their currency fluctuate within a narrow band of rates.

Various policies can be used in an effort to achieve either goal. For example, the policymakers of an economy could use monetary ease and lower taxes during a period of unemployment to improve an economy's level of employment and output by increasing spending. That would also tend to make the economy's a balance of payments worse by encouraging imports and outbound money flows to wherever interest rates are now higher.

On the other hand, tight money and higher tax rates may reduce total customer spending and end balance of payments deficits by discouraging imports and attracting money from abroad with the higher interest rates, but at the expense of causing unemployment and lower rates of growth and tax collections.

Conflicting policy objectives. The inherent problem of stabilizing an economy with fixed exchange rates both internally and externally is that the policies that work to solve one potential problem can make the other worse. For example, tight money to push up interest rates and attract money from abroad to cure a balance of payments deficit may also reduce total spending so much that unemployment results. Similarly, policies such as monetary ease to expand the level of spending in order to take the economy to full employment may result in lower interest rates and lead to balance-of-payments deficits as money then goes abroad in search of higher interest rates.

What this means is significant—that sometimes policy makers must choose between two conflicting outcomes: enough spending to eliminate unemployment or enough money inflows to eliminate a balance of payments deficit.

The situation is further complicated because there are various combinations of monetary tightness and fiscal restraints that yield full employment levels of spending and other combinations that will yield equilibrium in its balance of payments. In essence, the more an economy's fiscal activities such as higher taxes or lower government spending tend to restrain total purchasing and improve the balance of payments, the less that monetary restraint is needed to prevent demand-pull inflations and improve the balance of payments.

Similarly, the lower levels of spending that tend to be associated with greater degrees of fiscal restraint mean that fewer products will be purchased abroad (and domestically) and that the economy will tend toward a balance of payments surplus. On the other hand, less monetary restraint tends to not only result in lower interest rates but also increased spending. In other words, the lower interest rates will drive "hot money" out to other economies where it might earn a higher return while the increased spending tends to mean there will be more imports so that even more money goes abroad.

The policy implications. When an economy has fixed exchange rates there is only one combination of monetary restraint and fiscal restraint that will simultaneously result in both internal and external equilibrium.

All other combinations result in an undesirable level of spending or a balance of payments that is out of balance, or both. And that one combination can be an ever-changing target as things constantly change both at home and abroad. It means policy makers in economies with fixed exchange rates have a particularly difficult job—they must either constantly and accurately fine tune their monetary and fiscal restraints or periodically accept inappropriate levels of income or balance of payments problems or both.

The price an economy pays for choosing to protect its fixed exchange rate instead of having policies that generate enough spending can be quite high. For example, the Federal Reserve and Congress, following the lead of Britain and many of the world's smaller economies where exports are a more vital part of its total spending, spent much of the twentieth century implementing monetary and other policies designed to prevent the United States from having balance of payments deficits. They did not want the United States to run out of reserves and have to change it exchange rates. They acted because the Congress and the Federal Reserve somehow thought that defending a fixed exchange rate for the dollar was important to the maintenance of American prosperity.

The United States, for instance, did periodically succeed in defending the dollar's fixed exchange rate against other currencies via the periodic imposition of import taxes and tight money policies that discouraged dollars from flowing abroad. As might be expected, those periodic policies did help the balance of payments. But they also caused massive shortfalls in total spending and thus high levels of unemployment, slow rates of growth, and lower tax collections that resulted in budgetary deficits.

The absurdity of promoting prosperity with policies that periodically resulted in recessions, low growth, and deficits became so apparent that in 1973 the Federal Reserve governors finally quit attempting to run interest rates and the supply of money up and down in response to the balance of payments. Now the dollar's exchange rate is established in the world's money markets. That is important. It means the governors can concentrate on keeping the level of total spending at whatever levels are to generate full employment.

In other words, since they are no longer burdened with balance of payments considerations the policy makers of the United States are now free to choose any combination of monetary and fiscal restraint that will result in full employment without inflation. Of course, being free to choose does not mean that the right combination of policies will be chosen; if they aren't, there can be inflation from too much spending or unemployment and low levels of growth from too little.

The price that people and employers pay when their economies have fixed exchange rates can be quite high. Britain and the United States, for example, spent much of the twentieth century trying to prevent balance of payments deficits in order to maintain the fixed exchange rates. They did so because their financial advisors, including Keynes who was otherwise quite bright, somehow thought that fixed exchange rates were important to maintaining their economies' prosperity and the value of their currencies. They did succeed in defending their fixed exchange rates via the periodic imposition of high taxes and tight money policies—and that periodically resulted in such massive shortfalls in total spending that the British and American economies spent many years in deep recessions and depressions with massive unemployment. Worse, the American and British efforts to maintain a specific rate periodically failed so badly that their currencies had to be revalued to whatever rate would eliminate their payments deficit—the rate that would have occurred if their currencies had been free to fluctuate. Both the British pound and the United States dollar are now allowed to freely fluctuate against the currencies of other countries.

Depicting the dilemma. Figure 14-3 depicts the implications of the conflicting policy objectives. The "internal equilibrium curve" represents the various combinations of monetary and fiscal restraint that will yield a full employment level of spending. It depicts the reality that *the more an economy's fiscal activities such as higher taxes tend to restrain total spending, the less that monetary restraint is needed to prevent excessive levels of spending.*

More specifically, points to the right of the internal curve represent the various combinations of monetary restraint and fiscal restraint that are so great they will cause unemployment due to inadequate customer spending. Points to the left of the curve represent the various combinations of monetary tightness and fiscal restraint that result in excess spending and are, thus, inadequate to prevent demand-pull inflation. Only the monetary and fiscal policy combinations that are depicted by the curve will result in an equilibrium level of spending that will result in full employment.

Similarly, the "external equilibrium curve" represents the various combinations of tight money and fiscal restraint that will put the economy's balance of payments in equilibrium with neither a surplus nor a deficit.

More specifically, the lower levels of income that tend to be associated with greater degrees of fiscal restraint mean that fewer products will be purchased abroad (and domestically) and that the economy will tend to run a balance of payments surplus. On the other hand, lower levels of monetary restraint tends to not only result in lower interest rates but also higher levels of spending. In essence, the lower interest rates will drive money out to other economies and the excess spending will tend to mean more imports so that even more money goes abroad.

Accordingly, points representing monetary and fiscal combinations to the right of the external curve result in balance of payments surpluses and points to the left of the curve represent the fiscal and monetary combinations that will result in balance of payments surpluses.

Since various combinations of fiscal restraint and monetary restraint can lead to balance of payments equilibrium, the greater the fiscal restraint to discourage an economy's customers from spending, the less the necessity for monetary restraint to keep interest rates high in order to keep money from going abroad. The external equilibrium curve for the Figure 14-3 example economy depicts the various combinations of fiscal and monetary restraint that will result in the economy having its balance of payments in equilibrium with neither a surplus nor deficit.

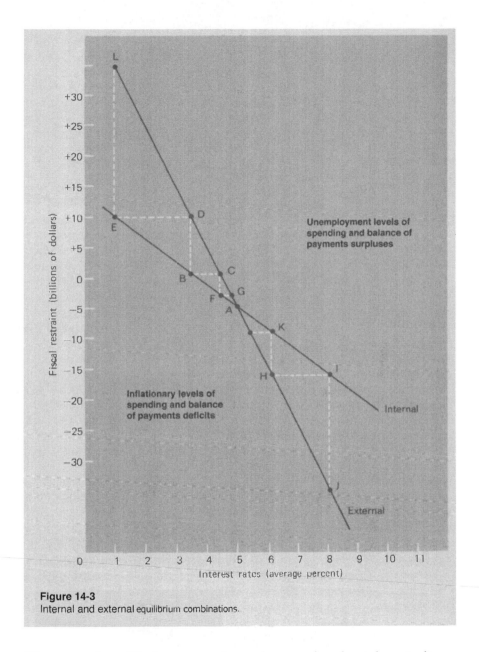

Figure 14-3
Internal and external equilibrium combinations.

The external equilibrium curve slopes down and to the right to indicate that a country's balance of payments can be in equilibrium with higher and higher degrees of monetary restraint when there are lower and lower levels of fiscal restraint to curb purchasing abroad and other expenditures.

An economy's external equilibrium curve tends to be more inelastic than its internal equilibrium curve. This occurs to the extent that money flows abroad are more responsive to interest rate changes than are changes in consumer and other spending to buy domestically produced goods and services. In other words, the external equilibrium curve is more inelastic because money flows abroad are more responsive to interest rate changes than domestic spending is responsive to interest rate changes.

The policy solution. The terrible impact on jobs and production that the United States and Britain efforts to defend their fixed exchange rates periodically caused was not inevitable; it was the result of poor policy choices—because there appears to be *one combination of monetary restraint and fiscal restraint that will simultaneously result in both internal and external equilibrium.* Had they chosen to keep adjusting their policies to continually move toward that one combination both countries would, at least conceptually, been able to retain their fixed exchange rates and avoided their periodic recessions and depressions.

In the Figure 14-3 economy, for example, the one and only combination of monetary restraint and fiscal restraint that will result in both a full employment level of spending and a balance of payments that has neither deficit nor surplus is that depicted by Point A; all other combinations result in an undesirable level of spending or a balance of payments that is out of balance, or both.

Identifying that one combination and moving to it is easier said than done. In the real world, conditions in the money and product markets of the world's economies are constantly changing at home and abroad. That means policy makers in economies with fixed exchange rates must either constantly change and fine tune their monetary and fiscal restraints or accept inappropriate levels of income or balance of payments problems or both.

Even more pernicious, however, is the very real possibility that an economy's domestic and international circumstances are such that the policy combination curves that depict them do not intersect. Then no combination of monetary and fiscal policies can simultaneously succeed in solving both problems

In any event, most economies, including the United States, have relatively recently (1973) opted for flexible exchange rates so that their decision makers can concentrate on getting the level of total spending to the correct levels without having to worry about their economy's balance of payments.

In other words, *since they are no longer burdened with balance of payments considerations the policymakers of the United States are now free to choose any combination of monetary and fiscal restraint that will result in an equilibrium level of spending that will yield full employment without inflation.* Of course, being free to choose does not mean that the right combination of policies will be chosen; if they aren't, there can be inflation from too much spending or unemployment and low levels of growth from too little.

Europe's euro zone policy dilemma. The tradeoff between balance of payments considerations and sufficient total spending was the euro zone's greatest policy problem during its sovereign debt crisis. The euro, like the dollar, is free to fluctuate in response to market forces. Thus the exchange rate between countries is fixed—they all use the euro. But what to do when some countries need more spending and others do not?

Germany consistently opposed efforts by the European Central Bank to increase the supply of euros in order to encourage spending increases—because its labor force was already fully employed; France, Spain, and Italy, on the other hand, had significant unemployment and needed more spending.

The German decision makers opposed increasing spending in the euro zone because they understood that more spending would bid up prices for German products and increase the demand for German labor—which would result in higher wages and permanently higher costs in Germany. They did not want inflation and they did not want higher costs so that German employers would have to charge higher prices and risk losing their export sales.

In contrast, other euro countries wanted monetary ease in order to increase spending and put their unemployed workers back to work (and because the easy money policies would make it easier for them to keep spending borrowed money instead of reforming their economies by eliminating the laws and regulations that discouraged the growth of their tax bases).

In essence, when they gave up their central banks and currencies and adopted the euro the euro zone countries abandoned their ability to conduct their own monetary policies and use exchange rate changes to affect total spending. All they had left was fiscal policy changes. Accordingly, those with both budget deficits and not enough total spending to yield full employment had to choose between increasing their deficits by cutting taxes and raising government spending to achieve full employment or raising taxes and cutting spending to eliminate their national deficits which would reduce their total spending and further increase their unemployment. They initially, at the suggestion of the IMF, tried to raise their taxes and cut government spending. It did not work; their unemployment grew as their total spending fell and this, in turn, reduced their tax collections to such an extent that their deficits got worse instead of better.

Why did they have such a dilemma? They had it because by adopting the euro they established a fixed exchange rate between one another. Little wonder that the more financially sophisticated of the European countries, Britain, Switzerland, Sweden, Denmark, and Norway wanted to keep their monetary and fiscal policy options open and refused to adopt the euro.

The relationship between total spending, production capacity, and investment spending.

How fast an economy's investment and other non-consumption spending must grow if the economy is to maintain full employment has long intrigued economists. It is an important question because the rate at which investment and other non-consumption spending must grow to maintain full employment also tends to be the rate at which the economy's production capacity and income can grow when there is full employment.

The question arises because investment spending has a dual role in an economy's prosperity. On one hand, sufficient investment and other non-consumption types of spending are necessary if an economy is to offset the savings that occurs and have enough total spending to keep its labor force and capital fully employed. On the other hand, the investment spending that helps generate full employment also results in additional capital goods being produced and tends to increase the economy's production capacity—so that in the future the economy will be able to produce more and, thus, need even more investment and other non-consumption spending to remain at full employment.

The impact and the full employment spending requirements of the dual role of investment have been analyzed by various splendid and pragmatic economists beginning with Sir Roy Harrod and Evsey Domar. To illustrate the implications of the dual role of the investment spending, consider an economy having the following characteristics: the investment portion of every four dollars of non-consumption purchasing acquires enough capital to replace the capital goods worn out in the production process. It also adds enough additional capital goods to economy's stock of capital to produce another one dollar's worth of additional goods and services in each subsequent time period; the average and marginal propensities to save are forty percent of the level of income so that investment and other non-consumption spending has a multiplier effect of 2.5; wages and prices are inflexible downward; $36 billion of investment and other non-consumption purchasing has just occurred; and the economy is in equilibrium with a full employment level of income of $90 billion.

Under the example conditions, the capital goods acquired with the investment portion of the $36 billion will then increase the productivity of the economy's employers by nine billion to a new and higher total of $99 billion in the subsequent time period because of the 4:1 non-consumption spending to output ratio. Then, since the capacity of the economy's employers has increased, merely repeating the $36 billion of non-consumption spending will not result in enough total spending to generate full employment levels of production. Instead, a new and higher level of non-consumption spending of $39.6 billion will be needed to generate the new and higher level of spending required for full employment.

Furthermore, the level of non-consumption spending will have to be even larger in every subsequent period if full employment is to be maintained. For instance, in the next time period the amount of non-consumption investment will have to be $43.56 because the $39.6 billion that preceded it will increase the economy's production capacity from $99 billion to $108.9 billion.

It is obvious from the previous example that, in the absence of other changes, in every subsequent time period the amount of investment and other non-consumption purchasing in an economy must be larger than the amount that preceded it if full employment levels of production are to be maintained. But how much larger? Astute analysts will notice that in the previous example, both non-consumption spending and the level of income increased ten percent each year. Thus, ten percent is the example economy's "natural rate of growth" *when full employment is maintained under the savings propensity and output ratios that were specified.*

The formula for determining the rate at which investment spending must grow to maintain full employment is R= s/Cr where R is the rate, Cr is the non-consumption purchasing to output ratio, and s is the average and marginal propensities to save. Thus in terms of our example economy:

$$R = s/Cr$$
$$R = .40/(1/4)$$
$$R = .10$$

In this example non-consumption spending will have to grow at the rate of 10 percent per year to keep the economy at full employment. That is also, of course, also the rate at which the economy will grow—its *natural rate of growth* if proper policies are implemented to influence total spending so that full employment is maintained.

It all sounds very elegant and wonderful, and it is. But it is also useless if the underlying conditions and relationships on which the full employment growth rate is based do not remain stable over time. An even more serious drawback, however, is the reliance on capital accumulation as the source of growth and the implicit assumption of a constant relationship between investment, foreign, and government spending.

In other words, on the supply side it ignores the possibility of changes in an economy's production capacity such as could be caused by major technological improvements such as improved techniques for the drilling of natural gas or changes in the size of the economy's labor force due to such things as improved health and longevity or a crisis in Mexico driving a huge number of immigrants into the U.S labor force; on the spending side it ignores the possibility that foreign and government spending might fluctuate, even if investment does not, and take the economy away from having enough total spending to cause full employment without causing so much spending that a demand-pull inflation results. It also ignores the possibility that other events will happen to cause inflation and unemployment and result in the need for other levels of total spending.

On the other hand, such an analysis may be quite valuable; after all, new technology tends to be embedded in new capital, population and labor force participation rate changes appear to occur slowly and at relatively stable rates, and demand can be kept at or near full employment with appropriate monetary and fiscal policies. At the very least, the concept of a "natural rate of growth" if full employment is maintained is another arrow of conceptual understanding for analysts to put in their quivers, if only because it reflects the tendency for an economy's capacity to grow over time and calls attention to the possibility of sustained levels of full employment.

Implementation of monetary and fiscal policies.

The residents of every economy have a vested interest in seeing that inflation and unemployment do not develop, that potential production occurs, and that growth is not thwarted. This self-interest tends to lead to the implementation of governmental fiscal policies and central bank monetary policies whenever the absence of such activities would result in the existence of undesirable economic circumstances. Certain problems and considerations must be resolved, however, before it is possible to determine the monetary, fiscal, and other policies that might be appropriate and viable for an economy under a given set of economic circumstances and political realities.

The choice of goals. There are areas of policy conflict regarding the goals which governments and central banks should try to attain with their monetary and fiscal policies. Needless to say, these conflicts necessitate the economy's choosing, inevitably via its political process, the goals that it considers to be most desirable before it can select the policies appropriate to attain them. For instance:

1. Is it more desirable that total spending rise or fall when there is inflation and unemployment due to higher costs or increases in the economy's non-competitive prices? More spending may be desirable because it means more production and employment, but undesirable if it means more inflation. On the other hand, less purchasing may be desirable because it counters inflation but undesirable because it means fewer goods and services will be purchased and, thus, less production, more unemployment, and lower rates of growth and tax collections.

2. Should balance-of-payments deficits be eliminated by monetary policies that cause interest rates to rise so that foreign funds are attracted? Such "tight money" policies not only tend to eliminate payments deficits and so solve certain international financial problems, but also tend to reduce the purchasing of goods and services and thus cause a decline in production, and increase in

unemployed labor and capital, and a reduction in the economy's growth.

3. Should the existence of unemployment caused by structural changes or frictional conditions lead to policies that expand to purchasing until all or some those unemployed are able to locate jobs? Or should more selective means such as increasing spending for "jobs training," "make work" employment, or increasing welfare expenditures be used to counter such unemployment?

4. Should taxes be raised and government expenditures reduced when an economy's sovereign debt becomes unfinanceable or should impediments to growth be removed so that the economy's tax base, its production and employment, grows.

5. Should there be tax rates, spending programs, and transfers that cause redistribution of income and wealth from low income people to high income people such as occurred in the United States in the early 21st century? Transfers to the favored few, special tax rates that encourage money to flow into financial assets instead of capital goods, inflation, and unemployment all may cause an income redistribution to occur. Redistribution from potential purchasers with a particular marginal propensity to consume or buy capital goods to other potential purchasers with different propensities may change total spending. It also might change peoples' and employers' incentives to work, produce, and invest and, thus, change the economy's level of income and rate of growth.

6. Should an economy produce for the present or the future? The establishment of tax incentives and lower interest rates may encourage employers to make investment purchases of capital goods and introduce new technologies that will allow even more goods and services to be produced in the future. But more investment purchasing in an economy already operating at maximum levels of production means both that there will be a demand-pull inflation and that fewer goods and services will be left over to satisfy the present needs of the economy's residents.

The experiences of the countries of the euro zone during the second decade of the twenty first century provide a graphic illustration of both the importance of the political process and the importance of macroeconomic knowledge. Their governments had previously surrendered control of their currencies and central banking powers to the European Central Bank and adopted the euro. Many of the governments then borrowed profusely until they reached unsustainable levels of sovereign debt—until they reached the point where they could not provide both normal government services to their peoples and pay the banks from whom they earlier borrowed.

In order to temporarily obtain the money they needed to refinance that debt (read save the big banks that had loaned money to them knowing they could not repay it) they were required by the European Central Bank, acting on the advice of the IMF, to impose severe restrictions on their economies, such as tax increases and spending cuts that result in severe levels of unemployment and recession.

Three things then happened: their deficits and unemployment rates grew instead of declining; their governments were thrown out by the voters in the next election; and the IMF received additional funding from the United States and others so it could continue providing temporary "help" to the euro zone countries (read big banks) with problems.

The United States had a somewhat similar experience in 2010. Americans were so distressed at the continuing recession and unemployment, for which they mistakenly blamed Congress instead of the Federal Reserve, that they voted out so many incumbents such that control of the House of Representatives passed to the Republicans.

Selecting monetary and fiscal policies that will work.

Some macroeconomists, but certainly not the more worldly of them, believe there may at times be conditions in an economy that will make it difficult for its decision makers to identify and implement policies that will generate sufficient levels of total spending. In other words, that under certain circumstances neither conventional fiscal policies nor conventional monetary policies will work.

This would certainly be the case if interest rates are as low as they can go and the primary influence of a monetary expansion is via interest rate reductions. Then there would be no change in the equilibrium level of spending as a result of a monetary expansion because the minimum level of interest rates already has been reached. Spending would not increase because the economy is in the Keynesian version of the "liquidity trap."

Under such circumstances, it is alleged, any additional money the Federal Reserve might place in the commercial banks via its open market and other activities will be held instead of being used to bid up the price of financial assets and cause their interest rates to fall. And if interest rates don't fall, it is alleged, there will be no increase in consumer and employer purchases. Thus, a monetary policy of expanding the money supply, or any other policy intended to drive down interest rates, will not increase the level of total spending and result in more production and employment. It follows, according to the Federal Reserve governors and Keynesians, that since monetary policy will no longer work fiscal policies are the only way to restore full employment levels of production.

An analysis providing the basis for their beliefs can be seen by examining the equilibrium conditions in the economy depicted by Figure 14-4. The IS and LM curves represent the possible equilibrium conditions in the economy's product and money markets.

When only fiscal policy will work. If the equilibrium conditions in the money and product markets are depicted by points that intersect along section "a" of the LM curve (IS1), monetary policies to encourage spending increases will not work because the economy is in the liquidity trap—only fiscal policies such as tax cuts and government spending increases can result in higher equilibrium levels of income whose effect would be reflected by shifting the IS curve to the right, such as IS2 and IS3.

In other words, policies of monetary expansion will not have such an effect on the equilibrium level of total spending *if the primary influence of a monetary expansion is via interest rate reductions as the Federal Reserve governors and many analysts have traditionally assumed.*

If the governors and regional presidents, and the Keynesians and their followers are correct, then the effect of a monetary expansion when interest rates are already as low as they can go. Then the effect of any subsequent monetary expansion would be depicted by a shift in the LM curve to the right—without changing the point ("a") at which the LM and IS curves intersect. There is no change in the equilibrium level of purchasing because the minimum level of interest rates already has been reached. Spending does not increase because the economy is in the "liquidity trap."

Under such circumstances, any additional money the Federal Reserve might flow into the commercial banks via its open market and other activities will be held instead of being used to bid up the price of financial assets and cause their interest rates to fall. And if interest rates do not fall, so the story goes, there will be no increase in consumer and employer purchases. Thus, a monetary policy of expanding the money supply under such conditions will not increase the level of income and result in more production and employment. It follows, according to the governors and Keynesians, that since monetary policy will not work, an expansionary fiscal policy is the only way to restore full employment levels of production.

When both fiscal and monetary policies will work. Both monetary policies whose effects are represented by shifts in the LM curve and fiscal policies whose effects are represented by shifts in the IS curve can increase an economy's total purchasing if the initial equilibrium conditions in the economy as similar to those represented graphically by section "b" of the LM curve and IS2.

Any move in one basic market of the economy under these conditions, however, will be at least partial offset by "secondary" automatic stabilizer effects in the other market. Thus, for example, lower taxes or more government spending tends to increase the equilibrium level of spending in an economy at every level of interest rates. This is depicted by a shift of the economy's IS curve to the right to IS2. But the increased demand for money at the higher levels of income may partially offset the expansionary effect of the initial fiscal change by causing higher interest rates and thus tend to at least partially offset the effect of the expansionary fiscal policy.

When only monetary policies work. Finally, only monetary policies can expand an economy's level of income if the size of the economy's money supply is so limited that any move towards increased spending is choked off by higher interest rates. Such a condition is represented by the inelastic "c" potion of the LM curve. This is the highest level of total spending that the economy's money supply can accommodate. When it is reached, only a monetary expansion will work—fiscal policies such as tax cuts and government spending increases can not further increase total spending. In other words, implementing an expansionary fiscal policy when all the economy's money is already being used for transactions purposes will merely cause the economy's interest rates to be bid up until total spending is choked back to the initial level.

In essence, all that will happen if spending increases such as to IS3 is that the level of interest rates will rise until the amounts of consumer and other spending desired by purchasers are cut back to the level at which all available money in the economy is used for transactions purposes. Then the only solution if more spending is needed is to increase the money supply to achieve conditions that would be depicted by a shift of the LM curve to the right.

The idea that only monetary policy will work when an economy has one of the "c" combinations of income and interest rates is also more than a bit unrealistic—because dollars and other monies would flow in from abroad in response to the high interest rates and the economy would begin using the newly arrived dollars and other currencies and money substitutes for its transactions. In other words, spending might at times be held back by a shortage of money, but never totally.

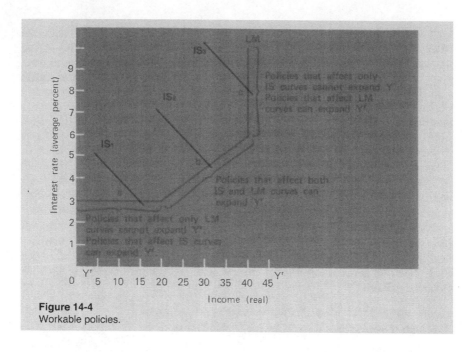

Figure 14-4
Workable policies.

The pragmatic dissent. Pragmatic economists totally disagree with the Keynesian liquidity trap analysis and its conclusions as unrealistic and unworldly. They maintain that in the real world the availability of credit and its repayment terms is much more significant to potential purchasers of goods and services than minor changes in its interest rate price.

They explain the governors' and Keynesian views as being the result of their unworldliness due to their use of overly simplistic models focused on interest rates and their traditional lack of business and commercial banking experience—which causes the governors to confuse the markets for financial instruments, which are highly responsive to interest changes, with consumer and employer spending in the product markets which are relatively insensitive to interest rate changes but very sensitive to the availability of credit and its repayment terms no matter what the rate of interest.

In essence, macro-pragmatic economists reject the Keynesian liquidity trap analysis because they do not think interest rates have to fall in order for a monetary expansion to encourage the increased purchasing of goods and services. They find no evidence that the existence of a minimum rate of interest, the basis of the liquidity trap of the Keynesians, eliminates the income-influencing effect of a policy of monetary expansion or contraction.

To the contrary, in terms of the basic model, pragmatic macroeconomists being aware of the conditions that actually exist in the real world, and having actually read Keynes so that they know his ideas primarily apply to Britain, see expanded total spending as the primary effect of an *appropriately conducted* monetary expansion. In terms of the model—an expansion of the money supply can have an effect depicted by the rightward shift of *both* the LM and IS curves.

On the other hand, pragmatic economists do see a form of "liquidity trap" that is not related to a minimum rate of interest. To the pragmatists the "liquidity trap" occurs in the real world when a monetary expansion does not increase total spending because the commercial banks and other depositories hold the additional money, instead of loaning it out—because they or their regulators fear their loans will default or because they and their regulators want them to hold more reserves and tier one capital.

This, the pragmatists say, describes the conditions that existed during the Great Recession and helps explain why the Federal Reserve's alleged (and relatively inconsequential) "quantitative easings" tended to have no impact on the economy's production and employment. In terms of the basic model, the effects of the pragmatists' liquidity trap is depicted by the IS curve *not* shifting rightward—because the absence of loanable funds and credit prevents additional spending at every possible rate of interest.

In essence, according to the pragmatists, it was not the existence of a minimum rate of interest that foiled expansionary monetary policies during the Great Recession. What foiled it, they say, was the arrival of new regulations and regulatory requirements, and the possibility of earning more income speculating with their deposits and depositing them at the Federal Reserve—they required and encouraged the banks not to make consumer and business loans. This was exacerbated by the huge contraction in the supply of money and credit created by the shadow banks. In a word, the monetary base and M2 did increase did increase during the Great Recession—but that part of the money supply which is outside the data generated by the Federal Reserve decreased even more.

Wall Street vs. Main Street.

Conventional Federal Reserve monetary policy is indirect. The Federal Reserve indirectly puts newly created money into the hands of consumers and other spenders by flowing it into and out of the real economy via the primary dealers from whom the Open Market Desk buys and sells federal bonds and other financial assets. The primary dealers then flow the money on into the financial markets (aka "Wall Street" where many of the buyers and sellers are located) by buying bonds for the Federal Reserve. The money that "Wall Street" receives from the primary dealers is inevitably deposited into a commercial or universal bank where it becomes available to be loaned out or held as reserves.

The Federal Reserve's buying of financial assets to increase the amount of money commercial and universal banks have available to loan to the consumers and employers of "Main Street America" (and others) is the essence of conventional monetary policy. And it often works—but not always.

It does not work when the banks decide or are forced to hold it as reserves or to use it to buy bonds or other financial assets—as they might do to "improve" their assets in response to "stress tests." It also does not work if the banks use the money for their own proprietary trading or to loan it to other traders instead of consumers and other potential spenders.

For example, a Federal Reserve policy of buying bonds when also tends to bid up their prices so that their owners tend to be able to sell them for a profit. These profits, in turn, encourage the universal banks and other traders and speculators to buy more bonds in the financial markets so that they can sell them to dealers and traders for a profit the next time bond prices rise.

Astute analysts will spot a potential pitfall in the previous scenario: the financial markets and the banks loaning them money are doing well but no money has gotten to the consumers and employers of Main Street America.

Moreover, if prices in the financial markets are booming because the Federal Reserve is buying, and is expected to continue buying because there is a recession, all the additional money plus some of the banks' existing funds that would normally be loaned to consumers and employers might be used for the banks internal operations or loaned instead to traders and speculators. Then the Federal Reserve's expansion of the money supply ("quantitative easing") would *reduce* the amount of money and credit available for Main Street consumers and employers to spend.

Moreover, shifting their loans from the long term loans typically sought by the consumers and employers of Main Street to the shorter term and more liquid loans to the financial traders and speculators of Wall Street is a rational thing for the universal and commercial banks to do, particularly if there is a recession, such that the consumers may lose their jobs and employers lose their revenues; and then be unable to repay their loans.

In other words, the Federal Reserve's policy of indirectly flowing newly created money to consumers and employers via its chain of primary dealers and traders and banks may work under normal circumstances— but fail when it is needed most.

The impact of such responses to a quantitative easing during a recession would be a *reduction* in the supply of money and credit in the real economy. That, in turn, would tend to result in consumers and employers having to pay higher interest rates to induce the banks to loan to them instead of using it for their own proprietary trading, using it to build up their own reserves and capital, and using it to make loans to the financial traders and speculators.

This appears to be exactly what happened throughout the Great Depression—the newly created money (and some of the old) was siphoned off along the way by the financial community and never reached the consumers and employers of the real economy. In terms of the basic model which depicts the economy, such a reality would be depicted by a *reduction* in the real supply of money.

Tax revenue maximization.

An oft-repeated suggestion by politicians in the United States and elsewhere for raising more tax revenues is "tax the rich" who have high incomes. But will higher income tax rates actually yield more revenues? The answer is maybe yes and maybe no. It depends on how the people and companies with large incomes and high levels of wealth will respond.

Every study that has been done suggests that, as tax rates rise higher and higher, more and more taxpayers will cease paying by either being discouraged from working and producing so they earn less taxable income or, more likely, move to jurisdictions with lower taxes. Thus it is that companies such a California-based Microsoft often establish residency in states such as Nevada which have no corporate income taxes; and thousands of United States companies and individuals claim legal residency in the Bahamas which levies no income tax at all. Similarly, many high income British citizens claim residency on the Island of Man and elsewhere.

In essence, higher and higher tax rates yield higher and higher tax revenues—until they reach some point at which revenues begin to decline. The suggestion that at some point higher rates will yield lower tax collections has been around for centuries even though in the United States it is often attributed to economist Arthur Laffer who allegedly first sketched it out for a journalist on a restaurant napkin.

An example Laffer Curve is depicted in Figure 14-5. Economists and politicians have long disagreed as to the shape of the curve for a given economy at a give point in time—those who want higher taxes say it peaks at tax rates higher than those in existence; those who want lower tax rates say it peaks at rates below the current rates.

Astute analysts note that in the real world the average rate of taxation at which collections peak will vary from state to state and country to country depending on how easy it is to shift taxable income to lower tax jurisdictions. And they particularly note that the effect on tax collections as a result of a change in tax rates will depend on whose tax rates are increased and whose are not. Thus, for example, a twenty percent increase in the tax rates on a person or business already paying a combined federal and state tax rate of seventy percent tax may cause them to avoid the tax increase by fleeing whereas a twenty percent increase on a person or company only paying five percent because they have a very low income may be so minor as to go virtually unnoticed.

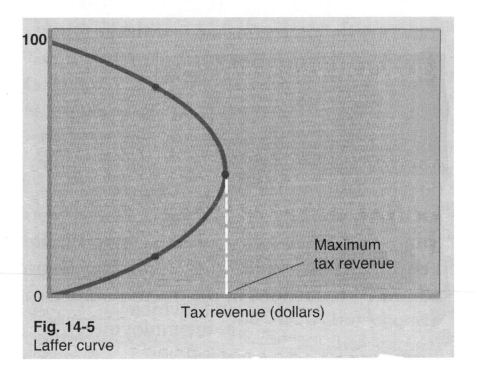

Fig. 14-5
Laffer curve

More policy complications.

Even if a monetary or fiscal policy is implemented which is basically workable, it still may be offset otherwise not able to achieve the desired results. The experiences of the United States during the Great Recession are proof certain that good intentions cannot offset unworldly incompetence when it comes to monetary and fiscal policies.

For instance, the implementation of a monetary policy designed to expand the excess reserves of commercial banks is no guarantee that the commercial banks will be able to lend out those reserves. That is exactly what happened during the Great Recession. The Federal Reserve engaged in "quantitative easing" to fight the recession by engaging in open market operations to expand the money supply by buying assets. But the intended expansionary effect on the level of income was more than totally offset by its simultaneous acquiescence to the higher reserve and capital requirements imposed on the commercial banks by its own bank regulators and the Federal Deposit Insurance Corporation.

Simultaneously with the adverse impact of the higher reserve and capital requirements, there was also "deleveraging" going on wherein lenders reduced their borrowing of funds to re-loan to consumers and employers in order to reduce their exposure to the risk of loan defaults. There was also a shift, encouraged by the regulators, to short term lending to investment banks and other traders gambling in the financial markets—because such debts could be more quickly liquidated than the longer term loans typically sought by consumers and employers.

All in all, the availability of credit and financing available to consumers and other product buying spenders collapsed and the recession continued to worsen for years—and all the while the Federal Reserve's governors were congratulating themselves for preventing a financial meltdown and claiming they had done all that could be done since interest rates banks were charging each other to borrow money for twenty four hours had hit all-time lows. It was a disgraceful performance.

Conversely, a decline in the availability of money designed to fight an inflation caused by too much spending may be offset by the introduction of new credit arrangements or the availability of loans from overseas banks and other intermediaries.

Similarly, changes in taxes or transfers are no guarantee that purchasing will change; purchasers are free to do as they please and may, for instance, increase their savings rather than increase their purchases. That is also what happened during the Great Recession; Congress cut the taxes paid by wealthy citizens and made large transfers to a handful of American and foreign financial institutions employing high income people with low propensities to consume. It did not work—they primarily used the money to buy financial instruments and their smaller competitors so the recession continue to worsen until it wiped out so many would be spenders that it morphed into a permanent depression.

Similarly, a workable policy being implemented to attain one goal might be offset by the implementation of other workable policies to obtain other goals. For instance, the United States Congress might increase taxes in an effort to reduce the federal deficit at the same time the Federal Reserve is increasing the money supply to encourage more spending in order to combat unemployment. This occurred during the Great Recession.

Alternately, as also happened during the Great Recession, the Congress, when it appropriated money to help a favored few of its big campaign contributors and effectively ignored everyone else, caused "everyone else" to dramatically cut their consumer and investment spending; they realized that neither the federal government nor the Federal Reserve was going to respond effectively to the recession so they began saving more so they could survive if they lost their jobs and customers, which many then did when spending fell as a result of their increased savings.

Time lags. There is no guarantee that otherwise workable policies can be put into effect in time to have any positive influence. The make-work "jobs bill" passed during the first year of the Obama Administration to fund "shovel ready" public projects that would employ people who would otherwise be unemployed due to the Great Recession is a good example: four years later signs began to appear in Chicago announcing street resurfacing projects funded by the program and the media was full of arguments about whether the new subway cars that would be funded by the program should be built in Illinois or in Canada.

In the real world of today's regulations and contract requirements there may be a tremendous time lag between the need for action and its arrival. First the problem has to be seen and analyzed and a policy formulated; then the political process of passing two houses of Congress and obtaining presidential approval has to occur; then the various environmental and other studies conducted and defended against the inevitable appeals and court cases; then contracts can be let and defended against another round of appeals and court cases; then can workers hired and the project put into effect until, finally and hopefully, economy gets the intended results. And that may take so long that the conditions are different by the time activities designed to eliminate a previously perceived problem begin to have their impact.

If the Great Recession fiscal policy of increasing government spending to provide jobs accomplished anything, it was to prove conclusively that in the United States there is no such thing as a "shovel ready" project that will quickly create jobs if it receives federal funding. It also proved that flowing newly created money into the financial markets to save cronies and political supporters does not have the same impact as flowing newly created money into the product markets to enable consumer and employer spending.

Temporary Changes. Certain things are obvious to analysts who understand the concept of an equilibrium level of income and the effect on it of "make work" federal spending projects. One of them is that the temporary changes in governmental fiscal activities historically employed in the United States to "prime the pump and get the economy going again" may not cause lasting changes in the level of purchasing and production.

In the real world, once the one-time temporary purchasing associated with "make work" projects ceases, the employment they create will disappear and their multiplier effect will be lost. In other words, in the absence of other changes, the economy will return to its original position of inadequate levels of total purchasing once the "pump priming" ends. Similarly, temporary tax and transfer increases or decreases may not influence consumption spending if such purchasing is primarily related to people's permanent or relative incomes.

Appropriate policies. Even when macroeconomic goals have been selected and there are workable policies to reach them, some policies are more appropriate than others. As suggested in the discussion of "Functional Finance" and elsewhere, it is inappropriate to change governmental purchasing and transfers merely to influence the level of total spending unless changes in taxation are impossible. The basis for this suggestion is the lack of relationship between the need for government purchasing and transfers to alleviate distress and provide products for public use, and the need for activity to affect total purchasing. In any event, monetary policies are a better choice to change total purchasing when there is inflation and unemployment because they can be accomplished more quickly—if the central bank is run by competent policy makers.

Just because policies are generally appropriate and can achieve one of an economy's major goals, such as fighting inflation or unemployment, does not mean they are the best way to go. For instance, monetary policies may be implemented to hold down spending to fight inflation. But such policies may hardly affect either established employers that internally generate the funds required for their expansion or public utilities whose higher interest rate costs can be passed on to their customers in their entirety.

On the other hand, such policies fall heavily on those sectors of an economy which traditionally depend on outside sources for financing: housing, state and local governments, and new and expanding employers that do not yet generate enough funds from depreciation and operations.

In other words, every policy tends to have its winners and losers and, thus, discriminates for and against some of those who it affects.

Political feasibilities and realities.

The whole area of implementing appropriate and realistic macroeconomic policies is complicated further because, as so many analysts in the academic world and Federal Reserve System do not seem to realize, the application of fiscal and monetary policies cannot be considered or advocated solely on the basis of technical considerations. Various politically oriented forces within an economy such as that of the United States shape the size and nature of the fiscal and monetary policies that are politically feasible for solving macroeconomic problems. These forces, though often based on irrational fears and misconceptions arising from a lack of knowledge and understanding, are nonetheless potent; failure to consider them can result in the advocacy of policies that cannot and will not be adopted.

Primary among the forces in the United States is the desire for balanced budgets. The reality is that a large proportion of the electorate and their representatives are unaware of the nature of debt creation, the difference between the debt of governments with central banks and those without them, and the effect of the existence of public debt; neither do they understand that the relatively insignificant procedures associated with refinancing the national debt is the price that may have to be paid periodically if an economy is to have full employment levels of spending without using monetary policies or having undesirable levels of government purchases and transfers.

The fact that deficits and surpluses may be deliberately brought into existence as a by-product of fiscal policies has already been discussed in some detail as has the fact that there is no upper limited to the size of the national debt or the ability to pay the interest associated with it. In other words, the concept of "bankruptcy" due to an inability to pay public debts as they come due does not apply to a national economy with its own central bank even though it does apply to all other governments.

The fact that a country with its own central bank is always able to pay its bills and will never be bankrupt is important—it means a national economy such as that of the United States with its own central bank can use fiscal policies to attain the optimum level of purchasing even though such policies consistently result in deficits or surpluses; government's without their own central bank can go bankrupt and thus have a limited ability to use fiscal policies to solve their problems of inflation and unemployment (sorry Greece, France, Italy and the other members of the euro zone. You'll have to do as the Germans require or go off the euro and get your own currency).

In addition to fears about deficits and national debt, many people seem confuse increased government spending with increased government regulation and to credit unbalanced federal budgets and/or government spending with causing inflation. Informed analysts know what might cause an economy's prices to rise and they know deficits and the national debt are not among them; additionally, they know how relatively insignificant federal spending is of total spending.

On the other hand, there is some validity in the concern that increased government spending, and particularly new federal spending programs, will result in increased and counterproductive regulations—the American political process is such that special favors for constituents and campaign contributors and new regulatory powers for government bureaucrats are routinely slipped into the voluminous pages of legislation that inevitably accompany a major spending bill.

In the real world a government which represents the people cannot and will not disregard their economic fears and concerns no matter how illogical and unwarranted they may be. That, and the fact that fiscal policy takes so long to implement and may be imperfectly crafted due to political pressures, and its authors lack of knowledge and experience, is why more and more analysts with an understanding of macroeconomics and real world experiences in business and commercial banking, are increasingly moving to the view that the price and employment stabilization efforts of economies such as the United States should be focused on the implementation of appropriate and timely monetary policies.

In other words, the pragmatists advocate *setting the federal tax rates to balance the federal budget at full employment and using Federal Reserve monetary policies to get the economy up to full employment levels of production and keeping it there.*

CHAPTER SUMMARY

I.   The historical relationships between wages and unemployment and prices and unemployment suggest that wages and prices increase more when unemployment is lower.

II.   The problem with such historical comparisons is that they might not be applicable to contemporary facts and situations when appropriate monetary and fiscal policies are pursued.

III.   The natural rate of unemployment is the proportion that frictionally and structurally unemployed workers are of the total labor force. They are always with us.

IV.   The natural rate of inflation is the rise in prices that needs to occur to prevent redistribution and maintain the natural rate of unemployment.

V.   Policy makers in economies with fixed exchange rates must consider both internal and external stability lest efforts to solve one problem makes the other worse. There may be only one level of monetary restraints and fiscal restraints at which an economy will be in equilibrium both internally and externally.

VI.   Price increases in an economy such as the United States tend have a "ratchet effect" in that, once they rise, they tend not to fall.

VII.   Investment spending to buy capital goods has two functions: it affects the total amount of goods and services purchased in a given time period and it affects the amount of production that can occur in subsequent time periods.

VIII. Economists have tried to identify the rate at which non-consumption spending must increase to provide full employment levels of total spending when the investment component of the non-consumption spending both affects total spending and increases the economy's production capacity. The rates they derive may not be applicable due to the complex and ever changing nature of modern economies.

IX. When implementing policies decision makers must often make choices between conflicting effects. Should there be more purchasing or less then there is both inflation and unemployment? Should interest rates be raised to eliminate balance of payments deficits or reduced via monetary easing when total spending is not high enough? Should structural and frictional unemployment be fought with policies that expand total purchasing or with selective programs or ignored? Should an economy produced primarily for the present or the future?

X. Newly created money the Federal Reserve attempts to indirectly make available to the consumers and employers of Main Street to encourage spending may be siphoned off by the financial institutions of Wall Street and not reach them.

XI. Laffer curves depict the relationship between tax rates and tax collections. Higher and higher tax rates yield higher and higher tax collections until at some point enough taxpayers change their behavior and location such that the higher rates yield lower revenues. This varies from state to state and country to country depending on the ease with which the taxpayers can shift jurisdictions and whose taxes are increased. There is no agreement as to what level of income will yield the highest level of tax revenues in countries such as the United States.

XII. Monetary and fiscal policy solutions to inflation and unemployment may not work under certain circumstances. Furthermore, there may be offsetting developments and time lags to consider. Decision makers must select policies that are both workable and politically feasible for the unique circumstances that actually exist.

XIV. The reality of the United States is that a lack of understanding about deficits and the national debt may keep the federal government from adopting appropriate fiscal policies. Accordingly, pragmatic analysts suggest that federal taxes and spending should be set so that the federal budget will be balanced when there is full employment and that full employment be achieved via monetary policies.

CHAPTER FIFTEEN

TRIGGERS, INDICATORS, AND GOALS

It would be wonderful if we all lived in an ideal world where everyone has perfect knowledge and there is perfect wage, price, and interest rate flexibility and no time lags and no market imperfections. Then we would always have instantaneous adjustments in the billions of prices and decisions that occur daily in an economy such as the United States, and they would always result in full employment and maximum rates of production and growth. But we do not.

Since perfect price stability and perfect full employment are impossible outside a nonexistent world of perfect markets and simple models, most pragmatic economists and analysts accept that the basic goal of an economy's decision makers is to limit the inflation that does occur to the natural rate which is inherent in the structural changes of a dynamic economy and to provide enough customer spending so that the economy's employers fully employ all of the economy's labor force except those in the process of moving between jobs and those left behind by structural changes.

Such an accomplishment, of course, requires that monetary, fiscal and other policies be selected that will induce customer spending neither so high as to pull prices up faster than would occur as a result of structural changes nor so low as to discourage future capacity growth or cause more unemployment than is inevitable as a result of frictional and structural changes. In any event, that's the plan even though to date it has rarely been achieved or even attempted.

Rarely may be charitable. To paraphrase economist Milton Friedman, the Congress and the Federal Reserve governors and regional presidents have been remarkably consistent in all their major price and income stabilization decisions—always wrong.

Complexities. When considering data and events to alert policy makers and trigger responses, analysts should keep in mind that it is often difficult to identify the precise cause of a problem because multiple causes can be occurring at the same time. Then no one single policy "solution" may be possible. For example, inflation can be of a demand—pull nature at one point in time and primarily the result of higher wages or other costs or regulatory actions or poorly chosen stabilization policies at another; or some or all of the above simultaneously. In other words, *decision makers need to examine a number of different facts before making a policy decision.*

Pragmatic analysts understand that there will always be a small amount of unemployment at the full employment level of income due to continuing frictional unemployment and the residual unemployed resulting from structural unemployment.

They also understand that it is absolutely impossible to totally stabilize prices because of the upward drift in the average level of prices that tends to occur as a result of ongoing changes in consumer preferences and the arrival of new products and other structural changes. Under normal circumstances in countries such as the United States the general level of prices will drift upwards two to four percent per year and unemployment will always be in the neighborhood of three to five percent.

The real world. During the Great Recession which started in 2008 the United States policy makers failed to keep the level of income stabilized at levels that would result in high and growing levels of employment. They failed despite the existence of a 1946 law directing that full employment be the major economic goal of the economy. Instead, they ignored the unemployment and the problems associated with it and pursued other goals such as maintaining the profits and bonuses of a handful of large trading-oriented financial institutions and bailing out part of the auto industry—the part that employed UAW members who had supported the president politically. As a result, the recession worsened and morphed into a permanent depression. Perhaps one reason nothing of substance was attempted for so many years thereafter was that the act left it to the members of the appropriate congressional committees and the Federal Reserve governors to determine when to act and what to do.

The 1946 act specifies full employment as the goal of United States income stabilization policies—not price stability, not income redistribution, and certainly not aid to cronies, political supporters, and a large financial firms who engage in proprietary trading with other people's money. The law was passed at time of a severe demand-pull inflation following WWII. Congress was adamant that Federal Reserve not begin to fight inflation and other problems at the expense of causing more unemployment. It is the law and the Federal Reserve governors consistently ignore it.

So what should have been done and when should it have started? And, more importantly, what policies should be pursued from here on out?

In the past, appropriate and timely income and price stabilization policies have been sadly lacking in many economies—their customer spending has been too high or too low. In the United States, for example, as much as sixteen trillion dollars of goods and services were not produced, that could have been produced in the first five years of the Great Recession which began in 2008. Instead, the members of the labor force and the capital goods that could have produced them were left unemployed due to inappropriate, or non-existent, monetary and fiscal policies that resulted in a lack of customer spending such that all that production was lost *forever*.

As a result of that totally avoidable event, millions of people and businesses went bankrupt and tens of millions of families were financially destroyed. In contrast, the personal conditions and public recognition of the policy makers responsible for the debacle improved—they continued to draw their salaries and bustled around making speeches and appearing on talk shows. Most of the important ones were even reelected and reappointed.

More specifically, as if to prove how little the White House and Congress understood the situation and why it continued, one of the four principal architects of the debacle was promoted by the new President to be Secretary of the Treasury; the second was reappointed as chairman of the Federal Reserve; the third was retained for years until her term expired, and the fourth returned to Wall Street to reap the rewards of his favoritism.

The Federal Reserve's victims, and that's how pragmatic analysts see them, were primarily the workers and businesses and banks of the private sector. But they were not the only ones to suffer. Many governmental employers at the state and local level also cut loose employees as their tax collections declined; and millions of people and businesses from every walk of life suffered mortgage foreclosures and bankruptcies. And everyone suffered—an estimated forty two percent of all privately held wealth in the United States was destroyed, primarily by the decline in the value of homes and businesses.

The failure of the policy makers occurred despite the law requiring that full employment be the major economic goal of the economy. Worse, the recession was totally unnecessary and would neither have happened nor continued until it morphed into a permanent depression—if the policy makers had been qualified in terms of education and experience. Then they would have known what to do and done it.

It also would have been helpful if the decision makers had been possessed of sufficient character and integrity such that they would stand up to the lobbyists and Treasury officials who advocated, and received, special help for themselves and their clients—or at least enough integrity so that after they finished helping the "favored few" they would have proceeded to do the right thing by implementing policies that would have helped the recovery of the economy as a whole. But they did not. And it really does not matter that they failed to do the right thing because they were unqualified or because they lacked the necessary character and integrity. The bottom line—they failed.

In the real world there is no reason for total customer spending in the United States' or any other economy to ever be at levels below those needed to bring forth full employment levels of production, or at levels so high that they cause demand-pull inflations. Just because misguided monetary and fiscal policies implemented by the Congress and the Federal Reserve has caused inflations and recessions to occur in the past does not mean that such misguided policies have to occur and continue in the future. To the contrary: properly applied monetary, fiscal, and other price and income stabilization policies can be implemented to ensure that total spending is neither too low nor too high—*if competent decision makers are elected and appointed and if they respond to the correct indicators.*

In essence, it is the view of pragmatic analysts that there is no reason for customer purchasing in the United States to ever be at levels below those needed to bring forth full employment levels of production and growth, or be at levels so high that it causes demand-pull inflation. *But what indicates that action is needed and how big should the response be and who should do it? And what is an "excessive" rate of inflation or unemployment or an overly slow rate of growth?*

FACTS THAT INDICATE ACTION IS WARRANTED

Pragmatic economists and analysts establish goals and look at a broad array of indicators before they suggest the income-affecting actions, if any, that might be undertaken. They attempt to relate them to the circumstances and realities of the economy they are analyzing. Primary among them are rates at which various prices level indices are changing, the various rates of unemployment, and the rates at which income, employment, and production appear to be growing or declining.

But which price levels, which unemployment rates, and which growth rates? And are there any components of the indices or surrogates that might provide early warnings of impending problems and, even more importantly, provide guidance as to the actual source and size of the problems so that effective and timely policies of an appropriate size can be selected? These are important questions because many millions of people can be terribly damaged if the policy makers get it wrong.

And they often get it wrong: In the midst of the Great Recession, for example, former Treasury Secretary Lawrence Summers famously said "Economic forecasters divide into two groups. There are those who cannot know the future but think they can—and then there are those who recognize their inability to know the future." Summers then went on to prove there is a third group, the grossly unworldly, who do not have a clue as to what is needed to keep the United States prosperous—by suggesting that the current Federal Reserve monetary policy based on maintaining the current Federal Funds target rate should continue and that "contingent (fiscal) policies" should adopted to immediately increase infrastructure spending and subsequently increase gasoline taxes to pay for them.

The spending and tax changes should be triggered and ended, Summers went on to note, based on the on the hopelessly inaccurate official rate of unemployment, an "expected" rate of inflation which can't be measured, and the use of the grossly irrelevant Federal Funds rate.

It was a cry for action in the midst of a terrible recession that effectively called for the maintenance of a non-expansionary monetary policy and the adoption of impossible-to-implement fiscal policies, all to be based on two grossly inaccurate indicators and one non-existent indicator.

If Summers' suggestions are fully implemented to the greatest degree imaginable, and without the inevitable years of time lags associated with public works projects, they would have effectively doomed the United States to even more years of recession and still no light at the end of the tunnel. It says something sad about American journalism and politics, and the declining influence of the former and declining public respect for the latter, that his views were taken so seriously that they were commented upon favorably by various members of Congress and appeared in a number of major newspapers without their absurdities being acknowledged.

The Rate of Inflation.

Inflation is an increase in the general or average level of prices of the goods and services being produced and sold in an economy. Not having an inflation is certainly a primary goal of policy makers because an inflation means, in the case of the United States, that the dollar loses some of its value or purchasing power—because the higher prices mean each dollar will buy less than it did before the inflation started. And the hit from inflation extends beyond its currency; it also reduces the value of bank deposits and other financial instruments that can be converted to dollars and of contracts and other obligations that require dollar payments.

Indeed, just the fear that inflation might be coming can cause behavioral changes. If people with money think higher prices are coming, they are likely to rush to use their money and go in debt to buy things now before prices go up and they have to pay even more; demand will increase. On the other hand, if sellers think higher prices are coming they may wait to sell things such as newly produced products until they can get the higher prices for them; supply will decrease.

Because inflation or the threat of inflation is important, the analysts and policy makers of most countries, including the United States, track inflation with various price indices. Among the most commonly cited indices in the United States are the Consumer Price Index (CPI) which tracks the prices consumers pay for consumer goods and services; the Producer Price Index (PPI) which tracks the prices manufacturers report they are charging retailers and is declining in importance as manufacturing declines as a percentage of total production; and the GDP and GNP deflators which attempt to track the prices of all newly produced goods and services produced and purchased in the economy. The CPI is used to calculate the automatic annual cost of living increases due Social Security recipients.

The Federal Reserve used to pay particular attention to the CPI but subsequently switched to the index of Personal Consumption Expenditures (CPE) because it excludes volatile items such as food and energy. Astute analysts look at them all and do not read much significance, if any, into monthly changes.

The indices are derived via the constant sampling of specific prices and are believed to be quite accurate even though they may fluctuate on a month to month basis. Monthly changes are insignificant to the point that anyone who makes much of a monthly change is more likely to define themselves as unqualified than as having anything worthwhile to say. What is more significant is when the various inflation indicators tend to track together *over time* so that each tends to reinforce the results reported by the others.

In essence, higher consumer prices tend to be associated with higher wholesale prices and higher goods and services prices. When indices of all three are generally going up together, it means the United States is having an inflation and that something should be done to stop it—and *perhaps* should have been done to prevent it from starting in the first place.

But even using the higher prices of a broad range of indices as an indicator of the need for price stabilization policies is fraught with danger: for example, the higher prices may be being caused by something very different than just too much spending because the money supply is too large. Thus policy makers must also know what is causing the inflation and the real world effects of the various price and income stabilization policies that might be implemented to combat or prevent it. This requires looking behind the basic price indices—at surrogates that can confirm the nature of the inflation; index components that can suggest both its size and nature; and leading indicators to see what subsequent price changes might be expected in the future.

For example, if both prices and unemployment are rising it may suggest that the inflation is being caused by something other than excessive aggregate demand. But if prices and unemployment are rising, and wages, oil prices, and utility prices are not rising, it might suggest that the inflation and unemployment is not of a cost-push nature. Thus, it could be a classic stabilization inflation wherein excise taxes, such as those levied on gasoline, have been increased to fight a nonexistent demand pull inflation.

Or perhaps it is a form of non-competitive price inflation occurring because increased ethanol subsidies have just been installed that have raised both the price of corn and the price of fuel at the gas pump—in which case, prices may continue to climb because the resulting tendency towards higher corn prices will subsequently increase the cost of meat products and thus affect Consumer Price Index so that analysts can expect cost-push increases in the future as wages responsive to increases in the cost of living push up production costs in the future.

In other words, *policy makers face complex realities in the real world and need to use a lot of indicators to guide their inflation-fighting policies.*

The rate of unemployment.

A second major goal of every economy is to have low rates of unemployment of its labor force and production capital. It is widely accepted in all quarters that involuntary unemployment is an undesirable state of affairs and a particular burden on those who unnecessarily suffer the condition as a result of poor or non-existent income stabilization efforts to prevent or eliminate it. Moreover, and something which should be of particular concern to policy makers seeking reelection to Congress or reappointment to the Federal Reserve chairmanship, unemployed workers and their families vote. Although most people cannot be expected to have the knowledge of trained and experienced macroeconomic analysts, they do have an instinctive feeling when something is terribly wrong, such as when they or members of their families and friends are unemployed and unable to find jobs.

Little wonder then, that the United States government collects date and attempts to make monthly estimates of labor and capital unemployment. Its Bureau of the Census also collects and reports monthly labor participation data for the different age and sex cohorts of the economy's population. This information is important because it can be used to generate much more accurate estimates of the actual rate of unemployment than are "officially" generated by the federal government's Department of Labor.

The "official government estimates," as might be expected, are carefully calculated in a way that will suggest unemployment rates are low—in order to make the government look good. For example, at times during the Great Recession and the depression that followed the official rate was reported by the federal government to be in the neighborhood of eight percent and falling. Simultaneously, pragmatic economists using the latest monthly *Current Population Survey* employment data and historical labor force participation rates during times of prosperity and full employment, were estimating the actual United States unemployment rate to be in the neighborhood of twenty percent and rising.

Undeterred by the reality of massive unemployment and the resulting economic distress of tens of millions of Americans suffering bankruptcy and foreclosure, the Federal Reserve governors and regional presidents in 2008 and again in 2009 and again in 2010 and again in 2011 and again in 2012, cited the stable official unemployment rate and stable Federal Funds rates and rising asset prices in the financial markets as reasons for not undertaking an expansionary monetary policy. In essence, the economy, they thought, was not declining—it just was not growing.

They also gave speeches explaining that an increase in the money supply would not work, even though the economy was operating far below capacity due to a lack of sales, because it could not cause a further decrease in interest rates. They also explained that they could not increase the money supply because it would cause inflation by increasing spending—thus overlooking the not so minor fact that the governors have the ability to instantly reduce the monetary base if they overshoot on a monetary expansion and put too much money in circulation such that total spending becomes excessive.

In essence, the governors and regional presidents looked at the wrong indicators and made bad decisions based on the Keynesian liquidity trap that did not apply to the United States, an obsolete theory of inflation, and a woeful ignorance of their own powers to control the money supply.

What causes the problem? Various possible causes and remedies exist when an economy has unnecessarily high levels of unemployment. But it depends on what is causing the problem. Is it inadequate aggregate demand or higher costs or increases non-competitive prices that is causing the unemployment? Or could it be structural changes or stabilization efforts or something else?

For example, the data might suggest that a rise in unemployment is being caused by falling auto sales and the subsequent multiplier effect of the decline on total spending. If auto sales are falling it might be because total spending is starting to fall and a strong indicator of the need to start implementing expansionary monetary or fiscal policies to expand the level of income.

But wait. Perhaps total spending is okay and the unemployment is concentrated on the auto industry because the FDIC has clamped down on banks making consumer and auto loans.

Whatever the cause, a *sustained* increase or decrease in an accurately estimated rate of unemployment is an indicator that something might be seriously amiss. Other indicators are then needed to illuminate the cause of the problem so the proper policy remedies can be introduced.

Rate of income growth.

The third goal of every economy is a growing production of goods and services, particular the growth of income on a per capita basis. Growth in an economy's production capacity tends to occur constantly as its working age population grows and new technology is introduced as its employers buy new capital goods. Whether the potential growth is actually realized, however, depends on total spending continually increasing enough to cover both the additional production and the general upward drift to higher prices that occurs in a dynamic economy.

In the United States it has been estimated that the nominal dollar amount of total spending must increase by at least four to six percent per year to maintain full employment—some to cover the higher prices and some to cover the increased capacity.

Because of the importance of the level of total spending, decision makers tend to keep a close watch on both the monthly reports of total spending (gross domestic product) and the income as it is received (national income). Both are important indicators and shifts away from a seasonal adjusted four to six percent need to be explained and understood in relation to the economy's labor unemployment and idled production capacity—so that appropriate policies can be implemented. In other words, *decision makers need to know if the economy is going to be short of total spending or have too much.*

Leading and lagging indicators

The basic indicators of the need for the implementation of a policy to stabilize an economy's income at a desirable level are well known: price level changes, unemployment rate changes, and growth rate changes. But there are other indicators and some of them are quite useful because they are "leading indicators"—those that tend to move prior to changes in the basic indicators; others are less useful because they are "lagging indicators" that show up after a basic move or problem has begun. Taken together, and particularly the leading indicators, they are helpful to analysts trying to determine the policies an economy should be pursuing.

Similarly, but in the other direction, some indicators routinely cited by journalists, Junior Chamber of Commerce luncheon speakers, and Federal Reserve governors as significant indicators are neither particularly significant nor particularly useful. Changes in the Federal Funds rates and stock prices are good examples of relatively useless and misleading indicators as to the condition and direction of the economy. Relying on them may lead to erroneous policy decisions. They may be interesting and sufficiently simple for journalists, "business economists," and members of Congress to understand, but the economy's prices, employment, and level of income tend not to track with them, particularly when there is a recession or depression—so they are not appropriate indicators of the need for fiscal and monetary policies.

On the other hand, the relatively meaningless indicators are useful because they help qualified analysts identify those claiming to be experts who are not. Here's a real-life example. Today a story in a well-known financial newspaper was quite optimistic about the future of the United States economy. It reported a surge during the month just ended of consumer borrowing as consumers added more than $16 billion in non-revolving debt for such things as student loans and car loans, almost $7 billion of additional debt from government loans, and over $5 billion in credit card debt.

According to the journalist this was good news because it was more than double what the newspaper said "economists" had been predicting. The article also noted that consumer confidence had remained "steady" which it suggested meant that people may be feeling more secure about taking on debt to finance purchases of things such as new cars which they had been delaying so that there was "pent up demand," and that approximately three hundred thousand new jobs had been created in the past two months. The story also noted that the White House was crowing over the fact that the unemployment rate had dropped slightly for the fourth straight month and annual income in the economy in money terms had slightly increased by a seasonally adjusted two percent

The story's solid and encouraging facts that seem to indicate the economy might be finally coming out of its Great Recession. But pragmatic analysts looking at more meaningful indicators knew that was not the reality of the economy. How can that be?

In fact, the credit card expansion may have been related to recent jump in the price of gasoline that occurred when the White House announcing it was opposing the construction of a new pipeline to bring oil from Canada to the United States; the student loan increases to the fact that last month was the month when students traditionally sign up to borrow money to pay for their educations in the coming school year.

In point of fact, the economy' monetary income growing at an annual rate of two percent is an absolute disaster that suggests the recession is getting worse—because, as pragmatic analysts know, there is a "natural" upward drift in product prices and an economy's production capacity tends to constantly increase as new technologies come on line and its labor force grows as a result of population increases and immigration.

If, as some suggest, the "natural" increase prices and productivity requires a four to six percent increase in total nominal spending for the United States economy to remain at full employment, then the two percent the White House and newspaper were touting actually suggests that production and employment in the economy had further receded by another two or three percent below its full employment level of production.

That the economy may have been getting worse and had sunk into a permanent state of depression, instead of getting better, tends to be confirmed by the employment data. The increase in the number of new jobs was not even enough to provide jobs for people entering the labor force for the first time.

Similarly, it appears by looking at other data that the official unemployment rate remained stable at about eight percent only because so many people had their unemployment insurance run out without finding jobs, or had become so "discouraged" by the lack of vacancies that they had not bother to submit any applications—and thus were not counted even though they desperately wanted jobs.

Pretending such people are unemployed may make Federal Reserve governors and regional presidents, and the White House officials and regional boards who appointed them, feel less guilty about their failures—but in the real world those people are unemployed and available to work. In other words, what the data indicators in the story actually suggested to pragmatic analysts is that the actual rate of unemployment which had been hovering in the range of twenty percent of the available labor hours was getting worse and that the recession was not only continuing to deepen but was morphing into a permanent state of depression with nothing on the horizon to increase customer spending and restore prosperity.

Useful indicators.

Consumer credit and *consumer confidence surveys*. Consumer confidence and the increased availability of consumer credit are significant because consumers are the economy's most important source of customer spending. They are leading indicators that suggest spending will be higher or lower in the future.

Mortgage rates. Mortgage rates and new housing sales are often used as policy indicators because new housing construction is both a major source of jobs and may be a good indication of consumer' view of the future state of the economy. But they may not be the best of indicators: First, because a decline in the rates may either be encouraging by signaling that more credit is available for home buyers or discouraging because it means there are fewer people looking for money because fewer people intend to buy new homes; second, because they are greatly influenced by the inventory and prices of existing homes for sale and, third, because they are influenced by buyer qualifications which may be changed by the FDIC and Federal Reserve. Pragmatic analysts need to look at the reasons behind changes in the rates and sales before reaching conclusions and making recommendations.

Non-financial business working capital and equipment loans. New plant and equipment purchases as reported by the commercial banks to the Federal Reserve are an important leading indicator. An increase in loans suggests employers across the country expect more customers in the future; a decrease suggests the opposite.

Changes in labor force participation rates. This is are very significant leading indicator of the direction an economy moving and how far it is from full employment. A decline in labor force participation strongly suggests that an economy is receding further below its full employment level of income; an increase strongly suggests it is moving towards full employment. Comparisons of the current rates with historical rates during times of prosperity give pragmatic analysts excellent estimates of the actual rate of unemployment by both sex and age cohort and, thus, an estimate of the increase in the level of income needed to achieve full employment.

Many macro-pragmatic economists consider these rates to be the most important of all the indicators that should guide the stabilization policies implemented by an economy's economic decision makers. In the United States they can be found in the monthly *Current Population Survey* published by the Census Bureau.

Car and truck sales and inventories. Data on these activities are lagging indicators of uncertain value, particularly on a month to month basis, because an increase can either mean increased consumer incomes and confidence about the future, or be influenced by special sales efforts to pump up sales at a time when both consumers and the manufacturers think the overall future looks bleak.

Inventory buildups. Information reporting that there have been inventory buildups is of questionable value. Analysts need to know more about why inventories are increasing or decreasing before they use them as an indicator—because buildups can occur either when employers are optimistic about future sales and want to have more stock on hand that they expect to be able to sell, or because they misjudged the future and bought too much. If it is the latter, it means they will be buying less in the future and jobs at their suppliers will disappear so that unemployment increases.

Manufacturing capacity utilization rates. This is a very important indicator. It is the capital equivalent of an accurate labor unemployment rate. An increase means employers are producing more because they expect more revenues in the future and will need more employees. An increase suggests the economy is recovering; a decrease that things are getting worse.

Hours in the average work week. This is an important leading indicator if it is seasonally adjusted. An increase tends to mean that business is picking up and that more and more workers will be hired as employers get closer to having to pay overtime rates. One does not want to make the recent mistake of the Federal Reserve governors and White House and crow about an increase in jobs and the work week and claim it means the economy is finally coming out of the recession—if the data is for the month of December when retailers traditionally add temporary help and ask employees to work more hours. Seasonally adjusted, it turns out the White House and governors were crowing about data that was worse than previous years and indicated the recession was worsening.

Purchasing managers surveys. This is an important leading indicator if it is seasonally adjusted. Purchasing managers are sophisticated buyers and tend to place bigger orders when they think sales will improve in the future; smaller orders when they think sales will decline.

Job vacancy indices. They can be important indicators of the state of the economy and the direction it is moving, but only if their numbers are accurate as they once were when most job vacancies were advertised in newspapers and could be counted by clerks beavering away in the Department of Labor. Today, however, the accuracy and direction of the numbers is not certain because job searches have moved heavily to the Internet and the data are not systematically collected. Ignore them.

Capital equipment loans. This can be a leading indicator; increases suggest employers expect their sales to increase and are gearing up to increase their production; decreases suggest there will be further moves away from full employment levels of production.

Foreclosure rates and bankruptcy filing rates. These are important leading indicators. Levels above those historically occurring when there is full employment suggest that they economy may be worsening and that it could be time to implement policies to increase the level of income.

Changes in labor productivity rates. An often misinterpreted indicator, useful only if properly understood. In essence, higher per-worker productivity tends to be the result of layoffs and increased unemployment as employers respond to declining sales by laying off their least productive workers. Similarly, a declining rate of labor productivity can be the result of employers adding more and more workers to an existing stock of capital as sales increase and an economy moves back to full employment.

Tax collections. Taxes are collected and reported after the work has been done, the products sold, and the profits earned. They are a lagging indicator as to how well an economy is doing.

Inconsequential and misleading indicators. The competency of those who take them seriously is suspect.

The official rate of unemployment. The rate of unemployment reported each month by the federal government is grossly inaccurate and totally misleading as to both size and direction. Pragmatic analysts know that accurate rates of unemployment, and the direction they are moving, can only be obtained by comparing the number people working today with today's population with historical labor force participation rates for each age and sex cohort during times of full employment with adjustments for part-timers who would work full time, the population's ever increase longevity, and the population's changed financial needs related to any preceding recession years.

Federal Funds rates. The Federal Funds rates are the rates a relative handful of large commercial banks charge each other to borrow reserves overnight. The banks borrow when they are short of reserves and lend when they have excess reserves. Only a Federal Reserve governor or someone with no real world experience in business or commercial banking could believe that a commercial bank will borrow money it must repay within 24 hours in order to make loans to consumers, employers and governments; or believe that the overnight rates track with the state of the economy, the availability of money and credit for consumers and employers, or the need for more spending.

The inappropriateness of the Federal Reserve's use of the Federal Funds rates to guide Federal Reserve policy is absolute. Using it as a policy indicator regarding the need for income increasing monetary policies is the Federal Reserve's single most damning failure. The Federal Reserve's reliance on the Federal Funds rates, more than anything else, explains why the Federal Reserve's monetary policies, if that's what they can be called, allowed the Great Recession to persist year after year until the economy finally morphed into a permanent depression wherein conventional monetary policies to increase the level of spending would no longer work.

A permanent depression exists when there is nothing on the horizon to sufficiently increase spending. This occurs when things get so bad for consumers and employers that the Federal Reserve's normal policy tools to increase spending are no longer sufficient even if they are finally adopted—because its previous policies have destroyed so many consumers and businesses that there are no longer enough qualified spenders left for their conventional policies to affect if they are finally put into place.

New unemployment insurance claims. These are potentially misleading indicators, particularly if the data are raw numbers instead of seasonally adjusted numbers. Seasonally adjusted increases and decreases suggest an economy's general direction and the magnitude of its unemployment problems; they are primarily useful in a minor supporting role to confirm other more significant labor force information such as labor force participation rates and the unemployment rates that are derived from them.

Monthly reports on the number of newly created jobs. These too are totally useless and potentially misleading indicators, particularly if they are raw numbers instead of seasonally adjusted numbers. They are also useless if they are not directly contrasted to job creation levels during times of full employment and to accurate estimates of the total number of people out of work. When seasonally adjusted they are primarily useful in a supporting role to confirm other more significant labor force information such as labor force participation rates and the unemployment rates that are derived from them. For example, reporting that three hundred thousand new jobs have been created in the past two months when four hundred thousand people enter the labor force every two months actually means that the economy is even further away from full employment and an even bigger increase in total spending is needed to restore full employment.

Stock market declines or increases. Over the long haul of time stock and bond market indices such as the Dow Jones and Nasdaq tend to reflect the profitability and prospects of the publically traded large employers in the private sector of the United States economy. Such employers, however, are not traditionally the main source of new jobs and economic growth—they are usually generated by smaller non-listed employers. Accordingly, how the big listed employers are doing is not a very good guide as to how the rest of the economy is doing.

At best, moves in the stock, bond, and other financial markets are lagging indicators that tend to overreact on a day to day basis as its investors "playing the markets" attempt to make knowledgeable gambles on stock price moves to obtain wealth from each other. As a result, even though financial assets such as stocks and bonds are an important part of wealth in the United States because they can be quickly liquidated (except when there is a catastrophic event such as the derivative meltdown), they are not a reliable indicator of the need or lack of need for policies to stabilize an economy's prices, employment, and growth.

All monthly data and particularly data that is not seasonal adjusted. Monthly data is not an appropriate guide to policy for a number of reasons: it may be influenced by one-off events; it may not be accurate so that it is subsequently significantly revised. Astute analysts particularly do not want to make the recent mistake of journalists and the White House by suggesting that employment numbers data the number of jobs increasing as a result of temporary Christmas season hiring suggested a recover was underway, only to be blindsided when season was over and the temporary workers became unemployed again.

Price level changes unaccompanied by relevant related data. Price level changes are a major indicator that suggests the implementation of stabilization policies may be appropriate. Astute analysts need more because they know that changes in the level of an economy's prices may be caused by other than too much spending caused by federal spending or the creation of too much money. Price level increases are particularly questionable as indicators when an economy is coming out of a prolonged recession or depression and its prices are in a one-time period of adjustment related to heretofore suppressed structural changes.

The observations and "expertise" of proven incompetents. Analysts and investors should be wary of the observations and recommendations of the International Monetary Fund; and, closer to home, former Treasury Secretaries and Federal Reserve Chairmen whose grasp of economics is such that they presided over inflations and recessions. Relying on them is the equivalent of relying on the advice of a heart surgeon whose patients keep dying on the operating table because he never studied medicine. Inexperienced and insufficiently trained journalists and faux "economic experts" and "business economists" are harder to identify—but it can be done because they reveal themselves by what they say and write. A list of comments that would never be made by a trained economist with real world experience is enumerated in the appendix at the end of this book. Analysts, politicians, and journalists can use them to identify people whose ideas and concerns can be safely ignored.

SUMMARY

I.   Price increases, unemployment increases, and slowing rates of income growth are the key indicators that an economy's decision makers may need to implement one or more stabilization policies.

II. There can simultaneously be multiple causes of multiple problems. Accordingly, decision makers need to look at a wide range of indicators.

III. Decision makers in countries such as the United States have caused massive financial and personal losses as a result of responding in the wrong way to the wrong indicators.

IV. Supporting data are typically needed to understand what a key indicator such as an increase in the general level of prices is actually indicating.

V.   The official rate of unemployment may be hopelessly inaccurate and misleading as to size of the problem and the direction it is heading. Unemployment estimates based on an economy's population and its current and historical labor force participation rates are much more accurate and meaningful.

VI. Income has fluctuated in "business cycles" in the past. There is no need for such cycles. Appropriate macroeconomic policies can stabilize an economy's level of income at full employment without causing inflation in excess of the natural rate associated with structural changes.

VII. Changes in its labor force participation rates may be the best indicator of an economy's future growth and unemployment. Among the other useful indicators are consumer credit and consumer confidence surveys, mortgage rates, the capital and equipment loans of non-financial businesses, hours in the average work week, purchasing manager surveys, job vacancy indices, and foreclosure rates and bankruptcy filings.

VIII. Certain widely used and cited indicators tend not to be used by trained economists and pragmatic analysts because they tend to be misleading and inaccurate. Among them: reports on new and expiring unemployment insurance claims, the Federal Funds rates, reports on newly created jobs that are not accompanied by information as to concurrent changes in the size of the labor force, financial market advances and declines, the official rate of unemployment, and all monthly data that are not seasonally adjusted.

Chapter Sixteen

CONVENTIONAL FISCAL POLICIES

Government spending, taxing, transfers, and borrowing are the principal fiscal activities that affect the level of total spending that occurs in an economy. Governmental budgets are balanced when they collect the same amounts of money from taxes as they disburse for transfers and purchases. Most people and politicians think national governments should follow a policy of balancing their budgets. Some of them even believe that problems such as inflation and recessions will somehow be abated if they do.

Unfortunately the mere existence of balanced budgets at the national level does not necessarily solve the problem of inflation or any other major problem an economy might encounter. In particular, even with a balanced budget it is still possible for the various types of spending in an economy to add up to a level of total spending that is significantly too high such that it causes inflation or too low so that it causes unemployment.

To put it bluntly, it's a fool's errand to think that a balanced budget has much to do with jobs, prosperity, economic growth, fighting inflation, or removing hurtful regulations. On the other hand, it is similarly a fool's errand to ignore the political reality that the public wants the budget balanced. Fortunately, both a balanced budget and high rates of growth are simultaneously achievable without inflation and unemployment caused by too much or too little total spending. How this can be accomplished will be considered in great detail in this chapter and the chapters that follow.

The fiscal choices.

The basic goal of using fiscal policy to influence total customer spending in potentially prosperous democracies, such as the United States, is to limit the inflation to the increases in the general level of prices inherent in structural changes and to provide enough total spending to fully employ all but the frictionally unemployed and that portion of the structurally employed who are unemployable.

The federal government has three basic policy alternatives when confronted with a situation in which its budget is balanced, the economy has either too much or too little total spending, and the government is buying and transferring exactly what its government wants to buy and transfer:

First, the government can accept the situation. Such a policy means that optimum amounts of federal spending and transfers occur and that they are financed by the collection of an equal amount of tax revenues. It also means that a level of total spending exists that will cause inflation or unemployment *unless the spending levels of the economy's customers are influenced in some other way* such as through monetary policies.

Second, the government can deliberately pursue a fiscal policy of changing the amounts of its purchases and transfers to generate the desired level of total spending with those expenditures and the subsequent multiplier effects they have on total spending. This may or may not be accompanied by a similar change in taxes so that budget balancing is maintained *but it certainly results in a level of government expenditures other than that which would occur in the absence of the government trying to keep the level of total spending in the United States from being too large or too small.*

Third, the federal government can maintain its purchasing and transfers at whatever Congress considers to be their optimum levels and adjust the level of tax collections until the desired level of total purchasing occurs. This means that the government's tax revenues may significantly differ from the amount of its outlays. In other words, it means that the government's decision makers, in order to cause the economy to have a level of total spending that is neither too small so that unemployment results nor too large so that a demand-pull inflation results, will either have to cope with budget surpluses or run deficits and be forced use other sources of financing to make up the difference—such as borrowing money or increasing fees.

Using government spending changes such as "jobs bills" to influence the level of income was the original Keynesian prescription from Keynes' *General Theory*. It was most recently used to rationalize the hundreds of billions of dollars spent to bailout the unions of America's legacy automobile companies and save the bonuses of the executives of non-bank financial institutions who made bad bets on mortgage derivatives. The transfers they were given were expected to "trickle down" to taxpayers and people generally as the relative handful of recipients of the welfare spent or deposited the money they were given.

Functional finance.

Since an ever-increasing level of total spending must occur in a growing economy if high levels of employment, production and growth are to be maintained, and since sources other than taxes exist to finance government outlays, the tax adjusting third alternative is the basic governmental fiscal approach favored by many of today's economists and analysts—but, for reasons to be discussed shortly, not all of today's macro-pragmatic economists and analysts agree.

The father of "functional finance," and the man who coined the phrase, is Abba Lerner. The essence of functional finance is to let government expenditures be used to achieve their primary function of providing whatever are the optimum amounts of transfers and government purchases; and let taxes carry out their primary function of holding down non-governmental spending to the extent necessary to achieve full employment levels of spending without causing inflation. Full employment levels of spending are thus achieved. The budgetary deficits or surpluses which result from having tax collections whose size is unrelated to the level of government spending is seen as, at most, a minor inconvenience that should not stand in the way of an economy having the best of all possible worlds—the optimum level of total spending and the optimum level of government spending.

In essence, the advocates of the *functional finance* approach to governmental fiscal activities prefer the existence of deficits and surpluses to the existence of unemployment and inflation. And instead of preferring that the government buy either unneeded military equipment and roads when total purchasing is too low or too few military items and roads when it would otherwise be too high, they prefer the deficits or surpluses that would result from adjusting the amount of taxes without changing the level of government outlays away from the levels that would exist if there were no economic problems to solve.

Stated yet another way, the advocates of functional finance consider the optimum level of taxes to be that which results in the optimum level of total spending rather than the level needed to finance government outlays; they prefer not to have labor and capital wasted by standing idle because there is not enough spending nor producing less desirable goods and services merely to "make work" for otherwise unemployed labor and capital."

On the other hand, functional finance may not work because its *countercyclical fiscal policies* changing government spending, taxes, and borrowing to counter changes in the level of spending may not occur in a timely manner or appropriate amounts. Indeed, such failures are virtually certain due to the checks and balances, time lags, and the lack of decision maker qualifications inherent in the American political system.

Moreover, such countercyclical fiscal actions may not work even in the unlikely event the political problems can be overcome. For example, if consumption spending is a function of relative or permanent income, a temporary tax decrease or one-time Social Security payment intended to increase people's disposable income and cause consumer spending to increase may be of little consequence because it only affects people's absolute levels of income; a temporary tax decrease for employers will increase their cash positions but it may not cause them to increase their investment spending to buy even more plant and equipment if they already have existing plant and equipment sitting idle due to a lack of customers.

Determining the optimum level of taxation.

Adding up the various types of spending can be used, at least conceptually, to identify the optimum level of taxes an economy needs to achieve full employment levels of spending without inflation. In essence, the level of tax collections needed to generate a desired level of total spending is determined by bringing together the "best available" estimates of the spending components and their relationships with one another and solving for the rate of taxation that will yield the desired level of spending. The resulting rate of taxation, when applied to the economy's full employment level of income, then determines the amount of taxes that will occur when the best level of total spending is reached—the spending level that is high enough to cause full employment but not too high so that it causes inflation from too much spending.

Consider an example economy with the capacity to produce $700 billion of goods and services whose equilibrium level of income is initially $600 billion. For the sake of an example, assume it has a balanced budget with $100 billion of taxes and $100 billion of government spending and transfers—because consumption spending unrelated to income is $10 billion, investment spending to replace capital worn out during the production of income is twenty percent of the level of income, investment spending for other than replacement purposes is $30 billion, retained earnings and other business savings are ten percent of the level of income, foreign spending is $20 billion plus ten percent of the level of income, government spending is $80 billion, plus make work government spending of $12 billion minus three percent of the level of income so that it goes away as income increases, transfer spending is $20 billion plus unemployment insurance and other income related transfers of $25 billion that go away at the rate of five percent of the level of income as it increases, taxes are $30 billion plus an income tax rate of 11.667 so that $70 billion of income related taxes are collected, and the marginal propensities to consume are eighty percent for transfer recipients and sixty percent for everyone else.

If $700 billion level of total spending is necessary for this economy to attain full-employment levels of production and the $100 billion spending increase to reach it is to be obtained through a reduction in income taxes, the income tax rate will have to be reduced from an average of 11.667 percent of the level of income to an average of 6.19 percent.

If you do the math you will find that the reduction in the rate of taxation to 6.19 percent will cause the level of total purchasing in the economy to rise from $600 billion to $700 billion. It will also move the economy's government from a situation involving $100 billion each of government outlays and taxes to an unbalanced budget involving a deficit of $26.67 billion.

In other words, cutting taxes can cause total spending to rise; and, if the cuts are done in the necessary amounts, a total amount of spending can be reached that is large enough to cause full employment but not so large as to cause inflation from too much spending.

In a sense, the acceptance of the resulting deficit and the need to finance some government outlays in a manner other than taxes is the price that must be paid by the example economy *if it is to use taxes to obtain fully employment levels of spending while retaining the optimum levels of government purchasing and transfers.*

This is a classic Keynesian response using fiscal policy to obtain a desired level of total spending. Whether it is the best or most effective way to go is another matter entirely. *It is not* and why it is not will be discussed in some detail. But it would work and it and increasing government spending and transfers is the Keynesians' solution to problems such as the United States' Great Recession.

Fiscal drag and the full-employment budget surplus.

The decision makers of the example economy could use some other policy such as monetary policy or selling more abroad to obtain the $700 billion of spending needed for full employment. Then the initial

11.667 rate of taxes would remain and be applied to the new and $100 billion higher level of income. That rate applied to that income would result in a budgetary surplus of $11.667 billion. According to some analysts and politicians, the potential surplus is a measure of the "fiscal drag" the government placed on the economy by its efforts to balance its budget at an income level below the level of spending needed for full employment.

On the other hand, the mere removal of the "fiscal drag" caused by efforts to balance the budget is not enough to insure an economy will reach full employment. For example, the reduction of taxes by the full amount of the example economy's $11.667 "full employment surplus" will only cause total spending to rise to $630.4 billion. Furthermore, the elimination of the drag of the full employment surplus may still result in a budgetary deficit.

For example, if the entire $11.667 tax cut was in the autonomous (non-income related) taxes, additional tax revenues from applying the original tax rate to the resulting higher level of income would raise tax collections from income related taxes by $3.55 billion for a net deficit of $8.117 billion.

Deficits are not inevitable if lower income tax rates are used to bring an economy up to its full employment level of income: at some high level of income in the future the lower tax rates will generate enough revenues to balance the budget. In the example economy the lower tax rate of 6.19 percent will generate enough tax revenues to balance the budget when the income level in the economy reaches $1184.65 billion. Below that level there will be deficits; above that level there will be surpluses.

The maximum size of government indebtedness.

Continued government borrowing caused by repeated deficits means the total amount of government debt and interest payments will rise to higher and higher levels. That's the United States' experience. But is there an upper limit to the size of government debt or the amount of interest that it can pay? The question is important because, if answered affirmatively, it means that there is a limit to how long the governments of an economy such as the United States can continue to run budgetary deficits.

The answer as to whether there is some limit on budgetary deficits, as analysts saw in earlier chapters, is that *it depends on the type of government.*

Governments that do not have their own central banks absolutely do have upper limits; Governments such as those of California, Detroit, and Greece have debt limits because at some level of indebtedness they will be unable to borrow enough to make the payments as they come due. They are like individuals and businesses in that they can keep running deeper into debt only so long as there are lenders willing to loan them the money to cover their current expenses and service their existing debts.

On the other hand, there is no debt or interest limit for governments such as the United States, Canada, and Sweden which have their own currencies and money-creating central banks. *They can always borrow because they can always pay*—because, if necessary, their central banks or the government itself can literally create new money and use it to make whatever payments must be made. That does not mean they are wise to run deficits and borrow to cover them or that they should do so. It means they can always borrow if they decide to do so.

No central bank with the ability to create money. Whether governments without their own money-creating central banks should borrow to fund spending is another question. Analysts will recall from earlier discussions that borrowing has several potential beneficial results. One is that it can be a rational way to cause the future beneficiaries of capital projects to help pay for them.

For example, Using a thirty year bond to pay for a new road or sewer system that will provide services for the next thirty years and levying a sewer or road tax for thirty years means that the beneficiaries will pay for the project as they receive its benefits. If such long-life projects are not debt financed they may not be built because people living at the moment may be unwilling to tax themselves to pay for benefits that will be primarily received by other people in the future. Borrowing to cover unexpected deficits or accumulating reserves from unexpected surpluses is also rational because it allows government spending activities to proceed smoothly when revenues unexpectedly fluctuate.

That leaves the basic questions for every government without its own central bank: do we tax now to cover our current spending or do we spend now with borrowed money and tax even more later to pay for the spending plus the fees and interest expenses resulting from the borrowing? And how much can we borrow before lenders refuse to lend us more money?

Central bank. There is no debt or interest payment limit on governments with their own central banks, such as those of the United States and Canada. According to the precepts of functional finance, the function of taxes in such countries is to hold down consumer and business spending so that employers and their labor and capital are available to produce for governments and their transfer recipients. And it is true that such an appropriate level of taxation may result in a deficit or a surplus. But not to worry if the result is a deficit because the government's central bank has both the power to create money to pay for it *and* the power to simultaneously remove money from circulation.

This is an important reality. It means a central bank can simultaneously take money out of circulation at the same time it is creating new money to finance its government's deficits. In other words, *federal deficits can be financed by the Federal Reserve without in any way increasing the economy's overall supply of money or in any way causing inflation or burdening its future.* But should the federal government do so?

The burden of deficits
and the national debt.

It is an article of faith in some quarters that the federal deficit and the resulting national debt are serious problems that somehow have to be solved so the national debt does not become a terrible burden on future generations of Americans. It makes for a steady stream of wonderful political speeches and, fortunately less frequently, inane congressional actions such as raising taxes in the midst of a recession in an effort to balance the budget. But in the real world are deficits and the national debt really the big problems politicians make them out to be?

The Secretary of the Treasury is responsible for coming up with the money needed to cover federal deficits and the redemption of federal bonds as the national debt comes due. The Secretary typically prefers to borrow whatever money is necessary from the Federal Reserve, if only because it is so much simpler than selling bonds to the public.

Whether the Federal Reserve will loan to the Treasury at any point in time to cover its deficit and redeem any bonds that are maturing, however, is totally up the Federal Reserve governors.

The Federal Reserve's decisions are, at least supposedly, made by its governors and the regional presidents totally independent from the wishes of the Treasury, White House, and Congress. In fact, there are constant discussions between them. And, as is particularly the case when the Federal Reserve governors, and particularly the chairman, have weak personalities and inadequate educations and experience and don't realize that they are more powerful and make all the decisions—they often give in to the inevitable financial-markets orientation of the Treasury Secretary.

But the relative ease in which deficits are financed and the national debt managed does not mean that federal borrowing and the resulting increase in the national debt has no impact. The impact depends on who does the lending and who ends up with the debt. There are many possibilities.

For example, if the Treasury borrows from the public or commercial banks instead of from the Federal Reserve it might take in money that would otherwise have been spent on consumer goods or to buy capital such as plant and equipment or, if the bonds are sold abroad, take in money that would otherwise been used to import American-made products. In other words, borrowing from the public tends to "crowd out" other borrowers. To the extent that happens, total spending tends to decline and cause a reduction in production and employment.

Crowding out is avoided if Treasury borrows the money it needs directly from the Federal Reserve. Then, to greatly oversimplify the process, the Treasury creates and sends the necessary amount of bonds across the street to the Federal Reserve and the Federal Reserve creates new money with the stroke of a pen and deposits it in the Treasury's account. That's it; the deficit is again financed. Done. No big deal and no one affected in any way.

But wait. There may be no problem financing a deficit or the national debt as it comes due, but what happens when the federal government spends all that new money? It would seem that the money supply would increase so total spending might increase and cause inflation. No problem. The Federal Reserve has a large staff that, at least allegedly, watches the money supply in the economy like a hawk. If the staff sees too much money coming into the economy the Federal Reserve can immediately remove any the governors deem excessive.

The Federal Reserve has several ways to do remove money from the economy in order to reduce the economy's money supply. Typically it, rightly or wrongly, that there is too much money in circulation it will *instantly* sell some of the trillions of dollars of bonds it has accumulated over the years at no cost to itself by creating new money. The money it receives in payment comes out of circulation and the overall size of the money supply becomes whatever level the Federal Reserve's governors' desire. Done. No big deal and no one affected in any way.

Paying off the debt. Finally, there is the important question of who would get the money if, for some reason, the Treasury and the Federal Reserve got tired of listening to the political speeches about the "burdens on future generations" and decided to pay off the national debt.

The biggest single holder of the debt is the Federal Reserve. The federal bonds the Federal Reserve owns could be torn up and no one would even know or care. Or the Federal Reserve could play silly games to placate Congress and create new money and use it to pay off the bonds by giving itself the money. Then, of course, the Federal Reserve would have a capital gains "profit" in that it would be selling bonds in which it has a zero cost basis because it bought them in the first place with newly created money. In other words, all the money the Federal Reserve would receive by paying off its own debt holdings would be profits—on which Federal Reserve pays a one hundred percent tax rate.

What all this means is that the big chunk of national debt owned by the Federal Reserve is not a real problem. In effect, the Secretary of the Treasury writes a very large tax payment check—and the Federal Reserve endorses it and sends it back to pay its taxes. Done. The debt paid. No big deal and no one is affected in any way. All that happens is that the official size of the national debt is reduced.

Similarly, much of the rest of the debt is owned by various federal agency trust funds and pension funds. They, like the Federal Reserve, have been required by congress to hold federal debt to "back" their activities and pension obligations. Paying them off with newly created money would have absolutely no impact whatsoever—except that the federal trust funds and federal pension funds would be more liquid and will have to use the money to buy other interest bearing assets if they wanted their assets to earn money.

Most of the rest of the debt is owned by American banks, insurance companies, pension funds, and the like. They would be a bit more liquid if the Federal Reserve created new money and used it to pay off the national debt they owned. But they would not be much more liquid because the federal debt is already very liquid in that it can be so easily bought and sold.

But would not paying off some of the national debt cause an increase in the money supply that might cause spending to increase and cause inflation? Not at all—once again, the Federal Reserve could instantly engage in open market and other actions and soak it *all* up. Done. The debt is paid and the money supply did not increase. So once again, no big deal and no one is affected in any way—except the pension funds and other financial institutions just became slightly more liquid liquid and will have to use the money to buy other interest bearing assets if they wanted their assets to earn money.

Perhaps the big impact would occur if the twenty percent or so of debt held overseas by people and governments in countries such as China and Japan were paid off? They would get the newly created dollars and give up the bonds. So they would be a bit more liquid. But so what? Perhaps they would use the dollars to buy shares of Deutsche bank or Greek bonds or Toyota cars, or maybe wheat and corn produced in Kansas or a building in Boston. Or maybe they would just squirrel it away the same as they squirreled away the bonds.

Obviously sooner or later some of the dollars would tend to return and be spent to the United States. And obviously that would increase the size of the money of the United States. But, once again, so what? The Federal Reserve would merely use its open market operations or other activities and soak it all up. Done. No big deal and no increase in the money supply and no one is affected—except the Chinese got more liquid and maybe buy some more wheat, Boeing planes, and Caterpillar tractors from the United States. Is that really a bad thing?

What's the point? The point is that in the real world *neither the federal government's deficits nor the national debt are great burdens that will now or later somehow threaten the United States with inflation or any other problem.* In essence, journalistic nonsense and political speeches to the contrary, the national debt is no big deal and certainly not a big deal compared to moronic monetary and fiscal policies that bankrupt tens of millions of people and businesses, cause tens of millions of people to lose their homes and jobs, and force tens of millions of people to be forced to liquidate their retirement assets in order to survive.

Despite its non-importance most pragmatic analysts do *not* recommend paying off or down the national debt at this time or any other time even though it could be done relatively easily and quickly. The main problem is that the public and politicians (and don't forget the Chinese) are not yet sufficiently knowledgeable about governmental debts and deficits. So they might panic in some unforeseen way. There is no reason to upset people and it is not a problem—so forget about it. It really is no big deal.

Fiscal alternatives to tax changes.

At times an economy's political situation is such that the tax adjustments required to pursue a policy of functional finance are not possible. Then a situation can exist wherein government outlays are optimum, the budget is balanced, and yet there are less than optimum levels of total purchasing. In such a situation, the non-pragmatic advocates of a fiscal response recommend expanding government transfers and purchasing past the levels that would exist if total purchasing were not a consideration.

They see such an expansion as appropriate even if the additional goods and services bought by the governments and their transfer beneficiaries are relatively less desirable than others that might be produced. They note that there will be a positive effect on the overall production of goods and services as a result of the multiplier effect as the initial government spending increases move through the economy.

For instance, an increase in government buying in order to obtain unneeded fighter planes and pave a few dirt roads simply to make work for the economy's unemployed because total purchasing is inadequate may, indeed, be a wasteful use of labor and capital. But the owners of the "wasted" labor and capital will earn incomes. And their purchases with those incomes can cause the production of additional goods and services that are desired. For example, a government purchase of a relatively useless road improvement means that the labor and capital employed to produce it are wasted.

But all is not lost. The owners of that wasted labor and capital earn incomes by the unnecessary "improving" of the road and they can use these incomes to buy the goods and services they prefer. If they prefer automobiles more autos will be produced; if they prefer houses more houses will be produced; if they prefer more haircuts and restaurant meals, then more hair will be cut and more food prepared.

And the multiplier effect does not stop there—the resulting increases in the incomes of auto workers, home builders, barbers and restaurant staff may lead them to buy things such as computers and cell phones. In other words, *even though the initial "make work" government spending is for relatively useless purposes, the government outlays will have a multiplier effect that expands the production of other, relatively desired goods and services.*

Budget surpluses may be appropriate.

Deficits and a growing national debt may *not* be a long-run problem in economies such as the United States—if they adopt the monetary and fiscal policies needed to have sustained periods of full employment without inflation. Instead, functional finance may require that the taxes the economy needs to collect to avoid demand-pull inflations may *exceed* the level of government spending. In other words, instead of running deficits, as the United States has in the past as a result of its inadequate policies that have not maintained full employment, it may well have to start running surpluses.

If such surpluses occur, as might well be the case if there is sustained prosperity and a desire for relatively "easy money" in order to encourage capital intensive modes of production, the country's politicians will be vulnerable to calls for a reduction in taxes and/or more federal spending in order to balance the budget. Such a move to a balanced budget by increasing spending or reducing taxes would then, of course, tend to cause a demand-pull inflation if the economy already has enough spending to be at full employment. Then non-fiscal activities, such as restrictive monetary policies or restricting export sales to foreigners, would be needed to hold down total spending and prevent the demand-pull inflation.

The problem of a demand-pull inflation caused by a move to a balanced budget when and economy is already at full employment is not an idle concern for pragmatic analysts. The tax rates needed to generate budgetary surpluses when there is full employment may already exist in the United States.

There is also the possibility that the public will want more government spending if there is a surplus when the economy is a full employment. Certainly the politicians would be under great lobbyist pressure to spend the money. Such an increase in government spending when the economy is already at full employment would also tend to result in a demand-pull inflation. Then the monetary and other policies to hold down spending would tend to have to be even more restrictive.

Moreover, the propensities to consume and invest in the economy may increase when the people and employers expect that full employment will continue permanently so that they do not feel so much pressure to save for precautionary purposes. This too might occur and require even more restrictive policies to hold down total spending.

Earmarks and incentives.

One of America's most cherished pieces of political theatre occurs when the members of Congress make their traditional speeches citing the need to reduce deficits "which are a burden on future generations" and vowing to oppose any increase in the national debt.

This usual occurs immediately after the speechmakers have larded a particularly large spending bill with hundreds of special "earmarks" and "tax breaks" on behalf of lobbyists representing special interest groups and their campaign contributors. Political theater aside, what do these fiscal actions do to an economy's price level, unemployment and level of income?

"Earmarks" are special pieces spending legislation directing that federal spending or tax cuts occur for some special purpose. The purposes inevitably range from relatively useless "bridges to nowhere" to spending projects that may be of great national interest.

But who is to say which spending is more valuable. And, in any event, each such expenditure, when it finally occurs, typically results in an employer or employers using labor and capital to produce the purchased product or service. In other words, the earmarks have the same positive effect as all other government spending in that they tend to increase the economy's level of income and the employment of its labor and capital.

Whether earmarks are the best use of the federal government's money is another matter entirely. In a sense they are: the United States has a government whose elected officials represent their constituents and answer to them for what they do. If the spending is what their voters want, then so be it. If it is not, they risk being defeated in the next election or reapportionment by irate voters.

The same basic case can be made for special tax cuts and tax breaks such as those given to hedge funds and oil companies. Perhaps there is a good reason they pay significantly lower taxes on their profits than most companies; and, then again perhaps not.

Debt limits and deficits.

Congress in its wisdom periodically sets a legal "limit" on size of the "national debt." The Treasury cannot issue more bonds when the limit is reached. It is thought that this will somehow force the government to stop spending money that the Congress has previously appropriated. Whether or not it will actually have to shut down some spending in order to live within its revenues then depends upon the Federal Reserve—because the Federal Reserve can buy newly created bonds and then, because it has a one hundred percent tax rate, simultaneously pay an equal amount of taxes on the resulting income it books by selling the bonds. Thus the debt need never grow beyond the limit and the federal government need never shut down any spending to live within in revenues. All that is required is for the Federal Reserve to pay its taxes in response to its mandate to conduct monetary policy so as to maintain full employment in the United States.

That does not mean that the Federal Reserve will do so or that it should do so or that its governors even know that they have the option to let federal spending continue. And even if the Federal Reserve acts, political gamesmanship will inevitably occur. For example, the President can seize upon the excuse of the debt limit to stop paying the government's wages and bills in order to embarrass the Congressional leaders;

members of Congress, in turn, get to give inspiring speeches about the evils of the national debt and the need to cut taxes, particularly those paid by their friends and contributors.

Temporary stabilization efforts.

The inevitable Congressional and White House reaction to a serious problem such as a major recession or inflation is to "do something." Typically what they propose doing is something temporary to "prime the pump" and "get the economy going again." Also typically, what actually ends up being done is less about improving the economy and more about garnering positive "ink" and TV interviews for themselves and special "help," always well-deserved and in the national interest, for a few of their political contributors and lobbyists. Rarely considered is a broad program of fiscal actions to fight the recession or inflation or whatever else might be among the nation's problems.

The response of Congress and the White House to the "Great Recession" is a good example. In a nutshell, the mortgage crisis and recession was used to justify actions to help a few of the politicians' favored friends and the economy as a whole was left to fend for itself. It did not fend very well and the recession lasted and deepened for years for the reasons enumerated in the previous explanations.

What the politicians did can be broadly divided into two overlapping sets of fiscal activities: large one-time actions allegedly for the purpose of increasing customer spending, so as to encourage production and employment, and small one-time actions to help the unemployed. Little, if anything, was done to permanently increase the level of spending and income or permanently help the unemployed even though, as pragmatic analysts know, one-time changes don't have a lasting impact.

One-time actions to encourage spending and income. Among the various fiscal activities that Congress and the White House undertook to counter the shortfall in total spending that was causing unemployment were temporary tax cuts, targeted tax credits, one-time tax holidays; one-time special aid to a few too-big-to fail financial institutions and a couple of the employers of staunch political supporters; and a one-time $200 payment to Social Security recipients. They all created a modest blip on the spending horizon and allowed some inspiring political speeches, and then their impact faded away.

One-time actions to reduce unemployment. Fiscal actions undertaken to fight unemployment included jobs bills to fund "shovel ready" projects that were not ready for years; job credits that meant little because employers were laying off employees instead of adding them; job retraining so that unemployed workers could be trained to fill job vacancies that didn't exist; and a bailout of those parts of the automobile industry that employed the Presidents' union supporters. They too had an insignificant effect and faded away. As one wag so aptly put it—most of the new jobs that were created were for the grant writers and program administrators associated with the "job training" industry.

CHAPTER SUMMARY

I. Because of the impossibility of perfect price and employment stability, policy makers basically aim to limit the inflation that does occur to the increases in the general level of prices inherent in structural changes and to provide enough customer purchasing to employ all but the frictional and that portion of the structurally employed who are unemployable.

II. Policy makers can use fiscal activities to affect the level of income—taxing, spending, transferring, and borrowing in ways that encourage spending or dampen it.

III. Balanced budgets can be expansionary and cause inflation because the purchasing multiplier is more positive than the tax multiplier is negative.

IV. In the face of undesirable levels of spending in an economy, a government can accept the situation and do nothing; change the amounts of its spending to generate the desired total level of spending; or maintain its purchasing and transfers at the optimum level and adjust the level of tax collections to achieve the desired total level of spending. Many economists prefer the tax change alternative because they see the function of taxes as being to hold down spending.

V.   The equilibrium income formula can be used to determine the tax levels and rates needed to obtain the desired level of total purchasing by setting the estimates of the values of the various components into the equation equal to the desired level of income, then solving for the rate of taxation that will yield the desired income level.

VI. The United States and other countries with their own currencies and central banks do not have limits on the size of their deficits and national debts. They can cover their deficits, and even fully pay them off if they so desire, with money created by their central bank. Thus, unlike state and local governments which can borrow only as long as lenders consider them good risks, the federal government can always borrow money and always repay it. Creating new money and using it to finance a deficit or pay off a debt does not mean that the money supply increases because existing money can be simultaneously withdrawn from circulation. Accordingly, the national debt is not a burden on future generations.

VII. When governments cannot adjust their taxes in a timely manner to achieve a desired level of total purchasing, they have to resort to either changing the amount of money they spend on purchases and transfers, or the use of non-fiscal policies. Though initial purchase and transfer changes to make jobs may be wasteful, recipients of higher incomes from the wasteful spending will spend them as they desire, causing valuable goods and services to be produced.

VIII. Pragmatic economists and many analysts think it unrealistic to look to tax changes and other fiscal policies for a solution when there is inflation or unemployment. They think there is too much misunderstanding and economic illiteracy to overcome, to say nothing of the time lags, distorted resource allocations, and counterproductive regulations that inevitably accompany fiscal legislation. They advocate having tax rates that balance the federal budget at full employment—and leaving the achievement of full employment and stable prices to the implementation of direct and indirect monetary policies.

Chapter Seventeen

CONVENTIONAL MONETARY POLICIES

Monetary policies implemented by the Federal Reserve System are one of the three major policy tools the United States uses to affect the level of spending in an effort to achieve full employment and stable prices. The others are fiscal policy and trade policy.

The basic monetary policy of the Federal Reserve during a recession is quite simple: expand the money supply and the banks will loan it out and spending to buy goods and services will rise. More specifically, increasing the money supply means the banks will have more money to loan out. Then the competition among the banks to attract borrowers will cause them to offer lower interest rates so that consumers and investors will be willing to borrow the new money and spend it.

The Federal Reserve's basic procedures and operations have not changed for about one hundred years. Its open market operations, the buying and selling of federal bonds in the open market, are still the principal way by which the money supply of the United States is increased and decreased. These operations are conducted continuously minute by minute during every banking day by the Federal Reserve's Open Market Desk.

The Desk ostensibly operates at the direction of the Federal Reserve's governors and a rotating smaller group of five of the presidents of its twelve regional banks, always including the president of the New York regional bank. Together they constitute the Federal Open Market Committee. Traditionally, perhaps because of the personalities inherent in academic and government bureaucracies and the members' uncertainty regarding their own qualifications and lack of business and commercial banking experience, they follow the leadership and guidance of their presidentially appointed chairman. The committee typically conveys its decisions to the Desk's staff by voting, inevitably as the Chairman suggests, to increase or decrease the Federal Funds target rate.

One of the great advantages of monetary policy is that it can be much more quickly implemented than fiscal policy—almost instantly. Another advantage is that the governors have fourteen year terms so that, once confirmed, they are not subject to the political pressures that campaign-contributing constituents and lobbyists can bring to bear. A third, and perhaps most important, advantage is that the governors, at least so it is claimed and intended, are selected for their expertise.

If there is a problem, and there certainly is most of the time, it is that those doing the appointing and confirming typically do not themselves have the educations and experiences needed to separate economic sheep from political appointee goats—because all are touted to the White House, Congress and the media as highly qualified. So the White House staff doing the vetting and appointing, in turn, typically and often unfortunately for the President they serve, tend to rely on the advice of senior Treasury officials and the president's financial supporters at a handful of large New York based investment banks. And therein is the "regulatory capture" problem from the perspective of a pragmatic analyst—*the problems and concerns of the big investment banks and the Treasury officials they sponsor and cultivate are not the same as those of the economy's commercial banks, employers, and people.*

The problem appears to be particularly true during a major recession when the Federal Reserve's creates new money and attempts to indirectly flow it through the financial system to Main Street's consumers and employers to encourage them to spend more—but much or all of it never reaches them because it is siphoned off along the way for use by the financial institutions.

Little wonder then that the resulting Federal Reserve appointees, and the policies they implement and the real world problems they ignore, all too often have a catastrophic impact on the real economy due to their lack of appropriate educations and lack of real world experiences in business and commercial banking. But that is the way the system works.

Interest rate-related efforts and open market operations are the monetary policy tools most often used the Federal Reserve in its efforts to control the money supply and affect total spending. But they are not the only tools the Federal Reserve governors and regional presidents on the FOMC have available to affect total spending and, thus, the degree to which the United States will have inflation, unemployment, and economic growth. The other tools include:

Reserve requirement changes.

The Federal Reserve specifies the proportion of each dollar of deposits that commercial banks and other transactions depositories must hold as reserves. If open market operations to increase the monetary base are the equivalent of a machine gun constantly firing money bullets into an economy, then a change in the reserve requirements is the equivalent of a massive one-time artillery barrage.

Consider, for example, an economy with a money supply of twenty trillion dollars because the reserve requirement is ten percent and the Federal Reserve has provided the economy with two trillion dollars that its banks and other financial institutions are holding as reserves. If the reserve requirements dropped to eight percent the existing two trillion of reserves would support a money supply of twenty five trillion.

The Federal Reserve rarely uses this potent tool, and did not do so during the Great Recession, both because of its massive impact and, more probably, because some of its governors and regional presidents and much of the public, member of Congress, and the federal bureaucracy misunderstand the role of the reserves—they see the purpose of the reserves as *not* being for the purpose of controlling the size of the money supply, but rather for the purpose of insuring that money will always be there for depositors to withdraw.

In contrast, central banks in countries such as China actively use reserve requirement changes to affect the size of their money supplies. Perhaps they do this because of their inability to engage in open market operations due to the lack of financial markets in which the Chinese national debt can be bought and sold.

Given that in the United States there is a viable alternative in the form of open market operations because financial markets do exist where government debt can be bought and sold, and given that changing reserve requirements might unnecessarily distress people who are not sophisticated enough to understand the real purpose of reserves and reserve requirements, pragmatic economists do not recommend changing reserve requirements to change the size of the money supply and affect total purchasing.

Interest rate changes.

Reducing the Federal Funds target rate was one of the Federal Reserve's first acts upon learning of the collapse of the derivative markets. The Open Market Desk instantly responded to the lower rate by buying federal bonds. But those who sold the bonds held the money they received in payment as each financial institution scrambled for money to cover their existing derivative losses and build up reserves to cover for the additional losses they rightly feared might come. Loans to consumers and employers quickly ground to a halt.

Quantitative easings indirectly increase the supply of money in the hands of lenders.

Somewhere along the line in the years after the beginning of the Great Recession in 2008 the Federal Reserve chairman and his governors and regional presidents finally realized that their reliance on the bailing out the "favored few" and using of the Federal Funds target rate as a guide to monetary expansion was, to put it charitably, not working. The Federal Reserve then three times over a period of five years engaged in programs of "quantitative easing" wherein it pursued open market operations and other smaller programs that indirectly poured hundreds of billions of newly created dollars into the financial markets via the purchase of federal bonds and other financial instruments. The additional dollars were expected to then be deposited in the various banks and depositories and available to be loaned to consumers and employers. It did not work.

The reduction of the Federal Fund target rate and the quantitative easings did put additional money into the banks. But they did not generate the expected increase in consumer and employer loans and spending not for several interrelated reasons: A significant one was that the Federal Reserve and FDIC simultaneously took steps that both increased and changed the reserve, capital, and lending requirements of the commercial and universal banks. This threw the newly created money into the "regulatory liquidity trap" wherein all newly created money flows into financial system and some of it ends up in the hands of the commercial and universal banks but is *not loaned out* to consumers and employers because of regulatory restrictions and uncertainty about the future. As a result the monetary expansions did not have their intended effect of causing more spending and employment.

More specifically, at the same time it expanded the monetary base the Federal Reserve went along with other regulators, particularly the FDIC, and simultaneously subjected the commercial banks to "stress tests" wherein the banks would be closed if they did not have enough reserves and capital. The commercial and universal bankers, not wanting to lose their jobs and banks, then held the additional money as reserves, or used it to buy federal bonds and other relatively liquid assets that were acceptable to the regulators instead of loaning it out to consumers and employers.

Moreover, the lack of funding for consumers and employers was exacerbated as deleveraging by the money market funds and others further reduced the overall supply of loanable dollars. As a result, the actual quantity of loanable funds and credit available to consumers and employers to borrow and spend did *not* increase despite the so-called "quantitative easings." It fell.

In effect, the monetary base and the supply of M2 went straight up by a substantial amount and the supply of all the rest of the money and credit went straight down by even more.

Directly assisting specific beneficiaries via special facilities.

The crash of derivative prices arrived very quickly in 2008. Within a few days the Federal Reserve and everyone else knew the big investment banks such as Goldman Sachs and Morgan Stanley were in serious trouble. So too were the big universal banks such as Citigroup and the Bank of America which had huge counterparty exposures—as a result of themselves taking trillions of dollars of risky proprietary trading gambles in the derivative markets and using their deposits to finance financial traders instead of consumer and employer spending.

The commercial and universal banks had access to the heretofore never used the discount process. After much prodding by the Federal Reserve many used it, including big traders such as Goldman Sachs and Morgan Stanley which were allowed to proclaim themselves to be commercial banks in order to access the money—albeit with each and every user publically claiming that it did not to need the money to survive. Each, it seems, only took the bailout money to show solidarity with all the others who, unlike them, desperately needed it. The smaller investment banks and the country's employers and consumers, however, had no such access to the discount process.

But it was soon clear that the discounting would not provide enough money. As a result of continued deterioration of the financial markets, and the desperate representations of the big traders and the Treasury Secretary, it was then quickly decided by the Federal Reserve and Treasury that a handful of the big financial traders and their insurers were "to big to be allowed to fail" should be directly provided with more money so they could meet their obligations. And that may have been a rational decision because they owed so much money to the each other and other commercial banks and other counter parties that the failure of any one of them might well have destroyed the entire United States commercial banking system.

Accordingly, it was decided to help the handful of investment banks and universal banks that were "too big to fail" and let the benefits of their continued prosperity trickle down to the rest of the economy. As part of their rescue, at the forceful recommendation of the Treasury Secretary, the Federal Reserve set up "special facilities" to channel large sums of money *directly* to the biggest investment banks and their insurers. This, it was alleged, would enable them to avoid defaulting on their obligations to the commercial banks which had loaned them money (and it would also let them pay their traders and executives who were due billions in bonuses for the "profits" they had made trading in the months before their trades collapsed).

Citibank was the biggest universal bank beneficiary and Goldman Sachs was the biggest single beneficiary. Goldman, for example, borrowed almost $600 billion to meet its debt obligations and pay billions in bonuses to the handful of traders whose gambles had successfully made Goldman insolvent. Meanwhile the Federal Reserve continued to ignore the impact of the financial collapse on America's consumers, commercial banks, and private businesses—but it did loan the federal government enough to bail-out a couple of UAW-organized auto manufacturers and send a one-time $200 to each Social Security recipient to "prime the pump" and get the rapidly sinking economy going again.

The fact that the Treasury Secretary who was the architect of the Federal Reserve's bailout plan had retired as Goldman's chairman to become Treasury Secretary and taken his entire retirement bonus in Goldman stock was never a factor in his recommendation that the Federal Reserve save Goldman and a few others, particularly those who owed money to Goldman, and, effectively, leave America's employers, smaller commercial banks, and consumers to fend for themselves.

The Secretary's recommendation was enthusiastically endorsed by the Federal Reserve's New York regional president—who, despite his lack of an education in the field of economics and no experience in business or commercial banking, was then successfully touted by then-Secretary and other executives of the New York based too-big-to-fails, particularly

Citibank whose rescue he led while president the Federal Reserve's New York regional bank, to be his successor as Treasury Secretary.

Term auction facilities.

In addition to its quantitative easings during the Great Recession and the special facilities and other monies it flowed to its "favored few," the Federal Reserve instituted "term auction facilities" wherein it created additional new money and allowed commercial banks to bid for the right to borrow it for a few weeks with interest rate offers.

The thinking of the Federal Reserve governors was twofold: first, that the banks which offered to pay the highest interest rates were the ones whose customers most needed money and credit as evidenced by the fact that they were the ones most willing to pay high interest rates to get it. And, second, that giving the commercial banks access to money they could hold to meet their reserve and capital requirements would allow them to keep making loans at a time when they would otherwise have to reduce their loan portfolios to meet the new and more stringent reserve and capital requirements being imposed by the FDIC and other regulators.

Unfortunately, as with its similar provision of inadequate amounts of new money on a day to day basis as guided by the Federal Funds market and its inadequately timed and sized quantitative easings, the term auction facilities also did not do much to encourage the commercial and universal banks to make loans to consumers and employers. Those who took the money instead tended to use it to make short term loans to the financial traders and to earn interest by depositing it as reserves at Federal Reserve.

What the governors and regional presidents apparently were not sufficiently professionally trained to realize, it seems, is that not many consumers would bother to borrow money for a few weeks in order to buy a new home or car; and few employers would borrow for a few weeks to buy new equipment and warehouses. To the contrary, in the real world, unlike the day to day or week to week monies that might be borrowed for trading purposes in the financial world, the requirements of bank borrowers in the real world typically exceed a few weeks. To this day, it apparently has not yet dawned on the governors and regional presidents that no commercial bank is going to borrow money that it has to repay in a few weeks in order to make loans to consumers and employers that will be repaid over a period of years.

As a result, even more billions flowed into the too-big-to-fails so they could increase their speculations on derivatives and currencies; the economy's level of income and employment remained depressed and continued to worsen; the commercial banks continued to stock up on reserves and reduce their loan portfolios to meet their new and higher reserve and capital requirements; and the Federal Reserve chairman and its governors, mistakenly thinking they had taken significant steps to end the recession, went home and slept soundly—and continued to do so year after year after year as the economy continued to slowly decline further and further into a permanent depression.

Changing the size and composition of assets and capital requirements.

In addition to establishing reserve requirements for banks and other transaction depositories, the Federal Reserve also establishes requirements as to the composition of bank assets and liabilities. It does this so that the banks will have assets they can liquidate or borrow against if they experience unexpected withdrawals or losses. It also does this so the owners of banks have their own money at risk when they accept deposits and use the money to make loans. For example, for some years the Federal Reserve has required that the deposits and other liabilities of commercial banks not exceed the lower of $25 for every dollar of paid-in capital (a "tier one" requirement of four percent) or $12.50 for every dollar of tier one capital plus other acceptable assets such as federal bonds and federally insured notes and mortgages (a "tier two" requirement of eight percent).

Other regulators such as the FDIC and the Treasury also set asset and liability requirements. In the real world, whoever's requirements are highest is the one that rules the behavior of the universal and commercial banks. It stopped being the Federal Reserve once the Great Recession began. The FDIC quickly set higher requirements and enforced them with "stress tests." This was a disaster for the economy for it literally forced the banks to stop making and renewing loans to consumers and employers. To the contrary, many of them reduced or eliminated personal and employer lines of credit, called for some of their existing loans to be immediately paid off, and refused to did renew loans and lines of credit as they came due—in order to reduce their potential loses to those that their regulators thought could be covered by their remaining capital.

In effect, the enhanced capital requirements immediately became a major reason why the Federal Reserves policy of indirectly flowing money into the economy via quantitative easings and special facilities did not work—because they were accompanied by regulatory encouragement pressures ("we'll close you if you don't") to improve the quality of their assets by increasing their holdings of federal debt and making short term loans to traders and financial institutions that could be easily liquidated if the commercial banks needed funds to cover withdrawals.

Even worse, the FDIC used its higher requirements and "stress tests" to force the closure of a number of smaller banks who could not cut back quickly enough on their consumer and business loans—and, incredibly, even loaned money to the to-big-to-fails to buy up the closed banks and other lenders. In other words, as a result of the FDIC, more and more banks failed and more and more of the economy's deposit monies were diverted to the "too-bigs" where they could be used to provide short-term loans for speculative trading instead of consumer and business loans.

It is worth noting that the world's central bankers took notice of the efforts of the Federal Reserve and the FDIC and, equally perversely, began their own efforts, centered in Basel, Switzerland, to phase in new and higher capital requirements, particularly for the big European universal banks which engaged in both commercial banking and investment banking. In order to be allowed to keep doing business with each other, the world's biggest banks, including those in the United States if they wanted to continue doing business with the big European banks, were required to change the way they measure the risks taken by their proprietary trading desks—to take into account the possibility of rare but damaging events such as another meltdown of the mortgage derivatives or the arrival of another sovereign debt crisis.

They were also subjected to stricter rules on when items could be moved from their trading books to their bank capital accounts. The American banks had to accept them or they could not continue to do business with their European bank counterparties. In a nutshell, the Basel rules are aimed at preventing banks from inflating the liquidation values of the reserves and capital assets they claim to have supporting their deposits and liabilities.

But the Basel rules were not implemented in a timely manner in the United States. The Federal Reserve delayed forcing the banks to comply because the "too-big" banks wanted to retain their proprietary trading desks and the profits they were again earning by buying, selling, and financing derivatives and other financial assets using their sophisticated trading platforms.

The "too-bigs" accordingly lobbied for delays because their models predicted they would earn more profits if they continued financing trading instead of making conventional loans to consumers and businesses. So for the first five years of the Great Recession they pushed back against the Basel rules, claiming to have come up with new and better mathematical models that would accurately predict risk—so that Basel-like rules to prevent them from gambling with their own money and their depositors' money were no longer needed.

The lobbying charge was led by JP Morgan Chase which claimed to be the only big American bank to come through the mortgage crisis relatively unscathed (it "only" took $25 billion of bailout funds but said it only did so to show solidarity with those who actually needed to be bailed out). It did not really need the money, so it claimed, because of its "scientific" low-risk trading practices based on its superior mathematical models. These, its executives said, insured that JP Morgan Chase did not put its depositors and counterparties at risk by funding its own and others' trading activities instead of consumer and business loans.

Alas, just before the first congressional hearing on an American version of the proposed Basel regulations to again separate banks' gambling and trading activities from their commercial banking activities, a single trader tucked away in the bank's London office and equipped with Morgan's latest highly touted mathematical model, found that it predicted the future so badly that he lost over six billion dollars of the bank's capital in the course of a few weeks. He lost it betting on the rate at which commercial bank loans would default.

The problem with such economic models is that they inevitably assume that past levels of experiences and relationships will persist and, thus, that with the right data they can be used to predict the future. In the real world, however, there are sooner or later "black swan" unexpected events and relationship changes. Pragmatic analysts understand this and use models to explain only the most basic of relationships, and only in the full knowledge that the world and its relationships continually change. In essence, once again, they know you cannot always drive the economic road ahead by looking in the rear view mirror. The resulting crashes are called recessions, depressions, and financial meltdowns. Whatever the name, they mean widespread business failures, unemployment, foreclosures, and bankruptcies.

Morgan's loss was not fatal, even though it further reduced the bank's ability to make conventional consumer and businesses loans. The bank's executives apparently knew the gambles were being made and let them continue so long as they were profitable—and only stopped them when the losses began piling up. Morgan, of course, has improved its model and resumed trading.

But what if Morgan's managers had been kept in the dark and the trader had continued for a few more weeks in a desperate effort to keep his job by continuing to bet in hopes that the model's numbers would finally came up? This is exactly what happened to England's centuries old Baring Brothers investment bank a few years ago when an obscure trader based in Hong Kong lost billions betting on currency exchange rates—and continued to double and redouble his bets in an effort to cover his loses before his bosses found out. As one might expect, Baring Brothers failed. A similar near-miss when a single trader kept going to try to cover his losses hit the huge Credit Suisse commercial bank for so many billions in losses that it too almost failed during the Great Recession.

Among those failing and exacerbating the Great Recession because they didn't have enough capital and salable assets to cover the losses generated by their "sophisticated" trading and risk management models were Lehman Brothers, AIG, Washington Mutual, Fannie Mae, General Motors Acceptance Corporation and a host of others. Coming close to failing were Citigroup, Goldman Sachs, and Morgan Stanley. They were saved so they could continue their proprietary trading and pay bonuses to their money-losing traders and executives. Each received ten billion from TARP plus many hundreds of billions of dollars in bailout loans from the Federal Reserve.

A similar, at least conceptually, direct financing effort by the Federal Reserve was undertaken to save millions of Americans from bankruptcy and foreclosure—if they were retired or disabled they each got $200. As a result, the "too-bigs" were saved and helped to grow larger; the "too-smalls" were not saved. *But, as analysts shall come to see, an important precedent was set when newly created money was flowed into circulation by going directly to potential spenders instead of indirectly via open market operations.*

Interest rate swaps.

Interest rate swaps occur when the Federal Reserve simultaneously sells short-term federal securities to drive down their prices and increase their yields, and uses the proceeds to buy long-term federal securities to drive up their prices and decrease their interest rate yields.

The Federal Reserve governors' "belief," unsupported by logic or the results but sincerely held, is that the resulting decline of a few basis points in the interest rate yields of long term federal bonds and mortgage derivatives will have a significant impact on long-term consumer loans for such things as houses and cars and long-term loans to employers for the purpose of buying capital goods such as plant and equipment. This will occur, the governors apparently think, because banks will switch their money from buying federal bonds and making short-term loans to financial traders to making long-term loans to consumers and employers. The additional supply of money available for such loans, it is alleged, will drive down their interest rates by a few basis points and significantly increase consumer and business spending.

The Federal Reserve governors tried this interest-oriented approach for years during the Great Recession. It did not work—because, in the real world, consumers and employers are more motivated by the availability of credit and the payments to service it rather than extremely modest tweaks in its interest rate cost.

Indeed, Federal Reserve's swaps may well have had a negative effect on total spending and caused the recession to worsen and morph into a depression. This occurred as more and more consumers and employers working and producing in the real world came to the conclusion that the Federal Reserve's leaders would not take steps to the recession. As a result, they reduced their expectations about future jobs and revenues and cut back further on their spending to buy consumer and capital products.

Paying interest on reserves.

During the long years of the Great Recession and the depression that followed, the great majority of commercial banks, those not involved in using their depositors' money to finance their own and others' gambling, were dismayed when the Federal Reserve engaged in open market operations to increase the quantity of money in the economy (QE1, QE2, and QE3) while at the same time the FDIC was encouraging them, under threat of closure, to hold more reserves and make better loans.

The banks pointed out that they needed their money to earn interest to help cover their recession-generated loses if they were stay in business. So the Federal Reserve obligingly agreed; it began paying interest on the reserves deposited at the Federal Reserve. Indeed, it paid higher rates than the banks could generally net by refinancing mortgages and renewing expiring business credit lines.

This, of course, resulted in some of the newly created money that reached the commercial and universal banks being returned to the Federal Reserve in the form of reserve deposits instead of being loaned out to consumers and employers. In other words, it made it even more difficult for people and employers to refinance their mortgages and buy more goods and services. So the number of foreclosures, bankruptcies, and layoffs continued to grow.

WHAT THE FEDERAL RESERVE IGNORED

As important as what the Federal Reserve did during a recession is what it ignored and the policies it could have implemented but did not. Its omissions and oversights were extensive during the Great Recession. They help explain why the Federal Reserve's quantitative easings and the other policies it implemented were not successful.

Benign neglect and reliance on business cycle theory.

If anything, the Federal Reserve's policy during the Great Recession was one of benign neglect of the real economy in the mistaken "conventional wisdom" belief that business cycles were inevitable and the economy would eventually turn around on its own. So the largest commercial and universal bank recipients of the newly created money not only held more of it in reserve and improved their capital ratios by using the money to buy federal bonds, they used much of the remainder to finance their own trading desk gambling and those of their investment bank and money market fund clients, the only ones willing to borrow money on the short term basis "encourage" encouraged by the Federal Reserve and other regulators. Only what was left went consumers and employers—and there was not enough left to make a dent in the continuing decline in total spending (aggregate demand) relative to the economy's ever growing production capacity (aggregate supply).

Yet another reason the quantitative easings did not work, and arguably the most significant in the end, was that the Federal Reserve waited too long to begin getting loanable funds into the banks and encouraging them to make loans to consumers and employers. By the time the Federal Reserve governors and regional presidents finished helping their cronies and sponsors in the financial markets and, more than five years later, began to turn their attention to the real economy, it was too late. The real economy was already long into such a deep and worsening recession that morphed into a permanent depression. So businesses and commercial banks continued to fail and millions of mortgages and loans continued to default as people and employers who would normally have paid lost their jobs and revenues.

As a result of the Federal Reserve's various failures and delays, so many people and employers were ruined by the time the third quantitative easing began that the banks were afraid to make significant amounts of loans at all at any interest rate to consumers and employers. So when some of the additional money did flow into the banks—it was then trapped there by the banks' fears and regulations or sent off to be deposited at the Federal Reserve or to buy federal bonds or, in the case of a handful of big banks, to finance their own and others' speculations and gambles in the financial and currency markets *instead of being loaned out* in the course of normal commercial banking activities to consumers and employers.

The Federal Reserve's delay in taking action is significant because during those years more and more businesses and banks failed and more and more people lost their jobs, homes, and retirement assets. In essence, fewer and fewer people and employers were left who were both willing to borrow and could qualify for loans and credit.

The economy's continual decline is significant for, at some point, it meant that the United States' economy had deteriorated so badly that finally making all the money and credit they want available to those who are left would not generate enough additional spending to pull the country out of its malaise. In other words, the recession morphed into a permanent long-term depression for which the Federal Reserve's conventional monetary policies aimed at lowering interest rates would no longer work.

In essence, as pragmatic economists know, and the Federal Reserve's governors and regional presidents apparently did not, there is a liquidity trap. But it does not only occur when interest rates reach some very low level as their early macroeconomics texts and models indicate. In the real world it also occurs when an economy reaches such dire straits that its lenders cannot find, or are discouraged by their regulators from finding, enough consumer and employer borrowers to provide with loans and credit no matter what interest rates they charge.

In other words, an interest rate-related liquidity trap exists in theory when interest rates reach a minimum and it exists in reality when an economy reaches such a depressed state that its commercial banks cannot provide enough loans and credit to get it going again even when they finally have the money to do so. *Conventional monetary policies then become ineffective.* That is what happened to the United States by the fourth or fifth year of the Great Recession.

**Separating investment banking
from commercial banking.**

The commercial bank failures associated with the United States "Great Depression" of the 1930s resulted in the 1933 Glass-Steagall Act. The Act established the FDIC to guarantee deposits and prohibited commercial banks and their subsidiaries from engaging in securities trading and speculation. The idea was to stop the banks from gambling in the stock market with their depositors' money—and losing their bets and going out of business. In essence, it required that the banks' money and deposits were only to be used for the normal loans and activities of commercial banks, not put at the risk of being lost when their speculations went bad.

In 1999 the Glass-Steagall Act was amended to effectively allow commercial banks to again engage in proprietary securities and currency transactions using bank assets—the capital and deposits that previously would have been used for loans to consumers, employers, and local governments. In effect, the repeal resulted in hundreds of billions of dollars being moved away from routine commercial loans to consumers and employers and into directly gambling on the movements of prices in currency and securities markets as well as loaning some of their deposits to those who do. In other words, commercial banks were allowed to become universal banks providing more services and engaging in more activities than just accepting deposits and making loans to consumers and employers.

The trading profits of the investment banks soared after the repeal, and so did those of the universal banks which both traded with them and funded them with their capital and the deposits they received—until 2008 when their buying and selling of mortgage derivatives and their creation and sale of "synthetic" (read fictitious) and other financial instruments resulted in many hundreds of billions of dollars of losses.

And yes, much of what they were selling was fictitious. Facing a shortage of real mortgage derivatives to sell that actually contained viable mortgages, the "too bigs" first created new mortgage derivatives containing unviable mortgages they encouraged their mortgage company suppliers to create for that purpose—by making and buying loans to unqualified buyers who could not possibly make the payments. Prior to their collapse in value these low grade mortgages were sold for high profits to gullible pension funds and foreign banks.

When the "too-bigs" still did not have enough derivatives to sell to the gullible pension funds and other buyers "playing the market," they created and began selling un-backed "synthetic" or "phantom" derivatives wherein buyers and sellers could bet on the direction of the prices of real derivatives and other indices. Las Vegas was jealous and the New York gambling commission and the SEC turned a blind eye—because, it appears, the firms issuing the phantom securities had paid rating agencies such as Standard and Poor's, Moody's, and Fitch in such a way as to encourage them to give the make-believe "synthetic" securities they created high credit-worthiness ratings.

In many cases the creators of the real and "synthetic" derivatives continued to be able to buy the highest possible rating—as high as that of the United States federal debt which is typically the highest rated debt in the world because it will always be repaid—right up until their prices collapsed and they became worthless. United States' law to this day requires all publically traded financial instruments to be "rated" by the "experts" at these rating firms to insure their buyers are not misled—and does not hold them responsible if they are bribed with big fees.

Interestingly, and perhaps significant for the future, the handful of big investment and universal banks whose failed speculations and gambling losses triggered the recession were provided with so much "bail out" money that, instead of loaning it out to consumers and employers to help get the economy going again, they promptly resumed proprietary trading and began buying up the smaller banks and other financial institutions which had not been "saved."

The "too-bigs" did so with the money they received to "save" themselves, and with additional money they were loaned for that purpose by the FDIC and the Federal Reserve. In essence, they were able to buy the too-small-to-save banks and institutions which did not receive the emergency aid and had been partially or totally ruined by the loan defaults and bankruptcies that accompanied the recession the bailed-out beneficiaries caused.

In other words, thanks primarily to the Federal Reserve, the "too-big-to-fail investment and commercial banks whose gambles and speculations caused the problems got rewarded and bigger—and the other commercial banks and the economy's ability to generate output and employment got smaller.

Wags have suggested, and only partially in jest, that the economy and the American people would have been better served if the Federal Reserve and the other bank regulators had outsourced their ratings requirements, regulations, and inspections to the Nevada Gambling Commission and concentrated their efforts on providing enough money and credit to keep Main Street Americans prosperous and fully employed.

Similarly, since much of that booking was centered in New York, some pragmatic analysts have long wondered why the New York State Gaming Commission does not act to regulate the financial gamblers, the new ways of gaming they create, and their "trading casinos." And they similarly wonder why the Las Vegas and other casinos do not open books for the commercial banks and others who want to bet on stock and derivative prices. And they particularly wonder what keeping the "too-big" traders and hedge funds alive has to do with jobs and production in the United States and why they are so important they should get special low tax rates.

The effect of deleveraging.

A financial institution's leverage is the ratio between its assets, including loans, to its liabilities. Its equity capital is the banks' "skin in the game." It is intended to be the financial cushion available to cover any loan loses so that the bank always has enough assets to insure its depositors will be safe and meet its other obligations. It is supposed to be large enough, even in rare but damaging events such as the collapse of mortgage derivatives and *market freezes* (wherein every bank is so afraid that the others will fail that no bank does any business with another financial institution.)

In the trading and speculation boom years preceding the mortgage derivative-induced Great Recession of the United States and the simultaneously occurring "sovereign debt crisis" of Europe, the commercial banks increased their lending to the financial sector without proportionally increasing their capital. They did so by borrowing money to loan with increasing exotic financial instruments that *appeared* to be available to be quickly liquidated to cover loan losses in the unlikely event mortgages and other loans defaulted. There were, after all, markets where the assets they were creating and buying could be instantly sold.

As the ratios of their liabilities to their asset cushions ratios grew and bigger and bigger, larger trading profits and employee bonuses resulted from the buying and selling of derivatives and other securities compared to the profits and bonuses generated by their loans to consumers and businesses. As a result, the commercial banks became increasingly vulnerable to quickly running out funds for their regular customers if smaller and smaller percentages of their loans and other portfolio assets were not repaid or collapsed in value.

Unfortunately, buyers in the markets for the derivatives and other securities being traded virtually disappeared overnight when the mortgage and sovereign debt crises and their attendant loan defaults arrived at the start of the Great Recession. As a result, the assets of many commercial banks and the "too-bigs" could not be sold for enough to cover their debts. So some commercial banks and investment banks were closed by regulators both in the United States and abroad—they became insolvent as the value of their remaining assets could not be sold for enough to cover their liabilities to their depositors and other creditors; others, particularly those "too-big-to-be-allowed-to-fail," were rescued by emergency advances from their governments and central banks.

Overall, supply or money and credit tended to dry up in the United States and Europe—so mortgages and lines of credit could not be obtained or refinanced. So income and employment declined and many economies including the United States suffered prolonged recessions, some of which, such as that of the United States, then slowly morphed into permanent depressions.

Governments could not respond to the rapidly growing crisis with a monetary expansion because they had delegated those powers to central banks they did not control. They also, at least in the United States, could not respond quickly with significant fiscal policies due to concerns about federal spending and deficits. So in an effort to "do something" they and their regulators rather quickly responded to the problems attributed to excess leveraging with various "accords" and "stress tests" wherein the commercial banks were forced or encouraged to "deleverage"—improve their ratios by raising additional capital and further reducing their loans.

Most commercial and universal banks then chose, or were forced, to reduce their exposure to possible losses by reducing their loans to consumers and businesses to the lower levels that could be supported by what was left of their capital. They had to do this because money for the additional capital they needed was difficult to find because financial institutions everywhere were cutting back. In this way, *without the central banks raising their reserve requirements*, there was a massive reduction in the supply of money and credit in both the United States and Europe.

That, of course, exacerbated the United States' recession so that even more loans defaulted and more banks got in trouble. So the banks cut back even more on making and renewing loans as the continuing losses cut into their capital.

In the United States, the decision makers at the Federal Reserve and FDIC naively claimed, and to this day still do, that the deleveraging and higher capital requirements they were requiring would help the United States economy recover from the recession by making bank deposits "safer" such that savings and deposits would increase. The additional savings, they suggested, would result in additional investment spending.*

Astute analysts will recognize this as the savings equals investment concept that is true when an economy's level of income is in equilibrium. They will also recall that the equality does not mean that more savings will result in more investment—because investment spending depends on a host of factors of which the amount or existence of savings is not one. To the contrary, had savings actually increased as a result of the "safer" banks there would have been even less spending and the recession would have worsened as a result of the reduced spending instead of being improved by more spending. In essence, they were twice wrong—savings and deposits did not increase and, if they had, total consumer and employer spending would have declined instead of increased.

In fact, the additional reserves and capital they required did not attract more deposits but, rather, created a "perfect storm" of credit destruction that destroyed the availability of money and credit for consumers and businesses and drove the United States deeper and deeper into recession. And instead of making banks and their deposits "safer," it caused a number of commercial banks to fail.

In essence, the governors and the regional presidents on the Open Market Committee drove the economy deeper into recession as the commercial and universal banks and other depositories responded to the requirements for more and better capital assets and higher and better loan to capital ratios by making even fewer consumer and business loans. In other words, instead of using the additional money provided by the Federal Reserve to make loans to consumers and employers, they used it to increase their reserves, buy more federal bonds to achieve the required increases the quality of their capital, and to fund their trading desks and loans to traders.

In effect, after meeting the regulators new requirements and funding their own trading desks and the trading activities of others, there just was not much money left in the commercial banks to loan to businesses and consumers. So the recession continued until it destroyed enough consumers and employers that it morphed into a permanent depression.

Shadow banks and systemic exposure to risk.

One activity of the regulated universal and commercial banks that affects both the supply of money and the amount of it available for conventional bank loans and credit is the ability of the banks to outsource lending risk and to unregulated shadow banks such as hedge funds, investment banks, and money market funds.

In essence, the banks accept deposits and, instead of using the money to make loans to consumers and employers, they use the money to make loans to hedge funds and similar searchers for big trading profits and employee bonuses, including their own subsidiaries and trading desks. These, in turn, make the risky loans and take the financial and trading gambles that the commercial banks cannot. As such they are merely conduits for the commercial banks' loanable funds which allow the commercial banks to take risks that they might not be allowed to take *instead of making conventional loans to consumers and employers.*

Unfortunately, as happened in the United States during the Great Recession, the risks taken by the hedge funds, trading desks, and lenders become systemic as the traders and gamblers interact with each other—become counterparties with each other in the search for trading profits at each other's expense as they buy and sell in expectations of price moves.

Normally the profits and losses even out as one institution's loss is another's gain so that their contribution to society as a whole is zero. But when things go bad for the financial system as a whole, as it did when the prices of mortgage derivatives collapsed, the result is that the traders will have such major losses if they sell their assets that, for some, they will not be able to pay off their debts. Then the losses that their counterparties, the other traders and banks to whom they owe money, will then suffer might well be so great as to bring them down also.

It was due to their projected inability to pay their debts by selling their derivative and other financial assets that almost caused Citibank, Goldman Sachs, Morgan Stanley, and a handful of other big U.S. and foreign investment and universal to fail and bring down the entire world financial system with them. If they had not been bailed out they might well have defaulted on their contractual obligations. Their potential insolvency and bankruptcy would have occurred, if they had not been bailed out, because the prices of their mortgage-based derivatives virtually collapsed when everyone suddenly stopped buying them.

To prevent this from happening again, the Basel agreements specify that the net exposure between any two of the six largest "systemically important" trading firms and universal banks is to be limited to ten percent of their capital; 25 percent between all other financial institutions. That sounds impressive—until one realizes that most investment and commercial banking institutions which lose ten percent of the monies due to them will be hopelessly bankrupt and default on all their obligations to their counterparties, bankrupting many of them in the process

When the large universal banks complained about such "onerous" and unnecessary restrictions now that they have improved their trading and risk models, a group of Stanford University professors said "to the extent that banks (including investment banks) find the single counterparty position limit onerous, this should only alarm us with respect to the great interconnectedness of the system."

They are right. The American banking system supervised by the Federal Reserve has come a long way away from the days of conventional banking wherein the banks accept deposits and use the money to make loans to consumers and employers.

Regulatory changes and regulatory malfeasance.

Another reason why the Federal Reserves policy of indirectly flowing money into the economy via quantitative easings and special facilities did not work was that it was accompanied regulatory encouragement pressures ("we'll close you if you don't") to improve the quality of their assets by increasing their holdings of federal debt and making short term loans to traders and financial institutions that could be easily liquidated if the commercial banks needed funds to cover withdrawals.

The Federal Reserve and other regulators similarly shot themselves in the foot when they looked the other way when the commercial and universal banks ignored the Community Reinvestment laws and regulations that effectively require them to use a significant portion of their deposits to make loans to consumers and employers in their service areas—instead of holding the money or diverting it to their trading desks and to traders and financial firms.

Similarly, The Federal Reserve and other regulators looked the other way when the commercial and universal banks inappropriately foreclosed on millions of mortgages with false claims and filings. This ruined the credit and spending abilities of millions of consumers. It occurred because the Federal Reserve and other regulators allowed the banks to engage in foreclosure processes that gave the third party agents of the large institutions that owned most of the mortgages a profit incentive to foreclose instead of reworking the mortgages to keep people in their homes.

What made the process particularly absurd, and raised serious questions as to the competency of both the regulators and the executives, was that the larger banks and other big mortgage owners typically had higher costs and booked bigger losses and capital write downs via the foreclosure and sale process than they would have booked by rewriting the mortgages. But the regulators allowed them even though the reduced consumer and employer spending that resulted from the unnecessary destruction of potential spenders creditworthiness caused the recession to deepen.

Similarly, the Federal Reserve encourage began paying interest on commercial bank reserves that were deposited at the Federal Reserve instead of being loaned out. Accordingly the commercial banks made even fewer loans and most of those they did make went to investment banks and other traders who would accept short term financing to support their financial and currency trading. Consumers and businesses got short shrift because they tend to need longer term repayments for their credit cards balances, mortgages, and working capital lines.

Yet another reason the quantitative easing did not work was that the amount of additional newly created money the Federal Reserve provided was seen to be hopelessly inadequate by everyone except, it seems, the Federal Reserve governors and certain journalists. The shortfall in the amount money and credit made available to consumers and employers to fund the buying of new goods and services was tremendous. This occurred because the Federal Reserve and other regulators took steps that effectively diverted the newly created money, and then some, to "safer" assets such as federal bonds and short term loans to the financial sector so its participants could continue buying and selling derivatives and other financial assets.

In other words, the quantitative easing amounts sounded large to the journalists and the untrained governors and inexperienced regional presidents but *what* was actually made available to consumers and employers was quite small and significantly less than was needed to rejuvenate the economy.

The commercial and universal banks and their customers quickly understood that there was not going to be enough new money created to stop the decline and turn the economy around—it was too little and too late. As a result, each commercial bank tended to prudently avoid extending credit making and renewing loans. This, in turn, caused a tragedy of the commons, in which sensible individual decisions to prepare for a worsening future by holding more money for precautionary purposes led to a collective tragedy in the form of spending being cut back instead of increasing.

WHY DID THE FEDERAL RESERVE FAIL?

The root cause of the inadequate sizes of the quantitative easings and loan-discouraging regulations appears to be that the Chairman and his governors and regional presidents actually believed that the economy's problems were not so bad because the official unemployment rate only went up a point or two; and because the stock markets and financial markets rallied when the large investment and universal banks were bailed out.

The governors and regional presidents, it seems, really thought what they had done was significant when they saw the financial markets recover as a result of the newly created money they supplied. They also naively and wrongly believed that the relatively minor interest rate changes were an effective way to achieve more consumer and employer spending.

And they also naively and wrongly believed that a significant portion of the newly created money would flow into the commercial and universal banks and become available for loans to consumers and employers.

And they also naively and wrongly believed that changing the Federal Funds rate would somehow significantly change the interest rates paid by consumers and employers.

And they also naively and wrongly believed the resulting lower rates of interest would motivate consumers and employers to substantially increase their spending

And they also naively and wrongly believed, and so did not require, that the relative handful of large universal banks and other intermediaries would use a substantial portion of the additional monies to provide mortgage relief and refinancing in order to minimize their mortgage-related losses.

They were also concerned about increasing the money supply because "everyone knows" that an increase in the money supply will cause inflation, later if not immediately. And the governors and their staff did not even know enough to concentrate on the labor force participation rates to get a feel for the magnitude of the problem—perhaps because that data comes from the federal government and does not appear in the Federal Reserve's in-house publications.

Yet another reason the various quantitative easings did not work was that the Federal Reserve and other regulators neither enforced the Community Reinvestment laws and regulations requiring banks to loan to their communities nor encouraged them to do so.

MAJOR MONETARY POLICY ERRORS

One lesson from the Great Recession is that policy makers are likely to make big mistakes if they are insufficiently trained and do not have enough business and commercial banking experience to understand the realities of the American economy and its monetary system. As a result, they respond badly and to the wrong policy indicators. It is worth looking at some of the most common monetary mistakes advocated by journalists and "business economists" and implemented by the Federal Reserve's governors and regional presidents, if only to know whose ideas and advocacies are worth ignoring.

Some of the mistakes are significant, most are interrelated, and all are indications that those who made them are neither experts nor qualified to make monetary policy decisions.

Among the mistakes of the media and the Federal Reserve's governors and regional presidents during the Great Recession and the depression that followed:

1. Thinking the Federal Funds rates reported by the banks reflect the availability of credit and using it as the key indicator of the degree to which the economy needs an increase or decrease in the money supply. Relying on the Federal Funds rates to guide their policies is arguably the Federal Reserve governors' biggest and most significant blunder. Anyone living in the real world knows that no commercial banker will ever borrow money that has to be paid back in twenty four hours and loan it out for months and years so people can buy houses and cars and businesses can buy plant and equipment. In the real world, moves in the Federal Funds rate are no indication whatsoever of the state of the economy's employment and production, the availability of money and credit for consumers and businesses, or the degree to which there is a need for open market operations to change the size of the money supply.

2. Believing that monetary policy acts primarily via interest rate changes. To the contrary, it is primarily the financial markets that respond to interest rate changes. In contrast, the producers and purchasers of goods and services in the product markets respond primarily to the availability of credit and its repayment terms, not its interest rate price. Belief that monetary policy primarily acts through interest rate changes is a particularly pernicious belief because it has led the Federal Reserve's governors to the erroneous conclusion that "there's nothing more we can do because the economy is in a liquidity trap" when the average Federal Funds rate and the rates on federal bonds reach historic lows.

    Many pragmatic macroeconomists and analysts believe a major source of the governors' misunderstanding, at least among the minority of the governors who had actually studied economics, was the use of inappropriate macroeconomics texts and their associated professorial lectures in the years following Keynes. The texts and lectures, based on Keynes' ideas, described the way the British central bank affects the commercial banks by setting a wholesale rate at which banks can borrow money to loan. The Federal Reserve does not do that. In essence, it appears many of today's journalists, "business economists," and Federal Reserve governors learned about a monetary system that does not exist in the United States—but are so unworldly and untrained that they think and act as if it does.

3. Confusing the conditions in the financial markets which are highly responsive to the short term availability of money and interest rate changes with employment and income conditions in the product markets of the real economy which are not.

4. Believing that if the Federal Reserve puts too much newly created money into the economy there will subsequently be an inflation from too much spending; In essence, forgetting, or not knowing, that the money supply never need be "too large" because they can use open market sales to instantly remove any money that turns out to be excess.

5. Not being aware of their regulatory and moral suasion duties and powers and, therefore, failing to use their powers and influence to affect the behavior of commercial banks and other lenders on matters such as mortgage foreclosures and mortgage revisions, community reinvestment, and the renewal of consumer and business lines of credit.

6. Believing there is a relationship between the Federal Funds rate and the economy's level of rates such that the Fed will be setting or influencing the economy's level of interest rates if it changes the Federal Funds target rate. It is in Britain that there is a relationship between the interest rate set by the central bank and the interest rates charged by banks, not the United States.

7. Relying on simplistic models using data from past experiences to project the future. The past when different conditions and policies prevailed is not necessarily a guide to the future. Journalists, "business economists," and central bankers relying on historical data are not likely to accurately see the road ahead by looking into the rearview mirror.

8. Believing that the special financial assistance provided by the Federal Reserve to a handful of large financial firms who created derivatives and lost money gambling on their prices will somehow trickle down to encourage total spending and thus benefit consumers and employers.

9. Misinterpreting the role of reserves to be that of insuring depositors can be repaid. Protecting depositors is the role of the banks' capital requirements and the deposit insurance provided by the FDIC. The most important role of reserves is to give the Federal Reserve a method of controlling the amount of money in circulation.

10. Standing idle and unaware while the FDIC usurped the Federal Reserve's role in establishing the capital requirements of the commercial banks and other transactions depositories. The FDIC effectively increased the banks' capital requirements and, in so doing, reduced the availability of loanable funds at the same time the Federal Reserve governors were trying to fight unemployment and low levels of spending by increasing the monetary base.

11. Standing idle and unaware while the FDIC usurped the Federal Reserve's role in establishing the reserve requirements of the commercial banks and other transactions depositories. The FDIC inspectors effectively increased the reserve requirements and reduced the supply of money in circulation and the availability of loanable funds at the same time the Federal Reserve governors were trying to pursue a monetary expansion.

12. Standing idle while the FDIC usurped the Federal Reserve's role in establishing borrower loan eligibility. The FDIC inspectors insistence that banks increase their reserves and hold more

liquid assets such as federal bonds and short term loans to safe borrowers such as the "too bigs" effectively increased bank lending requirements and, in so doing, reduced the volume of loans being made at the same time the Federal Reserve governors thought they were pursuing expansionary policies.

13. Defining the money supply so narrowly that it appears to be going up when, in fact, it is rapidly declining due to deleveraging, reductions in personal and business credit lines, and flows out of the country.

14. Being guided in their policy making by irrelevant interest rate comparisons such as that between the actual Federal Funds rates and the "target rate" set by the Fed, instead of by the economy's employment, production, price stability, and growth.

15. Confusing the well-being and prosperity of a handful of large financial firms with that of the economy as a whole and its commercial banks, consumers, employers, and governments.

16. Assuming that payments and subsidies to assist large financial firms which get in trouble gambling on the price movements of derivatives indices, and currencies will somehow "trickle down" to encourage production and employment in the labor and product markets.

17. Defining the money supply narrowly to include only that which is recorded in the Federal Reserve's own data. Thus the Federal Reserve data may show the money supply expanding while, in fact, it is contracting as dollars flow abroad and the credit lines of consumers and employers are contracting along with other generally accepted forms of payment.

18. Ignoring the arrival of Paypal and other generally accepted forms of digital payments in their calculations of the size of the money supply.

19. Raising the capital requirements of the banks and other financial intermediaries during a period of recession. They could not raise the capital so they deleveraged by reducing their loans to meet the new and higher ratio requirements.

20. Believing that all inflation was caused by an increase in the money supply so that it could be prevented by holding down increases in the money supply.

21. Not realizing that what the Federal Reserve thought to be a massive expansion of the money supply via open market operations (QE1, QE2, QE3) did not work because the banks and other intermediaries were simultaneously required and encouraged to hold it as reserves and change the composition of their capital and other assets.

22. Paying interest on reserves to encourage banks to deposit money with the Federal Reserve instead of loaning it out to consumers and employers during a period of inadequate total spending.

23. Thinking they were helping the economy as a whole when they directly channeled newly created money to Citigroup, Goldman Sachs and a handful of other institutions to cover their gambling losses and bonus payments when the value of mortgage derivatives they created and sold crashed.

24. Equating the health and welfare of the financial markets and their investment banks and other traders and speculators with the health and welfare of the product markets and commercial banks.

25. Ignoring the possibility that the United States economy could reach equilibrium at such a low level of income that the remaining creditworthy consumers and employers would no longer be able to respond with enough spending even if the money and credit they want reaches them.

26. Responding the state of the financial markets and effectively ignoring the state of the labor and product and housing markets.

27. Imposing higher capital ratios on banks. Instead of raising additional capital so they can maintain their current level of lending the banks may, and did, reduce the amount of their loans in order to attain the required new ratios.

28. Basing policy decisions on simplistic interest-oriented models that ignore both the effect of credit cards, digital dollars, overseas dollars, credit lines, and foreign bank money creation and, perhaps most importantly, the reality that the availability and repayment terms of loans and credit is often more significant to consumers and employers than the money's interest rate price.

29. Failing to put enough money into circulation during a time of high unemployment because they fear the additional money would cause inflation in the future—because they do not understand that there are many causes of inflation and are unaware they have the power to at any time in the future instantly remove from circulation any amount of money they find to be excessive.

30. Imposing higher creditworthiness and collateral requirements on borrowers at a time when total spending is inadequate instead of allowing the individual depositories to make their own judgments on a case by case basis.

31. Believing banks and other mortgage owners would minimize their losses by refinancing those mortgages that could be refinanced instead of taking bigger losses and ruining the creditworthiness of potential consumers by paying their agents more if they administered foreclosures than if they administered refinancings.

32. Failing to act in a timely manner. The ability of conventional monetary policies to stop a recession ends when the recession lasts so long that it devastates the creditworthiness and abilities of enough potential consumers and employers. Then conventional monetary policies, if ever implemented, will not affect a customer base sufficient in size and ability to generate enough of an increase in spending to result in full employment levels of production.

33. Believing that interest rate swaps will significantly affect total spending and engaging in them in lieu of undertaking income-increasing policies that would actually encourage an increase in production and employment

34. Allowing large financial traders such as Goldman Sachs to quickly obtain the status of commercial banks when they needed to be bailed out and then allowing them to quickly leave that status so they can avoid the Federal Reserve's reserve and reporting requirements.

35. Bailing out foreign commercial banks such as Deutsche Bank so they would have enough capital and reserves to cover their trading desk losses and unpaid bonuses while standing idly by while United States commercial banks failed because they did not have enough capital and reserves.

36. Bailing out domestic and foreign financial institutions on the condition that they use the funds to repay debts to companies in which the Treasury Secretary had a significant interest.

37. Attempting to influence the exchange rate between the yuan and the dollar even though it has been more than thirty years since such actions became unnecessary because the dollar is free to float against other currencies in response to market forces.

38. Emphasizing the importance of large financial firms and the financial markets instead of commercial banks and the consumers, employers, and governments buying and hiring in the labor and product markets.

39. Giving in to Treasury pressure to hold down interest rates in order to hold down the interest component of the federal budget. The goal of the Federal Reserve is to keep the economy prosperous, not to make the re-financing of the Treasury easier and make federal spending look smaller.

40. Standing idly by while the boards of the regional Federal Reserve banks appoint unqualified presidents who will sit on the FOMC with

the governors. Members of the FOMC need to be macroeconomic specialists with real world experience in business or commercial banking.

41. Implementing the self-dealing requests of Treasury officials even though they have blatant conflicts of interest.

42. Encouraging the federal government to channel funds created by the Federal Reserve to the IMF and World Bank whose real-world primary goals appear to be the funding highly paid bureaucracies and actions that encourage wasteful spending and useless reforms.

43. Listening to the Secretary of the Treasury who is traditionally a lobbyist from one of the large investment banking houses and who, inevitably, has neither any knowledge of macroeconomics nor any experience or interest in the real world of commercial banking and business.

44. Making policies to increase spending based on the grossly inaccurate official rate of unemployment instead of a significantly more accurate unemployment rate derived from labor force participation rates.

45. Considering stock and financial market levels and fluctuations to be significant indicators of the state and direction of the economy.

46. Ignoring the fact that foreign banks are increasingly accepting dollar deposits and using them as reserves in fractional reserve systems so that the overall supply of dollars increases without the Federal Reserve taking any action.

47. Ignoring the fact that the use of open market purchases with newly created money means the Federal Reserve will accumulate an ever growing stock of unearned assets on which profits could be periodically taken and taxes paid.

48. Ignoring that Federal Reserve open market purchases during a recession may make the financial markets thriving and prosperous

and encourage banks to divert their available loanable funds away from consumers and employers and towards traders and financial institutions.

49. Not understanding the concept of the liquidity trap or the relationship between interest rates and the borrowing of consumers for consumer goods and employers for plant and equipment. They erroneously concluded that expansionary monetary policies will not work once an interest rate minimum is reached because they believed the liquidity trap to be related only to interest rate minimums. In the real world, the provision of additional excess reserves to commercial banks and other profit oriented lenders tends to result in additional loans to consumers and businesses even if the rate of federal bonds approaches zero.

50. Imposing capital requirements that encourage banks to buy federal debt and make short term loans to financial institutions instead of long term loans to consumers and employers.

51. Supporting the continuation of universal banks so that commercial banks can continue to use their deposits and capital to trade and gamble in the financial markets instead of making loans to consumers and employers.

52. Directly flowing newly created money to a handful of specific recipients in the financial markets to protect them and encourage their trading activities instead of systematically increasing the money supply in the real economy by directly and permanently flowing a portion of the increase directly to recipients who are more likely to spend the money to buy newly produced goods and services.

53. Periodically providing one-time increases in the money supply instead constantly flowing new money into the economy as needed to keep it prosperous without shortfalls that result in unemployment or longfalls that result in demand-pull inflations.

54. Believing that new created money injected into the financial system indirectly via open market operations and other activities will actually reach potential lenders and then be used by them to provide money and credit to consumers and employers.

WHY THE FEDERAL RESERVE WENT WRONG.

Once they had bailed out their cronies and interest rates in the financial markets had reached the apparent minimums, the Federal Reserve's governors and regional presidents thought they had done all they could. They held to that view while consumers were losing their personal lines of credit, unemployment and government deficits were growing, employers could not get their working capital lines renewed at any rate of interest, new mortgages and refinancing were extremely difficult to find if they could be found at all; inflation was below the levels normally associated with structural changes, and inappropriate and often unnecessary and unprofitable foreclosures ruined the creditworthiness of millions of consumers.

What the governors actually did was to create many hundreds of billions of new dollars and simultaneously caused them to be deposited in the banks' interest-earning reserve accounts at the Federal Reserve and used to buy federal bonds instead of being loaned out. And much of what the banks did loan out went out as short-term loans to finance speculations and trading in the derivative and currency markets instead of to consumers and employers. And all the while the commercial banks and shadow banks were deleveraging so that the supply of money and credit was collapsing.

The Federal Reserve Chairman, who was reappointed for his efforts to help the "too-bigs" while the economy collapsed, has since claimed it was necessary to directly flow money to the handful of large banks and partnerships identified by the Secretary of the Treasury in order to prevent a "financial meltdown." And he is correct. Such a meltdown might have occurred had the "too-bigs" been forced default on their obligations. After all, their inability to pay their debts might have brought down other banks and institutions.

In any event, their victims and pragmatic analysts, knowing that properly implemented monetary policies can expand total spending and restore full employment without causing inflation, are entitled to ask why the Treasury and the Congress, and particularly the Federal Reserve, did so little for the rest of the economy for so long that the recession continued for years thereafter and finally morphed into a permanent depression.

Lack of qualifications.

The simple explanation of the failure of the Federal Reserve to end the Great Recession is that its governors and regional presidents simply did not know what to do. A majority of the governors were lawyers and administrators without professional training in economics and not a one had real world experience in business or commercial banking. So they accepted the idea that monetary policy worked by running interest rates up and down and that there is a minimum rate of interest at which point monetary changes stopped working and their hands were tied. They also accepted the idea that money supply increases would inevitably cause inflation.

What they failed to understand is the relationship between the commercial banks and their regulators, that money supply increases need not cause inflation, and that interest rate changes tend to have relatively little impact on consumer and employer spending.

They also failed to understand that the liquidity trap is not just an interest rate phenomenon—that it also occurs when commercial banks and other lenders receive additional money but do not loan it out to consumers and employers for regulatory reasons.

In essence, it was not the existence of a Keynesian interest rate liquidity trap caused by very low interest rates that was a major cause of inadequate consumer and employer spending during the Great Recession—it was the regulatory liquidity trap wherein loanable excess reserves and federal bonds must be held for regulatory reasons and capital requirements are imposed that favor government bonds and short-term loans to traders over long term loans to consumers and employers;

The effect of the regulatory liquidity trap was then exacerbated by the non-enforcement of community reinvestment regulations. That failure enabled the continued diversion of the banks' loanable funds to their own and others' trading activities; and the unemployment and the non-existent regulatory supervision of the ever-growing foreclosures and bankruptcies meant fewer and fewer consumers and employers could meet the regulators' loan requirements;

Moreover the governors were similarly wrong that interest rates had reached a minimum. They reached that conclusion by looking primarily at the rates on federal bonds, the federal funds overnight rates, and the growth of the excess reserves that were parked at the Federal Reserve instead of being loaned out. They thought what they observed meant that there were no borrowers for the additional money they had created.

The problem was that the things the governors and regional presidents looked at were not indicative of the seriously depressed state of economy or the desperate straits of millions of Americans seeking jobs and mortgage refinancing. The federal funds rates were low because banks did not need to borrow reserves—they were responding to the irrelevantly low target rates and the interest payments now being offered by the Federal Reserve by voluntarily holding excess reserves because of the stress tests and the fear of seizure by the FDIC.

Similarly, the federal bond rates were low because their price had been bid artificially and temporarily high—both by banks buying them at the insistence of regulators and because, among other things, federal bonds were considered as one of the few "safe havens" for wealth during Europe's sovereign debt crisis and uncertain future of banks and other financial assets. They were also being bought because they were considered acceptable assets by regulators outside the Federal Reserve conducting "stress tests"—which were frowning upon and carefully scrutinizing loans to consumers and employers.

Moreover, the governors were similarly wrong about the relationship between interest and consumer and business spending. They wrongly thought interest rates are a major determinant of consumer and investment spending. As pragmatic analysts know, it is the availability of credit and the repayment terms that dominate such employment generating spending decisions in the real world, not relatively minor changes in the level of interest rates.

Regulatory capture and other explanations of the Federal Reserve's failures.

The root source of the Federal Reserve's failures can be summed up as resulting from a combination of regulatory capture by the Treasury Secretary and the Federal Reserve staff; lack of experience in business and commercial banking; inadequate economic educations resulting in reliance on inaccurate "common knowledge" and inappropriate data; a lack of ethics that caused some to accept positions they knew they were not qualified to fill; and weak personalities such that they let equally unqualified and self-serving Treasury and Wall Street officials influence their decisions.

How could this happen? There are no educational or business or commercial banking experience requirements for a political appointment to be a Federal Reserve governor or regional president. Typically the governors come from the academic world or are political activists who have served in the Federal Reserve and Treasury bureaucracies and whose candidacies are supported by the leaders of handful of New York investment banks. Similarly, the regional presidents typically come from the regional bank bureaucracies. Rarely, if ever, have a majority of the governors been trained macroeconomists with real world business or commercial banking experience.

Traditionally the committee's decisions are dominated by the chairman of the governors who is appointed into that position by the President and confirmed by the Senate. The policy-setting Open Market committee traditionally adopts the Chairman's policies, however unworldly and inadequate the committee members think they might be.

Accordingly, in the real world it is the Chairman of the Federal Reserve governors (and those who influence him if he is weak or inadequately trained) who determines the monetary policies of the United States and, thus, the degree to which the country is prosperous *or not*. When the chairman is weak, untrained, or unworldly the governors and regional presidents inevitably make bad decisions and the United States has recessions, depressions, and inflations; when he or she is strong, trained, and worldly the United States has prosperity, growth, and stable prices.

Indeed, because the economy is so important both domestically and internationally, many pragmatic analysts consider the chairman of the Federal Reserve to be the most powerful person in the country, more important to the prosperity and international standing and wealth of the country than the President and Congress combined.

The central bank competency index.

Perhaps the best a pragmatic analyst or concerned politician can do to "scientifically" evaluate and compare the income changes and other macro problems caused by monetary policy incompetents is to develop an outcomes based index by which to evaluate their competency by comparing their score to those of their peers around the world and their predecessors. Here is such a competency index developed by Guenter Conradus to evaluate the competency of the President and the Chairman and governors he or she appoints:

GIR= 2(CPI) + 15(U-3) +15(4-Yr) + 60(71-LFP) + 5(20-BD) + 2(-1+TD) where GIR is the governors incompetency rating, CPI is the average annual percentage increase in the Consumer Price Index, LFP is the highest percentage of labor force participation in the past 20 years, U is the average annual unemployment rate accurately calculated using historical labor force participation rates during the latest period of sustained prosperity, Yr is the average annual percentage increase in per capita real income, BD is the percentage of real income going to the bottom twenty percent of the population, and TD is the percentage of real income going to the top one percent of the population.

Thus, for example, the incompetency index for the President and Chairman would be 409 if the actions of the President's governors during the past year resulted in the CPI rising five percent (10); the actual unemployment rate averaging sixteen percent (195); per capita real income rising two percent (30); the labor force participation rate averaging sixty nine percent (120); the bottom forty percent of the people ending the year with sixteen percent of the income (20); and the top one percent of people ending the year with eighteen percent of the income (34). Competent appointees would have a number rating close to zero.

The annual ratings of the Federal Reserve governors and regional presidents in office during the "Great Recession" were a series of record highs in the hundreds. This suggests to pragmatic analysts that if the individual governors and regional presidents were traded on a market as one of Goldman's "synthetics" they would be sold short; if they were sold in a store that was still open they would have been well past their sell-by date; if they were a business they would be bankrupt; and if they did not have bureaucratic sinecures they would be unemployed.

SUMMARY

I.   Policy makers do not have to depend on fiscal policies to achieve full employment levels of total spending. Monetary and other policies can be used instead. Macro-pragmatic economists prefer monetary policy because fiscal policy requires abilities beyond those of most policy makers and typically takes too long to implement.

II.   The implementation of monetary policy generally takes the form of open market operations wherein the central bank creates new money and flows it into the economy indirectly using newly created money to buy assets in the open market from any seller willing to sell. The newly created money is then inevitably deposited into a commercial bank or other transactions depository.

III. Reserve requirement changes are a potent weapon in terms of increasing and decreasing the excess (loanable) reserves of commercial banks. Such changes are rarely used in the United States because the primary function of reserve requirements is to control the supply of money and credit.

IV. Capital requirements are intended to give the bank owners "enough skin in the game" so they do not make excessive and risky loans.

V. Interest rate swaps occur when the Federal Reserve tries to encourage the lower long term interest rates its unworldly governors believe will encourage them to make loans to borrowers instead of buying government bonds. Basically the Federal Reserve sells short term federal debt and buys long term federal debt with the proceeds. Thus the interest rate on the long term debt tends to go down without an increase in the money supply. The results have ranged from inconsequential to negligible.

VI. Paying interest on reserves deposited with the Federal Reserve encourages banks to deposit money with the Federal Reserve instead of making commercial loans. It discourages spending to buy goods and services. Even so, "to help the banks" the Federal Reserve began paying interest during the Great Recession.

VII. The big banks' use of its capital and deposit monies to engage in proprietorial trading, instead of loaning it out to borrowers, is thought by analysts to be a major cause of the Great Recession and the slow recovery from it. It is again being banned because a handful of large banks suffered such huge losses when there were big and unexpected swings in the financial markets that they needed special assistance to avoid failing.

VIII. The Keynesian liquidity trap occurs when interest rates in an economy become so low that banks and lenders will hold any money they receive rather than use it to buy financial assets or make loans to consumers and employers; the regulatory liquidity trap occurs when lenders hold or disperse any money they receive to meet regulatory requirements rather than loan it out to consumers and employers.

IX. The Federal Reserve has periodically created new money and used it to bail out large financial firms who made bad bets gambling on the future prices of financial assets. Pragmatic economists think a portion of the annual increase in the money supply inherent in a dynamic economy could be better injected directly via transfers to high marginal propensity to consume recipients.

X.   The Federal Reserve governors and regional presidents mad numerous mistakes of commission and omission.

XI. The most likely explanation for poor monetary policies is inadequate economics training and regulatory capture resulting from weak personalities and the lack of real world experience in business and commercial banking.

XII. The Federal Reserve chairman is more important to the wealth and prosperity of the United States economy and its place in the world than the President and Congress combined.

XIII. An outcomes based competency index measures the degree to which the competency of one set of government policy makers compares to those of others.

CHAPTER EIGHTEEN

OTHER POLICIES TO FIGHT INFLATION AND RECESSIONS

Conventional monetary and fiscal policies are the traditional responses when an economy has problems such as inflation, unemployment and slow rates of growth. Inevitably, however, and usually when the monetary and fiscal policy decision makers fail to undertake appropriate actions in a timely manner, well-meaning and other politicians and "experts" rush to demand that "something be done." Sometimes this involves the implementation of conventional fiscal policies in the sense of general cuts or increases in taxes, transfers, and government spending; often, however, it involves pursuing other policies. Among them:

Manipulating international trade to increase total spending.

Selling more to foreigners and buying less from them is usually one of the first things politicians and economic decision makers consider when the level of spending in their economy is too low to generate full employment. And, if it is available to them, one of the first things they then think about is changing the exchange rate of their currency. In essence, any government controlling the rate at which its money exchanges with the money of other economies can change its exchange rate—to reduce the amount of their own money foreigners need to obtain the local money needed to buy local products.

Changing the exchange rate to *devalue* your currency makes your domestically produced goods and services less expensive to foreigners and their products more expensive to the people, employers, and governments in your economy. Countries such as the United States do not have this option open to them because their exchange rates are allowed to fluctuate in response to market forces. They can, however, attempt to force countries who do have fixed exchange rates, such as China, to change them.

Alternately, an economy might do various things to encourage or force its people and businesses to reorient their spending away from foreign-made goods and services and towards those produced by its own employers. For example, it might impose import quotas or raise its tariff barriers in order to encourage its purchasers to buy at home instead of buying imports.

At one time or another over the years United States and most other countries have attempted to pursue such "beggar thy neighbor" policies—trying to increase their domestic sales and put their unemployed workers back to work by selling more to foreign buyers and spending less abroad (beggar thy neighbor: our workers go to work; theirs go on unemployment). It sounds good and quotas and tariffs can actually help a particular business or industry whose foreign competitors are disadvantaged. But it rarely works for the economy as a whole—because the other countries retaliate with their own exchange rate changes and quotas and tariffs.

The United States had such experience in the early 1970s when the dollar still had a fixed exchange rate against other currencies. The federal government responded to a balance of payments deficit and a rise in unemployment by blaming it on imports from Japan and other countries—even though the United States at the time was selling more abroad than it was buying. So Congress took steps to "protect American jobs" by cutting imports. These involved putting a tariff surcharge on top of the tariffs already being levied on imports and engaging in a series of exchange rate changes to "devalue" of the dollar.

It did not work very well. The initial result was an even greater balance-of-payments deficit, a relatively modest increase in the level of sales to foreigners, and inflation as the higher prices Americans had to pay increased the cost of living and triggered cost of living wage increases that forced employers to raise their prices.

The payments deficit grew because American customers could not find similarly-priced substitutes for many of the now more expensive foreign-made products. In effect, the new exchange rates caused United States' customers to pay more dollars for the goods and services they purchased from the foreign employers who produced them. For example, the devaluation caused Americans to have to pay thirty percent more dollars for each Japanese and German car and caused them to buy about ten percent fewer cars; so in this industry alone the devaluation increased the total amount of dollars flowing to foreigners by about twenty percent, so the United States balance of payments got worse. In other words, devaluing a currency may worsen a balance of payments deficit and cause its consumers and other buyers to have to pay higher prices for what they buy—inflation.

There are two inflation-related results of such new and lower exchange rates: first, foreign-produced products cost more dollars to buy so the cost-of-living index rises. Second, the prices of American-made products rises because of the increased foreign demand for American-made products that occurs if foreigners respond to the new exchange rates by buying more. In effect, if devaluation works, consumers and businesses in an economy whose exchange rate is devalued are left to pay higher prices for fewer products. In other words, the general level of prices went up and the amount of goods and services available to Americans went down. Most analysts would not call that a good outcome.

On the other hand there may also be less unemployment as foreign spending increases and American buyers shift back to American-made cars and other products. Other unemployment-reducing forces may also be set in motion. For example, the United States' devaluation of the dollar in the 1970s motivated the Japanese to begin setting up assembly plants in the United States.

Similarly in effort and outcome, during Europe's "Sovereign Debt Crisis" recession in the early 21st century, virtually every country in the European Economic Community (EEC) undertook various actions to encourage its consumers to buy at home and its employers to export more to the other EEC countries and further abroad. The United States was in the midst of its own "Great Recession" at the same time and did the same thing. Greece's inevitable response is the most extreme—it will literally go off the euro and re-introduce its own currency in order to avoid making the reforms which might enable its economy to become more viable. In effect, by not engaging in the tedious job of making its economy more productive and prosperous, the Greek leaders appear are choosing for Greece have its own currency whose exchange rate they can change.*

Pragmatic analysts saw the Greek abandonment of the euro as inevitable, and not just because of its sclerotic government and economy. Initially Greece had trouble joining the euro block because its annual deficits and national debt were considered too high relative to its level of income to be able to service its debts. Europe resolved that problem by allowing Greece to submit a revised application which increased Greece's income by twenty five percent—by adding the value of the prostitution and money laundering services the economy produced.

In the past, the traditional way countries attempted to sell more abroad has been to change their exchange rates so that the products of their employers would require less foreign money to buy—in effect, making their currencies cheaper. A cheap currency giving an artificial boost to competitiveness is, after all, on balance more palatable than a recession. And it doesn't hurt anyone except tourists going abroad and those who want to buy foreign goods and services instead of buying domestic products. During the Great Recession this solution was not open to the United States because it had earlier adopted a freely floating exchange rate. It also was not open to the European countries which adopted the euro and so no longer have the power to change their exchange rates to increase their exports and decrease their imports.

The efforts of the United States to implement trade-related policies to increase its exports and shift Americans from buying abroad to buying at home did not stop after it allowed the dollar to float. In response to the Great Recession and the political pressures to "do something" Congress delayed approving bilateral trade agreements in fear that producers in the other country would end up selling more to the United States than United States employers would sell to them; and

A major effort was made to appropriate money to the government-owned United States Export-Import Bank so it could provide (read subsidize) low interest financing for exporters, particularly Boeing for the sale of new commercial airliners; and

Funds were made available to the IMF and ECB so they could loan them to countries that wanted more dollars to spend; quotas to limit the importation of items such as sugar were reaffirmed; and

Special financing was provided to countries such as Iraq and Israel so they could buy American-made fighter planes and military goods; and the list goes on and on.

Concurrently, to fight inflation by holding down energy costs and, particularly, the domestic price of gasoline, serious political pressure was put upon countries such as Saudi Arabia to increase their oil output so that the price of the oil the United States was importing would come down and the tariffs levied to keep out imports of energy, such as ethanol from Brazil, were eliminated.

Does it work? In the real world trade-related efforts to "export the recession" by getting foreigners to buy more from your country's employers, instead of from their own, tend to be zero-sum games designed to benefit a favor few beneficiaries with influential lobbyists—because the other countries almost always retaliate.

But they do not always retaliate when a currency is undervalued. For years China successfully fixed an under-valued exchange rate for the yuan against the dollar without an American response. This encouraged Americans to buy Chinese products because it took relatively few dollars to get enough yuan to buy them—and discouraged the Chinese from buying American products because it took lots of yuan to get enough dollars to buy them. Throughout the Great Recession Americans spent more than three dollars in China for every dollar the Chinese spend in the United States.

The Chinese were able to maintain the rate by accumulating the dollars that poured in to buy Chinese products instead of allowing them to be spent. The United States went along with the resulting trade imbalance both for political reasons and because it meant less expensive goods for the Americans to buy (Walmart and Apple were among the biggest importers and resellers of consumer goods made in China).

Overall, it has been suggested by some analysts, the undervalued Chinese yuan may have reduced domestic spending in the United States by about one percent. The reduction was heavily concentrated in United States consumer goods manufacturing. Estimates of the American jobs that would be lost from such a net loss of spending range from several hundred thousand to three million. But that is nothing to worry about because except with proper Federal Reserve monetary policies total spending to buy American-made goods can be increased to fully offset the loss. Then the United States would be even richer—it would have all its production plus some of China's.

One way to put the relatively inconsequential impact of Chinese imports in perspective, even if the Federal Reserve fails to act, is to note that American employers need a one percent increase in spending every 60 or so days just to keep up with America's productivity increases associated with its population growth, capital accumulation, and new technologies.

Another way to look the annual damage China's policy of exporting to the United States does to American jobs *if the Federal Reserve does not act does not increase spending* is that it is the equivalent of about five percent of the total unemployment caused by the poor policies of the Federal Reserve which result in too-low levels of total spending. The conceptual difference, of course, is that Americans get valuable products from China and only unemployment and ruination from the Federal Reserve's governors and regional presidents.

In other words, instead of the Federal Reserve's Chairman going to China to berate the Chinese into changing their exchange rates, he and the governors, and the president who appointed them and the senators who confirmed them, should look in the mirror and shout at themselves for not implementing proper monetary policies.

**Evaluating international trade as a solution
for recessions and depressions.**

Selling abroad is a major source of income for the employers of many prosperous smaller economies such as those of Sweden, Norway, and Denmark. Those economies that have not adopted the euro can change their exchange rates and, in so doing, significantly affect their spending and employment. Moreover, because they are relatively small, the larger countries are not so likely to be significantly impacted and retaliate.

The United States is different. Foreigners only buy about ten percent of the goods and services produced by the economy's employers. Thus, for example, if a major and hugely successful effort to sell more abroad produced a twenty percent increase in the dollar volume of sales to foreigners it would increase total purchasing in the United States by two percent—enough to buy the growth in output that occurs every 120 days or so.

To put that in perspective, the United States needs to increase its total spending in nominal money terms five or six percent per year just to stay even with its increased production capacity and the upward drift in prices as the structure of its economy evolves. In other words, more sales abroad is always helpful but it's hardly sufficient to pull an economy out of a Great Recession when twenty percent or so of the economy's production capacity is idled due to a lack of total spending.

Put yet another way, the maximum impact on total spending of all the trade agreements that Congress has debated so hotly for the past few years is probably, at its worst or best, the equivalent to about ten days of the spending growth needed to keep pace with the growth of the economy's production capacity. In other words, all the political angst and hot air and votes probably has less of an impact than the Federal Reserve chairman casually suggesting to the head of the Open Market Desk that he or she "go easy on loosening up for another day or two."

The European experience. Europe's sovereign debt crisis began with Greece running out of money. Successive Greek governments had been borrowing extensively to pay government salaries and the subsidies it offered to its extremely over-regulated and unproductive economy. Finally, Greece reached the point where it could no longer find lenders willing to loan it more euros; it could no longer pay its bills. The result was a real fear throughout Europe, and particularly at a handful of big European banks, that Greece would default on the euro bonds they bought and that such a sovereign debt default would contagiously spread to other euro-using countries; then they too would not be able to cover their budget deficits and finance their ever-increasing national debts.

To forestall the contagion, at least until their own banks' loans to Greece were repaid, the members of the euro block clubbed together to find money to loan to Greece so it could cover its current budget deficit and, more importantly, repay their banks. To make the new loans politically feasible to Germany, the most prosperous country in Europe and biggest source of the new monies, the lenders required Greece to cut its spending and increase its taxes—so that Greece would not need to borrow so much in the future.

The Greek government promised a lot and partially complied in order to keep getting euros to cover its deficit. As an astute analyst might expect, the reduced government spending and higher taxes caused total spending to fall. Greece then promptly sank into a severe recession with massive unemployment—which cut its tax collections and made its deficit and borrowing needs even worse.

At that point Greece was in a recession due to a lack of spending with no additional money for spending increases on the horizon. Worse, the Greek economy was literally paralyzed—because previous Greek governments effectively prohibited competition in virtually every industry, supported millions of make-work government jobs, and had a policy of preventing potential employers from starting new businesses and existing businesses from engaging in employee layoffs no matter what the circumstances.

Some idea of the magnitude of the problems the Greek leaders did not want to tackle is suggested by the fact that Greece still tries to protect virtually every public and private employer from competition. After years of painful cuts in spending Greece still has about nine times as many public employees per capita as bureaucratic Britain. That is why it is inevitable, unless Greece massively reduces its regulation-induced stagnation and allows its tax base to grow, that Greece is going off the euro and that its new currency will be devalued relative to the euro to cut the purchasing power of Greek salaries and the cost of doing business in and with Greece. Other similarly sclerotic euro-using countries are sure follow.

Incomes policies.

A government "incomes policy" attempts to prevent cost-push inflation by limiting wage increases. More specifically, it is a policy of tying wage increases that increase workers' incomes to the increases in their productivity. The basis for such a policy is the ill-founded belief that higher wages will not cause cost-push inflation and unemployment *if they are accompanied by sufficient increases in worker productivity.*

In the past the United States' government, in an attempt to prevent wage increases from causing cost-push inflation and unemployment, has at times estimated the average annual increase in labor productivity and then either attempted to persuade or to force workers and employers to agree to wage increases that do not exceed the productivity estimate. Supposedly, if workers receive wage increases that do not exceed the government's productivity estimates, there is no reason for employers to raise the prices because their costs per unit of production will not be higher.

The use of productivity estimates as guidelines for noninflationary wage increases, however, may be an exercise in futility which merely causes any inflation and unemployment that does occur to be wrongly attributed to factors unrelated to higher wage costs. In the real world, cost-push inflation might well occur because of differential gains in labor productivity.

For example, the productivity of an economy's hair stylists might not rise in a given year whereas the productivity of its autoworkers rises ten percent because of new capital investments and improved technologies.

Then, if the government's estimate of the overall productivity increase is estimated to be 3.8 percent both the autoworkers and the hair stylists will be urged (read pressured by the government) to accept increases that do not exceed 3.8 percent.

It sounds reasonable—but a 3.8 percent increase in the wages of the hair stylists without a productivity increase means a 3.8 percent increase in the labor cost of producing hair services. Then the hair styling shops will only provide such services if they can price their services higher to cover their higher costs.

On the other hand, a 3.8 percent increase for auto workers means no increase in the labor costs of each vehicle they produce but, due to the tendency for prices in the real world to be inflexible downward, the prices of cars may not fall. Then there would be inflation: because if prices hair dressers and others charge rise and the prices of automobiles and other products stay the same, then the average price in the economy will increase—inflation.

In the real world, wage-push inflation and unemployment can be avoided under an "incomes policy" only if increases in the prices of the goods and services experiencing higher labor costs are offset by reductions in the prices of products whose labor costs decline. In many industries, particularly those in the state and local government sector such as where employers produce such things as police services and street repairs, there apparently is not enough competition among employers to cause the required off-setting price reductions. Moreover, the government pressure typically has been concentrated on holding wage increases within the guidelines, not on encouraging price reductions where productivity has increased faster than the average.

In essence, any price increase that occurs because productivity has increased slower than the guideline rate may not be offset by price reductions where productivity has increased faster. In other words, *an economy's general level of prices may be pushed up by higher wages even if every wage increase is within the government's productivity guidelines.* Worse, the higher prices will tend to cause unemployment—unemployed hair stylists for example

Open Mouth Policies.

If you are a corporate executive, government official, or labor union leader there is nothing more painful than finding yourself or your organization publically pilloried by politicians and the media suggesting investigations and retribution because you have done something they or their supporters do not like, such as raising prices or laying off workers. No employer wants the bad press and notoriety; so quite often when politicians and regulators threaten and complain the initial price increase or whatever other action triggered the response is delayed or modified.

In the United States, for example, presidents and members of Congress have periodically browbeaten both union and business leaders into holding down wage and price increases. Under certain circumstances such "open mouth operations" can be just as effective as the Federal Reserve's open market operations in holding down price increases and preventing layoffs and plant closures that would otherwise contribute to inflation and unemployment.

And it plays both ways—employers looking for special benefits such as tax breaks and reduced regulations and price increase routinely threaten to pack up and move unless they get them. Similarly, the managers of government employers such as city bus lines and school districts often announce cutbacks and layoffs just before their budgets are submitted and the public votes on tax increases. Analysts interested in such events can search publications such as the *Economist* or the *Financial Times* or the *Wall Street Journal* and find a constant stream of them.

Interventions and controls.

The "open mouth" efforts of the 1960s were not particularly successful so by the early 1970s attempts were made to use rigid price and wage controls to stop inflation which by then had reached levels not seen since the Civil War. They were never fully carried out, perhaps because just the possibility that they might occur led to employers quickly increasing their prices, and sometimes wages, so that if they were frozen, they would be frozen at higher levels. Indeed, the possibility of wage and price controls caused one of the greatest periods of inflation in American history. (The greatest single monthly price increase in American history occurred in the month *after* the Nixon-Ford administration announced it would seek price controls to prevent inflation.)

A second and significant drawback to the use of controls is that they have the same impact as a serious recession—they tend to delay the changes in individual prices and wages relative to one another. These changes are important because they are needed to efficiently allocate labor and capital into the most efficient production processes and toward the goods and services that are most desired by purchasers.

And finally, the subsequent removal of the controls has the same effect as ending a severe recession—it tends to result in a burst of wage and price changes as the economy's subsequent recovery and growth releases the pent up changes inherent in the new products and technologies that are changing its structure—and that's not good if it causes decision makers in an economy to respond inappropriately to "fight" the inflation by cutting spending.

In the United States, for example, there is every reason to expect some individual prices to adjust upward when the United States finally gets out of its current Great Recession and prosperity and full employment are restored. Analysts can only hope that the knowledge of the Federal Reserve governors has been sufficiently updated by the time that occurs—so that they do not react to the one-time burst of structurally generated price increases with a general tightening of the money supply that causes yet another recession to further blot their reputations.

Targeted assistance programs.

Targeted assistance programs are efforts to reduce unemployment by helping specific employers and specific groups of unemployed workers. Quite often the primary government response to unemployment has been to succor those who are adversely affected rather than to implement monetary and fiscal policies to eliminate the problem and get them back to work.

Thus, for example, a complex unemployment insurance program has evolved to provide relief to unemployed people such as those who lose their jobs because of inadequate aggregate demand. During the Great Recession one of the primary responses of the United States government was to launch and expand a host of new programs to help the unemployed, both directly and by encouraging employers to hire more workers.

One such program involved substantially extending the number of weeks unemployed people could draw unemployment benefits. An unemployment insurance payment does partially alleviate the distress of an unemployed person. But it typically does not provide as much income as the individual was previously earning. Thus, reliance on such "direct assistance" programs in lieu of policies to increase total spending results in even less spending and, thus, fewer goods and services being produced than could be produced.

Other programs during the Great Recession involved retraining unemployed workers so they could find employment in new jobs. In 2010 over $14 billion was spent by 49 different federal job training programs administered by nine agencies—a fraction of the hundreds of billions provided to Citibank and Goldman but still a lot of money. Unfortunately the United States was mired in a recession so there were no jobs for most of the unemployed when their retraining was completed. The programs did, however, provide work for thousands of grant writers, instructors, and bureaucrats. In essence, recession-generated job training programs that actually put people back to work are hard to find—until monetary and fiscal policies are used to increase spending and put people back to work and they are no longer needed.

Numerous other specific programs were implemented or expanded during the Great Recession. The total fiscal effort according to the White House was $787 billion dollars of additional federal spending over and above the much bigger efforts of the Federal Reserve to help the "favored few." Among the things Congress and the White House provided in response to the need to "do something:" special subsidies to encourage consumers to buy cars that get better mileage; loans to solar energy companies that promptly went broke; assumption of the pension responsibilities of companies that would otherwise have lower profits or go broke; special tax breaks for drilling oil wells; increased payments not to grow crops and subsidies to buy the crops that are produced at higher-than-market prices; and special low income tax rates on hedge funds on the premise that they contribute something to the nation's prosperity. The actual list is very much longer.

Similarly, on the premise that it was "necessary to promote exports and remove a threat to the creation of American jobs" Congress funded the government operated Export-Import Bank to do such things as provide Chinese airlines the low cost financing they needed to buy long range Boeing airliners so they could compete against Delta Airlines on the long Mumbai to New York run; put up some of the money the Treasury used to bail out a handful of big banks such as Morgan Stanley and Goldman Sachs so they could pay the bonuses earned selling the derivatives whose prices crashed; sent money to the IMF so that it could help finance the bailout of the European banks that loaned money to Greece and keep advising countries to cut spending and raise taxes even though it would plunge them deeper into recessions; and gave money to the World Bank so it could hire more bureaucrats and help African officials provide jobs for their people and new Ferraris for their sons by providing them with more money to spend on the grandiose dams and railroads that rarely get completed but are so beloved of the World Bank's bureaucrats.

The total amount of money the federal government put into the stimulus effort is reported to be $787 billion. But would that much additional government money be significant even it did not take years to work its way into the economy? $787 billion sounds impressive—but it is not. During the first five years of the recession the shortfall in total spending needed to keep the economy at full employment appears to have been about fifteen trillion dollars—more than twenty times the amount of the one-shot "stimulus."

To put the situation in perspective, consider that during that during those years the economy's production capacity grew by trillions of dollars as the working age population increased and new technologies continually came on line. Accordingly, a one-time $787 billion and its multiplier effect on total spending looks to be short of even being putting the economy's increased production capacity to work—leaving the contribution of the stimulus toward the total spending increase needed to end the recession at *less than zero*.

In any event, pragmatic analysts are rather doubtful that most of such targeted assistance programs, with the exception of the unemployment insurance benefits, actually result in much income trickling down to the real economy to help reduce unemployment; but they do provide marvelous photo opportunities for the politicians who are "doing something" and a semblance of legitimacy under which Congress and the White House can reward their political supporters and contribution-generating lobbyists.

Confidence building activities to encourage spending.

In the real world expectations play a major role in the decisions of employers and consumers to buy goods and services. Little wonder then that the leaders of national governments go out of their way to see light at the end of the tunnel and prosperity right around the corner. Sometimes people even believe them and spend more money. Other specific actions are also possible to build buyer confidence. Among those that might be undertaken for the United States:

Increasing the size of the bank deposits covered by the FDIC's deposit insurance program might be helpful if people are concerned that their bank or savings and loans might close;

Guaranteeing that Social Security benefits and approved private pension benefits will always be fully and promptly paid could encourage seniors and disabled people to spend more today because they are less worried about having enough money to buy food and shelter in the future;

Monetizing (paying off) all or part of the national debt with newly created money could be helpful if people are concerned or confused about the size and significance of the national debt. For example, the Federal Reserve has accumulated a huge amount of unearned assets in the form of federal debt as a by-product of its creation of the additional money supply needed by the ever-growing American economy. The Federal Reserve could literally tear up a trillion or so of those bonds and dramatically reduce the national debt in an instant.

Or the Federal Reserve (or Treasury) could, if the United States really falls out with China, print one green piece of paper with a President's picture and a lot of zeros and mail it to China to pay off *all* the federal bonds China has accumulated by manipulating its exchange rate to encourage export sales to the United States and dollar inflows to China.

The Federal Reserve could conceptually take such an action with China or any other country. Pragmatic analysts do not necessarily recommend it—but it is a delicious thought that the Chinese people earned incomes, the Americans got inexpensive goods, and the Chinese Communist Party ended up with a single piece of green paper.

Fight inflation by increasing competition and deregulation.

Ever since Adam Smith wrote in the 1700s it has been recognized that cartels and government regulators can reduce competition and cause inflation by raising their prices. They do so by either restricting production to hold down supply or by setting the prices of goods and services higher. It therefore follows that encouraging competition and ending price fixing and price increasing regulations can fight inflation.

The United States' airline industry is a case in point. Until late in the twentieth century its prices were fixed by federal bureaucrats and competitors were not allowed to enter the industry. Then the depression-era price fixing agency was eliminated. We all know the results—ticket prices fell and employment in the industry boomed as the number of travelers doubled and redoubled and doubled again.

Other price reductions to fight inflation could be accomplished by similarly allowing competition for many of the other goods and services whose prices are currently fixed or influenced by the government—Milk? Local taxi and bus services? Hospitals that must get a certificate of necessity before they build? Cable television licenses that prevent new entrants? Requiring a law degree for the provision of various services that can be done by a typist? The list goes on and on.

All the prices the government fixes inevitably have something in common—their prices are always fixed and influenced under the guise of somehow helping the public. But in reality they are fixed and influenced to protect employers who don't want to compete. They are low hanging fruit for a fight against inflation.

Increase prices to fight unemployment.

Perhaps the silliest income stabilization policy ever undertaken by any government was the United States' efforts to end the depression of the 1930s by increasing product prices at a time when there was massive employment and people were literally starving to death. The economy was stuck in a great depression and many people were homeless and did not even have money to buy food. The policy to increase prices apparently came about because an advisor to the President pointed out that prices tended to be high when the country was prosperous. It therefore followed, it was thought, that the way to restore prosperity was to increase prices.

The National Recovery Administration (NRA) was set up in the 1930s to do just that. (Apparently the idea that higher prices would cause even fewer items to be purchased and result in even fewer workers being employed did not occur to the Congress, the White House, or the new NRA appointees.)

In one of its most famous failures among many, the NRA officials tried to set the prices of pigs higher. That failed because pig farmers, desperate for cash, were selling pigs to hungry people for prices below those which the NRA decreed. Something had to be done. So in the midst of starvation and massive unemployment caused by inadequate levels of total spending, the NRA began killing hundreds of thousands of pigs so they could not be sold.

The pig killings were so outrageous in the face of hungry people that it was stopped. But many other NRA price-fixing efforts continue even now. For example, to this day dairy farmers are required to sell their milk at prices set by regional "milk boards" whose members are charged with maintaining milk prices and protecting the profits and prosperity of each region's dairy operators.

In a famous 21st century case during the Great Recession, a milk board charged with setting the prices for all two of the dairies in its region, which prices were at the time apparently the highest in the United States, sued in Federal Court to stop a third dairy from being established in the region on the grounds that the additional milk it would produce would drive down the price of milk towards the national average and in so-doing hurt the incomes of the region's existing dairies. The law is still in effect—two dairies won.

Cutting entitlements.

One of the strangest suggested "cures" for 2008 recession and its attendant budget problems was the call by certain members of the Congress and other "experts" to cut "entitlements." Entitlements in virtually every case were the federal transfers that went to someone other than themselves and their supporters.

Social Security and Medicare are loudly pointed to by those who will not use them because they have significantly larger congressional retirement pensions and medical benefits in their future; farm subsidies by those who represented urban areas; tax breaks for hedge fund owners are routinely castigated by those who do not have money in them; food stamps are denounced by those who still have jobs; and mortgage and student loan relief is attacked as a "moral hazard" by the same banks which asked to be bailed out when their derivative speculations failed.

Each program, even though it is relatively small in a $20 trillion economy, is inevitably alleged to somehow be "unsustainable" without major cuts. And it is true such "entitlements" comprise a majority of all federal expenditures: Social Security and Medicare alone are each about twenty percent of all federal outlays and each is the equivalent of about three percent of total customer spending. But would cutting part of the three percent do much to help the economy prosper? They are, after all, estimated to keep almost half of all Americans over age 65 out of poverty.

Cutting back on programs such Social Security and Medicare would indeed have a major impact on an economy in a recession or depression—it would get worse as the spending of the recipients declines and ripples through the economy via the multiplier effect. As a result, unemployment would rise, production decline, tax collections fall, and more people forced to take early retirement and apply for disability assistance and food stamps. Offsetting that, of course, would be the impact of redirecting the "saved" money—with each advocate of cuts inevitably favoring something that would benefit himself or his supporters.

Forcing job openings to fight unemployment.

One of the prevailing views of some American unions and many left-wing European governments is that there is only so much work to be done. Under such circumstances, increased productivity means fewer workers will be needed. Accordingly, one of their answers to the existence of unemployment is to toughen up the "work rules" in union contracts and implement new laws and regulations to prevent the introduction of new technologies or the speeding up of the production process.

Among their other "job-creating" answers are reducing the number of hours in the work week, discouraging overtime by requiring higher wages, imposing additional paid holidays, and lowering the retirement age at which workers can begin drawing pensions. It is a long-standing European solution—the Luddites used it in medieval England, destroying weaving machines in order to save the individual weavers working in their homes.

Such policies can be help reduce employment and they can open up job vacancies to additional workers—but only until the employers can move to a new location where labor can be more efficiently utilized. Some employers, of course, cannot move. A retail store or police department or school district or church, for instance, needs to remain where its customer revenues are located. Such employers are forced to hire additional workers and raise their prices to cover the additional costs. They often do so secure in the knowledge that their competitors, if any, face the same increased costs and will respond with similar price increases; or they close and all their employees become unemployed.

Similarly, if their customers (such as the taxpayers in the case of school districts and police department) will not increase their spending, then layoffs will be forced due to the employer being financially unable to pay the now higher costs of providing services. In other words, unemployment may result from work sharing policies that are intended to create jobs.

The effect of such job creating policies is particularly devastating when employers can move. In the real world it may take a few years but, in the end, employers whose labor costs are significant are likely to relocate their plants and offices to where labor is less expensive. The American automobile industry is a good example. Over time, to escape productivity limiting union work rules and above-market wages, the factories and assembly plants moved out of the unionized and highly regulated Detroit to non-union southern states and to Mexico. And their suppliers then followed.

France provides a poignant example. A few years ago, to create jobs, its President proudly announced a thirty five hour work week in a speech in Northern France. It would, he promised "create more jobs." The very next day the largest employer in Northern France announced it was laying off all of its thousands of French workers and moving its operations to another country so its prices could remain competitive in the world market.

Overall, attempts to force employers to hire more employees by making the existing workers work fewer hours, or making them work less effectively, tend to cause inflation as prices rise to cover the higher costs of the additional workers. They also may cause more unemployment than ever before as fewer goods and services are bought at the higher prices and employers respond by moving to new locations or closing.

Wait for prices to fall and goods to wear out.

There is school of thought whose members think the best policy to restore a recession-afflicted economy to full employment is to adopt no policy at all. Their view is that sooner or later prices will adjust in response to the forces of supply and demand and the economy will recover on its own. This policy, as astute analysts will recall, was the considered in detail by both the Keynesians and their Austrian and Chicago-based opponents.

And the Austrians and Chicagoans are right. Deflation would work—but only occur in a world in which everyone is possessed of perfect knowledge and all goods and services are produced by perfectly competitive employers and bought in perfectly competitive markets by buyers who are perfectly competitive in response to perfectly flexible wages and prices. Their views go back to the days of primitive economies where there was always enough spending because barter occurred so that supply created its own demand. Or, in a slightly more advanced economy, where all savings go into banks and interest rates adjust to insure that all the savings is loaned out and only for the purpose of buying just enough goods and services to offset the depositors' savings. In other words, only imperfect economies, such as that of the United States and every other county in the world, need policies to prevent inflation and unemployment.

A slightly more advanced view is that if an economy waits long enough its capital and durable consumer goods will wear out and spending will then begin to recover because of the pent-up demand for replacements. Then the accelerator and multiplier effects will kick in and spending in the economy will increase. In essence, their position is that the ups and downs of the business cycle are inevitable so nothing, they say; just be patient and things will turn around. The not-so-minor problem with that approach, of course, is that there is no reason to think that the spending increase will start soon or be sufficient to restore full employment or that it will stay at that level if it ever gets there.

In any event, prices and wages in the real world tend to be inflexible downward, and any additional spending that occurs as things begin to wear out may never be enough. And that means there will be unemployment and less than maximum levels of production. The fact that the general level of wages and prices in the United States did not decline during its many years of the Great Recession is sufficient proof for pragmatic analysts to conclude that it is rarely a valid policy decision to do nothing or to wait for enough capital and consumer durable goods to wear our or for prices and wages to decline.

Restrict incoming money to encourage exports.

The simultaneous big recessions in Europe and the United States left their investment banks and hedge funds with significantly fewer opportunities to safely invest their euros and dollars. In search of higher returns and safe places to park their wealth, the investment banks, hedge funds and other traders turned to smaller economies such as those of Switzerland and Brazil which were prosperous and booming.

As a result, a literal tsunami of "hot money" flooded in to buy the Swiss francs and Brazilian reals needed to make local investments and be able to hold wealth in the form of assets that were not likely to depreciate in value. This, in turn, put both countries' exchange rates under pressure to appreciate. Should that have occurred it would have meant that the prices of the goods and services they were exporting would increase dramatically to buyers with foreign currencies and their export sales began to decline.

Switzerland responded, as it traditionally does under such circumstances, by requiring foreign depositors to pay in order to deposit money into Swiss banks; Brazil by levying a tax on incoming money. Switzerland's central bank, at no cost to itself, also created billions of new Swiss francs and exchanged them for foreign currencies so that the exchange rate of the Swiss franc would not rise and make it more difficult for Swiss exports to be sold.

In other words, both countries successfully restricted and soaked up the inflow of foreign currencies in order to prevent the appreciation of their own currency's exchange rate that would have hurt their export sales and caused unemployment. Pragmatic economists around the world saluted their competence; and they looked askance at the policy makers of the countries who screwed up their economies in such a way that the people of Switzerland and Brazil were enriched.

In one of the more amusing demonstrations of economic ignorance about central banks and exchange rates, a *Wall Street Journal* columnist looked at the hundreds of billions of additional foreign currency reserves the Swiss central bank (SNB) was obtaining for Switzerland by creating new Swiss francs and providing them to anyone who wanted them in exchange for the euros and other currencies they possessed. He wrote that the SNB's obtaining ownership of foreign money at no cost to itself in order to help Swiss exporters "reinforces the SNB's credibility in the short run, although if the crisis drags on, the balance sheet could balloon to extraordinary levels, raising risks."

The author never described what the "risks" would be to Switzerland for having more wealth and the world for having more Swiss francs—because he could not. There are none. In essence, the paper misled its readers because its reporter did not understand the role and powers of a central bank.

The *Financial Times* chimed in similarly. It said Switzerland would "pay a price" for getting so many euros in exchange for newly created Swiss francs. It explained that it would be hard for the Swiss to "off load" so many euros "fast enough . . . to rebalance its assets."

What the *Financial Times* did not explain was what the price would be or why a price would have to be paid or why the Swiss central bank would ever have to "offload" the euros or why having euros that it got for free by creating new Swiss francs was somehow a bad thing for the Swiss—it could not because there is no price would ever need to be paid, no offloading that would ever need to occur, and nothing wrong with getting richer. On the other hand, the story was correctly punctuated.

Where does the United States go from here?

After years of being mired in a slowly sinking economy it seems reasonable to conclude that conventional fiscal policies are politically impossible to implement, increasing exports and fiddling with the work week are not viable solutions, and conventional monetary policies will not work once an economy is stuck in a deep depression.

Does that mean the United States economy will never return and we are doomed to limp along forever under dismal auspices of the depression that morphed out of the Great Recession? The answer is an emphatic no.

The United States could quickly and easily, within a matter of a few months, leap forward to full employment and rapid growth—if one or two of the Federal Reserve governors and regional presidents get their act together and start thinking and acting outside their self-imposed policy box.

CHAPTER SUMMARY

I.   Using international trade changes is a traditional governmental response to inflations, unemployment, and low rates of growth.

II.   Changing its exchange rate allows an economy to devalue its currency. That makes its products cheaper to foreign buyers and foreign-made products more expensive to its own buyers.

III. An incomes policy attempts to prevent cost-push inflation by limiting wage increases to increases in productivity. It only works if the prices of products with above average productivity gains are flexible and decline.

IV.	Open mouth policies are efforts to use political and social pressure to prevent worker layoffs and price and wage increases.

V.	Wage and price controls may do more to increase wages and prices than they do to prevent the increases.

VI.	Targeted assistance programs such as "jobs" bills, retraining programs, and extended unemployment benefits are efforts to reduce unemployment by helping specific workers and employers. Except for the unemployment insurance, most take a lot of time to implement and are of little benefit to the economy as a whole or to the great mass of unemployed workers.

VII.	Inflation and unemployment can sometimes be fought by introducing competition and preventing hot money inflows.

VIII.	Programs to reduce unemployment by forcing job openings via requiring shorter work weeks, less overtime, and earlier retirements tend to only work when the employer cannot escape by moving and can charge higher prices to cover the resulting higher costs. Overall, such programs tend to cause both inflation and more unemployment as fewer items are bought at the higher prices and employers move to new locations.

Chapter Nineteen

PRAGMATIC POLICIES TO QUICKLY END RECESSIONS AND INFLATIONS

It is a fact of life that the economy of the United States has changed greatly over the years. One thing that has not changed is that periodically severe inflations and recessions arise and are confronted with the same old ineffective monetary and fiscal policies that yield the same old inadequate results that occurred in the past.

The tragedy is that the United States should not be using ineffective policies and getting inadequate results. Macroeconomic understanding has dramatically progressed in the last hundred years even if the fiscal and monetary policies of the federal government and the Federal Reserve's governors and regional presidents have not. Analysts know their policies are ineffective and their abilities defective because the unnecessary inflations and recessions keep coming.

Sometimes everything works out—extraneous events come to the rescue or the policy makers belatedly do the right thing and the economy recovers. But every so often the implementation of workable policies is not even attempted until it is too late. That occurs when long years of economic distress cause the economy to morph into a chronic condition of subnormal activity without any marked tendency towards recovery. It is called a depression—and there is nothing inherent in the United States' economy that will make one go away by itself.

More specifically, recessions become depressions when the underlying conditions in the economy deteriorate to such an extent that *conventional* monetary policies, should they finally begin to be implemented in sufficient amounts, are no longer capable of restoring what is left of the economy to full employment and high levels of production.

Such a sad and totally unnecessary state of affairs has existed several times in the modern era of the United States.

The first was the Great Depression of the 1930s which ruined the lives of an entire generation of Americans as it dragged on for years until an extraneous fiscal event, the huge increase in spending associated with World War II, finally got the economy fired up and moving again.

The second was the Great Recession which started in 2008 and morphed into the depression that continues to this day—with unemployment in the neighborhood of twenty percent and no big spending increases on the horizon to increase production and turn the country around.

In neither of these great depressions was appropriate monetary and fiscal policies deployed to quickly end them when they first began. But there is a tremendous difference between today and the 1930s. The analysis of entire economies and their problems and policies, macroeconomics, did not even exist as a separate field of study during the initial years of the 1930s depression. Indeed it only came about as a separate field of expertise because the Great Depression motivated economists to try to understand why recessions and depressions occur and what can be done to end them.

In the 1930s the Federal Reserve governors and the congressional makers of fiscal policy could not be expected to understand either the causes of recessions before they evolve into depressions or the policy alternatives available to end them. Today, the causes of recessions, depressions, and inflations are well known—except, it seems, to those who are responsible for preventing them and most of the journalists and "business economists" who write about them.

As a result, instead of enjoying the fruits of continuing prosperity, the United States today remains in the grip of a recession that has morphed into one of the worst depressions in its modern era. It has been going on for more than five years and the failure, both of the Congress and, particularly, of the Federal Reserve's governors and regional presidents, to appreciate the magnitude of the problem, let along to even begin to come to grips with it, is outrageous. Their failure to act has already destroyed the hopes and dreams of many tens of millions of Americans and the legacies of two presidents and the members of three Congresses.

One reason for these failures and the resulting periodic inflations and recessions is that for over one hundred years the Congress and the Federal Reserve System have, for all practical purposes, been getting the same old inadequate results because the same old types of untrained and inexperienced people have been using the same old inappropriate policies in response to the same old obsolete economic theories in the same old ineffective ways based on the same old misleading data. No wonder the United States has continued to have recessions and inflations.

Worse, the United States is now stuck in the second great depression of its modern era and the traditional monetary policies, which once might have quickly propelled the economy back to full employment, are no longer useful—because the Federal Reserve governors waited so long to act that the economy's commercial banks are now in the liquidity trap of regulator-imposed excess reserves and too few qualified spenders remaining. Now there are not enough creditworthy people and employers left who are willing to borrow in order to spend more money no matter what the interest rate or its availability and repayment terms.

So what can be done to end such a depression when an economy is also in the regulatory liquidity trap? And who should do it and who should not?

Those are not simple questions. The reality of a modern economy such as those of the United States and the Scandinavian countries is that it is enormously complex. It does not just have something called an aggregate supply that is being purchased by something called an aggregate demand. It has huge and constantly changing variety of specific goods and services that differ in innumerable ways and are produced by millions of public and private employers in response to hundreds of millions of public and private customers whose desires and abilities are themselves constantly changing.

Moreover, the production arrives at its final customer destinations after money-using processes that involve even more innumerable intermediate transactions that themselves involve the production and distribution of everything from raw materials to complex and interrelated intermediate products and services.

Restoring such a complex economy from the depths of a depression to full employment by picking and choosing a handful of key or too-big-to-fail participants to "help" is an absolute impossibility. In the United States it would require a President or members of Congress or Federal Reserve governors and regional presidents with such infallible knowledge that they can identify the crucial players and fix the entire economy with a few well-chosen regulations and lots of money to bail them out. In the real world such "key players" do not exist and, if history is any guide, neither do the "public servants" and politicians who would be capable of identifying them.

In other words, a one-time bailout of a couple of legacy automobile manufacturers and a handful of too-big-to-fail investment and universal banks is not sufficient to end a recession before it morphs into a major depression. And that is an established fact.

The further proof of the conclusion that neither key participants nor prescient congressmen and Federal Reserve governors and regional presidents exist is suggested by the impact, or lack thereof, that they had on the 2008 recession by effectively limiting their recovery efforts to their patrons, cronies, and political supporters.

To the contrary, because the economy's participants are so numerous and so intertwined, any solution has to be both *all-encompassing* and *massive* and *permanent*. The initial highly targeted one-time response to the beginning of the recession was not any of those things. So years passed and the recession that the Federal Reserve once could have quickly ended became a prolonged and permanent depression.

So the question remains: what can be done to end a depression when an economy is in the liquidity trap? And who should do it and who should not?

CONGRESSIONLY GENERATED POLICIES ARE NOT THE ANSWER

Congress is much more likely to be attuned to the pain and suffering caused by a prolonged depression than the Federal Reserve governors. Its members, after all, have to face the public in periodic elections and are constantly barraged by constituents, lobbyists, and the media. They know when there is a problem.

The Federal Reserve governors, in contrast, tend to have moved from one secure salaried position to another, to say nothing of their typically coming from relatively cloistered academic and bureaucratic environments with secure salaries and pensions and no knowledge or exposure to the real world of business and commercial banking. It is little wonder then that the members of Congress are more likely to feel the heat and want to "do something."

But what can they do? The traditional answer of the Keynesians is for Congress to legislate a massive and permanent increase in public spending—enough to get total spending in the economy up to the level required for full employment and keep it there. That is what Keynes recommended for Britain during the 1930s. And the return of Britain and the United States to full employment occasioned by the massive increase in government spending associated with World War II is proof of the concept's validity.

**More government spending is not a
realistic solution for the United States.**

A massive increase in government spending is conceptually a viable solution when the United States or any other economy is mired in a major depression. That is when conventional monetary policy will not work because any additional liquidity that might be provided will be trapped—held by financial institutions fearful of non-repayment or loaned elsewhere, instead of being loaned out to be spent by consumers and employers in the market areas the banks are licensed to serve.

The not-so-minor problem with a fiscal policy of massively increasing government spending, of course, is that in the real world of 21st century United States it would be politically all but impossible to achieve.

One reason more government spending will not work politically is that the sheer size of the required increase when an economy is trillions short of having enough total spending. That alone would raise political concerns about moving the federal budget into a permanent state of huge deficits and a rapidly increasing national debt. Pragmatic analysts know that such deficits and the ever-growing national debt that would result from them would not be a significant problem. But most congressmen do not know that at all. The realities and nuances of federal finance are beyond them. They know families, businesses, and state and local governments have to balance their budgets and, so far as they know, so does the federal government.

Another reason it will not be acceptable to Congress is that, for better or worse, big appropriations bills tended to be larded with new regulations and give even more powers to the unelected bureaucrats. Many Americans instinctively oppose governments telling them what to do and will demand their representatives support them in their opposition. Many will—if only so that they do not get voted out in the next election and join the unemployed for whom there are no jobs available.

Another reason it may not be politically acceptable is that the members of Congress know that every employer, government, lobbyist, and campaign contributor adversely affected by those regulations will spend months and years fighting the bill in the congressional halls and the courts. Others will spend months and years trying to get a bigger share for themselves and their clients.

In other words, in the real world it is likely to take years for enough members of Congress to come to agreement and pass such a spending bill, if it can be passed at all. And then it might take more years for the spending to actually occur and begin pulling the economy out of the depression.

It is only in a country such as Keynes' Britain where a Keynesian solution of more government spending can be successfully implemented. Fiscal actions move swiftly in Britain because it has a single legislative body and its leader is also the head of the government. In contrast, the United States has two legislative bodies with amending powers and a President with veto powers. In essence, the British political system can design a fiscal racehorse that can rush to victory and end the depression; the American political system is more likely to design a fiscal turtle that would stagger out of the capitol building and be run over by a car full of politicians and Federal Reserve governors on their way to a talk show.

In any event, most pragmatic analysts, after considering the motivations and abilities of the members of Congress, have concluded that trying to implement major spending legislation of a sufficient size is *not* a viable solution. Better, they think, to keep Congress and the federal government benign with taxes and spending that result in a balanced budget at full employment—and use other faster and surer policies to get the additional spending is needed for full employment.

Pragmatic fiscal policies.

The fact that spending and taxing changes are not politically feasible does not mean they would not work *if* they could be implemented. Just because pragmatic analysts accept the concept of a balanced budget at full employment does not mean they do not understand and accept the reasoning of "Functional Finance." To the contrary, they understand that, logically, the primary function of taxes at the national level is to hold down consumer and employer spending so there will be enough production capacity left to produce for the government and its beneficiaries. And they understand that the tax revenues collected to allow the optimum level of total spending may not be the same as the amount of money the government spends on federal purchases and transfers—in other words, that an economy is quite likely to have a budgetary surplus or deficit.

But pragmatic analysts are worldly enough to know that the American political process moves slowly and that that the limited macroeconomic knowledge and experiences of the public and the majority of the members of Congress and White House staff make it unlikely that a majority of them will ever be able to grasp the concepts of functional finance. And even if they did, it is unlikely that a majority of their constituents will understand the concept sufficiently to encourage them to pursue it. *Accordingly, pragmatic analysts reject the functional finance policies of the Keynesians and, instead, advocate what might be called a "pragmatic fiscal policy."*

The pragmatic fiscal policy is simple and non-Keynesian: set tax rates at whatever level will yield a balanced budget at full employment. In other words, do what is necessary to placate the politicians and then do something else to achieve that full employment level of income. It means accepting the twin realities that the American political process moves too slowly and that the average politician is not capable of understanding or implementing the fiscal activities required for functional finance. In other words, *the pragmatists think an economy's policy makers should not even consider trying to use government spending, transfers, and taxes to achieve full employment.*

Yes, fiscal policy would undoubtedly work if properly applied. But pragmatic economists believe it is a non-starter in the real world. It is not feasible because the level of sophistication needed by members of Congress to understand the role of federal taxes in the real world is totally beyond them. They see the members of Congress as generally good and caring people, but primarily trained as lawyers as are so many of the Federal Reserve governors, and, like the Federal Reserve's governors and regional presidents, without sufficient knowledge of economics and the real world of business and commercial banking to understand the implications of their actions and inactions.

Accordingly, pragmatic analysts support the concept of a balanced federal budget at full employment levels of income and look to other solutions, *particularly the "direct injection" policies of monetary expansion that might be implemented by the Federal Reserve System.*

**Other undesirable congressional solutions:
international trade and deflation.**

Congress has several other actions in addition to increasing public spending or cutting taxes that it might undertake in an effort to end a depression. One policy that was repeatedly attempted in the nineteenth and twentieth centuries is the adoption of laws and regulations that encourage foreigners to buy more American-made products.

Quotas and tariff barriers can be thrown up by Congress. If they are, Americans will tend to buy fewer foreign-made products and move their spending to domestically produced goods and services. Similarly, Congress can provide funding for foreigners so they can buy more American-made products. Typically this is done via organizations such as the Export-Import bank, the IMF, and the World Bank. Similarly, trade agreements with other countries can be negotiated and renegotiated and "foreign aid" grants can be given to countries so they can buy things such as wheat and fighter planes.

Conceptually a massive increase in foreign spending or a massive shift from foreign to domestic products would work. Foreign spending would rise, there would be a multiplier effect on total spending, and the depression would end—except for a few not-so-minor problems inherent in the way the real world works. One is that sales to foreigners comprise a relatively insignificant portion of total spending in the United States so that even a major percentage increase, even one whose size is beyond Congress's wildest dreams, is not likely to have much of an effect.

The biggest problem, of course, is that foreign governments will inevitably retaliate with their own quotas and tariffs if the United States tries to steal their customers away. In other words, selling more to foreigners is not a realistic solution.

Other undesirable congressional solutions: the promotion of deflation and lower wages.

It has been suggested by some particularly cloistered "experts" that full employment could be restored and that recessions and depressions could, at least conceptually, be ended if wages and prices fall sufficiently. Prices and wage levels did not generally decline during the Great Recession. But someday, the "experts" point out, they might.

They note that Congress could take steps to actively encourage prices and wages to fall. For example, it could outlaw unions and all contracts and agreements that require the payment of specific wages and prices; it could encourage anti-trust activities to increase price competition; and it could direct regulatory agencies to reduce their allowable rates of return and price fixing.

Unfortunately, analysts who have looked in detail at the alleged salutary effects of deflation do not see it as a viable solution. They have concluded three things: First, achieving deflation by forcing wages and prices significantly lower would be virtually impossible to achieve. Second, that deflation has the same effect as increasing the supply of money—so why not avoid the hassle and just increase the supply of money. And, third, that it would not work once an economy has been enmeshed in a depression for so long that there are not enough potential spenders left no matter how much loan money and credit is made available to them—so after lots of hassle and strife the country would probably still not have enough consumer and other customer spending to get out of the depression and back to full employment.

THE FEDERAL RESERVE IS THE ONLY ANSWER

Where does that leave pragmatic analysts? The inapplicability of everything else means that, by default, the American economy and its pragmatic analysts and politicians are left with the Federal Reserve. And here, despite all its horrendous blunders *of the past*, there may be hope.

The hope exists because the Federal Reserve governors are independent of the politicians once they are appointed and confirmed.

**Using generally unused
Federal Reserve powers.**

The powers and potential powers of the Federal Reserve are immense. So it is quite amazing that its governors and regional presidents stood idly by in 2008 and the years thereafter while the housing market tanked and the recession and unemployment and bank failures bloomed as total spending fell and loans defaulted. Many creative actions could have been undertaken.

For example, the Federal Reserve could have ordered the banks *and anyone else who owned mortgages and who wanted to be a bank borrower or use bank services* to offer all mortgagees the opportunity to rent their houses after foreclosure or to make interest only payments for a period of years;

Or it could have ordered them to reduce the interest rates on first and second mortgages to some maximum such as the then-current rates of interest;

Or it could have ordered them to temporarily reduce or eliminate the principal portion of the monthly payments for all who so requested;

Or it could have told the banks to maintain the same volume of consumer and business credit lines as it had previously issued;

Or it could have ordered the banks to maintain the level of local loans as required by the Community Reinvestment Act;

Or it could have given the banks a percentage quota for mortgage refinancing both for themselves and any mortgage company they banked.

The list of helpful things the Federal Reserve governors had the power to do, and did not do, is virtually endless.

Unfortunately the Federal Reserve governors and regional presidents were captured by Treasury Secretary, the obsolete theories of the Federal Reserve staff, and the "common knowledge" they gleaned from the media and listening to luncheon speakers. So they did not do any of these things or use any of the Federal Reserve's other explicit or implicit powers—so foreclosures skyrocketed, commercial banks took losses that ate into their capital and some banks failed, housing prices collapsed further, bankruptcies and foreclosures increased, businesses failed, and total spending and employment declined. In other words, *weak and unqualified Federal Reserve decision makers can be an incredibly costly burden for an economy.* They do not do much for reelection campaigns either.

Analysts have conjectured that the Great Recession would not have morphed into a permanent depression if the Federal Reserve had promptly used its regulatory powers to affect mortgage and financing relief while simultaneously delaying its "stress tests" and using its open market operations to provide the commercial banks with massive amounts of money to loan. We will never know because the Federal Reserve governors and regional presidents failed to act.

In any event, *the window of opportunity for the success of conventional monetary policies appears to be closed.* Today the United States is mired in the second great depression of its modern era—and in the pragmatic liquidity trap with no major increase in spending on the horizon to end it; not the Keynesian liquidity trap of minimum interest rates but rather the much more powerful liquidity trap of commercial banks and other lenders who are afraid or prohibited or diverted from using their deposits and capital to make conventional loans to consumers and employers at any rate of interest.

The possible use of monetary policy rules.

It has been suggested by some analysts that everything would be economically okay if decisions to increase or decrease the money supply are based on firm policy rules. Their reasoning is quite simple—the people who tend to get themselves appointed as Federal Reserve governors and regional presidents can not be trusted to voluntarily do whatever it is that needs to be done. History would seem to support that view. In essence, a bet that political appointees will do the right thing is never a safe bet in a lively democracy.

Supposedly the Federal Reserve governors and regional presidents act to ensure a supply of money that will cause and support the levels of spending needed to achieve high levels employment, stable prices, and constant growth. This requires that they expand the supply of money and credit when the economy's level of income is depressed below the level needed to generate full employment and contract it during a demand-pull inflation. Historically, however, the Federal Reserve has all too often done just the opposite.

But they might do the right thing if they had no choice but to follow a specific rule. There are several types of monetary rules which might be adopted: those that specify the types and sizes of the policies to be used, and those that specify when the policies are to be implemented.

During the United States' Great Depression of the 1930s, despite employment and production being far below the economy' potential, the Federal Reserve on at least one occasion deliberately reduced the money supply in order to fight a "future inflation" that did not exist—and made the depression even greater.

Similarly, during the Great Recession of the early 21st century several members of the FOMC similarly opposed further monetary ease because "everyone knows" a bigger money supply to fight the recession would "cause inflation in the future." They succeeded in holding off the implementation of necessary quantitative increases until the economy deteriorated to such an extent that it became stuck in the liquidity trap.

The present-day Federal Reserve opponents of an expansionary monetary policy are similarly undeterred by the facts—that the economy is in a massive depression; that their so-called QE1, QE2, and QE3 expansions of the money supply have been at least partially offset by higher reserve and capital requirements; that the requirements of regulators have caused banks to buy more federal bonds, increase their reserve deposits and make short term loans to the financial sector; and that allowing the recession continue will result in ever decreasing numbers of creditworthy borrowers.

More incredible than even their lack of responsiveness to the distressed state of the economy and their lack of empathy with the millions of people in distress, is that, as a group, the members of the Open Market Committee have such inadequate macroeconomic educations and real world experience that they apparently do not realize that they do not have to worry about over-expanding the money supply in response to the depression since they also have the power to immediately eliminate any excess.

In other words, the FOMC is dominated by governors and regional presidents who do not even realize that they have both the power to increase the supply of money in an effort to end a recession and, then, if they overshoot, instantly turn around and decrease it. Where did the White House staff and the regional bank directors find these people?

Unworldly and unqualified appointees are not new phenomena. The Federal Reserve decision makers similarly bungled things, but in the opposite direction, immediately after World War II. Then, in an effort to keep the interest expenses in the federal budget down, it engaged in monetary ease to prop up the price of federal bonds. That further fueled the demand-pull inflation that raged as the population spent their wartime savings.

The Federal Reserve did the same thing in reverse in the early seventies when its governors feared inflation and so tightened up on the money supply to such an extent that interest rates rose—causing the Consumer Price Index to rise and giving the economy the very inflation the governors feared. This occurred because the higher interest rates increased the monthly cost of housing, automobiles, and consumer durables. These are the products for which interest is often a bigger part of the monthly cost of buying them than their sticker price.

Some pragmatic economists in the 1940s and 1950s, such as Milton Friedman and other disciples of quantity of money theorist Irving Fisher, feared the continuation of such misguided policies by unqualified governors and regional presidents. They proposed removing the discretionary powers of the Federal Reserve to affect the money supply. They suggested, instead, that the Federal Reserve be required to follow a simple and easily understood "rule" wherein the money supply would be increased at a constant annual rate.

In other words, the early pragmatists proposed that the United States money supply no longer be altered by the whims and common knowledge of those who presently govern it or by the decisions of the commercial banks and other depositories to lend or not lend their excess reserves.

Over the years various other rules have been suggested for governing the economy's money supply. Among them: that the supply be increased at a constant rate or that it be changed only as needed to stabilize some index of prices or unemployment. One of the most seriously discussed rules is that the money supply be increased at some constant rate. Typically, this rate has been described as being the rate at which the demand for money would grow if there were full employment without inflation or full employment with only structural inflation.

Obviously, if the money supply of the United States is to only increase at some constant rate or, for that matter, to be governed by any rule, not only would the discretionary activities of the Federal Reserve have to be ended, but also the money-creating and money-destroying activities of the banking system would have to be eliminated as well as the flows of dollars to and from outside the economy and the creation of dollars outside the banking system.

The early proponents of the "rules" approach felt that such changes are possible. For instance, the ability of the commercial banks and other depositories to influence the money supply could be substantially reduced by requiring them to hold one hundred percent of their transactions deposits as reserves. All that means, say the advocates of the rule, is that the deposit of a given amount of cash will then merely change the composition and holders of the money supply, but not expand it.

Today the advocates of basing the size of an economy's money supply on strict rules, popularly known to pragmatic economic cognoscenti as the "Panglossians," still feel the United States would have the best of all possible economies if its money supply was only increased according to precisely specified permanent rules. They say temporary changes in the supply of money will not be needed to stabilize total spending once such rules are in effect. Instead, they argue, the security of knowing that neither incompetent central bank policy makers nor the banking system nor the Congress will be able to interfere adversely with the money supply will tend to eliminate cyclical fluctuations in total spending.

The spending fluctuations will be eliminated because they, so it is alleged, occur primarily in response to either changes in the policies of the banks and monetary authorities or because of changes in the public's expectations about future policy changes. In other words, these rules advocates feel that if the Federal Reserve would stop changing its policies when economic conditions change, then the conditions would not change. Pragmatic analysts, of course, recognize the naïveté of such a rule in the real world with its virtually infinite number of things that might influence the purchasing and financial decisions of the hundreds of millions of consumers, employers, and governments.

The huge drawback to accepting such rules, including the rule discussed immediately below, is that some external force such as a foreign war or trade war or a sovereign debt crisis might cause income fluctuations to occur despite the rules. And while it is true that at least the spending fluctuations would not be intensified by poor monetary policies such as occurred in the past, and are occurring now, it is also true that they also could not be countered by inappropriate policies if they did occur.

Today some pragmatic economists think it would be easier to introduce competency requirements to the Federal Reserve appointment and confirmation process than to introduce rigid monetary rules to a complex economy. That idea, in reality, is also a non-starter because of the political forces inherent in a vibrant democracy. Most pragmatists, however, do not rule out the use of some form of rules. To the contrary, they see the introduction of some form of governor-imposed Federal Reserve rules as the only way the United States is ever going to be able to get out of its current depression.

Rules related to targets. A more sophisticated and somewhat more useful version of monetary rules is for the Federal Reserve to engage in money creating activities in response to the rate of inflation or some other relevant metric such as an accurately estimated rate of unemployment. Thus, for example, the Federal Reserve might set a target rate of inflation of three percent for the average level of prices of the goods and services produced by American employers. Then the rule would require the Federal Reserve to increase the money supply and engage in other expansionary actions when prices were increasing at less than three percent and tighten up when prices are increasing faster than three percent.

Some pragmatic analysts have taken this one step further and suggested that the rate selected should be whatever is the "natural rate" of inflation, the upward drift in the general level of prices associated with the economy's ever-evolving structure.

There are several problems with such a rule. One is that extraordinary events will inevitably cause prices changes to differ from the long term trend. For example, "friends of business" might get elected to the Presidency and Congress and reward their supporters by relaxing anti-trust efforts to promote competition so that heretofore competitive industries gather together to keep out new competitors and increase prices; or "friends of labor" might get elected and reward their supporters with laws and regulations that encourage labor unionization and push up production costs so that businesses have to increase their prices to cover their now higher costs.

Another huge problem is that there are other causes of inflation and unemployment in addition to too much spending caused by there being too much or too little money in circulation. In other words, rules focused on controlling just one source of inflation and unemployment would leave the economy vulnerable to all the others.

Another possible problem with using a specific inflation goal to trigger monetary expansions is that the price increases associated with the never ceasing structural evolution of an economy may come in spurts. For example, during recessions and depressions customers may delay switching between products and technologies such that only one percent of the normal three percent or so increase in prices to occur, with the remaining two percent not arriving until full employment returns. This seems to be the American experience during the Great Recession and the subsequent depression into which it morphed—price increases appeared to be lower than those that normally occur in the United States each year for structural reasons, even though the structure of the economy continued to change with the on-going introduction of new products and technologies.

Conceptually, if "catch up" structural price increases occur when an economy comes out of a recession or depression, the economy's initial years of recovery and full employment would tend to see major increases. For example, after six years of recession the example economy described above would then tend to see a one-time fifteen percent rate of inflation—the normal three percent for the recovery year and the catching up of the repressed twelve percent (two percent per year for six years). Unsophisticated decision makers looking at the fifteen percent might then abandon the rule and tighten up in order to fight the inflation—throwing the economy right back into the depression.

A possible solution: expanding the scope of Federal Reserve operations.

Going in the opposite direction from rules that remove powers from the Federal Reserve are various reforms that the Federal Reserve might undertake on its own initiative if it is competently governed. For example, the Federal Reserve might make "voluntary tax payments" to the federal government in any amounts it deems appropriate. The governors could then choose to allow the federal government to partially or fully balance its budget during times of recession by buying non-interest bearing Treasury notes instead of the interest bearing notes. They could immediately send them to the Treasury as a required by the Federal Reserve's one hundred percent tax rate.

Public fears of a budget that is unbalanced would thus be allayed and the Congress might be less hesitant about fully utilizing its fiscal tools to stabilize the economy without the panic or uncertainty that might accompany a deficit. Such a reform would appear not to even require congressional approval. *It also would do nothing to insure that total spending is neither too large nor too small to generate full employment.*

Alternately, and in the same vein but much more simple and realistic, the Federal Reserve might annually identify that portion of its huge holding of treasury bonds that are excess to its open market buying and selling needs and simply turn them back to the federal government as a voluntary tax payment. In effect, as pragmatic analysts know, the actual national debt of the United States is significantly lower than the totals reported because much of it is in the hands of the Federal Reserve and various government agencies.

Similarly, the actual level of federal spending is significantly lower than is reported in the federal budget because a big item in the budget is interest on the national debt which is paid to the Federal Reserve and promptly returned because of the one hundred percent tax rate the Federal Reserve pays on its income. But, once again, *such a policy would do nothing to insure that total spending is neither too large nor too small to generate fully employment.*

The only viable answer: *directly* injecting money increases via targeted assistance.

The Federal Reserve has the power to create new money and flow it into the economy as its governors see fit. Normally the Federal Reserve gets newly created money to the economy's spenders *indirectly*—by using open market operations to flow newly created money into the financial intermediaries who then, in turn, flow some of it into commercial banks. The commercial banks then, in turn, loan the newly created money to consumers and employers who want to make more purchases.

But the Federal Reserve does have an option and it has used it before—it could create new money, bypass its primary dealers and the bond sellers and banks, and flow the newly created money directly to specific recipients. The recipients' spending and the multiplier effect it has would increase production and employment. It would also tend to move the federal budget from deficit to surplus by increasing tax collections and reducing the need for unemployment related welfare and make-work spending. *Pragmatic analysts see this as the only realistic option left when an economy has morphed a permanent major depression wherein conventional monetary policy will no longer work because the economy is in the regulatory liquidity trap and conventional fiscal policy won't work due to the realities of the political process.*

There are precedents for such direct injections. The Federal Reserve does such a direct provision of newly created money to a potential spender when it creates new money and uses it to buy bonds directly from the Treasury and the money is then spent by the federal government.

Similarly, the Federal Reserve created new money and directly flowed it to Citigroup, Goldman Sachs, and other big traders during the initial months of the Great Recession. Specifically, it established "special facilities" that sent newly created money to a handful of big trading firms and commercial banks so they could continue in business and pay the billions of dollars in "profit" bonuses their partners and traders earned selling the mortgage derivatives and fictitious assets that subsequently collapsed in value. *This is a very important precedent. Remember it.*

It may not say much for either the ethics of the then Treasury Secretary and the White House or the abilities and moral fiber of the Federal Reserve's chairman that a significant portion of the direct aid went to the Secretary's partners at Goldman Sachs, and much of the rest went to the companies that owed Goldman money and were required to pay it to Goldman as a condition of getting bailed out. But it was a great precedent and future generations of Americans can be thankful it occurred.

More specifically, the precedent of creating new money and flowing it *directly* to certain beneficiaries does open some very interesting possibilities regarding the use of monetary rules. Indeed, *it opens the door to a viable solution to quickly get the United States out of its current depression and budgetary deficits without increasing federal spending.*

**Monetary rules are part
of the pragmatic solution.**

An inherently dynamic and growing economy, such as that of the United States, will always need a dynamic and growing supply of money. Accordingly, the Federal Reserve could, without giving up its discretionary powers to respond as needed, adopt some version of the monetary rule wherein *a portion of the normal increase* is systematically flowed to recipients who society might consider a bit more worthy and deserving of receiving direct injections than the partners and traders of Goldman Sachs and Morgan Stanley—for example, the many millions of Americans who are Social Security recipients.

In essence, instead of creating new money and flowing it into the commercial banks indirectly via open market operations or directly via the likes of Goldman Sachs, the governors, on their own volition and without congressional approval, could decide that the Federal Reserve will create new money and directly flow a portion of it into the economy and banks through other recipients.

For example, the Federal Reserve could immediately and permanently begin creating and sending some amount such as $500 per month to every Social Security recipient. Then any additional money the economy needed to have each month could be created by the Federal Reserve and injected indirectly via its traditional use of open market purchases. A particular plus for such a money expanding rule is that Social Security recipients tend to have high propensities to consume such that total purchasing would tend to quickly increase as a result of the permanent increase in the recipients disposable incomes.

Other pluses of such a policy is that Congressional action is not be needed and that, because of its magnitude and permanency, it is not likely to cause the Congress to see the Federal Reserve as being open to the financing of other spending schemes.

Moreover, and unlike open market operations which may result in assets being bought from overseas owners and traders so that the newly created dollars go abroad or into the hands of those who would speculate with it, all Social Security payments now go into commercial banks via direct deposit. The Federal Reserve could even send the new money directly to the recipients' bank accounts and not even route it through the Social Security system.

Moreover, there is also a precedent for fighting an economic depression via directly channeling newly created money into the economy via Social Security recipients. Congress borrowed newly created money from the Federal Reserve and sent each Social Security recipient $200 at the same time it and the Federal Reserve sent hundreds of billions to Goldman and other big trading firms so they could cover their liabilities, pay their multi-million dollar bonuses, and continue trading without wiping out the value of the Treasury Secretary's Goldman shares.

Moreover, the law Congress passed years ago requiring the Federal Reserve to have a dollar's worth of "assets" to 'back' each dollar it creates should not be a problem. The Federal Reserve got around this in the course of a weekend in 2008 by proclaiming Goldman Sachs and several other large trading firms to be commercial banks. That made them eligible to use their derivatives and other assets as collateral for direct Federal Reserve funding. A few weeks later they were allowed to resign as banks so they would not be subject to the bank laws regarding their use of the bailout money for speculative trading.

Allowing recipients to become instant banks with the stroke of a pen in order to directly receive new created money from the Federal Reserve and then resign is also an important precedent. It means, the Federal Reserve, if necessary, could similarly proclaim Social Security recipients to be commercial banks some weekend and similarly accept their resignations a few days later.

Alternately, and mindful that personal debts expire when a person dies and that Congress requires a dollar of assets back each newly created dollar, the Federal Reserve could book the newly created money it sends to Social Security recipients to expand the money supply as ninety nine year loans. Then it could write them off, just as the government did for Chrysler's UAW pension fund when it died and could not pay.

FEDERAL RESERVE ACTIONS TO
END THE CURRENT DEPRESSION
AND PREVENT FUTURE RECESSIONS

However it might be accomplished, the United States will always need a constant stream of newly created money flowing into its economy to handle its ever growing number of transactions. There is no reason to believe that *all* of the required expansion of the money supply should only be done by indirectly via open market operations or directly by periodically bailing out the likes of Goldman Sachs and Citibank.

In essence, the Federal Reserve's governors and regional presidents have established the precedent of flowing money directly into the economy via specific recipients instead of indirectly via the banking system. Accordingly, there is no reason for them not to begin doing so in a systematic manner and in sufficiently large quantities to end the depression and keep it ended.

Pragmatic analysts and caring people everywhere can only hope that when the Federal Reserve's governors finally *begin* doing something significant to end the current depression, they will keep in mind that what was good for a handful of Goldman's geese ought to also be good for millions of current and future Social Security ganders—particularly if it is permanent instead of one-time and it constantly increases the money supply that will have to be constantly increased if the United States' economy is to continue to grow.

Three rules for the Federal Reserve
to adopt to end the depression.

The first rule would be to steadily and *permanently* flow a portion of the newly created money that the constantly growing United States economy will need into the economy via its many millions of Social Security or other worthy recipients. For example, a permanent addition of new money each month via a $500 per month payment from the Federal Reserve to each Social Security recipient would seem to be appropriate way to meet a prosperous and growing American economy's ever growing need for additional money. The resulting additional consumer spending and its multiplier effect would appear sufficient to quickly pull the United States out of its current depression and keep it out.

And the recovery would be almost instantaneous. It only took a few weeks for the $200 payments to hit the recipients' bank accounts once the President decided to send the checks. So there is reason to think first $500 could arrive in the banks equally quickly. Indeed, just the announcement of that the money would be quickly and permanently coming is likely to set off the massive spending increase needed to pull the United States out of its current depression.

Moreover, the people running the businesses and commercial banks of the United States are neither stupid nor inexperienced. They would instantly understand that consumer spending is going to quickly and permanently increase, and that the ability of tens of millions of consumers to service credit card debt, mortgages, student loans, and other consumer debt will dramatically and permanently increase. There is every reason to believe employers would rush to build up their inventories and to make the investments and employee hires needed to increase their production capacities.

State and local governments would similarly respond to the soon-to-arrive higher sales and income tax collections that would tend to turn their current deficits into surpluses. In other words, spending would quickly increase and end the depression.

The second Federal Reserve self-imposed rule would be to use open market operations to continue indirectly adding (or withdrawing) *additional* newly created money, over and above that provided via the direct funding, as needed to keep the economy within an acceptable spread between inflation and unemployment. For example, the governors might adopt a rule requiring the Federal Reserve Open Market Desk to keep adding creating additional new money and using it to buy bonds and other financial instruments so long as unemployment, calculated using historical labor force participation rates, is below some level such as six percent, and be allowed to stop adding it whenever the consumer price index exceeds some level such as a seasonally adjusted four percent.

In other words, in addition to the direct flowing of new money into the economy via worthy recipients, the Federal Reserve' Open Market Desk could be given a permanent order to engage in its conventional open market activities as needed to keep the economy within an acceptable spread of inflation and unemployment.

The third rule is to have qualified Federal Reserve governors and regional presidents who are professionally trained economists and capable of making the decisions necessary to establish and continue to carry out the first two rules. Once again, there is no need for Congress to act in any way for the necessary policies to be implemented. The governors could do it themselves, if necessary by suggesting or requiring that members of the Open Market Committee who have not been appropriately educated recuse themselves when policy votes are taken.

Alternately, the White House and the Senate could take it upon themselves to do something really different—only appoint and confirm appropriately educated governors with appropriate real world decision-making experience outside the bureaucracies of the federal government and the too-big-to-fail financial community.

It would also, of course, be particularly helpful if the appointees also had sufficient moral fiber to do the right thing for the country as a whole instead of pandering to the titans of the financial community and letting their common sense be swayed by the fallacious "common knowledge" purveyed by their unqualified colleagues and staff.

The pragmatic conclusion

The United States can very quickly, *within a few weeks*, end its current depression with Federal Reserve policies that do not require congressional or presidential approval. The necessary knowledge and precedents exist. What is missing is the President's appointment of a couple of qualified Federal Reserve governors, or the regional boards' appointment of a couple of qualified regional presidents scheduled for FOMC seats.

And they would not even have to be permanent appointments. There are qualified people who are more interested in public service than in bureaucratic careers. In essence, non-career recess appointees are all that is needed to adopt the rules and give the necessary orders. Then, once the expanded policy of direct money injections is in place, the President and the regional boards can go back to appointing their usual class of place holding appointees who will, if the past is any guide, leave the new rules and policies in place—both because they are under no pressure to make changes because economy is again at full employment and growing, and because the traditional governors and regional presidents have proven themselves time and time again to be incapable of making major decisions such as would be required to abandon the new rules.

Routing a constant stream of newly created money directly into the economy through the Social Security recipients, instead of via Goldman Sachs, the UAW, and the bond markets, would work and the governors and regional presidents would be under no pressure to make changes. *After all, to paraphrase the great Schumpeter, once a monument is erected it only requires caretakers to maintain it.*

SUMMARY

I.   The United States has unnecessarily suffered inflations, unemployment, low rates of growth, budgetary deficits, and recessions and depressions as a result of poor monetary and fiscal policies.

II.   Pragmatic economists are aware of the concepts of functional finance but believe congressionally generated fiscal policies such as tax and spending increases and decreases are not practical due to the time lags inherent in the decision making process, the lack of congressional expertise in budgetary matters, and the political pressures on decision makers to adhere to the prevailing "common knowledge."

III. Deflation and selling abroad are not viable solutions to reduce unemployment when the United States is in a recession or depression.

IV. The Federal Reserve's traditional monetary response to a recession or depression is to increase the money supply to get more money into the hands of consumers and other buyers of newly produced goods and services. It flows the money to them *indirectly* by creating new money and using it to buy federal bonds and other assets in the open market. The recipients of the money then deposit it in the commercial banks and the commercial banks then loan it to the consumers and other buyers.

V. The indirect flowing of money to consumers and other spenders via the bond markets does not work when the failure of the Federal Reserve to act appropriately in a timely manner is such that a recession morphs into a permanent depression. If the Federal Reserve waits too long so many potential consumers and employers will be ruined by the time it finally begins. Then there will not be enough potential spenders left to get spending up to the level required for full employment.

VI. The lack of appropriate training and experience on the part of the Federal Reserve's governors and regional presidents could be at least partially overcome by the adherence to monetary rules regarding the expansion of the money supply. This would be particularly effective if the rules were related to viable targets such as accurately calculated rates of inflation and unemployment.

VII. Monetary rules would have the Federal Reserve increase the money supply at some fixed rate. The problem is that adherence to the rule would leave the Federal Reserve powerless to further increase or decrease the money supply when it might be appropriate to do so.

VIII. A more modern version of the rules approach is for the Federal Reserve to expand the money supply as necessary to keep the rate of inflation at some acceptable level such as three percent or whatever rate is associated with the natural growth and evolution of the economy. But then what if there is a cost push inflation of four percent—does it then press down spending to cause inflation to drop to three percent even if that causes massive unemployment?

IV. The Federal Reserve is the only viable source of a solution when the United States has a recession or depression. One possible solution is for the Federal Reserve to use its generally unused regulatory powers to direct more of the loans and credit extended by commercial banks to consumers and employers.

VIII. The only option left when the indirect flowing of money via the financial systems to banks to consumers and employers is no longer sufficient is to *directly* flow newly created money to potential spenders. The Federal Reserve has periodically done this to assist specific large financial traders such as Goldman Sachs. It could do so more broadly by flowing much smaller amounts of money to a much larger group of recipients.

IX. The direct flows of newly created money could continue permanently to provide a major portion of the constantly increasing supply of money and credit that is required by a constantly growing economy. The Federal Reserve's conventional indirect flowing of money into and out of the economy via the financial markets could then be used to fine tune total spending in the economy as needed to achieve full employment without causing a demand-pull inflation.

X. Adopting a policy of directly flowing new money to additional recipients who are potential spenders would likely end the current United States' depression and massive unemployment in a matter of weeks. A secondary result would likely be such massive increases in tax collections that the federal and other governments of the United States would tend to run budgetary surpluses with their existing tax rates.

XI.   No congressional action would be required for the Federal Reserve to extend its *direct flow* program to recipients in addition to the too-big-too-fail financial traders. It only requires Federal Reserve governors and regional presidents with sufficient professional training and experience to do what must be done if the United States economy is to escape from its current depression and massive unemployment. Such experts are immediately available.

APPENDIX A

IDENTIFYING UNQUALIFIED "ECONOMIC EXPERTS"

To trained analysts the world seems to be full of qualification-challenged "business economists," journalists, and Federal Reserve governors and regional presidents. But how does a journalist or analyst separate the macroeconomic wheat from the chaff to know who is qualified by education and experience and who is not?

One way to do it is to use their statements and writings to *disqualify* those who merely repeat grossly inaccurate tidbits of common knowledge. Below are fifty or so inaccurate statements. They would never be uttered or written by anyone who has both studied macroeconomics at the professional level and had real world experience in business or commercial banking. In other words, anyone who repeats something like them as fact is likely to be an unqualified "expert" and should be ignored; if they have a journalistic or policy making position they should be ignored and replaced.

1. *Monetary policy primarily affects an economy's prosperity, spending and employment by changing interest rates.* Wrong. Interest rate changes primarily affect the financial markets. The availability of credit and its payment terms are infinitely more important to the spending levels of consumers and employers than interest rates.

2. *Increases in the money supply will sooner or later cause of inflation.* Wrong. There are many causes of inflation. Increases in the money supply are only one of the many causes of increased spending and increased spending is only one of the many causes of higher prices. Moreover, increased spending will not tend to cause inflation if

there is unemployed labor and capital or if the economy's capacity grows as the spending grows. Moreover, if the increase is too large it can be instantly reversed at any time.

3. *The Federal Reserve sets interest rates.* Wrong. Common knowledge to the contrary, the Federal Reserve does not set the level of interest rates in the United States. Interest rates are set in the financial markets by the supply and demand for dollars and credit. The Federal Reserve can change the supply and that will affect interest rates in the United States—if it is not offset by a change in the demand for money. The only interest rate the Federal Reserve actually sets is the discount rate at which commercial banks never borrow because to do so indicates to the bank regulators that the bank is in serious trouble and should be closed.

   The Federal Reserve also sets a suggested "target rate" for the overnight borrowing of reserves by large commercial banks. The Federal Reserve has historically used the relationship of the target rate to the actual overnight rates reported by the banks to guide its policies. Since the relationship is tenuous, at best, and does not exist at all during a recession when both the target and actual rates are at a minimum, the Federal Reserve's policies based on the target rates have frequently been inappropriate and unsuccessful.

4. *The Federal Funds target rate is significant.* Wrong. The Federal Reserve considers its federal funds target rate a significant indicator of the state of the economy and the direction the economy is headed. In the real world it is not significant in any way, shape, or form. Anyone who believes a commercial bank will borrow money that it has to repay in twenty four hours and loan it out so people can buy cars and houses is either incredibly naïve or holds an important position at a credit rating agency or the Federal Reserve. So too is anyone who believes that the Federal Funds rates, the interest rates large commercial banks report they charge each other to borrow reserves overnight, somehow track with the desires of the hundreds of millions of consumers and businesses to borrow money and the interest rates banks can charge for those dollars. So too is anyone who believes the desires of customers to borrow money to spend

and the interest rates they pay somehow tracks with the need for more or less total spending for the United States to achieve full employment without inflation.

5. *Sooner or later the Federal Reserve will have to unwind (dispose of) its asset holdings.* Wrong. The "chief economist" of Morgan Stanley actually warned its clients that the assets the Federal Reserve received in return for the bailout cash Morgan and others received means there will be economic troubles in the days ahead—because the Federal Reserve will sooner or later have to "unwind its position" by selling the assets in the open market. This, he suggested, will cause the money supply to contract and income to fall. He was wrong on all accounts.

   In its hundred years or so of existence the Federal Reserve has never once been forced to reduce or "unwind" its asset holdings. In the real world it does not have to so, never has, and never will. That is why the Federal Reserve's holdings of assets are now so large. In the real world the Federal Reserve only sells assets when it is pursuing a deliberate policy of removing money from circulation to stop a real or imagined demand-pull inflation. Since a growing economy tends to need more and more money the Federal Reserve has never taken steps to reduce the supply when it was appropriate to do so.

6. *The unemployment rate announced by the federal government each month is indicative of the state and direction of the economy.* Wrong. It does not indicate anything at all because it is so hopelessly inaccurate. It grossly understates number of available workers who want work and will go to work as soon as work is available. A much more accurate rate of unemployment is derived by applying labor force participation rates in full time jobs during times of prosperity to today's population in the various age/sex population cohorts and subtracting the number of people who are actually employed full time. The necessary data can be found in the *Current Population Survey.*

7. *A recession occurs when the level of income declines for two successive quarters.* Wrong. That is a journalistic rule of thumb of obscure

origins. In the real world a recession exists whenever the level of income in an economy has receded below the level of income needed for full employment.

8. *A recession ends when the level of income stops declining.* Wrong. It ends when the level of income is no longer below the level needed for full employment.

9. *The national debt is the same as other governmental and private debt. Wrong.* It is not the same. Private debt and the debts of state and local governments must be paid. For them the choice is to pay now or to pay later plus pay the accrued interest. In contrast, the national debt of the United States can be paid either by tax revenues or with money created by the Federal Reserve System. State and local governments do not have a central bank; the United States government does have a central bank with money creating powers. It also has a Treasury with money creating powers. Federal bonds will always be paid in full. Warnings to the contrary are an indication of gross incompetence on the part of those issuing the warning.

10. *The national debt is a burden on future generations.* Wrong. The national debt is never a burden on future generations because it can always be paid off or refinanced without the future generations having to come up with a single penny—because the federal government always has the Federal Reserve and Treasury available to pay off or roll over the debt. It is governments without a money-creating central bank, such as Greece and Spain, that are in the same position as Detroit and California. They must either tax and pay now or borrow money and pay later.

11. *Depression is another name for a recession.* Wrong. A recession is considered by pragmatic analysts to be a "temporary" problem of inadequate total spending that is solvable by conventional monetary policies. It occurs when spending in an economy recedes below the level needed to provide full employment. It can be prevented and reversed with appropriate monetary and fiscal policies.

Recessions can morph into depressions. A depression is a condition wherein an economy permanently has massive unemployment which conventional monetary policy can no longer cure. The Great Recession which started in 2008 morphed into a depression after years of Federal Reserve inaction. The depression arrived when the economy's consumers and employers became so debilitated that conventional monetary policies to expand the supply of money and credit would no longer suffice to end the recession—because there were so few creditworthy spenders left after so many years of bankruptcies, defaults, late payments, lost pensions, foreclosures, and forced retirements.

12. *We need to get countries like China to change their exchange rates.* Wrong. That would accomplish little except to cause Walmart and other major buyers of Chinese products to shift their buying of labor intensive products to other low wage countries. And they are doing that already in response to China's growing wages and lack of the rule of law. Presently millions of Chinese are working to produce things for Americans and we periodically pay them with bank credits exchangeable for little pieces of green paper with dead presidents' pictures on them. Pragmatic monetary policies can end our workers' unemployment without stopping the Chinese from also working for us. Then we would be wealthier because we would have the workers of both China and our economy producing for us. Moreover, it is possible that the elasticity of U.S. customer demand for Chinese products is such that an exchange rate increase in the dollar price of the yuan would actually cause even more dollars to flow to China.

13. *The Federal Reserve should move to strengthen the dollar by raising interest rates and pressuring countries with big balance of payments surpluses to change their exchange rates.* Wrong. The exchange rates for the dollar against all other currencies are set in the world's currency markets by the forces of supply and demand. The freely floating rates that result automatically adjust to eliminate any balance of payments surpluses or deficits. Because it has freely floating rates the United States balance of payments is always perfectly balanced

with the amount of money coming in exactly equaling the amount of money going out.

14. *The dollar would be worth more if it is backed by gold.* Wrong. The value of a dollar is what you can buy with it. "Backing" the dollar with gold or anything else would have no effect on its value because it would have no effect on the prices of the items that could be bought with it. Pork bellies are for eating and gold is for filling teeth and jewelry. Both are commodities and neither is accepted in payment by most sellers.

15. *Lowering the retirement age will open jobs up for young people and reduce unemployment.* Wrong. Such a policy is often advocated when there is a lot of unemployment. Pragmatic analysts consider it much better to increase total spending to end the unemployment than to make older people unemployed by giving their jobs to younger people. Increasing spending instead of forcing retirements means the economy will produce more. There will be more tax collections, and less welfare and budget deficits, if everyone, young and old, who wants to work is allowed to work.

16. *A shorter work week will create jobs.* Wrong, in the real world it would tend to reduce the number of jobs in an economy—because employers who can do so will tend to move their jobs to where labor is less expensive; those that cannot move will have higher labor costs and thus have to charge higher prices—and there will be even fewer jobs if the higher prices reduce the number of items that are purchased.

17. *Shovel ready projects are available to create jobs and reduce unemployment.* Wrong. If the relatively insignificant "jobs bills" of the Great Recession proved anything it is that there are no shovel ready jobs in the United States. In the real world, before people can be hired there will be delays while the projects are designed, the money is applied for and received, the projects obtain the various required regulatory approvals, and the workers are recruited. Then, usually years later when they are no longer needed, the jobs begin. Most "make-work" jobs take years to come to fruition.

18. *A one-time "jobs bill" funding additional capital projects will "prime the pump" and help get the economy going again.* Wrong. There will be an initial burst of employment when the projects finally get going years later and then the jobs will peter out as the projects winds down. Only a permanent increase in spending will result in a permanent increase in spending and employment.

19. *A one-time tax cut will "prime the pump" and help get the economy going again.* Wrong. There will be an initial burst of employment if and when the money that would have been paid in taxes is spent to buy new goods and services. Then the jobs will peter out as the one-time increase in spending winds down. Only a permanent decrease in taxes will tend to result in a permanent increase in employment.

20. *A one-time Social Security payment or tax credit will "prime the pump" and help get the economy recover.* Wrong. If history is any guide, most of it will be used to pay down credit card and other debts and any increase in spending that does occur will be temporary and soon peter out.

21. *More savings is required if the United States is to have more investment and growth.* Wrong. Just the opposite is more likely to be the case. The decisions to invest and to save are independent of one another. More savings means less spending and, therefore, reduced levels of production resulting in the need for less investment and the employment of even fewer workers.

22. *We need to balance the budget in order to fight inflation.* Wrong. Inflation is caused by many things. The existence or non-existence of a balanced budget has nothing to do with causing inflation or ending it. On the other hand, balanced budgets can be associated with excessive government spending that can cause inflation—the different impacts of taxes and government spending and transfers on total spending mean that an increase in government spending accompanied by an equal increase in tax revenues will cause total spending to increase. This will tend to cause a demand-pull

inflation if spending is already at the level needed to generate full employment.

23. *Federal government spending causes inflation.* Wrong. Federal spending is only a small and virtually irrelevant portion of total spending in the United States. Moreover, excessive spending is only one of the many things that can cause inflation.

24. *Deficits cause inflation.* Wrong. Deficits do not have anything to do with an increase in an economy's general level of prices or the money supply. Can anyone really believe that an employer hears about a deficit and thinks "deficit? I'll have to raise my prices." Common knowledge explains that the Federal Reserve will print money to pay for the deficit and the increase in the money supply will cause inflation. That, of course, is also not true—the money supply need not increase because the Federal Reserve can simultaneously use open market operations and other actions to remove any new money it creates and uses to finance the federal government.

25. *Cutting deficits by reducing government spending and increasing tax collections is necessary if a country like Greece is to recover from a recession and be able to pay its debts.* Wrong. Cutting spending and raising taxes will further reduce the economy's total spending, thus tending to make its recession, tax collections, and deficit even worse. The only thing Greece and similar countries can do to stay on the euro is increase their tax bases by removing the government laws and regulations that discourage the growth of its tax base by promoting inefficiency and stifling competition.

26. *The stock market has risen which indicates the economy is getting better.* Wrong. The stock market and the prices of financial assets are very poor indicators of an economy's economic state and direction. They are primarily based on expectations as to the future prices of the various financial assets and the general level of interest rates at which earnings and yields are capitalized.

27. *Business cycles are inevitable.* Wrong. Modern monetary and fiscal policies can and should make them totally obsolete. There is no reason for total spending to ever be too high or too low.

28. *Economic growth requires a population increase.* Wrong. It requires such things as education so that workers are more productive, investment in capital such as plant and equipment, economic freedom and the rule of law so that would-be producers can produce, and new technologies. Pragmatic analysts rate economies in terms of the growth of their per-capita production.

29. *Being a large or the largest economy in terms of total output is significant.* Wrong. The success of an economy is best measured by its per capita output. Sweden and Norway are small and prosperous with high per capita incomes and India and China large and poor with low per capita incomes. Which do you think operate under the rule of law and where do you think most people would prefer to live and work?

30. *Wage and price controls may be necessary to fight inflation.* Wrong. They not only do not work, they may make the inflation even worse because employers will tend to quickly set their prices higher so that if they are frozen they will be frozen higher. Moreover, they are not needed because modern monetary and fiscal policies are available that will work.

31. *Job retraining programs are a useful response to unemployment when an economy is in a recession or depression.* Wrong. Recessions and depressions are conditions when jobs are generally not available. Retraining workers for nonexistent jobs typically provides employment for grant writers and administrators, not for their trainees and students who graduate into a world with no job vacancies.

32. *Interest rate swaps will have a significant effect on jobs and unemployment.* Wrong. The relatively insignificant decline in long term interest rates caused by selling short term debt and buying long term debt have historically failed to have any significant effect

on income and unemployment. In the real world, people and employers respond to their expectations about the future and the availability of credit and its repayment terms. They do not respond to minor changes in interest rates, particularly when they expect a recession or depression to continue.

33. *Investment bankers and those with whom they are comfortable have the education and experience needed to be a Treasury Secretary or Federal Reserve governor.* Wrong. History suggests the reverse. The real economy is about customer purchases, production, and employment. It is not about buying and selling financial assets such as derivatives in the financial markets.

34. *Higher taxes and less government spending are the best way to fight inflation.* Wrong. Such policies might work if the inflation is being caused by too much total spending. But such policies will not work if something else is causing the inflation. Moreover, some higher taxes, such as gasoline taxes, will actually make the inflation worse.

35. *Income has increased by three percent this year which means the recession is over and the economy is recovering.* Wrong. The production capacity of an economy such as that of the United States normally grows three to four percent per year due to the accumulation of plant and equipment, the introduction of new technologies, and population growth. Moreover, its prices also tend to increase two or three percent due to structural changes. Thus a three percent increase in spending is an absolute disaster. It means the economy has slipped further below its full employment level of income.

36. *If need more investment we need to encourage more savings.* Wrong. Just the reverse is true. Pragmatic analysts recognize that more savings would mean less spending to buy goods and services and, thus, a reduction in the need for investment spending to obtain more plant, equipment, and inventory.

37. *A law limiting the size of the national debt is significant.* Wrong. It is totally insignificant political theatre designed to impress

congressmen and voters who do not know any better. In the real world, the law can be superseded and overridden by actions of the Federal Reserve.

38. *The Federal Reserve determines the amount of reserves and capital commercial banks must hold.* Wrong. It determines the minimum amount of reserves and capital commercial banks must hold. In the real world, other agencies such as the FDIC and Comptroller of the Currency can and do set higher levels.

39. *Having the dollar backed by gold would increase the value of the dollar.* Wrong. The value of the dollar is determined by what it can buy; the value of a dollar in exchange for a foreign currency is set in the financial markets where dollars are bought and sold. Sometimes countries attempt to use their reserves to buy and sell foreign currencies in order to have a specific fixed exchange rate. They can only fix a rate that is different than the rate would be in the financial markets until they run out of reserves or stop building them. Gold does not have anything to do with prices or exchange rates other than that it can be sold for the money to defend a specific fixed rate or accumulated as reserves so it can be subsequently sold for money that can be spent. So can other commodities such as wheat and pork bellies.

40. *Savings is necessary for investment.* Wrong. Investment spending can occur no matter whether there is an equal amount of savings or not.

41. *Supply creates its own demand.* Wrong. This is only true in a crude and primitive barter economy. Just because you have something to sell in a money using economy does not mean someone will want to buy it.

42. *Wage and price controls or freezes help prevent inflation.* Wrong. They are more likely to cause it by causing employers to quickly raise their prices before they get frozen.

43. *Lower taxes on wealthy people and those with high incomes are the best tax cuts to get the economy going.* Wrong. Exactly the reverse will be true if wealthy people have lower propensities to consume than people with less wealth and lower incomes. Most studies show that to be the case.

44. *The economy will come out of a recession or depression naturally if we wait long enough.* Wrong. Only an increase in customer spending will pull an economy out of a recession or depression. Such increases do not just happen. Moreover, even if a spending increase does occur it might not be enough to cause the economy to regain full employment or stay there. Instead, as the Great Depression of the 30s and the Great Recession show, if the policy makers wait to act the economy will decline until sooner or later enough people and employers will be ruined such that it sinks into a permanent depression wherein conventional monetary policies are no longer capable of generating a recovery.

45. *Saving failing business such as legacy automakers, Citigroup, and Goldman Sachs is good policy because it saves jobs.* Wrong. Businesses fail because customers do not value their products enough to be willing to pay for them and because they use resources inefficiently. These are the employers that should be allowed to fail so their workers and capital can be employed more efficiently by others. Temporarily helping a failing business is only justified when its failure is caused by a temmporary external force outside of its control—such as the failure to implement monetary and fiscal policies to keep the economy generally prosperous. Even then the answer is to get the economy going again, not to aid a small handful of the millions of employers and workers.

46. *Interest rates adjust so that savings are always equal to investments.* Wrong. It is the level of income that adjusts to equate them and there is no reason the resulting level of income will be enough to result in full employment.

47. *Social Security will run out of money sometime in the years ahead unless something is done to fix it.* Wrong. In 1969 Social Security

taxes began going into the general fund along with all the other major tax revenues the federal government collects. At that moment Social Security spending effectively became just one more of the Federal Government's major spending programs along with defense, agriculture, education, etc. None of these federal programs are funded years ahead and there is no reason that any of them should be including Social Security. There is no more danger of Social Security running out of money than any other federal program such as defense, education, and agriculture. Moreover, the federal government has the Federal Reserve ready to finance its spending if there is ever a shortfall of money for *any* federal program.

48. *Saving the big financial institutions prevented the economy from melting down.* Wrong. It prevented the big financial institutions from melting down. The real economy did melt down and millions of jobs and trillions of production were lost. Anyone making such a statement is confusing the meltdown of the financial firms with a meltdown of the economy's commercial banks and employers.

49. *Tight money may be needed to squeeze inflation out of the economy.* Wrong. Tight money may be needed to hold down spending to prevent a demand-pull inflation but it won't stop other types of inflation. The person credited with uttering this nonsense was the principal author of the stabilization policies that caused the very inflation he thought he was preventing.

50. *Monetary policy works by changing interest rates.* Wrong. This is the type statement frequently made by most unworldly analysts, untrained "business economists," and Federal Reserve governors. In the real world monetary policy primarily works via changing the supply of money to affect total spending, not the interest rate price of borrowing or holding it. Minor changes in interest rates affect financial traders, not commercial banks, employers, and consumers.

51. *Helping too-big-to-fail financial institutions trickles down to help the commercial banks and the economy.* Wrong. The too-big-to-fail institutions operate virtually independently of the real economy.

Protecting or subsidizing their profits has little to do with maintaining full employment or the profits of businesses and commercial banks or the revenues of non-profit employers.

52. *Someone who is employed as an economist by an investment banking firm or rating agency is an expert who knows what they are talking about.* Wrong. With rare exceptions most of them are former traders and stock brokers who, like the majority of Federal Reserve governors, never studied economics at the professional level or had experience in the real world of business or commercial banking. Within the financial and rating firms they are typically part of the marketing department—and charged with cranking out client-attracting press releases containing whatever inaccurate common knowledge and garbage-grade analysis is needed to impress gullible potential clients.

53. *Higher interest rates and higher taxes are needed to fight inflation.* Wrong. Most inflations are not demand-pull inflations caused by too much spending. Moreover, interest rates and some taxes are cost items that have to be covered by employers. Accordingly taking steps that increase them may cause an economy's employers to raise their prices—inflation.

54. *Investment spending is encouraged by lower taxes on high income people and financial institutions such as hedge funds and financial traders.* Wrong. Those who hold this view inevitably are confusing the buying of stocks and bonds in the financial markets with the buying of plant and equipment. The investment spending that results in jobs and production does not occur just because some person or financial institution has more money. It tends to occur for various other reasons—such as when employers expect the plant and equipment they buy will result in sufficient revenues in excess of the capital and non-capital costs they will bear as a result employing the capital. Indeed, lower taxes on high income people and hedge funds are not as likely to cause total spending to increase and motivate investment spending as would lower taxes on less-wealthy people with higher propensities to consume. In essence, lower taxes on hedge funds and traders appears more likely

to result in more financial trading and gambling than in the buying of more plant and equipment.

55. *The velocity of money is significant.* Wrong. What counts is where and how and when money is spent—not how frequently it changes hands. The concept of money "velocity" comes from the nineteenth and early twentieth century theories of inflation which assumed that all spending is to buy goods and services; that all inflation is caused by excessive spending; and that all excessive spending is caused by either too much money or an increase in its velocity. Many knowledgeable analysts consider the use of the word "velocity" to be the greatest single telltale sign that someone discussing or writing about the economy does not have a clue as to how an economy actually operates in the real world.

56. *The historical relationship between increases in the supply of money and increases in prices proves that increases in the money supply cause inflation.* Wrong. It is true that the money supply and prices have gone up in tandem over the years. But that does not mean the increased supply of money caused the higher prices. It is just as likely that the increase in the prices caused the Federal Reserve to increase in the money supply—because the Federal Reserve is charged with providing the economy with "enough" money to maintain full employment. Accordingly, the Federal Reserve tends to respond to higher product prices and the resulting increase in the amount of nominal money needed for transactions purposes by increasing the money supply so that the higher level of monetary transactions can occur.

57. *The unemployment rate has fallen from 8.1 percent to 7.9 percent. The economy may be turning around.* Wrong. The official rate is meaningless because it can be achieved by people giving up and no longer actively looking; one month changes in any rate may only be a cyclical move around a deteriorating long term position; and the initial numbers of any rate are often revised. Such an official monthly decline was frequently experienced during the Great Recession as the economy sank deeper and deeper into a permanent depression with unemployment in the twenty percent

range and labor force participation rates reaching lows not seen since the 1930s.

58. *The number of people filing for unemployment insurance has declined. The economy may be turning around.* Wrong. The decline may be subject to revision; and, most importantly, even if it is better than the preceding month the total may be so high as to indicate that it is the total number of people who are unemployed that is growing. Such a periodic monthly decline was frequently experienced during the Great Recession years as the economy sank deeper and deeper into a permanent depression.

And finally, a statement that is not wrong:

59. *The labor force participation rates for every age-sex cohort have risen every month for the past six months. The economy may be turning around.* Right. That is possibly an accurate conclusion. If so, it can be confirmed with other data. Many knowledgeable analysts consider an acknowledgement of the importance of the labor force participation rates as the best single telltale sign that a journalist or "business economist" can be taken seriously.